*The coward believes he will live forever
    If he holds back in the battle.
But in old age he shall have no peace
    Though spears have spared his limbs.*

*Cattle die, kindred die,
    Every man is mortal:
But I know one thing that never dies,
    The glory of the great deed.*

The Elder Edda, "Words of the High One"
(P.B. Taylor & W.H. Auden, trans.)

*O*f *possessions cattle and fat sheep are things to be had for the lifting,
and tripods can be won, and the tawny high heads of horses, but a man's
life cannot come back again, it cannot be lifted nor captured again by
force, once it has crossed the teeth's barrier. For my mother Thetis the
goddess of the silver feet tells me I carry two sorts of destiny toward the
day of my death. Either, if I stay here and fight beside the city of the
Trojans, my return home is gone, but my glory shall be everlasting; but if
I return home to the beloved land of my fathers, the excellence of my
glory is gone, but there will be a long life left for me, and my end in death
will not come to me quickly. And this would be my counsel to others also,
to sail back home again . . .*

The Iliad, Book IX (Lattimore, trans.)

WORLD

MYTHOLOGY

Second Edition

An Anthology of the Great Myths and Epics

Donna Rosenberg

NTC *Publishing Group*
a division of NTC/CONTEMPORARY PUBLISHING GROUP
Lincolnwood, Illinois USA

Acknowledgments

Cover: The Poseidon of Artemision, attributed to the Greek sculptor Kalamis. c. 460–450 B.C. The Romans removed this bronze statue from a temple dedicated to the Greek god of the sea. However, the ship carrying it sank before it reached its destination. The sculpture was found beneath the sea near Cape Artemision, Greece, in 1928. National Museum of Athens, Greece. Photograph by Richard Rosenberg.

Frontispiece: One of five carved wooden serpent heads found in 1904 in an Oseberg Viking royal ship burial. c. A.D. 850. According to some scholars, the heads were thought to protect against evil spirits. Viking Ship Hall, Oslo, Norway. Rendering by Lauren Wohl.

Page 2: Apollo. From west pediment of the temple of Zeus, Olympia, Greece. This temple, the largest of its time, was built by the architect Libon of Elis from 472 to 457 B.C.; however, an unknown artist designed its sculptures. Museum of Olympia. Photograph by Richard Rosenberg.

Page 148: Low-relief stone scene of the building of Noah's Ark. From Sainte Chapelle, Paris, France. Designed by Pierre de Montreuil for Saint Louis IX, the Crusader King (reigned A.D. 1226–1270). Archaeological excavations have revealed a layer of clay nine feet deep left by a great flood in Mesopotamia in about 2900 B.C. The Akkadian Utanapishtim in *Gilgamesh* is the counterpart of the biblical Noah, Greek Deucalion, and others. Photograph by Donna Rosenberg.

Page 204: Stone sculpture of a helmeted Viking warrior, who holds a battle-ax and a sword. 10th century A.D. Yorkshire Museum, York, England. Photograph by Richard Rosenberg.

Page 254: Stonehenge. This Stone Age structure was built in stages between 2800 and 1500 B.C. near Salisbury, in southern England. Long assumed to be an ancient religious site connected with the Celtic worship of the sun, Stonehenge may also have been used as an astronomical calculator. Photograph by Richard Rosenberg.

Page 324: Bronze Hindu sculpture of Shiva, Lord of the Dance. India, late 10th to early 11th century A.D. Shiva's "dance of the universe" consists of five movements: creation, preservation, destruction, reincarnation, and nirvana. The Art Institute of Chicago. Photograph by Richard Rosenberg.

Page 400: Bronze sculpture of a Yoruba warrior from the area that is now Nigeria. Mid-15th to mid-17th century A.D. Metropolitan Museum of Art, New York. Photograph by Richard Rosenberg.

Page 464: Thunderbird, symbolizing the vitality of life, perched at the top of a Kwakiutl totem pole. Pacific Northwest coast tribes carved many such poles, containing figures important in family history and tribal lore, from the trunks of cedar trees in the late 19th and early 20th centuries. Thunderbird Park, Provincial Museum. Victoria, British Columbia, Canada. Photograph by Donna Rosenberg.

Published by NTC Publishing Group
A division of NTC/Contemporary Publishing Group, Inc.
4255 West Touhy Avenue, Lincolnwood (Chicago), Illinois 60712-1975 U.S.A.
Copyright © 1994, 1986 by NTC/Contemporary Publishing Group
Printed in the United States of America
International Standard Book Number: 0-8442-5767-2
Library of Congress Catalog Card Number: 93-85887
05 QB 24 23 22 21 20 19 18 17 16 15 14

To Dick, my favorite hero.

Contents

Preface

W*orld Mythology* presents the major myths from around the world in a manner that preserves their appeal as fine literature. My retelling of each myth retains the principal plot, characterization, style and cultural values of the original, although a one-volume edition has made it necessary to shorten the longer epics. The myths are arranged geographically into seven major cultural groups: Greece and Rome, the Middle East, Northern Europe, Britain, the Far East and Pacific Islands, Africa, and the Americas. In order to facilitate cross-cultural comparisons and contrasts, I have included creation, fertility, and hero myths from each culture. An introduction to each myth includes historical background, literary analysis, and an evaluation of the myth's appeal. The student edition also includes interpretative questions.

Myths reflect human nature, with its needs and desires, hopes and fears. Myths reveal the human condition. Creation myths satisfy the need to have roots. Fertility myths respond to the need for economic stability in an unpredictable world. Hero myths provide models for human behavior. Myths reveal cultural responses to the ever-important questions: Who am I? How should I lead my life? Thus, they reveal the different ways in which human beings respond to the issues that unite them.

The study of world mythology leads readers to broaden their knowledge, understanding, and appreciation of others. Prejudice feeds on stereotypical views of cultural differences and on cultural bias. Students of world mythology study the distinctive qualities of each culture and, in the process, become more humane. They learn that human beings are remarkably alike through time and across space.

Equally important, the study of comparative mythology leads readers to gain insight into themselves and to evaluate the nature of their own lives. Like the heroes of every culture, all people today confront choices that force them to reconcile their personal wishes with their responsibility to others. Like these heroic figures, all people today must confront tasks in the course of their daily lives that appear to be insurmountable. They, too, must be courageous and determined if they are to achieve their goals. The study of the hero teaches that great character is as important as great deeds.

The world's myths continue to inspire many creative and intellectual pursuits. They enrich the appreciation of literature, art, and music and can lead to greater interest in history, religion, psychology, anthropology, and archaeology.

Introduction

Myths symbolize human experience and embody the spiritual values of a culture. Every society preserves its myths because the beliefs and world-view found within them are crucial to the survival of that culture. Myths usually originate in an ancient, oral tradition. Some explain origins, natural phenomena, and death; others describe the nature and function of divinities; while still others provide models of virtuous behavior by relating the adventures of heroes or the misfortunes of arrogant humans. Myths often include elements from legend and folklore. They depict humans as an integral part of a larger universe, and they impart a feeling of awe for all that is mysterious and marvelous in life.

Myths are an important way to understand ourselves and our connection to other people at a time when the welfare of each culture depends on the attitudes and actions of other cultures. Although most of the myths in *World Mythology* were created by people who lived in societies that were much less complex than our own, they address fundamental questions that each thinking person continues to ask: Who am I? What is the nature of the universe in which I live? How do I relate to that universe? How much control do I have over my own life? What must I do in order to survive? How can I lead a satisfying life? How can I balance my own desires with my responsibilities to my family and my community? How can I reconcile myself to the inevitability of death?

The answers to these questions have produced from diverse cultures a body of myths that closely resemble each other in subject, although the treatment of each issue naturally varies from one society to another. Despite the unique perspective of each culture, their shared concerns tie human beings to one another across the globe and throughout history.

The following themes are common in world mythology: The first parents are often the gods of sky and earth. The creator-god usually fashions the first human beings from parts of the earth—perhaps clay, trees, rocks, or plants. The gods destroy at least one world of mortals by causing a great flood. In the world as in nature, birth, maturity, and death are often followed by rebirth. Heroes are children of gods who have an unusual birth, possess extraordinary strength, kill monsters with the help of special weapons, embark on an arduous journey, descend into the Underworld as part of their tasks, and have an unusual death.

An inherent part of many myths is the belief in one or more divine powers who create life and control the direction of the universe. Throughout the world, these divinities, whether in human or in animal form, are anthropomorphic in that they think, act, and speak like human beings. They differ primarily in their attitude toward mortals. Some gods, like those of Greece, Egypt, India, and North America, appreciate the merits of human beings, are sympathetic to them, and try to help them. Other gods, like those of Sumer, Babylonia, and northern Europe (the Norse gods), tend to be indifferent to the fate of human beings.

The Purpose of Myths

Myths were originally created as entertaining stories with a serious purpose. Their broad appeal has enabled them to survive for hundreds and sometimes thousands of years. A myth's serious purpose is either to explain the nature of the universe (creation and fertility myths) or to instruct members of the community in the attitudes and behavior necessary to function successfully in that particular culture (hero myths and epics).

A particular culture may be interested in the creation of the entire universe, beginning with divine beings who separate earth and sky. Most of the major cultures start with the beginning of the universe—a chaotic, formless mass that a god or pair of gods separates. The gods multiply so that each can have his or her particular role in the universal scheme, and the creator-god brings life to earth in the form of plants, animals, and human beings.

On the other hand, some cultures are interested only in myths that explain the origin of their own people and enhance their nationalistic spirit. For example, the Navajos depict their journey upward through four worlds into a fifth world. Similarly, the Irish Celts are concerned with the settling of Ireland, the Japanese explain the creation of their islands, and the Yoruba explain the creation of life, their sacred city-state.

According to many myths, human beings are not perfect creatures even though a god created them. In many cultures, the creator-god must fashion and destroy, usually through a flood, a succession of races. This theme is found worldwide: in the Greek writer Hesiod, in the Hindu myths of India, and in the myths of the Maya of Central America and the Yoruba of Africa. One of the most elaborate flood myths comes from Sumer and Babylonia.

All cultures explain how human beings acquired particular foods and the agricultural tools that permitted them to become civilized. Some myths, like the Hittite myth of Telepinu and the African myth from Dahomey, involve gods who have been insulted and must be appeased for fertility to be restored. The Telepinu myth includes powerful, metaphorical incantations designed to enlist the god's aid. The Greek myth of Demeter and Persephone is a masterpiece of psychological complexity. The myths of other cultures involve a divine figure who teaches agricultural skills to human beings. Viracocha introduces the Aymara/Tiahuanaco peoples to a more complex and civilized way of life. Other myths, like the Zuñi, the Chinese, and the Indian, show a divine or semi-divine heroic figure rescuing humanity by killing a monster that has destroyed the fertility of the land.

The heroic myths and epics of a society teach its members the appropriate attitudes, behavior, and values of that culture. These myths are of particular interest and value to us. Not only are they exciting adventure stories, but in these myths we see ourselves, drawn larger and grander than we are, yet with our human weaknesses as well as our strengths.

Heroes are the models of human behavior for their society. They earn lasting fame — the only kind of immortality possible for human beings — by performing great deeds that help their community, and they inspire others to emulate them. Heroes are forced by circumstance to make critical choices where they must balance one set of values against competing values. They achieve heroic stature in part from their accomplishments and in part because they emerge from their trials as more sensitive and thoughtful human beings.

Yet heroes are not the same throughout the world. Achilles, Odysseus, Gilgamesh, Sigurd, and Sunjata, for example, come from cultures where individuals may earn fame in a variety of ways. This permits them to express their individuality. In contrast, Rama must always remember and follow dharma, the particular form of proper and righteous behavior that the Hindu culture expects of a person in his or her political, economic, and social position.

In spite of their extraordinary abilities, no hero is perfect. Yet their human weaknesses are often as instructive as their heroic qualities. Their imperfections allow ordinary people to identify with them and to like them, for everyone has similar psychological needs and conflicts.

Many of the greatest heroes cannot accept mortality. Gilgamesh so fears death that he undertakes a long and perilous journey in search of the secret of immortality. Ultimately, he learns to be satisfied with the immortality that comes from enduring accomplishments. Achilles must choose between death with honor and a long, undistinguished life. When he feels deprived of honor on the battlefield, he chooses life—and only the unforeseen ramifications of that choice cause him to change his mind. Hector and Beowulf are forced to choose heroic deaths because they cannot live with the stain of cowardice.

Unlike most heroes, Heracles knows that he will become immortal after he has accomplished his labors. His primary concern is to avoid the labors because he refuses to be ordered about by a cowardly king. Odysseus actually rejects the opportunity to become immortal because he cares more about the quality of life than its duration. He prefers his own mortal wife and the problems of governing a kingdom to marriage with a beautiful goddess and a life of boredom.

The hero myths examine the relationship between the individual's desires and his or her responsibilities to society. Often the choice is crucial but uncomplicated: whether or not to risk death to save the community. The hero who chooses to risk death acquires honor and lasting fame; the hero who chooses safety is denied both. Heracles and Beowulf make the world a safer place by killing many monsters. The hero of *Kotan Utunnai* helps his people by fighting valiantly against the enemy.

In the major epics, the issue is the same, but the circumstances are infinitely more complex. When a leader places his or her own desires before the needs of the community, both the community and the individual suffer. Agamemnon and Achilles quarrel over a slave girl because public honor is the key to self-esteem. Similarly, Lancelot and Guinevere place their love above their loyalty to King Arthur, thereby destroying the Round Table and putting Britain into the hands of power-hungry local rulers. Aeneas places the needs of his community above his personal desires but loses his own humanity. Similarly, Rama places the needs of his community above his love for Sita, causing great personal tragedy for both of them. On the other hand, Gassire earns fame by placing his personal desires before the needs of his community.

Heroes define themselves by how they relate to external circumstances. They acquire lasting fame by performing deeds of valor, but they acquire even greater heroic stature by winning an inner battle against their desires. Hector fights a greater battle because he first must overcome his fear of Achilles. Both he and Beowulf fight against a superior foe, knowing that they will die in the process yet choosing to die with honor rather than to live without self-esteem and public approval. Odysseus' greatest strengths—his clever intelligence and his self-confidence—cause his problems. He survives his homecoming only because he masters his need to assert himself and flaunt his superiority. In contrast, Quetzalcoatl is outmatched when Tezcatlipoca preys upon his vanity.

We should not be intimidated by the external characteristics of the hero: an immortal parent, unusual birth, aristrocratic social position, and divine sponsorship. We could say that Heracles can perform great tasks because his father is Zeus. We do this in our own lives whenever we attribute someone's success primarily to luck instead of to individual courage, perseverance, and ability. However, this attitude is not personally helpful. Although these heroes lived long ago in cultures very different from our own, they can still serve as models for us. We too must often risk our self-esteem and our reputation by making difficult choices and by attempting tasks where we fear failure. We too want to live in such a way that we are remembered for our good deeds.

The Matriarchal Society

A knowledge of the basic difference between Mother Earth–centered matriarchal religions and the Father Sky–centered patriarchal religions is crucial to an understanding of the symbolic content of many myths. The political, economic, social, and religious foundation of the matriarchal society was the agricultural year. The importance of agriculture fostered a cyclical view of life, emphasizing the progression of all living matter from birth to maturity to death to rebirth. Even in lands where the climate remained relatively stable from one season to the next, people could see the connection between the development of their own lives and the development of life among plants and animals.

In the matriarchal society, the Great Goddess or Mother Goddess personified Mother Earth and was the supreme deity. She was the source of all human life and the source of all food. To survive, societies needed to produce children and to produce food. They knew how dependent they were upon the blessings of the Great Goddess, and they worshipped her properly so they would receive those blessings.

The queen personified the Great Goddess, and she wielded great political, economic, social, and religious power. Other women were considered daughters of the Great Goddess. Thus, all women in the matriarchal society were highly valued, and many of them held important positions. Women were the heads of their families, and inheritance passed from a mother to her daughters, with the youngest daughter being most important because, presumably, she would be the last to die and thus would continue the family line the longest. Children were reared by their mother and her brother, while the father lived in the home of his mother and helped rear his sister's children. The children's primary moral obligations were to their mother and their siblings.

When the male's role in procreation became understood and valued, the queen took a husband, called the sacred king, for one year. At first, he was her brother or her son, but later he was a youth who symbolized her son. Many youths competed for the great honor of being sacred king. They had to win many contests involving physical strength and the skillful use of the bow. Heracles' tasks against the Nemean lion, the Cretan bull, the Erymanthian boar, and Artemis' deer represent typical contests. Odysseus' participation in an archery contest where the winner will marry Penelope is an echo of this tradition.

Each spring, when the seeds of the new crops were sown, the past year's sacred king would be sacrificed as part of a major religious ceremony. The priestesses of the Mother Goddess would eat his flesh in order to acquire his powers of fertility, and the fields and farm animals would be sprinkled with his blood so they too would become fertile. Then in a religious ceremony the queen would take a new sacred king for the coming year.

The sacred king gradually gained more power. He increased the length of his reign to eight years by choosing a substitute sacred king to die in his place. At the end of each year, the real king would retire from public view into a burial chamber or cave for one to three days, while the substitute king reigned in his place. The priestesses of the Great Goddess would sacrifice the substitute king in a sacred ceremony and use his flesh and blood to ensure the fertility of the community. Then the real king would resume his duties for the coming year. When Gilgamesh rejects Ishtar's marriage proposal, he relates the ways that she has destroyed previous mates. Ishtar retaliates by causing the death of Enkidu, who functions as Gilgamesh's substitute.

By 2400 B.C., aggressive tribes worshipping a supreme male god who was a father-figure or a successful warrior had begun to invade many matriarchal communities. They brought with them a new social and political order in which males dominated. Kings gained enough power to change the old social system to one in which kings ruled by heredity and animals were sacrificed to win the favor of the gods.

Some cultures depict a world view in which one generation of gods replaces another, the newer gods being more civilized and capable than the earlier ones. For example, Zeus conquers Cronus in Greek mythology, and Marduk conquers Tiamat in Babylonian mythology. The battle between one family of gods and another often reflects the political and religious conflict between the indigenous people, who were farmers and worshipped the Great Goddess or the Mother Goddess, and a warlike invading people, who worshipped male sky gods. Zeus' conquest of Cronus and the Titans reflects the political conquest of one people by another, and his liaisons with many Mother Goddesses in addition to Hera, his wife, represent a compromise in which the invaders' religion was united with each local religion. Similar changes are reflected in Babylonian mythology, where a religion in which Marduk is the principal god incorporates the older gods.

Academic Perspectives on Myths

Because myths are symbols of human experience, they can be analyzed in a variety of ways, depending upon the perspective of the scholar. Years ago, many scholars viewed myths as symbols of the external environment. Those who created myths were thought to have observed nature and interpreted the behavior of human beings in a parallel manner. For example, heroes were considered symbols of the sun. They wielded swords that symbolized the sun's rays against monsters that symbolized clouds and night, the enemies of the sun. Each hero story was thus a symbol of the conflict between day and night and, by extension, between good and evil.

In the 20th century, the symbolic interpretation of myths moved from the external environment to the internal environment of the unconscious mind. Sigmund Freud and his followers view myths as the expression of the individual's unconscious wishes, fears, and drives. For example, Otto Rank explains the characteristics of the traditional hero in terms of infantile hostility, childhood fantasies, and rebellion against one's father.

Carl Jung and his followers, among them Carl Kerenyi, Erich Neumann, and, more broadly, Joseph Campbell, view myths as the expression of a universal, collective unconscious. In their theory innate psychological characteristics, common to all human beings, determine how people throughout the world and throughout history experience and respond to the process of living. The contents of the collective unconscious are divided into archetypes — such as the mother, the child, the hero, the trickster, and the giant — but these are simply image frameworks. A particular individual's life experiences determine in what particular shape and form the archetypal images will be expressed. Thus, the fact that myths from around the world contain many similar themes reflects the existence of a common collective unconscious. The fact that they differ in their treatment of these themes reflects the influence of each culture's particular physical, social, economic, and political environment on the archetypes.

Scholars in this century have interpreted myths in other ways as well. Mircea Eliade, a historian of religions, views myths as the essence of religion, conceived from a genuine religious experience. It is the sacred experience that gives myths their structure and their utility. The ancient world contained a multitude of co-existing religious ideas and forms: different types of monotheism and polytheism (both female-dominated and male-dominated), nature worship, and ancestor worship. Consequently, numerous similarities and connections exist from one culture to another. This is evident from the study of various aspects of the religious experience, such as the nature of divinities, creation myths, sacrifices, rituals, death, and paradise.

The anthropologist Paul Radin views myths from an economic perspective. The individual's actual struggle for survival in the face of economic uncertainty, caused by an insufficient food supply and poor technology, creates fears that life will be unhappy and short. Religious leaders manipulate these fears for their own material benefit, often in concert with the political leaders of the community.

Anthropologist Claude Lévi-Strauss views myths as abstract constructions rather than narrative tales or symbols of experience. The structure of all human minds is identical and is revealed by the similar ways people solve their problems. Myths are identical products from identical minds, so myths from around the world possess a common structure. They reveal the conflict between opposing forces — such as life and death, or nature and culture. To discover the meaning of a particular myth, one must focus on its underlying structure rather than its narrative content or any symbolic meaning. This structure invariably reveals tensions in social relations or economic problems. The analysis of myths proves that human beings, no matter how primitive their technology, are not mentally inferior. Their myths demonstrate that they possess the intellectual capacity to understand the world in which they live.

Part of the fascination of mythology involves viewing it from a variety of perspectives simultaneously. Each discipline offers a valuable contribution, increasing our appreciation of the whole.

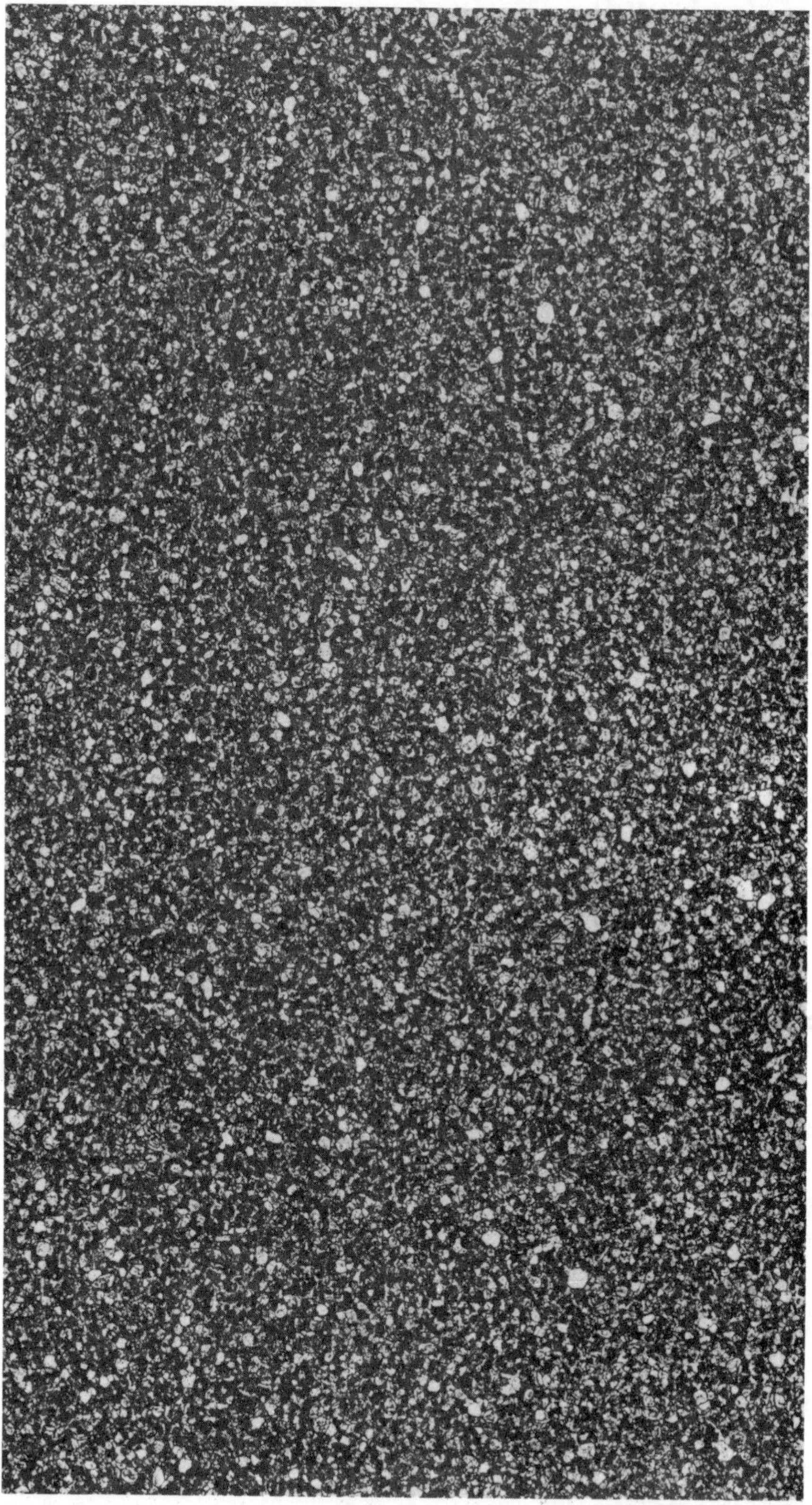

Greece and Rome

The myths of Greece have earned universal fame and popularity. Recorded as early as approximately 775 B.C. (Homer's *Iliad*), and approximately 725 B.C. (Hesiod's *Theogony*), they reveal a universe that closely resembles our own. Their gods, their heroes, and their depiction of the human condition are consistent with our own knowledge of human behavior.

The Greek gods are a large family, and each member of that family possesses a distinctive personality. Love, hate, jealousy, and pride motivate their behavior just as those feelings motivate human behavior. The gods who first rule the universe are overthrown by Zeus, who, with his brothers, sisters, and children, rules the world of human beings.

Zeus' sister, Demeter, and their daughter, Persephone, prefer the simple beauties of the earth to the majestic palaces of the gods on Mount Olympus. When Zeus' brother, Hades, abducts Persephone, we experience with Demeter the plight of every mother who has lost her beloved daughter.

Zeus expects human beings to conform to an unwritten code of respectable behavior. When King Lycaon and his nobility lose their respect for the gods and for other human beings, he destroys almost the entire race with a flood. However, he promises to create another race in its place, and he keeps his word.

According to Hesiod, Zeus also created five races

of human beings, each worse than the race that preceded it. People today speak of "the good old days" and wonder whether the human race will survive. Hesiod had the same attitude and the same concern. It is interesting to compare his description of his own generation with life today.

Heracles, whom the Romans called Hercules, is the most famous Greek hero. His accomplishments were so great that his name continues to be attached to any great task that humans face today. His courage, his strength, and his skill in the face of adversity provide a model of behavior for all of us.

Many other famous heroes walk through the pages of Homer's *Iliad*. Achilles and Agamemnon, among the Greeks, and Hector, among the Trojans, must choose between their own personal desires and the needs of their people. Their war is ancient, but their agony is modern. Once again, the courage with which they meet the challenges in their lives makes them impressive, yet very human, models of behavior for all of us.

Homer also follows the hero Odysseus as he returns home after the Trojan War, in one of the best adventure stories ever written. Anyone who has watched Odysseus escape from the blind Cyclops and, later, deceive the arrogant suitors who have invaded his palace will never forget this most ingenious of all heroes. Moreover, Odysseus' wife, Penelope, is one of the greatest women in all of literature. Her loyalty and creative intelligence match those of her husband.

The Romans adopted the Greek gods and their myths. Virgil wrote his own myth, *The Aeneid*, to glorify Augustus Caesar and the founding of Rome. *The Aeneid* begins shortly after Homer's *Iliad* ends, and it describes the adventures of the Trojan hero Aeneas. Because Virgil patterned his epic upon Homer's two epics, it is interesting to compare the works of these two great authors, particularly their concept of the hero. Virgil's dramatic portrayal of the destruction of Troy is one of the most powerful descriptions in all of literature, and Aeneas' love, Queen Dido of Carthage, is one of the world's most noble heroines.

Like *The Aeneid*, the myth of Romulus and Remus explains the founding of Rome. However, it is anonymous and older, and it owes much less to Greek traditions.

Introducing **The Creation of the Titans and the Gods**

Creation, according to the Greeks, moves from a mother-dominated society, in which the most important divinities are female, to a father-dominated society, in which the most important divinities are male. Just as the human family progresses through time from generation to generation, so the divine family, which was created in the image of the human family, moves from the rule of the parents, to the rule of the children, to the rule of the grandchildren.

Gaea, who is Mother Earth, is the first Great Goddess or Mother Goddess. The peoples who were living in

Greece when the Bronze Age tribes invaded the land worshipped the Great Goddess because they were farmers, and the fertility of the earth was of prime importance to them. Their survival depended upon their ability to raise enough food to sustain them through the nonproductive months of the year, and upon their ability to have enough children to assure the continuity of their clan. These people drew a connection between a woman's ability to give birth to children and the earth's ability to "give birth" to all plants. Therefore, the earth spirit was feminine, and the principal divinities that the early Greeks worshipped were also feminine.

When Uranus becomes ruler of the world, his son, Cronus, dismembers him—just as priestesses of the Great Goddess or Mother Goddess in the female-oriented religion dismembered the sacred king. They used his blood, which they considered to be a prime source of fertility, to fertilize the soil so that it would produce an abundance of crops. Uranus' blood, too, produces "crops," in the form of monstrous offspring. In the matriarchal, or mother-dominated, society, a son owes a greater loyalty to his mother than to his father.

When Cronus becomes ruler of the world, the divine family is in transition from the mother-dominated society to the father-dominated society that will follow under the rule of Zeus. Rhea is a Great Goddess or Mother Goddess, just as Gaea, her mother, is. In the contest for power between husband and wife, Cronus is winning until Rhea solicits the help of her mother. Then the females win. Yet, Rhea uses her son, Zeus, to carry out her plan, and with her approval, he becomes the next principal ruler, even though he is male.

He will rule with greater authority than either Uranus or Cronus did.

Cronus disposes of his infant children by eating them. Cannibalism is not unusual in history. Primitive people believed that they could acquire desirable characteristics—such as courage, strength, wisdom, and skill—by eating the important organs of another creature, often a fearsome enemy, who had possessed those characteristics. Consequently, early peoples might eat the meat of an animal they had killed, or they might drink the blood or eat the heart of the person who, until they killed him, had been a great enemy. In the matriarchal society, the priestesses would eat the flesh of the sacred king in order to acquire his fertility.

Hesiod tells this myth in the *Theogony*.

Principal Gods

The First Generation

GAEA: first Great Goddess or Mother Goddess in Greek mythology; Mother Earth, who nourishes all life

URANUS: son and husband of Gaea; ruler of the sky

The Second Generation: Children of Gaea and Uranus

HUNDRED-HANDED GIANTS: triplets; best known: Briareus

CYCLOPES: triplets; one-eyed metal-smiths; servants of Zeus

TITANS: thirteen; race of immortals who, with their children, ruled the universe before the gods conquered them:

CRONUS (Saturn)*: youngest child; god of the sky after Uranus and ruler of the Titans; father of the first six Greek gods: Zeus, Poseidon, Hades, Hera, Demeter, and Hestia

RHEA (Cybele): sister and wife of Cronus; a Great Goddess or Mother Goddess like Gaea; mother of Zeus, Poseidon, Hades, Hera, Demeter, and Hestia

HELIOS: god of the sun prior to replacement by Apollo in late Greek and Roman mythology

SELENE: goddess of the moon prior to replacement by Artemis in late Greek and Roman mythology

THEMIS: goddess of prophecy at Delphi before Apollo conquered her oracle

ATLAS: strongest Titan; condemned by Zeus eternally to hold up the sky

PROMETHEUS: most creative and intelligent Titan; created mortal man out of clay

EPIMETHEUS: brother of Prometheus; husband of Pandora (the first mortal woman)

The Third Generation: The Greek Gods

Children of Cronus and Rhea

ZEUS (Jupiter, Jove): youngest, most intelligent, and most powerful child; lord of the sky after Cronus; ruler of the gods; maintains order in the world of mortals; protects strangers and guests

POSEIDON (Neptune): brother of Zeus; lord of the sea; causes earthquakes

HADES (Pluto): brother of Zeus; ruler of the Underworld; lord of the dead

HERA (Juno): sister and wife of Zeus; queen of Olympus; goddess of marriage and childbirth

DEMETER (Ceres): sister of Zeus; a Great Goddess or Mother Goddess like Rhea and Gaea; goddess of grain

HESTIA (Vesta): sister of Zeus; kindest and most loved of the gods; guardian of the home

Immortal Children of Zeus

APOLLO: twin of Artemis; god of prophecy, medicine, archery, and music; god of the sun in late Greek and Roman mythology

ARTEMIS (Diana): twin of Apollo; goddess of the hunt; goddess of the moon in late Greek and Roman mythology

ATHENA (Minerva): goddess of arts and crafts and defensive war; helper of heroes; goddess of wisdom in late Greek and Roman mythology

APHRODITE (Venus): goddess of beauty and sexual desire

PERSEPHONE (Proserpine): wife of Hades; queen of the Underworld

THE FATES: CLOTHO, LACHESIS, and ATROPOS: determine the length of each mortal's life

ARES (Mars): god of war

HEPHAESTUS (Vulcan): husband of Aphrodite; metalsmith of the gods, famous for his creativity and skill

HERMES (Mercury): Zeus' messenger; guides travelers and leads shades of the dead into the Underworld; helps merchants and thieves

*Roman names of the gods are in parentheses.

The Creation of the Titans and the Gods

Out of the original emptiness, which was called Chaos, emerged the first three immortal beings: Gaea (Mother Earth), Tartarus, who ruled the deepest, darkest region of the Underworld, and Eros (Love), whose great beauty inspired the creation of many of the deathless gods. Then Gaea, without any partner, gave birth to Uranus (Father Sky). She made him her equal, so that he would surround her on all sides and would provide a home for the immortal beings. Gaea also gave birth to Ourea (Mountains) and Pontus (Sea).

Gaea then married Uranus, and he ruled over all that came into being. The first immortal children of Gaea and Uranus were the three Hundred-Handed Giants. Each Giant had fifty heads and fifty arms extending from each shoulder.

Their next immortal children were the three Cyclopes. Each Cyclops had only one eye, set in the middle of his forehead. They were expert craftsmen, and they later built the palaces for the gods on Mount Olympus.

Uranus feared the terrible strength of these six children, and he hated them because they terrified him. So as each child was born, Uranus took him from his mother, bound him, and hurled him deep into Gaea's being, the earth. Each child fell for nine days and nine nights, finally landing in the region named after its ruler, Tartarus, on the tenth day. There Uranus kept the Hundred-Handed Giants and the Cyclopes, far from the surface of the earth and the light of the sun. His eyes now shone with pride and satisfaction, for he ruled without fear of any challenge to his authority, and he expected to rule forever.

Gaea was outraged by her husband's actions. She longed for her children, and she hated Uranus for what he had done to them. However, she buried her feelings deep in her heart and quietly waited for the time when she could take revenge.

The next immortal children born to Gaea and Uranus were the thirteen Titans. They and their children became the oldest generation of Greek gods. Helios was the god of the sun and drove it across the sky in his chariot. Selene was the goddess of the moon. Oceanus was the god of the river that surrounded the earth. Like her mother, Gaea, Themis was the goddess of prophecy at Delphi. Cronus married his sister Rhea, who was a goddess of the earth like her mother, and in time they became the parents of the Greek gods. Later, Atlas, by far the strongest of the Titans, held up the sky so that it would not fall upon the earth. Soon thereafter, Prometheus, the most intelligent and clever Titan, created mortal man out of clay and water. His brother, Epimetheus, married Pandora, the first mortal woman.

Gaea decided to use her Titan children as her means of revenge against Uranus. She took a large piece of flint and shaped it into a huge, sharp, stone sickle. Then, she approached her sons and said, "I want you to punish your father, for he is very cruel. He has imprisoned your brothers in the land of Tartarus against my wishes and against their will."

Almost all of Gaea's sons were so terrified of Uranus that they listened to her command in silence and refused to obey her. But Cronus, the youngest Titan, was very similar to his father in temperament, and he was much more courageous than his brothers. When he saw their reaction, he said, "If no one else will help you, Mother, I certainly will! If our father has been cruel to you and to our brothers, we should take revenge!"

When she heard Cronus' words, Gaea's heart overflowed with pride and satisfaction. It was gratifying to have one son who had the courage to help her. Now, Uranus would learn what it was like to endure endless suffering!

So Gaea put the great, flint sickle into Cronus' hands. She warned him to be careful with its sharp, curved blade. Then she told him where to hide and what she wanted him to do. Later, when Helios had drawn the chariot of the sun across the sky and had retired for the night, Uranus joined his wife by the shore of the sea and lay down to sleep with her.

Selene shed the light of the moon upon the sleeping figure of Uranus as Cronus, from his place of hiding, raised the huge, stone sickle and emasculated his father. Then he quickly threw the severed pieces into the sea and said, "Your reign is over, Father! Now I shall reign in your place. You may challenge me, but my power is clearly greater than yours. So, I advise you to submit to your fate."

Uranus, being immortal, could not die. However, he screamed in agony, for his immortality did not prevent him from feeling excruciating pain. Part of his anguish came from the realization that his power had suddenly ended.

From Uranus' blood, which flowed into the earth, Gaea brought forth the three black-clothed Furies. With eyes that dripped poisonous tears and breath that was too foul to bear, these immortal goddesses drove to insanity any child who killed one of his parents.

From the same blood, Gaea also brought forth another group of terrible beings, who were simply called the Giants. They looked fearsome, with their hairy heads and faces and their dragon-like feet. When they wore their shining armor and carried their long spears, they appeared to be invincible.

The severed pieces of Uranus' immortal body remained in the sea, where a white foam surrounded them. In time Aphrodite, the goddess of beauty and sexual desire, was born from them, and she was often called the foam-born goddess.

Cronus became god of the sky, as his father had been before him. Like his father, he feared the Hundred-Handed Giants and the Cyclopes, so he ignored his promise to Gaea and kept his brothers bound and imprisoned in Tartarus.

Gaea, disappointed and angry, watched and waited for the next opportunity to free her children. Being a goddess of prophecy, she enjoyed informing Cronus that one day a son of his would overpower him just as he had overpowered his own father.

"I shall fool the Fates!" he exclaimed to himself, with a clever smile. "If I do not have any children, then I will be able to rule forever!"

However, it was not so easy to change his destiny. Cronus loved his wife, Rhea, and in time she gave birth to a lovely daughter, Hestia. When Rhea proudly presented their baby daughter to Cronus, the words of his fate screamed inside Cronus' head! His great fear of losing power brought a mad, distraught glint into his eyes. Without considering whether the baby was female or male, Cronus took the baby lovingly from his wife, opened his gigantic mouth, and swallowed the infant in one gulp. "Now," he thought with satisfaction, "I have cheated the Fates of their prophecy and my child of his throne!"

Four more children were born to Cronus and Rhea: Demeter, Hera, Hades, and Poseidon. Each time Cronus embraced the infant so lovingly that Rhea was certain he would accept this child. However, each time the glint of madness would steal across his eyes as the words of the prophecy roared in his ears, and each time he would open his gigantic mouth and swallow the infant in one gulp. Then, once again, Cronus would grin with satisfaction and think to himself, "I have cheated the Fates of their prophecy and my child of his throne!"

By this time, Rhea's heart was overflowing with grief. When she was about to give birth to her sixth child, she went to Gaea and said, "Mother, please help me! Cronus has robbed me of our children just as Uranus robbed you of the Hundred-Handed Giants and the Cyclopes. I cannot bear to let him steal this baby too! What can I do? Can we hide the infant from Cronus before he sees it? How can I trick him?"

Gaea replied, "My heart understands your pain, my daughter, and I think I can help you. I know that Cronus is destined to be overpowered by his son just as he overpowered his father before him. Surely the child about to be born to you is the son who is destined to take revenge upon Cronus for his treatment of his father, his brothers, and his own children.

"When your time to give birth arrives," Gaea counseled her daughter, "go to the island of Crete and take refuge in the deep, hidden cave high on the slopes of Mount Dicte. I shall see that nymphs nurse your infant son with goat's milk, and I will have them hang his cradle from a tree so that Cronus will not be able to find him on land, or sea, or in the air. Young boys, the Curetes, will march beneath his cradle, clanging their spears against their bronze shields to smother the sound of his cries.

"And as for how to trick Cronus," Gaea concluded, "he is so crazed with fear that an ordinary rock should be all you need to fool him!"

So it came about that Rhea gave birth to the infant, Zeus, in the cave of Mount Dicte, on Crete. She left her mother, Gaea, in charge of the baby and quickly returned home. She then found a rock about the size of her newborn infant and wrapped it in swaddling clothes as if it were an infant. Soon Cronus entered the room.

"How are you feeling?" he asked her sweetly. "Let me admire our latest child. Not every infant is born into such a royal family!"

Rhea forced herself to think of the fate of her other five children as she handed the well-wrapped rock over to her husband. As usual, Cronus took the bundle she gave him and lovingly embraced it. Then the words of the prophecy screamed in his head, and the look of madness shone forth from his eyes. Beside himself with fear of his destiny, Cronus opened his gigantic mouth and swallowed the rock in one gulp. "Now," he said to himself, smiling with the greatest satisfaction and relief, "once again, I have cheated the Fates of their prophecy and my child of his throne! I shall rule forever, after all!"

Years passed, and Zeus became a mature god. Cronus never realized that a son had escaped his eye and evaded his gigantic mouth. He ruled untroubled and unthreatened, never thinking that his destiny might be rapidly approaching.

One day when Cronus was thirsty, Rhea gave him a tasty drink. He was delighted and asked for more. A young stranger walked in and handed him the cup, and Cronus had swallowed the drink before it occurred to him that he had never seen the young man before.

"Who is he?" he wondered. "Why should *he* have brought me the drink? What if he has poisoned me! Why does my stomach feel so strange? Did I drink too much? Was the second drink different from the first drink?"

Suddenly, Cronus felt an excruciating pain in his stomach. He vomited up the rock, followed by Poseidon, Hades, Hera, Demeter, and Hestia, all of whom were fully grown by now.

Rhea then entered the room, with the young stranger, Zeus, by her side. "Your destiny is upon you, Cronus!" she exclaimed. "The Fates prophesied that a son would overpower you just as you overpowered your own father. That son, Zeus, now stands before you. You are reaping the fruits of the seeds you sowed when you swallowed our children and kept your brothers in chains in Tartarus! We will now see whether Zeus will rule with more intelligence and kindness than you did. Your mind has been as blind and your heart as hard as that rock you swallowed!"

"If this stranger, son of mine or not, thinks that he is going to take my kingdom from me, he is not as intelligent as you seem to think he is!" Cronus responded. "Anyone who wants to rule in my place will have to fight me, and all of the other Titans, too!"

So it came to pass that Zeus and his brothers and sisters, the first Greek gods, waged war against Cronus and the Titans who allied themselves with him. The gods and the Titans were so evenly matched in numbers and in strength that they fought for ten years without victory for either side.

Finally, Gaea, who has given Zeus the poisoned drink to give his father, helped Zeus once again. She told him about her lost children, the Hundred-Handed Giants and the Cyclopes, whom Uranus and Cronus had kept imprisoned beneath the ground at the borders of the earth, and how they were chained in grief and sorrow, far from the light of Helios and the companionship of the deathless gods. She prophesied that the gods would win their war if they brought the Hundred-Handed Giants and the Cyclopes up from Tartarus as their allies.

Zeus and his brothers went down to Tartarus to rescue Gaea's children and encourage their alliance. Once they had killed the guard, removed their uncles' bonds, and fed them, Zeus said, "Listen to these words from my heart. We have been fighting the Titans for ten years without success. If you will repay our kindness to you by fighting on our side, your great strength will make us victorious."

To these words one of the Hundred-Handed Giants replied, "We know that you are fighting to defend the deathless gods from the cruelty of Titan rulers. And we know what it is to be the victims of Titan power. Had you not freed us, we were doomed to face an eternity of darkness, bondage, and isolation. Uranus and his son Cronus do not understand suffering and know nothing of mercy. We know that you will rule the world with greater wisdom. Of course, we shall fight with you against the Titan tyrant!"

Then one of the Cyclopes said, "In return for our freedom, we present each of you with a special gift. To you, Zeus, we give the gift of thunder and lightning in the form of a thunderbolt, an invincible weapon against any enemy. We shall make more of these for you when we set up on Mount Olympus.

"To you, Poseidon," he continued, "we give the trident. Not only is it a superior fishing spear, but you will find it a most effective device for shaking the earth and creating waves at sea. Until then, its three barbed prongs will make it a useful weapon against the Titans.

"And to you, Hades," he concluded, "we give the helmet of invisibility. In time to come, the hero Perseus will need your weapon to kill the monstrous Gorgon, Medusa. Until then, it will serve you well against Cronus and his Titan allies."

With high spirits, Zeus and his allies returned to the upper world and renewed the battle. The Hundred-Handed Giants broke cliffs off the mountains until they had a huge crag in each of their multitude of hands. Then they pelted the Titans with their stone weapons.

The Titans responded with arrows and spears. The combatants could not kill each other, for they were all immortal beings. However, they could injure and overpower one another. The battle caused an upheaval across the earth and sea. The mountains quaked, and even Tartarus felt the impact of the mighty rocks upon the earth high above him.

Then Zeus hurled his invincible lightning bolt, which engulfed in flames whatever it touched. The earth resounded with the roars of mighty thunder as the blazing woods and the scalding sea scorched the air. Finally, the Hundred-Handed Giants hurled the Titans beneath the earth into Tartarus and placed them in chains for eternity in that dark, dismal land. Two of them volunteered to guard the hated Titans forever. The third, Atlas, because of his size and his strength, was forced to hold up the sky upon his shoulders. The war was over.

When the three male gods drew lots for their kingdoms, Zeus drew the sky, Poseidon the sea, and Hades the Underworld. In addition to maintaining peace and order among all of the immortal beings in the world, Zeus taught human beings to be just in their treatment of one another. Those who did not respect the deathless gods and other mortals were severely punished. Poseidon could use his trident to cause earthquakes as well as storms at sea, but he also taught mortals how to tame horses to work for them and how to build ships. Hades taught mortals to have respect for the dead by conducting proper funeral ceremonies and following certain burial practices.

Zeus married his sister Hera, who became the goddess of marriage and childbirth as well as queen of Olympus. Hestia became the guardian of the home and taught mortals how to build houses. Demeter became the goddess of grain. She taught mortals how to save the kernels of wild corn, plant them where they wanted corn to grow, and harvest the mature plants.

Zeus became the father of many other gods: Athena, the goddess of arts and crafts and defensive war; Apollo, the god of prophecy, medicine, and archery; Artemis, the goddess of the hunt; Hermes, Zeus' messenger; Persephone, the queen of the Underworld; Ares, the god of war; and Hephaestus, the renowned metalsmith.

The rule of the Titans had ended. The rule of the gods had begun.

Introducing **The Ages of Man**

After Homer, the next important Greek poet was Hesiod, who lived toward the end of the 8th century B.C. Hesiod wrote a number of myths based upon myths that already existed. He shaped this creation myth so that it would teach people how to lead satisfying lives in their own difficult age.

According to Hesiod, as human beings acquired more technology, their values deteriorated. Therefore, the first, golden race of mortals, which led the most simple life, was the most honorable and the happiest of all the races that Zeus created. They were a peaceful society of farmers, and they worshipped the Great Goddess or Mother Goddess (Mother Earth), who made them and their land fertile. In Greek history, this race conforms most closely to the peoples who inhabited

Greece before about 2600 to 2000 B.C., when the Mycenaeans invaded the land.

The bronze race of mortals lived in the Mycenaean Age. This was a time of many wars, including the Trojan War, which is the setting of Homer's *Iliad*. The Mycenaeans were more aggressive and acquisitive than the peoples they encountered when they invaded Greece. They worshipped Zeus, and in their society, the male was more important and more powerful than the female.

Hesiod's description in *The Works and Days* of the race of iron, "our" race, refers to the people living in his own time. You will find it interesting to compare his vision of life in his time with your view of life today.

The Ages of Man

Zeus, lord of Mount Olympus and father of the deathless gods, was also the father of human beings. The first generation of mortals to inhabit the grain-giving earth was known as the Race of Gold. These mortals were pure in heart and in deed. They respected both their fellow human beings and the deathless gods, and the immortals loved them in return. Because they treated one another justly, they needed neither written laws nor courts nor punishments. They lived carefree and easy lives, in freedom, safety, and peace. Since fear, grief, and hard labor never touched their lives, the passing years did not ravage their appearance or weaken their strength. Old age earned respect and gratitude.

The weather treated the Gold Race kindly, providing the warmth, beauty, and sustenance of an eternal spring. Mortals did not have to work to house or to clothe themselves. Flowing nectar and milk formed their rivers, and the leaves of dwarf oak trees dripped honey. They feasted by gathering the wild grains and fruits that grew abundantly about them, and they leisurely shepherded their flocks of cattle and sheep in lush, green pastures. They had the time and the desire to enjoy the wildflowers that radiantly blossomed in the sunshine and the stars that shone in the night sky.

The Race of Gold had no wish to possess more than it already had. It was neither acquisitive nor aggressive. These mortals did not fashion boats in order to discover what lay beyond the borders of their own land. They did not threaten other human beings, and in return, no one threatened them. They had no need to build defensive walls around their towns. They had no need to possess weapons. They had no armies, and they never heard the sound of a trumpet calling them to battle.

They died as peacefully as they had lived; death came in the form of a gentle sleep. After their bodies became part of the earth, their spirits roamed across the land, hidden by the mists. They protected the living from any danger and taught them how to lead a just life.

When the first generation had passed away, Zeus created a second generation of mortals. They were the Race of Silver, and they were far less virtuous than the Race of Gold. Although their bodies matured with the passage of time, the Silver Race remained juvenile in spirit. For 100 years each child stayed at home with his or her mother, isolated from the companionship and instruction of other human beings. During this time, these mortals devoted their lives solely to the pursuit of childish pleasures.

As a result, the lives of adults in the Silver Race were short and unhappy. They never learned to treat one another with kindness and consideration, and their selfish behavior created injustice and war. They did not respect the deathless gods and made no effort to please them.

Because the Silver Race honored neither gods nor mortals, Zeus became angry with them. The father of gods and mortals changed the weather from eternal spring to a year of four seasons, which ranged from the icy cold of winter to the blistering heat of summer. Caves and sheltered forest areas no longer provided sufficient protection from the weather, so the Silver Race built the first houses.

Food was now less plentiful. The people began to yoke oxen in pairs and drive them across their fields, toiling each day during the growing season, first to plant seeds of corn and later to reap the mature ears. Zeus brought their life on the earth to an early end, and when their bodies became part of the earth, their spirits entered the Underworld.

Then Zeus, father of gods and mortals, created a third generation of mortals, which became known as the Race of Bronze because their weapons and tools were bronze. These mortals were far inferior to the Silver Race because they were so cruel. They loved Ares, god of war, above all the other gods, and they lived by the sword. Their brute strength made them powerful, but their hearts were as unresponsive as the hardest rock.

Despite their strength and power, members of the Bronze Race died young. They brought black Death upon themselves through endless violence and war. When their bodies became part of the earth, their shades descended into the dark, dismal Underworld, and they left nothing of worth behind to give them a good name.

Next, Zeus created a fourth generation of mortals, which became known as the Race of Heroes. These human beings were more noble and virtuous than the members of the Silver or the Bronze Race. Some of them died in the war against Troy and in other wars, but Zeus placed those who survived upon the islands of the blessed at the ends of the earth. There, the heroes still live along the shore of Oceanus in a land that bears a harvest of honey-sweet fruit three times a year. Grief can no longer touch them; only the honor and glory they earned during their ordinary lifetimes survive. They are ruled by Cronus, whom Zeus freed from his bondage in Tartarus for this purpose.

The fifth generation of mortals that Zeus placed upon the grain-giving earth is our own, the Race of Iron. Now each day is filled with work and with grief, and each night many mortals die. The worst crimes in the history of humanity now occur throughout the world, and yet no mortal feels shame. Justice and faith have left the world; treason and fraud, violence and greed have replaced them.

The Iron Race does not think of others' needs and does not share the bounty of the earth. Instead, we have divided up the earth's surface into a multitude of private properties, and we keep as much as we can for ourselves. We feel that the earth has not provided enough wealth in the grains she gives, so we have built ships and sailed into the unknown in order to acquire more wealth.

We have torn into the grain-giving earth, searching for the riches she has hidden within her. We have found her secret treasure and have become powerful and wealthy from her deposits of iron and gold. The value of these metals has led to war, and mortal hands have become bloody as they greedily tried to grasp the golden treasures of victory.

If we do not change our ways, our behavior will destroy us. When the time comes that host and guest no longer act hospitably, when friend argues with friend and brothers are enemies, when children and their parents cannot agree with each other, when grown children forget what their parents have done for them and instead treat them with disrespect and dishonor, criticizing them and complaining bitterly because they have grown old and weak, when people who keep their word or are just or virtuous receive less respect than those who use their strength for violent and evil purposes, when those who are evil hurt those who are honorable, then Zeus will destroy our Iron Race, for we will have shown the father of gods and mortals that we are unfit to inhabit the earth that sustains us.

Introducing **Demeter and Persephone**

When the agricultural communities in Greece worshipped Mother Earth, different communities called the Great Goddess or the Mother Goddess by different names, including Gaea, her daughter Rhea, or Rhea's daughter Demeter. Most of the female divinities in Greek mythology were originally Great Goddesses: Athena in Athens, Hera in Argos, Artemis in Crete, and Aphrodite in Cyprus. Their roles changed when they were incorporated into the male-dominated religion of Zeus.

In an agricultural society, productive soil was of major importance, and the entire community was earth-oriented. The ancient farming peoples observed that plants, animals, and people were born, grew to maturity, and died, and that others like them were born again, often the following spring. This fact became the central focus of the matriarchal religion. Death was an accepted part of the life cycle, for it was followed by rebirth or new life. The people worshipped the Great Goddess to insure the fertility of their fields and themselves, for that would insure that their community would survive.

Demeter, Persephone, and Hades controlled the life cycle in nature. As the goddess of grain, Demeter taught mortals how to plant, raise, and harvest corn, wheat, and barley. Whether Persephone was living with her mother or her husband determined whether the season was one in which the seeds sprouted and the crops grew, or

whether it was the winter season when the seeds lay dormant. Hades was not only the god of the dead, from which new life would emerge, but he was also known as the god of wealth. (His other name, Pluto, was derived from *ploutos*, which means wealth.) The dead earth revived each spring to burst forth with new plant life; in addition, the earth contained the metals (copper and tin) from which bronze was made.

Consequently, the myth of Demeter and Persephone celebrates the arrival of springtime and the annual rebirth of nature. Although Demeter's sorrow at the absence of her daughter creates the barren winter season, the myth emphasizes the joy of their annual reunion and their happiness at being able to spend the greater part of each year together.

The most complete version of this myth is in *The Homeric Hymns*.

Demeter and Persephone

Demeter, the Great Goddess, bringer of seasons and giver of life-sustaining gifts, was the Olympian who most loved mortals and the earth that fed them, and they dearly loved her. She was delighted that farmers' wives set an extra place at the table in the hope that she would knock upon their door and join them in their evening meal. So she smiled when the gods teased her that she ate more meals in the humble homes of mortals than in the lofty palaces that Hephaestus had designed and the Cyclopes had built for the immortals on Mount Olympus. Demeter was kind, loving, and generous, but she was also the daughter of Cronus, feared ruler of the Titans, and the sister of Zeus, the Loud-Thunderer.

The joy of Demeter's eternal lifetime was her daughter, Persephone, whom she had borne to Zeus. Persephone loved sunshine, wildflowers, and laughter, and she had the gift of bringing what she loved into the lives of those who knew her. The wildflowers in Sicily were so beautiful that Persephone often roamed the fields there, carrying a large basket that she could fill with the beautiful blossoms. Bright-eyed Athena and Artemis, the archer goddess, usually accompanied her.

Aphrodite watched one day as Hades, lord of the dead, drove his chariot around the island of Sicily. As usual, the king of shadows was checking to see whether the unruly giant Typhon, who lay on his back under Mount Aetna vomiting fire and flaming ash, had created any cracks in the earth with his eruptions. Hades was quite relieved to find every piece of earth in its proper place, for he feared that if the earth opened above the Underworld and admitted the light of Helios' bright sun, his many subjects would tremble fearfully.

Calling her son, Eros, to her, golden Aphrodite said, "Few of the immortals have a high regard for our powers. Notice how Athena, Artemis, and Persephone all shun the idea of love. Zeus and his brother, the lord of the sea, have been subjected to our weapons, and it is time for us to rule the dark lord of the Underworld as well. Send one of your infallible arrows flying into Hades' heart, to make him fall madly in love with Persephone."

Eros' sure aim brought Hades to Zeus for permission to marry Persephone. "Of course, I would be delighted to give you Persephone, dear brother," Zeus replied, "but our sister, Demeter, would never agree to such a marriage. She would not permit me to exchange Persephone's freedom to roam through flower-filled fields, shimmering under the light from Lord Helios' chariot, for the opportunity to be queen in your dark kingdom. Power does not mean that much to the Great Goddess or to Persephone.

"However," the lord of Olympus concluded, "since you are my brother and the ruler of a mighty kingdom, if you insist on having Persephone, that would be a great honor for her. Although I cannot force my daughter to marry you, I shall secretly help you to seize her."

So it came about that one day, as Persephone was gathering flowers on one of the Sicilian meadows, she noticed in the distance an incredibly beautiful bloom that she had never seen before. Leaving her companions far behind, Persephone immediately ran over the fields toward this unusual flower. She had no way of knowing that her father secretly had commanded the earth to create this special flower as a lure in order to please Hades.

As Persephone reached toward the fragrant flower to add it to her collection, the earth suddenly opened wide, and out came a golden chariot drawn by black horses and driven by the dark lord himself. Keeping his left hand on the reins, Hades extended his right arm, lifted Persephone off the ground, placed her beside him in the chariot, and drove off at top speed before Persephone's companions realized that she had disappeared.

"Mother! Mother!" she screamed. "Help me! Father, help me!" But her mother was far away, and no one among the gods or mortals heard her screams. Only Helios, lord of the sun, observed the crime from his chariot as he traveled across the sky. By the time Artemis and Athena arrived at the meadow, the crevice had closed, the unusual flower had disappeared, and Persephone was gone. All that remained was the basket filled with flowers that the young goddess had dropped when she was snatched away.

Persephone continued to call for her mother as the chariot carried her through deep lakes and smoking pools. As long as she could see the grain-giving land, the swift-flowing sea, and Helios above her in his chariot, she hoped that someone would hear her cries. But when a sea nymph tried to stop Hades, he struck the earth, opened a crevice, and disappeared with Persephone into its dreary depths.

For some time after the earth had closed upon Persephone, the sound of her voice echoed from the mountain heights and issued forth from the depths of the sea. When the Great Goddess heard her daughter's cries, pain enclosed her heart in its mighty grip. From her lovely hair she tore its band, from her shoulders she loosened her dark cape, and freely she ran, like a wild bird, over land and sea, desperately searching everywhere for her lost child.

The deathless gods who knew where Persephone was remained silent. Mortals could not help the grieving and distraught mother. So that the darkness of night would not slow her search, the Great Goddess kindled two pine torches in the fiery crater of Mount Aetna. From that time on, neither Dawn nor the evening star found her at rest. But she searched the earth in vain.

At last, Demeter returned to Sicily, where Persephone had last been seen and her own fruitless search had begun. Not knowing who to blame, Demeter punished Sicily first. If no one could tell her what had happened to her daughter, she would withdraw her life-sustaining gifts. So she broke the plows, killed the oxen and the farmers who owned them, and commanded the earth to shrivel and mold the seeds it harbored. Soon the very land that had been famed for its fertility became barren. First, the country was plagued by drought. Then, blasting winds brought with them a deluge of rain. Corn that had not withered upon the stalk was devoured by greedy birds.

From Sicily, the Great Goddess wandered back across the earth, causing a year of drought and devastation for all of humankind. She so concealed the nourishing seeds within the earth that not one of them sprouted. Even when teams of oxen pulled curved plows over the fields so that the farmers following behind could plant white corn, golden-haired Demeter made all of their labor come to naught.

Then, still carrying her flaming torches, the Great Goddess approached the lord of the sun, who watched both gods and mortals. Placing herself in front of Helios' horse-drawn chariot, Demeter said, "I heard my daughter scream as if someone had seized her against her will, and yet I have been unable to learn what has happened to her. Since your chariot takes you high above the grain-giving land and the swift-flowing sea, did you see who took my child?"

To these words Lord Helios replied, "I shall tell you the truth, Great Goddess, for I pity you in your sorrow. Zeus, the cloud-gatherer, gave Persephone to the lord of the dead to become his queen. You heard her cries as Hades carried her down to his gloomy kingdom. Yet the marriage is a good one, since the dark lord is your brother and rules a mighty kingdom. Try to put aside your anger and your grief."

Demeter's heart now overflowed with a deeper and more savage sorrow. Torn between fury and anguish, the Great Goddess determined to punish Zeus and the other Olympians by causing all mortals to die of starvation. Then the deathless gods would no longer be honored with sacrifices and gifts, and grim Hades would gain more shades to honor him.

Zeus, fearing that such might be her intent, sent wind-footed Iris to command Demeter to return to Mount Olympus. When the Great Goddess did not respond, Zeus commanded the other Olympian gods, one by one, to approach her and offer her greater honor and glorious gifts. However, Demeter refused all but the last of them. To him she said, "Tell Zeus that I shall set foot upon fragrant Olympus in order to talk with him, but I shall not permit any seeds to sprout upon the earth until I have seen my beautiful child."

When the Great Goddess approached Zeus she said, "Father of gods and mortals, I come pleading to you on behalf of our daughter. Even if you do not care for me, surely you love Persephone! You know how she loves the light of the sun, the joyous sound of laughter, and the scent of flowers. How can you make her live in our brother's dark and dismal kingdom, ruling over the dead when she so loves life? And how could you permit her to marry someone who had to seize her against her will? Tell Hades that he must let her go!"

"Truly, Demeter," Zeus replied, "I share your love and your concern for our daughter. However, Hades seized Persephone because he loves her, and he is as great a god as I am. Only the drawing of lots gave the Underworld to him and Olympus to me. If our brother's love and power cannot make you put aside your anger and resentment, then I shall let Persephone return to you — as long as she has eaten no food in Hades' dark kingdom. But if she has consumed the food of the dead she is condemned to remain in that dismal land, for so the Fates decree."

To these words the Great Goddess replied: "I shall meet Persephone on the meadows she loves. Until then, the earth will remain lifeless and barren. Farewell."

As Demeter departed, Zeus sent his messenger Hermes, the Wayfinder, down to Hades' grim kingdom to persuade the dark lord with kind words to let Persephone return to her mother. Hermes found the lord of the Underworld in his gloomy palace and said, "Hades, kind uncle and lord of the dead, my father has commanded me to bring Persephone up to her mother.

"The Great Goddess," Hermes continued, "has threatened to destroy all mortals by withholding their source of food, thus removing from the gods their source of honor and sacrificial offerings. She has hidden all seeds deep in the earth where they cannot sprout, and not one of the Olympians has been able to soften the rage and grief that fill her heart."

At these words, Hades smiled grimly, but to Persephone he kindly said, "Go now with Hermes to seek your dark-robed mother. But, in your heart, know that I too love you and want you here with me.

"Think of me with kindness," Hades continued, "for I shall be a good husband to you. Remember that I am the brother of Zeus and my kingdom is also very great. While you are here, you will rule everything that lives and moves, and I shall see that you receive the greatest honor among the deathless gods. I shall punish for eternity anyone who wrongs you or who does not worship you with sacred rites and sacrifices."

When she heard her husband's words, Persephone's heart filled with joy. While the Wayfinder harnessed Hades' immortal horses to his golden chariot, the lord of the Underworld gave Persephone a honey-sweet pomegranate seed to eat so that his beloved wife could not remain forever in the upper world. Persephone, unaware of the consequences, swallowed the seed.

When she had mounted the chariot, Hermes took the reins and the whip into his hands, and they quickly left the palace. Once the deathless horses reached the upper air, neither the swift-flowing sea nor grassy meadows nor the peaks of mountains were any obstacle to Hades' swift steeds.

Demeter waited for Persephone in a meadow that should have been ablaze with the colorful flowers of summer. Now, however, this ground, like the lands that in prior years had produced rich crops of corn and wheat, lay barren and idle. As soon as she saw Hades' golden chariot, the Great Goddess rushed to meet her daughter. Hermes had barely halted the horses before Persephone leaped down from the chariot and threw her arms around her mother's neck in a long, happy embrace.

As Demeter held her dear child in her arms, her heart filled with fear, and she suddenly asked Persephone, "My child, tell me truly, when you were in Lord Hades' dark kingdom, did you taste any food? If you ate nothing there, you can live here where the sun shines with your father and me. But if you had any kind of nourishment you must return to your husband, for the Fates have decreed that anyone who eats the food of the dead must remain in the dismal land of death!"

Persephone's eyes filled with tears, and she replied, "I shall not attempt to deceive you, Mother. As Hermes was about to bring me to you, my husband gave me a honey-sweet pomegranate seed to eat. I swallowed it because I was hungry; I had no idea of the consequences."

Tears then flowed uncontrollably from Demeter's eyes, for it seemed that her visit with her dear child was doomed to be brief. Sorrow and despair threatened to push all the joy of their reunion from her heart. She felt she could not bear their eternal separation.

Suddenly, Demeter's spirits lifted with surprise and delight as she saw her own mother, Rhea, approaching them. With great love, the mother of the gods embraced her daughter and her granddaughter.

"Come, my child," said Rhea. "A mother must have the strength to bear pain as well as joy. Sorrow visits all of us. You must not let your grief destroy you.

"I have come from Mount Olympus," Rhea continued, "and I bring you a special message from your brother, Zeus. He wishes you to rejoin the Olympian family, where you will be highly honored among the deathless gods. He gives you his word that Persephone need spend only one-third of each year in Hades' dark and gloomy kingdom. When the time comes each year for the earth to bring forth the fragrant flowers of springtime, she will leave the kingdom of darkness and return to you. You will be together until all of the crops have been harvested and Helios, lord of the sun, has caused the days to become short and cool.

"So put aside your anger against Zeus, my child. Enjoy your lovely daughter for the seasons that you can be together, and make the earth once again yield the life-giving fruits that mortals need to sustain them."

Demeter heard her mother's words and smiled through her tears. She would have her daughter after all! These separations she could endure. Immediately, she caused the fertile land to blossom with leaves, flowers, and life-giving fruits. Then the goddesses joined the immortals on Mount Olympus.

Thus the pattern of the seasons became established. Each year, after the harvesting of the autumn crops, Persephone would return to her husband, the dark lord of the dead, for the winter months. Then, in her loneliness and sorrow, Demeter would allow the earth to lie leafless and idle.

As soon as Lord Helios once again warmed the earth with the sun, and the days became longer, the Great Goddess would see her beloved child joyously running toward her. Once again, in her great joy, Demeter would cause all flowers and seed-bearing plants to blossom upon the earth. Once again, she would bless the mortals she loved with her life-sustaining gifts.

Then people would often see a beautiful mother and daughter roaming together through sunny flowering meadows. Farmers' wives once again would set an extra place at their table for the evening meal, hoping that their beloved Demeter would join them to share the fruits of their labors.

Introducing **The Flood Cycle**

Sometime between 3000 and 2000 B.C., a great flood occurred in Mesopotamia. This event had such an impact upon the peoples who lived in that area that several flood myths of striking similarity developed. One is Sumerian, one is Greek, and one is Biblical.

In all three myths, a mortal is warned to prepare for a great flood. He builds an ark, stores the necessities of life on board, and survives. After the flood he lands safely on a mountainside, and the human race continues. Whether the flood arrives as a divine punishment for improper mortal behavior or as a capricious divine whim depends upon the nature of the divinity or divinities involved. Like the Biblical flood, the Greek flood is a punishment for immoral behavior.

In ancient Greece, principles of behavior were transmitted through myths instead of by divine commandment. The Lycaon myth is particularly important because it instructed the Greek people that their gods (with the exception of Artemis) *opposed* human sacrifice and cannibalism.

Human sacrifice is historically one of the oldest forms of religious sacrifice. As a community becomes more civilized, it moves from human sacrifice to the sacrifice of animals and food, and then to prayers and self-denial. In matriarchal societies, as part of the worship of the Great Goddess or Mother Goddess, the sacred king was killed and dismembered. His organs were mixed with meat and served to the worshippers to promote their fertility. Cannibalism apparently existed in Greece at one time, prior to the creation of the Lycaon myth.

Traditionally in the creation myths, the first humans were created from whatever materials were plentiful in the particular culture. In the mythology of the Navajo people, for example, First Man and First Woman were created from ears of corn. In Norse mythology, they were created from two trees. Because Greece is very mountainous and its soil very rocky, the use of stones for the creation of the new generation of human beings is very appropriate.

The Roman poet Ovid tells the following myth in *Metamorphoses*.

The Flood Cycle

Lycaon: The Cause

Early in Zeus' reign as lord of Olympus, a race of mortals lived upon the earth who cared only about themselves. When word reached Zeus that these human beings had no respect for anyone, either mortal or divine, he decided to see for himself whether what he had heard was, in fact, true. He chose to wander upon the earth in the disguise of an ordinary mortal traveler in order to learn the true nature of human beings.

Much to his dismay, Zeus discovered that mortals were even more wicked than he had heard. No matter where he wandered, he saw human beings commit crimes of every sort, for they had no sense of what it was to be humane. They were cruel to one another, they did not welcome uninvited guests, and they did not honor the deathless gods. However, Zeus continued on his journey, for he was certain that if he traveled long enough and far enough, he would find mortals who were sensitive, loving, and kind human beings and who feared the immortal gods.

Thus it happened that as Dusk pulled the chariot of Night across the evening sky, Zeus approached the palace of King Lycaon, which was located in the area in Arcadia famed for its pine woods. Seeing that the courtyard of the palace was deserted, Zeus followed the sound of human voices into the great hall, where the king, his family, and his nobles were eating their evening meal.

When Lycaon noticed that a stranger was standing in the entrance to his hall, he called out, "You, there! What are you doing in my palace? If you have come to beg for food, my servants will find some scraps for you. Wait outside by the gate."

To these words, Zeus replied, "It is appropriate for you to welcome the stranger among you, for the traveler and beggar are dear to Zeus, lord of Olympus. I have come from lands to the north and ask for your hospitality. I stand before you, both as the stranger and as Zeus, father of gods and mortals."

Some of the nobles immediately looked with respect and awe upon the stranger in the doorway. Lycaon, however, laughed and said, "Arcadians, you believe whatever you hear too readily! Why worship an ordinary stranger? If this god is what he claims to be, he will most certainly make that fact known to us.

If he is not, he deserves no special treatment within these halls. Watch how I test him; I have a way to prove beyond a doubt whether his flesh is mortal or divine. First, of course, I shall have him eat with us, for that is the proper thing to do.

"Bring forth a platter of some freshly prepared meats," he commanded one of the servants. "We cannot honor the king of the gods with cold food, can we! Meanwhile," the king said to the stranger, "the place at the head of the table will be yours, for it is the place of honor, and you say you are the great Zeus."

The servant soon returned with a platter of freshly cooked meats, some boiled, some roasted. As the king took the platter of meat, his eyes glinted with amusement and excitement. With a great flourish, he set the platter down in front of the stranger, who was now sitting at the head of the table.

"Zeus, lord of Olympus, and the acknowledged father of every god and every mortal man," Lycaon cried, "accept this sacrifice as a token of the great esteem with which we mortals, here in Arcadia, regard you!"

The stranger took one look at the meat upon the platter, and his being shook with revulsion and disgust. One piece of meat covered the bony structure of a young man's hand, while another appeared to be one of his feet. Strewn between them like pieces of stew were parts of the victim's heart and liver. This was indeed Lycaon's test of his guest's identity, for with the exception of Artemis, the archer goddess, no Olympian god would accept a human sacrifice.

Suddenly and without a word, the stranger pushed over the table and rose to his feet. As he looked at King Lycaon, his eyes blazed as bright as the chariot of Helios at midday. Suddenly a deafening roar filled the great hall, accompanied by a blinding flash of light. The wooden table burst into flames that seemed to touch the roof-beams. The nobles knocked over chairs and one another in their attempt to escape from the wrath of Zeus, but their efforts were futile. Only Lycaon was left alive.

The king could not take his eyes off the stranger, who stood within the blaze like a brighter flame in huge, human shape. The stranger seemed to be growing taller and taller as Lycaon looked at him. In fact, as the king stared, he felt his backbone bend so that it became too painful to stand upright. Only with his hands and feet upon the floor could he feel comfortable. When Lycaon finally withdrew his eyes from the stranger's gaze, he found that his head was now very close to the floor. There, beneath him he noticed two paws where his hands had been, attached to two long, hairy legs. Hysterical with fear, the king opened his mouth to scream, but the only sound that emerged was a long howl.

Lycaon tore from the room as fast as his four legs could transport him, howling again and again to warn the Arcadians of their danger. The air outside felt cool and refreshing, but now Lycaon was excruciatingly hungry. He could feel foam dripping from his mouth as he thought about the delicious taste of raw meat. Drawn to the sheepfold, he slashed into the nearest ram, delighting in the taste of its warm blood.

No longer did the king think with horror about his transformation. As he ran over the fields, he found the smell of the grass, the feel of the ground beneath his feet, and the taste of fresh, raw meat satisfying indeed.

Yet Lycaon had not changed very much. It is true that gray hairs, rather than rich garments, now robed his body, but his eyes were still red, his face was still fierce, and his thoughts were no more bestial than they had been when he was a king. Lycaon had always been a wolf.

The Flood: Punishment

Zeus, lord of thunder and black clouds, returned to Mount Olympus determined to punish all mortals for their evil ways. Although the deathless gods approved their king's decision to destroy the human race, they were concerned about the future. Without mortals, who would offer sweet-smelling sacrifices to the gods? Zeus calmed their fears when he assured them that he would create another, better human race once he had destroyed the present one.

Zeus prepared to destroy the earth with his lightning bolts. Then he realized that Mount Olympus also would ignite from such a blaze and put aside his weapons. Instead, he decided to release his black storm clouds and destroy the mortals by flooding the entire earth.

Zeus then sent his messenger, Hermes, to his servant Aeolus, lord of the winds, and commanded him to imprison in his cave the winds that dry the earth and bring clear weather, but to free all of the storm winds. Out flew the dreaded South Wind, shrouded in black clouds. His beard was swollen with showers, and rain poured from his wings and his clothing. As he flew, his hands made the heavens roar, for he crushed all the moisture out of the clouds around him, causing heavy rains to fall upon land and sea.

As the rains destroyed all of the corn and wheat, the farmers mourned the loss of their year's labors. Yet Zeus' anger still raged unappeased within his heart. He enlisted the aid of his brother Poseidon, who commanded the rivers and streams to overflow all barriers and rush upon the earth without restraint. The lord of the sea also shook the earth with his great trident, so that water had new cracks and crevices to fill and flood.

A blanket of water now unrolled upon the earth, covering the open fields, forests and orchards, cattle and sheep, houses, people and even the temples of the gods. Higher and higher the water rose, swallowing the tallest buildings, until the earth was one huge sea, with no shore in sight.

People tried to survive the catastrophe as best they could. Some climbed the highest hills. Others set off in boats, rowing over the land they had recently plowed or over their own drowned town or vineyard. Fish became entangled in the leafy branches of trees, and sea animals now rested where mountain goats had lately grazed. Sea nymphs busily explored cities, temples, and groves of fruit, while dolphins followed forest paths.

Wolves swam among the sheep, and lions and tigers together tried to stay afloat. The rabbit's swift feet could no longer help him, nor could the boar's dreadful tusks wound this new foe. Birds flew over the seas anxiously hoping to sight some place of refuge; finding none, they finally dropped into the endless waters, hopeless and exhausted. The ever-rising waters swam over the hills and washed the highest mountain peaks with their waves. The few people who escaped death by drowning starved to death.

Deucalion and Pyrrha: Rebirth

The creative Titan Prometheus had fashioned the first mortal beings, the race that Zeus was now destroying, out of earth and water. Because Prometheus had helped his humans by stealing fire from the forge of Hephaestus, the immortal metalsmith, Zeus had punished him by ordering Hephaestus to nail him to Mount Caucasus in Scythia (the area to the north and northeast of the Black Sea).

Prometheus could foresee all future events except those affecting his own immortal life. When he knew that Zeus, the Loud-Thunderer, was about to destroy the people whom he had created and whom he dearly loved, he called out to his mortal son, Deucalion, while Deucalion was asleep. In his dream, Deucalion heard his father counsel him to build a very large chest and to stock it with all kinds of provisions, such as food, clothing, and tools.

When the heavy rains came and their land flooded, Deucalion and his wife, Pyrrha, boarded their chest and floated away. They floated upon the swollen seas for nine days and nine nights.

When Zeus looked down from Mount Olympus and saw that the seas had swallowed all men and women except for Deucalion and Pyrrha, who were innocent, kind, god-fearing people, he commanded Aeolus to imprison the South Wind and to free Boreas, the North Wind, for Boreas would chase the storm clouds away and dry the seas. The lord of black clouds also directed Poseidon to lay aside his trident and calm the wild waves.

Poseidon, in turn, commanded Triton, a sea god, to blow upon his loud-sounding shell and order all the floods to retreat. As they obeyed, the seas again revealed their shores, the streams sank and stayed within the confines of their channels, and the hills rose once more above the water.

When the rains finally stopped, Deucalion and Pyrrha saw the twin peaks of Mount Parnassus, which had escaped the waters of the flood because they reached above the clouds and touched the stars of evening. The couple guided their chest in that direction and floated by the side of Mount Parnassus until the receding waters left their craft on solid land.

With the greatest joy the two set foot on land once more, but soon sorrow pushed away their delight. Without any living beings, the earth was deathly silent and desolate. They were all alone.

Tearfully, Deucalion said to Pyrrha, "Dear wife, you are the only one of all your sex still alive. As Helios drives his chariot across the sky, we are the only two people he can see, for the sea has swallowed everyone else. Nor can we be sure of living in safety even now, for the clouds above us are still black and threatening.

"However, at least we have each other!" Deucalion continued. "If Fate had kept you alive but taken me from you, what would you have done, being all alone in the world as we are? Who could calm your fears or soothe your sorrows? Where would you find comfort and companionship? I know that if the seas had swallowed you, I would have followed your path, for I could not have borne this isolation without you!

"Oh, how I wish that I had my father's creative talents!" he concluded. "Then I, too, would shape people out of clay and put living souls into their bodies. As it is, we are the last two members of our mortal race."

With these words, both Deucalion and Pyrrha wept and offered prayers of gratitude to the gods on Mount Olympus for saving their lives. Then they decided to seek the oracle of Themis, the Great Goddess of the Titans, who would know all that was to come.

The temple of Themis was slimy with moss and mud, and the fire that once had continually burned upon the altar blazed no more. The couple lay down upon the floor, kissed the cold stones, and prayed. "If the deathless gods are able to put aside their great anger, may they listen and grant our wish. Great Themis, tell us how to renew our race; they have drowned, and we who remain are in despair."

To these words the compassionate goddess replied, "When you leave my temple, loosen your clothing so that it flows freely around you. Then hide your faces, and throw the bones of your great mother behind you."

After a long silence Pyrrha said to Deucalion, "I may not obey the Great Goddess. I tremble as I beg her pardon, but my mother's shade would wander homeless if I disturbed her bones."

Surely, however, the Great Goddess was well aware of this problem, so Deucalion and Pyrrha slowly repeated the strange set of directions, hoping to find another meaning buried in those words. Finally, Deucalion said, "The deathless gods are just; they would not command us to do something evil. Unless I misunderstand the oracle, the earth is our great mother, and her bones are the stones and rocks around us."

Pyrrha then replied, "You may be right, Deucalion, but the idea makes no sense to me. However, it will do no harm, and we should trust the gods."

So Pyrrha and Deucalion unbelted their clothing, covered their heads, and gathered the stones that surrounded them, carrying them in the folds of their clothing. Then side by side they walked down the slopes of Mount Parnassus and looked straight ahead while they tossed the stones over their shoulders behind them.

Once they hit the earth, the stones began to lose their hardness. As they became softer, they began to grow larger and to assume the shape of human beings. Within a short time they already looked like rough-hewn marble statues that needed only the sculptor's finishing touches in order to appear alive. The solid part of each rock turned into human bone, while the part that contained soft, moist earth became flesh. The veins remained as they had been in the rock, only now they were human veins. The rocks that Deucalion threw became men; Pyrrha's rocks became women. Between the two of them, they created a race of human beings who possessed the strength and endurance of the material from which they had been formed.

The fertile earth herself reproduced all the other forms of life. When Helios once again brought the light of the sun to shine upon the earth, which was still very muddy and damp from the great flood, the Great Mother brought forth all the old forms of life, and some new ones as well.

Introducing **The Labors and Death of Heracles**

Heracles was the most famous and popular of the Greek heroes. He was often called the "defender of the earth." His labors took him to all parts of the known world, and, wherever he went, he made the land a safer place for people to live. He received very little help from the gods; his achievements were truly his own.

Heracles is an unusual Greek hero in that he does not seek the glory, fame, or power that he acquires. Initially, he refuses to perform the labors, even if they will make him famous, because he will not subjugate himself to a morally inferior person. He finally decides to perform the labors, not to achieve the reward of immortality—the fondest wish of mortals throughout human history—but only because it is a divine command.

The labors of Heracles indicate that he probably existed in the matriarchal culture. In that female-dominated society, the youth who aspired to become the sacred king and the companion of the reigning priestess of the Great Goddess had to compete against a number of other contenders for this, the greatest honor a man could achieve. Such a youth would have to win various contests that were similar to the tasks Eurystheus assigned to Heracles. Traditional competitions included: an archery contest in which the archer shot an arrow through a ring or a series of rings; fights with wild beasts, such as a lion, a boar, and a bull; a wrestling match with a mighty opponent; the plowing of a hill or field in one day; and the bridling of wild horses.

Apollodorus gives the most complete version of Heracles' labors in *The Library*.

The Labors and Death of Heracles

Heracles was the son of Zeus and a mortal woman. The lord of Olympus wanted to be certain that Heracles earned eternal fame, but he also wanted to please Hera, who hated his children by other women. Therefore, Zeus promised Hera that Heracles would have to perform for King Eurystheus of Tiryns whatever ten labors the king commanded. Only then would Zeus make Heracles immortal.

Heracles earned his name when he was eight months old, for Hera unintentionally caused him to win great glory (*Hera* + *kleos*: glory). Wishing to kill him, she sent two huge snakes into his nursery. As the snakes approached his bed,

Heracles gleefully extended his arms, grabbed a snake in each hand, and strangled both serpents.

Heracles continued to earn fame as he grew into manhood. He married a princess and became the father of three sons. Eurystheus, fearing that Heracles would become a threat to his power, commanded him to perform the labors. When Heracles refused to become Eurystheus' servant, Hera caused Heracles to become insane. In a fit of madness, he picked up his great bow and shot his children, thinking that they were enemies.

Upon recovering his sanity, Heracles withdrew from all society, became purified of his crime, and sought the advice of the oracle of Delphi. The oracle informed Heracles that he must obey the will of the gods by performing whatever ten labors Eurystheus commanded, and that he would then become immortal. Heracles obeyed the oracle and placed himself in the service of the king.

Eurystheus first commanded Heracles to bring him the skin of the lion of Nemea. Heracles knew that the beast could not be hurt by stone or bronze, so he would have to devise some other way to kill it. When he came upon the lion, he learned that his arrows and his huge wooden club were also useless. The lion responded to Heracles' attack by retreating into a cave that had two exits. Heracles blocked one exit with a huge rock and entered the cave through the other opening. He wrestled with the beast until, finally, he was able to put one arm around the lion's neck, tighten his grip, and choke it to death. Heracles left the cave wearing the lion's skin as a fearsome trophy.

When Heracles returned to Tiryns dressed as the Nemean lion, Eurystheus was so frightened by the sight that he ordered Heracles to remain outside the city gates. Thereafter, Eurystheus communicated with Heracles by having one of his servants act as his messenger.

For his second labor, Eurystheus commanded Heracles to kill the Hydra of Lerna. This monster lived in a swamp and scoured the nearby countryside in search of cattle to eat. It had nine snake-like heads upon its huge body, and the middle head was immortal. First, Heracles forced the monster out of the swamp by shooting blazing arrows at it. Then he grabbed the Hydra and tried to smash its heads with his club. But wherever Heracles destroyed one head, two new heads replaced it. Seeing that such schemes would only multiply his problem, Heracles ordered his nephew and traveling companion, Iolas, to put a log into a fire and create a white-hot brand.

Then Heracles cut off the Hydra's mortal heads one by one. As he severed them, Iolas immediately seared and sealed the monster's raw flesh before a new set of heads could sprout. Heracles cut off the one immortal head and buried it under a huge rock by the side of the road. Finally, he sliced the Hydra's body into pieces and dipped his arrows into the monster's blood, for a wound infested with the Hydra's deadly poison was incurable. When Heracles returned to Tiryns, Eurystheus declared that this labor did not count because Iolas had helped perform it.

For his third labor, Eurystheus commanded Heracles to bring to Tiryns the swift deer with golden horns that was sacred to Artemis, goddess of the hunt. Heracles realized that if he wounded the deer, he would anger Artemis. So instead of shooting it, he pursued it for an entire year. Finally, the deer lay down, exhausted, and Heracles captured it. He enclosed it in a net, slung the net over his shoulders, and returned with it to Tiryns.

Heracles' fourth labor involved capturing the Erymanthian boar and carrying it, alive, back to Tiryns. The wild boar was extremely dangerous because of its sharp tusks, and it was incredibly fast in spite of its short legs. Heracles chased it up a mountainside into deep snow, where it could no longer run swiftly. When the beast was too exhausted to challenge Heracles with its tusks, the hero bound its feet and carried it back to Tiryns on his shoulders.

For his fifth labor, Eurystheus chose to humiliate Heracles by ordering him to clean the stables of King Augeas in one day. If the stables had ever been clean, no one remembered it, and many herds of cattle had left dung piled high. To preserve his dignity, Heracles did not mention Eurystheus' command. Instead, he approached the king and offered to clean the stables in a day in return for some cattle.

When Augeas agreed, Heracles changed the course of two nearby rivers so that they ran through the stables and washed away the dung. However, when the king learned that Heracles had been ordered to clean the stables, he would not pay him. Also, Eurystheus would not accept this labor because Heracles had performed it in return for a promise of payment.

For his sixth labor, Eurystheus commanded Heracles to chase the hordes of Stymphalian birds away from the lake of that name in Arcadia. The birds were robbing the farmers of the fruits of their orchards and were dangerous as well, for they would shoot their feathers like arrows. Athena helped Heracles by giving him a bronze rattle that made such a dreadful noise it frightened the birds away.

The seventh labor required Heracles to journey to Crete and capture the bull that Poseidon had sent to King Minos for a special sacrifice. When the king did not kill the beautiful bull as he had promised, the lord of the sea turned it into a ferocious beast. Heracles caught the bull, brought it back to Tiryns, and set it free.

For his eighth labor, Heracles had to capture the mares of King Diomedes, which ate human flesh. He found them chained to their bronze troughs, feeding upon the arms and legs of strangers. Heracles was so angered by the king's savage nature that he killed Diomedes and fed his body to his mares. Once the horses ate the flesh of the man who had trained them to enjoy eating people, Heracles could control them. He took them to Eurystheus, who set them free. The mares then climbed Mount Olympus, where wild animals killed them.

In the course of performing this labor, Heracles stopped to visit his good friend King Admetus, whose wife, Alcestis, had just died. Heracles wrestled with Death for her life and won the contest, thereby restoring Alcestis to her husband.

For his ninth labor, Eurystheus commanded Heracles to bring him the belt of the Amazon queen, Hippolyte, because his daughter wanted it. The Amazons were an aggressive tribe of female warriors, and Ares, god of war, had given Hippolyte her belt. When Heracles arrived, Hippolyte met him; once she knew why he needed it, she gave him her belt. Hera felt this was too easy, so the goddess disguised herself as an Amazon and shouted that Heracles was abducting their queen. When the warrior women attacked him, Heracles thought Hippolyte had betrayed him, so he killed her, took her belt, and returned to Tiryns.

For his tenth labor, Eurystheus commanded Heracles to bring him the beautiful red cattle of the monstrous giant Geryon, who had the form of three men joined together at the waist. Guarding the cattle was a two-headed dog named Orthus. When Orthus attacked him, Heracles clubbed the dog to death and began to herd the cattle. Geryon met Heracles by the river and tried to stop him. Heracles moved to the giant's side, raised his mighty bow, and killed Geryon by shooting one arrow through his triple body.

On his way back to Tiryns with Geryon's cattle, Heracles stopped along the Tiber River and lay down to rest. A monstrous, fire-belching giant named Cacus saw the beautiful cattle and stole the best oxen. Craftily, Cacus disguised the path to his cave by dragging the oxen backwards by their tails. When Heracles awoke, he noticed that some of his cattle were missing. He found the nearest cave, but the only animal tracks he saw led away from the cave rather than into it. However, as he moved off with his cattle they mooed, and to his surprise, Heracles heard a response from inside the cave.

Heracles then took his great club and headed for the cave. Cacus, seeing him approach, lowered a gigantic rock into the doorway, sealing himself and the stolen cattle within the cave. Three times Heracles climbed above and around the cave, trying to find a way to reach the giant. Finally, he set his weight against a large rock that was part of the roof of the cave and, with all of his might, pushed it upon its side. As the rock moved toward the earth, the murky interior of Cacus' den was revealed.

Gazing down upon the roaring, fire-spewing giant, Heracles saw pale, decaying heads of men nailed to the cave's walls and smelled the foul odor of blood. First he hurled huge rocks and tree trunks upon Cacus. Then, undaunted by the clouds of black smoke that issued forth from the depths below, he jumped into the cave, threw his arm around the giant's throat, and squeezed with all his strength. When he had permanently extinguished Cacus' fires, and the giant lay dead upon the floor, Heracles moved the stone from the doorway. He dragged the giant out by his feet, led forth the cattle, and went on his way.

Eight years had now passed since Heracles had begun his labors. For his eleventh labor, Eurystheus commanded Heracles to collect the golden apples of the Hesperides, daughters of the Titan Atlas, who held the sky upon his shoulders. Gaea had given the apple trees to Hera as a wedding gift, and they were guarded by a hundred-headed, immortal dragon who spoke in many different voices.

In order to locate the garden, Heracles had to consult Nereus, the old man of the sea. When Heracles found him along the shore and grabbed him, the sea god tried to frighten Heracles away by turning himself into a series of fearful sights. He became a raging fire, a roaring lion, a slithery snake, and a torrent of water, but through every change in appearance, Heracles held on to the figure beneath the apparition. In the end, Nereus gave up and gave Heracles the directions he needed.

On his way to the garden, Heracles passed through Libya, which was ruled by a giant son of Gaea named Antaeus. Antaeus was an unusually strong and skillful wrestler and challenged every stranger to a wrestling match. Antaeus inevitably won and put the loser to death. Then he hung the head of his latest victim next to his other trophies on the temple of Poseidon.

When Antaeus forced Heracles to wrestle with him, Heracles noticed that whenever any part of the giant's body touched the earth, he immediately became much stronger. Heracles realized that, in order to win this contest, he would have to prevent Antaeus' mother from renewing her son's strength. Therefore, Heracles hugged Antaeus and, using his deathly grip and all his might, he lifted the giant into the air and held him there, strangling, until he died. Then Heracles killed all the wild beasts in the country, enabling farmers to plant olive orchards and vineyards.

Heracles continued his journey, which took him to the Caucasus. There he found the Titan Prometheus nailed to the mountain and helpless as Zeus' eagle tore out his liver. Heracles raised his giant bow and killed the bird; then he freed Prometheus. In return, Prometheus advised Heracles that he should find Atlas and take the sky upon his own shoulders, sending Atlas for the golden apples instead of attempting to deal with the dragon and gather them himself.

Heracles followed Prometheus' advice. Atlas returned with the apples but announced that he was tired of holding the sky upon his shoulders and that he would take the apples to King Eurystheus himself. Heracles immediately agreed to take over Atlas' task, but craftily asked Atlas to hold the sky temporarily while he put a pad upon his head to make the weight more tolerable. Atlas helpfully put the apples upon the ground and accepted the sky. Heracles quickly picked up the apples and left the gigantic Titan with his awesome burden.

For his twelfth and final labor, Eurystheus commanded Heracles to enter the Underworld and return with Cerberus, the monstrous, three-headed dog that guarded the entrance to the dread kingdom of Hades. Heracles was accompanied by Hermes, the Wayfinder, who leads the shades of the dead down to the Underworld.

Heracles approached Hades and asked his permission to take Cerberus to King Eurystheus. The lord of the dead agreed on the condition that Heracles must capture the monstrous hound without using any weapon. Hades' command challenged Heracles because, in addition to its three heads, Cerberus had a back covered with snakes and the tail of a dragon. Heracles covered himself with his protective lion skin, embraced the three-headed monster, and never let go. He carried the hound up to Tiryns, showed the monster to Eurystheus, and then returned it to Hades.

Heracles continued to have numerous adventures after he had completed his labors. Many years later, Heracles' wife, jealous that he might love another woman, sent her husband the gift of a tunic that had been soaked in the blood of the Hydra. An enemy of Heracles' had treacherously led her to believe that the tunic would cause Heracles to remain in love with her.

When Heracles put the tunic on, the heat of his body activated the poison, causing the tunic to stick to his skin and burn it. In agony, he immediately tore off the tunic, and with it his skin. Only death could relieve his misery, so he built a funeral pyre and lay down upon it. However, no one he asked was willing to put a torch to it and kill him. Finally, Philoctetes happened to pass by, and when he saw Heracles in such excruciating pain, he agreed to light the pyre. As a reward,

Heracles gave Philoctetes his great bow and arrows, which the young man, in later years, took to Troy.

Just as the burning torch touched the wood of the funeral pyre, a bolt of lightning flashed in the clear sky and struck the pyre. A cloud immediately descended into the roaring mass of flames, enveloped Heracles, and carried him up to Mount Olympus. After the fire had consumed the entire pyre, not even Heracles' bones remained among the ashes. Zeus had kept his promise; Heracles had become immortal.

Introducing **The Iliad**

Historical Background

The story of *The Iliad* occurs in about 1250 B.C., late in the Bronze or Mycenaean Age. The action is located in what is now Turkey, sometime during the last year of the Greek war against Troy.

As early as about 2600 B.C., Greek-speaking tribes from the north invaded the area of northern Greece known as Macedonia. Between 1900 and 1600 B.C., the descendants of these peoples moved southward to inhabit the rest of Greece. The golden age of their civilization occurred between 1450 B.C., when they conquered the island of Crete and adopted much of the technology and art of that advanced society, and about 1200 B.C., when their palace centers were sacked in civil wars.

Our knowledge of the Mycenaean civilization in Greece is based primarily upon what archaeologists have been able to discover. Fortunately, they have located and studied the ruins of a number of important sites in Greece and in Troy, the site of Homer's "Ilium" in Turkey. The material available to archaeologists is very limited, due to the ravages of time,

weather, fire, and theft. The materials that have survived include decorated objects—such as jewelry, pottery, and metal containers—and an assortment of war gear—shields, helmets, and various kinds of weapons. In addition, archaeologists have found a large number of clay tablets, inscribed with a language called Linear B, which they can read.

The Mycenaean civilization in full bloom far surpassed in complexity and wealth many of the Greek civilizations that followed it, including Homer's age. The Mycenaeans were an aggressive people who enjoyed fighting, hunting, and athletic contests. Except for the Peloponnese, their land was mountainous and their soil rocky and dry. Therefore, they took to the sea and became fearsome raiders of other communities. In this way they acquired extraordinary wealth. They lived and died with weapons by their sides; fortunately for archaeologists, they buried their dead in tombs along with the war gear and wealth they had possessed in life. The Mycenaeans loved decorated objects. Whether of gold, bronze, or clay, their arts and crafts reflected their interest in war and in hunting ferocious wild animals.

They constructed palaces that were fortified strongholds. For example, the palace at Mycenae, built in 1350 B.C., had walls twenty-three feet thick. The Mycenaeans who lived in these palaces were aristocrats, and each king's palace was the political, economic, and social center of his small kingdom.

Connected with the palace were the numerous nobles, artisans, scribes, farmers, and common laborers needed to keep the complex organization operating. The king had to be a strong, able, and aggressive leader who could protect the people in his palace community and gain wealth for its aristocratic members by sacking other communities.

Archaeological remains reveal very little about the religious practices of these people and nothing of their myths except the names of some of their gods. We can assume that the family was important because the dead are buried in family groups. We can assume that in an age of piracy and well-fortified palaces, hospitality was necessary for the traveler to survive, and yet people had to be very cautious about welcoming strangers.

Ancient Troy, Homer's Ilium, was located across the Aegean Sea from Mycenaean Greece, on the coast of what is now Turkey. Part of the city was built upon a large hill that, in modern times, has been called Hissarlik, or "Place of Fortresses." For six centuries, Troy was vitally important in the ancient world because of its unique location in terms of overland trade between Europe and Asia and marine trade between the Mediterranean and northeastern Europe.

Troy controlled the Hellespont strait (now called the Dardanelles), a narrow waterway that functioned as the gateway from the Aegean Sea to the Black Sea, with its access to three major rivers, the Danube from Germany, the Don from Russia, and the Dnieper from the Ukraine. The Mycenaean Greeks and other ancient peoples valued items such as pure copper that they could obtain in trade with those who inhabited the lands of northeastern Europe.

However, the prevalence of unfavorable wind and current patterns in the Hellespont strait usually forced ships en route to the Black Sea to wait for long periods of time in Troy's harbor, now known as Besik Bay, until favorable conditions permitted them to continue their journey. For hundreds of years, Troy took advantage of this situation by collecting a large toll for the privilege of using its harbor. Consequently, given its strategic location at the mouth of this major trade route, Homer's Ilium was an extraordinarily powerful and wealthy Mycenaean city.

Homer's Ilium was the sixth of nine cities that existed on the same site, and it is likely that the Mycenaean Greeks attacked the great walled citadel for economic reasons—either for unhindered access to the Black Sea or for Troy's fabulous wealth. The Mycenaean Greeks destroyed Troy VI in about 1250 B.C., shortly before the period of upheaval that marks the end of the Bronze Age in the Mediterranean world. However, as yet, no proof exists that the Trojan War actually occurred, and, if it did, its date is also uncertain. Moreover, until 1992, the apparent remains of Troy VI were trifling when compared to Homer's description of Priam's great city.

During the centuries between the collapse of Rome and the birth of the modern age, most historians and other scholars viewed the entire narrative content of the The Iliad as pure myth. However, in 1870 Heinrich Schliemann, a wealthy German merchant, decided to become an amateur archaeologist. He took his beloved copy of The Iliad in hand and let it lead him through the Homeric world for the next fourteen years. To everyone's amazement but his own, Schliemann first unearthed the remains of what is actually an earlier Troy, then Mycenae, then more of the earlier Troy, and finally Tiryns. Schliemann's Troy exists on the same site as the later city, Homer's Ilium or Troy VI. The earlier city contained such fabulous wealth that Schliemann mistook it for the city of legendary fame.

Carl Blegen, an archaeologist from Cincinnati, Ohio, discovered Troy VI in the 1930s. Although the time frame was consistent with Homer's Iliad and the walled fortress-city was impressive, the remains that he unearthed were too small to be as important as Priam's city was supposed to be.

In the late 1980s, for the first time in about fifty years, an international team of archaeologists began to work at Hissarlik once again, intending to apply the latest scientific methods to the known Troy and its surrounding area. In 1992, a geomagnetic survey suggested that a great outer wall, twelve to eighteen feet thick, surrounded an inhabited area that is nine times larger than the previously known site of Troy.

Preliminary analysis has revealed that the remains of the wall exist six to ten feet below the surface, that the wall originally enclosed well-planned streets and buildings that would support a busy, wealthy community, and that both the wall and at least some of the buildings that it protected were destroyed by a disastrous fire. Also, preliminary excavations have unearthed the remains of fifteen ancient fortifications, many other buildings, and many examples of Mycenaean pottery.

Analysis of this archaeological data has confirmed the date of these remains to be from the period of Troy VI, thereby possibly establishing the existence of a 13th-century, Bronze Age Troy that is consistent with the' Ilium of The Iliad. Consequently, the extensive excavations and analyses that are scheduled for the remainder of the 1990s and the early 21st century may finally turn myth and legend into fact.

However, historians and Homeric scholars want archaeologists to discover more than Homer's Ilium. In order to determine whether Homer's account of the Trojan War is historically accurate, archaeologists must find some remains of the Greek camp that would have existed near the shore of Troy's harbor during the period of Troy VI.

Homer and the Oral Tradition

One of the most important books in Western literature, The Iliad is also one of the two earliest examples of Greek literature, the other being its companion epic poem, The Odyssey. Most scholars attribute both works to Homer. However, we have no proof that Homer ever existed, and it appears that the ancient Greeks knew no more about him than we do.

Today, many Homeric scholars think that Homer lived and worked in about 760 B.C. and later. It is possible that he composed The Iliad as a young man and that he was much older when he composed The Odyssey.

The linguistic aspects of *The Iliad* and *The Odyssey* place the epics no later than the 8th century B.C. and connect them with the language of Ionia, the central part of the east Aegean coast that includes the large islands of Samos and Chios. These conclusions are consistent with the fact that, in about 700 B.C., Arctinus of Miletus wrote *The Aethiopis* to be the sequel to *The Iliad*, thus placing *The Iliad* in the 8th century B.C. or earlier. They also support the traditional idea, dating from the period between about 650 and 525 B.C., that Homer was a blind Ionian poet from the island of Chios or the city of Smyrna (now called Izmir) in Asia Minor.

In Homer's time, the Greeks possessed an elaborate oral tradition that had developed during the dark age that followed the collapse of the great Mycenaean civilization. Successive generations of professionally trained poets, called *rhapsodes*, learned, taught, and performed a wealth of literary material orally. A rhapsode chanted his tales to the accompaniment of his lyre (a small, harp-like instrument). If he was fortunate, he became attached to a particular king's household staff; otherwise, he traveled from house to house, earning his food and lodging with his tales. The best rhapsodes were highly respected, for they provided one of the major forms of entertainment in their day. They combined radio, television, movies, albums, history books, and novels all in one human being.

Rhapsodes served a far more important purpose as well. In times of political instability and war, they kept alive the heroic past of Greece. By recounting the great deeds of mortal men, they provided their listeners with heroic models of behavior. In a culture that had no code of ethics or body of laws, their tales presented standards and goals for living one's daily life. Courage, strength, skill, intelligence, loyalty, respect for all forms of life, moral responsibility, and hospitality were prime values; glory and honor were principal goals.

At this time, it was still the custom for a poet to create narratives without attaching his name to them. As the opening lines of *The Iliad* and *The Odyssey* reveal, Homer viewed himself as the anonymous voice of the Muse of Epic Poetry, a daughter of Mnemosyne, the goddess of memory. Homer was the last and greatest of these anonymous poets, eclipsing all who preceded him and casting his shadow upon all who followed him in the ancient world, including the next great epic poet, Virgil. Toward the turn of the 8th century B.C., the concept of anonymity was replaced by the concept of authorship, and the 7th century epic poets, such as Hesiod, speak in their own voice.

At this time, also, the Greeks had once again developed a civilization that was complex enough to need writing, and they were in the process of adopting the Phoenician alphabetic script for their own, mostly economic purposes. Therefore, we do not know whether Homer, himself, put *The Iliad* and *The Odyssey* into writing, or whether he dictated them to someone else, or whether other poets memorized and performed *The Iliad* and *The Odyssey* as Homer had created them until they were eventually written down.

Many contemporary Homeric scholars think that one poet, who was probably illiterate, dictated both *The Iliad* and *The Odyssey*. *The Iliad*, which is longer and more complex in its structure, is organized as if it were going to be recited rather than read. Moreover, all of the existing ancient copies agree in terms of dialect and plot details, thus reflecting the existence of one original *Iliad*.

Homer is first mentioned in writing that scholars date at 660 B.C. By the middle of the 7th century (about 650 B.C.), *The Iliad* and *The Odyssey* were well known throughout Greece and the Greek Aegean. The writer of one of the *Homeric Hymns* refers to himself as a blind poet, and when the ancient Greeks attributed these poems to Homer, they decided that he must therefore have been blind. Late in the 6th century (about 525 B.C. or later), Chios had a guild called the *Homeridai* ("the descendants of Homer") that trained rhapsodes. By this time, *The Iliad* and *The Odyssey* were considered an important part of a Greek student's education.

Until late in the 4th century B.C., students usually memorized *The Iliad* and *The Odyssey* by listening to others recite them. It is possible that an authoritative edition of *The Odyssey* existed in Athens in the 6th century B.C.; however, few copies of *The Iliad* have been found that were written prior to about 455 to 400 B.C.

In the 4th century B.C., books became more plentiful in Athens, and a larger segment of the Athenian public could read. Thus, it is not surprising that numerous fragments of both epics have survived from this period. In addition to being written on papyrus, which was scarce and expensive, the early copies were also written on rolls of leather or on wooden tablets. Athenian authors of the 4th century B.C. often quoted Homer in their writings. According to Plato, one of the great 4th century B.C. Greek philoso-

phers, Homer was the teacher of every Greek.

Many contemporary Homeric scholars think that Homer created *The Iliad* and *The Odyssey* with the knowledge of other epics in mind. Homer's choice of subjects, the related knowledge that he obviously expected his audience to possess, and the existence of six other ancient Greek epics on the Trojan War all reveal that Homer and the other rhapsodes of ancient Greece knew a larger body of myth on the subject of the Trojan War.

In *The Iliad*, for example, Homer chose one event from the last year of the ten-year Trojan War and developed it in depth. He assumed that his listeners would know the complete story of the war with Troy, the stories of all the families of the major heroes in that war, and the stories of the Olympian gods that determine their ways of relating to one another.

In keeping with the oral tradition, Homer created *The Iliad* and *The Odyssey* by taking traditional building blocks of material from the poets who preceded him and reshaping them to form the foundations of his artistic creation. These blocks included: various myths about the gods and about the heroes of old (the fathers of the heroes of the Trojan War); myths about the war with Troy and its various participants, from long before the start of the war until the last of the heroes had returned home; folk tales; set passages describing scenes of sacrifice, fighting, and funerals; and particular descriptive phrases, called *epithets*, that described people and nature. From these blocks of material, Homer created two dramatic tales that were new in the important sense that each had a focus that was uniquely his own. Although Homer was trained to work within a particular framework, like all rhapsodes, he was also free to manipulate much of the material so as to reflect his own artistic vision and to please a particular audience.

The Muse of Epic Poetry gave Homer the power to remember the heroes' exact words and to describe their actions as if he had personally observed them. Often Homer would repeat descriptions and speeches, sometimes exactly and other times with slight variations. Repetition not only made the storytelling process easier, but it reminded listeners about what the poet had been telling them, for these were always very complicated tales. Approximately one-third of the lines in The Iliad and The Odyssey are repeated, often more than once.

Homer designed his tale in the form of a tree. The principal plot forms the trunk of the tree, and many other stories branch off from the trunk. Some of the auxiliary stories are included in order to instruct particular characters in the major plot; others are inserted artistically as comic relief or as parallel subordinate plots that reinforce the theme of the principal plot. Given the extensive connections among stories, Homer invariably begins his tale in the middle and moves in many directions simultaneously.

The Iliad and The Odyssey became incorporated into a group of six other Trojan War epics that had been written by various poets in the 7th and 6th centuries B.C., and this group of eight epics became known as the Epic Cycle. The later poets were so impressed by The Iliad and The Odyssey that they made no effort to deal with the subject of either epic. Instead, each poet chose to supplement both epics by telling a part of the Trojan War narrative that Homer had chosen to omit.

By the 6th century A.D., all of these supplementary epics had disappeared. However, a writer by the name of Proclus had summarized them, and summaries of his work have survived to this day, along with 120 more-or-less scattered lines from the original epics. By studying this material, it is possible to discover details about the Trojan War that Homer does not include in The Iliad and The Odyssey, and it is also possible to see what Homer undoubtedly contributed to the traditional version of that narrative.

For example, it is interesting to note that Patroclus' death and funeral in The Iliad are very similar to Achilles' death and funeral in The Aethiopis. Whether Arctinus copied Homer or both poets followed the earlier oral tradition is open to conjecture.

Being a rhapsode himself, it is probable that Homer performed other epics than his own. Particular details in The Iliad and The Odyssey reveal that he may well have been familiar with the older epic literature from the Middle East, such as Gilgamesh from Sumer and Babylonia and the Babylonian creation epic, the Enuma elish. (Both of these are included in World Mythology.)

Achilles and Gilgamesh can be shown to follow the same heroic pattern. Moreover, Homer apparently found the close friendship between the two heroes in Gilgamesh to be such an appealing idea that he increased Patroclus' importance in The Iliad in order to create a relationship between him and Achilles that parallels the relationship between Enkidu and Gilgamesh. Patroclus does not appear to have the same relationship to Achilles in the plot of The Cypria, which chronologically precedes the plot of *The Iliad* in the Epic Cycle.

Consistent with Homer's treatment of Patroclus in *The Iliad* is his creative addition of a second shield for Achilles. In both *The Aethiopis* and the *Little Iliad*, Odysseus and Ajax (Telamon's son) compete for Achilles' shield. Consequently, it appears that, traditionally, Achilles only needed and possessed one shield.

The survival and fame of *The Iliad* and *The Odyssey* confirm that Homer was the supreme poet of ancient Greece. Because these epics are unusually long, they made great demands both on the rhapsode and on his audience. Performing *The Iliad* must have taken between six and ten three-hour sessions and, therefore, was a form of entertainment that would continue for a three- to four-day period. Homer profoundly influenced Greek civilization for a thousand years, for the people of ancient Greece knew and valued his words as people continue to know and value the Bible. In fact, students of every generation have studied *The Iliad* and *The Odyssey*, for something in Homer speaks to every human being across time and space.

Appeal and Value

Without the existence of writing, it is amazing that information about any event could survive the gap of more than 400 years between the Trojan War and the first written version of *The Iliad*. Yet archaeologists have confirmed a surprising number of Homer's details, such as the existence of most of the communities he mentions and his descriptions of war gear. Homer memorized lists of communities that no longer existed in his own day. He also retained the use of chariots as a means of transportation across battlefields, even though chariots no longer existed in Greece when he created *The Iliad*, and he did not know their real purpose. Homer's distance in time from the events he described resulted in some inaccuracies. For example, the Mycenaeans buried their dead; they did not cremate them. Homer also describes palaces that appear to have no historical basis at all.

But Homer is not read primarily for his history. The universal appeal of Homer resides in his heroes. What survives of the other epics in the Epic Cycle reveals that Homer was a literary giant among poets. Unlike those who came after him, Homer was a born psychologist and was far more interested in creating heroes who thought and acted like real people in time of crisis than in repeating the multitude of factual details that traditionally described the events in the Trojan War. Unlike the earlier heroes of Greek myth and the traditional heroes of world myth, the heroes in Homer's epics do not achieve fame or immortality by killing evil human beings or monsters. In *The Iliad*, many good men, due to circumstances beyond their control, find themselves called upon to kill other good men in battle. They win honor and glory, but at the cost of suffering and death.

The details of the Trojan War may no longer command attention, but the characters in Homer's epics still seem vitally alive, as if yesteryear were but yesterday. When we watch Homer's characters react to the problems in their lives, we realize that the people who lived in 800 B.C. are basically the same as we are. We have the same needs and the same kinds of conflicts, and we must cope with the same ultimate fate, death. The Homeric hero becomes so real to us that we identify with him, gaining insights into our own feelings and goals. This examination of our own attitudes and values may help us to exert more control over the course of our own lives.

Human behavior and the emotions that cause it obviously fascinated Homer, for the opening lines of *The Iliad* state that his focus will be the anger of Achilles and the devastation it caused all the Greeks who were fighting in the war against Troy. In keeping with his perspective, Homer's style is dramatic rather than narrative. He does not tell us what his characters are like; instead, he reveals their personalities by actively involving us in their moments of crisis. Homer enables us to listen to their private thoughts and public statements and to watch them interact with other characters. Often, two characters who are quite different in attitude and behavior react against one another.

This approach lets us see each major character from a variety of perspectives. Each hero becomes a vital, complex person who possesses a range of emotions and whose behavior varies as his emotions change. The issues he faces are complex and important, so the decisions he must make are never obvious or easy. Given a particular hero's values and attitudes and the very human limitations of his personality, it is as difficult to categorize him as good or evil as it would be in real life. Homer almost always leaves the interpretation of his heroes' personalities and the evaluation of their behavior to the other characters and to us.

Homer's characters vividly stand out from the story of the Trojan War as a sculpture stands apart from its background. He gives us no idea of the timing of his story beyond its duration of a few days; neither the year nor the season interests him. He tells us that the Greek ships are swift, black, and "hollow," that men row them and that they have sails, but we still cannot picture them in our minds. We have even less of a feel for the appearance of the Trojan wall and of Troy itself. Homer is interested primarily in human beings, and anything else is included in the story only to the extent that it enhances his portrayal of the individual.

Homer's extended comparisons, known as *Homeric similes*, function in this way. In these comparisons Homer relates the appearance, emotions, or actions of one of his characters to something or someone in the natural world—a particular wild animal or bird, a forest fire, flood, or storm, or a farmer or artisan working. The scenes Homer describes in his similes provide additional emotional depth by showing, for example, how much fear, anger, grief, or happiness a particular character is feeling at that particular moment. In this way the Homeric simile increases the significance of human emotions and actions.

The Homeric Hero

The principal characters in *The Iliad* are heroic aristocrats. Homer examines their attitudes and their behavior in crucial wartime situations. These aristocrats are no strangers to the demands of war. On the contrary, their families reared them to assume a major role in the warrior culture that dominated their age. In fact, many nobles were much happier fighting on the battlefield with their friends than living at home in peaceful isolation.

The Greek nobility in the Mycenaean age valued strength and skill, courage and determination, for these attributes enabled the person who possessed them to achieve glory and honor, both in his lifetime and after he died. The Mycenaean hero never forgot that death was his ultimate fate. Faced with a grim view of life after death, he chose to concentrate on the aspects of his existence he could control, notably the quality of his life and the manner in which he died.

The striving for excellence in particular areas of human behavior, called *aretē* by the ancient Greeks, is an integral part of the Homeric hero's life. Strength, skill, and determination are necessary and admirable attributes both on the athletic field and on the battlefield. Courage and moral responsibility are obviously components in the *aretē* of the warrior. *Aretē* in the form of intelligence, insight, or ingenuity is more common in the older hero. Years of experience in the warrior culture have made the older generation of heroes more expert in this area, and one of their major roles is to counsel the younger men.

The Homeric hero strives to be the best among his peers. His goal is to achieve the greatest glory in order to earn the highest honor from his peers, his commander, and finally from his warrior society. He has the opportunity to exhibit the greatest *aretē* and thus win the greatest glory on the battlefield, for armed conflict presents the ultimate challenge to his abilities. How well the Homeric hero fights, how heroic his adversary is, and how well he faces death all combine to determine how well he will be remembered and honored, not only by his companions but by society and posterity. Given that suffering and death are an inevitable part of the human condition, honor, glory, and lasting fame compensate the Homeric hero for his mortality.

The Homeric hero judges his own *aretē* by what his warrior society thinks of him. Public approval is crucial to the Homeric hero's self-esteem. Thus, the greatest insult one can confer upon the Homeric hero is to withhold the honor he has earned. The hero then feels robbed of his proper status in society, and he feels the intolerable shame of public disgrace. The Homeric hero feels dishonored if he does not receive enough wealth or appropriately impressive prizes for his contributions in battle, or if he is judged the loser in a competition that he thinks he deserved to win.

The Homeric hero achieves honor when the various members of his society praise his accomplishments. His commander confers a more tangible honor by rewarding him with wealth and prizes that represent in material terms the amount of honor he has earned. Such wealth includes gold and bronze, valuable objects and animals, land and the power to rule those who inhabit it, and female slaves captured when their cities were raided. The highest and most honored prize is called the prize of honor, and in *The Iliad* this prize is the most attractive, intelligent, and skilled female captive.

Moreover, once the Homeric hero achieves his goals of glory and honor, the poets will sing about his great accomplishments, conferring wide and lasting fame upon him. Such fame is the ultimate honor, for it is the only form of immortality that any mortal can acquire. Lasting fame places the Homeric hero lower than the gods but higher than ordinary men.

Ultimately every Greek warrior must choose between dying as a hero and dying an obscure or disgraceful death. Despite his values, the choice of how to die is never easy, for the warrior loves life and believes that death will be an eternally dull existence. Moreover, his decision inevitably involves the welfare of his society, whether in the form of his companions on the battlefield or the people of the city he is defending. Sometimes he must choose between his loyalty and responsibility to the individuals he loves most and the loyalty and responsibility he owes to the larger community. The Homeric hero's decision to accept death in order to give significance and value to his life gives him a dignity, a nobility, and a grandeur that do not tarnish with the passage of time. When he is most vulnerable, most aware of his situation, and most alone, he is most noble.

The principal focus of The Iliad is on the consequences of a quarrel between Agamemnon, the commander of all the Greek forces, and Achilles, his greatest warrior. In a very human but very juvenile, arrogant, and callous act, Agamemnon publicly humiliates Achilles by taking away his prize of honor. Achilles retaliates by withdrawing from battle. His decision cripples the Greek forces and results in needless suffering and death among the Greeks, eventually including the death of his best friend, Patroclus. The Iliad demonstrates how the actions of these two great Greek heroes cause great harm to their community (the army) when each thinks only of himself. Homer's own attitudes toward war and its heroes are reflected in the values of Agamemnon, Achilles, Patroclus, and Hector.

The issues in The Iliad are not simple ones by any means. The removal of Achilles' prize of honor is a blow to his reputation as well as to his pride. Moreover, Achilles knows that if he chooses to fight in the Trojan War, he will die an early death but will be remembered as a great hero; whereas if he refrains from fighting, he will lead a long but insignificant life and will not be remembered at all. He understandably vacillates between choosing life and choosing death.

Achilles personifies what is best and worst in human nature. As he moves from one crisis to another, he is at his best when he stands apart from his warrior society and questions the values by which he and they live. He is also at his best when he offers compassion and consolation that reveal his profound understanding of the human condition. However, at his worst, Achilles behaves like a selfish child and acts like a brutal beast. With striking psychological realism, Homer portrays the two sides of Achilles' nature as they exist in the human personality, like the two sides of one coin.

Achilles is considered to be the first tragic hero in literature, and his tragedy has many possible causes. He may be a tragic figure because he must sacrifice his life in order to achieve the lasting fame that confers immortality. He may be tragic because, given his values, he is not ultimately free to choose either life or death. His tragedy may also lie in the fact that his reason for reentering the war has nothing to do with his argument with Agamemnon, the principles for which he stood, or the Greek cause. Finally, it may be tragic that his view of his fellow warriors condemns him to be honored by those whose values he does not respect. Because Homer presents all these factors, he permits us to evaluate Achilles' situation for ourselves.

Homer changed the traditional Trojan War myth wherever necessary in order to create a psychologically cohesive narrative. For example, in *The Aethiopis*, Zeus permits Thetis to rescue Achilles from the funeral pyre and take him to White Island in the Black Sea, where he lives forever. The ability of a god to grant immortality to a favored mortal occasionally occurs in the earlier, traditional body of Greek myth, and, given Achilles' heroic stature, it is likely that he would have received this highest accolade.

However, by permitting Achilles to die, Homer makes both *The Iliad* and *The Odyssey* more stimulating intellectually. It is interesting to consider whether Odysseus' attitudes and behavior would have been different in *The Odyssey* had he not talked with the shade of Achilles in the Underworld. It is also interesting to consider how Homer's audience would have responded to *The Iliad*, since they would have known the story of Achilles' later rescue.

Homer's treatment of the Greek and Trojan heroes is unbiased. Although the Trojans are the enemy, in Homer's epic they are not villains. They are as human and heroic as the Greeks. The greatest of the Trojan warriors is Hector, whose sense of responsibility to his people stands in sharp contrast to his brother Paris' selfishness, and to Achilles' selfishness as well. Like Achilles, Hector knows that he will die fighting in the Trojan War. He too vacillates between choosing life and choosing death, even though an honorable death will bring the immortality of everlasting fame. His

death at the hands of Achilles shows only that Achilles is the greater warrior. Hector's humane values and his ultimate courage reveal that he is the greater human being.

Yet, like Achilles, Hector is not perfect. At the base of his single-minded devotion to his people is the fact that above all else, above even his wife and child, he values his reputation. Therefore, in this respect, the motivating force behind Hector's behavior is similar to that behind Achilles' behavior. Hector's fear of disgrace, with its accompanying shame, causes needless death among the Trojans, including his own.

The ancient Greeks were fond of two precepts: "Know thyself" and "nothing in excess." However, the Homeric hero, in striving for excellence or *aretē*, was such an accomplished individual that it was easy for him to forget his human limitations and to think that he was even greater than he actually was. The ancient Greeks called such excessive pride and arrogance *hubris*. Hubris would lead the hero to think that he was greater than the heroes who were his peers and that he had the limitless power that he attributed to his gods.

As a result of this attitude, the hero inevitably would say or do something excessive, without thinking of the consequences. The ancient Greeks called such action *atē*, which means blind, rash behavior. *Atē* would inevitably lead to retribution, or *nemesis*. Sometimes the gods would punish the hero directly; sometimes other human beings would punish him. Either way, the Homeric hero brought his fate, which was often death, upon himself. The reader can follow the pattern of *aretē*, hubris, *atē*, and nemesis in the behavior of Agamemnon, Achilles, Patroclus, and Hector.

Women in The Iliad

The Iliad is dominated by men, since it is set during the Trojan War. However, the Homeric heroes clearly place a very high value upon women. The aristrocratic woman in Mycenaean society also possesses aretē, consisting of beauty, intelligence, loyalty, and excellence in handicraft work (usually weaving). Although the queen's place is in the home instead of on the battlefield, as mistress of the royal household she wields great power during her husband's frequent absences.

The Homeric hero's most honored prize is the female captive who possesses the greatest aretē. The heroes reveal, by both their actions and their words, that they cherish these women both as individuals and as symbols of honor. It is worth noting that the abduction of Helen caused the Trojan War, and that the anger of Achilles over the seizure of Briseis, the female captive who was his prize of honor, is the focus of The Iliad.

However, Homer also depicts this situation from the female point of view. Through Andromache, Homer eloquently expresses the plight of all aristocratic Mycenaean women who become war's victims. The woman who is so valued as to become a prize of honor is actually enslaved by the victorious nobleman who wins her. She is carried off to a new land, where she is relegated to a life of servitude and deprivation.

Female divinities play a major role in The Iliad. Athena, the goddess of defensive war, is the favorite child of Zeus, the ruler of all the Greek gods, because she is so intelligent and clever. She is also the favorite divinity of the Homeric hero, whom she inspires and guides. Since the ancient Greeks gave their gods the qualities they themselves possessed, the fact that Athena is a superlative being is another indication that they esteemed women highly.

The Role of the Greek Gods

Because The Iliad is the earliest written work from ancient Greece, it is the earliest presentation of the Greek gods. The Homeric gods are ageless and immortal, can possess great knowledge of the future, and are influenced by the pleas of one another and the prayers of mortals. They have not given any moral code to mortals, and they do not live by such a code themselves. In practice, they are simply a divine aristocratic family whose members possess the same variety of feelings and attitudes as mortals. Their behavior is often angry, jealous, deceitful, and, in some instances, amusingly juvenile. It is clear that the ancient Greeks did not require perfection, either in themselves or in their divinities.

The Homeric gods are not all-powerful. Unlike divine power in the earlier, traditional body of Greek myth, fate and death are beyond the control of even Zeus, who may talk as if he could control when a mortal dies, but never tries to do so. While mortals live, however, the gods may participate in their lives by giving advice (both good and bad), by supplying thoughts and ideas, strength and skill, courage and determination, and by causing weapons to hit or miss their mark. They may appear as their divine selves, or they may disguise themselves as any human being they choose, depending upon the purpose they have in mind.

The Homeric hero feels the presence or absence of his gods. He often attributes all of his success on the battlefield to them or blames them for his failures and bad luck. However, he always accepts the fact that the gods cannot prevent his death when it is his time (his fate) to die.

The relationship between the Homeric hero and his gods is complex. The Homeric gods clearly have their favorites among mortals and make an effort to help them. However, a mortal must earn divine esteem and goodwill by the way he treats both the gods and other mortals. The gods are particularly partial to heroes because they appreciate and enjoy heroic deeds. Their help enhances the heroic stature of those warriors who receive it.

Homer attributes to the gods powers that today we ascribe to science, human nature, human skill, luck, and fate. The Homeric gods do surprisingly few things that we can explain in no other way. Certainly only a god could whisk Paris off the battlefield and into his palace bedroom. Only a god could lure Hector into a direct confrontation with Achilles and then instantly disappear. However, a god need not be present to cause the strap of Paris' helmet to break, or to tell Achilles that it is better to hurl sharp words at Agamemnon than to stab him with his sword.

The Homeric gods do not change a mortal's personality or fate. Even though the gods may give advice or help, a mortal's actions in response to any given situation are determined by his or her own personality and ability. Consequently, a mortal's fate is created by the interaction between personality and situation. Because the Homeric gods are not all-powerful, mortals can be dignified, morally responsible, and important. The world of ancient Greece contains no puppets.

Principal Characters

The Greeks

AGAMEMNON: son of Atreus; older brother of Menelaus; king of Mycenae; commander of all the Greek forces; husband of Clytemnestra; father of Iphigenia, Electra, and Orestes

CLYTEMNESTRA: daughter of King Tyndareus and Queen Leda of Sparta; wife of Agamemnon; queen of Mycenae; mother of Iphigenia, Electra, and Orestes

MENELAUS: son of Atreus; younger brother of Agamemnon; king of Sparta; husband of Helen

HELEN: daughter of Zeus and the goddess Nemesis; reared by King Tyndareus and Queen Leda of Sparta; wife of Menelaus and queen of Sparta until abducted by Paris and taken to Troy

NESTOR: king of Pylos; old, wise Greek leader

ACHILLES: son of the hero Peleus and the sea-goddess Thetis; leader of the Myrmidons; greatest Greek warrior

PATROCLUS: best friend of Achilles

PHOENIX: Achilles' tutor

AJAX: son of the hero Telamon; second greatest Greek warrior

ODYSSEUS: son of the hero Laertes; king of Ithaca; master of strategies

CALCHAS: chief prophet of the Greeks

The Trojans

PRIAM: king of Troy; husband of Hecuba; father of Hector, Paris, Deiphobus, and Cassandra

HECUBA: wife of Priam; queen of Troy; mother of Hector, Paris, Deiphobus, and Cassandra

HECTOR: son of Priam and Hecuba; husband of Andromache; father of Astyanax; brother of Paris; commander of the Trojan forces; greatest Trojan warrior

ANDROMACHE: wife of Hector; mother of Astyanax

ASTYANAX: son of Hector and Andromache

POLYDAMAS: Hector's good friend and wise counselor

PARIS: son of Priam and Hecuba; brother of Hector; abductor of Helen

DEIPHOBUS: son of Priam and Hecuba; brother of Hector and Paris

CASSANDRA: daughter of Priam and Hecuba; sister of Hector and Paris

AENEAS: son of Aphrodite and Anchises

PANDARUS: a respected Trojan spearman

BRISEIS: Achilles' prize of honor

CHRYSEIS: daughter of Chryses, a priest of Apollo; Agamemnon's prize of honor

For a list of the gods, see pages 5–6.

Introducing **the Prologue to The Iliad**

Because of the particular focus of *The Iliad*, Homer excludes many myths that relate to the Trojan War. He relates parts of them in *The Odyssey*; later ancient Greek writers, along with a Roman, Hyginus, tell many more of them.

Aspects of the birth of Paris, his survival, and his judgment are related by Euripides (5th century B.C.) in *Andromache*, *Helen*, and *The Trojan Women*; by Proclus in his summary of *The Cypria* (by Stasinus of Cyprus or Hegesinus of Salamis, in the 7th or 6th century B.C.); by Apollodorus (2nd century B.C.) in the *Epitome*; and by Hyginus (late 1st century B.C. to early 1st century A.D.) in the *Fabulae*.

The circumstances of Helen's marriage to Menelaus are related by Hesiod (700 B.C.) in *The Catalogue of Women*, by Apollodorus in *The Library*, and by Proclus' summary of *The Cypria*.

Apollodorus, in the *Epitome*, tells the tale of Odysseus' attempt to avoid the war. Hyginus, in the *Fabulae*, tells the corresponding tale about Achilles.

Euripides, in *Iphigenia at Aulis*, and Apollodorus, in the *Epitome*, tell about the departure of the Greek forces for Troy.

Exploring an unusual and provocative version of the legend of the Trojan War, Euripides, in *Helen* and in *Electra*, relates how Hera retaliates for

Paris' choice of Aphrodite by creating a phantom Helen who goes with him to Troy. Meanwhile, Zeus orders Hermes to transport the real Helen to Egypt, where she spends the ten-year period of the war as the faithful wife of Menelaus.

Prologue to The Iliad
The Birth of Paris

Hecuba, the wife of King Priam of Troy, was about to give birth when she had a dreadful nightmare. She dreamed that instead of a baby, she gave birth to a flaming torch crawling with snakes. When she told her dream to the prophets, they told her that the baby must be killed, for if he lived he would cause the destruction of Troy.

As soon as he was born, Priam and Hecuba obediently gave the baby, whom they had named Paris, to two of their trusted servants and ordered them to kill him. The servants did not have the heart to kill Paris, so they left him exposed upon a mountainside, expecting that he would die of starvation or would be mauled by wild animals. Instead, Paris was found and raised by a shepherd couple. He grew to manhood as their son.

Many years later, when this shepherd boy's favorite bull was chosen by King Priam's servants to be a prize in funeral games commemorating Paris' death, the young man went to the games and won all of the contests. Priam's daughter Cassandra, to whom Apollo had given the gift of prophecy, announced that this young man was, in fact, the son they thought had died. Then his parents welcomed Paris home.

The Judgment of Paris

While Paris was still living with the shepherd family, an event occurred that led to the eventual destruction of Troy. Zeus, lord of Olympus, held a royal wedding celebration to honor the sea goddess Thetis and the great mortal hero Peleus. He invited all the gods except Eris, goddess of discord, for a wedding is no place for arguments. Highly insulted, Eris came anyway. When she was not permitted to enter, she threw a golden apple into the hall and announced that it was a gift for the most beautiful goddess.

Every goddess wanted the honor of receiving the apple, but finally all of them gave up except for Hera, Athena, and Aphrodite. They asked Zeus to decide which of them was most beautiful, but he refused to choose among his wife and two of his daughters. So he ordered Hermes, the Wayfinder, to take the golden apple and the three goddesses to Mount Ida and to have Paris, who was herding sheep there, judge among them. Each goddess thought Paris would have an easier time if she promised him a special gift.

Hera said, "If you give the apple to me, Paris, I shall give you extraordinary wealth and shall make you ruler over all mortals."

Athena said, "If you give the apple to me, Paris, I shall make you the bravest and wisest of mortal men, victorious in war, and skillful in every craft."

Finally, Aphrodite said, "If you give the apple to me, Paris, I shall give you Helen, the daughter of King Tyndareus and the most beautiful woman in the world, as your wife." (It did not matter to Aphrodite that Helen was already married to King Menelaus of Sparta.)

Paris liked Aphrodite's gift best of all, so he awarded the apple to her, and from that time on Hera and Athena hated all Trojans. Paris then sailed to Sparta, where he was the guest of Menelaus and Helen for nine days. Then when Menelaus left on a trip, Paris convinced Helen to return to Troy with him. She left her nine-year-old daughter at home, took all of her possessions, and sailed away on Paris' ship that night.

The Marriage of Helen

Helen's marriage to Menelaus had involved an unusual circumstance, which also contributed to the eventual destruction of Troy. Because of Helen's beauty, many of the greatest kings in Greece approached her father, King Tyndareus, for her hand. He was afraid to choose one of them for fear that the others would be furious enough to attack the chosen suitor and destroy the marriage. Odysseus, Ajax, Menelaus, and Patroclus were among the suitors.

Odysseus looked at his competitors and decided that Helen would never choose him, for he was not handsome. He approached her father and offered to help the king solve the problem of the suitors if, in return, King Tyndareus would help Odysseus win Penelope, who was the king's niece, for his wife. Odysseus suggested that before announcing his choice, the king should make all the suitors swear that they would punish anyone who tried to break up the marriage. Once the suitors had taken the oath, King Tyndareus chose Menelaus to be the husband of Helen and Odysseus to be the husband of Penelope.

Preparation for War: Odysseus and Achilles

When Menelaus returned to Sparta and heard that Paris had carried Helen away, he went to wide-ruling Agamemnon, his powerful brother, and asked him to raise an army to bring her back. He then sent heralds to many of the Greek kings, including Helen's former suitors, to remind them of the oath they had sworn. Many kings were delighted to have an occasion for heroism and adventure; Odysseus felt otherwise.

An oracle had warned Odysseus that if he went to Troy, he would return home, alone, twenty years later. So when Agamemnon and Menelaus came for him, he pretended to be insane by harnessing a horse and an ox, instead of two oxen, to his plow. Knowing that Odysseus was a man of many schemes, the two brothers tested him by taking his infant son, Telemachus, out of his cradle and putting the baby down in front of the plow. To avoid killing his son, Odysseus had to stop pretending to be insane. He made arrangements for organizing the soldiers who would go with him to Troy, and then he left with Agamemnon and Menelaus to find Achilles.

Achilles' mother, the sea goddess Thetis, could not accept the fact that Achilles was doomed to die since his father, Peleus, was mortal. (In order to be immortal, one must have both an immortal mother and an immortal father.) When Achilles was an infant, she tried to burn away his mortality by secretly placing him in a fire at night. However, Peleus suddenly awakened in the middle of the night, found his wife holding the baby in the flames, and commanded her to stop. Thetis was so infuriated that she abandoned her husband and returned to her home in the sea to live, leaving Achilles to be reared by his father.

(A Roman poet writing more than 1,000 years after the Trojan War adds more detail to this story. He says that Thetis then took the infant Achilles down to the River Styx in the Underworld. There she held onto him by the heel of one foot and submerged the rest of him in the water. The river water protected from injury every part of his body it touched, so Achilles could be wounded only in the back of one heel — the Achilles tendon. Homer, however, does not indicate that he knew this story.)

Thetis knew that Achilles would die if he fought in the Trojan War, so she hid him in the palace of a king who was a friend of hers. The king dressed fifteen-year-old Achilles as a girl, gave him a feminine name, and housed him with his daughters.

Agamemnon, Menelaus, and Odysseus heard that Achilles was in the palace, but the king would not admit it. He did agree to let them search the palace, but they could not find Achilles anywhere. Odysseus, a man of many schemes, then pretended to be a peddler. He returned to the palace with a tray of beautiful scarves and jewelry, plus a spear and a shield. When the daughters of the king and their handmaidens came into the forecourt of the palace to examine these beautiful articles, he had the servants sound an alarm and shout that the palace was under attack. Achilles immediately tore off his woman's clothing, grabbed the spear and the shield, and went looking for the attackers. Instead he found Odysseus, who told him of Helen's abduction. Achilles then promised the Greek kings that he would bring his soldiers to Troy.

Departure for Troy

The Greek kings, with all of their soldiers, gathered at Aulis and prepared to sail across the Aegean Sea to Troy. Time passed and the fleet remained beached, for the winds would not blow in the right direction. Finally, the prophet Calchas announced that favorable winds would blow only when Agamemnon appeased Artemis, the goddess of the hunt, by sacrificing his most beautiful daughter. Agamemnon had killed a deer that was sacred to Artemis and then bragged that he had killed a deer the archer goddess could not have hit. Therefore, he would have to soothe her rage.

Agamemnon sent Odysseus to his wife, Clytemnestra, with the false message that their daughter Iphigenia should come to Aulis in order to become the bride of Achilles. When Iphigenia arrived, her father let Calchas place her upon an altar. As the prophet was about to kill her, Artemis secretly substituted a deer and carried Iphigenia off to become one of her priestesses. The winds shifted, and the Greeks set sail for Troy. But Clytemnestra never forgave her husband.

The Iliad

Chapter 1

Agamemnon insults the priest of Apollo, causing Apollo to punish the Greeks. In order to correct the situation, Agamemnon must give up his prize of honor. Achilles and Agamemnon argue, and as a result, Agamemnon takes Achilles' prize of honor. Achilles, in turn, retaliates by withdrawing from battle.

Sing, goddess, of the time when wide-ruling Agamemnon and godlike Achilles parted in anger. The wrath of Achilles brought numerous troubles upon the long-haired Greeks and sent down to Hades the shades of many brave warriors, while dogs and birds feasted upon their dead flesh.

Who set Agamemnon and Achilles against each other? Apollo, god of the silver bow, caused the argument when Agamemnon dishonored Apollo's priest. Agamemnon had been awarded the priest's daughter, Chryseis, as a prize of honor, but soon the priest arrived with a rich ransom. He spoke to Agamemnon, his brother Menelaus, and all the other Greeks. "May the Olympian gods permit you to destroy Troy, Priam's great city, and return safely to your homes if you will accept my ransom and free my daughter. Do this out of reverence for the son of Zeus, far-shooting Apollo."

All of the Greeks agreed to honor the priest of Apollo, except for Agamemnon, whose heart beat with resentment. The wide-ruling king warned the priest, "Do not let me find you by our hollow ships, old man, or even Apollo will not be able to protect you! I refuse to free your daughter. Instead, Chryseis will grow old in my house in Argos, far from you and her country. There she will weave on the loom and serve me. Go peacefully now, without arousing my anger."

Agamemnon's words put fear into the priest's heart. Silently he walked some distance along the shore of the salt sea. Then he prayed to Apollo, "Hear me, god of the silver bow! If I have ever pleased you, let your arrows repay the Greeks for my sorrow."

So he prayed, and Apollo heard him. Down from the peaks of Mount Olympus, the Far-Shooter came like night, with anger in his heart and his bow and arrows upon his shoulders. Each invisible arrow carried a deadly disease. First he shot the mules and dogs, and then he killed so many Greek warriors for nine days that funeral pyres were burning continuously everywhere.

On the tenth day the goddess Hera felt sorry for the Greeks and put into Achilles' heart the idea of calling the Greek leaders together in council. When everyone had assembled, godlike Achilles took the speaker's staff into his hands and said, "Agamemnon, son of Atreus, we are now being destroyed by plague as well as by war. Let us ask some priest or prophet to tell us why Apollo is so angry with us. Then perhaps if we appease him with a sacrifice of lambs and goats he will end the plague."

When Achilles had finished speaking, the prophet Calchas, to whom Apollo had given knowledge of the past and the future, rose and took the speaker's staff. "Achilles, dear to Zeus," he began, "I will speak out if you will promise to defend me against the anger of the one who rules over all the Greeks."

To this Achilles replied, "Be brave, Calchas, and reveal what you know. I swear by Apollo, the dear son of Zeus whose gift you possess, that as long as I live and see, no man will harm you—not even if you fear Agamemnon himself, who states that he is by far the greatest of the Greeks."

Then Calchas revealed, "The Far-Shooter is punishing us because Agamemnon has dishonored his priest by not accepting his ransom and returning his daughter. Now Apollo will not remove the plague until we have returned Chryseis freely, without accepting any gifts in return."

Agamemnon rose angrily. With rage in his heart and fire in his eyes, he grabbed the speaker's staff and exclaimed, "You prophet of evil! You never reveal any good thing! Why must you blame me for Apollo's anger just because I want to keep Chryseis in my own house? I prefer her to my wife, Clytemnestra, and Chryseis is certainly Clytemnestra's equal in beauty, intelligence, and skill with handiwork.

"Yet even though I love her," Agamemnon continued, "if it is necessary, I will return Chryseis to her father. I prefer to see the Greeks safe rather than dead. Just give me another prize so that I am not the only noble Greek without this symbol of my rank and honor, for it is not appropriate for a person of my stature to have his prize of honor taken from him."

Achilles then took up the staff and answered him. "Great son of Atreus, most greedy of all men, how can the great-hearted Greeks give you a prize of honor? We have already distributed everything of value from the cities we have raided, and it is improper to take back what we have given. However, if you give up Chryseis, we will give you prizes worth three or four times her value when Zeus lets us sack well-defended Troy."

Agamemnon replied, "Brave you are, Achilles, but do not try to deceive me. Do you think that you can keep your own prize of honor while making me return mine? No! If the great-hearted Greeks give me another prize that pleases me, I shall accept it. Otherwise, I shall seize a prize of honor from you, or from Ajax, or from Odysseus, by force. However, I will deal with this later. Now let us return fair Chryseis and make suitable sacrifices to Apollo, the archer god."

Then Achilles, his eyes glaring, exclaimed, "Oh, you shameless, cunning man! How is any Greek willing to obey you? I did not come here because the Trojans had injured me. They have never bothered my pigs or horses or my fields of grain, for great distance separates the rich soil of Phthia from Troy—shadowy mountains and the salt sea. Rather it was for you, shameless one, dog-face, for you and for your brother Menelaus that we came to wreak vengeance on the Trojans.

"Yet now," Achilles continued, "you threaten to take away my prize of honor, which I earned and which the Greeks gave to me. Whenever I sack a town, my prize is never as great as yours, even though I am the greatest Greek fighter. Even so, my small prize is my own. So now I will return to my homeland. I refuse to stay here, dishonored, in order to win greater wealth for you!"

To these words wide-ruling Agamemnon replied, "Run away if you wish! I will not ask you to stay. I have many others who honor me, even Zeus, lord of Olympus. Of all the kings Zeus favors, I hate you most of all, for you are too fond of arguing and fighting. You are strong only because a god has given you that gift. So take your men and your black ships, and go home.

"I do not care about you or your anger," Agamemnon continued, "but know this. Because Apollo has taken my Chryseis from me, I will come to your hut and take your prize of honor, fair Briseis, from you. Then you will understand how much more powerful I am than you are, and in days to come, no other king will think that he can argue with me and treat me as his equal."

As Agamemnon said these words, Achilles debated within himself whether he should draw his sword and kill this arrogant son of Atreus, or whether it would be better to control his anger. While his hand was on his sword hilt, Hera sent Athena down to him, for Hera loved both Agamemnon and Achilles. Athena stood behind Achilles and pulled his golden hair, making herself visible to him alone.

Startled, Achilles turned and recognized the bright-eyed goddess. "Why are you here, daughter of Zeus?" he asked. "Have you come to watch how this insolent king will lose his life?"

To these words Athena replied, "Hera has sent me here to ask you to control your anger, for she loves both you and Agamemnon. If you will use words against Agamemnon instead of your sword, in days to come you will receive three times as many gifts."

"No matter how angry he is," Achilles replied, "a man must obey the two of you, for the gods will listen to those who obey them." So the son of Peleus leashed his fury, took up the speaker's staff, and attacked Agamemnon with strong words instead.

"You drunkard!" Achilles exclaimed. "You with the face of a dog but the heart of a deer! You have never been brave enough to arm yourself for battle with your countrymen or to take part in an ambush with the other Greek kings. You are as afraid of that as you are of dying! Instead, you much prefer to seize for yourself the prize of any Greek who disagrees with you. You must rule over mice, not men; otherwise you would not think that you could treat other people in this way."

Achilles then announced, "By the staff I am holding in my hands, I swear before you a mighty oath. When hundreds of Greeks fall to their deaths before man-slaying Hector and you cannot defend them, all the Greeks will long for

Achilles' help. Then you will sorrow in your heart, knowing that by refusing to honor the best of the Greeks, you have caused their destruction."

Then sweet-speaking Nestor, the aged and wise king of Pylos, rose, took up the speaker's staff, and spoke. "Shame upon both of you!" he cried. "It is sad to see the Greeks divided like this. Surely Priam and his sons are delighted to have such strife between the two Greeks who are greatest in counsel and in fighting. Listen to me, for I am older than both of you, and long ago even better men than you paid attention to my words."

Nestor then advised, "You, Achilles, should not think that you can fight against a king. Although you are the mighty son of a goddess, Agamemnon is greater than you are, for he is king over more people. As for you, Agamemnon, powerful as you are, do not take Briseis, for the Greeks gave her to Achilles as his prize of honor. Control your anger, for Achilles is the Greeks' great defense in this war."

Then Agamemnon replied, "You are right, old sir, but this man thinks that he is the chief commander whom everyone should obey. The immortal gods made him a spearman, but did they also give him his insulting tongue?"

Achilles interrupted him. "Yes, for people would call me a coward and a mouse if I gave in to your demands. Order others if you will, but not me, for I will obey you no longer. I will not fight you for Briseis because you gave her to me. However, if you attempt to seize anything else that is mine, my spear will invite your dark blood!"

With these words, the two leaders rose and disbanded the assembly. Agamemnon sent Chryseis homeward, with Odysseus as captain. Then he commanded the Greeks to purify themselves in the salt sea and to sacrifice bulls and goats to Apollo.

Achilles returned to his huts, where he gave up Briseis to Agamemnon's two heralds. As they were about to leave, he announced, "Let the two of you be my witnesses before the immortal gods and mortal men and before that foolish king when the day comes that the Greeks need me to save them from destruction. For the wide-ruling son of Atreus does not have the sense to look ahead and see the consequences of his actions."

Chapter 2

Achilles' mother agrees to persuade Zeus to restore
Achilles' honor by showing the Greeks that, unless he
rejoins the war, the Trojans will defeat them. Zeus
sends Agamemnon a false dream that tells the king to
attack Troy now, for the attack will be successful.
When the Greeks and Trojans meet on the battlefield,
Menelaus and Paris fight one another but neither
warrior is clearly victorious.

Then godlike Achilles sat down alone beside the shore of the loud-sounding sea and cried. Stretching out his hands, he prayed to his mother, silver-footed Thetis. "Seeing that my life will be so brief," he began, "surely Zeus, the Loud-Thunderer, should permit me to be honored. Yet wide-ruling Agamemnon has dishonored me by seizing Briseis, my prize of honor."

Thetis heard Achilles' prayer deep in the salty sea. Quickly she emerged like a mist, comforting her son as she listened to his tale of sorrow.

When he had finished, Achilles said, "As I was growing up in my father's house, I often heard you brag about how, of all the immortal gods, you alone saved Zeus of the storm-clouds when the other gods united against him and bound him up so intricately. You brought Briareus, one of the Hundred-Handed Giants, to rescue him, and in this way you earned his eternal affection and gratitude.

"So please help me now," Achilles pleaded. "Go to Zeus, lord of counsel, and ask him to help the Trojans for my sake, letting the Greeks die by their ships. Only through disaster will Agamemnon, that arrogant son of Atreus, discover how blind he was when he refused to honor the best of the Greeks."

Tearfully, Thetis replied, "Knowing how short your life will be, I wish that you could have been spared this grief. Instead, you bear sorrows that are too great for any one man. Do not attempt to leash your anger. Avoid all battle, and stay instead by your swift black ships. Meanwhile, I will go up to snow-covered Olympus and plan to convince Zeus to support us."

Achilles obeyed his mother's instructions. He no longer attended the council sessions where men win glory, and he remained idly by his ships, far from the battlefield. Yet he sorely missed the war cry and the fighting.

As she had promised, Thetis approached Zeus as he sat alone upon the highest peak of many-ridged Olympus. "Father Zeus," she prayed, "if ever I have helped you by word or deed, hear my plea. Bring honor to my son who is fated to die so young, for Agamemnon has dishonored him by taking his prize of honor. Please help the Trojans until the Greeks restore my son's honor and compensate him for their insult. Bow your head in agreement, or else deny my prayer and show me how little you honor me."

Zeus, the Cloud-Gatherer, replied, "You are making my life with Hera more difficult by asking this of me. She already complains that I have given the Trojans too much help in battle. Yet I will do as you wish."

While gods and mortals slept, Zeus considered how he could best bring honor to Achilles and kill many of the Greeks beside their black ships. He decided to send wide-ruling Agamemnon a misleading dream. Calling Dream to his side, he commanded, "Go, harmful Dream, and tell Agamemnon to rouse the long-haired Greeks to battle since now they can conquer the well-defended city of the Trojans. Hera has convinced all the gods to side with the Greeks."

So Zeus spoke, and Dream went to Agamemnon, appearing in the form of Nestor, king of sandy Pylos, whom of all the elder Greeks Agamemnon most honored. "Why are you asleep, Agamemnon?" Dream asked. "A leader in your position, in charge of the entire Greek army, should have too much on his mind to sleep the night away. Now listen carefully, for I bring you a message from Zeus, lord of Olympus, who cares for you.

"Quickly rouse all the bronze-coated Greeks to arms because now is the time to take Priam's great city. Hera has won the support of all the deathless gods, and by the will of Zeus, Troy is doomed. Do not forget these words once you awaken." So Dream spoke to Agamemnon and departed.

Once wide awake, Agamemnon foolishly believed his dream to reflect reality. He put on his tunic, cloak, and sandals, and hung his sword around his shoulders.

He took his father's sceptre, fashioned by Hephaestus, in his hand and had his heralds call the Greeks to assembly.

When Agamemnon had explained to the council of elders the nature of his dream, wise Nestor spoke, "Friends, kings, and leaders of the Greeks," he began, "if any other Greek had had such a dream, we might think it false and therefore ignore it. However, since Agamemnon, who states that he is by far the greatest of the Greeks, has heard these words, let us prepare to attack."

Meanwhile, Zeus sent Iris, his wind-footed messenger, to the place where the Trojan forces had assembled. There she appeared in the form of the Trojan's principal watchman. "Old sir," Iris said to Priam, "I have been a part of many battles, but I have never seen such a large and impressive army marching across the plain to attack us. In numbers they are as great as the leaves in the woods or the sands along the salt sea!"

Then Iris turned to Hector of the shining helm. "Hector, godlike son of Priam, I place you in command of all the Trojans and our allies. Because those who have come to our aid speak many different languages, let each chieftain inform and lead his own countrymen out to battle." So Iris spoke, and Hector knew her true voice and obeyed her advice.

The horse-taming Trojans marched upon the field as noisily as cranes fly up into the sky toward the ocean when they flee from the heavy rains of winter. The bronze-coated Greeks silently approached them, each man with courage in his heart and eager for battle.

Just as the south wind spreads a mist over mountain peaks — a mist that the shepherd dislikes but the robber loves, for it hides the land and a man can see no farther than he can throw a stone — so the feet of these hundreds upon hundreds of marching men created a heavy cloud of dust over the armies as they moved quickly across the plain.

As the Greeks approached the Trojans, Paris became the Trojan champion. Carrying a bronze-tipped spear in each hand and upon his shoulders a panther skin, his curved bow, and his sword, he challenged the Greeks. "Come forth, any of you who think you are the best of the Greeks!" he announced. "I challenge you to fight me face to face to the death!"

Menelaus was pleased in his heart to see Paris emerge from the Trojan throng. Just as a hungry lion is delighted to come upon the carcass of a great horned stag or a wild goat, and he eats the tasty flesh even though he senses that young hunters with their pack of dogs are swiftly coming upon him, so Menelaus was delighted to see Paris, for the war-loving king of Sparta was anxious to take vengeance upon the Trojan prince who had taken fair Helen from her home and had carried her across the sea to Troy.

But when Paris saw Menelaus leap from his chariot in order to accept his challenge, Paris suddenly became terrified. As a man turns pale, trembles, and reels backward when he spies a snake on his mountain path, so did Paris shrink fearfully away from war-loving Menelaus and hide among the Trojan ranks.

When Hector observed this behavior, he criticized his brother with strong words. "Evil Paris! You are so handsome that women cannot resist you. It would have been far better for the Trojan people had you never been born, or had you died unwed. As it is, your behavior is shameful. Your countrymen scorn you, and

Greeks must be laughing indeed to see that the Trojan champion, for all his beauty, lacks courage and strength in his heart."

Hector then asked, "Are you the same man who crossed the salt sea to a strange land and returned with a beautiful woman, bringing sorrow upon your father, your city, and your countrymen, and shame upon yourself? Do you really intend to evade Menelaus? You should learn what kind of man he is whose wife you took. You will find no help in your lyre or in the gifts Aphrodite has bestowed upon you, for Menelaus is a respected warrior who would send you, defeated, into the dust. The Trojan people must share your cowardice, or they would have stoned you to death long before this, for all the evils you have brought upon them."

To these words, Paris replied, "Hector, you are right to criticize me, but do not blame me for golden Aphrodite's gifts. Instead, command all the Greeks and Trojans to stand aside while I fight Menelaus hand to hand for fair Helen and all her treasure. Then our people and their allies can return to their homes, and the Greeks can return to their lands in peace."

All the Greeks and Trojans were overjoyed to hear Hector's announcement, for the war rightfully was a conflict between Paris and Menelaus, and few were enthusiastic about continuing the fighting into this tenth year. The leaders of both forces united in prayer to Zeus and the other immortal gods, swearing to the terms of the agreement.

Wide-ruling Agamemnon raised his arms and prayed, "Father Zeus, observe our oaths. If Paris kills Menelaus, fair Helen and all her possessions will be his, and we will return to Greece empty-handed. But if fair-haired Menelaus kills Paris, then the Trojans must return Helen and her treasure along with suitable compensation for inciting us to war. Otherwise, I will remain on Trojan soil and continue to fight until I win what is rightfully mine."

When Paris and Menelaus had armed themselves, they entered the clearing between the seated Trojan and Greek forces, approaching each other with glaring looks and ready spears. Paris was the first to throw his far-shadowing spear, which bent its bronze point upon meeting Menelaus' round shield.

As Menelaus raised his spear, he prayed, "Zeus, lord of Olympus, permit me to punish Paris for stealing my wife so that any guest hereafter will fear to commit an offense against his friendly host." His spear penetrated Paris' armor, but it did not draw blood, and when he smashed his sword upon Paris' helmet, the sword fell to the ground, broken into four pieces.

So war-loving Menelaus jumped upon Paris, grabbed the thick horse-hair crest of his helmet, pulled him around, and began to drag his body backward toward the seated Greeks. Paris would have strangled to death, bringing Menelaus endless glory, if Aphrodite had not observed Paris' plight and cut his helmet strap, permitting him to break loose from Menelaus' grasp. When Menelaus leaped after Paris with his bronze spear he could not find him, for Aphrodite had lifted him up, hidden him in a dense mist, and returned him to his bedroom in Priam's great city.

Agamemnon shouted, "Hear me, all you Trojans and your allies. Obviously Menelaus has won the duel, so return Helen and her treasure to her rightful husband, and compensate the Greeks for Paris' offense." So he spoke, and all the Greeks shouted in agreement.

However, Hera and Athena were still angry with Paris for choosing Aphrodite's beauty over their own. This meant that Zeus could keep his word to Thetis without offending them, and the immortals agreed that Athena should cause the battle to resume.

Athena chose the Trojan Pandarus and appeared to him in the form of a respected Trojan spearman. "Why don't you shoot Menelaus with one of your arrows?" she suggested. "Then you will win fame and honor in the eyes of all the Trojans, especially Paris. He surely will reward you most handsomely for killing Atreus' war-loving son!"

So bright-eyed Athena persuaded the foolish Pandarus to draw his bow upon the unsuspecting Menelaus. However, because Athena at heart was a friend to the king of Sparta, she directed Pandarus' arrow through Menelaus' belt, where it wounded but did not kill him.

Agamemnon was so outraged at the injury to his brother that no one could accuse him of reluctance or cowardice as the Trojans resumed the battle. Leaving his chariot, he went by foot through the ranks of the bronze-coated Greeks, eagerly cheering them on to battle and the winning of glory. "Father Zeus will not help those who do not keep their word," he cried, "so be of good strength and courage. Vultures will feed on Trojan flesh, and many Trojan wives and children will sail home with us once we have taken Priam's well-defended city."

Just as the waves of the salt sea pound the shore, one after the other, driven toward by the west wind, so did the Greeks return to the battle, group after group, in endless succession; and each chieftain commanded his respectful, silent men, gleaming in their armor.

The Trojans, on the other hand, were as noisy as herds of sheep impatiently waiting to be milked, for they included peoples from many lands who did not share a common language. Bronze clashed upon bronze until untold numbers of Greeks and Trojans remained upon the plain, intermingled, with their faces buried in the dust.

Chapter 3

Hector returns to Troy. He urges Paris to join the Trojan warriors and then he bids farewell to his wife and son.

Hector of the shining helm decided to leave the plain of battle and enter Priam's great city in order to ask the women of Troy to pray to the deathless gods for help. The bronze-coated Greeks were clashing against the horse-taming Trojans with a mighty uproar, and Hector was no longer confident of a Trojan victory. Louder than the waves of the sea as they crash upon the shore when they are driven from the ocean's depths by the harsh blowing of the north wind; louder than the roaring of a fire that rages among the trees of a forested mountainside; louder than the howling wind among the highest branches of the oak trees were the Greeks and Trojans as Hector left them.

When his mother spied him, she cried, "My dearest child, why have you left the dreadful battle to return home? Do you wish to offer prayers to Zeus, lord of Olympus? Stay while I bring you honey-sweet wine for the prayer, and then relax and have some wine yourself." So Queen Hecuba spoke to her godlike son.

Man-slaying Hector replied, "Mother, do not bring me any honey-sweet wine unless you want to weaken me and make me forget my strength and my courage. I am so covered with the dirt and blood of battle that it is wiser for you and the other women to pray to Athena than for me to petition Zeus of the storm clouds. I am here to call Paris to battle if he will listen to me."

Hector found his brother at home in his bedroom aimlessly handling his shield and his bow while Helen sat among her servants and their handiwork. Again he addressed Paris with contempt. "Strange man! Your countrymen are dying in battle upon the wall and within the city, and here you sit! And yet you are the person responsible for the raising of the war cry around Troy. You yourself would be very angry with any coward you caught shrinking away from this hateful war. So arise and help defend your city before it is burned to the ground!"

"You are right, as usual, Hector. Even Helen has been urging me to join the fighting. So either stay with us while I put on my armor or else go on your way. I shall follow, and I will probably overtake you before you leave the city."

When Hector did not reply, Helen softly spoke to him. "I wish that on the day I was born, a great storm wind had carried me away to some lonely mountainside or to the shore of the loud-sounding sea, where the waves would have washed me away, for then this hateful war never would have occurred. Or, considering that the deathless gods determined these events, I wish that they had married me to a better man than Paris, one who could feel the anger and hatred of his family and his people. Paris will never change, so I fear that he will reap the bitter fruit of the seeds he has sown. But come and sit down, dear Hector, since Paris' foolishness and my shame have laid the heaviest burden upon your shoulders."

Hector replied, "Do not ask me to stay, Helen, even though you love me. I am most anxious to rejoin the Trojan forces, whom I know miss my help while I am within the city walls. Try to make Paris move quickly so that he will be able to overtake me. Meanwhile, I shall go home to see my dearest wife and baby, perhaps for the last time."

With these words, Hector went searching for his wife and child. They met near the Scaean Gates, the entrance to Priam's great city, for Andromache had been standing upon the wall of Troy, weeping as she searched the battlefield for him. Hector smiled wordlessly as he gazed upon his infant son, but Andromache tearfully approached her husband, took his hand in hers, and pleaded with him.

"Oh, Hector," she cried, "your courage and your skill in battle will destroy you! You lack any pity for your baby son, who will become an orphan, or for the woman who will soon be your widow, for the bronze-coated Greeks will soon kill you.

"It would be better for me to die than to lose you," she continued, "for swift-footed Achilles has made me an orphan. He killed my kingly father in his armor and murdered my seven brothers as they were tending their sheep, and then Artemis killed my mother. So, dear Hector, you are my father, my mother, and my brother, as well as my husband. Have pity upon me, and remain here upon the wall of Troy."

Finally Andromache advised her husband, "Position the Trojans by the wild fig tree, for there the wall is most easily accessible. Three times already the greatest warriors among the Greeks have tried to enter there."

Hector responded, "Dearest wife, I too have thought of this, but our people would look upon me with shame if I were to shrink like a coward from battle. My own heart cannot tolerate such behavior. I was taught to be courageous always and to lead the Trojans into battle to win great glory for my father and myself.

"My heart and my soul tell me that the day will come when the Greeks will destroy our fair city and its people. Yet I do not grieve for anyone in my family as much as I do for you when some Greek steals your freedom and leads you across the salt sea against your will.

"There," Hector added, "as a slave in some Greek household, you will work at the loom as some mistress directs you, and you will carry water from the spring as part of your sad burden. And when he notices your tears, some stranger will say, 'Look. There goes the wife of man-slaying Hector, who was the greatest in war of all the Trojans in the days when man fought against man at Troy.' May I be dead and may the earth cover my body before the Greeks enslave you."

With these words, Hector stretched out his arms to his little son, but Astyanax, terrified by his father's shining bronze helmet with its wildly waving horsehair crest, tearfully withdrew from his embrace. Then Hector and Andromache laughed together, and Hector removed the helmet from his head and placed it upon the ground.

Taking his infant son in his arms, Hector kissed Astyanax and prayed. "Zeus and all you other immortal gods," he began, "permit my son to live and grow to be as I am: courageous and strong, and foremost among the Trojan people; and grant that he will become a great king of Troy. Then one day may someone say of him as returns from war, 'He is better far than his father!' and his mother will be glad in her heart."

Hector then placed Astyanax in his mother's arms, and she held him, smiling through her tears. This sight brought pity to Hector's heart, and he caressed Andromache as he said, "Dearest, please try not to be too unhappy. I shall not die before my fate sends me down to Hades, and I share the same fate as every other mortal; neither the courageous nor the cowardly can escape it.

"So return home," her husband concluded, "and keep busy with your daily chores. War is the responsibility of the men of Troy and, therefore, mostly mine." Hector put his crested helmet upon his head and returned to his men.

Andromache walked home, frequently looking back tearfully. When she arrived, all the women of the household cried for Hector, even though he still lived, for in their hearts they knew that he would never return alive from this battle with the Greeks.

Paris did not dally long at home. Just as a well-fed horse breaks his rein and goes galloping across the field, anticipating a swim in the fast current of the river, and rejoices in his strength and splendor as he carries his head high and feels his mane waving upon his neck, so Paris in his sparkling armor moved through the streets of the city on his swift feet, laughing with the pure joy of being alive.

He met his brother as Hector was leaving the place where he had talked with Andromache. "Hector," Paris apologized, "I'm sure that I delayed you and did not come as soon as you wished."

To these words Hector replied, "No one who is observant can criticize your skill in battle, Paris, for you are courageous and strong. But you are also irresponsible, and it makes me sad to hear the Trojans say truly that you are the cause of their troubles. However, let us go on our way. We will deal with this later if Zeus lets us drive the Greeks from our land."

Chapter 4

Agamemnon's advisers counsel him to apologize to Achilles. He offers Achilles many gifts if he will rejoin the Greeks and keep Hector from burning their ships, but the warrior refuses.

The Trojans were fighting with skill, spirit, and success. They and their allies summoned from many lands frustrated every attempt of the bronze-coated Greeks to subdue them.

Without Achilles to lead his countrymen, the Myrmidons, and without the gods to help them, the Greeks were not equal to Hector and the Trojan army. Just as farmers and their dogs force a lion out of the cattle pen so the wild beast cannot capture the fattest of the herd, and they remain on watch throughout the entire night and when the lion returns, skillful hands send arrows and dreadful flaming torches to frighten it away, and with the coming of rosy-fingered Dawn it finally retreats in anger, so the Trojans sent the Greeks back across the plain toward their hollow ships.

There Agamemnon, with sadness in his heart, commanded his heralds to call the Greek leaders to assembly. When everyone had arrived, the wide-ruling king rose and addressed them. As a waterfall pours down the face of a cliff into the dark stream below, so Agamemnon stood weeping before the gathering.

"My friends, leaders, and chieftains of the Greeks," he began. "Cruel Zeus, lord of Olympus, has blinded me. Long ago he promised me, and he bowed his head to it, that I would not return home until I had destroyed well-defended Troy. Obviously he was deceiving me. So let each of us gather our countrymen into our hollow ships and return to our homeland, for we cannot hope to capture Troy. We need not feel ashamed to run from ruin, even in darkness, for it is better to escape and live than to be captured or killed."

Those assembled before him sat in complete silence. Finally, Odysseus rose. "Son of Atreus, do you mean these words you have just spoken? If so, it would be far better if you commanded some ordinary army. Do you really wish to leave Troy now, after we have fought here for nine years to destroy it? Remain quiet so that no other king will think to follow your poor example. You must have lost your senses to speak to us in this way in the midst of battle. Your advice would be the dearest wish of the Trojans."

Agamemnon replied, "Your words have touched my heart. I would not have the bronze-coated Greeks withdraw against their will. I welcome other opinions on this matter."

Nestor, the wise king of Pylos, rose. "Great son of Atreus, wide-ruling Agamemnon, I will begin and end with you, for Zeus has enabled you to rule all the men gathered here. It seems best to remind you of the day long ago when, against my advice and the consent of all gathered here, you took from godlike Achilles' hut his prize of honor, fair Briseis. By giving your pride free reign, you dishonored a mighty warrior whom the deathless gods honor. Consider how best to apologize, with what word to entreat him, and with what gifts to persuade him to rejoin us."

Agamemnon replied, "Old sir, you are right to remember my foolishness. I do not deny that I was blinded by my strong feelings. As a result, Zeus honors Achilles, whom he loves in his heart, and is destroying us. To atone for my insult, I shall give the son of Peleus an overwhelming number of impressive gifts.

"I shall give swift-footed Achilles seven new tripods, untouched by fire; the weight of ten talents in gold; twenty shining cauldrons; and twelve strong, swift, prize-winning horses. I shall also give him seven beautiful women who are skilled at handicraft, among them Briseis, whom I have never touched."

Agamemnon added, "Later, if the gods permit us to seize well-defended Troy, let Achilles pile gold and bronze into his hollow ships and choose for himself the twenty most beautiful Trojan women next to Helen. And if we return to the rich land of Argos, I will honor Achilles as I honor my son Orestes. Let him choose any one of my three daughters to be his wife, and he need offer none of the usual courting gifts. Finally, I will give him seven large cities near the salt sea on the border of sandy Pylos, cities that are rich in sheep and cattle, whose people will honor him as if he were a god.

"All this I shall do for Achilles if he will put aside his anger. Only Hades, lord of the dead, is unrelenting, and he is, therefore, the god whom mortals hate most. The son of Peleus should agree to my proposal because I am older than he is, and I am a greater king."

So spoke Agamemnon, and everyone was pleased with his words. Nestor then said, "Great son of Atreus, no one could find fault with the gifts you are offering Achilles. So let us choose who will approach Achilles in your name. First let Phoenix, Achilles' tutor, lead the way, followed by Ajax and Odysseus."

The three men walked along the shore of the loud-sounding sea with prayers in their hearts that Poseidon, the Earthshaker, might help them persuade Achilles to their cause. When they arrived, Achilles greeted them warmly. "Welcome!" he cried. "Even in anger, you are my dearest friends! The bronze-coated Greeks must desperately need my help that they have finally sent you to me."

After Achilles had fed them, Odysseus discussed why they had come. He explained the successess of the Trojans under Hector's leadership, and he repeated the list of gifts that Agamemnon was offering Achilles if he would forget his anger and return to the war.

When he had finished recounting the gifts, Odysseus said, "But if you hate the son of Atreus and his gifts too much, then at least have pity for the rest of us! We will honor you as a god, for you will win great glory. Now you may easily kill Hector, for he thinks there is no one who can match him among the Greeks."

Achilles replied, "Odysseus, man of many wiles, I shall say exactly what I think so that you will not think you can argue with me. I hate a man who thinks one thing but speaks another.

"Neither Agamemnon nor any other bronze-coated Greek will persuade me to rejoin the battle, for it seems that no one appreciates the warrior who fights without rest. He who remains at home receives the same gifts as he who fights his best; the coward is honored equally with the brave man; and death is the fate of both the man who is idle and the man who works hard. I have spent many a bloody day in battle and many a sleepless night in watch. I destroyed twelve Trojan cities from my ships and eleven more by land. I took much treasure from these cities and gave all of it to Agamemnon. He remained behind, beside his hollow ships, and from the treasures I gave him, he distributed a few and kept the rest. Some he gave to kings and chieftains, and they have been allowed to keep them. Only from me did he take a prize of honor."

Achilles went on to say, "Agamemnon has led all of us here to bring Menelaus' wife, fair Helen, back to Sparta. Are the two sons of Atreus the only mortal men who love their wives? Surely I love mine with all my heart, even if she is a captive I won with my spear.

"I know Agamemnon too well. He does not keep his word. He will not deceive me again, not will he persuade me to come to his aid. Even his gifts are hateful to me; I would not accept them if they were as many as the sands of the salt sea and the dust of the earth, and I would not marry his daughter if she were as beautiful as Aphrodite and as skilled in handiwork as Athena.

"What are gifts compared to life!" Achilles concluded. "My goddess mother has told me that if I stay here and fight at Troy, I will never live to return home, although I will have gained eternal fame. On the other hand, if I return to my homeland, I will lose all fame but live a long life. I am choosing life, and I advise you to do the same. You will not conquer the great city of Priam, for the horse-taming Trojans are a courageous people, and Zeus is watching over them. So let the arrogant son of Atreus plan the best way to keep man-slaying Hector from burning the Greek ships. The wall and the ditch will not be sufficient to stop him, so courageous and confident is he now that I am not fighting. Return to Agamemnon with this message, but let Phoenix sleep here tonight so that he can sail home with me tomorrow if he chooses."

For a few minutes after Achilles had spoken, everyone remained silent, overwhelmed by what he had said and the strength of his feeling. Then Phoenix spoke through his tears. "If you are indeed determined to return home and will not help protect the Greek ships from Hector's fire, then I must return with you.

"I have loved you and reared you as I would my own son, Achilles. I ask you now to rule your pride, and let pity enter your heart. Even the deathless gods bend, and they are far greater than you are. If Agamemnon were not offering you gifts, I would not ask you to put aside your anger and help the Greeks in their need. But he is amply rewarding you, and he has sent the best warriors, your dearest friends, to plead with you. Do not look arrogantly upon their words or upon their visit here.

"Until now," Phoenix concluded, "no one could blame you for your anger, but the time has come for you to relent. It will be much harder to save the hollow ships once they are burning. So agree to help the Greeks while they are offering you gifts, and they will honor you as a god. If you enter the battle later, you will have given up the gifts, and you will have lost much honor even if you save the ships."

Achilles replied, "Phoenix, old sir, Father, I do not need the long-haired Greeks to honor me. Zeus, lord of Olympus, has honored me, and his honor will be mine as long as I live. Do not annoy me by taking Agamemnon's part against me, or I will hate you as I hate him. Let the others return to the son of Atreus with my message. Meanwhile, spend the night with me, and in the morning we will discuss whether we should remain here or return home."

Ajax then said to Odysseus, "Let us be on our way, for we should quickly deliver Achilles' message, even if it is not a good one. The son of Peleus has no pity for his friends who have honored him above everyone else. A man accepts payment from the one who kills his brother or his son, and for a great price, the one who killed can continue to live in his own country.

"But you, Achilles, will not bend because of one woman, when we have offered you seven of the best women and many other gifts besides. Respect yourself and us, for we would like to be your dearest friends."

Achilles answered, "I would agree with you, Ajax, except that I am furious to think of how the arrogant son of Atreus has dishonored me among the Greeks as if I were some worthless stranger. So return with my message. I shall not join the fighting until Hector brings fire to my own ships, and there I shall stop him."

Ajax and Odysseus returned to Agamemnon. When Odysseus repeated Achilles' message, the hearts of the Greek leaders and chieftains were sad. They realized that the son of Peleus would fight only if and when his heart moved him to do so. Until then, the bronze-coated Greeks would have to rely upon their own courage and strength.

Chapter 5

Patroclus convinces Achilles to let him lead the
Myrmidons into battle. Wearing Achilles' armor,
Patroclus pushes the Trojans away from the Greek
ships and back toward Troy. Finally, Hector kills him.

When Dawn, the rosy-fingered, shone forth upon gods and mortals, the war resumed. Just as reapers push into one another as they move through a rich farmer's field of wheat or barley, and many handfuls of grain quickly fall about them, so the bronze-coated Greeks and the horse-taming Trojans leaped upon each other and cut one another down, with no thought of retreat. Neither side gave in to the other, and they tore on like wolves.

Achilles stood at the stern of his black ship, watching the return of injured Greeks. Calling his closest friend to him, Achilles said, "Good Patroclus, dearest to my heart, I think the Greeks soon will be praying at my knees for me to help them, for they appear to be in great trouble. Go ask Nestor whom he has brought wounded from the field; I fear it is our doctor, and that, indeed, would be a cause of fear and grief."

When Patroclus questioned Nestor, the king of Pylos asked him, "Does Achilles suddenly pity the Greeks? Does he care that many of our greatest warriors are lying by their hollow ships sorely wounded by arrows or spears?"

Nestor then told Patroclus, "I remember that when Odysseus and I came to Phthia to ask Achilles to join wide-ruling Agamemnon and the other Greek leaders, your father told you to be your dear friend's adviser. Although Achilles is stronger than you are, you are older and, therefore, wiser than he is. Counsel him now. Perhaps he will take your words into his heart.

"And if, perhaps, some prophecy of his mother is restraining Achilles from fighting, let him place his armor upon you and permit you to lead the Myrmidons into battle. With godlike Achilles' armor upon you, the Trojans may think that you are indeed he, and they may retreat in fear."

Then Nestor concluded, "The Greeks need a chance to rest, for they are weary with fighting. Your countrymen are so well-rested that it will be easy for you to push the tired Trojans back from our huts and our ships across the plain toward Troy." So Nestor of sandy Pylos, in his wisdom, put fire into the heart of good Patroclus.

The Trojans, who had been fighting by the wall the Greeks had constructed to protect their huts and their ships, suddenly pushed forward. Just as a great wave upon the salt sea is forced by the fury of the strong wind into a mighty swell, and rushes down upon the decks of a ship and engulfs it, so the Trojans, with a loud war cry, drove their chariots over the defensive wall to the sterns of the Greek ships. They fought the Greeks there face to face.

As a starving mountain lion courageously enters a well-built sheepfold to seize its prey, and although it sees that the shepherds are prepared to defend the sheep with their swift spears and their dogs, it is determined to capture a sheep or else die in the attempt, so did man-slaying Hector, of the great war cry, put courage into the hearts of the Trojans and lead them to set fire to the hollow ships of the Greeks.

By the time Patroclus reached Achilles, he was in tears. The son of Peleus pitied him and asked, "Patroclus, dearest of friends, why are you weeping like a little girl who runs by her mother's side and slows her down by pulling at her robe and tearfully crying up at her until her mother picks her up? Have you heard that your father or mine has died? Or are you grieving for the bronze-coated Greeks who are being killed beside their black ships because of their arrogance?"

Then did great-hearted Patroclus foolishly relate to Achilles the plight of the Greeks and his wish to lead the Myrmidons into battle in Achilles' place, for he did not realize that he was, in fact, pleading for his own death.

Patroclus' words weighed upon Achilles' heart, and he replied, "Dear Patroclus, it is not my mother's prophecy that keeps me from battle. I simply could not let a man who is my equal seize my prize of honor just because he is more powerful than I am. I did not intend to be angry forever, but I did say that I would not rejoin the Greeks until Hector threatened my own ships.

"However," Achilles relented, "put my shining armor upon your shoulders, if that is your wish, and lead the war-loving Myrmidons into battle yourself. Drive the Trojans from the hollow ships, for if they burn the ships, the Greeks will have no way to return home. Win enough glory that the Greeks will return Briseis to me along with many impressive gifts, but not so much glory that your success will lessen my own value and my own honor. Although you love the war cry, once you have cleared the Trojans from the ships and have sent them in retreat across the plain toward Troy, return to me."

When Patroclus, wearing the armor of Achilles, was ready to depart with the Myrmidons, Achilles prayed to Zeus. "Lord of Olympus, in the past you have heard my prayers. You have honored me, and you have brought destruction upon the Greeks. Now hear my prayer again. I am sending my dearest friend into war with my Myrmidons. Grant him success and glory, but when he has driven the Trojans from the hollow ships, let him return uninjured to me."

So Achilles, son of Peleus, prayed, and Zeus, lord of counsel, heard him. He permitted Patroclus to drive the Trojans from the swift black ships, but he did not permit him a safe return from battle.

With Patroclus in the lead, the war-loving Myrmidons marched into battle. Patroclus cried, "Myrmidons, friends of Achilles, courageously win honor for the son of Peleus, so that wide-ruling Agamemnon will realize how blind he was when he dishonored the best of the Greeks."

So Patroclus put strength and courage into the hearts of the Myrmidons as they joyfully prepared to attack the Trojans. Like wasps along the wayside that swarm angrily from their nests when young boys foolishly torment them for the fun of it, so the Myrmidons swarmed upon the Trojans with a great war cry.

When the Trojans saw Patroclus in Achilles' shining armor, fear entered each man's heart, for they thought that godlike Achilles himself would soon be upon them. They gave way before the Myrmidons and considered how best to escape total destruction.

Just as a winter rainstorm at its peak causes swift, swollen rivers to wash away whatever lines their banks, so Patroclus raged across the plain, causing many Trojans to fall beneath his sharp spear. If he had remembered to return to the ships, as Achilles had counseled him, he would have avoided his fate. However, blind in his heart, he forgot the words of his dearest friend and foolishly pressed on across the plain toward Troy.

Then the bronze-coated Greeks would indeed have captured high-gated Troy under the leadership of Patroclus, but Apollo came down from Mount Olympus to stand upon the well-built wall and help his favorites. Three times Patroclus climbed upon a corner of the high wall, and three times the lord of the silver bow raised his immortal hands, pushed against Patroclus' shining shield, and threw him back.

When Patroclus, undaunted, made a fourth attempt to climb the wall, Apollo stopped him with a terrifying cry. Then he said, "Give up, Patroclus! It is not your fate to sack the great city of Priam with your spear; nor will swift-footed Achilles destroy this city, and he is a far better man than you are." Patroclus obeyed Apollo's command, having no intention of angering the Far-Shooter.

Meanwhile, Hector of the flashing helm was standing at the Scaean Gates and wondering whether it would be better to continue the fighting or to summon the Trojans inside the well-defended walls. Apollo assumed the form of Hector's uncle and said, "Godlike Hector, why are you not fighting? It is not honorable to stand about idly while others are winning glory for themselves and their fathers. If I were strong enough, I would punish you for your cowardice. Now drive your horses toward Patroclus and kill him; then Apollo, the Far-Shooter, will give you glory." So spoke Apollo, and Hector returned to the battle.

As long as the sun was high in the sky, the spears and arrows of Greeks and Trojans took an even toll. But when the sun revealed that the time had come to unyoke the oxen and stable them for the evening, then the bronze-coated Greeks took the lead.

Three times Patroclus, shouting the great war cry, killed nine men. As he raged on for the fourth time, far-shooting Apollo enveloped himself in a thick mist and came up behind Patroclus. Unseen, the lord of the silver bow took his immortal hand and struck the warrior on the back with such a mighty force that his eyes whirled in his head. Then he knocked Patroclus' helmet to the ground, where it clattered as it rolled beneath the feet of the horses, and its horsehair crest became covered with blood and dust.

Still Apollo was not finished with Patroclus. The warrior's bronze-tipped, far-shadowing spear broke apart in his hands, his shield fell to the ground, and his armor loosened. Then his mind became blind, and as he was standing senseless, a Trojan came up behind him and speared him in the back. However, even this wound did not kill Patroclus.

Man-slaying Hector then approached and drove his spear clear through Patroclus' stomach. Just as a mountain lion overpowers a mighty boar when the two fight upon a mountaintop for the right to drink from a little spring, so did Hector, godlike son of Priam, end good Patroclus' life.

Standing over the fallen body of his enemy, Hector said, "Patroclus, you thought that you would sack Troy! You wanted to make slaves of our women and return with them to your homeland. You were a fool! Instead, vultures will feed upon your flesh. Even your dear friend, Achilles, with all his courage, strength and skill, could not help you. He must have commanded you to kill me. He muddled your good sense!"

The dying Patroclus replied, "You can boast about my death only because Zeus and Apollo first subdued me. Otherwise, if twenty Hectors had attacked me, I would have killed them all with my spear. You were not first but third in my slaying.

"And remember this well," Patroclus concluded. "You yourself do not have long to live, for it is your fate to be killed by Achilles. Even now, your death is very close at hand." With these words Patroclus' shade left his body and went down to the kingdom of Hades.

Hector replied to the dead Patroclus, "Why do you prophesy my death? Maybe I will kill the son of Peleus!" He then removed Achilles' shining armor from Patroclus and took it for himself. He would have dragged off Patroclus' body as food for the dogs of Troy, but Ajax took his shield, which was like a wall, and defended the corpse.

The bronze-coated Greeks then fought the horse-taming Trojans for the body of Achilles' friend. All day long the battle raged. Just as a man gives the hide of a great bull, soaked in fat, to his people to stretch, and they arrange themselves in a circle, where they stand and pull it until the moisture evaporates, the fat penetrates the skin, and the hide is completely stretched out, so the Greeks on one side and the Trojans on the other pulled the body of Patroclus first this way and then that until, at long last, the Greeks were able to carry his corpse back to the hollow ships.

Chapter 6

*As soon as Achilles hears that Hector has killed
Patroclus, he is determined to kill Hector. He and
Agamemnon formally settle their quarrel, and Achilles
shows his skill on the battlefield. Hector flees from
him, and Achilles chases Hector around the walls of
Troy.*

Meanwhile, back at his hut, Achilles was filled with foreboding. "Why are the Greeks being driven back again?" he asked himself. "My mother once told me that I would live to see the best of the Myrmidons felled by Trojan hands. Great-hearted Patroclus! My dearest friend! How foolish of him to ignore my words and fight against man-slaying Hector."

While he was thinking such thoughts, the son of Nestor arrived in tears and announced, "I am so sorry to bring you very sad news, Achilles. Hector has killed Patroclus and has taken his armor. Now our warriors are fighting the Trojans for his very body!"

These words enveloped Achilles in a black cloud of grief. With both hands he covered his head and clothing with black soil. Then he lay himself in the dirt and tore his hair.

As he moaned in grief, silver-footed Thetis appeared before him. "My child, why are you crying?" she asked. "Zeus, lord of counsel, has indeed granted your wish, and the bronze-coated Greeks are sorely in need of you."

Achilles replied, "Mother, even if the deathless gods have heard my prayer, what joy can I have when Patroclus, dearest of all to me, is dead? I no longer care to live unless I slay the godlike son of Priam who killed my friend!"

"You are then fated to die soon," Thetis replied, weeping, "for your own death will rapidly follow the death of Hector."

"Let me die, then," responded Achilles, "since I was not able to stand with Patroclus against Hector. I now realize at what great price I sat uselessly by my ships, enjoying anger far sweeter than honey against wide-ruling Agamemnon. Hector has killed good Patroclus and many other friends. May such anger, which upsets even the wisest, no longer afflict the deathless gods and mortal men!"

Achilles then announced, "I shall go forth to slay Hector, who killed the man I loved. I shall accept my fate whenever Zeus and the other immortals bring it upon me. Until then, may I win great fame and glory, and may every Trojan realize that the greatest of the Greeks no longer remains apart from battle. If you love me, Mother, do not attempt to prevent my return to battle."

"I shall not try to dissuade you, my child," Thetis replied. "I ask only that you wait until Dawn has brought early light. Then I will return to you, bringing you new armor forged by Hephaestus himself. You will enter battle wearing shining armor that will bring glory to the immortal craftsman who fashioned it and to you."

When the Greeks finally had carried Patroclus' body back to the hollow ships, wise Polydamas advised Hector. "Godlike son of Priam, listen to my thoughtful counsel. I think that we should return to Troy. It was safe for us to remain by the Greek ships, far from our well-defended city, as long as Achilles was angry with wide-ruling Agamemnon. Now, however, I fear the wrath of the swift-footed son of Peleus. He will fight relentlessly to destroy our city and to capture our wives. If we remain here, many of us will become food for dogs and vultures, and we will weaken the defense of Troy. We can fight Achilles far better if we take a stand upon our walls."

To this advice, Hector of the flashing helm angrily replied, "Polydamas, your words do not please my heart. Are you not tired of being confined within walls? I shall not permit any Trojan to listen to you! We shall fight the bronze-coated Greeks at their hollow ships. If Achilles enters the battle, I will fight him face to face, and one of us will win great glory."

So Hector commanded the horse-taming Trojans. His countrymen foolishly supported him, for bright-eyed Athena robbed them of their good judgment. They praised man-slaying Hector for his poor counsel and refused to listen to wise Polydamas.

When rosy-fingered Dawn brought light to gods and mortals, Thetis appeared before Achilles as she had promised, with Hephaestus' shining armor. Following her advice, the son of Peleus then called the Greeks to assembly in order to end his argument with Agamemnon.

Once they had gathered together, Achilles rose and said, "Agamemnon, did we gain anything by fighting in this way over a woman? Would that Artemis the archer had slain her when I captured her! My mighty anger has caused the deaths of my dearest friend and many other Greeks and has brought great glory to Hector and the Trojans. Now it is time for us to put aside the past and unite once again against our enemy. Few will escape the fury of my spear!"

Agamemnon replied, "Often the long-haired Greeks have criticized me, even though I was not at fault. The evil goddess Ate blinded me and Zeus stole my judgment on the day that I seized your prize of honor. Therefore, I am willing to compensate you for the injury I have caused you. I offer you, once again, all of the gifts that Odysseus promised you in my name when he came to your hut."

Achilles answered, "Great son of Atreus, wide-ruling Agamemnon, whether you give the gifts, as is proper, or whether you withhold them is your decision. But let us put an end to this talk. Instead, we should quickly prepare for battle, for that is an unfinished task. Let everyone watch as I destroy the Trojans with my far-shadowing bronze spear!"

Soon the plain shone with shining bronze as the Greeks met the Trojans in battle. Achilles' desire for revenge combined with his courage, strength, and skill to ravage the Trojan army. Swift-footed Achilles pushed ever onward to win glory. As a wildly raging fire sweeps through the parched forests on a mountainside, and the wind scatters flames everywhere, so the godlike son of Peleus raged among the Trojans, causing the black earth to swim with Trojan blood.

Now that Patroclus was dead, Achilles could feel no pity. When one of the Trojan warriors begged for his life, Achilles explained, "Until Patroclus died, I enjoyed sparing Trojan lives. Many I captured alive and sold across the sea. But now no Trojan who comes into my hands will avoid death. Great-hearted Patroclus died, and he was a far better man than any of you. Even I, goddess- and hero-born, and as skillful as I am, shall die in this war, either by some Trojan spear or by an arrow from a well-aimed bow."

Hector was standing near the Scaean Gates of Troy with his father when they saw Achilles approaching. "My dearest child," Priam pleaded, "do not go forth to meet Achilles alone lest he kill you, for he is a far better warrior than you are. Cruel man! I wish the immortals valued him as I do! I would let the dogs and vultures ravenously feed upon him as I left him, unburied, upon the dirt. Do not bring great glory to the swift-footed son of Peleus by offering him your life!"

As Hector of the shining helm watched Achilles come toward him, he thought to himself, "If I retreat within the walls of Troy now, Polydamas will remind me that I have caused our troubles. After I killed Patroclus, I ordered the Trojans to remain near the Greek ships. Thinking that we had nothing to fear, I was quick to criticize Polydamas' wise counsel. How blind I was to think that we could defeat the bronze-coated Greeks once godlike Achilles returned to the battlefield!

"Now Achilles has sent the shades of many fine Trojan warriors down to the kingdom of Hades, and I feel ashamed in front of the armored men and long-robed women of Troy. I fear they will say I brought destruction upon my people because I was too confident in my ability to fight Achilles. It would be far better to face Achilles man to man and either kill him or die with honor.

"On the other hand," Hector thought, "what if I lay down my shield and crested helmet, rest my far-shadowing spear against the wall, and go forth unarmed to meet Achilles, promising to return Helen and all the treasure that Paris took from Sparta? We could give the sons of Atreus half the treasure of Troy as well.

"But how can I even consider this? If I approach Achilles in a submissive way, he will neither respect me nor pity me but will kill me as I stand unarmed before him. No, the first approach is the better one: to fight it out and learn which of us will gain glory."

As Hector stood thinking, Achilles approached him. The godlike son of Peleus was a terrifying sight as his father's ash spear rode upon his right shoulder and his bronze armor blazed like the fiery sun. Fear grabbed Hector's heart, and he fled. Swift-footed Achilles immediately pursued him. As a falcon in the mountains, the swiftest of birds, swoops easily after a trembling dove and pursues it with shrill cries, so Achilles chased Hector.

Around the walls of Troy they ran, past where the Trojan people sat upon the wall, past the observation post, past the wild fig tree, along the wagon track, and by the two springs that feed the Scamander River, the one steaming hot and the other icy cold. As swiftly as Hector ran, a faster man ran after him, for they were not running a race to win a beast of sacrifice or a bull's hide as a prize. They were running to see who would win Hector's life!

Three times around the walls of Troy they ran, as all the deathless gods watched from Mount Olympus. As when a hunting dog stirs a fawn from its den and chases it through woods and meadow, and though the fawn escapes for a while by hiding in thick underbrush, yet the dog tracks its scent and follows it until he finds it, so swift-footed Achilles pursued man-slaying Hector.

Whenever Hector tried to come close enough to the Scaean Gates for the Trojans upon the wall to shoot at Achilles, the son of Peleus would take an inside track and drive Hector back toward the plain. Apollo helped Hector for the last time by increasing his strength and hastening his feet so that swift-footed Achilles could not overtake him.

Meanwhile, Achilles signaled the Greeks that they should not try to kill Hector. The godlike son of Peleus wanted to win that glory for himself.

Chapter 7

Athena tricks Hector into fighting Achilles face to face. It is Hector's time to die, and Achilles kills him. Hector reminds Achilles that his own death will soon follow.

As the race around the well-built walls of Troy continued, the lord of Olympus commented, "I pity Hector, whom I love, but Achilles is a good man too. Should we save Hector from death, or good as he is should we let Achilles kill him?"

Bright-eyed Athena replied, "Oh, Father, lord of the bright lightning and of the dark cloud, how can you suggest that we have a choice? Do you intend to change the fate of a mortal that was set long ago? Save him if you wish, but know that all of us do not agree with you."

As Hector and Achilles were approaching the hot and cold springs for the fourth time, Zeus raised his golden scales and set the two fates of death upon them: on the one hand, that of swift-footed Achilles; on the other, that of man-slaying Hector. When he held the scales in the middle to see how they would balance, the scale bearing Hector's fate sank. Now Apollo would have to leave him, for a god may not help a mortal on the day he or she is fated to die.

Athena went down to Achilles and said, "Great Achilles, dear to Zeus, now we shall kill Hector. He can no longer escape from us, no matter what Apollo may try to do to save him. Rest here while I persuade the son of Priam to fight you face to face."

When the goddess left Achilles, she appeared before Hector in the form and voice of his dearest brother, Deiphobus. "Dear brother," she cried, "let us stand here together and deal with Achilles as he deserves!"

Hector of the shining helm replied, "Deiphobus, you have always been the dearest of my brothers to me, but now I honor you in my heart even more because you have left the safety of the walls for my sake, while everyone else has remained within."

The bright-eyed goddess then said, "It is true that our father and mother and many friends pleaded with me to remain there, so terribly afraid are they of Achilles, but my heart was with you. So let us now attack the son of Peleus with all of our strength and skill, and learn if, in fact, he will kill both of us or whether your spear will put an end to him." In this deceptive fashion Athena tricked godlike Hector into confronting his fate.

Hector approached the son of Peleus and said, "I shall no longer run from you, Achilles, but will fight you man to man until one of us has taken the life of the other. But first, let us call the deathless gods to witness this pledge: I will treat you fairly if Zeus, lord of Olympus, gives me the strength to slay you. Once I have removed your splendid armor, I shall return your dead body to your countrymen, and I want you to promise to do the same."

Achilles angrily replied, "Do not talk to me of promises, Hector. Just as lions and men do not make pledges to one another, nor do wolves and lambs agree but rather continually plot evil against each other, so it is impossible for you and me to treat one another as friends and promise anything at all.

"Instead," Achilles continued, "summon all your courage, strength, and skill as a spearman, for you are about to die. You can no longer escape your fate, for by my spear Athena, bright-eyed daughter of Zeus, will take your life. Now you will finally pay for all the sorrow you brought me by slaying good Patroclus with your bronze-tipped spear."

With these words Achilles raised his own far-shadowing spear and hurled it at Hector. The son of Priam accurately judged its path, and moved so that the spear flew over his head and lodged in the earth behind him. Unseen by Hector, Athena removed the spear and returned it to Achilles.

As he prepared to hurl his swift spear, Hector announced, "You missed me, Achilles! You have also missed knowing my fate, sure as you were of it. You tried to frighten me into losing my courage and my strength and fleeing, but I will not give you that chance to drive your spear into my back. You will have to plunge it straight through my chest. Now, avoid my spear if you can!"

Hector's spear hit Achilles' shield as planned, but then it bounced off and fell to the ground out of Hector's reach. He called upon his brother for another spear, but Deiphobus was nowhere in sight.

Then in his heart Hector understood the truth. He thought, "The deathless gods have indeed brought me to my death! I thought that Deiphobus was by my side, but he is within the walls of Troy. Athena has deceived me! The lord of Olympus and his far-shooting son must long have intended this, even though they have usually been quick to help me.

"My death now awaits me," Hector concluded. "I see no way to avoid it. At least I will die with honor, so that men in times to come will hear of my valor."

He drew his great sword from his side and rushed upon Achilles. As a mighty eagle soaring high into the sky spies a little lamb or rabbit far below and, swiftly changing its course, swoops down through the dark clouds to the meadow to seize its trembling prey, so Hector of the shining helm attacked the son of Peleus.

Achilles met Hector's attack with rage in his heart. In his right hand, his spear shone like the brightest evening star. He paused briefly while he studied his old bronze armor in order to find the best place to strike. He had given that shining armor to great-hearted Patroclus, but now it was protecting man-slaying Hector. Hector's only visible flesh was at his throat, where he would die most quickly. There Achilles plunged his bronze tipped spear.

As his foe lay dying in the dust, the son of Peleus cried joyfully, "Hector, slayer of men, while you were busy killing Patroclus, you were foolish to give so little thought to how I would repay you for your evil deed. Good Patroclus will receive a proper burial, but your body will be ravaged by dogs and birds!"

Hector replied with the last of his strength, "I plead with you, do not take me to your hollow ships to be consumed by dogs. Instead, accept the gifts of bronze and gold that my father and mother will give you for my body so that the Trojan people can bury me with honor."

Achilles furiously responded, "Do not implore me, you dog! So great is my anger at what you have done to me that if I could, I myself would tear apart your flesh and eat it raw. Therefore, no one can keep the dogs away from your head, not for ten or twenty times the proper ransom, not even if Priam were to pay me your weight in gold. Your mother will not be able to mourn before your body, for you will be completely devoured by dogs and birds far from Priam's great city."

The dying Hector then said, "I knew that I could not hope to persuade you. Your heart is truly made of iron! Be careful, though, for I may bring the wrath of the deathless gods upon you on the day when, in spite of your courage, your strength, and your skill, my brother Paris and far-shooting Apollo will kill you at the Scaean Gates."

With these words, death came upon him. Godlike Hector's shade left his lifeless body and went down to the kingdom of Hades.

Achilles spoke to the dead Hector. "Lie dead, Hector! As for me, I shall accept my death whenever Zeus, lord of Olympus, and the other deathless gods bring that fate upon me."

Then the son of Peleus withdrew his bronze spear from Hector's neck and put it aside. He removed from Hector's body the bloody armor that had been his own.

The bronze-coated Greeks then approached the lifeless Trojan. As they stood admiring their greatest foe, they took their bronze spears and, one by one, each warrior drove his spear into godlike Hector's corpse.

Achilles announced, "Come, let us return to our hollow ships singing our song of victory, and let us take with us this warrior who has brought so much evil upon us. We have won great glory, for we have killed Hector of the shining helm, whom the horse-taming Trojans worshipped as if he were a god."

The son of Peleus then punctured the tendons of Hector's feet between the ankle and the heel, inserted a narrow strip of oxhide through each slit, and tied Hector's body to his chariot, leaving the hero's head to trail behind in the dust. After that, he put the shining armor into his chariot, climbed into it, and drove his horses forward at top speed, dragging Hector's body behind him.

Chapter 8

The Trojans mourn Hector's death and are angered that Achilles will not return his corpse. Finally the gods order Achilles to accept Priam's ransom and surrender Hector's body. After Priam returns to Troy, the Trojans conduct a royal funeral.

Hector's father and mother agonized over the death of their dearest son and his foul treatment at the hands of Achilles. Priam cried, "My friends, although you love me, let me leave the city by myself and go across the plain to the Greeks' hollow ships. There I will plead with this evil man for the body of our son. Perhaps he will be ashamed before his companions and will pity me in my old age, for he himself has a father like me."

Andromache, who heard the cries and wailing from the wall while she was at home weaving, reached the wall in time to see Achilles' horses swiftly dragging Hector's body off toward the Greek's hollow ships. Darkness like night came over her eyes and she collapsed, tearing from her head the veil that golden Aphrodite had given her on the day she had married Hector.

When Andromache regained consciousness she cried, "Oh, Hector, you have left me in deep grief, myself a widow and our infant son helpless without you. Even if he survives this war, he is now doomed to a hard, sad life, for other men will seize his lands.

"Once a child becomes an orphan," she continued, "his friends leave him. With a bowed head and tears on his cheeks, he approaches his father's friends, tugging at their coats. The one who pities him will offer him a cup for a moment, enough to wet his lips but not enough to fill his mouth. And a child whose parents still live strikes him and pushes him away from the table, saying: 'Go away! No father of yours is eating with us!' So the needy child tearfully returns to his widowed mother. Poor Astyanax, who has known only the best of love and care!" So Andromache spoke, weeping, and all the Trojans wept with her.

That night, Achilles mourned for Patroclus until he finally fell asleep by the shore of the loud-sounding sea. Then the shade of his dearest friend appeared before him, looking and sounding exactly as he had when he was alive.

"You have forgotten me," Patroclus admonished Achilles. "Bury me quickly so that I may enter the kingdom of Hades! Until you do this, the shades will not let me cross the River Styx and join them. You, too, are fated to die beneath the well-defended walls of Priam's city. When that time comes, let our bones lie together in the golden urn with the double handles which your mother gave you."

Achilles replied, "I shall do just as you wish, dearest friend, but come closer that we may clasp our arms about each other and grieve over our separation."

The son of Peleus reached toward Patroclus with his hands, but he could not touch him. Like a mist, the shade of his friend disappeared into the earth. Achilles proceeded to hold the funeral ceremonies and games in honor of Patroclus as he had promised.

Many days after the funeral, Achilles still kept the body of Hector, unburied, by his hollow ships. Whenever he felt the desire, he would attach Hector's body to his chariot, drag it around and around Patroclus' tomb, and then leave it lying face down in the dust. Since Apollo loved Hector even in death, he preserved Hector's corpse from decay and destruction.

The god of the silver bow finally prevailed upon his father, Zeus, to convince Hera and Athena that Achilles should not be permitted to have his way with Hector's body. This was not an easy task, for even Hector's death had not softened the hatred that Hera and Athena felt for the Trojans. The insult of Paris' choice of Aphrodite's beauty and gift over their own had not faded with time. Nevertheless, they finally permitted Thetis to counsel her son.

When Thetis entered Achilles' hut, he was sitting with his head upon his arms, still mourning for Patroclus. She sat down beside him, stroked his head, and said, "My child, how long will you continue this sorrow? Since your life will be so short, I would like to see you enjoy it. I have come as a messenger from Zeus, lord of Olympus. All the deathless gods are angry because you have not returned Hector's body for proper burial. Accept the ransom for the dead and give him up."

While Thetis was persuading Achilles to return Hector's body, the lord of Olympus sent wind-footed Iris down to advise King Priam to go alone to Achilles' hut with ample ransom. In order to calm his fears, Hermes, the Wayfinder, would be his guide.

Great-hearted Priam collected a wondrous array of gifts. As the eternally young god and the old king made their way together across the plain of Troy toward the hollow ships of the Greeks, Hermes reassured Priam that the immortals had protected Hector's body from both the ravages of time and Achilles' harsh treatment. Once they reached Achilles' hut, Hermes took leave of Priam and returned to Mount Olympus.

The old king entered the hut, took Achilles by the knees, and said, "Remember your father, godlike Achilles, who, like me, will soon become an old man. While you are alive, his heart is joyful. As for me, although I fathered fifty sons, you and war-loving Ares have killed the best of them. And for none do I mourn as I do for my son Hector, who guarded Troy and its people. I have come to you with numerous gifts as ransom for his body. Pity me, for I am forced to beg the man who killed my valiant sons."

Achilles wept in sympathy with Priam in his sorrow. Then the swift footed son of Peleus asked, "How did you have the courage to come alone to the hollow ships and look into my eyes when I have killed so many of your brave sons? Surely your heart is made of iron!"

Achilles continued, "The deathless gods spin the threads of mortals' lives to bring them grief, while the gods themselves live free of pain. Zeus, lord of the thunderbolt, sits between two urns, one filled with blessings and the other containing evils. The one to whom Zeus gives only evil gifts is despised both by mortals and by the gods. That man wanders upon the earth searching for honor but finding none. However, the one to whom Zeus gives gifts from both urns at some times finds good and at other times evil in his life.

"So it is with you. In the past the deathless gods gave you great gifts: the blessings of land, wealth, and many fine sons. Now, with this hateful war, the gods have brought evil upon you. The bronze-coated Greeks have killed many of the sons you loved. However, you must endure the pain. A heart overflowing with sorrow will not help you, for grief will not return the dead to life. So come now and sit down. Together we will put an end to our tears."

Priam replied, "Do not ask me to sit down while my son Hector lies unburied and away from Troy. Instead, bring him to me immediately so that I can look upon him, and accept the great ransom I have brought you."

Achilles angrily replied, "Do not incite me to fury, old sir, or I may harm you even while you are a guest inside my hut and, in doing so, anger Zeus. I intend to give your son back to you, for Zeus, lord of counsel, sent my mother to advise me.

I know in my heart that some god must have led you to my hut. No mortal, no matter how young and strong, would have had the courage to come into the camp of the bronze-coated Greeks, nor could he have done so without arousing the guards."

Then Priam became frightened and silent. Achilles, however, leaped forth like a lion, accepted the ransom, and prepared to return the body of Hector to his father. He also agreed to halt the war for eleven days so that the Trojans could prepare and hold a proper funeral for Hector. He shook the old king's hand to confirm his promise.

With Hermes to guide him once again, Priam returned to Troy with Hector's body. Andromache, Hecuba, and Helen led the women in wailing over the death of Hector, recounting his loss to them as husband, son, and dear friend.

The gathering of wood for the funeral pyre took nine days. On the tenth day, as rosy-fingered Dawn shone forth, the people of Troy assembled at the pyre. They laid godlike Hector's corpse upon it and set fire to his body. When Dawn next gave light to gods and mortals, they quenched the flames, gathered Hector's bones, and put them into a golden urn. They wrapped the urn in purple robes and placed it in a hollow grave. After they had covered the grave with large stones, they built a mound and set a watch upon it to protect it from the Greeks. The funeral concluded with a great feast in the palace of King Priam.

In this way the horse-taming Trojans held the funeral of godlike Hector of the shining helm.

Introducing **the Epilogue to The Iliad**

Arctinus of Miletus (late 8th century B.C.) relates the death of Achilles in his epic, The Aethiopis, and the defeat of Troy in another epic, The Iliūpe'rsis (The Sack of Troy).

Lesches of Pyrrha or Mitylene (mid-7th century B.C.) relates the death of Paris and the defeat of Troy in his epic, the Little Iliad.

The most famous rendition of the sack of Troy is told by Virgil (1st century B.C.) in Book II of The Aeneid.

Epilogue to The Iliad
The Death of Achilles

With the help of Apollo, Paris killed Achilles at the Scaean Gates by shooting an arrow into his heel. A great battle for Achilles' corpse followed. While Odysseus fought off the Trojans, Ajax was able to pick up Achilles' body and, through a shower of Trojan arrows, carry it back to the Greek ships. The Greeks burned the body of Achilles and placed his bones with those of Patroclus as they both had wished. However, Thetis actually rescued Achilles from the funeral pyre and took him to White Island in the Black Sea, where he is immortal.

After the funeral games, the Greeks decided to award Achilles' armor to the warrior who had contributed the most to the Greek effort. Odysseus, the best strategist, and Ajax, the best fighter, competed for this prize. Odysseus, with the help of Athena, won the votes of the Greek leaders. Ajax was so humiliated by his defeat that he went insane. Thinking that the Greeks' cattle were the warriors who had voted against him, he killed them. When he realized what he had done, he was so ashamed that he killed himself.

The Death of Paris

When the Greeks sailed for Troy, Philoctetes accompanied them carrying the bow that Heracles had given him before he died. At one of their island stops, he was bitten by a snake. The wound smelled so terrible that the Greeks left him behind on the island. Ten years later, the prophet Calchas, or the Trojan seer Helenus, whom Odysseus captured, told the Greeks that they needed Heracles' bow in order to defeat the Trojans. So Odysseus and Diomedes returned to the island and brought Philoctetes and the bow to Troy. There his wound was healed and he shot Paris in single combat.

The Defeat of Troy

After the death of Paris, his brother Deiphobus married Helen. Odysseus brought Achilles' son, Neoptolemus, to Troy and gave him his father's armor. Athena taught Epeius to build a great wooden horse, whose body would accommodate the greatest of the Greek warriors. Meanwhile, Odysseus, in the disguise of a beggar, entered Troy. Helen recognized him and plotted with him to capture Troy. However, she later changed her mind and tried to expose the men who were hiding inside the horse.

The Greeks left the horse outside the walls of Troy and hid on a nearby island. The Trojans were suspicious of the horse, but when two serpents attacked the priest of Apollo, who had warned against accepting a Greek gift, they took it inside. Then, certain that the war had finally ended, they celebrated their great victory.

Later that night, while the Trojans slept soundly, the Greeks who were hiding inside the horse, including Odysseus, Menelaus, and Neoptolemus, disembarked and opened the Trojan gates to the Greek armies, who had secretly returned. The Greeks then looted and burned the great city.

Menelaus killed Deiphobus and recovered Helen. The women in Hector's family became enslaved, as he had known would be their fate if Troy lost the war. The greatest Greek warriors were entitled to special prizes of honor, which, now, were the greatest of the Trojan women. Agamemnon claimed Hector's sister Cassandra, who had received but had spurned Apollo's love. Odysseus claimed Hecuba. Neoptolemus, who had killed Priam, chose Andromache. Hector's son

Astyanax was grabbed from his nurse by either Neoptolemus or Odysseus and thrown to his death, either from a tower or from the Trojan wall.

Introducing **The Odyssey**

Since *The Odyssey* is closely related to *The Iliad* in subject matter, and both were written by Homer, most of the introduction that precedes *The Iliad* applies to both epics. That introductory section contains a complete discussion of historical background, Homer and the oral tradition, the appeal and value of Homer, the Homeric hero, the role of women, and the role of the Greek gods in Homer. It is followed by the Prologue, which summarizes the myths leading up to the Trojan War.

Differences Between The Iliad and The Odyssey

Certain basic aspects of *The Iliad* and *The Odyssey* are so different that some scholars think two different poets created them. Most scholars, however, believe that Homer created both epics, the first being the product of his youth and the second arising out of his old age.

The principal difference between the two epics is that *The Odyssey* is primarily a superb adventure story, perhaps the greatest in literature, whereas *The Iliad* is a serious, dramatic portrayal of human personality and the conflicts that arise between a person's own wishes and his or her responsibility to the needs of the community.

Thus, the plot of *The Odyssey* has a narrower focus than that of *The Iliad*. Instead of presenting the heroic deeds

and psychological conflicts of Greek and Trojan heroes, *The Odyssey* describes the long and difficult journey of Odysseus, one of the heroes in *The Iliad*, as he returns from Troy and struggles for control of his kingdom. Odysseus' voyage introduces him to characters based in folklore, including monsters, giants, and a sorceress— another difference from *The Iliad*, which remains in the real world.

In *The Odyssey* the Homeric hero needs different strengths than he does in *The Iliad*, because he must face a different set of challenges. The hero of *The Odyssey* has left the battlefield. He still needs *aretē* in courage and determination, but *aretē* of the mind is even more necessary and replaces the warrior's emphasis on strength and skill. The achievement of glory and the reward of honor that play such a prominent role in the plot of *The Iliad* fade into the background in *The Odyssey*, where basic survival is the major issue.

In addition, the moral issues in *The Odyssey* are clearer than they are in *The Iliad*. Many characters in *The Odyssey* act more like heroes or villains, whereas more of the characters in *The Iliad* have complex personalities and display a combination of good and bad traits. In keeping with Homer's attitude toward good and evil in *The Odyssey*, the heroes survive, the gods punish the villains by killing them, and the story ends happily. In contrast, the best among the heroes in

The Iliad make mistakes and die, and the story has an unhappy ending.

Moreover, the characters in *The Odyssey* represent a greater cross-section of Mycenaean society than those in *The Iliad*. In *The Odyssey*, Homer devotes as much attention to a beggar and to the servants who herd animals as to the nobles who are living off Odysseus' possessions, and he gives a number of the servants important roles.

Furthermore, in many sections of *The Odyssey*, women are in positions of power and clearly dominate the action. For example, the goddess Calypso holds Odysseus captive on her island for seven years, and the goddess Circe is a powerful and terrifying sorceress. Odysseus' wife, Penelope, is one of the great women in literature. She is intelligent, creative, beautiful, and loyal to her husband and family. She remains faithful to Odysseus for twenty years, outwits her suitors, and accepts Odysseus as her husband only after testing him. In *The Iliad*, Homer concentrates on the warrior noblemen rather than on women. He emphasizes how armed attacks and wars make captives of even the highest-ranking women.

Finally, in *The Odyssey*, Homer employs the concept of divine justice. While in *The Iliad* a god rewards or punishes mortals according to the god's own personal bias, in *The Odyssey* the gods punish those who behave improperly. Poseidon prolongs Odysseus' journey because Odysseus blinds Poseidon's son, the Cyclops Polyphemus, and then boasts about it. Later, Athena insists that Odysseus and Telemachus kill all of Penelope's suitors. In *The Iliad*, a particular hero or army is frequently assisted by one god and harmed by another, because of the particular god's personal feelings of love or hate toward the Greeks or the Trojans.

The Return from the Trojan War

After the Greeks sacked Troy, all of those who had survived the war sailed homeward. The Homeric heroes had been away from home for ten years, and in times of political instability, kings had reason to fear important changes at home during their absence. Therefore, it is not surprising that Odysseus' returned to great danger.

However, Odysseus' difficulties in returning home cannot be attributed to political instability. On his way to Ithaca, Odysseus behaves in a way that antagonizes Poseidon, and Poseidon punishes him. Meanwhile, Athena, who had always been Odysseus' mentor, does not befriend him until he reaches Phaeacia.

Athena tells Odysseus that she would not challenge her uncle Poseidon's wishes. However, it is possible that her attitude is also based on an incident that is part of the larger tale of Troy. In Lesches' *Little Iliad*, Odysseus learns that the Greeks cannot conquer Troy as long as the Palladium, the statue of Athena's friend Pallas, remains within its walls. Therefore, Odysseus and Diomedes secretly enter the city and steal it. Arctinus states at the end of *The Iliūpe'rsis* (*The Sack of Ilium*) that Athena plans to punish the returning Greek leaders for its theft.

Principal Characters

ODYSSEUS (Ulysses)*: son of the hero Laertes; king of Ithaca; husband of Penelope; father of Telemachus; hero of the Trojan War who returns home after many years and a long, difficult journey; master of strategies

PENELOPE: loyal wife of Odysseus; mother of Telemachus; queen of Ithaca

TELEMACHUS: son of Odysseus and Penelope

EURYLOCHUS: second in command to Odysseus on the return voyage

AEOLUS: keeper of the winds

POLYPHEMUS: a Cyclops; son of Poseidon

TEIRESIAS: blind prophet who reveals the future to Odysseus

AGAMEMNON: commander of all the Greek forces in the Trojan War

ACHILLES: greatest Greek warrior in the Trojan War; father of the warrior Neoptolemus

AJAX: second greatest Greek warrior in the Trojan War; son of Telamon

HERACLES (Hercules): most famous Greek hero prior to the Trojan War; known for his twelve labors

ANTINOUS: principal suitor of Penelope

*Roman names are in parentheses. For a list of the gods, see pages 5–6.

The Odyssey

Chapter 1

Odysseus leaves Calypso and is honored by the Phaeacians. He agrees to tell his adventures.

Sing, goddess, of Odysseus, man of many schemes, who was forced to wander far after he sacked well-defended Troy, Priam's great city. Many were the men he met in these travels, but many more were the sorrows he felt in his heart as he sailed the salt sea. His goal was to return home safely with his companions. He achieved this goal himself. But he was unable to save his shipmates despite his good counsel, for they sorely angered Helios, lord of the sun, by eating his cattle. Blind to the consequences, they paid for their foolishness with their lives.

Ten years had passed since the bronze-coated Greeks had captured and looted Troy. Those who had survived that ten-year war and their voyage home were now safe and at peace. Only Odysseus, man of many schemes, still remained far from his homeland of Ithaca. For over seven years the goddess Calypso had held him captive on her island, hoping that her beauty and her offer of immortality would make him forget his wife and marry Calypso, but she could not tempt him. Each day Odysseus would sit alone upon the shore of the wine-dark sea and weep with longing for his wife and home.

Seasons had come and gone and come again, finally bringing with them the year the deathless gods had willed that Odysseus, man of many trials, should return home to Ithaca. Yet he was still far from freedom, far from contentment, and far from his family.

All of the gods pitied Odysseus except for Poseidon, the Earthshaker and lord of the sea, whose hatred did not cease until Odysseus reached the shores of Ithaca. Odysseus had blinded godlike Polyphemus, the mighty Cyclops who was Poseidon's son. Poseidon could have avenged this injury by killing Odysseus, but instead he chose to force Odysseus to wander from land to land, ever a stranger.

In the eighth year of Odysseus' stay with Calypso, bright-eyed Athena told Zeus, lord of Olympus, "My heart aches for wise Odysseus, that unfortunate, unhappy man. Calypso has confined him against his will to her wooded island. Why are you so angry with him that you permit Calypso to restrain him? Did he not offer you generous sacrifices in the land of the horse-taming Trojans?"

To these words her father, the Cloud-Gatherer, replied, "I would not forget godlike Odysseus, who honors the deathless gods and surpasses all mortal men in wisdom. However, like many other mortals, Odysseus may be quick to blame the gods for misfortunes that he has rashly brought upon himself through his own foolish behavior. By blinding Polyphemus, he incurred the unrelenting anger of my brother Poseidon. But let us plan to start the long-suffering Odysseus on his journey homeward. It is time for the lord of the sea to soften his heart; he will not be able to defy the will of all the gods."

Zeus then called his son Hermes, the Wayfinder, to him and said, "Go command the nymph Calypso to permit Odysseus of the stout heart to build a raft and depart. On the twentieth day and after much suffering, he will arrive at the land of the Phaeacians. It is his fate that they will honor him as if he were a god and send him home with more gifts of gold and bronze than he earned for himself at Troy."

When Hermes reached Calypso's island, he was able to converse freely with her, for great-hearted Odysseus sat alone and wept upon the shore of the loud-sounding sea. As a woman tearfully embraces her dying husband, who has given his life for the people of his city, postponing with his courage, his skill, and his strength the day when they will be captured and enslaved, and her tears express the pain in her heart as the proud conquerors prod her in the back with their spears and forcefully take her captive, eager to introduce her to her new life of labor and sorrow, so Odysseus wept tears of grief and despair over his endless captivity.

When Hermes had departed, Calypso approached Odysseus and said, "Weep no more, unhappy soul, for I shall let you go! But if you knew the troubles still before you, surely you would choose to remain here with me."

Odysseus replied, "I know that my wife, being mortal, cannot compare with you, and yet I long to return to her. Even if some god makes my journey across the wine-dark sea difficult, I shall bear it, for I have a steadfast heart that has already endured much suffering."

For seventeen days stout-hearted Odysseus sailed across the salt sea upon his raft. He had spied the pale shadows of the mountains of the Phaeacians, the oar-loving people, in the distance when the Earthshaker took note of him. Recognizing his last opportunity to torment Odysseus, Poseidon collected storm clouds to blacken the sky, gathered the strongest winds, and created mighty waves with his trident.

"Now I shall surely die!" Odysseus exclaimed. "How much better it would have been to have died a hero's death at Troy than to die here, alone and without honor. Then I should have had a proper funeral, and men would have sung of my great deeds."

As Odysseus clung to his raft, he was tossed this way and that by the waves. Seeing that he was powerless against the storm, a sea goddess came to Odysseus' rescue. "Take my veil," she advised, "and swim with it upon your chest. When you reach land, toss it back into the wine-dark sea."

For two days and two nights Odysseus swam upon the waves of the loud-sounding sea. When rosy-fingered Dawn shone forth upon the third day, he found himself close to shore. Still he would have perished upon the jagged rocks that lined the coast if bright-eyed Athena had not put it into his mind to swim out beyond the surf, where the water was more peaceful, and to search in greater safety for a harbor or a beach.

In time, Odysseus located the mouth of a peaceful river and swam to land. Once he had returned the goddess' veil as she had directed, he found a dry, sheltered place in the woods, and fell asleep upon a bed of leaves.

Meanwhile, Athena appeared to the princess of Phaeacia as her dear friend and led her and a group of companions to the river to wash their clothes. When Odysseus awakened and found them, the princess kindly invited the stranger to the palace to speak with her mother and father.

For the remainder of his time in Phaeacia, Odysseus was treated as a highly honored guest. After a good night's sleep, he was invited to a royal feast, where a fine minstrel sang stories about the war against Troy to the accompaniment of his lyre. When the king noticed that these tales brought tears to the eyes of his guest, he suggested athletic contests to brighten Odysseus' spirits and to exhibit Phaeacian skills in boxing, wrestling, and running.

After Odysseus had admired the prowess of the young men of Phaeacia, the king's son asked him, "Sir, stranger though you are to us, will you also show whatever skills you possess? A man earns great glory through excellence in athletic contests. Your effort will lift your cares from your heart. And be at ease about your departure. Even now, one of our swift black ships is ready to take you home."

Odysseus responded, "Kind prince, do not expect me to accept your invitation. My mind is filled with grief and exhaustion, not with athletic contests, and my heart is set only upon returning to my homeland."

Hearing Odysseus' reply, a friend of the prince who was an unusually fine wrestler said, "Stranger, you do not accept our invitation because you lack the skills to compete! You certainly do not look like an athlete. More than likely you are simply the captain of a merchant ship, one whose mind thinks only of freight and whose heart is set only on profit!"

"Young man," godlike Odysseus replied, "your words are rude, insulting, and foolish. The deathless gods do not endow each mortal with identical gifts, in either appearance, intelligence, or eloquence. One man may be nothing special to gaze upon but may speak words of such wisdom that he delights those who hear him. Another may be as well formed as a god but may speak like a simpleton. You, for example, are unusually handsome, but you lack judgment!

"I am by no means unskilled in athletics, as you suggest," Odysseus continued. "Although I am tired in body and spirit, your taunts have so angered me that I am willing to show my skills."

Then, without even bothering to remove his cloak, Odysseus chose a discus that was far larger and heavier than those used in contests and, with a light flick of his wrist, sent it flying down the field. The Phaeacians of the long oars, famous for their swift black ships, gazed upon the discus with awe as it sped far past their most distant marker. The young wrestler stood by, speechless.

"Match that, now, young men!" exclaimed Odysseus. "Or, if any one among you prefers, come try my skill in boxing, wrestling, or even running. I will compete against any among you except my host, for it is not appropriate for a guest to compete against the person who is entertaining him. You will find that I can hold my place in anything.

"With the exception of Philoctetes, who used the bow of godlike Heracles at Troy, I am by far the best bowman of any mortal who presently walks upon the earth. And I can send a far-shadowing spear farther afield that any man can shoot an arrow. Only in running may a Phaeacian surpass my best effort, for my journey here by raft has taken a sorry toll upon my legs."

The king, however, suggested other entertainments: dancing exhibitions, songs by their famous minstrel, and fine food, so that their long-suffering guest would remember his stay among the Phaeacians of the long oars with admiration and pleasure.

After the royal family and other nobles had presented Odysseus with a rich array of friendship gifts, including a silver sword from the young man who had taunted Odysseus about his lack of skill, the king said, "Let us now hear from our honored stranger, dear as a brother to us, who finds such sorrow in the tales our minstrel sings of the war with Troy.

"Tell us your name and the name of your country, the destination of the swift ship that will soon transport you across the wine-dark sea. Tell us of the places you have seen and the people you have met. Speak of those who are wild and without welcome, and also of those who befriend the stranger in their midst and honor the deathless gods. And tell us why tales of the bronze-coated Greeks and the horse-taming Trojans bring tears to your eyes. Did death come upon some dear relative or friend of yours as he shouted the war cry? The gods spin the thread of a mortal's life to create a song for others to hear, even those who are as yet unborn."

Chapter 2

Odysseus relates his adventures with the Lotus-Eaters
and the Cyclopes to the Phaeacians.

So the king of Phaeacia, land of the oar-loving people, entreated Odysseus to tell his tale. The man of many schemes began his story.

I am Odysseus, son of Laertes, and Ithaca is my homeland. I am known among the bronze-coated Greeks and the horse-taming Trojans for my many schemes. Even the deathless gods are aware of my deeds. Since your poet sings to you about the war the Greeks fought at Troy, I shall tell you about my travels as I have tried to return home to Ithaca from Priam's great city.

Upon leaving Troy, we tried to sail homeward with our twelve ships, but Zeus, the Cloud-Gatherer, turned day into night with a fearful storm. The winds were our captain, leading us where they chose.

On the tenth day we arrived at the land of the Lotus-Eaters, where the inhabitants eat the fruit of the lotus plant. When we stopped to acquire fresh water, I sent three of my men to investigate the area. The Lotus-Eaters, being friendly and hospitable, gave them the honey-sweet fruit of the lotus to taste. But as soon as they ate it, they lost all desire to rejoin their companions and to return home; they only wished to remain among the Lotus-Eaters and eat the lotus fruit.

I had to find them, drag them tearfully back to our ships, and tie them securely beneath the benches in order to take them with us. Fortunately, we were able to leave that land before anyone else among us tasted the lotus fruit.

Next we came to the land of the Cyclopes, a one-eyed race who live easily off their rich land. They spend their time gathering wild wheat, barley, and grapes, and tending their sheep and goats. The people themselves are as free as their plants. Each family lives high in the mountains in a hollow cave and makes its own laws. There we anchored our ships and feasted upon the local mountain goats.

When Dawn next shone forth upon us, I said to my comrades, "Stay here while I take my ship and my men over to the Cyclopes to see whether they are wild and without welcome or whether they befriend the stranger in their midst and honor the gods."

We had not gone very far when we spied a high cave very close to the shore, which appeared to house goats and sheep at night. Choosing twelve of my best men to investigate with me, I ordered our companions to remain behind and guard our ship. As a precaution against a cold welcome, I carried with me some food and a large goatskin container filled with sweet wine.

We could leisurely examine the large cave, for the Cyclops who lived there was probably out pasturing his flocks. At least, he was nowhere to be seen. When we noticed many crates of cheese, one of my comrades asked, "Why don't we simply take this cheese down to our ship? We can return for the goats and sheep and then leave this place."

I had no desire to leave so soon after our arrival, so we kindled a fire and ate the Cyclops' cheese while we waited for him to return. When it was time for the unyoking of oxen, a giant of a man entered the cave. He stood above and apart from other men as a lone, lofty mountain peak towers in isolation above lower ridges. At the sight of this monstrous being we fled toward the darkest part of the cave, where we hoped we would be safe from his gaze.

The giant Cyclops brought into the cave a huge armful of firewood and the animals that needed to be milked. He left the males outside in the high-walled stone courtyard he had built. Then he closed the entrance to his cave with a rock so huge that twenty-two four-wheeled wagons could not have moved it. Yet, he picked it up and set it in place with no apparent effort.

He had performed his evening chores and kindled his dinner fire before he noticed us watching him from the deep recess of the cave. "Who are you strangers?" he asked. "Have you come with some good purpose, or are you troublesome pirates?"

Although we were terrified by his enormous size and his deep voice, I replied, "We are Greeks returning home from Troy. The winds have driven us here, and we seek your hospitality in the name of Zeus, patron god of strangers."

"We Cyclopes do not honor Zeus," he responded, "because we are far better than those gods. How I treat you will depend upon how I feel about it. Tell me, where did you moor your ship?"

I was clever enough to spot a trap, so I answered, "Poseidon, the Earthshaker, destroyed our ship on your rocky coast. We were fortunate to escape with our lives!"

His only reply was to leap to his feet, grab two of my companions, and kill them by slamming them upon the floor of the cave. Then he tore them apart and ate them—flesh, bones, and all—drank his milk, and lay down to sleep on the floor of the cave among his sheep.

We gave up all hope of sleep. Weeping with fear, grief, and sheer horror, we waited for Dawn to appear. My mind devised a clever plan whereby I would stealthily approach the sleeping giant and slay him in the chest with my sharp sword. Fortunately, however, further thinking pushed my hand from my weapon, for if I had killed him, then Death would soon have come for us as well. Who besides the mighty Cyclops could move the rock that sealed the entrance to the cave?

As soon as rosy-fingered Dawn shone forth upon gods and mortals, the giant Cyclops awakened, rekindled his fire, and milked his animals. When he had completed his morning tasks, once again he grabbed two of my men, tore apart their limbs, and ate them—flesh, bones, and all.

He easily moved aside the huge stone that blocked the entrance to the cave, drove his flocks of sheep and goats into the courtyard, and then replaced the stone as easily as a man covers his quiver. We heard his whistling as he headed toward the mountain pastures, and once the sound had faded into silence, I knew that I had better use this time to plan some way to punish him and yet escape. I prayed that bright-eyed Athena would grant me such glory!

Finally I devised what seemed to be a satisfactory plan. The monstrous Cyclops had left a huge, green, olive-wood shepherd's staff upon the floor of the cave next to the sheep pen to dry out for later use. It was so large that it could have been used as the mast of one of the large black merchant ships of twenty oars that were built to cross the salt sea. I cut off about a fathom's length from the staff and ordered my companions to make it smooth. Then, I sharpened one end of the six-foot-long poker to a point, which I hardened in the blazing fire. Finally, I concealed the poker by burying it beneath the large piles of dung that littered the floor of the cave.

Next, I asked my companions to choose by lot who among them would help me to raise the poker and twist it into the monstrous shepherd's lone eye once he had fallen asleep. Fortunately, the lots fell upon just the four men I would have chosen.

In the evening the giant Cyclops returned to the cave, this time driving all of his goats and woolly sheep into the interior, the rams as well as the ewes. As usual, he effortlessly raised the huge boulder, set it in place, and then went about performing his customary evening tasks.

However, when he grabbed two more of my men in preparation for his evening meal, I was prepared. Offering him a bowl filled with my sweet red wine, I addressed the monstrous shepherd. "Cyclops," I said, "wash down your meal of human flesh with this tasty red wine. I brought it with me from the ship in the hope that you would accept it as a gift and help us get home."

The Cyclops listened to my words, took the bowl from my hands, and drank the container dry. He was so pleased with the taste that he asked for more. "Give me more with a great heart, and tell me your name. Then I will give you a gift in return. We Cyclopes have rich wine-giving plants, but your wine must be the ambrosia and nectar of the gods!"

So the monstrous shepherd spoke and drained the second bowlful of wine as he had drained the first. Three times I brought him wine, and three times he foolishly drank the bowl dry.

By this time the wine had muddled his mind, so I craftily said to him, "Cyclops, I shall tell you my name as you have asked, but in return I want the stranger's gift that you promised me. Noman is the name by which my mother, my father, and all my companions address me."

"Then, Noman," replied the Cyclops, "I shall tell you what my gift to you will be. I shall choose to eat you last of all!" With these words he collapsed upon the floor of his cave and lay there in a drunken stupor while wine trickled from his gaping mouth.

I immediately withdrew the poker from its hiding place beneath the dung and pushed it deep under the hot coals of the fire until it was white-hot. Meanwhile, I tried to strengthen the hearts of my companions with words of encouragement. When the pointed tip of the olive-wood poker glowed with heat, I withdrew it from the fire.

With stout hearts my companions plunged the point of the poker into the giant Cyclops' solitary eye, while I twisted the pole round and round as a man drills a hole in the timber of a ship. Blood poured out from around the poker, and as the eyeball burned, its roots crackled as a white-hot axe hisses when a smith submerges it in cold water.

The Cyclops screamed in agony, causing the walls of the cave to echo with his cries. We ran from him in terror as he wrenched the bloody poker from his eye and threw it to the floor. We hoped he would not find us as we huddled against the rear wall of the cave, for he was jumping wildly about, swinging his arms in fury.

The monstrous shepherd called upon the neighboring Cyclopes for help, and they were quick to come to his aid. As they stood at the blocked entrance to the cave, they asked, "What terrible thing has happened to you, Polyphemus, that you have awakened us in the middle of the night with your screams? Is some man stealing your flocks? Or is someone using trickery or force to kill you?"

In his anguish, from inside his cave the giant Polyphemus cried, "Noman is killing me, but with cunning and not with strength."

His friends replied, "Well, then, if no man is hurting you, you are alone. You must be ill. All you can do is pray to your father, Poseidon."

With this advice they left, for they saw nothing else that they could do to help him. My heart filled with laughter at the success of my devious name.

Then Polyphemus blindly felt his way to the entrance of his cave, removed the huge stone that blocked the doorway, and sat there with outstretched arms, expecting that he would touch me if I attempted to leave with his sheep.

I thoughtfully considered how, in fact, my companions and I were going to escape almost certain death. As I gazed upon the Cyclops' well-fed rams, each wearing a coat of thick fleece, I devised a scheme that I thought would be successful. Quietly I collected the braided willow twigs Polyphemus slept upon and tied the rams together in groups of three across. I tied one of my companions beneath the body of each middle ram; the other two rams protected him from the monstrous shepherd's blind touch.

I myself chose the best ram of all. Clutching his back, I stretched myself beneath his body, burying my fingers in his thick fleece. In this way we waited the rest of the night. When Dawn next brought forth light, Polyphemus sent the males in his flocks out to pasture. As the sheep passed him, he slowly ran his fingers across the fleece on their woolly backs, but he failed to discover my companions. The rams carried them forth to safety.

Finally, the ram I had chosen passed beneath the giant's touch. "Why are you last, good ram?" Polyphemus asked. "Each day you are the first to feed upon the grass, the first to drink from the stream, and the first to return home in the evening. Pity your poor shepherd for his blindness!

"Noman is most cruel and cunning," he continued, "to have used wine as a weapon against me, for surely no other device could have conquered me. If only you could speak, I know that you would tell me where he is hiding. Then I would hurl him to the ground with such force that his brains would splatter across the floor of my cave. Yet, even now, Noman has not escaped my wrath!"

With these words Polyphemus sent my ram out to pasture with the rest. As soon as I felt we were safe from the Cyclops, I freed my companions, and we drove his fine rams straight toward our ship. As welcome as we were to those we had left behind, they wept for the men Polyphemus had eaten. I had no liking for their tears and ordered them to load our new cargo quickly so that we could speedily set sail upon the wine-dark sea.

However, I would not leave that monstrous Cyclops without a final word. When I knew that I could safely shout and still be heard, I cried, "Polyphemus, the man whose companions you captured and ate in your hollow cave was indeed equal to your great strength! Zeus has now punished you for so cruelly mistreating your guests!"

Polyphemus responded to my words by tearing off the peak of a great mountain and hurling it toward us. The Earthshaker must have given sight to his son's hand, for the gigantic rock crashed into the salt sea right in front of our ship, creating an enormous wave that forced us back toward the shore. Quickly I grabbed a long pole and pushed us off to sea before we met with further danger. Then, from twice as far, I prepared to shout another message.

"Foolish captain!" my companions exclaimed. "Why must you continue to incite that monstrous Cyclops! Did not his first attack upon our ship bring us close enough to death?"

Their words did not convince me to be more cautious. I comforted my angry heart by shouting, "Cyclops, if any mortal asks who blinded you, tell him that Odysseus, raider of cities, is to blame."

Polyphemus groaned when he heard my words. "Then the prophecy of long ago has come to pass!" he cried. "I have expected my fate in the form of some large and impressive visitor. I was completely misled by how small and weak you are. Never did I imagine that wine would destroy my sight! But return to me, Odysseus, raider of cities, so that I can give you a warmer welcome and pray to my father to grant you a fast journey home. The Earthshaker will hear my plea on your behalf. In fact, if he chooses, he has the power to restore my sight."

"I wish I were as sure that I could end your life and send your shade down to the kingdom of Hades as I am certain that the Earthshaker will never be able to heal your eye!" I responded.

Then Polyphemus raised his arms and prayed to his father. "Poseidon, lord of the sea, if you are indeed my father and I am your son, prevent Odysseus from reaching his homeland. Yet if it is his unalterable fate to return to his home and his friends, may it be long before that day arrives. May he return alone and after much suffering, having lost all of his companions. May he be forced to arrive in a ship that is not his own, and may he find great trouble in his house."

So the mighty Cyclops prayed, and the lord of the sea heard his prayer. Then, with all of his strength, Polyphemus hurled a far larger rock at us. It fell into the sea just behind our ship, and the enormous wave it produced carried us toward the far shore.

There we rejoined our other ships. We divided the Cyclops' rams into equal portions, and I sacrificed my ram to Zeus, lord of Olympus. When rosy-fingered Dawn next shone forth upon gods and mortals, we continued our journey. Our hearts grieved for our lost companions, but we were happy to have escaped death.

Chapter 3

*Odysseus tells the story of his encounters with Aeolus,
the Laestrygonians, and Circe.*

Next we came upon the homeland of Aeolus, one dear to the deathless gods. Zeus has made Aeolus keeper of the winds, and he can provoke or calm whichever winds he chooses. He and his large, happy family live on a floating island. A bronze wall surrounds the island, and steep cliffs rise from the salt sea to the metal wall. Aeolus entertained us for an entire month, and he was eager to hear all my tales of the war with Troy.

When we were ready to continue our journey, Aeolus put into my hands a large bag made of oxhide, which contained all the storm winds. With the destructive winds confined in this manner, we would be able to proceed safely and quickly to Ithaca. He tied the bag so securely with bright silver twine that not even the smallest breeze could escape. Then he stored the bag in my hollow ship, caused the west wind to blow upon us, and sent us on our way.

We sailed upon the wine-dark sea for nine days and nights. When Dawn shone forth on the tenth day, we were so close to Ithaca that we could see people tending their fires on land. Then my heart felt at ease, and I let sweet sleep enfold me. My limbs were weary, for I had been so eager to return home quickly that I had insisted on controlling the mainsail myself.

I did not know that my companions had decided that the bag Aeolus had given me contained gold and silver that I would not share with them. As soon as they were certain that I would not hear them, they said to one another, "Look how well-loved and honored Odysseus is. Wherever we go, he receives worthy gifts! Our ships are already filled with great treasures he took from Troy, and now Aeolus has given him even more gifts. Meanwhile, we are returning with no gifts at all! While he is asleep, let us open the bag from Aeolus and see how much silver and gold it contains."

With that they opened the oxhide bag, and all the storm winds tumbled forth and blew us far out to sea. The tossing of the ship awakened me. At first the grief in my heart tempted me to jump into the loud-sounding sea and so let my shade go down to the kingdom of Hades. But soon my heart counseled me more wisely, and I chose to accept my fate.

The winds blew our ships back to Aeolus, much to the dismay of my companions. We put ashore to obtain fresh water, and I went, once again, to visit Aeolus.

"Why have you returned, Odysseus?" he asked me with surprise. "What heartless god is punishing you? We sent you on your way with such a kind gift that you should have arrived home without a problem."

With sorrow in my heart, I replied, "My companions brought trouble upon us while I slept. But I know that you can send us smoothly on our way once more, if only you will consent to do so."

Then Aeolus spoke words of wrath instead of welcome. "Leave this island immediately!" he cried. "You have become the most despised of all living creatures! The fact that you have returned here proves that the immortals detest you, and I may not help anyone whom the deathless gods hate." Then he drove me from his palace.

With grief in our hearts, we sailed on. Because of our foolish behavior, not even a breeze would help us with our journey, so each man had to pull his oar. In this manner we sailed for six days and nights.

When rosy-fingered Dawn next shone forth upon gods and mortals, we had come to the land of the Laestrygonians. Here the night is so bright that someone who needs no sleep can earn twice as much pay by herding cattle all day and sheep all night. We could see a fine harbor, with steep cliffs rising on each side. Two jutting points of land reached toward one another at the mouth of the harbor, creating a very narrow entrance from the salt sea.

Eleven of my ships entered the sheltered harbor waters, where their captains moored them close by one another since there was no need to fear the action of waves in such a well-protected area. I decided to moor my black ship outside the harbor where the open sea met one of the cliffs.

Once we had fastened our ropes to a projecting rock on the lower part of the cliff, I climbed up to a towering height to investigate the area. The land appeared devoid of cultivation, for I could see neither people nor oxen working the fields. Only smoke drifted up from the land. I returned to my ship and ordered three of my companions to go ashore and see what sort of people lived here.

The men walked along a wagon road until they came to a spring that was clearly the source of fresh water for the townspeople. There they introduced themselves to a maiden and asked about the king of the community. She directed them to her parent's house. Upon entering, they were horrified to see that her mother was the size of a mountain peak. The girl's mother immediately called her husband, who was even larger. As soon as he arrived, he grabbed one of my men and ate him. My other two men ran swiftly back to our ship.

The king then gave a mighty shout that echoed throughout the city and brought forth a multitude of giants. As they stood upon their towering cliffs, they hurled tremendous rocks upon those of our ships that were moored in their harbor. They speared my comrades off the decks as if they were fish and carried them, dead or alive, back to their homes to eat.

Without waiting for the giant race to discover my ship, I quickly cut the cables with my sword, ordered my companions to their oars, and headed out to sea. Our hearts were filled with both joy and grief. We were very glad to have escaped death once again, but we had left to the kingdom of Hades all of our comrades on our other eleven ships.

At the next good harbor we found, we stopped to rest. At dawn I armed myself with sword and spear and went to see if the island was inhabited. I climbed to a high point and could see smoke rising from a building in the wooded area below. I decided that it would be unwise for one person to investigate that house, so I returned to my ship.

There I divided my companions into two groups, one under the command of great-hearted Eurylochus and one under my command. We drew lots from a bronze helmet to see which group would investigate the house in the woods. Eurylochus drew the lot and set off with his twenty-two men. They were weeping with anxiety, which was no surprise given the experiences we had had so far on our journey.

Soon they came to the gateway of a house built of polished stone, situated in a clearing in the middle of the forest. Mountain lions and wolves stood around the building. Instead of attacking Eurylochus and his men, they wagged their tails and licked the strangers' hands in a most friendly fashion. Just as dogs fawn around their master when he returns from a meal, knowing that he has brought back chunks of food for them, so these lions and wolves fawned around my companions. Eurylochus and his men stood as still as death, their hearts filled with terror to have such ferocious beasts at their hands.

"Friends, listen!" one of the men commanded. "You can hear the lovely singing of some woman or goddess as she weaves. Let us call to her."

When they called, the singer immediately opened her doors and invited them inside. She was so beautiful and friendly that all of the men foolishly joined her — except Eurylochus, who was more cautious. The captain watched and waited, but not one of the men reappeared. So he quickly returned to our swift black ship and tearfully told us what had happened.

When he had finished, I quickly slung my bow across my chest, picked up my great bronze sword, and asked Eurylochus to lead me to the woman's house.

"Oh, do not make me return to that place," he pleaded. "No one who goes there will ever leave! Instead, those of us who are still alive and free should leave this island as quickly as we can!"

I decided that it would be best, after all, to leave Eurylochus with my men at our hollow black ship and confront the woman myself. I was approaching the stone house when Hermes, the Wayfinder, came toward me in the form of a young man.

He shook my hand and said, "Unlucky man! Do you still wander alone through places you know nothing about? Where are you going this time? The feared goddess Circe lives in that house. She is the daughter of Helios, who gives light to men, but unlike her father she is no friend to mortals. She likes to use evil drugs to transform the nature of beasts and men who walk the earth."

Hermes continued, "Fair-haired Circe has given your friends food concealing a drug that has made them forget their homeland. The touch of her wand has transformed them into pigs, and she has confined them in sties. Your comrades now have the shape, appearance, and voice of swine, though their minds remain unchanged. They are inside that house now, locked in their pens with the kind of food that swine enjoy, weeping at their misfortune.

"Have you come here to free them? If that is your hope, I assure you that, un-aided, you yourself would not return, for Circe would make a pig of you and confine you with your companions."

Then Hermes said, "I will protect you and save you from that fate. Take this powerful herb and follow my advice. Eat the drugged food Circe sets before you, for the herb I have given you will protect you from its power. Then, when the dread goddess touches you with her wand, draw your sword and act as if you intend to kill her. She will have such fear in her heart that she will be willing to swear a sacred oath by the immortal gods not to hurt you."

With these words he gave me the herb and returned to Mount Olympus. I continued on my way, became dread Circe's guest, and carefully followed the Wayfinder's advice.

When her magic did not affect me and I had thrust my sword upon her as if to slay her, Circe asked, "Who are you, and what city are you from? You must be Odysseus, the man of many schemes, who Hermes told me would come with his swift black ship on his return from Troy. I swear by the River Styx in the dark kingdom of Hades, the oath most sacred to all the deathless gods, that I will not harm you."

Then the goddess treated me like a most honored guest, providing me with a bath, fresh clothing, and rich food. However, my heart was so filled with grief for the men who were captive in her pens that her food could not tempt me. "If you wish me to eat," I advised her, "you will have to free my companions and show me that they are well."

Fair-haired Circe then picked up her wand, went over to the pigpen, and opened the gate. When the twenty-two pigs surrounded her, she touched each of them with another magical device. Instantly, each man resumed his human form, only he was now younger, taller, and much more handsome than he had been before. My companions sobbed with joy as they recognized me and realized that they were free.

When the goddess invited all of us to remain with her as her guests, I agreed. We pulled our swift hollow ship onto the land and placed our things in caves, as she advised. Of the companions I had left behind at the ship, only Eurylochus spoke against my plan.

"Foolish men, think about where we are going!" he exclaimed. "Do you enjoy trouble so much that you want the dread goddess Circe to transform us into pigs or wolves or lions so that we can protect her house? Odysseus is simply being reckless once again, as he was when he took us to the giant Cyclops' cave. Because of that foolish venture, some among us were killed!"

When I heard those words, I was minded to draw my long sword and separate Eurylochus' head from his body, but my companions soothed my anger. They suggested leaving him behind to watch over our ship and our possessions, but he chose not to anger me further and came along with us.

The seasons of a full year came and went while we enjoyed an easy life with Circe. Finally, my companions came to me and said, "Strange man! Have you forgotten your homeland? If it is indeed your fate to return to Ithaca and your high-roofed home, it is time to leave this goddess."

Circe was indeed willing to send us home. "Odysseus, man of many schemes," she began, "I shall not force you to be a guest in my house against your will, but before I can send you homeward, you must enter the kingdom of Hades and speak with the shade of the blind prophet, Teiresias.

"The North Wind will guide your swift ship, but once you have crossed the stream of Oceanus, you must beach your ship upon the dark shore and enter the Underworld alone. At the rock where two rivers flow into the third, dig a pit and honor the dead by pouring into it first milk and honey, then wine, and finally water. After your prayers, sacrifice a ram and a black ewe. Turn their heads toward the dark place of the dead, but you yourself must turn your back and face the rivers instead.

"Then," Circe counseled, "many shades of those who have died will approach you. Use your sword to keep them from drinking the blood of your sacrifice until Teiresias has spoken to you. He will warn you of the troubles ahead of you and how to deal with them."

Chapter 4

*Odysseus tells the Phaeacians about his adventures in
the land of Hades.*

So we took leave of Circe, daughter of Helios, lord of the sun, and went forth to the kingdom of dread Hades. I did not expect the fear that flooded my heart as shades of the dead in countless numbers surrounded me, drawn as they were to a living visitor in their dark, hopeless land. But my fear turned to grief when the shade of my mother approached me. She had been alive when I left for Troy. Even so, I would not let her come near the dark blood until I had talked with Teiresias.

Then the shade of the blind prophet came up to me. "Odysseus, man of many schemes," he began. "Why have you come to view the dead and this dark, joyless place? Withdraw your sword and move aside so that I can drink the dark blood and speak with you."

When I had obeyed his wishes, Teiresias said, "I think that there will be no honey-sweet journey back to Ithaca for you, since the Earthshaker's heart overflows with anger against you. He will not forget that you blinded his son, Polyphemus. Yet, if you control your companions and yourself and do no harm to the sheep and cattle of Helios, who sees and hears all, you will bring your swift black ship safely home.

"However, if any one of you harms the flocks and herds of the lord of the sun, then your companions will be destroyed along with your black ship. You will return home after many seasons have passed, alone and in a strange ship. You will find your house occupied by men who wish to marry your godlike wife and who are wasting your household goods. You must reward their rude behavior by slaying them and sending their shades down to the kingdom of Hades.

"When you have slain the suitors in your house," Teiresias concluded, "you must take a well-shaped oar and journey forth until you come to a people who know nothing of the salt sea, or of ships, or of oars like wings. When you meet a stranger who tells you that your oar is a fan to blow the chaff from the grain, you must plant the oar in the earth and sacrifice a ram, a bull, and a boar to Poseidon, lord of the sea. Then you may return home. Death will come peacefully to you from out of the salt sea when you are old and living in the midst of your prosperous people."

To his prophecy, I replied, "Teiresias, surely the gods themselves have spun the words you have spoken to me. Now advise me. The shade of my mother is sitting near this blood, but she will neither look at me nor speak with me. How can I get her to know me?"

Teiresias counseled, "If you wish to speak with any shade of the dead, permit him or her to approach the dark blood and drink some of it. The shades you deny will withdraw into the kingdom of Hades."

The blind prophet retreated into the dark land of the dead, and my mother's shade approached me again. She swallowed the dark blood and cried, "My child, how did you enter this dreadful region with life in your limbs? Are you still on your way home from Troy?"

I told her the purpose of my visit and something of my troubles, but I was more interested in hearing what she had to tell me. "How did you die?" I asked. "How are my father and my son, Telemachus? And tell me about my wife. Has Penelope waited with a faithful heart for my return, or has she married another?"

My mother answered, "Your wife weeps for your return as she lives within your house with a loyal heart, and your son has kept your kingdom whole. But your father has withdrawn into the country, where he lives like a peasant in his sorrow, longing for your kindness and your counsel. My heart, too, overflowed with sadness, and it was that grief over your absence that crushed my honey-sweet life."

When she had spoken, I tried three times to embrace her shade, but each time she escaped my arms as if she were a shadow or a dream. Finally I said, "Mother, why won't you let me hold you so that we can comfort one another? You act as if you are merely an apparition and have no substance to your form."

My mother replied, "Oh, my son, this is the way one exists after death. As soon as the spirit of life leaves the body, it becomes this dreamlike shade and departs for its new home in Hades' dark kingdom." Then her shade withdrew from me so that I might offer the dark blood to other shades with whom I wished to speak.

When the shade of wide-ruling Agamemnon approached me, I wept and hastened to offer him the blood to drink, for I had last seen him in good health by the hollow ships that lined the shore at Troy. "Most honored son of Atreus," I cried, "why are you here? Did Poseidon destroy your ship with a mighty storm while you were homeward bound? Or were you slain while raiding some wealthy city?"

"No," he responded, "although it would have been far better to lose my life as you suggest. Clytemnestra helped her new husband slay my companions and me while they entertained us at a rich feast. As white-tusked pigs are slaughtered in some wealthy lord's house to provide meat at a marriage feast, so we were attacked at our table, causing the floor to flood with our blood. In this vile manner did my wicked wife devise my death.

"And so, I have words of counsel for you, Odysseus," Agamemnon concluded. "Your wife has a wise and understanding heart, and I am sure that she will truly welcome your return. Nevertheless, it is best to be cautious. It is far more prudent to return to your homeland in secret than to announce your arrival openly. And do not reveal all of your innermost thoughts to your dear wife, for one can no longer trust even the most loyal woman."

As we concluded our sad conversation, I noticed nearby the shades of godlike Achilles, his great-hearted friend Patroclus, and Ajax, the most impressive-looking of the long-haired Greeks after Achilles.

When I offered the dark blood to Achilles, he said, "Odysseus, your visit here is the greatest plan you have yet devised! Why have you come? And how did you ever reach this dark land where the useless shades of dead men dwell?"

"I needed to see the prophet Teiresias," I replied. "I hoped he could tell me how I might return home to Ithaca, for I have had nothing but troubles since leaving Priam's great city, and I have yet to set foot upon my homeland.

"You, on the other hand, should not be sorry that you are dead. No man has ever been more blessed than you. When you were alive, the long-haired Greeks honored you as if you were one of the deathless gods; even here, in Hades' dark kingdom, you rule with some power over the dead."

"Do not talk to me about the pleasures of death," swift-footed Achilles answered. "I would much prefer to be a servant or a very poor man, and yet be alive, than to rule over all the shades in the Underworld. But what can you tell me about my father and my son? Is Peleus still honored in his old age? Did Neoptolemus become a leader in the war against the Trojans?"

"I have heard nothing about your father," I replied, "but it was I who brought Neoptolemus to Troy to join the bronze-coated Greeks. He stood third, next to godlike Nestor and myself, in the gift of thoughtful speech. Upon the plain of Troy, he was a mighty slayer of the horse-taming Trojans and always fought at the forefront of the Greek lines. Later, he fearlessly stepped from the body of the Trojan horse, eager to begin destroying Priam's great city. When I last saw him, he was on board his hollow ship, in good health, and well-honored with his share of the Trojan treasure."

With these words, the shade of swift-footed Achilles happily left me, for he was content to learn that he could be proud of his son. But the shade of Ajax, who still stood nearby, was not pleased with me at all.

"Ajax," I called, "will you not forget our contest for Achilles' armor now that you are dead? Must your heart still overflow with anger toward me because I won it?

"I wish that we had never competed for such an honor, and that I had never won it," I admitted. "Surely Zeus must be to blame, for when you died, we lost our great strength against the might of the horse-taming Trojans. And we mourned for you as we mourned for godlike Achilles. Won't you put aside your anger and talk with me?" However, the wrath of Ajax was unrelenting, and he chose to rejoin the shades who had left me.

Before I returned to my black ship, I saw Tantalus, whom the gods have condemned to an eternity of agonizing thirst and hunger. Although he stands in water that reaches his chin, whenever he lowers his head to drink it the water dries up so completely that he looks down upon the barren, black dirt at his feet. Then, as soon as he raises his chin, the clear water sparkles beneath it once more.

Tantalus also stands beneath trees that bear honey-sweet fruits — apples, pears, pomegranates, figs, and olives — upon their branches. But whenever he stretches forth his hands to grab one of these ripe fruits, a gust of wind suddenly blows that branch out of his reach. Then, as soon as he lowers his arms, the branch swings back into place above his head.

Not far from Tantalus I found Sisyphus, whom the lord of Olympus has condemned to another kind of eternal suffering. Sisyphus must continuously strive to push an enormous boulder up and over the top of a steep hill. I watched him gather all the strength in his arms and his legs to move the mighty rock slowly up the incline.

Just when it looked as if Sisyphus would indeed be able to thrust the gigantic boulder over the crest of the hill, the great weight of the rock became more than he could endure, and he could no longer move it. He was forced to use all of his remaining energy to scramble out of the boulder's path as it came tumbling back down the hill to the dusty plain below.

Then, as the sweat poured from his dusty limbs, Sisyphus began to push the rock up the hill once again. I wondered what he was thinking, or if he were thinking at all. Did he know that he would never be able to push the boulder over the crest of the hill? Or did he hope that, this time, he would have the strength to succeed?

Finally, I saw the shade of godlike Heracles, although Heracles himself lives among the immortal gods upon Mount Olympus as the husband of Hebe, daughter of Zeus and Hera. Even his shade terrified the dead, for he stalked the dark kingdom of Hades with an arrow in place upon the string of his giant bow, ready for action. He wore a golden sash across his chest from shoulder to waist, decorated with scenes of his many feats: wild boars, bears, lions, and death-dealing conflicts between mortal men. Wherever he moved, the shades of the dead flew from his path as frightened birds scatter in panic at the sight of an approaching predator.

When Heracles recognized me, tears ran from his eyes. "Odysseus, man of many schemes," he cried. "I see that you, too, endure wretched burdens like those I bore in the days of old when I walked the earth. Although Zeus is my father, it was my fate to serve a man far inferior to me and to perform the difficult labors he devised. The greatest task he demanded was that I enter the dark kingdom of Hades, capture the three-headed dog that guards the gates here, and return to him with it. Bright-eyed Athena and Hermes, the Wayfinder, helped me," he concluded, and with these words he walked on.

At this point I decided to hurry back to my ship before Medusa approached me. Even in the kingdom of Hades I was afraid that one look at the Gorgon's monstrous face would turn me to stone.

Chapter 5

*Odysseus concludes his tale by telling the Phaeacians
about Circe's advice, the Sirens, Scylla and
Charybdis, the cattle of Helios, and Calypso.*

We sailed back to Circe's island to bury one of my men, who had fallen to his death as we were leaving on our journey to the Underworld. The fair-haired goddess welcomed us again and said, "You are valiant men to have entered the kingdom of Hades. All other mortals need to face death but once. So take your fill of food and drink, and when Dawn next shines forth upon gods and mortals, I shall send you on your way."

Then Circe said to me, "Listen while I explain the course of your journey so that you will know how to proceed without further suffering. First of all, you will come upon the two Sirens. Anyone who is foolish enough to approach them will never return. They sit upon their island and tempt those who sail nearby with their beautiful songs, and anyone who cannot resist them becomes their victim. He joins the decaying bodies and mounds of bones that surround them.

"Before your swift ship comes upon the Sirens, you must fit soft wax into the ears of all of your men so they cannot hear the Sirens' sweet voices as they row past. If you wish to hear their songs yourself, stand with your back against the mast of your black ship and command your companions to tie your hands and your feet to it, fastening the ropes to the ends of the mast beyond your reach. Tell them that when you plead with them to untie you, they must instead bind you even more securely.

"Once you have passed the Sirens," Circe continued, "you will be faced with a difficult and dangerous choice. One way will take you between the clashing rocks, where mighty waves rush this way and that as they crash into the steep cliffs that line the narrow channel. Not even birds can survive a flight between these crags.

"With one exception, no ship has ever escaped destruction there, for the tossing waves tear apart the timbers of the strongest ship and send the bodies of those on board headlong into the fearsome waters, where they quickly perish. It is true that Jason's ship, the *Argo*, passed safely through on its return with the Golden Fleece, but it too, would have been smashed upon the mighty rocks had not the goddess Hera loved Jason and saved his ship."

Circe then said, "The other way will take you through another very narrow channel. On one side, a mountain rises so high above the water that its sharp peak is always shrouded in clouds. No mortal can set foot upon its cliffs, for the rock has been worn smooth and slick. Halfway up the cliff is a cave where the hideous monster Scylla lives. The sound of her dog-like bark is enough to terrify anyone who hears it, and her appearance is even more horrifying.

"She has twelve dangling legs and six heads. Each head contains a mouth filled with three rows of sharp teeth, and can reach out with ease to claim its victims, for it rests upon a very long neck. Scylla hides her feet in her hollow cave, but her snake-like necks permit her to extend her heads away from the mountainside and out into the middle of the narrow channel. There she fishes for dolphins and any other food that the waves toss within the reach of her gaping mouth."

Circe added, "Scylla's cave is high enough above the salt sea that the arrow of even the strongest and most skilled mortal could not approach it. Therefore, she lives in safety. However, I cannot say as much for those who sail by her. Not even the swiftest ship passes her way without losing at least six men to her gnashing teeth.

"Now I will tell you about the problem with the other side of the channel," the fair-haired goddess said. "An arrow's flight across from Scylla, a huge fig tree grows upon another, lower cliff. Its heavy branches reach out above the whirlpool called Charybdis. Three times each day Charybdis swallows the black water, and three times each day she spits it out again. If you should happen to be there when Charybdis is sucking in the water, not even Poseidon could save you from disaster! So I advise you to sail past Scylla instead. It is better to lose six of your companions to monstrous Scylla than to lose everyone to Charybdis."

I replied, "Both of your choices are dreadful, Circe! Tell me, is there not some way I can fight off Scylla and also escape the clutches of Charybdis?"

"No, Odysseus. To flee from Scylla is the best thing that you can do. She is a powerful and evil enemy, and she is immortal. You cannot use a weapon against her, and the longer you remain nearby, the more often she will reach out and seize six of you at a time. So your only defense is to row past her with as much speed as your strength will permit.

"Finally," Circe concluded, "after you have passed Scylla and Charybdis, you will come to the island where Helios, lord of the sun, pastures his immortal cattle and sheep. Do not harm them, and all of you will reach Ithaca safely. However, if you injure any of Helios' animals, your ship will be destroyed, your companions will die, and you will return home only after many years and much suffering."

When rosy-fingered Dawn made the new day light, my companions and I set forth once more upon our journey. As my men sat upon their benches and rowed over the wine-dark sea, Circe sent a good wind to hasten us along our way. I repeated to my companions the advice that the fairhaired goddess had given me. I had just finished when the wind quieted down, and the water became so calm that it seemed as if a god had put the waves to steep. We were approaching the island of the Sirens.

As my men furled and stowed the sail and then started rowing, I used my sharp, bronze sword to cut a large round of wax into many small pieces. I softened the pieces of wax and placed them in the ears of all of my companions, and they tied me to the mast as the goddess had counseled.

The Sirens noticed our swift black ship when we were about a shout's distance from their island. "Come to us, noble Odysseus, honored one among the long-haired Greeks! Listen to our song and become a wiser man, for we sing about things yet to come as well as about things that are past."

As I heard their lovely voices, I motioned with my head for my companions to untie me, but instead two of my men bound me more closely with other ropes, while the rest rowed steadily past the Sirens. Once I could no longer hear their singing, I motioned for my men to remove the wax pieces from their ears. When they had done this, they removed my bonds. We finished just in time, for I could see that our next problem lay just ahead of us.

The smoke and sound of the crashing waves so terrified my companions that they stopped their rowing. I walked among them and tried to encourage each one. "Surely what lies ahead of us now is no worse than what we lived through when the Cyclops, Polyphemus, confined us in his hollow cave! My intelligence, advice, and courage saved us then, and they will save us now. So listen well to my counsel.

"Rowers, stay seated and row with as much strength and speed as you can," I commanded. "Steersman, keep our hollow ship close to the sheer cliff that rises across from the smoke and the crashing waves. Let us hope that Zeus will permit us to escape this danger!"

I did not dare tell my companions about Scylla, for I was certain that they would be so terrified they would stop rowing and simply sit crouched together in the hold of our hollow ship. However, in spite of Circe's advice, I put on my glorious armor. Then, armed with a spear in each hand, I searched the misty mountain for the monstrous creature. I looked until my eyes became weary, but I could not see her anywhere.

So we ventured up the narrow channel. We kept our eyes upon the far side, where Charybdis was actively stirring up the salt sea. Whenever she spewed forth the water she had swallowed, she would first boil and bubble like the contents of a cauldron over a high fire. Then she would burst forth with such strength that a misty spray would drench the clifftops on both sides of the channel.

Her eruption was frightening enough, but our hearts overflowed with terror as we watched her suck into herself all the surrounding sea. The sheer cliffs resounded with a mighty roar as the loud-sounding sea rushed inward upon itself, revealing the black, sandy earth at the bottom of the channel. As our minds were fixed upon the hope that Charybdis would not swallow our hollow ship, Scylla's mouths fastened upon my six strongest companions. In desperation, they cried out for my help. But by the time I noticed them, their arms and legs were waving high above me, and my bronze spears were useless.

As a fisherman standing on a rocky ledge lowers his long pole into the sea to attract small fish, then gets a bite and tosses the squirming fish behind him upon the shore, so Scylla caught my six companions, lifted them up to her den, and threw their writhing bodies behind her into her hollow cave. Even as they screamed and reached toward me with their hands, begging me to the last to save them, I watched the monster sit in the doorway of her den and devour them. In all of my wanderings upon the salt sea, that was the most pitiful sight I ever saw!

Once we had left Charybdis and Scylla behind, we reached the island where Helios, who gives joy to mortals, keeps his immortal herds of cattle and flocks of sheep. We heard the animals long before we saw them, and I remembered the warnings of the blind prophet Teiresias and of fair-haired Circe.

When I told my men of the counsel I had received and suggested that we row our swift black ship past the island of Helios, Eurylochus responded with great anger.

"Clearly, Odysseus, you are much stronger than any other mortal, for your arms do not tire. Your heart, too, must be made of iron since you will not permit your companions, weary as they are with hard work and fatigue, to set foot on Helios' land. Black night is quickly coming upon us. We will be safer on shore than at the mercy of the loud-sounding sea if mighty stormwinds, which are destroyers of ships, come upon us in the darkness."

When all of my companions agreed with Eurylochus, I became certain that one of the gods was plotting against us. "I will consent," I replied, "only if each of you swears a sacred oath that you will not harm any of Helios' cattle or sheep, and will eat only the food fair-haired Circe has given us."

When they agreed, we anchored our well-built ship in the hollow harbor of Helios' island near a spring of sweet water. In the middle of that night Zeus, the Cloud-Gatherer, sent a mighty wind upon us and covered the salt sea and the island with clouds. At dawn we dragged our swift black ship ashore and sheltered it in a hollow cave. Then I reminded my companions, "Let us eat and drink from the stores upon our ship and do no harm to the cows and sheep of Helios, who sees and hears all things."

My men agreed, and they kept their word as long as our stores of grain and wine could feed us, for they did not want to endanger their lives. However, the South Wind blew upon us continuously for a month, and in time we consumed all the food we had brought with us. Then their hunger forced my companions to search Helios' island for whatever sources of wild food they could find — fish, fowl, and game. Meanwhile, I found a place to pray to the deathless gods for help, but instead of sending a source of food, they put me to sleep.

While I was asleep, Eurylochus counseled my men. "No one wants to die, but the worst form of death is starvation. So let us capture the best of Helios' cattle and sacrifice them to the gods. If we ever reach Ithaca, we will build a fine temple for Helios. But if the lord of the sun wishes to destroy us, I would rather drown quickly in the loud-sounding sea than waste away slowly from starvation."

My companions agreed with him and proceeded to make the sacrifice. They were roasting the meat when I awakened.

Later Calypso told me that Helios had complained to the immortals on Mount Olympus and then threatened them. "I expect you to punish Odysseus' companions for killing my cattle," he announced. "If you refuse to do so, I shall leave this world and shine upon the shades of the dead in Hades' dark kingdom instead of upon the grain-giving earth."

To these words, Zeus had replied, "Have no concern, for I shall destroy the swift ship of these men with my thunderbolt when they are far out on the wine-dark sea."

When I returned to my companions, I chided them for what they had done, but I could not bring Helios' cattle back to life. The gods made sure my men did not enjoy their six-day feast with fearless hearts. While the meat was roasting, we could hear the sound of cattle lowing, the hides crawled, and the meat upon the spits bellowed as if it were still alive.

During those six days the storm winds blew upon us continuously, but when rosy-fingered Dawn made the seventh day light, we were able to set sail upon the loud-sounding sea. When we could see nothing but the salt sea and the sky, Zeus sent a black cloud hovering above our swift black ship. Then the mighty West Wind attacked us, screaming in its fury as it broke our mast, which crushed the steersman as it fell upon him. Next, Zeus struck us with his lightning bolt, shaking us so violently that my comrades tumbled to their deaths from our blackened, shattered ship.

I lashed the broken mast to the keel and hung on as the South Wind came and pushed me back to Scylla and Charybdis. At dawn I could see that the tireless wind was driving me into Charybdis' whirlpool. Just as Charybdis was about to swallow the salt sea, and the remains of my ship with it, I gathered all my strength and jumped.

With my arms outstretched, I leaped toward the closest overhanging branch of the large fig tree that grew upon the top of the cliff. I grabbed it and clung with my hands and feet, swinging back and forth like a bat. The branch extended so far from the trunk of the tree that I could not safely climb upon it. I could only hope that my arms and legs were strong enough to support my weight until Charybdis spewed forth the remains of my swift ship.

My heart overflowed with joy when the wreckage reappeared with the surge of the loud-sounding sea. I dropped from the branch and fell into the salty water not far from the keel of my ship. Climbing upon it, I rowed away, using my hands as oars. The lord of Olympus kindly did not let Scylla see me, for if she had, I never could have escaped her. I drifted in this manner for nine days.

I reached Calypso's island on the tenth night. This fair-haired goddess rescued me and welcomed me into her home. She would have made me immortal if I had chosen to remain with her. But my heart constantly longed for my homeland and my dear wife, Penelope. Even so, I was forced to remain with Calypso for seven long years. When the eighth year arrived, the goddess suddenly decided to let me go. She even sent me forth on my raft with food, wine, clothing, and a soft breeze. I do not know whether a message from Zeus, lord of Olympus, changed her heart, but it would not surprise me if that were so.

This ends the tale of my wanderings over the wine-dark sea.

The words of Odysseus were greeted with silence and awe in the Phaeacian palace.

Chapter 6

Odysseus returns to Ithaca. He receives guidance
from Athena and meets his son Telemachus.

As Odysseus enjoyed the feast in his honor that evening, he often turned to watch the journey of the fiery sun. The sooner it set, the sooner his journey homeward would begin, and his heart was filled with thoughts of his family and his homeland. As a farmer hungers for his evening meal after he has spent the long day driving his oxen to plow a fresh field, and with joy in his heart watches the sun set so he can drag his weak legs home to dinner, so Odysseus longed for his return home and happily observed the setting sun.

Then he said to the king, "You have given me what my heart has wished for: gifts of friendship and a swift passage home. May the deathless gods grant me these gifts. May I find, upon my return home, that my wife has been faithful and my family is well. May the gods permit you to prosper in every way, and may they keep all harm from your people."

When Odysseus went on board the swift Phaeacian ship, he lay down upon the rug spread on the deck for him and went to sleep. As four yoked horses spring forward together beneath the lashes of the whip, so the swift ship leaped forward upon the wine-dark sea, leaving in its wake waves of foaming white. The ship moved so quickly that even a hawk could not have kept up with it. Odysseus, who was the equal of the gods in counsel and who had endured count-less trials both in the war with Troy and in his wanderings upon the salt sea, slept peacefully at last, confident that he would return home safely and soon.

However, with anger in his heart, the lord of the sea confronted the lord of Olympus. "I was kind enough, Brother, to honor your promise that Odysseus would return home," Poseidon complained. "Yet for all the suffering that he has endured, Odysseus has landed in Ithaca with more bronze, gold, and other gifts than he ever earned for himself in the war with Troy! How will the deathless gods continue to honor me when my own people, the Phaeacians of the long oars, show so little respect for my wishes?"

Zeus replied, "The gods would never dishonor you, for you are the oldest and best of the immortals. You should feel free to punish any mortal who dishonors you."

"I would have done so," the Earthshaker confessed, "but I did not wish to anger you. On its return voyage I would like to strike the ship that has taken Odysseus to Ithaca and then remove the city from the coast so that the Phaea-cians never again will be able to transport strangers across the wine-dark sea."

"Then do so," the lord of black clouds responded. "When the Phaeacians gather by the shore to welcome their sailors home, turn the swift ship to stone as it approaches the harbor and raise a ring of mountains around their fair city."

So it came to pass that the Phaeacians of the long oars, famous for their swift black ships, became a landlocked people. And Poseidon finally put aside his anger against the long-suffering Odysseus.

When Odysseus awoke, he stood upon the soil of Ithaca, but he did not recognize his homeland. Athena had shrouded the country in mist so that she could talk with him before he proceeded on his way.

"Surely I must be the most unfortunate of men!" Odysseus exclaimed. "What land have I come to this time? Are the people who live here wild and without welcome, or do they befriend the stranger in their midst and honor the deathless gods? What should I do with my possessions? And where should I go myself?"

As he walked this way and that along the shore of the loud-sounding sea, the bright-eyed goddess approached him in the form of a well-born young shepherd boy. Odysseus greeted her warmly and asked what land this was.

Athena replied, "If you do not know where you are, either you must be a foolish person or you hail from some distant land, for even the horse-taming Trojans have heard of Ithaca."

Odysseus, man of many schemes, responded with a long, false tale of how he had just arrived from his native land of Crete.

When he had finished his story, the goddess of the flashing eyes smiled and put her hand on his arm. Transforming herself into a beautiful woman, she said, "Only the cleverest among the deathless gods can surpass your ability to scheme and to deceive! You are a shrewd and daring man, and such a lover of misleading fabrications that you continue to create them even when you have returned to your homeland.

"But let us talk of other matters," Athena continued. "I am very surprised that you did not know me when you saw me, especially since I am always by your side and protect you whenever you are in danger. Did I not make all the Phaeacians love you?"

Odysseus replied, "Goddess, it is hard for any mortal to recognize you, for you appear in whatever guise you choose. I know that you befriended me during the years I fought against the horse-taming Trojans, but since we sacked Priam's great city and set sail for Ithaca, I have never seen you, either on board my hollow ship or on land.

"In fact, I have wandered from land to land, and from one disaster to another, with my heart overflowing with grief. If you have made any effort to lessen my suffering, I am certainly unaware of it! By the time you reappeared in Phaeacia, my troubles were behind me.

"Tell me," he then asked, "am I really in Ithaca?"

"I knew that you would have to come home alone, as you have," Athena explained. "I simply could not oppose Poseidon when you angered him by blinding his son, the Cyclops. And now I shall prove to you that this is indeed Ithaca." With these words, the goddess caused the mist to disappear.

Odysseus was so glad to be home that he kissed the grain-giving earth. Athena helped him store his gifts deep within a hollow cave, sealing the entrance with a large rock. When they had finished, she said, "I admire you because you are intelligent and careful. Any other man, upon returning home after twenty years, would immediately seek out his wife and children. Yet you will test the loyalty of your wife before you are at ease in your homeland.

"You will find that Penelope is the same faithful wife you remember," the goddess said. "But you will have to punish the arrogant suitors who for three years have been living without shame in your house, consuming your goods, and offering your godlike wife marriage gifts."

"Without this knowledge, I would have met the same fate as wide-ruling Agamemnon," said Odysseus, "for surely the suitors would have plotted against me in my house as Clytemnestra and her new husband devised his death. If you will help me I can fight the suitors, even if there are 300 of them!"

"Be assured that I shall help you," Athena responded. "The blood and brains of these men will spill upon the earth! However, first I shall disguise you so that no mortal will recognize you. I shall wither your skin with the wrinkles of old age, spoil your blond hair, and dress you in such disgustingly dirty and tattered clothing that you will be repulsive to gaze upon. Then I shall dim your shining eyes so that even your wife and your son will not know you.

"Stay with your loyal swineherd," the goddess counseled, "while I bring your steadfast son, Telemachus, home from Sparta. He has been visiting wise Nestor and now Menelaus, seeking knowledge about you."

Athena touched her wand to the long-suffering Odysseus. When she had completed his transformation, she gave him a staff to lean upon and an old, ragged bag to carry by its twisted string. Then they parted.

Odysseus and the swineherd were preparing their breakfast in the swineherd's hut when Telemachus quietly entered. As a father, his heart overflowing with love, greets his only son upon his return from a distant land after an absence of ten years, so the swineherd embraced the prince.

"Father," Telemachus said to the swineherd, "please go quickly and tell my mother that I have returned safely from Pylos and Sparta. Be certain that no one else hears your words, for there are many in my father's house who are contriving to bring death upon me."

When the swineherd had put on his sandals and left for the city, Athena appeared as a beautiful woman whom only Odysseus could see. She motioned him to join her outside and said, "Now is the time to reveal your true self to Telemachus, so that the two of you can plan how you will bring black death upon the suitors. Then you can proceed into the city. I shall remain near you, for I intend to be present at the battle."

The bright-eyed goddess placed her golden wand upon Odysseus. She exchanged his old clothes for clean ones, then made him much taller, younger, and more handsome.

When Odysseus reentered the hut, Telemachus exclaimed, "You suddenly look quite different, stranger. Before you were a shabby old man, and now you look like a god!"

The long-suffering Odysseus replied, "I am not a god, Telemachus. I am your father, whose absence has brought you great grief and has forced you to live with cruel men in your house. I have returned home after twenty years of pain and wandering." Odysseus kissed his son and let a tear roll down his cheek, for the first time permitting himself to express some emotion.

Wise Telemachus could not yet believe that this stranger was his father. "No mortal could transform himself in this way," he said. "I cannot help but think that you must be one of the deathless gods."

"It is easy for a god to transform a mortal," Odysseus explained. "Athena causes me to appear sometimes as a beggar and sometimes as my true self."

Then Telemachus threw his arms around his great father and wept for all the years that he had not known him. Odysseus, too, wept for all the years that he had been deprived of his son. Just as birds tear the air with shrill cries when they return to their nests with food, expecting to feed their hungry young chicks, and find their nests empty because farmers have stolen their young, so Odysseus and Telemachus cried for the years they had lost.

When they had had their fill of weeping, and Odysseus had told Telemachus of his travels, the man of many schemes said, "Now tell me how many suitors there are and what kind of men they are. I must decide whether the two of us alone can deal with them or whether we will need to enlist the aid of others."

Wise Telemachus replied, "Father, your friends have told me what a mighty warrior you were and how wise in counsel, but I question your judgment here. Do you really expect the two of us to conquer more than 100 strong men? We will need help."

"All right, then," Odysseus responded. "Will Athena and Zeus be help enough, or should I try to think of others also?"

"They are enough, of course," Telemachus said, "except that they spend their time on Mount Olympus."

"I think they will be with us when we need them," his father replied. "But for the time being, go home and join the arrogant suitors. I will come later as an aged beggar. No matter how I am treated, I want you to wait patiently, even if someone throws something at me or hits me or drags me by my feet out the door.

"When Athena puts it into my mind, I will nod my head as a sign that you should remove all the weapons and armor that line the walls of our great hall and hide them in the storeroom. If any suitor questions your actions, simply tell him that, over the years, they have become covered with soot from the fire that burns in the center of the great hall.

"Leave a sword, a spear, and an oxhide shield behind, for you and me," the man of many schemes concluded, "and if you are truly my son, you will tell no one, not even your mother, that I have returned."

Just before the swineherd returned from the city, Athena transformed Odysseus so that the swineherd would find the same old stranger he had left in his hut. As loyal as the swineherd was, he had so much love in his heart for Odysseus and for the steadfast Penelope that Athena was not sure he would be able to keep the knowledge of his master's return locked safely in his heart.

Chapter 7

Odysseus returns to his palace, where he meets the
suitors, his old nurse, and Penelope.

When rosy-fingered Dawn next shone forth upon gods and mortals, wise Telemachus returned to the city. Shortly thereafter, the swineherd led Odysseus, in his form as a raggedy old beggar, into the city also. When they approached Odysseus' palace, he said to the swineherd, "You go inside, and I will stay here. I have suffered so much from the war and the waves of the salt sea that no matter how I am treated, I shall endure it."

As Odysseus spoke these words, an old dog that lay in the courtyard of the palace lifted his head and pricked up his ears. Odysseus had raised Argos but then had gone off to Troy, and the dog had patiently waited twenty years for his master's return. At first, young men used to take him with them when they went off to hunt wild goats, rabbits, and deer. But, soon, without his master to care for him, he lay ignored among the piles of mule and cattle dung that always littered the courtyard until slaves collected it to fertilize the fields.

Argos recognized Odysseus immediately. He wagged his tail but was too weak to approach his master. Realizing that to pet his dog would reveal his identity, Odysseus turned away from the swineherd to wipe the tears from his eyes. Then black Death took Argos, for he had lived beyond his years to see his master's safe return.

Odysseus followed the swineherd to the palace and sat down in the doorway. Once he had finished the bread Telemachus passed to him, bright-eyed Athena counseled him to walk among the suitors and beg for more food. When the man of many schemes came to Antinous, the leader of the suitors, he asked, "How about a gift from you, my friend? You appear to be the best of the suitors here, in bearing even like a king, so you should give me the best gift of all."

"Indeed I shall give you a gift that is fitting and proper!" Antinous replied. He grabbed his footstool and threw it at Odysseus, hitting him in the shoulder.

The man of long suffering stood firm as a rock and then silently returned to the doorway. "Antinous has struck me because I am a beggar," Odysseus murmured. "If the gods protect those who are forced to beg for their food, may Death come for him before he marries."

Soon another beggar arrived at the palace, one known throughout the city for his endless appetite. Although he possessed little strength, he appeared impressive, for he was a very large man.

"Get away from the doorway, old man!" he shouted. "You are blocking my way!"

"Clearly there is room for both of us," Odysseus replied. "Do not provoke me unless you want a fight."

"If you want to fight a younger man," said the beggar, "I shall spatter your teeth upon the ground as if they were kernels of corn scattered by some pig!"

Antinous, hearing this exchange of words, announced, "As a prize, the beggar who wins the fight will always eat with us. The loser will have to beg somewhere else."

Long-suffering Odysseus replied, "Only an empty stomach encourages an old man like me to fight a younger one. Swear that none of you will interfere between us."

"Have no fear," wise Telemachus said, "If your mind and your heart lead you to take on this beggar, any suitor who strikes you will have to contend with me!"

Odysseus then arranged his tattered clothing so that his great arms and mighty thighs were free. The suitors marveled at the stranger's apparent strength, which his rags had concealed. The young beggar was sorry that he had ever opened his mouth. Odysseus debated whether to kill the young beggar with a mighty blow or simply knock him out with a lighter punch. He decided on the weaker blow, for then the suitors would not be too impressed with his strength.

So the man of many schemes struck the young beggar upon the neck, driving him to the ground. He dragged him by the feet into the courtyard of the palace and leaned his body against the wall by the gates. "Now, frighten away the dogs and pigs!" Odysseus said. Then, he returned to the doorway of the great hall and sat down again.

The suitors cheerfully called out, "Stranger, may Zeus and the other deathless gods grant what you most wish, since you have gotten rid of that bothersome beggar."

When the suitors had returned to their homes for the night, wise Penelope asked to speak with the stranger, even though he was a beggar. "Who are you?" she asked him. "And where are you from?"

"Ask me anything else, Lady," Odysseus replied, "but these questions fill my heart with sorrow, and I do not want to weep in your house."

The steadfast Penelope replied, "My heart, too, overflows with sorrow as I long for the return of my husband. While these suitors have pressed marriage upon me, I have fought them off by scheming against them. Some god put the thought in my mind to set up a great loom in my hall and to weave a large robe with very fine thread.

"I said to them, 'Since my lord, Odysseus, is dead, I am weaving this shroud for Laertes, his father, so that Death will not find him without a suitable covering. Although I know you are eager to marry me, just be patient until I finish this wrap.'

"The suitors agreed," Penelope continued, "so every day I wove the shroud, and every night by torchlight I unraveled what I had woven that day. Thus I have tricked my suitors for the three years they have sat in the great hall. But then one of my maidservants told the suitors my secret, and they caught me unraveling the thread. So I have had to complete the shroud, and now I can think of no other way to postpone choosing one of the suitors to marry.

"Now, tell me about yourself," she concluded. "Surely your parents are mortal and not some oak tree or stone."

Odysseus proceeded to tell his loyal wife one of his fabulous tales about his life in Crete. He incorporated into the story the fact that he had heard of Odysseus' return. He even went so far as to describe the episode with Helios' cattle and Odysseus' arrival in Phaeacia.

"You may stop your weeping," he counseled Penelope, "for I have heard that Odysseus is nearby. He would have been here by now, but he is wandering about gathering more riches. In fact, I shall swear a sacred oath by Zeus, lord of Olympus, that Odysseus will return to Ithaca within this month."

"May your words come true," wise Penelope responded, "but I have no confidence in my heart that they will. However, even if we cannot welcome you as we would if the lord of this house were here, my maidservants will still bathe your feet and prepare a fine bed for you."

"My lady," Odysseus replied, "I have no interest in a fine bed. However, if you have some great-hearted maidservant who has lived long enough to have suffered as much as I, if you wish, she may wash my feet."

Penelope answered, "I have such a servant, an old woman whose heart overflows with understanding. She nursed my husband on the day his mother gave birth to him, and she has loved him ever since then. As old as she is, she will wash your feet."

The old nurse rose and prepared to do as Penelope had asked. As she studied the stranger, she said to him, "We have welcomed many strangers in these halls, but you look and sound more like great-hearted Odysseus than any man I have ever seen. Even your feet are like his!"

"Everyone who has seen the two of us remarks that we are very similar," replied the man of many schemes.

Suddenly the thought occurred to him that, as the old nurse was washing his feet, she might notice the scar of an old wound located just above his knee. Then she surely would know him. So he seated himself away from the light of the fire and turned his face toward the dark part of the room.

Just as Odysseus had feared, as soon as the old nurse took his leg in her hands to wash it, her hands felt the scar and recognized it even in the dark. Remembering the wound Odysseus had once received from the tusk of an enormous wild boar, she abruptly dropped his leg. The bronze basin tipped over, and the water spilled upon the floor.

With tears in her eyes, the old nurse placed her hand under the stranger's chin and said, "You are indeed Odysseus, my dear child, although I did not recognize you until I took your leg in my hands."

As she spoke, the old nurse looked toward Penelope, hoping to signal to her, but Athena had turned Penelope's thoughts to other matters.

Odysseus clapped his hand over the nurse's mouth and said, "You will surely be the death of me unless you keep silent! My presence in this house must be kept a secret."

"You know how strong I am," she replied. "I shall remain as silent as a rock or a piece of iron."

When the old nurse had finished bathing his feet, Odysseus pulled his chair close to the fire once again and arranged his tattered garments to cover his scar.

Wise Penelope then said to him, "The time is coming when I will have to hold a contest to determine which suitor I shall have to marry. I plan to use the twelve ceremonial axes that Odysseus liked to use for practice with his great bow. Telemachus will line up the axes in a row with their handles upright, as his father did, so that the hole in the handle of each axe will be in line with all the others.

"First, I shall have the suitors compete against one another to see who can string my lord's bow most easily. Then they will compete to see who can shoot an arrow from a great distance through the holes in all of the axe handles."

The man of many schemes replied, "I see no reason for you to postpone this contest any longer, for Odysseus will be in your house before these suitors can even string his polished bow!"

Chapter 8

Odysseus fights the suitors and is recognized by Penelope. Finally, peace comes to Ithaca.

When rosy-fingered Dawn next shone forth upon gods and mortals, the suitors gathered in the great hall of Odysseus' palace. One gave the man of many schemes a gift similar to the one Antinous had chosen to give; he threw the hoof of an ox at Odysseus' head. However, Odysseus quickly moved his head aside to avoid it, and it hit the wall instead.

Telemachus said to the suitor, "If you had struck the stranger with that hoof, I would have run you through with my bronze spear. Then your father would have to hold a funeral rather than a wedding feast for you. I want no more of this behavior in my house!"

Then the prophet Theoclymenus spoke. He had arrived from Pylos with Telemachus and was his guest. "Oh, unhappy men!" he cried. "What kind of evil sits upon you? Your heads are shrouded in night, and tears fall from your eyes. Blood spatters the beams and the walls. Ghosts crowd the porch and the courtyard. An evil mist has veiled the sun, and in the darkness, the ghosts hurry down to Hades' dark kingdom."

"This stranger surely is out of his mind!" exclaimed one of the suitors. "We'd best take him outside if he finds it so dark in here!"

"I need no one to help me leave," Theoclymenus replied. "Nor do I intend to stay. I see evil approaching all of you, and no suitor will be able to escape it." And with these words he left the great hall.

Penelope then appeared with Odysseus' great bow, his quiver of arrows, and a chest containing the ceremonial axes. "I am putting before you the polished bow of Odysseus," she announced. "I will marry whoever among you most easily strings this bow and shoots an arrow through the holes in all twelve axe handles."

"Come, all of you!" Telemachus encouraged them. "Surely I do not need to praise the prize of this contest. Even I will try the bow. I would like to be able to use my father's weapon."

He jumped up, dug a trench, and arranged the axes with their handles upright in a straight line. Then he tried to string his father's great bow. When it looked as if he would succeed in his fourth try, Odysseus signaled to him to stop. "Obviously I cannot do it," Telemachus said. "I am either too young or too weak. You are much stronger than I am, so it is your turn to try!"

However, not one of the suitors could string Odysseus' mighty bow. They tried warming it and waxing it, but nothing helped. One of the men complained, "I am sorry to lose a woman like Penelope, but there are many other fine women in

Greece. What distresses me most is that not one of us is as strong as godlike Odysseus. Men to come are sure to think less of us because of our weakness."

Then Odysseus, man of many schemes, called out, "Suitors of good Penelope, give me the polished bow so that I can see whether I still have the strength I had before my wanderings began and I had to start begging for food."

Antinous replied, "Is it not enough for you to eat in our presence and listen to our conversation? What other beggar is treated so well? Besides, if you do manage to string the mighty bow, we shall quickly ship you to some other land, where you will not fare as well as you have in Ithaca."

Another suitor said, "And how would it look if a wandering beggar could string the bow that younger men cannot?"

Wise Penelope replied, "You suitors have already injured your reputations by your behavior in this royal house. What more do you have to lose? This stranger is well born and well built. If he strings the bow, I shall not marry him; surely he can have no hope of that. But I shall give him a set of fine clothes and good weapons to use in his own defense."

Telemachus then counseled, "Mother, I am in charge of the bow, and I will give it or withhold it as I choose. If I decided to let the stranger take it away with him, no one has the right to stop me. This is a matter for men, not women, so I ask you to return to your rooms and take up your usual tasks at your loom."

Penelope left the great hall, and the swineherd approached Odysseus with the polished bow and put it into his hands. Odysseus then quietly told the old nurse to bar all the doors.

He picked up his great bow and inspected it carefully, testing it this way and that. Then, with no effort at all, he lifted the bow and strung it. As a man skilled in the use of the lyre easily stretches the string of twisted sheep gut around a new peg and then fastens the string at each end, so godlike Odysseus strung his polished bow. While Zeus, lord of Olympus, set forth a loud clap of thunder, Odysseus stood by his chair, set one of his arrows upon the string, and sent it flying through all twelve holes in the axe handles.

Then the man of long suffering said to Telemachus, "See, the stranger you have fed and housed is as strong as he used to be, and he has not shamed you in any way. Now it is time to feed the suitors, for the sun has not yet set." These words signaled Telemachus, who armed himself with spear and sword and joined his father.

Odysseus then tore off his tattered clothing and said, "The contest is over, but I have other targets in mind. May Apollo, lord of the silver bow, grant me glory if I hit the mark!"

He aimed his first arrow at Antinous, who was lifting a golden wine cup to his lips. The arrow pierced his throat. Terror filled the hearts of the suitors as they ran this way and that through the great hall, searching for the weapons that used to line the walls but were now concealed in the storeroom.

"You dogs!" Odysseus exclaimed. "You were so sure that I would never come home from Troy! You sat here day after day for over three years, wasting my goods and wooing my wife, without fear of gods or mortals. Now black Death will come upon each and every one of you; you cannot escape."

When Odysseus had used all of his arrows, he, Telemachus, the swineherd, and another loyal servant armed themselves with bronze weapons and continued the attack. But the goatherd, who was a loyal supporter of the suitors, brought arms to them, for Telemachus had inadvertently left the storeroom door open.

Even weapons could not protect the suitors, for Athena now entered the great hall. Disguising herself as a swallow, she flew up to the roof beam and surveyed the battle from there. Thereafter, every spear Odysseus or his men hurled hit its mark, while the suitors' spears always flew far and wide of their targets. Finally, all of the suitors lay dead, and the floor of the great hall swam with their blood.

Unseen by mortal eyes, Hermes then appeared with his golden wand, which he uses to awaken or put to sleep whomever he chooses. He awakened the shades of the dead suitors and led them all down to Hades' dark kingdom. As in the deepest depths of a hollow cave bats fly about and squeak when one among them falls from the rock that they have clung to, so the shades of the suitors babbled to one another as the Wayfinder led them down past the streams of Oceanus and the gates of the sun into the land where the shades of the dead live on forever.

When Telemachus brought the old nurse into the great hall, she found Odysseus standing with the corpses of the suitors surrounding him. As a lion returns all covered with blood and frightful to look upon, from feeding upon an ox it has ravaged in the farmyard, so Odysseus was stained with blood and gore.

Before she could say anything, her master advised, "Your heart can overflow with joy, Nurse, but it is wrong to exult over the dead. The suitors were blind to the consequences of their own rash behavior. They honored no one who came among them, and the gods have punished them dearly for it."

While the servants were cleaning and purifying the great hall, the old nurse went up to Penelope's room and cried, "Wake up, dear child, to see what you have waited for so long. Odysseus has returned, and he has killed all of the arrogant suitors!"

Penelope replied, "Dear Nurse, your mind is usually quite sound, but the gods can both make the simple-minded wise and rob the wise of their understanding. They appear to have made you witless. Why tell me such a fantastic story?"

"Odysseus is the very stranger that the suitors taunted in the great hall," the old nurse explained. "He confided in Telemachus but no one else, so that they could surprise the suitors with their attack."

Penelope jumped out of bed, hugged the nurse in her joy, and asked, "If this is true, how did Odysseus manage to slay over 100 men with so few to help him?"

"I did not see it until it was over," the nurse replied, "but his vengeance was swift and complete."

"No, Nurse," Penelope replied. "Clearly it was the gods who killed the suitors. And as for Odysseus, he is somewhere far from home."

"It is you who are wrong, my child," the old nurse replied. "When I washed the stranger's feet, I saw the wound the boar made so long ago above Odysseus' knee. When I tried to tell you, your lord closed my mouth with his hand and told me I had to remain silent. Come with me, and see for yourself."

As Penelope went to meet her husband, she wondered whether to stand apart and question him or to embrace him warmly. When she entered the room, she simply sat down and silently observed him. Odysseus also sat silently, waiting to see if his wife would speak.

Finally, Telemachus became impatient and said, "Mother, your heart is as hard as rock and cruel besides! Why do you not sit next to my father and talk to him? No other woman would greet her husband in such a manner after he has been away from home for twenty years and has suffered so much."

Wise Penelope replied, "My son, I am too amazed to speak! If this really is my husband, then I must be more certain of it, for we two share knowledge that is known to us alone."

Then the long-suffering Odysseus smiled and said to his son, "Telemachus, let your mother test me, to be certain of my identity. Meanwhile, have everyone in the house dress for a festive occasion and make merry in our halls. This will mislead the people in the city and the suitors' families about what has really taken place here."

Great-hearted Odysseus then bathed and dressed. Bright-eyed Athena made him taller, stronger, and more handsome. As a skilled artisan overlays gold upon silver and creates objects of great beauty, so Athena made Odysseus appear as striking as a god.

When he returned to his wife, Odysseus said, "Strange woman! No other wife would remain apart from her husband after an absence of twenty years and so much suffering. It appears that nothing can soften your heart. So, Nurse, prepare a bed out here for me, for my wife has an iron heart."

Penelope added, "Come, Nurse. Move the bed out of the bridal chamber and cover it with fleeces, sheets, and blankets."

To this direction Odysseus responded with great anger. "Penelope," he cried, "I am losing both my patience and my sympathy! Who has moved my bed? Only a god would possess such skill. Certainly no mortal, no matter how young or strong, could budge it. I built our bridal chamber around the trunk of an olive tree and then removed all the branches, smoothed the trunk, and fashioned it into one of the bedposts. You know this as well as I do. Has someone cut the bedpost from the tree trunk and moved our bed?"

Penelope's heart softened at this, for she knew that this was her husband. Tearfully she embraced him and said, "Forgive me, Odysseus, for not welcoming you like this when I first saw you. I have always been afraid that some man would come and fool me into thinking that he was you. But your knowledge of our secret has convinced me that you are my Odysseus."

As the sight of land is welcome to shipwrecked swimmers, whose swift hollow ship Poseidon destroyed by sending tumultuous waves and mighty winds to attack its strong frame, and with hearts overflowing with relief and happiness, they finally set foot upon that land, so was the long-suffering Odysseus welcome to Penelope. Once she embraced him she could not release him, and Odysseus wept as he finally held his dear, loyal wife in his arms.

Rosy-fingered Dawn did not bring light to gods and mortals until bright-eyed Athena gave her permission. The goddess extended the night and delayed Dawn at the streams of Oceanus in order to give Odysseus and his Penelope time to weep, and to love, and to exchange tales of the past twenty years. And only when the last of the tales concluded were they content to fall asleep.

When Dawn finally shone forth upon gods and mortals, word of the fate of the suitors spread through the city. Each family collected its dead, and the corpses from far lands were sent home. Then the men of Ithaca assembled to discuss whether or not to take vengeance upon Odysseus.

The father of Antinous blamed Odysseus for the deaths of all his companions who left the land of the horse-taming Trojans aboard their twelve hollow ships as well as for the deaths of the suitors. Two of Odysseus' servants explained how the gods had taken Odysseus' side in the battle in the great hall. Finally, a prophet told the men of Ithaca that it had been their responsibility to curb the suitors' behavior, but they had been too cowardly to take action against their children and their countrymen.

Half of the speakers decided against vengeance and returned home, but the other half decided to attack. Zeus, lord of counsel, then directed his bright-eyed daughter to bring peace to Ithaca. When Odysseus and his small group of armed men faced the armed group from the city, Athena joined Odysseus disguised as a family friend.

Odysseus and Telemachus set upon the armed men with their spears and would have killed all of them, but Athena terrorized the group by calling out in her immortal voice. "Men of Ithaca," she shouted, "spill no more blood! Quickly return to your homes with your lives and live in peace with one another."

The long-suffering Odysseus ignored her words and started after the frightened men like an eagle diving down upon its prey. Zeus, lord of the bright lightning and the dark cloud, then hurled his blazing thunderbolt at the feet of his flashing-eyed daughter.

"Odysseus," Athena counseled, "drop your weapons! Put aside what is past and love your people. Then you will be king the rest of your life and will live peacefully and well. If you cannot obey, you will arouse the anger of mighty Zeus."

When Odysseus heard these words, his heart filled with joy. Thus Athena, in the form of a loyal friend, brought lasting peace between Odysseus and his people.

Introducing **the Epilogue to The Odyssey**

Because of the particular focus of *The Odyssey*, Homer excludes many myths that relate to the aftermath of the Trojan War. However, he relates the return of Menelaus and Agamemnon in Book IV of *The Odyssey*. Hegias or Agias of Troezen (7th or 6th century B.C.) wrote an epic, *Nostoi* (*The Returns*), that relates the fate of all of the major Greek heroes except for Odysseus, and Apollodorus (2nd century B.C.) deals with Hegias' material in the *Epitome*. Aeschylus (6th to 5th century B.C.) deals with the return of Agamemnon and the results of his murder in the *Oresteia* trilogy. Both Sophocles (5th century B.C.) and Euripides (5th century B.C.) deal with the subject in their two plays both entitled *Electra*. Euripides relates the return of Neoptolemus in *Andromache*.

Eugammon of Cyrene (mid–6th century B.C.), in his epic *The Telegony*, continues the story of Odysseus' life from the end of *The Odyssey* until his death.

Epilogue to The Odyssey

The Return of Other Greek Heroes

Upon the conclusion of the Trojan War, Nestor and Menelaus left immediately for their kingdoms. Nestor arrived safely in Pylos and found that his family and his subjects had loyally awaited his return. However, Menelaus spent over seven years attempting to return to Sparta, most of that time in Egypt. When he finally succeeded, he ruled until his death. Then the gods conferred immortality upon him, because he was the immortal Helen's husband, and both husband and wife were transported to the Elysian Fields, often called the Islands of the Blessed.

Agamemnon left Troy somewhat later. He arrived safely in Mycenae but was murdered upon his return by his wife, Clytemnestra, or by her lover, Aegisthus (who also had good cause to hate Agamemnon), or by both of them.

The Final Adventures of Odysseus

Odysseus did not remain long in Ithaca after he had reclaimed his kingdom from the suitors. As soon as he had put his affairs in order, he went to Thesprotis, where he took the queen, Callidice, as his wife. In time he led the Thesprotians in an unsuccessful war. Nine years later, after Callidice died, their son became king of Thesprotis, and Odysseus once again returned to Ithaca.

Meanwhile, Telegonus, Odysseus' son by Circe, was searching for his father. He landed on Ithaca without recognizing the identity of the island and proceeded to raid it. When Odysseus defended his kingdom, Telegonus inadvertently killed his father with his spear.

After learning of his tragic mistake, Telegonus took Penelope and Telemachus back with him to his mother's island, where they buried Odysseus and where Circe made them immortal. Then, in a double ceremony, Circe married Telemachus, and Telegonus married Penelope. The death of Odysseus brought the Heroic Age to an end.

Introducing **Romulus and Remus**

At the time of the Roman emperor Augustus Caesar (63 B.C.–A.D. 14), a person's ancestry was of great importance. Similarly, in order for Rome to be considered a major city, it had to have had an auspicious origin. Consequently, a number of gifted authors undertook to document the founding of Rome.

The Roman historian Livy (59 B.C.–A.D. 17), devoted his life to writing *The History of Rome*, in which he describes Aeneas' travels as an exile from Troy (a prestigious location) to Italy and then the founding of Rome by Romulus and Remus. The Roman poet Virgil (70–19 B.C.), in his *Aeneid*, also wrote about the founding of Rome, describing it as the divine mission of the Trojan hero, Aeneas. Virgil pays little attention to Romulus and Remus in *The Aeneid*. Plutarch, who lived in Greece approximately a generation after Augustus Caesar (c. A.D. 50–125), wrote *Parallel Lives of Greeks and Romans*, in which he devotes a biography to Romulus. He did not write about Aeneas.

The myth of Romulus and Remus is appealing because of its miraculous elements. First, like many famous Greek heroes (Perseus, Oedipus, and Paris, to name a few), Romulus and Remus are abandoned to die of starvation, attack by wild animals, or exposure. As is always the case with such infants, they are rescued and live to do deeds worth remembering. In addition, Romulus and Remus are fed by a wolf and a bird. Finally, Romulus disappears within a cloud and returns as an immortal being with a message for his people. These miraculous elements relate the Romulus and Remus myth to the heroic myths of many other cultures. Miracles traditionally accompany great leaders and testify to their greatness.

Romulus and Remus

After Aeneas, Ascanius, and Aeneas' grandson, Silvius, died, the kingdom of Alba Longa passed from father to son until the time of Numitor and Amulius, who were brothers. The brothers agreed to divide their inheritance and to choose their portions by lot. One would draw the kingdom of Alba Longa, and the other would keep the Trojan wealth of gold, silver, and jewels that had come down to them. Numitor drew the kingdom, but Amulius seized the throne and exiled his brother from Alba Longa.

Amulius then murdered Numitor's sons and made his daughter a Vestal Virgin in order to prevent her from marrying and having children who could inherit the throne. She became pregnant anyway and gave birth to twin sons, Romulus and Remus. Her declaration that the god Mars was their father saved neither them nor her. King Amulius imprisoned his niece and ordered her infants drowned in the Tiber River.

At this time, rains had caused the Tiber River to overflow its banks. The servants entrusted with drowning the infants decided that it would be just as effective to drown them in the flooded overflow as to try to reach the actual riverbed of the Tiber. They left the twins at the edge of the overflow in a basket.

When the flood waters receded, the basket containing the twins rested upon dry land. A wolf discovered them when she came down from the hills to drink from the river. The wolf mothered them by giving them her own milk to suck. A bird also helped to nourish them by placing little crumbs into their mouths.

The king's herdsman accidentally came upon the infants and found the wolf there, tenderly licking the babes with her tongue. He brought the twins back to his hut for his wife to nurse, and the couple reared the boys to manhood. They grew to be good, strong, and courageous young men. They spent much of their time farming and hunting. They also began to earn fame by attacking robbers and sharing with their shepherd friends the goods they retrieved in their raids.

The robbers retaliated by choosing a local holiday as the occasion for laying a trap for Romulus and Remus. Romulus defended himself successfully, but the robbers caught Remus and brought him before his uncle, King Amulius. They charged Remus and his brother with the crime of stealing Numitor's cattle. When King Amulius heard their accusation, he sent Remus to Numitor for punishment.

The king's herdsman had always suspected that the boys he had reared were of royal blood. He knew that the king had exposed two royal infants at just the time that he had found these two boys. Now he told Romulus of his suspicions.

When the robbers brought Remus before Numitor and announced that he was one of twins, Numitor also guessed the truth. Remus' age and his noble bearing made it likely that he was Numitor's grandson. Therefore, the king asked Remus about himself and his parents. Remus explained that he had thought his brother and himself to be the children of the king's herdsman, but that he had heard strange tales of his infancy, involving danger by water and rescue by wolf and bird.

Aided by Numitor, Romulus and Remus each gathered a group of herdsmen, quietly met at the king's house, and killed Amulius in a surprise attack. Numitor then explained to the people how King Amulius had usurped the throne and had tried to kill anyone who would succeed him. Amulius had been an unpopular king, so the people of Alba were not saddened by his murder. They unanimously acclaimed Numitor their king.

Romulus and Remus then decided to found a town at the spot where, as infants, they had been left to drown. Since they were of the same age, they could not agree on who should rule the town. They decided to ask the gods of the countryside to reveal the answer. In order to receive the divine revelation, Romulus and his followers stood upon the Palatine hill, and Remus and his followers stood upon the Aventine hill.

Remus saw the first sign, six vultures. Romulus then saw twelve vultures. Remus claimed the kingship because he had been given the first sign. Romulus claimed kingship because his sign was twice as strong as his brother's. Angry words led to death-dealing blows, and Romulus killed Remus. Romulus became the king of the new town and named it Rome after himself.

Romulus increased the population of Rome by opening the settlement to poor people, slaves, and banished men who wanted to begin a new life. However, they had few women. Neighboring communities refused to let their women intermarry with the Romans because they did not want their neighbor to become too powerful. They also felt socially superior to the inhabitants of Rome.

Romulus decided to hold a great celebration on a holiday sacred to the god Neptune. Hundreds of people from the neighboring communities took advantage of the occasion to see the new town. At a prearranged signal, the Roman men suddenly seized all of the visiting young women, including the daughters of the powerful Sabines. The parents of all of these women were outraged, but they were forced to return home without their daughters.

Romulus assured the young women that they would have loving husbands and many privileges in the Roman community. Their husbands lived up to that commitment, and the women accepted their new families and homes.

However, the Romans could not stop the relatives of these women from taking revenge for their abduction. For a number of years, Romulus and his army defended Rome against a series of attacks by neighboring communities. Finally, in order to acquire peace for themselves and their Roman families, the Sabine women took a stand against their relatives and forced them to come to peaceful terms with their Roman husbands.

Through his military skill and strength, Romulus brought a forty-year period of peace to his city. He made good laws, and everyone appeared to love him: the common people, the army, and the senators.

One day, Romulus was standing among his senators and reviewing his troops when a violent storm burst upon them. Dark clouds obscured the sun, making the day as black as night. Resounding thunder and crashing lightning sent many people scurrying for shelter. A thick cloud descended and completely enveloped Romulus so that no one could see him. When the storm blew over and the cloud disappeared, Romulus had disappeared also.

No one could say what had become of him. Most of the senators, soldiers, and townspeople decided that Romulus had become a god. After all, he was the son of Mars. But some suspected that a group of senators had secretly murdered him because he appeared to favor his army over the Senate.

In order to pacify the townspeople, Julius Proculus, a man known for his wisdom, addressed the Roman Assembly. "This morning, the shade of Romulus, the father of our city, came before me," he announced. "He commanded me to tell you that he has become the patron god of Rome and that the gods have destined Rome to become the greatest city in the world. He advises you to become soldiers so that Rome will never be conquered by another power."

Once the Romans received this assurance that Romulus had gained immortality and that their city had a glorious destiny, they felt at peace and turned their attention to thoughts of the next king.

Introducing **The Aeneid**

Historical Background

The founding and destiny of Rome are the focus of The Aeneid.

The same peoples who invaded Greece from the north between approximately 2600 and 1000 B.C. also invaded Italy. The first tribes who arrived brought copper and bronze into the area; much later, a second wave of invaders brought iron tools and weapons. In time, these two groups intermingled and inhabited all of the Italian peninsula.

Tribes who became known as the Latins settled in the lower valley of the Tiber River, called the plain of Latium. According to archaeologists, small Latin settlements existed on many of the seven hilltops there by 753 B.C., which, legend says, is the year Romulus founded Rome. (According to the chronology of The Aeneid, Aeneas founded Rome in 1176 B.C., eight years after the end of the Trojan War.)

Archaeologists think that the small Latin villages united sometime between 800 and 700 B.C. They know that by 700 B.C. at the base of their hills the Latins had built a common Forum area for commercial purposes, including a cattle market. By 625 B.C., many huts had sprung up around the Forum. The Latins could not use much of the lowland area, because the waters of the Tiber often flooded it. The lowland remained swampy, malaria-infested, and largely uninhabited until the Etruscan peoples, who possessed an advanced technology, invaded the area.

Between approximately 900 and 800 B.C., the Etruscan people left their homeland in Asia Minor to invade Italy. They brought with them the idea of the city-state. When they conquered the Latin villages in 607 B.C., they built sewers leading into the Tiber and drained the lowland areas at the base of the seven hills, making a city in that location possible. In about 575 B.C., the Etruscans leveled the existing primitive huts and constructed the large public Forum (the Forum Romanum) as the commercial and political center of a new, large city, which they named Rumlua. Romulus (the legendary first ruler of Rome) and Roma (Latin) are both derived from the Etruscan Rumlua.

Meanwhile, in approximately 800 B.C., the Phoenicians established the city-state of Carthage on Numidian land, on the coast of North Africa to the southwest of Sicily. By 750 B.C., the Greeks had begun to establish colonies on the island of Sicily and on the Italian peninsula.

The Etruscans were an enterprising people who learned whatever they could from the cultures with whom they came into contact. They adapted many religious and artistic ideas and much of their technology from the Greek colonies — including the Greek gods and the phonetic alphabet. They also made a political alliance with Carthage in about 545 B.C., a time when Carthage was wealthy and powerful and controlled the western part of the Mediterranean Sea.

From 509 to 133 B.C., Rome developed into a major power. By 270 B.C., it had conquered the Italian peninsula, including the Etruscans and the Greek colonies. Then it conquered Carthage, Greece, and part of Asia. The three wars with Carthage (the Punic Wars) have remained famous because of the amount of blood spilled and because of the unusual strategic skills of two of the generals involved. After Hannibal, a Carthaginian general, led 40,000 men, 9,000 cavalry troops, and African elephants over the Alps from Spain into Italy, it took the Romans almost twenty years to find a general (Scipio) who could defeat him.

At home, the Romans established a more democratic form of government than their original monarchy, giving the common people many rights and displaying the laws of Rome on twelve tablets in the Forum. The Romans were also more democratic than many of their neighbors in the treatment of the countries they conquered. Unlike the Greeks and many other peoples of that time, the Romans did not kill or enslave most of their enemies. The defeated countries had to pay taxes to Rome and supply troops to defend all of the provinces, but they remained free to govern themselves in most respects. In return, Romans brought their roads and other technological advances, their legal system, and their language and culture to all of their provinces.

The wars of conquest left Rome with numerous social and economic problems at home, provoking civil wars between 133 and 30 B.C. In 59 B.C., Julius Caesar was elected Consul for a nine-year term; he then made himself ruler for life. His greatest achievement was to conquer Gaul (France), for this brought Roman culture into northern Europe. He was murdered in 44 B.C. by those who felt that he had turned the Roman republic into a dictatorship.

Julius was followed by Mark Antony and Octavian, who ruled the empire together at first. When Antony fell in love with Cleopatra, the queen of Egypt, and gave her Roman provinces as a gift, Octavian went to war against him. Octavian's forces won the famous sea battle of Actium, in 31 B.C., and conquered Alexandria, in Egypt, the following year. With the victory against Antony, 100 years of civil wars came to an end.

Octavian inherited a dismal economic, social, and moral scene. Roman aristocrats were accustomed to being unpatriotic, selfish, and lazy. In addition, Rome was plagued by hordes of unemployed people from other levels of society — such as displaced farmers, dissatisfied war veterans, and

slaves from foreign countries — who were accustomed to free bread, free entertainment, and little work. From this economic shambles, Octavian created a professional civil service (a core of trained workers that anyone of ability could join) and a permanent, professional army, which would remain on the borders of the empire and defend them.

The Roman Senate named Octavian "Augustus" (the revered), and the nature of his rule supports such a tribute. Augustus created the Golden Age of Rome. Under his leadership all Roman lands were governed as one large empire, and he instituted conditions under which the Roman world lived in peace for 200 years (the Pax Romana).

Augustus worked with the Roman Senate to rule Rome and the empire. He gave the Senate the power to make laws, and he consulted its members. However, he alone controlled the Roman army so that no one could overthrow him.

Under Augustus, the Romans built an elaborate system of roads throughout their empire and numerous cities. Self-government under Roman law brought a long period of prosperity and peace. This stable environment encouraged the various races and cultures of the many Roman provinces to intermingle freely. The Romans took whatever they valued from the various cultures, synthesized it, and spread this greater knowledge, expressed in their Latin language, throughout the empire along with their public buildings, aqueducts, roads, and bridges.

Augustus also worked to revive the Roman values of a strong family dominated by the father, a respect for ancestral customs and current laws, a strong sense of justice, self-control, piety, and loyalty both to family and country.

The Romans took their cultural heritage from the Greeks. They adopted the Greek pantheon of gods, giving most of them new Roman names. They also adopted Greek myths, architecture and sculpture, and literature. Greek tutors taught them the Greek language, and a Greek slave translated Homer into Latin between 250 and 200 B.C. The poet Ovid (43 B.C.–17 A.D.) told many of the Greek myths with such skill that his stories provide the basis for most of the versions read today.

Virgil, who has for centuries been acknowledged as the greatest Roman poet, used The Iliad and The Odyssey as the basis for his great epic, The Aeneid, in which he glorifies Rome. Indeed, almost every significant event in The Aeneid — including the Trojan War, the dangerous adventures of Aeneas, the befriending of Aeneas by Dido, and the slaying of the Latin warrior Turnus — has a parallel in either The Iliad or The Odyssey.

Virgil and The Aeneid

Publius Vergilius Maro (Virgil) was the son of a farmer in Mantua, but like many young men of his time, he was educated in the larger cities of Milan and Rome. Augustus recognized Virgil's great literary talent and became his patron.

Augustus had been adopted by his great-uncle, Julius Caesar; through him, Augustus traced his ancestors back to the Trojan hero Aeneas, and thus to Aeneas' divine mother, Venus. Romulus had been the legendary founder of Rome according to the Latin tradition. However, after the Romans had defeated the other Latin peoples, they decided to accept Aeneas as the founder of their principal city.

Aeneas had been considered the heroic founder of Rome within the Etruscan culture, and he was also part of the Greek historical and literary tradition. The Romans felt that the Greeks had traditionally been more civilized than the other Latin peoples, and they did not want to have arisen from barbaric ancestors. So they created close political and cultural bonds between themselves and the Greeks in whatever ways they could.

The atmosphere of Rome at the time of Augustus and Virgil was optimistic and patriotic. The people felt that they were personally witnessing the dawn of a new age, one of peace and prosperity unprecedented in the history of the world. The fact that Rome had risen to become the major world power in such a relatively short time and from such ordinary beginnings encouraged their belief in a divine destiny for their nation. It was natural for Virgil to choose the myth of Aeneas' founding the city of Rome as the subject of an epic poem, to base the epic's content and structure upon The Iliad and The Odyssey, and to design it to glorify Augustus and his period in Roman history.

Unlike Homer, Virgil created his epic for a literate audience. The fact that he was writing for readers rather than listeners removed certain limitations and permitted a new set of standards. Virgil was not bound to an elaborate oral tradition that dictated his subject matter and many aspects of its treatment. For his audience, repetition was a liability. He could add much more detail to his plot and description, and he could afford to pay very careful attention to his choice of words and the structure of each line.

Virgil began *The Aeneid* in 29 B.C., two years after the battle of Actium, and he continued to work on it for the next (and last) ten years of his life. First he wrote the entire story in prose. Then he began the intense process of molding it into the style of an epic poem. Each day he created a few lines of poetry, concentrating on the structure of each line and the particular words that would best create the effect he wanted to achieve.

In 19 B.C., Virgil set out for Greece and Asia, where he intended to spend three years revising the entire poem. In Athens he met Augustus, who convinced the poet to return to Italy with him. In Megara Virgil contracted a fever, which got steadily worse; he died of it at the age of fifty-one. As he was dying, Virgil requested that *The Aeneid* be burned, but Augustus ordered the work to be published in spite of Virgil's wishes.

Appeal and Value

The Aeneid has been valued throughout the ages, both for the nature of its story and for its style. Many historical periods have considered it the single greatest work of literature in the world after the Bible. Students have studied it, adults have appreciated it, and poets have imitated its style. The great Italian poet Dante Alighieri (A.D. 1265–1321) idolized Virgil and immortalized him in his own great epic, *The Divine Comedy*. Even the Anglo-Saxon poets were influenced by his style. The Christians of the early Middle Ages, who ignored many of the ancient writers because they were pagans, continued to read *The Aeneid*. They were paricularly sympathetic to the virtue of Aeneas, to the higher purpose of his life, and to the conflict in the ex-ternal world between the forces of good and evil, because these ideas were also present in Christianity.

The decisive event of *The Aeneid* occurs when Aeneas leaves Dido in order to found Rome. He leaves the woman he loves and sacrifices his personal desires to fulfill his destiny. His act causes a great personal tragedy, for Dido commits suicide. Although Aeneas mourns for her, his resolve to pursue his historical mission never weakens.

The central role that Aeneas' divinely sanctioned and prophesied destiny plays in *The Aeneid* is lacking in both *The Iliad* and *The Odyssey*, where human motivations predominate. For example, Odysseus leaves Calypso as Aeneas leaves Dido—but he does it simply because he wants to go home, rather than to fulfill his divinely sanctioned destiny.

The portion of *The Aeneid* with the greatest current appeal is Virgil's vivid and eloquent dramatization of the fall of Troy. However, most people agree that, like Homer and Shakespeare, some aspect of Virgil speaks to every generation.

The Virgilian Hero

The Virgilian hero theoretically has the power to create history by the choices he makes in life. Yet at the same time he is a pawn of the gods and, beyond them, of Fate, the mysterious power that directs and controls all events. Although some of the gods may know the hero's destiny and may be able to postpone it, even the most powerful among them cannot alter it. Prophets and deceased relatives may also know the hero's destiny, and they or the gods may reveal aspects of it to him. However, the hero's knowledge of his destiny is always limited by how much those who reveal it know and how much they choose to tell him.

The Virgilian hero must cope with beings who help him on his way, as well as with beings who deter him. Presumably, the hero is free to reject both their help and his own destiny. In reality, the nature of the hero's personality and the persuasive powers of those who reveal his destiny to him combine to make it unlikely that he will disobey their directions.

In *The Aeneid*, the Virgilian hero's destiny is good for the world in which he lives or for the world of the future. Therefore, the beings who help him are good, and those who deter him are evil. The Virgilian hero usually has one or more divine beings on his side, including his own patron god or goddess. These gods appear to him directly or in dreams and give him advice. The hero also receives advice from his deceased relatives.

In addition to beings who help him, the Virgilian hero also must cope with beings who hinder him. Various non-Virgilian heroes act as deterrents, or as forces of evil. They are being guided by their patron gods just as the Virgilian hero is being guided by his own patron divinity. The gods' intervention sometimes causes the plot of *The Aeneid* to resemble a highly competitive chess game, one in which each divinity directs his or her favorite pawns across the board. The gods may take time out from the chess game to try to manipulate one another, for like the various heroes, each immortal is either Virgilian or non-Virgilian in temperament and attitude. The gods may also influence the natural environment by sending good or bad weather to help or hinder their particular heroes.

The Virgilian hero and his divinities represent the forces of order, self-discipline, rational thinking, and constructive behavior. Opposed to them — in the world of human beings and nature, and in the world of the gods as well — are the forces of disorder, passion, irrational thinking, and violence. *The Aeneid* examines the interplay between passion and reason, war and humanity, the primitive and the civilized. Even when the Virgilian hero is destined to create order and civilization out of disorder and chaos, when his victory is preordained, Virgil forces his readers to evaluate the worth of that hero's sacrifices and the nature of his victory.

Principal Characters

The Trojans

AENEAS: son of the goddess Venus and Anchises; founder of what becomes the Roman people

ANCHISES: husband of Venus; father of Aeneas

ASCANIUS: son of Aeneas and his wife Creusa (daughter of Priam and Hecuba)

ACHATES: close friend of Aeneas

PRIAM: king of Troy; husband of Hecuba; father of Hector, Paris, Cassandra, Creusa, and Helenus

HECUBA: queen of Troy; wife of Priam; mother of Hector, Paris, Cassandra, Creusa, and Helenus

HECTOR: son of Priam and Hecuba; commander of the Trojan forces; greatest Trojan warrior

PARIS: son of Priam and Hecuba; abductor of Helen (wife of King Menelaus of Sparta)

HELENUS: son of Priam and Hecuba; prophet

LAOCOON: priest of Neptune in Troy

The Greeks

AGAMEMNON: older brother of Menelaus; king of Mycenae; commander of all Greek forces in the Trojan War

MENELAUS: younger brother of Agamemnon; king of Sparta; husband of Helen

HELEN: wife of Menelaus and queen of Sparta until abducted by Paris and taken to Troy

ULYSSES (Odysseus): master of strategies for the Greek forces

NEOPTOLEMUS: son of Achilles; great warrior in his own right

SINON: Greek spy who deceives the Trojans

The Carthaginians

DIDO: founder and queen of Carthage

ANNA: Dido's sister

The Italians

LATINUS: king of Latium; husband of Amata; father of Lavinia

AMATA: queen of Latium; wife of Latinus; mother of Lavinia

LAVINIA: daughter of Latinus and Amata; destined wife of Aeneas

TURNUS: king of the Rutulians; betrothed to Lavinia; greatest Italian warrior

EVANDER: king of Pallenteum; ally of Aeneas against the Latins

PALLAS: son of Evander; heroic young warrior

SIBYL: priestess of the oracle of Apollo in Italy

The Romans adopted the Greek gods and gave them Roman names. For a list of the gods, see pages 5–6.

The Aeneid

Chapter 1

Venting her hatred of the Trojans upon Aeneas and his group of Trojan refugees, Juno forces them to travel stormy seas on their way to Italy. Finally, they land near the city of Carthage, on the coast of North Africa, and meet Dido, its great queen.

I sing of arms and the man, Aeneas, who, after many years of wandering, came to Italy and the shores of Lavinium. Fate forced him to leave his homeland of

Troy when the Greeks sacked Priam's great city. Then cruel Juno, with unrelenting hatred for all Trojans, forced him to endure stormy seas and war in Italy before he could build a city there and bring his gods into Latium, thus establishing the Latin race, the lords of Alba Longa, and high-walled Rome.

Goddess, tell me why the queen of Olympus forced such a good man to endure so much suffering and danger. Was it not enough that the Trojans were defeated by the Greeks and pitiless Achilles? Yet Juno has kept them wandering for seven years, driven over all the seas and always far from Latium. Why does one of the immortal gods harbor so fierce an anger?

Above all other lands Juno loved the ancient city of Carthage. The city had been founded by its queen Dido and other settlers from Tyre (in Phoenicia) and was famed for its wealth and its skill in war. However, Juno knew that some day an aggressive people of Trojan descent, who ruled many other lands, was fated to conquer her fair city. Moreover, the queen of Olympus had not forgotten Paris' judgment against her beauty, and even the Trojans' defeat at the hands of the Greeks had not satisfied her hatred.

"Why should I allow their fate to prevent me from punishing the Trojans before they reach Italy?" Juno thought. "If Minerva can sink Greek ships and drown their sailors because of the arrogance of one Greek leader, surely I — the queen of the gods, and the sister and wife of Jupiter — should be able to subdue this people."

With such thoughts enraging her heart, Juno came to Aeolia, homeland of storm clouds, where King Aeolus confines and soothes the struggling winds and the roaring gales deep in a dreary cave. "Aeolus," she greeted him, "a people whom I hate are sailing the Phoenician seas, bringing Troy's household gods into Italy. I want you to arouse your mighty winds and hurl them furiously upon these Trojans, sinking their ships and strewing their bodies upon the waves of the sea."

"I shall do as you wish," replied Aeolus, "for you and Jupiter have made me lord of clouds and storms." He struck the side of the cave with his spear, commanding the winds to emerge and attack the Trojan ships with mighty waves and great gales.

As the Trojans watched, clouds suddenly turned day into night. The men cried out with dread as flashes of lightning illuminated the clouds and the rumbling of thunder surrounded them. Aeneas stretched his arms toward the heavens and cried, "Compared to us, three and four times blessed are those who were fated to die before their fathers' eyes upon the plain of Troy!"

His words were followed by a shrieking gust of wind that struck his sail full force and raised mountainous waves, causing the oars to snap and the ship to turn broadside to the waves. As water cascaded into the ship, the sailors were washed overboard. Some were carried high upon the crests, while others could glimpse the ground between the swells. The storm drove three ships upon concealed rocks; three others were forced upon a shallow sandbar. One was completely swallowed by a swirling whirlpool of waters. The sea now wore the planking of ships and the bodies of men intermingled with its collection of weapons of war and Trojan treasure.

When Neptune became aware of this wild turbulence, he raised his head above the waves in order to learn more about the storm. He immediately recognized his sister Juno's anger behind the destruction of Aeneas' fleet, so he summoned the East Wind and the West Wind and said, "How dare you raise such a tempest without my command? Return quickly to your king and remind him that I, and not he, am the lord of the sea!"

Neptune calmed the sea and sent the clouds away, letting the sun shine forth once more. As when argument and strife tear apart a great country, and the common folk rage at one another until suddenly they see a man honored for his good character and worthy service, and they become silent and listen attentively while he soothes their passion with his words, so the sea sank into silent submission as the lord of the sea drove his chariot over the waters.

Aeneas and his remaining companions, weary from battling the sea, headed for the coast of Libya, which was the closest shore. Upon finding a good harbor, the seven remaining ships pulled into the sheltered waters. The Trojans disembarked, glad to feel firm ground beneath their feet.

Aeneas and his companion, Achates, set off to see what they could learn about their missing ships. From the edge of a nearby cliff they had a good view of the sea, but they could see no sign of the ships. They did see three huge stags, each leading a herd of deer, grazing along the shore. Aeneas took his bow from Achates and shot the three leading stags and four other large deer, providing one deer for each of the ships. Then the two men descended the cliff, picked up the deer, and carried them back to the ships, where Aeneas divided them among his company.

As Jupiter looked down upon them, Venus approached him, her eyes brimming with tears. "Oh, ruler of the gods, what terrible crimes have Aeneas and the Trojans committed that they cannot reach Italy? You promised that from their lineage would be born the Romans, a people who would rule both land and sea. Is this how you reward my son's virtue?"

The father of gods and mortals smiled and replied, "Have no fear, Daughter. I have not changed my mind, nor has the fate of your Trojans changed. You will see the city of Lavinium and the fame of great-souled Aeneas. Then his son, Ascanius, will move the capital to Alba Longa, where for 300 years Hector's race will rule Italy. Finally, the priestess Ilia will bear twins to Mars, and one of them, Romulus, will found Rome.

"The Romans will rule with no divine limit upon either the extent of their lands or the duration of their power. The day will come when the Roman descendants of the Trojans will conquer Phthia, the city of Peleus and Achilles; Argos; and Agamemnon's famous Mycenae.

"Augustus Caesar will be born from this noble line of Trojans," Jupiter continued. "Only the oceans will limit his empire, and the stars alone will limit his glory. This renowned Caesar will close the temple of Janus, imprisoning within it savage Rage. Sitting on his death-dealing weapons, with his hands tied in 100 bronze knots, this Fury, powerless, will shriek with ghastly, bloodstained lips. Then wars will cease, and an age of law will reign on earth. In spite of her present anger, Juno, too, will cherish the Roman people, who will rule the world. Fate has willed it so."

With these words Jupiter sent his messenger, Mercury, down to Carthage, so that Dido, ignorant of her fate, would welcome the Trojans. Because it was the will of Jupiter, the people of Carthage put aside their warlike thoughts, and their mighty queen became compassionate toward the Trojans.

With the light of morning, Aeneas concealed his ships within the shelter of a hollow rock and, with Achates, set forth to explore the strange country. Soon he saw his mother, Venus, disguised as a young huntress, come across his path.

"Tell me, young men," she began, "have you seen my sister hunting in this area?"

"I have neither heard nor seen your sister," Aeneas replied, "but who are you? You look and sound like a goddess. Please tell us, if you will, where we are. We were driven here by a storm at sea and have no idea who lives here."

"A people native to Tyre live here in the city they are building, called Carthage," Venus explained. "The powerful kingdom of Libya surrounds them. Dido, their queen, founded this city when she fled from her brother after he killed her husband. But who are you? Where are you from? And where are you going?"

"I am from ancient Troy, goddess, if the name means anything to you," Aeneas replied. "I am Aeneas the good, and my fame is known on Mount Olympus. I am carrying with me my household gods that I saved from enemy hands, and I am heading for Italy, my new country. Of the twenty ships I started with, only seven remain, and these have been heavily damaged by wind and waves."

"Whoever you are," Venus said, "the immortal gods must favor you, or you would not have survived to reach this city. Just follow the path, and go to the queen's palace. Unless my parents only pretended to teach me the art of prophecy, you will find that the winds have driven your missing ships and the men who sailed upon them safely into Carthage."

Venus concealed Aeneas and Achates in a thick fog so that they could enter the city without being seen or questioned. Their path took them to the top of a hill from which they could survey the city below. Aeneas marveled at the impressive buildings and the paved roads. Everywhere workers were busy with more construction. As bees in early summer go about their tasks of making honey, some busy in the sunshine gathering nectar from fields of flowers and others storing the liquid in cells bursting with sweet honey, so the people of Tyre were hard at work building their new city.

Concealed in the fog, Aeneas and Achates entered the majestic temple dedicated to Juno. As soon as Queen Dido arrived and seated herself, their lost shipmates came forward to speak with her.

"Oh, Queen, whom Jupiter has permitted to found this new city," their spokesman began, "we unhappy Trojans ask you to spare our ships and our lives. We have not come to attack you or to rob your homes. We have been driven by storms from sea to sea and have lost our king, Aeneas, greatest of all men in virtue and in deeds of war. Allow us to beach our storm-shattered ships while we fashion new planks and oars. If we find our king and our comrades, we shall sail to Italy and Latium. If not, we shall return the way we came to those among our people who have settled near the straits of Sicily."

Dido replied, "Put all fear from your hearts, Trojans. We are aware of Aeneas' people, of Troy's brave soldiers and their deeds in the war against the Greeks. If you wish to return to Sicily, I shall send you forth with an escort for your safety and with wealth to sustain you. If you prefer, you may remain in my city. I shall not distinguish between Tyrian and Trojan. Meanwhile, beach your ships while I send scouts along the coast and through Libya. Aeneas may have been shipwrecked along the way."

The mist suddenly disappeared, revealing Achates and godlike Aeneas, whom Venus made radiant. "Here I stand before you," Aeneas said, "Aeneas of Troy, snatched from the Libyan waves. Neither words nor deeds can thank you, Dido, for offering to share your home and your city with us. If the immortal gods respect virtue and justice, may they reward you."

"What fate drives you through such dangers, Aeneas?" Dido asked as she led him inside the palace. "Unhappy fortune has driven me also through evil times, but at last I have found peace in this land."

While Dido sent a feast down to Aeneas' comrades in the harbor, Aeneas asked Achates to bring his small son, Ascanius, to the palace, along with gifts snatched from the flames of Troy.

At the same time, Venus decided that it would help protect Aeneas against Juno's schemes if Dido were passionately in love with him. So the goddess called her son Cupid to her side and said, "For just this one night, pretend to be Ascanius, and when Dido hugs you at the feast, breathe into her the hidden fire and poison of passion."

Everything went according to Venus' plan. As Dido listened to Aeneas and embraced Cupid, thinking him to be Aeneas' young son, her love for her dead husband faded, and a living passion for Aeneas invaded her sleeping heart. To prolong the evening, Dido continued to question Aeneas about Priam, Hector, and Achilles. Finally, she said, "Tell us, from the beginning, about the strategy the Greeks devised to capture Troy, about the suffering of your people, and about your wanderings over land and sea for these seven long summers."

Chapter 2

*Aeneas tells Dido about the Trojan horse and the
destruction of Troy.*

The Tyrians sat in hushed silence, all eyes directed upon Aeneas as he began to speak.

Words cannot express, oh Queen, the grief you are asking me to remember: how the Greeks overthrew Troy's great and wealthy kingdom and the sickening sights I saw. Even a warrior like Achilles or stern Ulysses could not refrain from tears as he told such a tale! However, if you wish to hear about Troy's destruction, I shall tell you, though my mind shudders to remember the events and recoils in pain from the details.

Being unable to conquer Troy through the skills of war in nine years of fighting, the Greek leaders decide to follow Minerva's instruction and build a horse of mountainous bulk from the wood of the fir tree. They pretend that it is a religious offering and let such a rumor spread throughout Troy. Meanwhile, deep inside the horse's cavernous belly, the devious Greeks secretly hide a group of armed warriors, chosen for their courage and skill.

We think that the Greek forces are sailing back to Mycenae, but, in fact, their ships are hidden upon the barren shore of Tenedos, an island near Troy. So we rejoice to be free of war at last. The Scaean Gates are opened to all, and the people venture forth to see where Achilles camped, where the Greek ships were beached, and where the battles were fought.

Many stare in wonder at Minerva's deadly gift. Some among us are certain that we should drag the horse within our walls, but others, who are wiser in counsel, advise us to hurl this strange Greek gift into the sea, or to heap flames beneath it to feed upon it, or, at least, to explore its hollow belly by piercing its wooden sides with our spears. Noisily the crowd argues, this way or that.

Then the priest of Neptune, Laocoon, comes running down from the fortress, calling to us from afar, "Oh wretched citizens, you must have lost your senses! Do you believe the Greeks have sailed homeward? Do you imagine that any Greek gifts are without guile? Do you not know Ulysses? Either Greek warriors are hiding within the wooden body of this beast, or this is a war device that can look beyond our walls and into our homes. Some evil surely lurks within its belly or will descend upon our city from above. Do not trust the horse, Trojans. No matter how it appears, I fear the Greeks, even when they bear gifts."

With these words the priest hurls his great spear with mighty force into the curved side of the horse. As the spear quivers in the wooden belly, the cavernous interior emits a hollow, groaning sound. If the gods had supported us and our judgment had been sound, Laocoon would have convinced us to destroy the Greek sanctuary with our bronze weapons. Then Priam's great city would still be standing. However, the priest's counsel falls upon deaf ears.

Meanwhile, the shouts of some Trojan shepherds draw our attention toward a young man they are dragging before Priam. With his hands tied behind his back, the prisoner is so obviously at our mercy that we do not question his honesty. It does not occur to us that he has courageously chosen to place himself where we would discover him, and that he is prepared to deceive us with his lies or to die as our prisoner. Our youth immediately approach him from all sides and taunt him. But as soon as he speaks, he will teach all of you how treacherous the Greeks are.

The prisoner stands among us, unarmed and afraid. "Alas!" he cries. "What land or sea will take me? What fate will next befall me? The Greeks have cast me away, and the Trojans angrily clamor for my death."

With these words he arouses our sympathy. "Tell us who you are and where you are from," we reply, "and why you are here."

When he is no longer afraid, he says, "I shall tell you the truth, oh King, come what may. I, the most unfortunate of men, am called Sinon, and I am of Greek birth. But I do not want to tell you a tale that does not interest you. If you hate all Greeks just because of their birth, then kill me now. Ulysses would be pleased, and Agamemnon would pay you to do it!"

Then, of course, we cannot wait to hear his story. Trembling, the prisoner begins his tale, speaking with guile and with false feeling.

"Often the Greeks wished to retreat, being weary of the tiresome war and longing for home. How I wish that they had done so! Many times a severe tempest at sea frightened them and kept them on Trojan soil. Then, when the wooden framework of this horse had already been built, storm clouds rumbled throughout the sky. The soldiers could not interpret the omen, so they asked the oracle of Apollo. The god responded, 'In order to reach the shores of Troy, oh Greeks, you had to appease the winds with the blood of a maiden's sacrifice. Now, in order to return to your homeland, you will have to please the winds with the blood of a warrior's sacrifice.'

"When the Greeks heard these words, their hearts froze and a cold shudder ran through them. Whom was Apollo choosing? Ulysses dragged the prophet Catchas forward and told him to discover Apollo's will. Calchas sat speechless in his tent for ten days, refusing to proclaim a warrior's death. Finally, the demands of the Greeks overcame his reluctance, and he announced my doom. Of course no one objected, for each was relieved that my fate was not his own.

"When the day I dreaded arrived, I ran from death. I broke my bonds and hid for the night in a marsh. I hoped that the Greeks would sail away without discovering me, and they did. Now I can never hope to see my homeland, my loving children, or my dear father. I am sorry that the Greeks may make my family atone for my crime by demanding the life of one of them in my place. But I ask you, by the gods above, to pity me, for I do not deserve such suffering."

We cannot resist the prisoner's plea. We not only pity him, we grant him life. Priam commands that his bonds be removed and then addresses him with kind words.

"Forget that the Greeks were your people," the king tells him. "From this time forth, you are one of us. Now explain to me truthfully: Why have the Greeks constructed this monstrous horse? Who designed it, and why? Is it a weapon of war? An offering to one of the gods?"

The young man raises his arms to the heavens and replies, "May I be free to put aside my loyalty to the Greeks and hate them for the suffering they have caused me. I am no longer bound by the laws of any country, so surely I can reveal their secret purpose. Only keep your promise, Trojans, and save me in return for the help I am giving you.

"From the beginning of the war, the Greeks could count on Minerva to help them. But this year the Greeks captured your prophet and forced him to tell them how they could win. The clever Trojan told them that they first would have to remove from Troy the statue of Minerva. So Ulysses, the contriver of crime, and the ungodly Diomedes secretly enlisted the help of Helen and stole the statue from its shrine, defiling it with their bloody hands. From that time on, Minerva ceased to favor the Greeks, and their strength was broken.

"As soon as they placed the statue in their camp, its eyes flashed with flames, salty sweat ran down its body, and three times the goddess herself leaped from the ground with her shield and quivering spear. Their prophet then told them that they would not be able to take Troy unless they first returned to Argos and found new, favorable omens there. So the Greeks are sailing for Mycenae, but they will return.

"Meanwhile, the Greeks have followed Calchas' counsel and have left this huge wooden horse here in order to atone for their insult to Minerva. The prophet commanded them to build it so large that you Trojans could not bring it through your gates and have it protect you. For if you move the horse into your great city, then you are fated to take the war across the sea to the cities of the Greeks and destroy them. On the other hand, if you harm this gift to Minerva, then Priam's country is doomed to utter destruction."

So well does Sinon tell this tale that we believe him. His guile and tears conquer us when ten years of Achilles could not! Then we see the most dreadful omen: Laocoon is sacrificing a mighty bull upon the altar of Neptune when, over the peaceful sea from Tenedos—I shudder to remember—we see two snakes with countless coils glide through the waters side by side and head for our shore. Their heads rise high above the wave, and the rest skims along the surface of the water behind them in endless coils, causing the sea to foam and roar. Their eyes blaze forth with blood and fire, and quivering tongues dart from their hissing mouths. We watch them as they cross the land and head directly for Laocoon. Then, terrified, we run from the site.

Upon reaching the altar, the two snakes coil themselves around the bodies of Laocoon's two young sons, enfolding them in a deadly embrace and sinking their fangs into the children's soft flesh. Then, as their father raises his weapons against them, the serpents entwine themselves around him, twice winding themselves around his waist, twice encircling their scaly bodies around his throat, and raising their heads high above his own.

Laocoon is covered with their poisonous black venom and gore. He strains his hands to tear their deadly coils from him, and he screams to heaven, as a wounded bull bellows as it shrugs off a poorly aimed axe and runs from the altar, but he is helpless. With the death of the priest, the serpents glide away to Minerva's shrine, where they take refuge under the goddess' feet and the curve of her shield.

This omen horrifies us. "Laocoon has been punished for his crime," some say. "He hurled his spear into the sacred body of the horse and angered Minerva."

"Pull the horse within the walls to Minerva's shrine," everyone cries. "We must atone for our priest's deed!"

So we make an opening in our walls, clearing the way into the city. Everyone takes part in the work. We place sliding rollers under the horse's feet, tie ropes around its neck, and then pull the monster up our walls. As it moves forward, boys and maidens sing hymns and happily handle the rope halter. So the horse glides dangerously into the very center of Priam's great city. Oh, Troy, famous in war!

Four times the horse halts near the gates to the city, and four times armor sounds within its cavemous belly. Yet, with ears that do not hear and eyes blinded by fright, we push it ever forward, until the ill-omened monster finally rests within our city walls. Even when Priam's daughter Cassandra reveals to us our coming doom, we do not believe her, for Apollo's angry gift to her was to be able to predict the future but not to be believed. And at the close of day, never aware that it is our last, we joyously decorate the shrines of the gods with colorful wreaths and begin an evening of celebration.

In time, night rises from the sea, wrapping in its mighty robe earth and sky and the scheming Greeks. While we sleep in comfort, unaware of our fate, the Greek ships leave the island of Tenedos and return to the familiar shores of Troy. Then, when Agamemnon's royal ship sends forth a flaming signal, Sinon quietly approaches the monstrous horse and opens its secret hatch.

Joyfully the Greek leaders, one by one, leave the monster's belly and slide down the lowered cable into the night air. Dreadful Ulysses, Menelaus, Neoptolemus, who is the son of Achilles, and Epeus, who designed this devious device, are among them. They kill our guards, open the gates to our city, and welcome back their thousands of companions. Then they attack while we sleep.

Chapter 3

Aeneas continues his story, describing to Dido the destruction of Troy.

While I am asleep the figure of Hector, weeping, appears before my eyes. His hair is coated with blood, his body is black with gory dust, and his swollen feet are still punctured with the thongs Achilles used to drag his body around the walls of our city. "Run, goddess-born!" he cries to me. "Save yourself from the flames! The Greeks hold our walls, and Troy is burning to the ground. You have done all you can for Priam and our country. If strength could have saved Troy, the Greeks would never have breached our walls. Troy now gives to you her holy things and her household gods. Take them with you as you search for the place you will establish a city." With these words he brings forth the cloth bands, the eternal fire, and the Great Goddess Vesta from their inner shrine.

As I force myself to awaken, I fear that I recognize the sounds of war in the distance — screams, cries, the clash of armor on every side. I climb up to the roof of my father's house and strain my ears to learn more, for land and trees stand between our house and the rest of Troy. As a lone shepherd high upon a rocky peak hears the far roar of a swollen mountain stream as it buries the crops and hurls down the forest, so I become aware of Troy's destruction. Now I understand the meaning of Sinon and the monstrous wooden horse. The Greeks' treacherous scheme has succeeded.

I rush inside and grab my weapons. I know that I shall not have time to use them, but my heart blazes with rage and resentment. I long to gather a group of my comrades and fight the Greeks to the death, for that is the most honorable way to die.

At my door I find Panthus, priest of Apollo and father of Hector's friend, the wise Polydamas. He holds his grandchild with one hand and carries the sacred articles and the household gods in the other. "Troy's last hour is upon us!" he cries. "Troy is dead, the Trojan people are dead, and our great glory is dead. Jupiter has given everything to the Greeks, who now are lords in our burning city. Armed warriors issue forth from the monstrous horse, and Sinon, arrogant with victory, spreads flames wherever he goes. Thousands of Greek warriors are everywhere among us, guarding our wide-open gates and barring passage on our narrow streets."

I take the sacred objects from him and prepare to do my part for my country. I go out to the moonlit streets, and my companions gather around me. When I see that they, too, are eager for battle, I tell them, "Men, if your hearts lead you to be courageous in this hopeless cause, follow me. The fate of our people is clear. The gods who supported our kingdom have left us, and our city is in flames. Let us die fighting!"

Who can describe to you the chaos of that night? Who can describe its bloodshed? Whose tears can equal our troubles? Like ravenous wolves in a black fog, whose hunger drives them blindly forth and whose cubs wait back in their den with tongues that already taste the food they expect, so we go forth, sheltered by black night, into the heart of our city to meet certain death. We gaze upon the queen of cities, now fallen. We step among the piles of lifeless bodies that litter the streets. Not all the corpses are Trojan, however. We who have been conquered summon enough strength and courage to take many of our Greek victors on man's long, last journey. Most of my companions are killed. Pain is everywhere; panic is everywhere; and Death is everywhere!

The clash of weapons draws us to Priam's palace, where a terrible battle rages. Ladders cling to the walls; Greek warriors clutch them with one hand and in the other hand hold a shield against an attack of arrows. Meanwhile, Trojans are on the roof, tearing down the towers and ripping up the roof, using whatever objects they can find as weapons for their final self-defense. We make our way to the roof to help the defenders. Below, other Trojans guard the doorways to the interior of the palace.

From the roof we see Neoptolemus, Achilles' son, leading a group of warriors to Priam and Hecuba's private rooms. As a snake fed on poisonous plants casts off its old skin and emerges from its hole with the warm days of spring, shining with the splendor of youth, and flicks its three-forked tongue from its mouth, so Neoptolemus shines in his father's lustrous, bronze armor. Using his battle axe, he bursts through the doorway, tearing the bronze-plated doors from their hinges.

Neoptolemus forces his way into the confusion with the strength of his father. Neither bolts nor guards can stop him. A foaming river that bursts its banks and overflows, its violent motion tearing away all barriers as it rushes furiously over the fields, sweeping herds and pens away, is more calm than this son of Achilles.

I also see Hecuba, with her 100 daughters, and Priam. The old king has put his long-abandoned armor upon his aged shoulders, grabbed his useless sword, and is preparing to meet his death among the invading Greeks. Hecuba and her women have tried to take refuge among the household shrines. They press together there, clutching the statues of the gods, like doves driven forth by a black tempest.

When Hecuba sees her husband in the armor of his youth, she asks him, "What madness moves you to put on your old armor? Where do you intend to go? Even if Hector were here, you could do nothing to save us. Come join me. Either this sacred altar will protect us, or we shall die together. "

Then one of Priam's sons comes running toward his parents. Through enemies and arrows he desperately tries to escape Neoptolemus' sword. Finally, Achilles' son spears him through the back, and the boy falls dead at the feet of his parents.

Being face to face with death does not silence the old king's fury or his tongue. "May the gods reward you as you deserve for making a father view the murder of his son!" he exclaims. "Achilles, the warrior you falsely claim as your father, treated his enemy Priam more respectfully than this!" The old king hurls his spear at Neoptolemus, but his arm is so weak that the spear merely catches upon a bronze decoration on Achilles' great shield and hangs there harmlessly.

Neoptolemus replies, "I shall send you to my father with a message. Tell him how poorly I fight and how shameful I am! Now die!" He pulls the trembling old king toward the altar. When Priam slips in the pool of his dead son's blood, Neoptolemus grabs Priam's hair in his left hand and with his right hand plunges his flashing sword into the old king's side.

So ends the life of one of the great kings of Asia. He was doomed to live long enough to see his sons murdered and his city in flames. His corpse now lies by the shore of the sea, a headless, nameless body.

As I gaze upon the dead king, in my mind I see my own father, my wife and son, and our plundered house. When the vision leaves me, I find that I am alone. The women have either leaped to the ground far below or have thrown themselves into the fire.

Suddenly, in the light of the fires, I notice Helen quietly hiding by the shrine of Vesta. The hateful woman is at a loss. She knows the Trojans despise her for causing the destruction of Troy. On the other hand, she fears the vengeance of the Greeks and the anger of Menelaus, whom she abandoned. My heart blazes with resentment as I gaze at the source of all our woes, and I want to make her pay for all of the death and destruction. For her sake, Troy has burned. For her sake, Trojan land is soaked with blood. For her sake, our good king has been murdered.

Without thinking, I say aloud, "How will Helen pay for her crime? Will she sail back to Sparta without injury, a queen returning in triumph from a major victory? Will she have the pleasure of returning to her father's house and living among her family? There is no honor in killing a woman, yet it will bring me great satisfaction to avenge the ashes of my family."

Suddenly, my mother appears before me in all of her divine radiance. "My son," she says, "it is not Helen or Paris who is to blame; the gods have destroyed Troy. Now return home and see if your father, your wife, and your child are still alive. If my love of your family had not prevented it, Greek swords would have drunk their blood, and flames would have consumed their bodies."

My first thought when I return home is to carry my aged father to the safety of the hills. But he steadfastly refuses my pleas. "You are young and strong enough to flee," he tells me. "I shall take my own life and leave my possessions to the Greeks."

I look at my father aghast. "Do you expect me to flee and leave you here?" I ask him. "If the gods intend to burn our great city to the ground and you firmly intend to remain here, then Neoptolemus, who is already bathed in Priam's blood, who murders the son in front of his father by a sacred shrine, that Neoptolemus will bring death here.

"Is this why you brought me home, Mother? Did you save me from the sword and the fire so that I could watch the Greeks enter my house and murder my father, my wife, and my son? Never! I shall die fighting the Greeks and avenging our people!"

I have put on my sword and have my shield upon my arm when my wife holds up our little son and pleads with me. "If you are leaving here to die," she says, "then take us with you, for you are abandoning us to the Greeks. Otherwise, use your armor to defend your own home."

And as my wife stands there weeping, a wondrous omen appears. Upon the head of our little son, Ascanius, flames that do not burn suddenly play upon his hair, illuminating his face with their ruddy glow. Frightened by the blaze, we quickly quench the holy fire with water.

But my father joyously raises his eyes and his arms to the heavens and prays, "Jupiter, father of gods and men, if we deserve your favor, confirm this omen with some sign." He has hardly finished speaking when we hear a sudden crack of thunder and see a star shoot down from the heavens into the forest, leaving a trail of light in the evening sky. "Now I shall go with you, my son," Anchises tells me, "wherever you lead us. Gods of my fathers!" he prays. "Save my house and my grandson. If you have sent this omen, then Troy must remain under your protection."

By this time, I can hear that the roaring flames are closer to us. "If we do not leave here quickly, we shall be engulfed in a flood of fire," I tell my family. I then spread a lion's skin over my shoulders and neck, stoop down, and say, "Come, father, climb upon my shoulders, and hold onto my neck. Carry with you the sacred objects and Troy's household gods. It is not right for me to carry them until I have washed off the blood of battle in a bubbling stream. Whatever happens, you and I shall endure it together. Little Ascanius, take my hand and try to keep up with me. Wife, follow us quickly! "

We pass through burning Troy, protected by the darkness. As we approach the gates, my father cries, "Run, my son! I see the bronze shields of the Greeks drawing near!"

Fearing for my father and my son, I head for the back streets and a more devious course, forgetting that my wife is behind us. So I lose her to Troy's shadows. I never know whether she stops, or whether she tries to follow and loses us. I do not even think to look back for her until we reach the mound sacred to Ceres, where we find our household servants.

Then, of course, I am frantic! I leave Anchises and Ascanius in a hidden spot and run back home, trying to retrace my steps. I do not see my wife, but towering flames are devouring our house. In a mad frenzy I rush among the city's ruins, calling her name again and again.

Suddenly the sad form of my wife appears before my eyes. As I stand speechless, the vision says, "Do not sorrow, dear husband. The lord of high Olympus will not permit me to join you on your journey. Years of wandering are your fate, followed by kingship, a royal wife, and satisfaction in the rich land that surrounds the Tiber River. I shall never be a slave to some Greek woman, but shall stay here with Cybele, the great mother of the gods. Love our child. Farewell."

I stand there, weeping, with so much I want to say to her. Three times I try to embrace her, but each time the vision escapes my grasp, drifting away like a light breeze. Finally, with the coming of dawn, I return to my family.

To my surprise a large number of Trojans have joined us and are prepared to follow me wherever I lead them. Since Greeks are guarding the city gates, we leave by back roads toward the mountains.

Chapter 4

Aeneas finishes his tale by telling Dido about his wanderings.

Once we have built our ships, we leave our homeland and set out to sea. We sail for days through tempests and for nights without a star to guide us. We are now far off our course. Finally, I see mountains and rising smoke ahead, so we sail in that direction.

Leaving our ships in a good harbor, we move quickly to spear some of the untended cattle and goats that we see scattered about us. As we sit down to a feast of fresh food, we call upon Jupiter and the other gods to share it with us.

Suddenly, we hear the noisy clanging of large wings. Looking up, we see huge winged creatures swooping down toward us from the mountains. The Harpies are upon us! These monstrous birds have the face of a woman — but thin and drawn with hunger — bronze feathers, clawed hands, and a dreadful scream. As they fly above our food, they snatch whatever they wish and spoil all the rest by dropping their foul-smelling filth upon it.

We then notice a deep, recessed area beneath an overhanging rock that is surrounded by bushes. Since it looks well-protected, we set up a fresh feast there. However, from some hidden home in the opposite direction, the noisy birds dive upon us once again, snatching and spoiling our food as before.

In hungry desperation, we hide our shields and keep our swords deep in the grass ready for their next assault. When the filthy birds arrive, we are waiting for them. But we have little success. Swords cannot wound their bodies and blows do not injure their wings. We chase them away, but they have fouled our food once again.

Then I notice that one Harpy has remained behind, perched on a high rock. "Are you bringing war upon us, Trojans? Would you drive innocent Harpies from their homeland? You have butchered our cattle and have fought us. Now plant these words in your heart. What Jupiter told Apollo and Apollo told me, I, the first-born of the Harpies, shall reveal to you.

"You are bound for Italy, and her harbors will welcome you," the Harpy foretells. "However, because of your violence toward us, you will not build the walls of your fated city until you are so famished that you chew and swallow your tables!" With these shrill words, the bird-like monster flies off into the forest.

My companions become so frightened that their blood freezes. With prayers to the gods, we hastily leave this country. We sail past Ulysses' kingdom of Ithaca and curse the land that sustained him. Eventually, we reach the city where Priam's son, the prophet Helenus, now rules.

After we have been warmly welcomed, I ask Helenus about the Harpy's prophecy. "Oh, goddess-born," he replies, "do not fear the chewing of your tables, for the Fates will find a way to help you. Meanwhile, since Jupiter is in charge of your destiny, I shall tell you how to travel safely over the seas.

"You are close to Italy," Helenus begins. "But you must sail past Circe's island and avoid the shores of Italy that are washed by the tide of our own sea, for evil Greeks dwell there. When you reach the coast of Sicily, sail to the left even though the route is a long one. By all means avoid the shore and the water on the right, for that marks a narrow channel between Sicily and Italy. The monster Scylla guards the right side of the strait, while greedy Charybdis guards the left.

"Three times each day, Charybdis swallows the sea and then hurls it into the heavens, lashing the heavens with water. Scylla lives in a deep cave. Above the waist she has a human form; below she is a monstrous sea-dragon, with dolphin's tails joined to her stomach, which is covered with wolves. With her mouths she pulls ships upon the rocks. It is far better to travel the long way around than to meet Scylla in her huge cave above the rocks.

"When you reach the shores of Italy," Helenus concludes, "find the town of Cumae, for a prophetess lives deep in a rocky cave there, chanting prophecies and writing them on leaves. She will tell you about the nations of Italy, future wars, and the proper way to perform or avoid every labor. In the end, she will grant you a good voyage. Finally, I advise you always to honor Juno first in your prayers, and try to win her favor with gifts."

Having received this prophecy from Helenus, we sail forth once again. In time, we can see Mount Aetna on Sicily. In the distance, we hear the roar of the waves upon rocks. We are certain that we have reached the channel of Scylla and Charybdis, so we head into the tossing sea to our left. The winds have stirred up the waves to lofty heights. First our ships seem to climb up to the heavens upon a mountain of water, and then they swiftly drop down to the depths of the sea.

Finally we enter a large, safe harbor and go ashore for the night. Nearby, Mount Aetna terrifies us with its thunder and hurls blazing rocks into the heavens. We hide in the forest and try to forget the monstrous noises that seem to surround us all night long.

The next morning, when Dawn has brushed the shade from the sky, a strange man comes out of the woods and stretches forth pleading hands to us. He seems starved for food. His face is as pale as death, his beard is unshaven, and from what remains of his tattered clothing, he appears to have once been a Greek warrior.

As soon as he notices our Trojan clothing and weapons, he becomes afraid. But his desperate need overcomes his fear, and he rushes toward us, asking us to take him away with us. Once my father assures him that he is safe with us, he tells us what has happened to him.

"I come from the country of Ithaca, and I was a comrade of the unfortunate Ulysses. I went to Troy with him and left with him, but he abandoned me here in the huge cave of the Cyclops Polyphemus.

"That den is as dark as it is vast," he continues, "and its floor and walls are littered with the remains of bloody feasts and gore. The giant who lives there strikes the sky with his head when he stands upright — may the gods remove this monster from the earth! — and one cannot safely speak with him, for he feeds on human flesh and blood. Before my eyes, he seized two of my companions in his monstrous hand, crushed their bodies upon the rocky wall of his cave, and ate them.

"Yet Ulysses would not let the Cyclops' bloodthirsty deeds remain unpunished. When Polyphemus had gorged himself upon his human feast, Ulysses offered him such great quantities of tasty wine that he sank to the floor of his cave in a drunken sleep. While pieces of flesh mixed with blood and wine dribbled from his mouth, we prayed to the gods and treated him with the same kind of courtesy he had shown our companions. Together, we raised a large, pointed pole and pierced the one great eye that lies beneath his savage brow.

"My companions managed to escape, but in their haste, they forgot that I was not with them. By the time I escaped from the cave, they had already sailed."

The Greek then counsels, "We should quickly board the ships and leave this terrible place, for 100 other monstrous Cyclopes shepherd their flocks upon these mountains and live along these shores. I have been hiding from them in the forest for three full moons, in constant fear of the sound of their footsteps and their voices. I have lived on nuts, berries, and roots, all the time hoping to see a ship pass by. I prefer to die by your hands than to be eaten by one of the Cyclopes!"

The Greek has barely finished his tale when we see Polyphemus heading down to the shore from the mountaintop with his flocks. The blind monster is terrifying as he steadies himself with his staff, even without sight, he moves swiftly and surely down the familiar trail. When he reaches the sea, he walks into the waves and washes away the blood that constantly oozes from his eye socket, groaning and grinding his teeth with the pain. Then he strides through the open sea, whose water reaches only as high as his waist.

We make every effort to leave the harbor quickly and silently, but Polyphemus hears the sound of our oars. He turns toward the sound, and when he cannot see us to grab us, he gives a mighty roar. The other Cyclopes, hearing him, run down from the mountains and out of the woods. We watch them gather upon the shores of the harbor and glare at us, but we seem to be safely out of their reach.

In our terror, our first thought is to sail in any direction as long as we move quickly, but we remember Helenus' warnings about Scylla and Charybdis and avoid their channel.

My final trial before reaching Carthage is the death of my dear father. Neither the Harpy nor Helenus had mentioned that sorrow to me.

With these words Aeneas concluded the tale of his wanderings and was silent.

Chapter 5

Dido and Aeneas love each other, and for a time
Aeneas forgets his obligation. Aeneas leaves Carthage
and Dido commits suicide.

Dido was so in love with Aeneas that all she could think about were his appearance, his words, his deeds. When Dawn lighted the earth with the lamp of Apollo, the queen confided in her sister.

"Anna," she said, "my dreams frighten me. This Trojan stranger who is our guest is so noble and brave that I fear I might marry him in spite of my firm decision never to marry again. Aeneas has rekindled a flame within me, and I must confess that he is the first man to weaken my resolve since my dear husband died."

"Oh, dearest," Anna replied, "do you intend to live your entire life lonely and sad, without ever enjoying love and motherhood? Do you think that the buried shade of your husband would appreciate such a sacrifice?

"I think the Trojan ships have been directed here by Juno," she continued. "What a great city would result from your marriage to Aeneas! With Trojan weapons to help us, what glory we could win! I advise you to make pleasing sacrifices to the gods, give Aeneas the warmest welcome, and delay his departure as long as possible. It is to your advantage that his ships are shattered and winter passage upon the sea is stormy."

Her sister's words relieved Dido's guilt, put hope into her heart, and fanned the passions that burned within her. As a deer is struck with an arrow from the bow of a shepherd, who is hunting from such a distance that he does not know it has reached its target, and the deer is forced to run through woods and meadows with the deadly shaft clinging firmly to its side, so Dido wandered with Aeneas through the city of Carthage with Cupid's arrow burning within her.

She could not hear the sad story of Troy too many times, and even when she was not with Aeneas, in her mind she saw him and heard his voice. Meanwhile, with Dido's attention distracted, many activities in Carthage lay idle. Training for war and the building of defenses ceased, and partly constructed buildings remained unfinished.

One day Dido and Aeneas went hunting together. Stags crossed the open meadows and wild goats walked over the mountain ridges, both providing good challenges. When a sudden storm caused the streams to swell with swift-running currents, Aeneas and Dido took refuge in a cave. There they consummated their love, and fires flashed in the sky to mark the gods' approval. But the event ushered in grief and death. Dido honored the divine ceremony as a legal one, and Rumor told the story far and wide.

Rumor is the fastest of all evils, and she gains strength and energy as she travels. She is as fast on foot as she is in the air. Monstrous in appearance, she has as many observant eyes along her belly as she has feathers on her wings and back, and her ears and her mouths each equal her eyes in number. She may be afraid at first, but in the end she walks the earth with her head in the heavens. She never sleeps. At night she goes squawking through the darkness. By day she sits on top of buildings, shouting lies disguised as truths.

When Rumor entered Libya with tales of Dido's passion for Aeneas and her neglect of her kingdom, she infuriated King Iarbas, whom Dido had rejected. Iarbas complained to Jupiter. "Dido has built Carthage on valuable land that I removed from my own rule and allowed her to buy. Since she has refused to marry me, how can you permit her to take Aeneas as her lord and thereby give to him all the benefits that by right are mine? Do you possess the power we mortals have believed, or are our sacrifices in your temples useless?"

Jupiter heard his words and sent Mercury, his messenger, down to Aeneas. "Tell him," the lord of Olympus commanded, "that it was not for this that we chose his mother's son to rule over Italy, nor was it for this that we rescued him twice from death at the hands of the Greeks. Moreover, if he has no interest in acquiring such fame and glory for himself, he should not steal his son's future. He must set sail at once!"

When Aeneas saw Mercury facing him in the clear light of day, he was speechless with fright. Jupiter's message so terrified him that he wanted to leave Carthage immediately, but he was reluctant to tell Dido. After much thought, he decided that it would be best to prepare the ships for departure in secret. This would give him time to find the right words and the best occasion for breaking the unwelcome news.

Rumor, however, quickly informed Dido, and she immediately confronted Aeneas with a torrent of questions and pleas. "You hypocrite!" she began. "Did you expect to leave here secretly? Can neither our love nor our promise keep you here? Are you choosing to leave me, or do you wish to acquire more fame? Would you choose to return to Troy in stormy winter weather? Pity me, and stay. Because of you, the tribes of Libya, the Nomad chieftains, and even my own Tyrians hate me. For you I have given up honor, fame, and the political security of my country. What is left for me except death? At least if I could bear your child, you would leave me with some meaning in my life."

As he listened to Dido's reproach, Aeneas kept Jupiter's command in his mind and struggled to bury his anguish deep in his heart. "I admit that you deserve the best from me," he began, "and I shall cherish my memories of you as long as I live. I would not have left without telling you — but remember, I never married you.

"If the Fates had permitted me to design the course of my own life," he continued, "I would have remained in Troy and rebuilt it. But Apollo has told me that my love and my country are in Italy. You have chosen Carthage; I can choose Italy. In my dreams, my father warns me not to sacrifice the destiny of my son, and now Jupiter has sent his messenger to me in the light of day to command me to leave. So spare yourself, and spare me your anger. I am sailing for Italy because I am not free to choose what I do with my life. My destiny is to found a great country. I may not satisfy my personal wishes as other people do."

Dido angrily replied, "False one! You are no son of goddess and mortal, but of some rocky mountain! You have no pity. You cannot even spare a tear or a sigh for me! Why have faith in the gods, when they are unjust? I welcomed a shipwrecked, homeless man and gave him love and part of my kingdom. I saved his ships and his companions. Now the gods tell him to leave. So, go to Italy! But if the gods are just, you will suffer for it! And when I am dead, my shade will torment you. I shall make you pay for what you have done to me!" With this curse, Dido left Aeneas.

Good Aeneas longed to comfort her, for his heart overflowed with his great love for Dido. However, he followed Jupiter's command and returned to his ships, where the Trojans were already preparing to leave. As a black column of ants crawls over the plain, through the grass, and along a narrow path with its plunder, and some strain with their shoulders to shove the huge grains of corn while others push them from behind and lament the delay, so some of Aeneas' men set their ships afloat while others carried branches from the forest to make into oars, each busy with some necessary task.

Meanwhile, Dido was observing their activity from the palace. "Anna," she said to her sister, "do you see how happy the Trojans are to leave? I can muster the strength to bear this sorrow, for I could foresee it. But do me one favor. Aeneas is your friend; convince him to wait and depart with good winds. I shall not plead with him to stay beyond that."

However, Aeneas refused Anna as he had refused Dido, for Fate had closed his ears to tearful pleas. As roaring winds descend from the heights of a mountain and try to uproot a mature oak tree, but the tree continues to cling to the rock, so Aeneas rejected pleas from every side. Although his heart was sad, he remained determined to leave.

Then Dido planned her death. Pretending to have a strategy for returning Aeneas to her or freeing herself of her love for him, she commanded her sister to prepare for the fatal occasion. "Construct a funeral pyre in the inner courtyard," she said, "and place upon it our bridal bed, Aeneas' weapons, and everything else that he has left here. I intend to destroy everything associated with that traitor as the priestess advises." As this was just what Dido had done when her husband had died, Anna obeyed her directions.

That night, when all the tired creatures on the earth were sleeping, Dido lay awake, tormented by choices. "What shall I do?" she asked herself. "Shall I find marriage among my old suitors, who will laugh at me, or among men I have thought beneath me? I could follow the Trojan ships, but who would accept me? Or should I gather my Tyrians about me and drive the Trojans from Carthage, forcing them to sail the stormy seas? No, I should die by the sword, for I have broken my vows to my dead husband! "

While Aeneas was asleep that night, Mercury appeared in his dream and said, "Goddess-born, how can you sleep when you are in such danger? Dido is considering all kinds of dangerous plans. Quickly leave these shores while favorable winds make your escape possible!"

Frightened by his dream, Aeneas forced himself awake and called, "Quickly, men, awake and set sail! A god from high Olympus has come down and ordered us to leave immediately! As we joyfully obey your command, oh Jupiter, please be with us and help us."

When early Dawn was spreading her rays upon the earth, Dido saw that Aeneas had departed. Filled with grief and dismay, she said to herself, "That vile stranger has made a fool of me! I should have grabbed him, torn him apart, and strewn his pieces upon the waves when I had the chance. I should have killed his men and even his son, and served Ascanius to his father as part of my welcoming feast.

"I summon you, Apollo, and Juno, and you avenging Furies," Dido continued. "Hear my prayer. If that traitor must reach Italy, then may he be faced with war, driven from his land, and torn from his son, and may he witness the death of his friends. Then, when he has agreed to an unfair peace, may he die early and lie unburied upon the shore.

"And this last prayer I make with my blood. May you Tyrians, my people, honor me by hating the race of Aeneas now and for all time to come. May a peace treaty never exist between our people and his. May the Trojans, their children, and their children's children be faced with war."

Then Dido turned to her husband's old nurse and said, "Dear Nurse, I am going to begin the ceremony. Ask my sister to come and bring with her the offerings."

Feverish with determination, Dido entered the inner courtyard, climbed upon the high pyre, and unsheathed Aeneas' sword. "Release me from my troubles!" she prayed. "I have built a great city, and now my queenly shade will pass beneath the earth. Happily do I enter the darkness. Let the hard-hearted Trojan witness these flames from sea and take with him the omen of my death." With these words, Dido fell upon the sword and died.

Screams and wailing tore from the palace. Rumor flew through Carthage, shocking the Tyrians with the dreadful news. Anna, hearing about her sister's death from Rumor's mouth, rushed back to the palace. Tearing at her face and beating her chest, Anna cried, "By taking your own life, you have also destroyed me, your city, its government, and its people!"

Aeneas was far out to sea when he saw funeral flames rising from within the walls of Carthage. He sensed, with great sadness, that Dido was dead.

Chapter 6

A storm forces Aeneas to return to the land where his
father, Anchises, died. The shade of Anchises directs
Aeneas to let many of his people settle there. Aeneas
then consults the Sibyl, who leads him into the
Underworld to talk with his father. There, Anchises
reveals to Aeneas the future of Rome.

"The winds are against us," the helmsman advised Aeneas. "If we allow them to guide us, we can reach Sicily, where our people live."

"Then let us direct our ships in that direction, for I long to revisit my father's ashes," Aeneas replied.

Once on land, Aeneas held athletic contests in memory of his father. While the men were participating in the games, Juno decided to delay further Aeneas' journey to Italy. She sent her messenger, Iris, down among the women, who after seven years of wandering wanted to establish a permanent settlement. Under Iris' leadership, the women set fire to the Trojan fleet.

Aeneas was dismayed at the sight. "Great Jupiter," he prayed, "if you have any regard for the Trojans, save our ships. Or, if I deserve your wrath, kill the few of us who are left with your mighty thunderbolt! " As he finished speaking, black clouds gathered overhead, bringing with them a raging thunderstorm that poured torrents of rain upon the burning ships and extinguished the flames. Thus the Trojans were able to save all but four of their ships.

That night, the shade of Aeneas' father appeared before him. "Dearest Son," he began, "Jupiter has sent me to tell you to leave the aged, the weak, and the fearful here, and take only the bravest Trojans with you to Italy, for there you will have to fight a strong people. But first seek the Sibyl in Italy, and let her lead you down to the kingdom of Pluto, where you will find me among the blessed in Elysium. There I will reveal to you the future of all your race. Farewell."

Aeneas immediately summoned his company and informed them of Jupiter's command. As soon as their ships were ready, they set off for the shores of the Sibyl and the oracle of Apollo in Italy. They found the Sibyl's cave concealed high in the mountains. The huge cavern where she was seated contained 100 interior entrances, so that her words echoed from one to the other. As soon as they entered, the prophetess commanded, "It is time to ask the god! Pray, Aeneas!"

"Apollo," Aeneas began, "you have always been kind to the Trojans. You guided Paris' hand and arrow as he killed Achilles. Protect us when we reach our destined shores of Italy. Sibyl, I ask for no more than the destiny I have been given."

Through the 100 openings in the cavern came this reply: "You will reach Lavinium, Trojans, but you will fight grim wars there and the Tiber will run red with blood. In Latium, you will fight a goddess-born hero like Achilles, and Juno will set herself against you, forcing you to seek help from many peoples in Italy. As with Helen, the cause of Trojan suffering will be a foreign bride and a foreign marriage. Yet face your destiny with steadfast courage. Your help, surprisingly, will come from a Greek city." Thus the Sibyl voiced her prophecies, hiding the truth in words of darkness.

Aeneas replied, "Thank you, Sibyl. Now, the shade of my father wants you to help me find him in the Underworld. He told me that the gate to Pluto's kingdom is not far from here."

"Goddess-born," the Sibyl responded, "it is easy to enter the gloomy Underworld, for the gates are always open. The difficult task is to leave the kingdom of death once you have entered it! Only a few sons of the gods favored by Jupiter have been able to do that.

"If you have such love for your father in your heart," the Sibyl counseled, "then you first must find within the forest a bough bearing golden leaves that is sacred to Proserpine, for Pluto's queen requires this gift. If you are destined to have this bough, you will be able to break it off, and it will follow you. Then, when you have made a sacrifice of black cattle, you will be able to enter the kingdom of the dead while you are still alive."

Aeneas entered the forest and wondered how he would ever discover the golden bough buried among so many branches. However, as soon as he wished to see it, twin doves — his mother's birds — landed on the grass in front of him. They led him to a tree within whose green leafy branches Aeneas could see the shimmer of gold. At his touch, the branch broke off in his hand. Once Aeneas possessed the golden bough, he returned to the Sibyl and sacrificed the black cattle.

With the first rays of dawn, tremors deep within the earth caused the ground beneath them to tremble, the forests to shake, and dogs to howl. "Run, run!" the Sibyl cried. "All of you who are not sacred must now leave! You, Aeneas, unsheathe your sword, gather your courage, and follow me."

The Sibyl rushed deep into the cave, and Aeneas fearlessly followed her. At the entrance to Pluto's dark kingdom, he came upon the evils that afflict human beings — Cares, Distress, Diseases, Old Age, Grief, Fear, Famine, Discord, War, and Death.

There, too, he found many famous monsters: the half-human, half-horse beings called Centaurs, the Hydra of Lerna with its hissing heads of snakes, and the triple-bodied giant called Geryon, all of whom the great Hercules killed; the flame-breathing Chimera, whom Bellerophon killed; Medusa, the serpent-haired Gorgon with the face that turned mortals to stone, whom Perseus killed; the six-headed Scylla, who ate six of Ulysses' companions; the Hundred-Handed Giant Briareus, who saved Jupiter when the Olympian gods revolted against him; and the Harpies. Aeneas turned his sword upon them and would have killed them, but the Sibyl reminded him that these were only the monsters' shades.

From there Aeneas followed the Sibyl toward the River Acheron, where the aged Charon, grim ferryman of the shades of the dead, stood guard in his boat. The flames blazing forth from his bony eye sockets, his untended beard, and his filthy clothing knotted upon his shoulders, terrified the shades as Charon tended the sails, poled his boat, and chose which beings could journey across the Acheron.

Aeneas watched as a crowd of shades rushed toward the arriving boat, clamoring to be taken aboard. As many as the autumn leaves that fall in the forest with the first frost, and as many as the birds that flock to warm lands when cold winds bring winter upon northern shores, the shades stood, arms outstretched, pleading with Charon to take them across to the opposite shore. The gloomy boatman carefully chose his passengers, taking some and pushing others away.

Aeneas asked the Sibyl, "Why do all of these shades crowd here at the river's edge? Why does Charon accept some but reject others?"

"Aeneas," the Sibyl replied, "You see before you the river on whose waters the Olympian gods swear their sacred oaths. Charon ferries across it the shades of those who have been properly buried so that they can enter the kingdom of Pluto. Those he denies have not received a proper burial. The unburied must wander upon this shore of the river for 100 years before they can gain entrance into Pluto's dark kingdom."

As he walked toward the Acheron, Aeneas met the captains of the ships that had been swamped in the storm that had washed the rest of his company ashore near Carthage. He talked with the helmsman of his own ship, who had fallen overboard and had drowned in stormy seas.

Charon spied Aeneas and the Sibyl before they reached the shore. "Who are you," he asked, "who, living and bearing arms, approaches the land of Shadows, Sleep, and Night? Stop where you are, and tell me your purpose. I may not ferry the living across this river in my boat. I took Hercules, Theseus, and Pirithous across only because their fathers were gods. Hercules carried off Cerberus, Pluto's three-headed watchdog, and the other two tried to steal Pluto's queen."

The Sibyl replied, "Have no fear. We do not come to cause any harm. Cerberus may continue to frighten the bloodless shades with his endless barking, and Proserpine will remain here in safety. The goddess-born Trojan, Aeneas, famous for his virtue and his skill in war, must see the shade of his father. If you do not believe me, this golden bough surely will convince you."

Gazing with wonder upon the golden bough, Charon cleared his boat and made way for Aeneas and the Sibyl to climb aboard. The boat groaned under Aeneas' weight and water leaked through the cracks in its seams, but it carried Aeneas and the Sibyl safely across the Acheron.

Cerberus, crouching in his cave, howled with all three heads. Upon seeing the snakes entwining his necks rise with anger, the Sibyl tossed the dog a cake soaked with sweet honey and sleep-inducing drugs. Greedily, all three mouths swallowed the sweet food, and the monstrous dog immediately fell alseep. Aeneas left the banks of the Acheron and entered the kingdom of Pluto.

Among the first shades he passed were the victims of love, with Dido among them. Lovingly, Aeneas addressed her. "Poor Dido! I swear to you by all that is sacred that I did not want to leave you! The gods, who now force me to make this journey, drove me from Carthage. I never thought my departure would cause you to take your own life!"

Dido ignored Aeneas' tears and his soothing words. She kept her eyes fixed upon the ground and showed as little emotion as a rock. Finally, she turned away from Aeneas, whom she still regarded as her enemy, and ran back to her loving husband. Aeneas, dismayed by her unjust fate, wept with pity as she left him.

Continuing on their way, Aeneas and the Sibyl came upon the shades of war heroes. Aeneas' Trojan friends were happy to see him. But as soon as the Greek heroes saw Aeneas, with his sword glittering in the gloom, they trembled and fled.

Next they came to a fork in the path. "Your father and Elysium are to the right," the Sibyl said. "To the left, behind that triple wall and encircled by the flaming Phlegethon River, is the castle where great criminals are punished. Each of them has committed some monstrous offense. Even if I had 100 mouths and a voice of iron, I could not relate to you all of their crimes and all of their punishments. Imprisoned there are those who killed a parent or who hated their relatives, those who refused to share their wealth, those who committed adultery, and those who engaged in civil war."

The Sibyl continued, "One king accepted bribes to change the laws and then sold his country to a tyrant for a payment of gold. One is condemned to shout: 'I warn you to be just and not to slight the gods.' Sisyphus continually rolls a huge boulder up a steep hill; Ixion hangs outstretched upon an endlessly revolving wheel of fire; Pirithous sits eternally upon the stone chair of forgetfulness, to which he is bound and attached. But come, let us find your father and achieve your purpose here. I see the arched gates where we are to place the golden bough."

Then Aeneas and the Sibyl entered the Happy Forest, a land of woods, meadows, and rivers on which a special sun and special stars shone. Some of the shades were wrestling, some were dancing, and others were singing. Here Aeneas saw Dardanus, the founder of Troy, as well as the greatest heroes who died defending their country, and the greatest priests, poets, and philosophers.

When Anchises saw Aeneas approaching, tears streamed down his cheeks. He stretched out both hands and cried, " At last you have come! Your love for your father has given you the courage to make this fearsome journey. What dangers have befallen you? I was afraid that Carthage would harm you."

"Your sad shade, father, often came to me and directed me along the right path. So I have come to find you in this kingdom. Let me clasp your hand and embrace you!" So Aeneas, weeping, spoke to Anchises. Three times he tried to embrace him, but three times his father's shade fled from his grasp like a light breeze. "Who are all of those people?" Aeneas then asked.

"They are spirits who are waiting for Fate to give them second bodies," Anchises replied. "When they have been here 1,000 years, they drink from the River Lethe and forget their entire past. Then they return to the world above in a new body. I have long wanted to show them to you, for they are the future beings of your race. With this knowledge, you will be more pleased about your destiny in Italy.

"Come now and see what glory your Trojan line will achieve, what fame and honor your Italian children will bring our name," Anchises said. "There is Silvius of Alban, who will be the last child born to you and your Italian wife, Lavinia. He will be a king and a father of kings, and through him our race will rule in Alba Longa.

"Then Romulus, a child of Mars and Ilia, will join his grandfather, Numitor. You can see how Mars has marked his son with a twin-plumed helmet like his own, so his place upon the earth is even now assured. Under his rule, a single wall will enclose Rome's seven hills. His empire will encompass the earth, and Roman spirit will equal the gods' Olympus.

"Now look at your Roman race. Here are Julius Caesar and all his children, who also are destined to appear on the earth above. That is Augustus Caesar, son of a god, who will bring forth the Golden Age in Latium and extend the Roman Empire to lands that lie beyond the stars and beyond the paths of the sun. Not even Hercules traveled over so much of the earth, although he captured the Arcadian deer, brought peace to the woods of Eurymanthus, and killed the Hydra of Lerna.

"There is Numa, the second king of Rome, called to kingship from a poor land, who will give the city a code of law. And there are Mummius, who will be famous for the Greeks he slays and the conquest of Corinth, and Aemilius Paulus, who will destroy Argos and Agamemnon's Mycenae, thus punishing the Greeks for destroying Troy. There, too, are great Cato, Cossus, and the mighty Fabius Maximus, who will restore the Roman state.

"Finally, there are the two Marcelluses; the first will defeat the Carthaginians and the Gauls, and then the gifted young Marcellus will so reflect the nobility of his Latin ancestors in virtue, honor, and skill in war that the Fates, fearing his potential power, will not let him live long. Remember, Roman, that your great contribution will be to rule the nations in your empire in peace under law, to tame the proud through war, and to treat the conquered with mercy!"

When Anchises had kindled in Aeneas the love of future glory, he told him about the wars he would have to fight, about the Laurentine peoples and the city of Latinus, and he instructed him how to avoid or face each trial.

Then Anchises took Aeneas and the Sibyl to the gates of Sleep, where he dismissed them. Aeneas quickly returned to his ships and rejoined his companions, and they continued on their way.

Chapter 7

*Aeneas and his companions arrive in Italy. As
prophesied, they must fight the Latin people, led by the
warrior Turnus. Aeneas is helped by Pallas, whom
Turnus slays. Finally, Jupiter forces Juno to put aside
her anger. Aeneas and Turnus fight in single combat,
and Aeneas kills Turnus when he sees him wearing
Pallas' sword-belt.*

With favorable winds, Aeneas and his companions set sail on a moonlit night.
They passed Circe's island, where they heard the daughter of the Sun singing as
she wove upon her loom. They also heard the roaring of her chained lions, the
raging of her boars and bears in their cages, and the howls of her wolves. With
magic herbs, the cruel goddess had transformed men into all of those monstrous
beasts. Neptune filled the Trojans' sails with strong winds to move them safely
past this dreaded land.

As the rays of dawn painted the sea red, Aeneas saw a great forest with the
Tiber River running through it to the sea. Colorful birds sang as they flew among
the trees. Joyfully, Aeneas directed his ships into the wide mouth of the peaceful
river; there they moored the ships and went ashore.

When the travelers set forth their food, Jupiter inspired them to use their
grain cakes to keep the wild fruits they had gathered off the ground. After they
had eaten the fruit, they ate the cakes. Young Ascanius laughed, "Look! We are
eating our tables, too!"

Aeneas immediately remembered the prophecy of the Harpy and said, "Hail to
the faithful gods of Troy! Here is our home; here is our country."

King Latinus welcomed the Trojans, for an oracle had pronounced that his
daughter, Lavinia, would marry a stranger, and their children would beget a race
that would establish a great empire. Juno, still unwilling for Aeneas to have his
Latin destiny, directed a goddess from the Underworld to go forth among the
people of Latium and create war.

First she inspired Amata, Lavinia's mother, to remind her husband of his
pledge to marry Lavinia to the warrior Turnus. Then she appeared in Turnus'
dreams and inspired him to defend Italy against Aeneas and the invading
Trojans. Finally, she caused a fight between a group of Latins and some of the
Trojans. Popular sentiment now opposed the Trojans.

Although King Latinus steadfastly tried to avoid war with Aeneas by refusing
to open the twin doors of the Temple of Janus, which would have declared a
state of war, Juno came down from Olympus and opened them herself. Turnus
then raised the flag of war and marshaled his troops.

As Aeneas slept on the bank of the Tiber, worried about the coming war, the
river god came to him and counseled, "Arise, goddess-born. Your home is here,
and your gods support you. Do not fear these threats of war. In thirty years,
Ascanius will found the great city of Alba. Meanwhile, seek King Evander in
Pallenteum. He perpetually wars with the Latins, and he will become your ally."

With two ships and a group of chosen men, Aeneas then rowed up the peaceful Tiber River to the city of Pallenteum, which would one day become the renowned Rome. As Aeneas arrived, the king, his son Pallas, and the city officials were offering sacrifices to the mighty Hercules and the gods in a grove near the city. When he heard the purpose of Aeneas' visit, King Evander welcomed him warmly, remembering Anchises and King Priam from his own youth. Then he explained to Aeneas the history of the rites honoring Hercules, who had killed the giant Cacus at the base of the cliff where they were presently sitting.

Evander told Aeneas that he would support him against the Latins, although his resources were few. He would send Pallas and 400 men. Then Venus signaled Aeneas with thunder in the sunny sky that she would bring him armor fashioned by her husband, Vulcan, the famed metalsmith of the gods. Afterward, Aeneas and Pallas led their men to fight Turnus and the Latins.

Meanwhile, in Aeneas' absence, the Latins attacked the Trojans. Many on both sides died. After Ascanius killed Turnus' brother-in-law, Apollo said to him, "Be satisfied, son of Aeneas, that Apollo grants you this glory. You have the courage and skill of the son of gods and the father of gods to be. Now refrain from further fighting." Eager as the boy was to continue, he obeyed the command of the great god.

The Trojan captains marshaled their men against Turnus, who stood alone against them. As a furious lion faces the spears of a band of hunters and reluctantly retreats, backing up because its courage and anger will not let it turn around yet unable to force its way through the armed hunters, so Turnus retreated toward the river, with rage blazing in his heart. Pressed upon by the Trojans, Turnus found his weapon was useless. Darts, stones, and finally a storm of spears attacked his helmet and his armor. With a leap, he jumped into the Tiber in full armor, and the water supported his body and carried him back to his men.

The fighting was in full force when Aeneas arrived with his allies. Pallas killed many Latins. Then Turnus decided to rescue the warrior Lausus and fight Pallas in single combat. Turnus left his chariot as a lion rushes down from the mountain to attack a bull it has spied upon the plain. Pallas, aware of how much mightier Turnus was than he, prayed to Hercules, "By my father's welcome, help me to strip the bloodstained armor from Turnus' dying body, and may Turnus' last sight be of his conqueror."

When Hercules wept to hear this prayer, Jupiter soothed his son. "Each mortal has his or her fated day to die," the father of the gods counseled, "and none has a long life. The courageous man performs deeds that will give him lasting fame, for fame survives after death. Turnus, too, is fated to die when his time comes."

Pallas' spear grazed Turnus' shoulder. Then Turnus' spear tore through the center of Pallas' shield and pierced his heart. Standing over Pallas, Turnus cried, "Greeks, tell Evander that I grant him Pallas' corpse and a proper burial." He then stripped Pallas' heavy sword-belt as a trophy of victory, unaware of how soon he would regret that gesture.

Juno, afraid of Aeneas' vengeance, received Jupiter's permission to rescue Turnus and postpone his inevitable fate. From the mist, she fashioned a shade of

Aeneas in his war gear. The phantom appeared at the front of the Trojan forces, provoking the enemy with its spear and its defiant cry. When Turnus attacked it, the spirit turned and fled, and Turnus pursued it, sword in hand.

The phantom took refuge on a moored ship. As soon as Turnus followed it on board, Juno broke the anchoring cable, causing the ship to float out with the ebbing tide. The phantom then became a black cloud and drifted into the sky, leaving Turnus helplessly being blown out to sea.

"Father Jupiter!" Turnus cried. "Why are you punishing me like this? I am ashamed to have left my companions to face their deaths without me. I wish that the earth would open and swallow me! Winds, pity me, and destroy this ship, or take me where no one will ever hear of my shame."

Upon receiving the corpse of Pallas, Evander sent Aeneas a message that it was now his duty to avenge Pallas' death by slaying Turnus. Meanwhile, the battle continued to rage. With Turnus absent from the Latin forces, the Trojans were victorious.

When Aeneas received envoys from the Latins asking for a truce in order to bury their dead, he said, "I favor peace for the living as well as for the dead. Fate brought me to your shores, and I never desired war. If Turnus was so set on war, it would have been far better for him to fight me in single combat than to cause the deaths of so many people."

By this time Turnus had returned, and the Latins had become divided. Some wished to continue the war, but others said, "Turnus, pity your countrymen and surrender. We have seen enough of death! If you are determined to win glory or a royal wife, then fight Aeneas in single combat. Why should we die, unburied and unwept upon the plains, for your own private gain and glory?"

Turnus replied, "Many of you speak well but fear the battlefield. If the Trojans call me to face Aeneas in single combat, I shall confront him with courage even if he surpasses the great Achilles and wears armor fashioned by Vulcan!"

The argument was cut short by the arrival of messengers, who announced that the Trojans and their allies were marching from the Tiber across the plain to their city. "Citizens!" Turnus cried. "You sit here in the council praising peace while the enemy rushes to attack our walls!"

When Turnus realized that the Latins were defeated and that they lacked further spirit to fight, he became furious. As a lion becomes aroused to anger once it has been wounded in the breast, and it defiantly tosses its shaggy mane, roars with its bloodstained mouth, and snaps the implanted weapon, so Turnus blazed with rage. "Arrange for me to fight Aeneas in single combat," he told King Latinus. "Either I will remove our nation's shame or the Trojan will win Lavinia as his bride and be our conqueror."

The Latin people were dismayed by the prospect of the unequal contest, and even those who had longed for rest and safety wished for weapons and a way to avoid Turnus' unjust fate. Therefore, one among them broke the truce. As war resumed, Aeneas cried, "Curb your anger! Honor the truce! I shall enforce the treaty. Peace will reign in Italy!" But Turnus ignored Aeneas' words and fought his way across the field, killing many. Aeneas, too, brought death to many, causing the field to turn red with blood.

Venus then inspired Aeneas to realize that he could conquer the city. Queen Amata, watching the course of the fighting from the roof, saw the Trojans advance without opposition, scale the walls of the city, and toss blazing torches into the houses. Frantically, she searched the plains for Turnus, but she could not find him. Thinking that he had been killed and blaming herself for her people's destruction, she hanged herself. Latinus, faced with the death of his wife and the conquest of his city, tore his clothes, covered his head with dirt, and walked the streets in stunned horror.

When Turnus heard about the disasters, he turned to gaze upon the burning city, and his heart filled with the conflicting emotions of shame, grief, and anger. "I am determined to fight Aeneas," he said. "I shall bear the bitterness of death; no longer shall I stand ashamed."

Turnus leaped from his chariot and rushed past his enemies' weapons to the city walls. As a great rock rushes headlong down the steep mountainside and bounces upon the ground, crushing trees, herds, and men, so among the scattered troops Turnus rushed to the city walls, where the earth was drenched with blood and the sound of clashing spears clamored in the air.

"Withdraw from battle!" he shouted. "Whatever my fate, it is better that I take upon myself the outcome of this war and decide it with my sword."

Hearing his words, Aeneas left the fighting to approach him. They attacked each other as two bulls charge into deadly conflict head to head, while their herders retreat in terror, the entire herd stands in quiet dread, and the heifers wonder who their next leader will be. As the bulls viciously gore each other with their horns, their necks and shoulders swimming in blood and the forest echoing their bellows, so Aeneas and Turnus clashed shield to shield, filling the air with a mighty clamor.

Jupiter, high above, picked up his balanced scales and placed the fate of each hero upon a scale to see whose life the battle would doom, for the loser's impending death would cause his scale to sink with the weight of his destiny. Turnus' sword blade broke off like brittle ice upon meeting Vulcan's armor. Regretting that he had hastily left his father's sword behind, Turnus ran from Aeneas. The Trojan, despite an arrow wound in his knee, pursued him.

As a hunting dog chases at the hooves of a stag that is confined by a stream, the stag running frantically this way and that while the dog clings close to those hooves, his greedy jaws ajar in anticipation of the tasty flesh, so Aeneas chased Turnus. Turnus called among his countrymen for another sword, but Aeneas threatened death to the one who supplied it.

Five times they ran full circle, and as many times they ran in reverse. They were racing not for a mere trophy but for Turnus' life! When another goddess restored a sword to Turnus, Venus helped Aeneas retrieve his spear from the tree in which it had lodged.

Then Jupiter said to his wife, "You know that Olympus claims Aeneas as the hero of Italy. We have come to the end, so stop grieving and do not contend against me. You have chased the Trojans over land and sea, started this evil war, brought death into a royal home, and caused the bride great grief. I forbid you to interfere further."

"Knowing your feelings," Juno replied, "I have remained aloof here with you, when I would have chosen to be fighting the Trojans myself on the battlefield. I now yield completely to your wishes. I ask only that when Aeneas and Lavinia marry, you permit the Latins to keep their ancient name and language. Preserve Latium, let Alban kings rule, call the race Roman, and let Troy's name die with its city."

Jupiter smiled and replied, "In the depths of your anger, you prove that you are my sister and Saturn's child. I hereby grant your wish. From Aeneas and Lavinia I shall create a blended race of one people, one language, and one set of laws and rituals. They will surpass all mortals and gods in virtue and in your worship."

Aeneas pressed on against Turnus with his great spear. "Why delay further?" he asked. "Let us fight hand to hand with our weapons instead of foot to foot."

"Do not think that you are my mighty enemy, Aeneas," Turnus replied. "Jupiter and the other gods are my greater foe!" With these words, Turnus spied an ancient, massive boulder that twelve strong men could hardly have lifted upon their shoulders. This he quickly grasped and tried to hurl at Aeneas. But as he raised and threw the stone, his knees trembled, his blood froze, and the rock, falling short of its goal, failed to wound his target. The dread goddess, Fate, had denied Turnus success, and the hero trembled with fear at the approach of Aeneas' spear and certain death.

Seeing Turnus falter, Aeneas aimed his deadly spear and hurled it upon his enemy. The spear pierced Turnus' shield and armor and then passed through his thigh. The huge warrior sank to the ground upon his injured leg. "I do not beg for mercy," Turnus said. "But think of your father and give my body back to my family. You are the victor, and Lavinia is yours to wed. Do not press your hatred further."

Aeneas, awesome in his armor, relaxed his sword arm and felt compassion for his fallen foe until he saw upon Turnus' shoulders the sword-belt of young Pallas. Memory of the courageous boy revived Aeneas' great grief and overwhelming anger. "How can you expect to win my pity when you wear as a trophy the belt of my dear friend whom you mercilessly killed?" he roared. "It is Pallas who demands this payment of your blood and here strikes you dead!" Aeneas furiously buried his sword deep in Turnus' chest. Turnus' limbs grew limp and chill and, with a moan, his life fled resentfully down to the shades below.

The Middle East

The myths from the Middle East, which date from 2500 B.C., are the oldest recorded literature in the world. Yet they reveal a universe of gods and heroes who react to the human condition as we know it today.

The gods of Sumer and Babylonia have human personalities. They enjoy helping a favorite mortal. However, many of them are most memorable for their quick tempers and rash behavior. These gods are unpredictable.

In the Babylonian creation epic, a male divinity, Marduk, overpowers the original female divinity, Tiamat, and becomes the new ruler of the universe. In ancient Middle Eastern cultures, the ability to perform magic tricks was considered proof of the ability to govern the world. Consequently, when Marduk and Tiamat pit their great magical powers against each other, Marduk wins because he possesses stronger magic.

The myth about Telepinu is interesting in that its plot addresses the problem of fertility without psychological complexity. The reason for Telepinu's anger is not explained; the myth simply describes how the god must be appeased in order for life on earth to continue to flourish.

The Egyptian myths are quite unlike those of Babylonia and Sumer, reflecting the fact that Egyptians were an isolated culture. The ancient Egyptians' view of the universe included predictable, helpful divinities who combatted an evil that could never be permanently conquered. The Egyptians also believed in resurrection for deserving human beings. The Egyptian gods have human feelings and human needs. Isis, for example, is a loyal and loving mother figure, one who casts a great shadow in the mythology of the region.

The Babylonian epic of *Gilgamesh* presents what may be the first tragic hero. Gilgamesh wants what many other human beings wish to possess, everlasting life, and he undertakes a perilous journey in the hope of achieving his wish. In the course of his journey, he hears about the great flood, which left its impact upon a number of Mediterranean cultures. Gilgamesh is dismayed to learn that everlasting life is not the destiny of human beings. He comes to value the ordinary pleasures in life and to perform deeds that will give him lasting fame, the only immortality available to human begins.

Introducing **The Enuma elish**

Historical Background

The Babylonian creation myth is the epic known as the *Enuma elish* from its opening words, which mean "when on high." It was recorded in cuneiform (wedge-shaped) script upon seven clay tablets that were found by British archaeologists in the 1840s in the course of their excavations at Nineveh, in what is now Iraq. These tablets were part of the library of King Ashurbanipal, who ruled from 668 to 627 B.C.

German excavations at Ashur (not far from Nineveh), begun in 1902, uncovered another version of the *Enuma elish*. This version is identical to the one at Nineveh except for the substitution of the name of the Assyrian national god (Ashur) for the Babylonian national god (Marduk). Therefore, this epic appears to have been important to the Assyrians as well as to the Babylonians.

Although these cuneiform tablets only date back to about 1000 B.C.,

their content and style indicate that the story recorded on them may have existed as early as 1900 B.C. In the introduction to his famous legal code, Hammurabi, who ruled the Babylonians from 1728 to 1686 B.C., refers both to the *Enuma elish* and to Marduk: "At the time when Anu, king of the gods, and Enlil, lord of heaven and earth and the god who determines the destiny of the land, first made Marduk supreme among the gods, then assigned to Marduk Enlil's role as king over all human beings, and finally made Babylon supreme among the nations of the world, at that time Anu and Enlil chose me, Hammurabi, the religious and god-fearing prince, to enrich the lives of the people by causing justice to shine upon the land like the sun, thereby destroying all that is evil."

Each year in Babylon, the *Enuma elish* was solemnly recited and dramatized as part of the ten-day New Year festival, which marked the beginning of the autumn season. The holiday was a serious one that emphasized the re-establishment of order in the universe, the renewal of life, and the determination of all human destinies for the coming year.

Scholars believe that the Babylonians enacted in pantomime the battle depicted in the *Enuma elish* between the forces of chaos and the forces of order. Chaos would reign in the streets of Babylon until Marduk was freed from his imprisonment. Then he would lead a procession, symbolizing the forces of the gods, against Tiamat and her demon forces. After Marduk had defeated Tiamat and her rebellious forces in a mock battle and had established order in the universe, the Babylonians would carry his image in a triumphant parade through the streets of Babylon. In this magical way, the people hoped to influence the gods who controlled human destinies and prevail upon them to usher in a year of fertility, abundance, and good fortune.

The people of Babylon may also have considered this myth to have magical power over the Tigris and Euphrates rivers. These rivers overflowed their banks each spring and often ravaged the countryside with severe flooding. People used the magic of incantation and dramatization to try to protect their community against the devastation of these terrible spring floods.

The myth honoring Marduk glorifies both the patron god of Babylonia—who had created the universe and had brought order out of chaos—and the city of Babylon, for the gods built the temple of Marduk in Babylon to be their earthly home. The myth thus combines both a religious aspect and a secular, political aspect. Just as the

destinies of human beings were determined in the course of the New Year holiday, so, too, the political destiny of Babylonia was being decided.

Thus, the *Enuma elish* epic is more than a creation myth. The Babylonians took the traditional Sumerian creation myth and reshaped it to serve new national, religious, and political purposes. The explanation of the creation of the universe became the story of the rise to supreme power of the storm god Marduk and the glorification of his earthly city of Babylon.

Babylonian Religion

The three greatest Sumerian divinities— Anu, god of the sky, Enlil, god of the air, and Ea, god of the earth—still existed among the Babylonian divinities. Then Marduk, who possessed both a great birthright as Ea's son and extraordinary abilities of his own, was born. Once Marduk entered the assembly of the gods, they gave him Enlil's role in the universe, so that Enlil became a god in name only, without function or power. Marduk became the supreme god. He was given the honor of creating the universe, of keeping it functioning, and of being responsible for the creation of human beings, whose purpose it was to serve the gods. All gods and all mortals obeyed Marduk's will.

Marduk achieved power by means of a religious revolution, and his victory established a new order and a new way of looking at the universe. The Sumerian gods had been an integral part of the substance of the universe, actually being the land, the water, and the heavens that they represented. When Marduk gave them new roles, he created the universe as the Babylonians recognized it. He organized the elements that already existed (the gods) in such a way that order emerged out of chaos.

It is also significant that Marduk built the new order upon the ruins of the older order. His was the victory of a new male-dominated, patriarchal religion over a female-dominated, matriarchal religion. Tiamat, who originally was the Great Goddess or Mother Goddess and who had given birth to all of the original gods, now became the enemy of the gods. She who originally was good and protected the lives of her children now became evil and attempted to destroy those children. She who originally had given birth to the best of the gods now gave birth to monsters and demons. She who originally was more powerful than her husband and her sons now was easily defeated by a new god who was immune to her potent magic.

Under Marduk, order emerged out of chaos, life emerged from dead matter, and nature was renewed each year. Nevertheless, even under Marduk, the universe and the gods within it were not predictable or reliable. Even the most powerful king was always dependent upon the goodwill and the help of the gods for success. Life after death promised no rewards for earthly achievements, just darkness, dust, deprivation, and eternal boredom. Therefore, the Babylonians believed that human beings had to make the most of their lives, in a world that lacked security and hope.

Principal Gods*

TIAMAT: *Babylonia:* Great Goddess or Mother Goddess; Mother Earth, who nourishes all life; wife of Apsu; mother of Anshar and Kishar; ruler of salt waters. *Sumer:* counterpart of Nintu

APSU: *Babylonia:* husband of Tiamat; father of Anshar and Kishar; ruler of all the gods and sweet waters. *Sumer:* counterpart of Anu

MUMMU: *Babylonia:* son of Tiamat and Apsu; god of mist

ANSHAR: *Babylonia:* son of Tiamat and Apsu; brother and husband of Kishar

KISHAR: *Babylonia:* daughter of Tiamat and Apsu; sister and wife of Anshar

ANU (An): *Babylonia:* god of the sky; son of Anshar and Kishar. *Sumer:* god of the sky; husband of Nintu; father and ruler of all the gods

NINTU (Ki): *Sumer:* a Great Goddess or Mother Goddess like Tiamat; wife of Anu; mother of all the gods; created the first human beings out of clay

ENLIL: *Babylonia:* god of the air between earth and sky. *Sumer:* son of Anu and Nintu; god of air and agriculture; became ruler of the gods along with Anu

ISHTAR (Inanna): *Sumer:* first, daughter of Anu, later of Sin; a Great Goddess or Mother Goddess; goddess of love and war

EA: *Babylonia:* son of Anu; husband of Damkina; father of Marduk; ruler of all the gods and sweet water after Apsu; god of wisdom, arts, and crafts. *Sumer:* son of Nintu; ruler of the earth; god of wisdom, arts, and crafts

DAMKINA: *Babylonia:* wife of Ea; mother of Marduk

MARDUK: *Babylonia:* son of Ea and Damkina; wisest and most accomplished god; becomes ruler of all the gods. *Sumer:* counterpart of Anu and Enlil

KINGU: *Babylonia:* commands Tiamat's forces against Marduk

SIN: god of the moon; father of Shamash

SHAMASH: son of Sin; god of the sun; protects the poor, the wronged, and the traveler

*For the most part, the Babylonians adopted the earlier Sumerian gods. Important distinctions between the Babylonian and Sumerian gods are noted.

The Enuma elish

In the beginning, only water and the mist that hovered above it existed. Father Apsu personified and ruled the sweet waters, Mother Tiamat personified and ruled the salt waters, and both waters flowed together as one. Mummu, their son, existed in the mist that covered them. Neither the heavens high above nor the firm earth below existed yet. Neither marshland nor pastureland had as yet appeared upon the waters. As yet, no huts of matted reeds had been fashioned.

Then the gods Anshar and Kishar were formed within the sweet waters of Apsu and the salt waters of Tiamat, and they emerged from the waters. In time, Anshar and Kishar became the parents of Anu, who became god of the heavens. Anu, in turn, became the father of Ea. Ea surpassed both his father and his grandfather, for he was wiser, more understanding, and stronger than they, and he was skilled in the use of magic. He became god of the earth, and he had no rival among the great gods.

The young gods joined together and had merry times. They were so rowdy that they disturbed Tiamat as they surged back and forth, and their exuberance caused her to resent their presence. As time passed the Mother Goddess came to hate their behavior, but she did not know how to deal with them. She asked Apsu to talk to them, but when he tried they ignored him.

Apsu, Tiamat, and Mummu sat down together to discuss the problem. Apsu announced, "I cannot abide the way the gods are behaving! Their clamor continues incessantly both day and night, so that I can never get any sleep. I desperately need peace and quiet! Since they will not listen to my pleas, I shall have to stop their raucous activities the only way I can, by destroying them!"

Her husband's words angered Tiamat. She replied, "I understand exactly how you feel, Apsu. You know that I have complained about the same problem. However, your solution is evil! Shall we destroy the children that we ourselves created? Their manners are rude, and their activities are annoying, but we must try to be understanding."

Mummu, however, supported Apsu. "I advise you to ignore Tiamat's opinion in this matter," he counseled. "Proceed with your plan and destroy the gods, for they show no respect for your authority. They are unruly both day and night, and their behavior gives you no peace." Apsu's face glowed with pleasure when he heard Mummu's opinion, for he enjoyed the evil plan that he had in mind.

The gods quickly learned of Apsu and Mummu's plot against them. When they first heard the news, they cried. Then they sat in silence, unable to think of a way to avoid their fate.

But Ea, who was the wisest, the most clever, and the most accomplished of the gods, soon thought of a way to spoil the scheme of Apsu and Mummu. First he created a magic circle to protect the gods and placed them safely within it. Then he recited a sacred spell upon the deep waters of Apsu, causing Apsu to fall into a sound sleep and Mummu to remain powerless.

Ea then placed Apsu in chains, removed his crown and halo, and placed them on his own head. When he had taken the symbols of kingship, he killed Apsu. He then bound Mummu, leading him about wherever he wished by a rope drawn through Mummu's nose.

Once he had conquered his enemies, Ea established his dwelling upon Apsu and the sweet waters that had belonged to him. There, deep within the waters, he rested peacefully with his wife, Damkina. His splendid house became the house of destinies; his sacred room became the room of fates.

In time Ea and Damkina became the parents of Marduk, the wisest and most able of all of the gods. Even though he was born fully grown, goddesses fed Marduk from the day of his birth and made him awesome to behold. From the beginning, Marduk appeared to be a natural leader, and as soon as Ea saw his son, his paternal heart filled with gladness. Ea made Marduk a double god so that he would surpass all the other gods in form and in strength. Four sparkling eyes shone forth from Marduk's face, enabling him to see everything, and four large ears extended outward, enabling him to hear everything. Whenever Marduk moved his lips, fire blazed forth from his mouth.

"Our son is the sun of the heavens!" Ea exclaimed. Indeed, Marduk wore the halos of ten gods upon his head, so that the brightness of his rays was awesome to behold. He inspired terror as well as majesty in all who beheld him.

Meanwhile, Anu created the winds of the north, south, east, and west, and these tempests violently disturbed Tiamat's waters. When some of the gods suffered in the dreadful windstorms and could find no rest, they designed evil within their hearts.

Led by Kingu, they said to their mother, "When Ea and the gods who helped him killed Apsu, our father, you allowed them to do it. Now Anu has created this terrible fourfold wind, which disturbs your body and keeps us awake, and you have allowed him to do it. Our eyes are weary from lack of sleep! Apparently you do not love us, for you do nothing! Think about your husband and Mummu, whom those gods defeated. You have been left all alone! Why not rouse yourself and avenge Apsu and Mummu by attacking the gods? We will support you!"

Tiamat was very pleased to hear these words of encouragement. "You have given me good counsel," she replied. "I will create monsters to help us, and then we will fight against those gods!"

The rebellious gods now felt free to express their anger. They met in assembly, both day and night, in order to plan their revolt.

Meanwhile, Tiamat created monster serpents as her invincible weapons. She filled their bodies with venom instead of blood and gave them sharp teeth and long fangs. She fashioned terrifying dragons and crowned them with halos like the gods, so that anyone who looked upon them would perish from fright. Once the serpents stood upright, no one would be able to stand against them. She created eleven monsters in all: the viper, the dragon, the sphinx, the great lion, the mad dog, the scorpion-man, three mighty storm demons, the dragonfly, and the centaur.

Then Tiamat chose Kingu to be commander-in-chief of her monsters and the rebellious gods. "I have cast my spell upon you, Kingu," she told him. "I have given you the power to counsel all the gods in the assembly. You now rule supreme and are my only companion. Your command will be everlasting, and your word will endure!" With these words, Tiamat fastened the Tablet of Destinies upon Kingu's chest.

In this way, Tiamat prepared to fight against her children in order to avenge the death of Apsu. Knowing nothing of fear, the monsters gathered around her and marched at her side. They were angry and ready for battle. Tiamat exclaimed, "May your great poison conquer our enemies!"

As soon as Ea heard that Tiamat and Kingu were leading a revolt against the gods, he went to Anshar, his grandfather, and informed him of their preparations for battle. Anshar was very concerned. "Ea, you have killed Apsu, and now you must kill Kingu, who marches at the head of Tiamat's forces!"

Ea tried his best to please his grandfather. But as soon as he saw Tiamat and her forces, his heart filled with terror, and he could not summon the courage to face them. Ashamed of his cowardice, he retreated and returned to Anshar. "Tiamat, Kingu, and Tiamat's monster serpents will never respond to my magic!" he exclaimed. "They are much more powerful than I am!"

Then Anshar turned to Anu and said, "You are both courageous and strong! Take a stand against Tiamat. Surely you can resist Kingu's attack!"

Anu obeyed his father's command and took the road to Tiamat. However, when he saw her terrifying forces, he did not have the courage to face her. Like Ea, he returned to Anshar in shame. "I am not strong enough to carry out your wishes," he confessed.

Anshar, Anu, and Ea sat in silence. "No god," they thought, "can face Tiamat and her forces in battle and survive!"

Finally Anshar joyfully exclaimed, "Marduk, the hero, will avenge us! He is very strong, and he is great in battle! Ea, bring your son before us!"

When Marduk stood before them, he announced, "Do not be concerned. I shall go and carry out your heart's desire! After all, it is not as if a male has come against you. Tiamat, for all her weapons, is only a woman! So, father of the gods, rejoice and be happy. Soon you will be able to tread upon Tiamat's neck!"

"My son," Anshar replied, "you are the wisest of the gods. Calm Tiamat with your sacred spell. Take your storm chariot and go quickly. Kingu and Tiamat's monster serpents will not be able to drive you away. Defeat them!"

Marduk rejoiced to hear the words of Anshar. He replied, "Anshar, if I am to avenge you, conquer Tiamat, and save the lives of the gods, then call all of the gods to assembly and proclaim my supreme destiny! Let my word determine the fates! Let whatever I create remain fixed. Let my command be everlasting, and let my word endure!"

Anshar called his adviser to his side and said, "Tell all the gods about Tiamat's revolt against us, and explain how Marduk will surely succeed where Ea and Anu have failed. Tell them to assemble here. After we have feasted upon good bread and wine, we will decree the destinies for Marduk, our avenger."

So it came to pass that the gods met in assembly and glorified Marduk. First they built a princely throne for him, from which he presided. Then they said, "You, Marduk, are the most important of the great gods. Your rule is unrivaled. It has the authority of Anu, god of the sky. From this day forth, when we gather in assembly your word will be supreme. Your decrees will be everlasting. No one among the gods will disobey your word. We grant you kingship over the entire universe. It will be within your power to raise or to bring low, to create or to destroy."

Then the gods brought forth a garment, placed it before Marduk, and said, "To prove your power, make this garment vanish and reappear. Now, reveal the extent of your power!"

Marduk then commanded the garment: "Vanish!" And it disappeared. He commanded: "Appear!" And it reappeared in one piece. When the gods saw the power of his words, they joyfully announced, "Marduk is king!" Then they gave him his throne, his sceptre, and his ceremonial robes. Finally they gave him matchless weapons to use against his enemies.

"Your weapons will not fail; you will indeed destroy your foes," they said to him. "Spare the life of the one who trusts you, but pour out the life of the god who is evil. Go now and cut off the life of Tiamat. May the winds carry her blood to secret places. May you return successful, having accomplished your purpose."

Marduk then constructed a great bow for himself, attached an arrow to it, and hung it at his side. In his right hand he grasped his mace. In his left hand he held a plant that destroyed poison. At his side he carried a net he had created to enclose Tiamat when he captured her. In front he set lightning. He filled his body with a blazing flame. Then he placed the winds of the four directions about him so that Tiamat could not escape.

Marduk then brought forth the evil wind, the whirlwind, the hurricane, the fourfold wind, the sevenfold wind, the cyclone, and the matchless wind and sent all seven winds to stir up the inside of Tiamat, goddess of the salt waters. He harnessed his team of four beasts—the Destroyer, the Relentless, the Trampler, and the Flier—to his invincible storm chariot, which inspired with terror anyone who gazed upon it. Marduk mounted his chariot, and Smiter, who was fearsome in battle, took up position at his right, while Combat, who could repel the most ardent fighters, took up position at his left. Both monsters possessed sharp teeth and tongues that dripped venom.

Finally, Marduk encased himself in a terrifying coat of armor and placed his fearsome halos upon his head. He smeared red paste upon his lips as a magical protection against the forces of evil. Last of all, he called forth the flooding rain-storm, his mighty weapon. Then he set forth to meet the raging Tiamat.

The sight of Marduk sent terror into Kingu's heart and distracted his mind. Kingu's forces could not face Marduk's brilliance and turned away in fright.

Marduk then raised his mighty weapon, the flooding rainstorm, against the enraged Tiamat and said, "Why have you begun such an evil conflict? You are attacking your own children! Do you not love them? Sons are fighting against their fathers, and you have no cause to hate them! You have conferred upon Kingu a rank to which he is not rightfully entitled. Although you are armed with weapons and surrounded by your forces, I ask you to stand against me in single combat!"

At these words, Tiamat lost her senses. Her legs shook and she cried aloud, using all of her magic. Then Tiamat and Marduk fought in single combat. Marduk spread out his net to enfold her. When Tiamat opened her mouth to consume him, Marduk drove the evil wind into her mouth in order to keep it open. The other winds entered Tiamat's body, broadly extending it. Marduk then shot her with his bow. The arrow tore into her stomach and ripped through her body, splitting her heart and killing her.

Marduk then threw down Tiamat's body and stood upon it. Once she was dead the gods who had marched at her side retreated in terror, desperately attempting to save their own lives. But Marduk's forces encircled them and permitted no escape. Marduk took the rebellious gods prisoner, smashed their weapons, and confined them in his net. Then he imprisoned them in cells.

Marduk bound with chains the band of eleven demons who had marched on Tiamat's right, then trampled their bodies. He imprisoned Kingu, took from him the Tablet of Destinies — which was not rightfully his — sealed the Tablet, and fastened it upon his own breast.

Once Marduk had subdued all his enemies, he returned to Tiamat, stamped on her legs, and crushed her skull with his mace. When he had severed her arteries, the north wind bore her blood to the secret places. Marduk then divided Tiamat's body into two parts like a shellfish. Half of Tiamat he set up as the sky; the other half he formed into the earth. From Tiamat's saliva, he created the clouds and filled them with water, but he himself took charge of the winds, the rain, and the cold. He put Tiamat's head into position to form the mountains of the earth, and he caused the Tigris and the Euphrates rivers to flow from her eyes.

Marduk then directed Anu to rule the heavens, Ea to rule the earth, and Enlil to rule the air between heaven and earth. He divided the year into months and days. He caused the moon, Sin, to shine at night in various phases as a way of marking the days of the month. He created the sun, giving the days to Shamash as he had given the nights to Sin.

When he had created order in the universe, Marduk handed over the shrines he created to Ea. The Tablet of Destinies he gave to Anu. He restored the bound gods who had helped Tiamat to their fathers. Finally, he turned Tiamat's eleven monsters into statues to remind the gods of the futility of revolt.

When he returned to Anu, Enlil, and Ea, Marduk announced, "I have hardened the ground in order to build a luxurious house and temple where you will spend the night whenever you descend from heaven and meet in assembly. I will call my temple Babylon, which means 'the houses of the great gods.' Skilled craftsmen will build it."

The gods asked Marduk, "Who will have authority in the temple you have built? Who will have your power on the earth that you have created? Establish Babylon as our home forever! Let someone bring us our daily ration, and we will continue to perform the tasks that we have always performed. Let Ea, who is skillful in all crafts, prepare the plans for Babylon, and we will be the workers."

Marduk's heart filled with joy to hear their response. "I will collect blood and create bones," he said to Ea, "and from them, I will create a savage and call him 'man.' His job will be to serve the gods so that they may rest at ease."

Ea, the wise, replied, "Call the gods to assembly. Tell them to give us the god who led Tiamat to rebel. Let that god perish so that human beings can be formed out of his blood."

When Marduk had assembled the gods, he said, "Declare under oath who among you devised the revolt and led Tiamat to rebel. Deliver him to me to take the responsibility, the blame, and the punishment upon himself. The rest of you will then be able to live in peace."

The gods who had rebelled revealed that the instigator of their revolt had been Kingu. Then they bound him and presented him to Marduk and Ea.

Ea killed Kingu, severed his blood vessels, and fashioned the first human beings out of Kingu's blood. Then Ea explained to them that the purpose of their lives was to serve the gods.

The gods had now been freed for a life of ease. But first, in order to honor Marduk and thank him for saving them, they worked for two years to construct Babylon, their earthly home. When the temple was completed, the gods gathered within its walls and celebrated. Then they praised Marduk's destiny.

"May Marduk rule unsurpassed among the gods," they declared. "May he shepherd the human race that he created. May he establish for them the rites of religious worship: the food to be offered, the incense to be smelled, and the sacred spells to be recited. May all human beings remember to praise and revere Marduk to the end of days. May they serve and support their gods and tend their sanctuaries without fail. May they improve their lands, build their shrines, and remember the Mother Goddess."

The gods concluded their celebration by proclaiming the fifty names and qualities that Marduk possessed, for they wished to honor their supreme god's glorious ways and deeds. Finally they said, "Let the shepherd and the herdsman rejoice in Marduk so that their lands may be fertile and they may prosper. The command of Marduk is unalterable; whatever he says, no god shall change. Vast is his mind, and broad is his sympathy. Yet when Marduk is angry, no god can withstand his wrath. Let Marduk's command be supreme, both in the heavens above and upon the earth below, for Marduk has destroyed Tiamat and has achieved everlasting kingship."

Introducing Osiris, Isis, and Horus

Historical Background

Civilization developed in Egypt between 4000 and 3000 B.C. The years between 3500 and 2500 B.C. were a Golden Age in which Egypt flowered politically, economically, and artistically. In about 3000 B.C., Upper Egypt and Lower Egypt united, becoming the first great nation of the Western world. About that time the Egyptians invented *hieroglyphics*, a kind of picture-writing, which permitted them to record their thoughts and thus establish a written heritage. By 2500 B.C., Re, the sun god, was the principal god, and the belief in Osiris, god of life, death, and resurrection, was widespread and of major importance. The great pyramids also had been constructed by that period, and the *Pyramid Texts* recorded important religious ideas.

In the years between 3500 and 2500 B.C., the political, economic, and religious climate in Egypt was very different from that in Mesopotamia, the other great ancient civilization of the West. Separated from the rest of the ancient world by large expanses of desert and by the Mediterranean Sea, the Egyptians lived in cultural isolation for many hundreds of years.

Until about 1700 B.C., civilization in Egypt proceeded without serious disruptions or significant outside influence. Egypt was more politically stable than Mesopotamia, so the people could concentrate on improving the quality of their lives. The Egyptians also kept to themselves economically. While the cuneiform (wedge-shaped) script of the Mesopotamians was adopted by many of the communities with which they traded, Egypt's economic isolation meant that its system of writing was not adopted by other peoples.

The differences between the physical environments in which the Mesopotamian and Egyptian civilizations developed led to profound differences in religion. In Egypt, the Nile River flooded and subsided with a predictable regularity. In Mesopotamia, the Tigris and Euphrates rivers would flood fiercely and unpredictably, widely changing their course from one year to the next and destroying everything in their paths. While Egyptians feared that these waters would dry up permanently and wither their culture, their fears had much less substance than the fears of those who lived in Mesopotamia. Thus, the Egyptians envisioned gods who were inevitably more benign than those of the Mesopotamians.

Egyptian Religion

Religious ideas permeated Egyptian politics, science, art, and literature. Like most ancient peoples, the earliest Egyptians prayed to their gods for children, success in farming and hunting, and success in war. However, from earliest times, the Egyptians also believed in the divine aspect of human beings and in the idea that when a human being died, he or she left life on earth and began life in another world. In addition, the ancient Egyptians believed that their king, the pharaoh, was god and man combined. He was both king and priest, both a human being and the son of the sun god.

The great pyramid tombs of the kings and queens of Egypt have survived to this day to testify to the Egyptian belief in the afterlife. The tombs contained not only mummified corpses but everything the ruler would need in the next life. The tomb of King Tutankhamen, a tomb that had been fortunate enough to escape grave robbers, revealed an incredible wealth of material: sculptures, wall paintings, and writings describing daily life, furniture, household utensils, wigs, jewelry, games, and musical instruments. Many of the golden and jeweled burial objects reveal a beauty and intricate design unequaled among the civilizations of the ancient world—and unsurpassed to this day.

The Nile was the lifeblood of the ancient Egyptians. Its waters created lush, fertile farmlands. Vegetation flourished along the banks of the mighty river, supporting the lives of animals and human beings.

In contrast, the desert was the great environmental enemy of the ancient Egyptians. It represented death, for human beings could not survive in such a hot, dry wasteland. It sheltered wild, poisonous animals and many evil spirits. The desert appeared to lie in wait, threatening to grasp the Egyptians in its clutches. Every summer, the intense heat and desert winds would cause the Nile to become slow and narrow. Although their river's flood cycle was predictable, the fear of death from famine haunted the earliest Egyptians. The nearby desert reminded these people that their existence was fragile. So the annual flooding of the Nile caused great relief and celebration. Water brought the rebirth of the land and provided sustenance and survival to human beings.

From earliest times, Osiris was the god of grain and of the Nile; like the Nile, he nourished all life. In his own and neighboring lands, he taught people what grains to cultivate, how to irrigate the land, and how to prevent unwanted flooding. Just as the Nile flooded, dried up, and flooded again, so Osiris lived, died, and was reborn. His death represented the death of vegetation when the Nile dried up. (The fact that Set dismembered Osiris is not significant, for that was a common ancient burial custom.) Osiris' regeneration represented the rebirth of vegetation when the Nile flooded in the spring.

Osiris was both god and man. The son of a god, Osiris was king of Egypt and the earth, and he caused both to be fertile and to prosper. Osiris lived and died, just as all human beings do. After Osiris' death his father, Re, who was the great god of the sun, made Osiris king of the gods and king of the Other World. Osiris' resurrection gave the ancient Egyptians the hope that they could share his destiny. Just as the gods had helped Osiris return to life, so they would help human beings who had led good lives gain life after death.

The worship of Osiris was particularly significant because it turned the ancient Egyptian people away from cannibalism. Once they came to believe that the human being was part divine, they viewed living humans with more respect and the human corpse as sacred. Once they came to believe that the key to immortality was to have lived a good life on earth, the quality of their relationships with one another improved immeasurably.

Osiris was a particularly appealing god because he had also been a man.

Because he had suffered and died, he could understand and sympathize with the suffering and death of each human being. Because he was a god, he could help people in both this world and the next. Osiris began as the example of a man who, with the help of the gods, regained life after death. In the course of time, he became the god who caused the person who died to achieve resurrection.

Horus, Osiris' son, became Osiris' counterpart on the earth once Osiris became lord of the Other World. In effect, Horus was a form of the resurrected Osiris. He inherited his father's kingdom and restored the order, justice, and prosperity that had existed under his father's reign. Horus was called the avenger of Osiris because he had performed the tasks involved in resurrecting his father's body. As Osiris' son, Horus acted as an intermediary between Egyptians who were destined to die and Osiris, who could grant them immortality.

The spirit of the newly dead person would appear before Horus and tell the god all of the good deeds that he or she had performed in life, to show why that individual deserved resurrection. Osiris would then take the person's heart (symbolizing conscience) and place it on one side of a great balance scale, with a feather (symbolizing law) on the opposite side. A jury would watch the balance of the scale, and the god Thoth, lord and maker of law, would record the result.

A person who had led a good life would have a heart lighter than the feather and would be granted new life in Osiris' kingdom, where he or she would live just as on earth. If the heart weighed more than the feather, the jackal that was sitting near the scale would eat the person's heart and

mummy, and he or she would remain dead. Thus, Osiris was also the god of truth and judge of the dead. He conducted this trial, which rewarded the virtuous and punished evildoers.

Isis, Osiris' sister and wife, was the greatest goddess in Egypt. She was called the Great Goddess, the Mother Goddess, the lady of green crops, and the lady of abundance. She represented both the loving and loyal wife and the loving and nurturing mother. As an earth goddess, Isis created every living thing and nourished and protected all that she had created. Like Osiris, Isis was a human being as well as a goddess. Her persistent search for the body of Osiris and her trials while she reared Horus in the papyrus swamps endeared her to the Egyptian people. Once Isis was reunited with Osiris, she remained in the Other World with him, giving life and food to the dead.

Set, Osiris' brother and enemy, represented the evil in the universe: natural catastrophes—such as earthquakes and storms—darkness, destruction, and death. He was the god of the desert through which he wandered. Naturally, Set plotted against Osiris, Isis, and Horus because they represented the forces of good. Good triumphed over evil in that Set could not destroy Osiris and Horus, no matter how cleverly he tried. Yet the gods did not destroy Set either. Evil would continue to exist in the world.

Between 2500 and 1500 B.C., Osiris gradually became as important as Re, the god of the sun. By 1850 B.C., the great religious festival of Osiris was held annually at Abydos, in Upper Egypt, where Isis had found Osiris' head. The focus of the Abydos festival was the dramatic presentation of the story of Osiris: his death and dismemberment, the finding of the pieces of his corpse, and his return to life. There Horus had resurrected Osiris' body, and there the door to the Other World was located. Therefore, the dead person was judged at Abydos and was either permitted to enter the Other World or condemned to eternal death. Wealthy Egyptians chose to be buried there.

Appeal and Value

It is clear from the earliest existing writings of the Egyptians that the story of Osiris, Isis, and Horus was very well known. Numerous references to parts of the story exist in ancient Egyptian sources, the *Pyramid Texts* and *The Book of the Dead*. However, either the ancient Egyptian writers saw no need to retell such a popular tale, or the narratives that once existed have long since disappeared. The only existing narrative of the entire story is that of the Greek Plutarch, who wrote *De Iside et Osiride* in about A.D. 70. Considering that the story may well have been 4,000 years old by that time,

it is amazing that Plutarch's Egyptian sources were so accurate.

The fact that this myth continued to live in a form so close to the original for many thousands of years testifies to the appeal of the values it contains. The love and loyalty a wife feels toward her husband have appealed to countless generations of human beings in cultures across the face of the earth. These values are as alive today as they were in ancient Egypt and in Plutarch's day. Equally appealing and enduring are the love and protection that a mother gives her child.

Moreover, throughout history, human beings have had to confront the forces of evil in the universe. Like Set, evil can be conquered temporarily, but it cannot be destroyed permanently. Our history books and our own experiences confirm this to be true. Finally, people have always feared their mortality and wanted to avoid death. The myth of Osiris provided Egyptians with hope for life after death.

Osiris, Isis, and Horus

Nut, goddess of the sky, was very beautiful and kind. She was married to Re, god of the sun and creator of all. But she also made love to her brother, Geb, god of the earth, and Thoth, lord of divine words. When Re discovered that Nut had secretly slept with Geb, his heart filled with rage and he cursed his wife. "You will not give birth to the child that is within you in any month of any year!" he exclaimed.

Nut's kind heart filled with sorrow at the thought that she would not become a mother. Tearfully she approached Thoth and said, "Re has cursed me so that I cannot give birth in any month of any year! Is there anything you can do to help me? Surely, one of the children within me is yours!"

Thoth replied, "Do not spoil your beauty with your tears. Instead, let good cheer chase your grief from your heart. Trust me to find a way to help you. I promise that before the next year begins, you will be called Mother of the Gods!"

Thoth's eyes sparkled as he left Nut and went off to find Moon. "Since you love to play games," he said to Moon, "I will agree to play as many games as you like if you will help me. Every time I win, I want you to give me a small part of your illumination. You will never miss the light, but it will be very useful to me. Do you agree?"

"I do not mind at all," Moon replied, "as long as you take very little light each time."

So it came to pass that Thoth and Moon played many games in the course of the next months. As they had agreed, whenever Thoth won a game he took from Moon a small part of her illumination. He then put this fragment of light aside and saved it.

Finally, Thoth had collected so many fragments of light that, when he put them together, they created five complete days. Thoth then added the five days he had won from Moon to the normal solar year of 360 days.

In this way, Thoth avoided the curse that Re had placed upon Nut. When the solar year came to an end, Nut gave birth to five children, one on each of the extra five days that Thoth had created. As Thoth had predicted, from that time on Nut was known as Mother of the Gods.

Re was the father of both Osiris, who was born on the first of these five days, and Horus the Elder, who was born on the second day. At Osiris' birth a voice called out from the heavens, "The good and great King Osiris, lord of all the earth, has been born!"

Geb was the father of both Set, who chose to be born on the third day, and Nephthys, who was born on the fifth day. Set showed his aggressive spirit from the moment of birth. While Nut's four other children were born at the proper time, Set chose the time and manner of his own birth. He cut an opening in his mother's side and forced his way into the world. In time, he married his sister Nephthys.

Thoth was the father of the Great Goddess Isis, lady of green crops, who was born on the fourth day. Thoth was the most intelligent of the gods. He was called lord of divine words because he possessed the magical power to compel whomever he chose to listen to and obey the words he uttered. Thoth taught his daughter something of this power. Isis and Osiris loved one another from the time they shared their mother's womb. In time, they became husband and wife.

Osiris became king of Upper and Lower Egypt and earned lasting fame for himself and his subjects. When he began his rule, his people were nomads. They lived a simple life, wandering from place to place and gathering the fruits of the earth. Osiris united these tribes and taught them to be a highly civilized people. First he made his subjects more industrious. He taught them the arts of farming so they could acquire more and better foods from the earth. Then Osiris gave his subjects a body of laws so they could live and work together in peace. Finally, he taught his subjects to revere and worship the gods. Osiris was the ideal king, and his rule created a Golden Age in Egypt.

When Osiris had improved the lives of his own people in these ways, he traveled to other parts of the world to convince the inhabitants to accept his ideas. He persuaded his listeners by entertaining them, setting his ideas to music and singing hymns and songs.

While Osiris was away from Egypt on these ventures, Set searched for an opportunity to take over the country. He was unable to succeed, for Isis and her father sensed his ambition and watched him carefully.

After Osiris returned, Set became even more determined to rule Egypt. One night, while Osiris was asleep, Set secretly measured the king's body. He then commanded his craftspeople to construct a wooden box that would fit Osiris. He ordered the best artists in the land to decorate it so beautifully that it would be a work of art. Finally, he convinced seventy-two of Osiris' subjects to join him in planning a revolt.

Soon thereafter, Set entertained the conspirators and Osiris at an elaborate feast. At the end of the meal, he had his servants bring the beautiful wooden box into the dining hall. As he had anticipated, the box was admired by all of his guests.

Pretending to jest, Set announced, "Whoever among you would like to own this beautiful box should climb into it. I promise to give it as a gift to the person whose body is a proper fit. However, your body must fit exactly when you lie down. If you are so tall that your head or your legs overhang the box, or if you are so short that your body leaves a space at the head or foot of the box, then you will not qualify for the gift."

As Set had planned, his dinner companions eagerly gathered around the beautiful box, each awaiting his turn to try it. One after another, each guest climbed inside the box and attempted to lie down as Set had directed. But no one fit exactly. Some were too tall; others were too short. Finally Osiris took his turn. He climbed into the box and lay down inside it. He was an exact fit.

Osiris had hardly settled himself inside the box when the conspirators quickly picked up the cover, placed it upon the box, and nailed it down, imprisoning the unsuspecting king. To make certain that Osiris would suffocate, they poured melted lead over the box. Then they carried the box to the Nile River and dumped it into the water. The current carried the box to the mouth of the Nile, where it became lodged in the papyrus swamps in the eastern part of the delta.

The people who lived near the city of Chemmis were the first to hear about the murder of Osiris, and they spread word of Set's terrible deed. When Isis heard about Osiris' death, her heart overflowed with grief. She immediately cut off one of her locks as a sign of mourning and put on the clothing worn by a woman whose loved one has died. Then she set off in search of the box.

As the Great Goddess wandered tirelessly from place to place throughout Egypt, her mournful cries interrupted farmers laboring in their fields, craftspeople working in their shops, and even those who slept soundly at night. Isis walked from town to town, questioning everyone she met. Finally, she found a group of children who had watched the box drift into the papyrus swamps at the mouth of the Nile, and they told her the direction it had gone.

Isis eventually learned that the box finally had become lodged among the branches of a tamarisk bush in the papyrus swamps near Byblos. This bush had grown into a very large tree, and the box had been completely enclosed within the tree's trunk.

The king of the country, Melcarthus, was unaware of the box. When he heard of this large tree, he had his servants chop it down and bring it to his palace. Trees of great size were rare in his country, and he had a specific use for its huge trunk. He placed it in the center of his dining hall to help support the roof of his palace. The use of this tree trunk as a column was talked of far and wide.

So it came to pass that Isis heard about the fate of the large tamarisk tree. She traveled to the town near King Melcarthus' palace and seated herself beside the fountain where women came to draw water for their households. The goddess sat there in silence until Queen Astarte's handmaidens arrived for water. Then she spoke with them in a very kind, friendly fashion. She braided their hair for them and perfumed them with the aroma of her own body.

The handmaidens returned to their queen with the exciting news of the strange woman they had met by the fountain. Queen Astarte immediately announced to her servants, "I want to meet this marvelous stranger who can transfer her own perfume to the hair and skin of other people! Go to the town fountain quickly, before she leaves. Find her, and bring her to the palace at once!"

So it came to pass that Isis entered King Melcarthus' palace and met the queen. Queen Astarte was so delighted with Isis that, before long, she asked the Mother Goddess to become the nurse of one of her sons. In time, Isis told the queen her story and asked for permission to cut open the pillar that supported the roof of the palace. With the queen's permission, she did so and removed the box without harming the ceiling.

Once Isis was alone, she fell upon the box with loud cries of mourning. Then she took leave of the royal family and returned to Egypt, taking the sealed box with her.

Upon reaching a remote place in the desert, Isis stopped and opened the box. The sight of her beloved husband, lying still and lifeless, was more than her heart could bear. The Great Goddess placed her face against the face of Osiris, embraced his body, and wept with grief. Then she placed the wings of a bird upon her arms and hovered over Osiris, flapping her wings in order to create air for him to breathe.

Finally, using knowledge that her father, Thoth, had taught her, she skillfully uttered the magical words of power in a way that she knew would bring temporary life to Osiris. Osiris returned to life! With delight, Isis embraced her great love and enjoyed him for as long as she could. Then, when Osiris once again lay lifeless and still, Isis replaced his body in the box. She carefully hid the box in a remote, isolated place where it would be safe from harm.

In time, Isis gave birth to Osiris' son, whom she named Horus. As she gazed upon her newborn child, the Mother Goddess' heart overflowed with joy. She hoped that one day Horus would avenge his father's death and would inherit his kingdom.

Shortly thereafter Thoth, lord of divine words, visited his daughter. "Listen to my counsel, Isis, and obey me," he said. "Those who follow the advice of another live and prosper. You must now escape from the eye of Set, and I shall help you. If you will hide your child from Set until he is grown, he will become doubly strong. Then he surely will avenge the death of his father and will sit upon his father's throne.

"However," Thoth continued, "until that time comes, Horus will never be far from danger. Therefore, I shall teach you the words of power that will protect Horus from death on earth, in the world above, and in the Other World."

Isis obeyed her father's counsel. That evening, she left the house with Horus and seven scorpion-helpers. The Mother Goddess said to them, "My child and I are all alone in the world. Because of the death of my husband, my sorrow surpasses the grief of anyone in Egypt. So turn your faces to the ground and take me to a hidden place where I may rear my child in safety and in peace."

With three of the scorpions leading the way, Isis brought Horus to an island in the papyrus swamps of the Nile delta. There she secretly nursed and reared her child. Isis would often hide Horus among the papyrus plants while she went into a nearby city to acquire food for herself and her child.

"Have no fear, dear Horus, my glorious son," she would croon. "Your grandfather and I shall keep every evil thing from you, for you are the father of all that is yet to be created. You shall be in no danger, either on land or in the water. The sting of the most poisonous snake will not kill you, nor will the strongest lion be able to crush you. For you are the son of Osiris and Isis, and in time you will become lord of all the earth as your father was before you!"

Yet one day when Isis returned from the city, she found Horus lying lifeless and still with the mark of a scorpion bite upon him. She immediately recognized the treachery of Set. Isis leaned over the body of her baby son and carefully began to chant the magical words that Thoth had taught her. As she intoned the words, the color gradually returned to Horus' face, and his limbs began to stir. By the time Isis finished, Horus was smiling up at his mother. The infant had been restored to life. He grew up to be a healthy young man, skilled in the arts of medicine that his mother taught him.

It came to pass that Set was hunting in the desert by moonlight one night when he accidentally came upon the box that Isis had hidden. He recognized it instantly and opened it at once. As he gazed upon the corpse of his rival, Set's heart filled with implacable hatred and rage. In a mad fury, the evil god tore the corpse of Osiris into fourteen pieces. Then Set traveled throughout the kingdom of Egypt, scattering the pieces of Osiris wherever his whim led him.

Not long thereafter, Isis heard about Set's latest attack upon Osiris. Her sister Nephthys, although married to Set, was always loyal to Isis. Therefore, Nephthys accompanied Isis and Horus on the search for Osiris. They sailed up and down the Nile in a papyrus boat, and wandered throughout the country until they had located the various fragments of Osiris' body. Wherever they found a piece, Isis collected it. Then she buried a small figurine of Osiris at that spot and placed a tomb over it. She hoped that this device would mislead Set and give them the time they needed to find and heal Osiris.

When Isis found Osiris' head at Abydos, she possessed all fourteen pieces of his body. With Nephthys to help her, Isis set to work at once. First, they arranged Osiris' head, torso, limbs, heart, and organs as they would be in life. Next, the goddesses connected the various parts with wax. Then, they prepared a long piece of linen cloth by smearing sweet-smelling ointments upon it and sprinkling it with spices that would preserve Osiris' body from decay. Finally, they wrapped Osiris' body in the treated linen cloth and buried it.

Once Osiris was properly buried, Horus prepared to do his part to return his father to life. He led Isis and Nephthys to the world of the dead, where they found Osiris. Then the two goddesses pronounced the magical words of power that would bring Osiris new life. Gradually, the dead god came back to life; he began to breathe, his eyelids fluttered, and he moved his limbs.

Horus then removed his eternal eye, placed it in his father's mouth, and directed him to swallow it. Osiris immediately became much stronger and regained the ability to see, speak, and walk. With the help of Re, Horus set up a ladder so tall that it reached from the Other World up to the world of the gods above the earth. Osiris slowly climbed up to join the gods, with Isis leading the way and Nephthys behind him. The gods welcomed Osiris warmly, for they were delighted to have him living among them once again.

Once Osiris had rejoined the gods, Re made him king of the gods and king of the Other World. Horus then became king of Upper and Lower Egypt in his father's place.

Now that Horus had taken his place among the gods, Osiris decided that the time had come to deal with Set. He tested Horus' readiness to avenge his father's murder.

"What is the most glorious deed a man can perform?" Osiris asked his son.

Horus replied, "To take revenge upon one who has injured his father or mother."

"What animal is most useful to a warrior?" his father asked.

"A horse," said Horus.

"Why not a lion?" his father asked in surprise.

Horus replied, "A lion is more powerful, but a horse is much quicker. Therefore, a horse can help a warrior capture a fleeing enemy better than a lion can."

Osiris was pleased to hear his son's responses, for they showed that he was mature enough to fight Set. Osiris then taught Horus how to use weapons of war and encouraged his son to take vengeance upon Set.

Horus and Set did fight each other, first in the form of two men and then in the form of two bears. The battle was so fierce that it lasted for three days and three nights. Osiris, Isis, and Thoth watched its progress. Joy flooded their hearts when Horus finally won and took Set prisoner.

But once Horus had conquered Set, Isis suddenly felt great pity for him. In her sympathy for her fallen enemy, Isis used her father's magical power with words. "Drop your weapons, Horus!" she cried.

Horus found himself powerless to resist. In spite of his own intentions, his weapons fell to the ground. Set was free!

Horus' heart filled with sudden rage and hatred toward his mother. "How can you do this to me, Mother?" he cried. "How can you let her do it, Grandfather?

Father, did you train me to win, only to see me lose in my moment of victory? Set has been our enemy for so long! He is evil, and his ways are cruel beyond imagining!"

No one replied to Horus' accusations. He watched, helpless, as Set ran away. In a fury, Horus then tore after Isis like a panther chasing its prey. When he caught her, he fought as fiercely as he had fought with Set. Finally, Horus cut off her head.

Thoth immediately used his magical words of power to change his daughter's head into the head of a cow, and he quickly attached it to her body. Horus then knew that Set would have to remain free, at least for the time being. He would conquer him, but in some other way.

Set was still determined to become king of Upper and Lower Egypt. He next tried to acquire the throne by accusing Horus of being Isis' illegitimate child and, therefore, not the legal heir to the kingdom. However, when the gods met in assembly to discuss the matter, Thoth convinced them that Horus was indeed the legitimate child of Isis and Osiris. The lord of divine words brought forth a great balance scale and weighed the testimony of Set on one scale and Osiris' defense on the other. When the balance registered in favor of Osiris, he, Isis, and Horus were recognized as speakers of truth, while Set was unmasked as a liar. As a result, Osiris became judge of the dead in the Hall of Judgment, weighing their testimony on the great balance scale just as Thoth had weighed his.

But Set did not give up. Twice more he challenged Horus, and twice more he lost in combat. At last he accepted Horus' right to rule Osiris' kingdom.

So it came to pass that the assembly of gods formally acclaimed Horus to be lord of all the earth as his father had been before him. Horus once again established order and justice, and with his reign prosperity returned.

Since he had been born from the seed of his dead father, Horus was chosen to be the intermediary between the living and the dead. Men and women would pray to him while they were still alive, asking him to notice their good lives and plead with Osiris for their resurrection after death.

Once Horus had inherited his father's kingdom, Isis remained with Osiris in the Other World and always accompanied him. She was satisfied and happy. Her husband had returned to life and love. Her son had avenged his father. The gods had proclaimed the truth of their words against Set's accusations. The kingdom of Upper and Lower Egypt was in good hands, and all was well.

Introducing **Telepinu**

This Hittite nature myth fits the pattern of the god who disappears, causing the earth to become barren. It contains the ritual for restoring the presence of the god and, with his presence, fertility.

Like other myths of its pattern, the Telepinu myth could account for the changing seasons in nature because it emphasizes the cycle of birth, death, and rebirth. If this is the myth's purpose, then it is not necessary to know the specific cause of Telepinu's anger, for presumably Telepinu will disappear whenever he becomes very angry, and something will anger him each year before the arrival of the winter season. (The first third of the Telepinu tablet was broken off and has never been found. Possibly that is why the story never reveals the cause of Telepinu's anger. However, at a later point in the story, Telepinu is given the opportunity to explain his behavior and chooses not do so.)

Some scholars think this myth was retold and the rituals reenacted whenever the Hittites wanted to expel the forces of evil from their communities. In many cultures, such "housecleaning" rituals were performed before the beginning of the new year or the spring planting season.

Telepinu

One day Telepinu, the god who made living things fertile, became furious and shouted, "I am so angry! No one should come near me!" He was so upset that he tried to put his right shoe upon his left foot and his left shoe upon his right foot. This made him even angrier.

Finally he fixed his shoes and stalked off. He took with him the ripening grain, the fertile winds, and the abundant growth in fields, meadows, and grassy plains. He went into the country and wandered into a secluded meadow that was sheltered among a grove of trees. There exhaustion overcame him, and he fell asleep.

Telepinu's rage upset the entire world of nature. Mist swirled over the countryside, fogging the windows of houses. Smoke invaded people's homes. In their fireplaces, the logs smoldered and would not burn. The sheep in the pens and the cattle in the barns ignored each other. The lambs and the calves were even neglected by their mothers. Cattle, sheep, and people no longer conceived. Even those already pregnant with new life could not give birth.

Corn, wheat, and barley no longer grew in the fields. All vegetation withered and died. Without moisture, the mountains and hills dried up. The trees also dried up and could bring forth no fresh growth. The pastures became parched, and the springs evaporated. Famine arose in the land; both human beings and gods feared that they would all die of starvation.

The great sun god prepared a meal and invited the thousand gods. They ate but could not satisfy their hunger; they drank but could not quench their thirst.

Tarhun, the storm god, looked among the many gods and became anxious about his son. "Telepinu is not here," he announced. "He has become angry and has taken with him every growing thing!"

The great gods and the lesser gods began to search for Telepinu. They wandered over hill and dale. They crossed lakes and streams. But they could not find him.

The sun god then sent forth the swift eagle, saying, "Go look for Telepinu. Search every high mountain! Search the deep valleys! Search the blue waves of the sea!"

The eagle searched far and wide but could not find Telepinu. Finally it returned to the sun god and said, "I have looked everywhere for Telepinu. I have soared over the high mountains, I have dipped into the deep valleys, and I have skimmed over the blue waves of the sea. I found no trace of the noble god Telepinu!"

The storm god became worried and angry. He went to his father and said, "Who has offended my son so that the seeds have dried up and everything has withered?"

His father replied, "No one has offended him but you. You are the one who is responsible!"

Tarhun responded, "You are wrong! I am not responsible!"

His father then said, "I will look into the matter. If I find that you are guilty, I will kill you! Now go look for Telepinu! "

Tarhun then approached Nintu, the Mother Goddess, and said, "Telepinu has become so angry that the seeds have died and everything has dried up. My father tells me that it is my fault. He intends to look into the matter, and he will kill me. What has happened? What shall we do? If Telepinu is not found soon, we shall all die of hunger!"

Nintu replied, "Calm yourself and do not be afraid. If it is your fault, I will correct it. If it is not your fault, I will also correct it. Meanwhile, go and search for Telepinu! Your winds can travel far and wide."

So Tarhun began to search for Telepinu. He went to his son's city and knocked at the gate of his house, but no one responded and the gate remained closed. Then he lost his temper and broke into Telepinu's house, but he still could not find his son. So he gave up and returned to Nintu. "I cannot find him at home," he said. "Where else should I search?"

Nintu replied, "Calm yourself. I will bring him to you. Bring me the bee. I will instruct it, and it will search for Telepinu." Tarhun did as Nintu requested and soon returned with the bee.

Nintu said to it, "Little bee, go and search for Telepinu! When you find him, sting his hands and his feet. Sting him until he springs to his feet! Then take some of your wax, and wipe his eyes and feet. Purify him and bring him before me!"

As Tarhun watched Nintu with the little bee, he said, "The great gods and the lesser gods have searched for Telepinu without finding him. How do you expect a bee to do any better than we did? Its wings are very small and weak, and it is a very small and weak creature. How can it succeed where the gods have failed?"

Nintu replied, "Despite your doubts, Tarhun, the bee will find Telepinu. Just wait patiently, and you will see!"

The bee left the city and searched everywhere for Telepinu. It searched the streaming rivers and the murmuring springs. It searched the rounded hills and the rugged mountains. It searched the barren plains and the leafless woodlands. The length of its journey was a great strain, and as the little bee flew it began to consume the honey and the wax within its body.

Finally, the bee found Telepinu as he lay asleep in a meadow amid a grove of trees. It stung his hands and his feet and finally aroused Telepinu from his deep sleep. Once he stood up, the bee took some of its wax and wiped Telepinu's eyes and his feet. After it had purified him, it asked him what he was doing sleeping in the meadow.

Telepinu replied furiously, "I simply became very angry and walked away. How dare you awaken me from my sleep! How dare you force me to talk to you when I am so angry!"

Telepinu grew still more enraged. He stalked about, causing further damage. He dammed whatever springs still bubbled. He made the flowing rivers overflow their banks, creating devastating floods. Water now flooded houses and destroyed cities. In this way, Telepinu caused the death of sheep, cattle, and human beings.

The gods became very frightened and asked, "Why has Telepinu become so angry? What shall we do? What shall we do?"

The great sun god then declared, "Let the goddess of healing and magic calm Telepinu's anger with her sacred chants! And fetch a male human being. Let him use his magic to purify Telepinu!"

The goddess of healing and magic chanted: "Oh, Telepinu, here lies sweet and soothing essence of cedar. Let what has been deprived be restored! Here is sap to purify you. Let it strengthen your heart and your soul! Here lies an ear of corn. Let it attract your heart and your soul! Here lies sesame. Let your heart and your soul be comforted by it! Here lie figs. Just as figs are sweet, even so let your heart and your soul become sweet! Just as the olive holds oil within it and the grape holds wine within it, so may you, in your heart and soul, have good feelings toward the king and treat him kindly!"

Telepinu came to her in a stormy rage. Lightning flashed and thunder rumbled upon the dark earth as he arrived.

Then the goddess of healing and magic chanted: "When Telepinu was angry, his heart and his soul burned like brushwood. So let his rage, anger, wrath, and fury burn themselves out! Just as malt is barren and cannot be used for seed or for bread, so let his rage, anger, wrath, and fury become barren! When Telepinu was angry, his heart and his soul were a burning fire. As this fire was quenched, let his rage, anger, wrath, and fury be quenched too!"

She concluded, "Oh, Telepinu, give up your rage, your anger, your wrath, and your fury! Just as water in a pipe cannot flow upward, may your rage, anger, wrath, and fury not return!"

When the gods gathered in assembly under the tree, the male human being said, "Oh, Telepinu, when you left the tree on a summer day, the crops became diseased. Oh Telepinu, stop your rage, anger, wrath, and fury! Oh, tree, you wear white clothing in the spring, but in autumn your clothing is blood red. When the ox goes beneath you, you rub off its hair. When the sheep goes beneath you, you rub off its wool. Now rub off Telepinu's rage, anger, wrath, and fury. When the storm god arrives and is fearfully angry, the priest halts his progress. When a pot of porridge starts to boil over, the stirring of a spoon halts its progress. May my words halt Telepinu's rage, anger, wrath, and fury!

"Let Telepinu's rage, anger, wrath, and fury depart!" the man prayed. "Let them leave the house, the window, the courtyard, the gate, the gateway, and the road of the king. Let them stay far removed from the thriving field, the garden, and the orchard."

He continued, "Let them go the way the sun god travels each night, into the Netherworld. The doorkeeper has unlocked the seven bolts and opened the seven doors of the Underworld. Bronze containers with metal lids and handles stand deep within the dark earth. Whatever enters them does not leave them because it perishes there. Let these containers receive Telepinu's rage, anger, wrath, and fury, and let them never return!

"I have purified Telepinu!" the man concluded. "I have removed the evil from his body. I have removed his rage, his anger, his wrath, and his fury!"

And so it came to pass. Telepinu returned to his house and cared again for his land. The mist left the windows, the smoke left the house, and the fire burned on the hearth. Telepinu let the sheep enter the fold and the cattle enter the pen. The mother cared for her child, the ewe cared for her lamb, and the cow cared for her calf. Telepinu cared for the king and the queen, giving them both long life and strength.

A pole was set up before Telepinu, and from it the fleece of a sheep was suspended. It signified abundance: plentiful grain and wine, fat cattle and sheep, and successive generations of children. It signified fruitful breezes and fertility for every living thing.

Introducing **Gilgamesh**

Historical Background

The epic of *Gilgamesh* was written down on clay tablets in cuneiform (wedge-shaped) script at least 1300 years before Homer wrote *The Iliad* and *The Odyssey*. However, the first of these tablets was not discovered until excavations at Nineveh, begun in 1845, uncovered the library of Ashurbanipal, the last great king of Assyria (668–627 B.C.). Among the 25,000 tablets was the Assyrian version of *Gilgamesh*.

The epic gained international importance in 1862, when an expert in cuneiform published an outline of *Gilgamesh* along with his translation of part of the Assyrian version of the flood. The similarity between the flood story in the *Gilgamesh* epic and the description of the flood in the Bible led archaeologists to intensify their search for more cuneiform tablets.

Today scholars have available tablets containing portions of the *Gilgamesh* epic from many of the ancient countries in the Middle East, dating from 2100 to 627 B.C.—including some recently found in the library of Ebla, the latest ancient kingdom to be discovered. Scholars believe that stories of the adventures of Gilgamesh that existed in the oral tradition of Sumer were first written down in approximately 2100 B.C.

Between 1600 and 1000 B.C., the epic had been inscribed in Akkadian (Babylonian), Hittite, and Hurrian translations, some following the Sumerian versions and some branching off into wider variations, but all keeping the Sumerian names of characters and gods. A priest by the name of Sin-leqi-unninni, who probably lived during this time, is given credit for creating the late Akkadian version of the epic. Scholars think that he took the available Sumerian tales and imposed a uniform focus upon them, so that a series of separate adventures became the dramatic story of Gilgamesh's search for immortality. Sin-leqi-unninni integrated the Sumerian flood story into the epic and also created the friendship between Gilgamesh and Enkidu.

Gilgamesh apparently was a real king of Uruk, in southern Mesopotamia, sometime between 2700 and 2500 B.C. At that period Sumer had city-states, irrigation, laws, and various forms of literature. The writings of the time reveal that the people valued justice, freedom, and compassion. The strong walls of Uruk are attributed to Gilgamesh, and he may well have ventured into the wilderness in order to bring timber to his region, for wood was a valuable building material that this region lacked.

The Sumerian view of the gods as unpredictable and therefore frightening reflects the unpredictable and disturbing nature of the world in which they lived. For example, the Tigris and the Euphrates rivers often radically changed their paths from season to season, a phenomenon that must have wreaked havoc on the farms and cities in the area. The flood in Gilgamesh is probably the specific, catastrophic flood that scholars think occurred in southern Mesopotamia in approximately 2900 B.C. It became a popular subject in the literature of the time.

Traces of an earlier, matriarchal religion remain in Gilgamesh as well as in the Enuma elish, the Babylonian creation epic. For example, the Temple of Anu and Ishtar belongs to Ishtar alone. The priestess from the temple who is chosen to civilize Enkidu is highly esteemed in her society. Her role in the temple closely connects her with the Great Goddess or Mother Goddess and sanctifies her sexual relationships.

In addition, Gilgamesh depicts Ishtar as a Great Goddess. When she wants Gilgamesh to marry her, he refuses because he knows that marriage to the Great Goddess will bring him certain death. He further insults Ishtar by listing the ways she has killed many of her previous mates. Ishtar becomes furious with Gilgamesh and retaliates by contriving to cause his death. However, his friend Enkidu dies instead, unwittingly serving as a substitute sacred king.

The Earliest Hero

Gilgamesh is an unusual hero in that his major quest has an intellectual purpose: the acquisition of knowledge. In addition to possessing courage, he must have great determination, patience, and fortitude in order to reach his destination. After enduring physical hazards, he must wage a battle against despair when he learns that he cannot become immortal. He must find experiences that make life worthwhile, and he must find ways of perpetuating his name. Later heroes start by accepting what Gilgamesh questions; they are born into societies that have already determined the acceptable ways in which a person can achieve fame and an immortal name.

Appeal and Value

Gilgamesh is the earliest major recorded work of literature, and Gilgamesh is the first human hero in literature. The epic has universal appeal among Western cultures because it reaffirms the similarities in human nature and human values across time and space. The epic reveals the importance of friendship and love, pride and honor, adventure and accomplishment, and also the fear of death and the wish for immortality. It speaks as clearly to us as it spoke to those who lived when it was written, almost 4,000 years ago.

Gilgamesh learns that the only type of immortality that he or any other mortal can achieve is lasting fame through performing great deeds and constructing lasting monuments. He also learns that life is precious and should be enjoyed to the fullest. What Gilgamesh discovers during his long and arduous journey, we too must learn in the course of our own lives.

Like Gilgamesh, we must fight the despair of failure and death. Like Gilgamesh, we must choose what we will value in life and have the freedom to make those choices.

Principal Characters*

GILGAMESH: king of Uruk who searches for immortality

LUGALBANDA: heroic father of Gilgamesh; earlier king of Uruk

NINSUN: goddess mother of Gilgamesh; priestess of Shamash

ENKIDU: best friend of Gilgamesh

HUMBABA: giant who guards the Cedar Forest of Lebanon

SIDURI: fishwife whom Gilgamesh meets on his journey

UTANAPISHTIM: king of Shurippak; survivor of the Sumerian flood

URSHANABI: Utanapishtim's boatman

*For a list of the Sumerian gods, see pages 152–53.

Gilgamesh

Chapter 1

Gilgamesh angers his people with his arrogance and selfishness. The gods create Enkidu to teach him humility.

Notice the strong walls of our city of Uruk! These walls were built by Gilgamesh on a foundation created in ancient times by the seven wise men, who brought great knowledge to our land. The top of our outer wall shines with the brightness of copper, but it is made of burnt brick. Now study the inner walls of our city. Examine the fine brickwork. These walls, too, surpass all others! No human being, not even a king, will ever be able to construct more impressive walls than Gilgamesh built around our city of Uruk! Now approach the majestic Temple of Anu and Ishtar. No mortal, not even a king, will ever be able to build a structure as beautiful as the one Gilgamesh created! Climb up and walk upon the walls of Uruk. Examine the fine brickwork. Admire the majestic Temple of Anu and Ishtar. Gaze upon one man's supreme achievement!

Who was the Gilgamesh who built these walls of lasting fame? Who was the Gilgamesh who built this most majestic temple? Gilgamesh was the renowned king of the city of Uruk. To his people, Gilgamesh was a tyrant who became a great hero.

Gilgamesh left his city to learn how to avoid death, and he returned having learned how to live. In the course of his travels, he saw everything throughout the land. Because he thought about what he had seen, he came to know everything that makes a person wise.

When Gilgamesh returned, he inscribed his travels and his thoughts upon stone tablets and placed these tablets on the strong walls of Uruk. He described the time before and during the great flood. He described his long, tiring journey in search of everlasting life. And he revealed the hidden mysteries of life and death that he had discovered. He wanted his knowledge to help his people improve their lives.

Read what Gilgamesh inscribed in stone upon the strong walls of the city of Uruk so that you, too, may gain wisdom.

Gilgamesh was two-thirds god and one-third man. His mother was the wise goddess Ninsun. His father was the noble Lugalbanda, a mortal who had also been king of Uruk.

Gilgamesh was such a godlike person that his people knew the gods had favored him. Nintu, the great Mother Goddess who had fashioned the first human beings out of clay, had also created Gilgamesh. Radiant Shamash, god of the sun, had given him great beauty. Adad, god of storms, had given him great courage. Ea, god of wisdom, had given him the capacity to learn from his experiences and to become the wisest of men. Yet, despite his goddess mother and all of his divine gifts, Gilgamesh was not a god, but a man. Therefore, he was doomed to share the common fate of all human beings, which is death.

When Gilgamesh was a young king, he was as willful and fearsome as a wild bull. He was the supreme wrestler and warrior. He knew no fear. He had no respect for tradition. He used the sacred drum as he wished. He did whatever he wished even when it hurt others. The fact that his behavior disturbed his companions did not restrain him.

Finally the nobles in Uruk became very distressed by Gilgamesh's behavior. They complained to one another, "Gilgamesh is incredibly arrogant, both day and night. Is this the way our king should act? It is true that the shepherd of our strong-walled city should be bold, but a king should also be majestic and wise! Gilgamesh interferes in the lives of his subjects beyond his right as king. Even in the households of his nobles and warriors, he intrudes between husband and wife, between mother and daughter, and between father and son."

The heavenly gods heard the complaints of the nobles of Uruk and met in assembly to discuss Gilgamesh's behavior. Anu, father of the gods, called the Mother Goddess before the assembly and said, "You created the hero Gilgamesh, mighty and wild bull of a man that he is! Now create an equally strong and courageous man, Enkidu, to be just like Gilgamesh. Make the spirit in Enkidu's heart like that of the warrior god, Ninurta, so that it will match the untamed spirit in Gilgamesh's heart.

"Then send Enkidu into Uruk, and let these two giants among men fight with one another. Enkidu will teach Gilgamesh his proper place in the world. Gilgamesh must be forced to recognize that, godlike though he is, he is not a god. Once he learns that he has limitations like all human beings, then the people in the strong-walled city of Uruk will be able to live in peace."

When she heard these words, Nintu conceived in her mind the image of a second heroic man, whom she created in the form of the god Anu. She washed her hands and pinched off a hunk of clay. Very carefully she drew the design she had envisioned upon it and threw the clay upon the broad, grassy plain a three-day journey from Uruk. Thus she created the hero Enkidu.

Enkidu came to life as a fully grown man. In some ways he looked as much like an animal as like a man, for his entire body was covered with shaggy hair. Long hair sprouted abundantly upon his head like rich fields of wheat. Like the god of cattle, he clothed himself in animal skins. Enkidu lived like a wild creature, away from the company of human beings and among the animals of the plain. He was aware of neither people nor land. Like his companions, the gazelles, he fed upon the grass of the plain. Along with the wild beasts at the watering place, he pushed for his turn to drink.

One day a hunter, who lived by trapping the wild animals, discovered Enkidu drinking at the watering place with the wild beasts. Amazed by the sight of such a strange human being, the hunter returned to the watering place on each of the following three days. Each time, he stared in fascination when he saw Enkidu among the wild animals. Each time, the sight of the mighty savage so frightened the hunter that he took his hounds and returned to his home, where he sat in silence, terrified of the wild man.

Finally the hunter said to his father, "For the past three days, I have seen a wild man at the watering place who appears to have come out of the hills. He is so strong that surely he is the mightiest in the land. In fact, the spirit of Anu, father of the heavenly gods, must live within his body! From what I have been able to observe of his habits, he seems to wander over the hills. He feeds with the gazelles on the grass of the plain, and he drinks at the watering place with the wild beasts who gather there.

"I am too afraid to approach him," the hunter confessed, "and yet he is robbing me of my livelihood. He fills in with dirt the pits I dig, and he tears up the traps I set. He releases the beasts and the smaller creatures of the plain whenever my devices catch them, and I can no longer capture any game!"

His father replied, "My son, the heroic King Gilgamesh lives in the strong-walled city of Uruk, which is only three days' journey from here. No one is mightier than he is! Even this wild man of whom you speak cannot possibly equal his strength! Gilgamesh is so strong that the spirit of Anu must live within his body!

"Therefore, you must go to the strong-walled city of Uruk and tell Gilgamesh about this mighty wild man. Bring back a priestess from the temple and let her educate this savage man in the ways of human beings. Let her meet him at the watering place. He will be attracted by her beauty. Once he embraces her, the beasts on the plain will regard him as a stranger and will associate with him no longer. He will be forced to become a human being."

The hunter took his father's advice and followed the road to the strong-walled city of Uruk. As soon as the king heard the hunter's tale, he sent a priestess from the temple to teach the wild man how to act like a human being.

After a journey of three days, the hunter and the priestess reached the home of the hunter. They spent the entire day sitting by the watering place, but Enkidu never appeared among the wild beasts. Early on the second day, the hunter and his companion returned to the watering place. They watched as the wild beasts and the creeping creatures came there to drink. Finally Enkidu, the mighty savage who was accustomed to feeding upon the grass of the plain with the gazelles and drinking at the watering place with the wild beasts, arrived.

"There he is!" the hunter exclaimed. "That is the savage man I have brought you to see! As soon as he sees you, he will approach you. Do not be afraid, for I am certain he will not hurt you. Let him get to know you, and teach him what it is to be a human being."

Enkidu was fascinated by the woman, and he spent six days and seven nights with her. He forgot the grassy plain where he had been born, the hills where he had roamed, and the wild animals that had been his companions. Later, when he was ready to rejoin the wild beasts of the plain, they sensed that Enkidu was now a human being. Even the gazelles drew away from him in fright.

Enkidu was so surprised by their change in behavior that, at first, he stood completely still. When he tried to rejoin them, he found that he could no longer run with the speed of a gazelle. He was no longer the wild man that he had been. However, he had gained something in return for the speed that he had lost, for he now possessed greater understanding and wisdom. He returned to the woman, sat down at her feet, and looked into her face attentively.

Chapter 2

Enkidu and Gilgamesh fight and become friends.

The priestess said, "Enkidu, when I look upon you now, I can see that you have become wise like one of the heavenly gods. Why do you still want to roam over the grassy plains with the wild beasts? Leave this wild country to the shepherds and the hunters, and come with me. Let me take you into the strong-walled city of Uruk, to the marketplace and to the sacred Temple of Anu and Ishtar. In Uruk you will meet the mighty King Gilgamesh. He has performed great heroic deeds, and he rules the people of the city like a wild bull. You will love him as you love yourself."

Enkidu's heart longed for a friend, so he said, "I shall do as you suggest. Take me to Uruk, where the mighty king Gilgamesh rules the people like a wild bull. I shall boldly address him and challenge him to a wrestling match. 'I am the strongest one!' I shall shout. 'I was born on the grassy plain, and my strength is mighty!'"

"Come then, Enkidu," the woman replied. "You must give up your wild ways and prepare to live like a man among other men. You must learn to eat the food other men eat, to wear the kind of clothes other men wear, and to sleep upon a bed instead of on the ground."

Placing her cape upon his shoulders, the woman took Enkidu's hand and, as a mother leads her child, led him into the nearby shepherd's hut. A number of shepherds immediately gathered around and offered him some of their bread and beer. But when Enkidu saw that the shepherds expected him to eat and drink as they did, he could only stare in embarrassment and gag at the unfamiliar refreshments. He could not bring himself to taste such food, for he had lived by sucking the milk from wild animals, and the strange smell and appearance of the bread and beer repelled him.

When Enkidu refused to eat the bread and drink the beer, the priestess said, "You must learn to eat this bread, for it sustains human life, and you must learn to drink the strong drink, for that is the custom in this land."

Enkidu accepted her advice, and when he had eaten and drunk he was happy. He then cut his hair, oiled his body, and put on the customary clothing of a man. He became truly human, and he looked like a young noble. "Before we leave for Uruk," he said, "I shall use my weapon to kill the wolves and the lions so the shepherds can rest at night."

Once Enkidu had done what he could to make the life of the shepherds easier, he and the woman began their three-day journey. "You will like the city of Uruk," she said to him. "The people dress in festive clothing as if each day is a holiday. The young men are strong and athletic, and the young women are perfumed and attractive.

"I shall point out Gilgamesh to you," she continued, "although you should recognize him. Like you, he enjoys life. He glows with manhood, and his whole appearance reveals his strength. He is stronger by far than you are, for he leads an active life both day and night. If he ever rests, no one is aware of it!

"Enkidu, you must curb your arrogance," the priestess warned. "Do not be too bold with Gilgamesh! Shamash, god of the sun, loves him. Anu and Enlil, who rule the heavenly gods, and Ea, god of wisdom, have made him very wise. Even before we arrive from the country, Gilgamesh will be expecting you, for he will have seen you in his dreams."

Meanwhile, Gilgamesh approached his mother, the wise and beloved goddess Ninsun, and told her his dreams so that she could explain them to him. "Mother," he began, "I dreamed last night that I walked among the nobles on a beautiful evening. As the stars in the heavens sparkled above me, one star, in form like Anu himself, fell out of the sky. This star-being landed right at my feet and blocked my path.

"When I tried to lift it," Gilgamesh continued, "it was much too heavy for me. When I tried to push it away, I could not move it. There the star-being stood, unconquerable, right in the middle of our strong-walled city! The people of Uruk rushed from their homes and gathered around it, while my companions, the nobles, kissed its feet. Much to my surprise, I loved this star-being! I placed my carrying strap upon my forehead, and with the help of my companions, I was able to lift it upon my back and bring it to you. However, when I placed it at your feet, you made it fight with me!"

Ninsun replied, "This star of heaven, in form like Anu himself, which suddenly descended upon you, which you could not lift and could not push away, which you loved, and which you placed at my feet and I made fight with you — this is, in fact, a man just like you, named Enkidu. He was born on the grassy plains, and the wild creatures have raised him. When Enkidu arrives in Uruk, you will meet him and embrace him, and the nobles will kiss his feet. Then you will bring him to me.

"Your heart will be joyful," Gilgamesh's mother continued, "for Enkidu will become your dearest companion. He is the strongest man in the land, with the strength of heavenly Anu. He is the kind of friend who will save his friend in time of need. The fact that you loved him in your dream means that he will always be your dearest friend. This is the meaning of your dream."

Then Gilgamesh said, "Mother, when I lay down again, I had another dream. This time, a strangely shaped axe lay upon the street within our strong-walled city, and all of the people of Uruk stood gathered around it. I loved it as soon as I saw it, so I picked it up and brought it to you. But when I placed it at your feet, you made it fight with me."

His wise mother replied, "Your second dream means the same as your first dream. The axe is the heroic Enkidu, who possesses the strength of heavenly Anu. When he arrives in Uruk, he will become your companion and your dearest friend."

Then Gilgamesh said, "It surely seems that, by Enlil's command, a dear friend and counselor has come to me, and I shall be a dear friend and counselor to him in return."

When Enkidu and the priestess were not far from the city, a strange man approached and looked as if he wished to speak with them.

"Please bring that man to me," Enkidu said to the woman. "I would like to know his name and why he has come."

The stranger said to Enkidu, "Our king, Gilgamesh, lives without any self-restraint. He thinks that he has the right to do whatever he chooses, without considering the rights of others and the traditions of our land. The assembly of the heavenly gods decreed at his birth that, as the king of Uruk, Gilgamesh would have the right to sleep with a bride on the first night of her marriage. Yet Gilgamesh has abused and extended this privilege. Therefore, the people of our city fear and resent him!"

When Enkidu heard this, his face became pale with anger. He said to himself, "When I meet this king who rules the people of Uruk like a wild bull, I shall teach him to know his proper place and to respect the rights and wishes of other people! "

Soon Enkidu entered the strong-walled city of Uruk, with the woman following close behind him. As he stood in the marketplace, the people of Uruk immediately gathered around the heroic-looking stranger and blocked his path.

"Why this man looks just like our king!" they exclaimed. "Look how similar his build is! He is not as tall, but his bones look stronger. The milk of the wild creatures has given him prodigious strength. Surely he is the mightiest man in our land! Now the clamor of weapons in contests of arms will echo throughout Uruk!"

The nobles rejoiced. "A godlike hero has appeared in our city as a match for our own great king! Godlike Gilgamesh has met his equal!" they proclaimed.

That night, when Gilgamesh was walking toward the Temple of Anu and Ishtar, the two great men met in the marketplace of the land. As the king approached the temple, Enkidu placed himself in the middle of the gateway, gathered his strength, and stuck out his foot to prevent Gilgamesh from passing through the gate. Amazed and angered, Gilgamesh wrestled with the presumptuous stranger. For a long while, the two giants fought one another like two bulls. They shattered the gateposts and made the wall shake.

Finally, Gilgamesh bent his knee to the ground and turned away from Enkidu. His fury suddenly left him, for he realized that this presumptuous stranger must be the Enkidu of his dreams. His dreams had revealed the truth, for Gilgamesh knew that he had indeed met his match in Enkidu.

When he saw that Gilgamesh had turned away, Enkidu said with the greatest respect, "Hail to you, Gilgamesh, whom Enlil has made king of the people! Your mother, the goddess Ninsun, has given birth to a great son! You tower over those you rule!"

The two men then embraced each other and became the dearest of friends.

Chapter 3

Gilgamesh and Enkidu prepare to travel to the Cedar Forest and to meet the evil giant Humbaba.

One day Enkidu's eyes filled with tears, for his heart was sad. Gilgamesh, hearing his friend sigh bitterly, said to him, "Enkidu, my friend, why do your eyes fill with tears, and why do you sigh with such bitterness?"

Enkidu replied, "I am crying for my lost strength. When I lived among the animals upon the grassy plain, I was swift and strong. Here in the strong-walled city of Uruk, my arms hang useless by my side. Inactivity has turned me into a weakling!"

"I know how to heal the grief in your heart," Gilgamesh replied. "The fierce giant Humbaba lives at the base of the Cedar Mountain, home of the heavenly gods in the Cedar Forest of Lebanon in the land of the living. Come with me to slay him, and then we shall have banished all evil from the land."

"You cannot mean what you are saying," Enkidu replied. "You can speak with great courage because you have never seen Humbaba. Although I have never seen him either, I learned from the wild creatures about the Cedar Forest and the evil giant who guards it.

"The forest extends over an area of 30,000 square miles," Enkidu explained. "Its span is so great that a person can enter it and never find his way out again. And as for Humbaba, the very thought of fighting that monstrous giant fills my heart with horror! Enlil, ruler of the heavenly gods, has appointed him watchman. He preserves the Cedar Forest by terrifying anyone who dares to enter it.

His face is as fearsome as a lion's. His dreadful roar resounds throughout the forest like a river that is swollen with flood. His teeth are those of a dragon, and flames issue forth from his mouth. With each breath he consumes every reed and tree in his path. Nothing that burns can escape being devoured by that monster! Why would you choose to pit yourself against a being who is more powerful than you are?"

"I know that it is my fate to die, sooner or later," Gilgamesh explained. "Before my life comes to an end, I would like to make a name for myself. So I intend to climb the Cedar Mountain! When those in time to come remember the great names of the past, I would like my name to be among them. I will bring the names of the heavenly gods with us, so that they too will be remembered."

"We cannot enter the Cedar Forest," Enkidu repeated. "Humbaba watches over the forest without ever resting. He can hear the wild cows when they are 200 miles away."

Gilgamesh responded, "My friend, who can reach heaven? Only the gods live forever with radiant Shamash. The days of human beings are numbered, and whatever they achieve is like the wind! Why do you fear death when, like all human beings, it is your fate to die? What has become of your heroic strength? Is it not better to do your best to gain fame than to wait patiently and quietly for the day of your death? Fame and glory will give life to your name even after your death.

"If you are still afraid to fight Humbaba," Gilgamesh continued, "then let me walk ahead of you while you encourage me to be brave. Even if I fail, I shall have made a lasting name for myself. People will say of me, 'Gilgamesh died fighting the fierce giant Humbaba!'"

"I shall not walk behind you, my friend," Enkidu replied. "While you are traveling toward the land of the living, I shall remain in the strong-walled city of Uruk. I shall inform your mother of your great glory. Let the wise goddess Ninsun proclaim your fame to all the people! I shall inform your mother of your impending death. Let the wise goddess Ninsun weep bitter tears as she grieves for her lost son!

"As for me, I do not choose to die," Enkidu continued. "I do not wish to be destroyed by fire. I am not ready to have the three-ply shroud cut. I am not ready to make that journey upon the Euphrates River."

Gilgamesh said, "Your fear fills my heart with sadness. With my own hands I shall kill Humbaba, cut down the cedars, and bring their fragrant wood to strong-walled Uruk. In this way, I shall make a lasting name for myself. I shall order the smith to forge new weapons for us: axes to chop and blades to shape the wood, and mighty swords to use against Humbaba. I wish to see this giant whose name fills our land with terror. I will overcome him in the Cedar Forest! Then all peoples will know how strong the King of Uruk is!"

Enkidu replied, "Oh, Gilgamesh, if your heart is set upon such an adventure and you are determined to enter the land of the living, then I will reluctantly accompany you. However, you must tell radiant Shamash. He is in charge of the Cedar Forest, and surely you will need his help."

So Gilgamesh chose two young goats, one white and one brown, and offered them to Shamash with a prayer. "Oh, heavenly Shamash, I wish to enter the

Cedar Forest of Lebanon in the land of the living, and I wish that you would help me."

"I know that your strength is great, Gilgamesh," radiant Shamash replied. "You are, indeed, a great warrior. But why are you attempting such an adventure? Why does the land of the living interest you?"

Gilgamesh tearfully answered, "Oh, radiant Shamash, please listen to my words. We human beings are not as blessed as the heavenly gods, for we cannot live forever. Every day in my city of Uruk, people die! When I look over the strong walls of my city, I see the Euphrates River bearing their dead bodies.

"Sooner or later even I, king though I am, shall have to face that fate. Even I shall have to make that last journey. Death makes the human heart heavy with grief. No matter how tall he is, a mortal cannot reach heaven. No matter how wide he is, a mortal cannot stretch over the earth.

"Yet before my life comes to an end," Gilgamesh concluded, "I would like to make a name for myself. I would like to enter the land of the living and climb the Cedar Mountain. When future generations remember the great names of the past, I would like my name to be among them. I will bring the names of the heavenly gods with me, so that your names too will be remembered."

Shamash heard Gilgamesh's words and accepted his tears as a sacred offering. The radiant god felt pity for Gilgamesh's human fate and was merciful to him. "I shall be your ally against Humbaba," he told Gilgamesh. "I shall confine in mountain caves the snake that poisons with its tongue, the dragon that scorches with its fire, the raging flood that destroys the land, and quick flashes of lightning that cannot be conquered. They will not be able to cause trouble for you during the course of your adventure."

When Gilgamesh heard the words of Shamash, his heart filled with joy. He called the elders of Uruk to assembly and informed them of his plan. They were not convinced by his enthusiasm.

"Your youthful spirit fills your heart, Gilgamesh," they said to their king, "but it has blinded your eyes to what you are doing. Listen to our counsel. We hear that the Cedar Forest extends over an area of 30,000 square miles. Who among human beings is brave enough to enter it? We hear that Humbaba is a creature to be feared. Who among human beings can face his weapons? The monster roars like a river swollen with flood, and his fiery breath brings death.

"Why do you want to face such a foe?" they asked. "You could not choose a more unequal contest! However, if we cannot convince you to change your mind, then go with our blessing. May your god, Shamash, protect you and bring you safely back to strong-walled Uruk! "

Gilgamesh knelt before radiant Shamash. Raising his hands in prayer, he said, "Heavenly Shamash, I am on my way. Guard my soul. Protect me and bring me safely back to Uruk. I am taking a road I have never traveled. I want to walk with joy in my heart."

Gilgamesh then set about recruiting some of his countrymen. "He who is responsible for a household, stay home!" he commanded. "He who is responsible for his mother, remain with her! However, if you are a single man and you would like to join me on this greatest of heroic adventures, I invite fifty of you to come along with me into the land of the living, where Humbaba guards the Cedar Forest. There we shall slay the monster and banish all evil from the land!"

The men of Uruk obeyed Gilgamesh. Those who were the support of their families stayed behind, while fifty youths prepared to accompany Gilgamesh upon the great adventure.

Gilgamesh ordered the metalsmiths to cast the enormous bronze axe that he would call his "might of heroism," along with axes and swords for all his companions. Then he ordered servants to cut wood from the apple, the box, and the willow trees to be fashioned into other weapons and tools. When all of the adventurers had been properly equipped, Gilgamesh's servants brought their king his weapons. They gave him his bow, a quiver full of arrows, and an assortment of cutting and shaping tools, and they placed his axe, the "might of heroism," and his sword upon his belt.

When the group was ready to leave, the people cried, "May you return safely to our city!"

Then the elders gave Gilgamesh their final counsel. "Do not put too much faith in your own strength, Gilgamesh. Permit Enkidu to travel the road in front of you, for he knows the way to the Cedar Forest and he is experienced in battle. Let Enkidu precede you through the forest and over the mountain passes. Let his eyes see clearly that he may protect himself and you, for the person who treads first protects the friends and companions who follow behind him.

"At night," they advised, "before you rest, you must dig a well so that the water in your waterskin will always be fresh. Remember to offer cool water to radiant Shamash, and never forget to honor your father, Lugalbanda. Then, after you kill Humbaba, you must remember to wash your feet as the gods require.

"May your god go with you, Gilgamesh," the elders concluded. "May Shamash heed your prayers. May he open before your feet the obstructed path, the closed road, and the formidable mountain. May the night bring you nothing to fear. May your father stay with you and protect you. May you live to attain your wish."

Then the assembled elders addressed Enkidu, saying, "We, the assembly, entrust our king to you. Protect your friend and companion, and return him to us safely."

Once they had received the blessing of the assembly of elder nobles, Gilgamesh said to Enkidu, "Let us go before my mother, priestess of Shamash. The great queen Ninsun, who possesses broad knowledge and great wisdom, will surely send us forth with her blessing."

Hand in hand, the two friends entered Ninsun's chamber. Gilgamesh said, "Mother, I have determined to make a great journey that will take me upon a strange road to the Cedar Forest and the home of Humbaba. There I face a battle whose outcome is uncertain, for I shall attempt to kill Humbaba in order to remove all evil from the land. Each day that passes from the day of my departure until the day of my return, pray to Shamash on my behalf, for he too hates evil."

Ninsun put on her ceremonial robe, placed an ornament upon her breast, and put a diadem upon her head. She climbed the stairs to the top of the temple-palace, where she stood upon the roof and offered incense to radiant Shamash.

Raising her arms to the god of the sun, Ninsun cried, "Why have you given me a son like Gilgamesh? Why have you given him such a restless heart? Why would you have him make such a journey upon a strange road? Why must he face Humbaba in the Cedar Forest?"

She prayed, "Oh, Shamash, I ask you to protect my son each day that passes from his departure until his return. And when at the end of each day you go to your rest, commend my son to the watchers of the night! Protect him in the Cedar Forest as he slays the fierce Humbaba, for he will remove all evil from the land, and you also hate evil."

Ninsun then smothered the incense and called to Enkidu, "You are not my own child as Gilgamesh is, mighty Enkidu, but I am now formally adopting you. Go with my blessing, and return safely to Uruk."

Chapter 4

Gilgamesh and Enkidu reach the Cedar Forest and kill Humbaba.

Enkidu then said to Gilgamesh, "Let us be on our way. Follow me, and have no fear in your heart. I know the road that Humbaba travels and the place where he lives."

Gilgamesh, Enkidu, and the young men walked a distance that would usually take six weeks in only three days. After sixty miles, they stopped to eat. When they had traveled another ninety miles, they prepared to spend the night. Then, before radiant Shamash they dug a well. They walked 150 miles each day and crossed seven mountains. Finally they arrived at the gateway to the Cedar Forest, which was guarded by Humbaba's watchman, whom they killed.

There Gilgamesh fell into a deep sleep. Enkidu prodded the king's body, but he did not awaken. He spoke to Gilgamesh, but he did not reply. "Oh, Gilgamesh," Enkidu cried, "how long will you lie here asleep? The young men of Uruk who have accompanied us are waiting for you at the base of the Cedar Mountain!"

At last Gilgamesh heard Enkidu's words and rose quickly to his feet. He stood upon the earth like a great bull, put his mouth to the ground, and bit the dust. Then he stood erect and clothed himself with words of heroism as if he were putting on his robe. "By the lives of my father, Lugalbanda, and my mother, Ninsun, who gave birth to me," Gilgamesh swore, "I shall not return to the strong-walled city of Uruk until I have entered the Cedar Forest in the land of the living and have fought with Humbaba, whether he is a man or a god! By the lives of my father, Lugalbanda, and my mother, Ninsun, who gave birth to me, may I achieve such glory that all who look upon me will view my deeds with wonder!

"Let us call the young men and hurry, Enkidu," Gilgamesh continued. "We want to find Humbaba before he travels beyond our reach."

Enkidu replied, "Oh, let us not walk deep into the Cedar Forest! When I opened this gate, my hands became weak. I no longer have the strength to protect either you or myself!"

"Do not be afraid, Enkidu," Gilgamesh assured his friend. "You know how to fight, and you are experienced in battle. If you will just touch my robe, you will not be afraid of death, and your hands and your arms will regain their former strength.

"Now, come!" Gilgamesh commanded. "Let us go forward and face this adventure together. Be of good courage! When we come face to face with Humbaba, if we are afraid, we will conquer our fear. Even if we feel terror, we will conquer our terror. The man who walks in front protects himself and his companion. Even if he dies in the process, he has made a lasting name for himself. The man who is a coward is not at peace with himself and leaves nothing behind to give him a good name."

They found themselves at the green mountain. Without further conversation, they stood still and looked around them. When they looked at the entrance to the Cedar Forest, they noticed the tremendous height of the cedar trees. They saw that the path that Humbaba was accustomed to walking was straight and clear. They looked upon the Cedar Mountain, which was the home of the heavenly gods. The face of the mountain was covered with a luxurious blanket of stately, shade-bearing cedar trees.

That night, Gilgamesh awakened Enkidu at midnight and said, "I had a strange dream, Enkidu. A mountain crumbled and fell upon me. Then a fine-looking man appeared. He pulled me out from under the mountain, gave me water to drink, and then helped me to stand upon my feet."

Enkidu replied, "Your dream is good, Gilgamesh. Humbaba is the mountain that fell upon you. We shall seize him, kill him, and toss his body upon the plain."

The next day, when they had walked sixty miles in the Cedar Forest, they stopped to eat. After another ninety miles, they prepared to spend the night. Then they dug a well before Shamash. Gilgamesh approached the mountain with an offering of a fine meal and said, "Mountain, bring me a dream."

Gilgamesh fell asleep with his head upon his knees. Once again he found himself wide awake in the middle of the night. "Enkidu, my friend," he said, "I have had an awesome dream! It is so disturbing that surely it is not favorable! I dreamed that I seized a wild bull of the plains. When I grabbed it, the bull stirred up so much dirt that the dust made the sky dark. Then the bull seized me and sapped my strength so that I was forced to retreat before it. But once I was at its mercy, the bull gave me food to eat and water from its waterskin to drink!"

Enkidu replied, "The wild bull of your dream, my friend, is really heavenly Shamash. When we need his help, he will hold our hands. It is he who let you drink from his waterskin. He watches over you, and he will bring you honor. In your dream, radiant Shamash is encouraging us to accomplish one thing that will be remembered after we have died. Certainly the deed must be to slay the monstrous giant Humbaba! "

Gilgamesh then said to Enkidu, "When we approach Humbaba, what should we do about his servants?"

Enkidu answered, "My friend, first capture the mother bird, for without their mother, where can the chicks go? Therefore, let us first kill Humbaba. We can find and kill his servants later, for like chicks, they will run frantically around in the grass."

Gilgamesh listened to the counsel of his friend. In order to attract Humbaba's attention, he lifted his axe and cut down one of the cedars.

Although they were more than two miles away from Humbaba's cedar house, the giant heard the noise and became furious. He left his house and fastened his eye, the eye of death, upon the two friends. He shook his head warningly and roared, "Who has come here? Who is damaging the precious trees that grow upon my mountains? Who has cut down one of my cedars?"

At the sound of Humbaba's roar, Gilgamesh suddenly trembled with fear. Enkidu saw the terror in his heart and said, "My friend, remember the words you spoke to the people of Uruk! Remember why we have made this journey! Now let courage enter your heart, and prepare to kill this monstrous giant!"

Gilgamesh gathered his courage and called out to Humbaba, "I, Gilgamesh, king of Uruk, have felled your cedar! By the lives of my father, Lugalbanda, and my mother, Ninsun, who gave birth to me, I have come to the Cedar Forest in the land of the living in order to fight you to the death and banish all evil from the land!"

Then Shamash from high in heaven spoke to Gilgamesh and Enkidu. "Approach Humbaba, and have no fear. Just do not let him enter his house." Shamash then hurled mighty winds upon Humbaba. Eight winds — the great wind, the north wind, the south wind, the whirlwind, the storm wind, the chill wind, the tempestuous wind, and the hot wind — arose against the fierce giant and beat against him from all sides so that he was unable to move in any direction.

Meanwhile, Gilgamesh, Enkidu, and the young men began to fell the cedars, trim their crowns, bundle them, and lay them at the foot of the mountain. When Gilgamesh had felled the seventh cedar, he found himself face to face with Humbaba.

Gilgamesh pushed the monstrous giant against the wall of his house and gently slapped his face as if he were pressing a kiss on him.

Humbaba's teeth shook with fear as he pleaded, "Heavenly Shamash, help me! I know neither my mother, who gave birth to me, nor my father, who reared me. In this land of the living, it is you who have been my mother and my father!

"Gilgamesh!" Humbaba then entreated. "I swear by the life in heaven, the life upon the earth, and the dead in the nether world that I shall subject myself to you and become your servant. I shall let you cut down my trees and even build houses with them."

As he listened to Humbaba's pleas, Gilgamesh felt pity for the giant. To Enkidu, the king said, "Should I not let the trapped bird flee the cage? Should I not let the captured man return to his mother?"

Enkidu said to Gilgamesh, "Do not listen to Humbaba's pleas! Do not let him talk you into freeing him, for he is a clever and dangerous enemy. He must not remain alive! The evil demon Death will devour even the greatest of human beings if he does not use good judgment. I assure you that if you let the trapped bird flee the cage, if you let the captured man return to his mother, then you most certainly will not return to Uruk and the mother who gave birth to you!"

"Enkidu," complained Humbaba, "you are only a servant and yet you have spoken evil words about me!"

However, Gilgamesh listened to Enkidu's wise counsel. He took his axe, the "might of heroism," and his sword from his belt. Then he struck Humbaba upon the neck. Enkidu also struck the monstrous giant upon the neck. With the third blow Humbaba fell to the ground, and Enkidu sliced off his head. For six miles round about, the cedars echoed the sound of Humbaba's body hitting the earth. Gilgamesh and Enkidu stood amazed that they had actually killed the watchman of the Cedar Forest of Lebanon.

Gilgamesh then continued into the forest, where he cut down Humbaba's cedar trees. The young men of strong-walled Uruk cut and tied them in preparation for their return to the city.

Chapter 5

Gilgamesh refuses to marry Ishtar, the goddess of love and fertility. She retaliates by sending the ferocious Bull of Heaven into Uruk. Gilgamesh and Enkidu kill the bull. Enkidu insults Ishtar and then becomes ill and dies.

When Gilgamesh returned to strong-walled Uruk, he cleaned and polished his weapons. He unbraided his dirty hair, washed it, and threw it back loosely over his shoulders. He then changed into clean clothes. Finally, he wrapped his royal, fringed cape about his shoulders, fastened it with a sash at his waist, and placed his crown upon his head.

When the goddess Ishtar saw Gilgamesh dressed in his royal clothing, she admired his great beauty and said to him, "Come marry me, Gilgamesh! You will be my husband, and I will be your wife."

She added, "I shall harness for you a jeweled and golden chariot, with golden wheels and brass borns. Storm demons will be your mighty steeds and will pull your chariot. The fragrance of cedar will greet you when you enter our house. Kings, princes, and nobles all will bow before you, kiss your feet, and bring you the fruits of the plains and the hills as tribute. Even the mountains and the plains will pay tribute to you. Your goats will give birth to triplets, your sheep to twins. Your colts will have the strength of burden-bearing mules. The horses that pull your chariot will be famous racers. The ox that pulls your plow will have no equal."

"And why should I marry you?" Gilgamesh asked. "You have harmed everyone you have ever loved! Listen, for I am happy to list your lovers for you. You loved Tammuz when you were young, but you left him and caused him to weep year after year. You struck the spotted shepherd-bird that you loved and broke his wing. Now, year after year, he stays in the orchards and cries, 'My wing! My wing!' Then you loved a stallion that was famous in war. First you whipped and spurred him into galloping twenty-one miles, and then you made him drink muddy water, causing him to die! His mother still weeps for him.

"Then," Gilgamesh continued, "you loved the herdsman who placed piles of ash-cakes at your feet, and every day he killed the finest of his goats for your pleasure. You rewarded his love by striking him and turning him into a wolf! His own shepherd boys drove him away from the flocks, and his hounds bit into his legs. Then you loved your father's gardener of the palm trees. Every day he brought you baskets of ripe dates for your table. You turned him into a mole and buried him in the earth, where he cannot move either up or down! If I let you love me, you would only treat me as poorly as you have treated all of your other lovers!"

Gilgamesh added, "You are like a pan of white-hot coals that go out in the cold. You are like a back door that fails to keep out the blasts of a tempest. You are like a palace that crushes the king within it. You are like a headdress that does not cover the head. You are like an elephant that shakes off its carpet. You are like pitch that blackens the one who carries it. You are like a waterskin that soaks the person who carries it. You are like a limestone rock that falls from the stone wall. You are like a shoe that pinches the foot of the one who wears it."

Ishtar became enraged as she listened to his words. She went up to heaven and tearfully complained to her father, Anu. "Father," she began, "Gilgamesh has hurled great insults upon me! He has recounted to my face all of my wicked deeds!"

Anu replied, "I believe that you started the quarrel and caused Gilgamesh to tell you of your shameful deeds."

Undaunted by his criticism, Ishtar pleaded, "Father, please give me the Bull of Heaven and let me use it to kill Gilgamesh. If you refuse, I shall break the bolts and smash the gates of the Underworld, letting them stand open. I shall cause the dead to rise to the world above, where they will eat among the living and outnumber them."

Anu replied, "If I give you the Bull of Heaven, there will be seven years of famine in the land of Uruk. Have you gathered and stored enough grain to feed the people through those lean years? Have you grown enough grass for all the animals?"

Ishtar said, "Yes, Father, I have stored grain for the people, and I have provided the beasts with grass to last seven lean years."

Then Anu gave Ishtar the Bull of Heaven, and the goddess led the bull into the strong-walled city of Uruk. When the bull snorted, pits opened in the earth and 200 young men of Uruk fell into them and died. With its next snort, more pits opened in the earth and 200 more young men of Uruk fell into them and died. With its third snort, the bull sprang upon Enkidu.

Enkidu leaped up and seized the Bull of Heaven by its horns. The bull foamed at the mouth and blew its foam into Enkidu's face. Then it struck him with the tassled end of its tail. Enkidu held fast, and Gilgamesh came to his aid. As the two heroes fought with the bull, Enkidu chased it and hung onto the thick part of its tail. Gilgamesh finally killed it by thrusting his sword between its neck and its horns. Then the two friends tore its heart from its body and dedicated it to Shamash.

Ishtar then climbed upon the strong walls of Uruk and shouted, "Woe to Gilgamesh, for he has insulted me by killing the Bull of Heaven!"

Upon hearing these words, Enkidu tore off the right thigh of the Bull of Heaven and threw it in the goddess' face. "If I could capture you as I captured this bull," he shouted to Ishtar, "I would treat you as I have treated it!"

Ishtar then gathered the temple women and mourned over the right thigh of the Bull of Heaven. Meanwhile, Gilgamesh gathered the armorers, the crafts-people, and the artisans and told them to take the parts of the bull they could use. Gilgamesh himself kept the valuable horns and hung them in his bedroom. He then made an offering of oil to honor his dead father, Lugalbanda.

Then the two friends washed their hands in the Euphrates River and rode together through the market street of Uruk. The people gathered to gaze upon them, and singers sang praises. Gilgamesh asked, "Who is the best of the heroes? Who is the most noble among men?"

The people replied, "Gilgamesh is the best of the heroes! Gilgamesh is the most noble among men!"

That evening Gilgamesh held a joyous celebration in the palace to mark their victory over the Bull of Heaven. During the night Enkidu had a dream. He awak-ened Gilgamesh and said, "My friend, listen to my dream. The great gods, Anu and Enlil, wise Ea, and radiant Shamash took counsel together. Anu said to Enlil, 'Because Gilgamesh and Enkidu have killed Humbaba and the Bull of Heaven, the one who removed the cedars from the mountain must die!' Enlil replied, 'Gilgamesh will not die, but Enkidu should die.'"

Enkidu's dream made him ill with fear. With the coming of day, he raised his head and wept before radiant Shamash. With tears streaming down his face also, Gilgamesh said, "Oh, dear Brother! Why would the gods spare me and punish you? Shall I sit down at the door of the spirits of the dead and never be able to see you, my dear brother, again?"

Enkidu cursed the events in his life that had brought him to the point of death. Raising his eyes, he said, "Oh, you gate to the Cedar Forest that hurt my hands! How I admired your size and your beautiful, fragrant cedar! Your wood is unsurpassed in all the land! Surely a master craftsman built you. But if I had known, oh gate, that your beauty would bring about my death, I would have set upon you with my axe and destroyed you!

"And Shamash," Enkidu continued, "I ask you to destroy the power and wealth of the hunter. May his life displease you. May the beasts escape from the traps he sets. May his heart be sad."

Enkidu then said, "I curse you, young woman of the temple, most of all and for all time to come! May you never have a house that pleases you. May you eter-nally be forced to live in the dust of the crossroad. May the desert be your bed. May you be unwelcome where other women gather. May the shadow of a wall give you your only comfort. May thorns and brambles tear your feet. May the ref-use of the road, the dirty and the thirsty, strike your cheek. May the drunkard soil with his vomit any place you enjoy."

When radiant Shamash heard these words, he called down from heaven. "Enkidu, why do you curse the young woman of the temple? She gave you food worthy of the gods and drink worthy of royalty. She clothed you with fine garments and led you to your best friend, Gilgamesh."

The god continued, "And has Gilgamesh not treated you like a king? He has given you a royal bed on which to sleep. He has seated you in comfort at his left hand. He has honored you and has encouraged the princes of the earth to kiss your feet. When you die, he will make the people of Uruk weep over you. Sorrow in their hearts will then overcome any thought of joy. He will make his people serve you even after your death. When you depart, Gilgamesh will let his hair grow long and will wander over the grassy plains clad in a lion skin."

When Enkidu heard the words of Shamash, his heart became calm. "I who have cursed you shall now bless you, woman of the temple," he said. "May kings, princes, and nobles love you. May you receive jewels and gold. May anyone who does not respect you be punished. May poverty find his storehouse and his home. May the priest let you enter the presence of the gods."

Still feeling sick, Enkidu lay down all alone. The next morning he said to Gilgamesh, "My friend, last night I had another dream. The heavens groaned, and the earth replied. While I was standing alone between heaven and earth, a young man with a very dark face and with claws like the talons of an eagle leaped upon me and overpowered me. Then he transformed my arms into the wings of a bird. He led me along the road of no return into the House of Darkness and Dust, which no one can leave once he has entered it."

Enkidu continued, "Those who live there dwell in eternal darkness, and there is no way to return to the land of the living. Their food consists of clay and dust. They are clothed with wings, like birds. I saw many people there who had been royalty during their lives on earth. All of the rulers I saw had removed their crowns, for they are of no use in the House of Darkness and Dust."

By the end of the day following Enkidu's unfavorable dream, he was ill. For the next twelve days he remained in bed, and his suffering increased. Finally he called Gilgamesh to his side and said, "The goddess Ishtar has cursed me! I shall not die honorably like one who falls in battle."

Gilgamesh cried, "May the bear, the hyena, the panther, the tiger, the deer, the leopard, the lion, the oxen, the deer, the ibex, and all the wild creatures of the plain weep for you. May your tracks in the Cedar Forest weep for you unceasingly, both night and day. May the Ula River, along whose banks we used to walk, weep for you. May the pure Euphrates, where we used to draw water for our waterskins, weep for you."

Gilgamesh continued, "May the nobles of strong-walled Uruk weep for you. May the warriors of Uruk weep for you. May those in Uruk who praised your name weep for you. May those who provided grain for you to eat weep for you. May those who put salve on your back weep for you. May those who put beer in your mouth weep for you. May the young woman of the temple who put fragrant oil upon you weep for you."

Gilgamesh's heart overflowed with grief and loneliness when Enkidu died. The king said, "Oh, elders of strong-walled Uruk, listen to me! I weep for my friend Enkidu. I moan bitterly like a wailing woman. An evil demon has robbed me of my dearest friend. He was like the bow in my hand, like the dagger in my belt, like the axe and the sword at my side, like the shield that protects me, like my ceremonial robe, and like my glorious royal decorations.

"Oh, Enkidu," Gilgamesh said to the body of his dead friend. "You chased the wild creatures of the hills and the panther of the grassy plains! Together we conquered all things! We climbed the mountains. We seized and killed the Bull of Heaven. We overthrew Humbaba, who lived in the Cedar Forest. What kind of sleep has come upon you, Enkidu, that you cannot hear me? You do not lift your head. When I touch your heart, it does not beat!"

Gilgamesh covered his friend in rich clothing and veiled him as a bride is veiled. First he roared over Enkidu's death like a lion. Then he cried over him like a lioness deprived of her cubs. Back and forth before Enkidu's body he paced, tearing out his hair and flinging off his clothing as if it were unclean.

With the first glow of dawn, Gilgamesh issued a summons throughout the land for coppersmiths, goldsmiths, jewelers, and engravers. "Create a statue of my friend Enkidu," he commanded. "Choose jewels for his breast and fashion his body from the purest gold."

Then Gilgamesh said to his friend, "Oh, Enkidu, I gave you a couch of honor on which to lie. I seated you on a seat of ease at my left, so that the princes of the earth would kiss your feet. I shall make the people of strong-walled Uruk weep over your death. These once joyful people will now lament and be sad, and they will perform services for you. And once you are gone, I shall let my hair grow long and roam over the grassy plains clad in a lion skin."

Chapter 6

Gilgamesh goes to Utanapishtim, the survivor of the great flood, to learn how a human being can gain immortality. He travels through a long, dark tunnel, receives advice from the fishwife Siduri, and finally is taken by boat to Utanapishtim.

Gilgamesh wandered the grassy plain, bitterly weeping over the death of his dearest friend. "When I die," he said to himself, "my fate will be just like Enkidu's! Grief tears at my heart, and fear of death gnaws at my stomach. I must travel as quickly as my feet will take me to the home of Utanapishtim (*uta:* he found + *napishtim:* life), who is called the Faraway. He is a human being just as I am. Yet he has found everlasting life and has joined the assembly of the heavenly gods. Surely he can teach me how to live for days without end!"

Gilgamesh traveled alone across the grassy plain and the scorching desert. One night, upon a mountain pass, he was confronted by two lions. The sight of them flooded his heart with terror. Raising his head to the moon, Gilgamesh prayed, "Oh, Sin, god of the light that brightens the night sky, protect me!"

Then Gilgamesh courageously drew the dagger from his belt and raised the axe in his hand. Approaching the beasts as straight as the flight of an arrow, he killed them, skinned them, and chopped them into pieces. He wrapped his body in their warm skins, for his own clothing had already become torn and tattered. He ate some of their flesh, for the food he had carried with him no longer could sustain him.

After many weeks of travel over land and sea, Gilgamesh came to Mount Mashu, whose twin peaks reach to the roof of heaven and guard Shamash as the sun rises and sets each day. There he found scorpion-men guarding the gate to the mountain. The halos around their heads dazzled the mountain itself, and their glance could kill any human being their eyes fixed upon. The sight of these guards caused Gilgamesh's heart to flood with terror. However, he forced himself to gather his courage and continue forward.

When they saw Gilgamesh approaching, one of the scorpion-men called to his wife, "This man who has come before us has flesh like the heavenly gods! He must be one of them!"

The scorpion-woman replied, "No, only two-thirds of him is god; one-third is human. The man who stands before you is Gilgamesh, king of strong-walled Uruk."

The scorpion-man then addressed Gilgamesh. "Child of the gods, why have you made such a difficult journey to this distant place? Tell me why you have wandered so far over land and sea."

Gilgamesh replied, "I have come to find Utanapishtim, the Faraway. I know that he has found everlasting life and has joined the assembly of the heavenly gods. I wish to talk with him about life and death."

The scorpion-man said, "Gilgamesh, no human being has ever found Utanapishtim! It is beyond the courage of any human being to make the journey! In order to reach the Faraway, you must first travel through a tunnel deep within the mountains. The tunnel extends for thirty-six miles in darkness black as pitch. From one rising of the sun to the next, no light penetrates that darkness."

Gilgamesh took the words of the scorpion-man into his mind and into his heart, but he was not dissuaded from making the journey. "I intend to take that path," he said. "Neither pain, nor sorrow, nor tears, nor extreme cold, nor scalding heat will stop me! Open the gate of the mountain so that I can continue my journey!"

The scorpion-man replied, "I shall open the gate of Mount Mashu to you, Gilgamesh. Go in safety, and may your feet bring you a safe return as well!"

Gilgamesh entered the tunnel of Mount Mashu. He kept the words of the scorpion-man alive in his mind and in his heart so that knowledge of what lay before him would lessen his fear of the darkness.

Gilgamesh traveled from east to west as the sun travels each day. When he had walked three miles, so thick was the darkness that he could see nothing ahead of him and nothing behind him, for there was no light. When he had walked nine miles, so thick was the darkness that he could see nothing ahead of him and nothing behind him, for there was no light. When he had walked eighteen miles, so thick was the darkness that he could see nothing ahead of him and nothing behind him, for there was no light.

When he had walked twenty-four miles, he was weary and impatient, and he cried out in protest. So thick was the darkness that he could see nothing ahead of him and nothing behind him, and still there was no light.

When Gilgamesh had walked twenty-seven miles, so thick was the darkness that he could see nothing ahead of him and nothing behind him, for still there was no light. But he could now feel a wind blowing into his face, so he quickened his steps. When he had walked thirty-three miles, he saw the rose color of dawn in the sky in front of him, and by the time he had walked thirty-six miles, the sky ahead of him was bright from the light of the sun.

Upon leaving the tunnel, Gilgamesh came upon an orchard of jewel-bearing trees. The jeweled fruits and foliage dazzled his eyes as they sparkled in the sunlight. A light wind helped show off their beauty by leading them in a graceful dance among their branches. Gilgamesh gazed in fascination at the glorious garden. For a short while, he forgot his grief and his pain, his fatigue and his fear. He was certain that he had entered the garden of the heavenly gods.

While Gilgamesh gazed in wonder at the orchard, radiant Shamash looked down from the sky and saw a human being clothed in animal skins. When he realized that the figure he saw was that of Gilgamesh, he became concerned. Shamash approached Gilgamesh and said, "Where are you going? You will not find the life for which you are searching."

Gilgamesh replied, "After wandering over the grassy plain and the scorching desert, must I lay my head in the heart of the earth, where there are no stars and no sun, and sleep the endless sleep? I want my eyes to feast upon the sun! I want its light and its warmth to fill my heart with joy! Light drives away the darkness!"

Shamash then left Gilgamesh to his journey, and in a short time, Gilgamesh reached the sea. There he saw the fishwife Siduri living in a cottage by the shore of the deep sea.

Siduri was sitting in her yard, gazing into the distance, when she noticed the haggard-looking, shaggy-haired stranger clothed in animal skins. When she saw that he intended to talk with her, Siduri's heart flooded with fear. She said to herself, "This man looks like a murderer! I wonder where he is going!" Obeying the counsel of her heart, she got up, locked the door of her house, and barred her gate with the crossbar.

Gilgamesh, watching her, picked up his pointed staff and placed his hand on the gate. Then he said, "Fishwife, what do you see that has made you bolt your door and bar your gate? Tell me, or else I will shatter your gate and smash your door!

"I am Gilgamesh, king of strong-walled Uruk," he continued. "I have overthrown and killed Humbaba, who guarded the Cedar Forest in the land of the living. I have seized and slaughtered the Bull of Heaven, and I have slain the lions who guarded the mountain passes."

Siduri said, "If you are indeed the hero you say you are, then why are your cheeks so pale and your face so gaunt? Why do you look like a stranger who has traveled here from afar with the ravages of heat and cold seared upon your face? Why does grief tear at your heart and fear gnaw at your stomach? And why do you roam over the grassy plain and the scorching desert searching for the home of the wind?"

Gilgamesh replied, "Oh, Fishwife, I have crossed the mountains from the east, as the sun rises, and I have roamed like a hunter over the grassy plain and the scorching desert. I have had to kill the bear, the hyena, the lion, the panther, the tiger, the stag, and the ibex. I have eaten the flesh of wild beasts and crawling creatures, and when my clothing hung about me in tatters, I had to wrap my body in their skins.

"Why should I not look as I look and wander as I wander?" Gilgamesh continued. "Enkidu, my friend, whom I dearly loved and who endured all kinds of hardships with me and helped me conquer all things, has met the fate of all human beings. Ever since Enkidu died, I have felt that he took my life with him on his journey to the House of Darkness and Dust!"

Gilgamesh concluded, "Because Enkidu has died, I fear my own death! How then can I be silent? How then can I be still? My friend, whom I dearly loved, has returned to clay! In time, must I also lay my head in the heart of the earth, where there are no stars and no sun, and sleep the endless sleep? Oh, Fishwife, now that I have seen your face, do not make me see my death, which I dread!"

Siduri replied, "Gilgamesh, where are you roaming? The life that you are seeking you will not find. When the heavenly gods created human beings, they kept everlasting life for themselves and gave us death.

"So, Gilgamesh, accept your fate," Siduri advised. "Each day, wash your head, bathe your body, and wear clothes that are sparkling fresh. Fill your stomach with tasty food. Play, sing, dance, and be happy both day and night. Delight in the pleasures that your wife brings you, and cherish the little child who holds your hand. Make every day of your life a feast of rejoicing! This is the task that the gods have set before all human beings. This is the life you should seek, for this is the best life a mortal can hope to achieve."

"You may have given me wise counsel, Fishwife," Gilgamesh replied. "Nevertheless, tell me, which is the way to Utanapishtim, the Faraway? Living on the shore of the sea as you do, you must be able to tell me the signs that mark the way. If necessary, I shall cross the deep sea. Otherwise, I shall continue to roam like a hunter over the grassy plain and the scorching desert."

Siduri replied, "Gilgamesh, there is no way to cross this deep sea! Since the beginning of time, no one who has come here has been able to travel over these waters."

Then Siduri added, "I have thought of one possibility. Perhaps Urshanabi, the boatman of Utanapishtim, would be willing to help you. He possesses sacred stone figures, which he keeps in the forest. If he will permit you to accompany him, I advise you to cross the deep sea with him. If not, you must withdraw and return to your strong-walled city of Uruk."

When Gilgamesh heard these words, anger flooded his heart. He drew the dagger from his belt and raised the axe in his hand. He entered the forest and sought to threaten the boatman who possessed the sacred stone figures. He found the sacred images, but not the boatman. He approached the images as straight as the flight of an arrow and in his rage he shattered them.

Urshanabi, who was close by, saw the gleam of Gilgamesh's dagger and heard the sound of the destruction. He ran to Gilgamesh and asked, "Who are you, and what are you doing here? Why do you look like a traveler from afar, with the ravages of heat and cold seared upon your face?"

Gilgamesh replied, "You must be Urshanabi! Gilgamesh is my name, and I am king of the strong-walled city of Uruk. I have crossed the mountains from the east, as the sun rises, and have come a long way. My friend, whom I dearly loved, has returned to clay. I am afraid that, in time, I also must lay my head in the heart of the earth and sleep the endless sleep.

"Urshanabi, show me the road to Utanapishtim, the Faraway!" Gilgamesh pleaded. "If necessary, I shall cross the deep sea. Otherwise, I shall continue to roam like a hunter over the grassy plain and the scorching desert. Oh, Urshanabi, take me to Utanapishtim!"

Urshanabi replied, "Your angry hands have hindered the sea journey. In your rage, you have destroyed the sacred stone images that enable me to cross the deep sea without touching the Waters of Death. Go into the forest, cut 120 poles, each 100 feet long, and bring them to me."

Gilgamesh took the dagger from his belt, raised the axe in his hand, and went into the forest. After he had returned to Urshanabi with the poles, the two men climbed into the boat, cast off into the waves of the deep sea, and drifted away. In three days they covered the distance it would have taken another craft a month and a half to cover. Then they found themselves at the Waters of Death.

Urshanabi said to Gilgamesh, "Take one of the poles and push us forward, but be careful not to let your hand touch the Waters of Death!"

Gilgamesh could use each pole only once if he wished to keep his hand completely dry, so it was not very long before he had used up all 120 poles. Then he pulled up his tunic and held it aloft as a sail.

While they were sailing upon the Waters of Death, Utanapishtim spied them far in the distance. "Why have the sacred stone images of the boat been broken?" he asked himself. "Why is someone riding in the boat who is not her master?"

When the boat landed, Utanapishtim, the Faraway, looked upon Gilgamesh and said, "Who are you, and why have you come here? And tell me, why are your cheeks so pale and your face so gaunt? Why do you look like a traveler from afar, with the ravages of heat and cold seared upon your face? Why does grief tear at your heart and fear gnaw at your stomach? And why do you roam over the grassy plain and the scorching desert searching for the home of the wind?

Gilgamesh replied, "My name is Gilgamesh, and I am king of the strong-walled city of Uruk. I have crossed the mountains from the east, as the sun rises, and have come a long way. Why should my cheeks not be pale and my face drawn? Why should I not look like a traveler from afar, with the ravages of heat and cold seared upon my face? Why should my heart not be torn with grief and my stomach gnawed by fear? And why should I not roam over the grassy plain and the scorching desert searching for the home of the wind?

"Enkidu, my dear friend, who chased the wild creatures of the hills and the panthers of the plain, who scaled the mountains with me, who endured all kinds of hardships with me and helped me conquer all things, who helped me seize and slaughter the Bull of Heaven and overthrow and kill Humbaba in the Cedar Forest, Enkidu, whom I dearly loved, has met the fate of all human beings."

Gilgamesh continued, "I wept over Enkidu's body for seven days and seven nights. I hoped that my sorrow and my pleas would arouse him from his endless sleep. The burden of my friend's death weighs heavily upon my heart. Ever since Enkidu died, I have felt that he took my life with him on his journey to the House of Darkness and Dust.

"Because Enkidu has died, I fear my own death! How then can I be silent? How then can I be still? My friend, whom I dearly loved, has returned to clay! In time, must I also lay my head in the heart of the earth, where there are no stars and no sun, and sleep the endless sleep?

"My eyes have seen little of sweet sleep, and my joints have felt much pain," Gilgamesh concluded. "I have roamed like a hunter over all lands, including the grassy plain and the scorching desert. I have crossed high mountains and choppy seas to come face to face with you, Utanapishtim. I wish to talk with you about life and death. I know that you have found everlasting life and have joined the assembly of the gods. I too wish to live on earth forever. Teach me what you know, so I can live as you do!"

Utanapishtim, the Faraway, replied, "Oh, Gilgamesh, do we build a house that will last forever? Do we seal arguments forever? Do brothers divide property into equal shares forever? Does hatred persist forever? Does the river rise and flood its banks forever? Should no one experience death? Since ancient times, nothing has been permanent. The shepherd and the noble have an identical fate — death."

Utanapishtim concluded, "When the heavenly gods gather in assembly, they decree the fate of each human being. The gods determine both life and death for every human being, but they do not reveal the day of anyone's death."

Chapter 7

Utanapishtim tells Gilgamesh about the great flood:
how it came about, what it was like, and how he
survived.

Gilgamesh said to the Faraway, "I know that you can live for days without end, Utanapishtim, but your features look the same as my own. Nothing about you looks strange; you resemble me in every way. I had expected that you would wish to do battle, but here you are, lying lazily upon your back. You appear to feel as I do, no longer interested in contests with the sword or with the bow. Tell me, how did you acquire everlasting life? How did you join the assembly of the heavenly gods?"

Utanapishtim replied, "Gilgamesh, I will reveal to you a secret of the gods." And so he began his tale.

You are familiar with the city of Shuruppak, on the banks of the Euphrates River. When both the city itself and the gods within it were already old, the gods decided to bring forth a great flood. Enlil, ruler of all the gods, called them together in assembly.

"The people who live upon the broad earth have become numerous beyond count, and they are too noisy," he complained. "The earth bellows like a herd of wild oxen. The clamor of human beings disturbs my sleep. Therefore, I want Adad to cause heavy rains to pour down upon the earth, both day and night. I want a great flood to come like a thief upon the earth, steal the food of these people, and destroy their lives."

Ishtar supported Enlil in his wish to destroy all of humanity, and then all the other gods agreed with his plan. However, Ea did not agree in his heart. He had helped human beings to survive upon the earth by creating rich pastures and farmland. He had taught them how to plow the land and how to grow grain. Because he loved them, he devised a clever scheme.

When Ea heard Enlil's plan, he appeared to me in a dream and said, "Stand by the wall of your reed hut, and I will speak with you there. Accept my words and listen carefully to my instructions. I will reveal a task for you."

I found myself wide awake, with Ea's message clearly etched in my mind. So I went down to the reed hut and stood with my ear to the wall as the god had commanded. "Utanapishtim, king of Shuruppak," a voice said. "Listen to my words, and consider them carefully! The heavenly gods have decreed that a great rainstorm will cause a mighty flood. This flood will engulf the cult-centers and destroy all human beings. Both the kings and the people whom they rule will come to a disastrous end. By the command of Enlil, the assembly of the gods has made this decision.

"Therefore," Ea continued, "I want you to abandon your worldly possessions in order to preserve your life. You must dismantle your house and construct a giant ship, an ark that you should call *Preserver of Life*.

"Make sure the ship's dimensions are equal in length and width," Ea counseled. "Build it of solid timber so the rays of Shamash will not shine into it. Take care to seal the structure well. Take aboard your wife, your family, your relatives, and the craftspeople of your city. Bring your grain and all of your possessions and goods. Take the seed of all living things, both the beasts of the field and the birds of the heavens, aboard the ship. Later, I will tell you when to board the ship and seal the door."

I replied, "Ea, my lord, I will do as you have ordered. However, I have never built a ship. Draw a design of this ark on the ground for me, so that I can follow your plan. And when the people of Shuruppak ask me what I am doing, how shall I respond?"

Ea then replied to me, his servant, "I am drawing the design of the ship upon the ground for you as you have asked. As for the people of Shuruppak, tell them, 'I have learned that Enlil hates me so that I can no longer live in your city, nor can I place my feet anywhere in that god's territory. Therefore, I will go down to the deep and live with my lord Ea. However, Enlil intends to shower you with abundance. After a stormy evening, you will find the most unusual birds and fish, and your land will be filled with rich harvests.'"

With the first glow of dawn, I began to construct my giant ship. The people of Shuruppak gathered about me with great interest. The little children carried the sealing materials, while the others brought wood and everything else I would need. By the end of the fifth day of hard labor, I had constructed the framework for my ship. The floor space measured an entire acre. The length, width, and height each measured 200 feet.

I divided the height of the ark so that the interior had seven floors, and I divided each level into nine sections. I hammered water plugs into it and stored supplies. I made the craft watertight. Every day I killed cattle and sheep for the people and feasted the workers with red wine, white wine, and oil as though they were water from the Euphrates. We celebrated each day as if it were a great holiday!

Finally, on the seventh day I completed my preparations and moved the ship into the water. When two-thirds of the ship had entered the water, I loaded into it whatever remained that I intended to take with me. This included what silver and gold I possessed and what living things I had. I put aboard my family and relatives. I put aboard all of the craftspeople. I put aboard animals of the field, both wild and tame.

Ea had given me a time by which I had to be ready to depart. He had said to me, "When Adad causes the heavens to darken with terrible storm clouds, board the ship and seal the entrance."

So I watched the heavens carefully. When they looked awesome with the gloom of an impending storm, I boarded the ship and sealed the entrance with clay. Long before the storm began to rage upon us, we cast off our ship's cables and prepared to let the sea carry us wherever it would.

The people of the land watched, bewildered and quiet, as Adad turned all that had been light into darkness. The powerful south wind blew at his side, uniting the hurricane, the tornado, and the thunderstorm. It blew for a full day, increasing speed as it traveled, and shattered the land like a clay pot.

In order to observe the catastrophe the heavenly gods lifted up their torches so that the land might blaze with light. But the storm wind raged furiously over the land like a battle. It brought forth a flood that buried the mountains and shrouded the people. No person could see another, and the gods looking down from heaven could not find them either. Its attack ravaged the earth, killing all living creatures and crushing whatever else remained.

As the heavenly gods watched the flood waters pour forth upon the land and destroy everything that inhabited the earth, they too became frightened. They took refuge in their highest heaven, the heaven of Anu. There they crouched against the outer wall, trembling with fear like dogs. Nintu, the Mother Goddess, wept for the people who lived on the earth.

The goddess Ishtar cried out for the victims of the flood like a woman in labor. "All that used to exist upon the earth in days of old has now been turned to clay," she moaned, "and all because I added my voice to Enlil's in the assembly. How could I agree with the order to attack and destroy my people when I myself gave birth to them? Now the bodies of my people fill the sea like fish eggs!"

Humbled by the enormity of their deed, the heavenly gods wept with Ishtar. For seven days and seven nights the stormy south wind raged over the land, blowing the great flood across the face of the earth. Each day and each night, the windstorms tossed my giant ship wildly about upon the tumultuous sea of flood waters. On the eighth day, the flood-bearing south wind retreated, and the flood waters became calm. Radiant Shamash ventured forth once again. He spread his sunlight upon the heavens above and the earth below and revealed the devastation.

When my ship had rocked quietly for awhile, I thought that it would be safe to open a hatch and see what had happened. The world was completely still, and the surface of the sea was as level as a flat roof. All humanity except us had returned to clay. I scanned the expanse of the flood waters for a coastline, but without success.

As Shamash brought his rays of light and warmth inside my ship, I bowed my face to the ground before the powers of the universe. They had destroyed the world, but they had saved my ship. I knelt in submission and respect before Shamash, who nourishes human beings with his healing rays. In gratitude for our survival, I sacrificed an ox and a sheep to the heavenly gods. Then I sat and wept, letting my tears course freely down my face.

My ship floated upon the waters for twelve days. When I next opened the hatch and looked outside, far in the distance in each of the fourteen regions a mountain range had emerged from the surrounding waters. In time my ship came to rest, secure and stable, upon the slopes of Mount Nisir.

For the first seven days, Mount Nisir held my ship fast, allowing no motion. On the seventh day, I set free a dove and sent it forth. The dove could find no place to alight and rest, so it returned to the ship. Next I set free a swallow and sent it forth. The swallow could find no place to alight and rest, so it too returned to the ship. Then I set free a raven and sent it forth. The raven could see that the waters had receded, so it circled but did not return to my ship.

Then I set free all living things and offered a sacrifice to the heavenly gods. I set up fourteen cult-vessels on top of the mountain. I heaped cane, cedarwood, and myrtle upon their pot-stands, and I poured out a libation to the gods. They smelled the sweet aroma and gathered around me like flies. I prostrated myself before Anu and Enlil.

Then Ishtar arrived. She lifted up the necklace of great jewels that her father, Anu, had created to please her and said, "Heavenly gods, as surely as this jeweled necklace hangs upon my neck, I will never forget these days of the great flood. Let all of the gods except Enlil come to the offering. Enlil may not come, for without reason he brought forth the flood that destroyed my people."

When Enlil saw my ship, he became furious with the other gods. "Has some human being escaped?" he cried. "No one was supposed to survive the flood! Who permitted this?"

Ninurta, the warrior god, said to Enlil, "Do not be angry with us. Only Ea knows everything. Only he could have devised such a scheme!"

Ea then said to Enlil, "You are the ruler of the gods and are wise. How could you bring on such a flood without a reason? Hold the sinner responsible for his sin; punish the person who transgresses. But be lenient, so that he does not perish! Instead of causing the flood, it would have been better if you had caused a lion or a wolf to attack human beings and decrease their number! Instead of causing the flood, it would have been better if you had caused disease to attack human beings and decrease their number! Instead of causing the flood, it would have been better if you had caused famine to conquer the land. That would have weakened human beings and decreased their number!

"It was not I who revealed the secret of the great gods," Ea said craftily. "Utanapishtim, the most wise, had a dream in which he discovered how to survive your flood. So now, Enlil, think of what to do with him!"

I bowed my face to the earth in fear and submission before Enlil. He took my hand, and together we boarded my ship. Then Enlil took my wife aboard the ship and made her kneel at my side. He placed himself between us and touched our foreheads to bless us.

"Until now," Enlil said, "Utanapishtim and his wife have been human beings. From this time forward, they will live like the heavenly gods. I have brought down for them everlasting breath so that, like the gods, they may continue to live for days without end. Utanapishtim, the king of Shuruppak, has preserved the seeds of humanity and of plant and animal life. He and his wife will live far to the east, where the sun rises, at the mouth of the river in the mountainous land of Dilmun."

Utanapishtim concluded the story of his adventure. "That is how it came to pass that my wife and I became like the heavenly gods and will live for days without end. Enlil himself conferred everlasting life upon us. But Gilgamesh, king of strong-walled Uruk though you are, who will call the heavenly gods to assembly for your sake so that you can find the everlasting life you are seeking?"

Chapter 8

Utanapishtim challenges Gilgamesh to go without sleep for a week. When Gilgamesh fails the test, Utanapishtim gives him a magic plant and sends him on his way home. Gilgamesh loses the plant before he arrives in Uruk, but he returns home safely.

Utanapishtim, the Faraway, said to Gilgamesh, "If you wish to become like the heavenly gods and live for days without end, you must first possess the strength of a god. Even though you are mighty, I will show you that, like all human beings, you are weak. Starting with this night, I want you to remain upon your feet and stay awake for seven nights and six days."

Gilgamesh obediently squatted down and tried to stay awake. Despite his best intentions, sleep blew upon him like a soft mist and conquered him.

Utanapishtim said to his wife, "Look at this hero who wants everlasting life! Sleep fans him like a soft mist!"

Utanapishtim's wife counseled her husband. "Touch Gilgamesh so that he will awaken and return safely to his strong-walled city. See to it that he will be able to return to his land the way he came, entering through the gate by which he left."

The Faraway responded, "In time, I shall do as you advise. Meanwhile, Gilgamesh will try to deceive you by telling you he has not slept at all. We must devise proof of his slumber to show him how weak he really is. Each day, I want you to bake him a loaf of bread and place it by his head. And record how long he sleeps by placing a mark upon the wall behind him each day."

So each day that Gilgamesh slept, Utanapishtim's wife put a loaf of bread by his head and made a mark for that day upon the wall behind him. By the morning of the seventh day, Gilgamesh was still asleep. Six loaves of bread were lined up in a row by his head and there were six marks on the wall. The first loaf had dried out, the second had spoiled, the third had become soggy, the crust of the fourth had turned white, the fifth had a moldy cast, the sixth was still fresh in color, and the seventh was warm, having just been removed from the oven.

Utanapishtim touched Gilgamesh as his wife placed the seventh loaf of bread next to the others. Gilgamesh awoke and said, "I had hardly fallen asleep when you touched me and awakened me!"

Utanapishtim replied, "Gilgamesh, count the loaves of bread by your head so that you will realize how many days you have slept! Your first loaf is dried out, the second has spoiled, the third is soggy, the crust of the fourth has turned white, the fifth has a moldy cast, the sixth is still fresh in color, and I awakened you just as my wife put the seventh loaf, still warm from the oven, by your head."

Gilgamesh groaned in resignation and said, "What should I do now? Where shall I go? Now that the robber Death is holding my limbs, I know that Death hides in my bedroom and I shall never escape it! Wherever I place my feet, Death will be there with me! I shall never become like the heavenly gods and live for days without end!"

Utanapishtim replied, "Let your heart not despair, Gilgamesh. It is true the heavenly gods have decreed that you, like all other human beings, cannot live for days without end. They have not granted you life everlasting. But Anu, Enlil, and Ea have granted you other gifts.

"The power to be unsurpassed in might they have granted you. The power to be skilled in wrestling they have granted you. The power to be skilled with the sword, the dagger, the bow, and the axe they have granted you. The power to be like a devastating flood in battle they have granted you. The power to lead attacks from which no one can escape they have granted you.

"The power to be unrivaled in heroism they have granted you. The power to seize and slaughter the Bull of Heaven they have granted you. The power to enter the Cedar Forest in the land of the living, to overthrow and kill Humbaba, and to fell the cedars they have granted you. The power to make the long, difficult, and dangerous journey to meet with me they have granted you.

"And as if extraordinary might and heroism were not sufficient gifts, the power to be supreme among human beings they have granted you. The power to rule your people as king and to be the greatest of leaders they have granted you. The power to bring light or darkness upon your people they have granted you. The power to free people or enslave them they have granted you. The power to teach your people and lead them to wisdom they have granted you.

"Therefore," Utanapishtim counseled, "cast away fear and sorrow. Rejoice in your heart that the heavenly gods love you and have smiled upon you!"

Utanapishtim then turned to his boatman and said, "Urshanabi, take Gilgamesh to the washing place that he may cleanse himself. Let him wash his long hair until it is as clean as snow. Let him remove his animal skins and let the deep sea carry them away, so that the beauty of his appearance may be seen. Let him replace the band around his head with a new one, and let him put on a new cloak to cover his nakedness. Then accompany him on his journey back to strong-walled Uruk."

Urshanabi took care of Gilgamesh as the Faraway had directed. When Gilgamesh was clean and newly clothed, the two of them climbed into Urshanabi's boat and prepared to sail away.

Utanapishtim's wife then said, "Gilgamesh made a long, difficult, and dangerous journey to meet with you. In appreciation of his effort, what gift will you give him to take back with him to his city?"

Utanapishtim asked Urshanabi to bring the boat close to the shore. Then he said, "Gilgamesh, because you have made a long, difficult, and dangerous journey in order to meet with me, I shall send you back to strong-walled Uruk with a secret thing created by the heavenly gods. The plant that you see growing deep in the water there is like the rose. Its thorns will prick your hands when you try to pick it. However, if you can gather that plant, you will hold in your hands the gift of everlasting youth. This plant cannot make you live forever, but it will keep you young and strong all the days of your life."

Gilgamesh replied, "I can gather the plant if you will give me two heavy stones." He tied one stone to each of his feet and placed his dagger between his teeth. Using a pole to push the boat out into the deep water near the plant, he jumped overboard. The stones pulled his body down into the deep water where he could reach the plant. He picked it successfully even though it pricked his hands. Then he cut the heavy stones from his feet and let the water carry him up to the surface of the sea.

Gilgamesh climbed into the boat once again, stowed the plant safely, and set off with Urshanabi. They successfully crossed the waters of death; in three more days, they covered the distance that would have taken another craft a month and a half.

In time they saw the cottage of Siduri and knew that the first part of their journey was behind them. Being tired and hungry, they steered the boat toward an inviting shore and beached it.

To protect his plant, Gilgamesh removed it from the boat and carried it with him. He wandered over the land, enjoying the freedom of moving about on firm ground and stretching his legs. He followed a freshwater stream inland until it formed a pool. There he put the plant upon the ground along with his clothes and went for a refreshing swim.

A serpent in the water smelled the appealing fragrance of the plant. It glided out of the water, slithered up the bank, took hold of the plant with its mouth, and carried it back into the water. As it returned to the water it shed its skin, emerging younger and fresher looking.

By the time Gilgamesh noticed what had happened, it was too late to save the plant. He sat down and wept. Then he took the hand of Urshanabi and said, "For whom have my hands labored? For whom does the blood of my heart work? I have obtained nothing for myself. I have only helped the serpent! Now the tide will carry the plant back into the depths of the sea!"

After composing himself Gilgamesh continued, "Since it is impossible to retrieve the plant, I must become resigned to my loss. We shall leave the boat on the shore as we had planned and continue our journey overland toward strong-walled Uruk."

When they had walked sixty miles, they stopped to eat. After another ninety miles, they prepared to spend the night. After many days and nights they saw the strong walls of Uruk in the distance. As they walked toward the city, Gilgamesh explained to Urshanabi, "Uruk is composed of four sections: the city, the orchards, borderland, and the precinct of the Temple of Anu and Ishtar."

As they entered the gates, Gilgamesh said, "Urshanabi, I want you to notice the strong walls of our city of Uruk. I built these walls on a foundation created in ancient times by the seven wise men, who brought great knowledge to our land. The top of our outer wall shines with the brightness of copper, but it is made of burnt brick. Now study the inner walls of our city. Examine the fine brickwork. These walls, too, surpass all others! No human being, not even a king, will ever be able to construct more impressive walls than I have built around our city of

Uruk! Now approach the majestic Temple of Anu and Ishtar. No mortal, not even a king, will ever be able to build a structure as beautiful as the one I have created! Climb up and walk upon the walls of Uruk. Examine the fine brickwork. Admire the majestic Temple of Anu and Ishtar. Gaze upon one man's supreme achievement!"

Gilgamesh inscribed these travels and these thoughts upon stone tablets and placed these tablets on the strong walls of Uruk so that his people could gain wisdom and remember him.

Northern Europe

The myths of Northern Europe were recorded primarily in Iceland in the 13th century A.D. They reflect a universe in which the physical environment often threatens human survival. Consequently, Norse (Germanic) myths are populated with evil giants and monsters that heroes—both divine and mortal—combat.

The oppressive environment in the myths is understandable in a society that faced long, cold winters, short growing seasons that often yielded a less than abundant harvest, and a lack of sophisticated medical knowledge. The Norse myths emphasize an unrelenting Fate. According to these tales, everything in the Northern peoples' existence is predetermined, so they must accept their destiny without question or rebellion.

The Norse gods possess human personalities, and they interact with one another and with the giants in many delightful myths, such as "The Theft of Idun's Apples" and "The Theft of Thor's Hammer." However, unlike the gods of the Greeks and the Sumerians, they involve themselves with human beings only on rare occasions.

The Norse gods share the same unalterable fate that mortals do. When Ragnarok, the last great battle, occurs, famous human warriors will fight alongside the gods against the giants. Nevertheless, the gods will be defeated by the giants. Odin, ruler of the gods, knows their fate, but he can do nothing to change it.

The Norse creation myth introduces the major concept of the conflict between the forces of good and the forces of evil. The myth describes the destiny of the universe from its creation to the destruction and inevitable death of the gods and mortals.

The fertility myth of Balder is an integral part of the creation myth. Like other Norse myths, it has been lifted from its earlier, agricultural culture and has been transplanted into the more aggressive Viking age, with an increased emphasis on death.

The myth of Sigurd provides the basis for the story of Siegfried in Richard Wagner's famous cycle of operas, *The Ring of the Nibelungen*. Like *The Odyssey*, it is one of the world's great adventure stories. The idea of a curse on a gold ring that destroys whoever possesses it is the root of many a modern tale, such as J. R. R. Tolkien's *Lord of the Rings*, and Sigurd's great love, Brunhild, is the original Sleeping Beauty. As in the other major Norse myths, unalterable Fate dominates *Sigurd the Volsung*. The saga's characters shine brilliantly against the blackness of their fate, but they are doomed and they know it.

Introducing The Creation, Death, and Rebirth of the Universe

Historical Background

The acceptance of Christianity in Iceland in A.D. 1000 formally brought pagan beliefs to an end in that country. However, many of the monks enjoyed the old poems and stories enough to record them.

During the next few centuries, many people thought that Odin and Thor really existed as evil spirits who tempted human beings with evil thoughts and deeds. In response to such ideas, in about 1220 Snorri Sturluson wrote *Gylfaginning (The Deluding of Gylfi)*. It tells the story of the creation of the world and other myths from the Norse, or Germanic, tradition.

Norse Religion

The Norse gods reflect the nature and values of the people who worshipped them. Not only do the Norse gods speak and act like human beings, but they too are subject to the Norns (the Fate Maidens) and face the inescapable destiny of death. Like human beings, the Norse gods know and accept their fate and are determined to face it with courage and dignity. Like many of the human beings who worship them, they choose to die in battle. They kill the evil giants to make the world a better place for future generations.

Except for Odin, who occasionally helps a great hero like Sigurd, the Norse gods do not protect human beings from the dangers of living. They usually keep to themselves, and their adventures involve the giants rather than humans. Similarly, the tales of human heroes do not usually include the gods.

The hierarchy of the Norse gods reflects the class divisions of Norse society. The Norse kings, as members of the warrior aristocracy, claimed Odin as their patriarch. Odin is both the god of war and the god of poetry. He brings both victory and defeat to warriors, and he inspires the court poets who create epics and songs about heroes and their battles. A fierce god, Odin demands human sacrifice from those who worship him.

Thor is the son of Odin and Frigg. Second to Odin among the Norse gods, he was worshipped by the peasant farmers, who needed his strength and dependability. Thor's hammer, Mjollnir, causes thunder and lightning, and is therefore related to the rain that helps produce abundant crops. Thor also uses his hammer to protect both Asgard, the home of the gods, and Midgard (Middle Earth), the home of mortals, from the evil giants.

Frey is the third most important Norse god. He is the son of Njord, god of plenty from the sea, and he is a fertility god like his father. Frey determines when the sun will shine and when the rain will fall. People prayed to him, his father, and his sister, Freya, for bountiful harvests and children. Like Odin, Frey demands human sacrifice from his worshippers.

Frigg and Freya are the most important Norse goddesses. Both are Great Goddesses or Mother Goddesses and are worshipped for their powers to bring fertility to the land and to people.

Appeal and Value

The appeal of the Norse creation myth is its broad cast of characters and great adventure. We recognize the giants, dwarves, and elves from our fairy tale heritage, which has Norse, or Germanic, roots. The concepts of gods who die and a world that is destroyed and reborn are fascinating. Readers of J. R. R. Tolkien will recognize that many names in The Lord of the Rings trilogy derive from Norse mythology, as do the names in C. S. Lewis' Chronicles of Narnia series.

Principal Gods

ODIN (also, Woden, meaning "wild" or "filled with fury"): ancient Indo-European god of wind; son of Bor and Bestla; oldest and greatest of the gods; father and ruler of the gods; father of mortals, giving life and soul; god of war

FRIGG: originally, a Great Goddess or Mother Goddess; wife of Odin; mother of the gods; most important goddess; knows everyone's fate but does not reveal it

THOR: son of Odin and Frigg; second greatest god; strongest of all gods and mortals; god of thunder

BALDER: son of Odin and Frigg; most gentle and best loved of the gods

HODER: son of Odin and Frigg; blind brother of Balder

HERMOD: courageous son of Odin and Frigg

BRAGI: son of Odin and Frigg; husband of Idun; god of wisdom and poetry

IDUN: wife of Bragi; keeps the golden apples of eternal youth

NJORD (meaning "enclosing ships" or "the sea"): god of fertility; ruler of the winds and the sea

FREY: son of Njord; god of fertility of the earth and of mortals; ruler of the sun and rain; third most important god

FREYA: originally, a Great Goddess or Mother Goddess; daughter of Njord; gives advice about love; second most important goddess

HEIMDALL: ancient Indo-European god of fire, similar to Agni, the Hindu god of fire; watchman of the gods

HOENIR: ancient Indo-European god; son of Bor and Bestla; brother of Odin; along with Odin, father of mortals, giving intelligence and emotion; after Ragnarok, ruler of the surviving gods

LOKI: son of two Frost Giants, but considered a god; evil mischief-maker

HEL: monstrous daughter of Loki; ruler of the dead in Niflheim

---

The Creation, Death, and Rebirth of the Universe

In the days when King Gylfi ruled the land that is now known as Sweden, he transformed himself into an old man called Gangleri and visited the great gods in their hall in Asgard, in order to learn about the nature of the universe. Because Gylfi came in disguise, the gods did not reveal their true selves to him. They called themselves High One, Just-as-High, and Third.

"I am searching for the wisdom of the gods," Gangleri announced. "Is any one among you knowledgeable?"

"Ask of us whatever you will," High One replied, "and you will leave here wiser than when you arrived."

Gangleri asked, "Tell me, if you can, how did all things begin?"

High One explained, "In the beginning, nothing existed but Ginnungagap, which was an open void. In that ancient time, neither the heaven above nor the earth below, neither sand, nor grass, nor the cool, tossing waves of the sea had been fashioned."

Just-as-High added, "The first world to come into existence was Muspelheim (destroyers' home). It is a hot, bright, flaming world in the southern part of Ginnungagap and it sends forth sparks and glowing embers. It is guarded by the giant Surt, who possesses a flaming sword."

Third said, "The second world to come into existence was Niflheim (fog home), in the northern part of Ginnungagap. In the middle of Niflheim is a spring called Hvergelmir (bubbling cauldron), from which eleven fast and fearsome rivers arose and flowed far from their source. The foamy venom from their waves hardened and turned into ice. As it cooled, a drizzling mist arose from the venom and fell upon the firm ice, forming a second layer of heavy ice over the first. All this ice makes Niflheim cold, foggy, and harsh."

Gangleri asked, "Did anyone exist before human beings? Tell me about the giants and the gods."

High One replied, "The Frost Giants lived during the time of endless winters before the earth was formed. Where the soft, warm air from Muspelheim met the ice from Niflheim, the ice thawed. Life first grew from the drops of melted foam venom and developed into the first being, a Frost Giant named Ymir. The venom from which he was created made him wild, fierce, and evil. Then from the thawed ice a cow, Audhumla (nourisher), arose, and Ymir fed upon the four rivers of milk she produced."

Just-as-High added, "While Ymir slept, he sweated. From the moisture in the armpit under his left arm, a man and a woman emerged. Ymir became the father of all the families of Frost Giants. Like their father, they were evil creatures."

Gangleri said, "That is certainly a strange tale! How then did the gods first come to exist?"

High One explained, "Audhumla constantly licked a salty block of ice. By the evening of the first day, a head of hair had appeared. By the second day, the male's entire head had become visible. By the end of the third day, the whole male, called Buri, had emerged from the block of ice. Buri was tall, handsome, and strong, and he became the grandfather of the gods. He had a son called Bor, who married Bestla, the daughter of one of the giants. Bor and Bestla had three sons who became the first Norse gods: Odin,who was the oldest, then Vili, and finally Ve."

"Were the gods and giants friends or enemies?" asked Gangleri.

High One replied, "Odin, Vili, and Ve killed Ymir. So much blood poured from his wounds that, except for Bergelmir and his wife, all of the other Frost Giants drowned in the flood of Ymir's blood. Bergelmir escaped with his wife by quickly climbing into a boat he had made from a hollowed-out tree trunk. Thus, they became the parents of the next race of giants, who were also Frost Giants and evil creatures."

Gangleri asked, "How was the earth fashioned?"

High One replied, "The three gods took the corpse of Ymir, carried it into the middle of Ginnungagap, and made the world from it. From his flesh, they molded the earth. From the blood that poured from his wounds, they made the salt sea and laid it around the earth. From his mighty bones they fashioned the mountains, and from his smaller bones, jaws, and teeth they formed rocks and pebbles. From his hair they created the forests."

Just-as-High added, "They gave the lands along the shores of the salt sea, Jotunheim (giants' home), to the giants and their families. However, they wanted to protect the folk who would live in the inland part of the earth, called Midgard (Middle Earth), from the evil giants. So they used Ymir's eyebrows to build a barrier that separated the two groups of beings."

Third said, "From Ymir's skull, they made the sky and set it in the form of an arch over the earth, with a dwarf holding up each of its four corners. Then they tossed Ymir's brains into the air to create storm clouds."

Gangleri said, "I did not know that dwarfs existed before human beings. How did they come to be?"

High One replied, "Originally, the dwarfs came to life as maggots in Ymir's flesh. The gods gave them the appearance of people and also gave them human understanding. The dwarfs still live in dark places in the earth and in rocky caves in the land called Nidavellir."

Just-as-High added, "The gods fashioned the burning embers and the sparks that blew out of Muspelheim into stars and placed them in fixed locations in the midst of Ginnungagap to give light to heaven above and the earth below."

Third said, "They arranged for the sun and the moon to travel through the sky every day in order to create day and night and the seasons. The sun travels quickly because a wolf is chasing her. When this world comes to an end, at the time of Ragnarok (doom of the gods), he will catch her. Another wolf runs in front of the sun, chasing the moon. In the end, at Ragnarok, the moon too will be caught."

Gangleri asked, "How did human beings come to inhabit Midgard?"

High One replied, "When the three gods were walking along the shore of the salt sea, they found two trees, an ash and an elm. They created the first man, Ask, from the ash tree and the first woman, Embla, from the elm tree, and clothed them to give them dignity. Odin gave them blood and the breath of life. Vili gave them understanding and power of movement. Ve gave them shape and the ability to see, hear, and speak. Ask and Embla became the parents of the race of human beings, like yourself, who live in Midgard."

"What can you tell me about Yggdrasill? Is it not some kind of tree?" Gangleri asked.

High One replied, "The branches of this great ash tree spread throughout the whole world and extend over heaven. Three great roots support the World Ash Tree: one among the Aesir (the gods) in Asgard, a second among the Frost Giants, and the third over icy Niflheim."

Just-as-High added, "The root in Asgard is nourished by the sacred spring of Urd. There live the three Fate Maidens, called Norns. Their names are Urd (Past), Verdandi (Present), and Skuld (Future). They establish the laws that determine the lives of all human beings and seal their fate."

Third said, "There are other Norns as well. Some are the daughters of the elves; others are the daughters of the dwarfs. Those who come from good beings shape good lives — long, wealthy, and famous. Evil Norns confer short, poor, unfortunate lives."

High One added, "The root among the Frost Giants is nourished by the spring of Mimir, which is the source of wisdom and understanding. Like Mimir, who owns the spring, anyone who drinks that water will become wise. However, it is not a simple task. Odin, the All-Father, wished to have just a single drink; he had to sacrifice one of his two eyes before he could take it."

Just-as-High said, "The root over Niflheim is nourished by the spring of Hvergelmir, the source of the world's great rivers."

Gangleri then asked, "What did the gods do after they created human beings?"

High One replied, "Odin, Vili, and Ve built a stronghold for themselves in the middle of the world, called Asgard, where they and their families would live. There Odin sits on his high seat and surveys the entire world, seeing what everyone is doing and understanding everything. Two ravens, Hugin (thought) and Munin (memory), sit upon his shoulders. Each day, Odin sends them out at dawn to fly over the world. When they return, they tell him all that they have seen and heard."

"What is the most interesting palace in Asgard?" Gangleri asked.

High One replied, "That is surely Odin's golden-bright Valhalla (hall of the slain). It is roofed with spear shafts and golden shields. Valkyries (choosers of the slain), the valiant daughters of Odin, ride down to Midgard to award victory to certain warriors and to choose those who are destined to die. They bring the dead warriors up to Valhalla to fight on the side of the gods against the giants when Ragnarok arrives."

Just-as-High added, "Every day the dead warriors entertain themselves by fighting one another, eating an endless supply of boar meat, and drinking endless cups of mead."

Third said, "There are 640 doors built into Valhalla, and when Ragnarok arrives 960 warriors will leave to fight the fearsome wolf Fenrir."

Gangleri asked, "How can one travel between Asgard and earth?"

High One replied, "The gods built the Bifrost (quivering roadway) Bridge, which human beings see as the rainbow."

"In your opinion, what gods should human beings believe in?" asked Gangleri.

High One replied, "There are twelve gods and twelve powerful goddesses. Odin is the oldest and greatest of the gods. He is called the All-Father because he is the father of both gods and humans. He is also called many other names, such as High One and Father of the Slain, since he is worshipped by many different clans in Midgard and has had many adventures."

Just-as-High added, "Thor is the son of Odin and his wife, the earth goddess Frigg. Thor is the strongest god. He drives a chariot drawn by two goats. He owns three precious possessions: his hammer, Mjollnir; his mighty belt, which doubles his strength; and his iron gloves, which he wears when he wields Mjollnir."

Third added, "Another son of Odin's is Balder. He is as beautiful as he is good, and he is the best loved of the gods. He is the most wise and the most kind. Whatever he says can never be changed."

Gangleri asked, "Which other gods are most important?"

High One replied, "Njord is also very important. He was originally from Vanaheim, the home of the Vanir gods, who make the land and sea fertile. He is very important to sailors and fishermen because he controls the wind and the sea. He is wealthy and makes those who worship him prosperous also."

Just-as-High added, "Njord has two important children, Frey (lord) and Freya (lady). Frey is third in importance, after Thor and Odin. Frey decides when the sun will shine and when the rain will pour. Therefore, he is responsible for the fertility of the earth. Human beings pray to him for peace and prosperity, and for their own fertility as well as that of their fields."

Third said, "Freya is as important a goddess as Frigg. People ask her for help in matters of love."

High One added, "Of course, there are many other important gods and goddesses. Idun keeps the golden apples that the gods eat in order to remain young. Bragi, her husband, is known for his wisdom and skill in poetry."

Third said, "Heimdall is the watchman of the gods. He can hear the wool growing on the backs of sheep and the grass growing in Midgard. He can see farther than 300 miles, even at night."

Gangleri asked, "Is Loki a god?"

High One replied, "Loki is the son of a giant, so evil flows in his blood. He is considered a god, but he is a mischief-maker. He is very clever, but he also lies and cheats. Some call him the Father of Lies and the Disgrace of Gods and Men. He often gets the gods into trouble — or out of it. He is the father of three monstrous children: the wolf Fenrir, Hel (goddess of the dead), and the World Serpent. He will be the enemy of the gods when Ragnarok comes upon us."

Just-as-High added, "Hel is a grim creature. Hunger and Famine are her companions. People who die from old age or disease live with her behind high walls in the land of Niflheim."

Gangleri asked, "What can you tell me about Ragnarok? Is there any way to escape it?"

High One replied, "The death of Balder will be the first indication that Ragnarok is approaching. Loki will be instrumental in causing both Balder's death and his confinement with Hel. As punishment, the gods will imprison Loki in a cave until Ragnarok arrives."

Just-as-High added, "Next, for three winters bloody wars will be waged throughout the world. Brother will strike brother with sword and axe, and both will die. Incest and adultery will become common. No mortal will show another mercy. Evil will run wild upon the earth, destroying relationships among family, friends, and clans. Finally the world will lie in ruins."

Third added, "Then three terrible winters, each lasting for an entire year with no summer between them, will bring biting winds, severe frost, and endless snow."

High One continued, "The wolf Hati will finally catch and swallow the sun, and the wolf Skoll will finally catch and swallow the moon. The giant Surt will tear apart the heavens with his scorching flames, causing the blazing stars, bursting with fire, to fall upon the earth. The earth will shake so forcefully that the trees of the forests will become uprooted and the mountains will collapse. This tremendous tumult will release Loki, Fenrir, and the monstrous dragon called the World Serpent, which lies deep in the salt sea that surrounds Midgard. The serpent will thrash about, poisoning the sea and the sky with its spurting venom and causing tidal waves to wash upon Midgard."

Just-as-High added, "Flames will flare forth from Fenrir's eyes and nostrils as he moves toward the plain of Vigrid with his mouth gaping in readiness. There he will meet the gathering of Frost Giants, the World Serpent, and all other creatures of evil. Heimdall will alert the gods to Ragnarok."

Third said, "Odin will fight against Fenrir; Thor will pit himself against the World Serpent; and Frey will battle Surt. The wolf will swallow Odin whole, but Odin's son Vidar, the fiercest of warriors, will tear Fenrir's jaws apart and kill him. Thor will slay the serpent, but its poison will kill him. Heimdall and Loki will kill each other, and Surt will slay Frey. Thus the high ones will be destroyed."

High One concluded, "With the fire from his flaming sword, Surt will set the entire earth ablaze. People will flee their homesteads in fear. With death as their destiny, the doomed and trembling human race will walk the road to join Hel. Finally, the charred and devastated earth will sink into the sea."

Gangleri exclaimed, "How horrible! What will happen after the whole world has been burned, and the gods and human beings are dead?"

High One replied, "The earth will rise out of the sea once again, fresh and green. The eagle will again fly down from mountain crags to capture fish. The daughter of the sun will travel the old paths of her mother and will brighten heaven and earth with her light. Fields will produce grain where seeds were never sown."

Just-as-High added, "After Surt's flames have destroyed the homes of the gods, Odin's sons Vidar and Vali will live where Asgard once was. Odin's grandsons Modi and Magni will join them and will claim Mjollnir, their father's hammer. Finally Balder will return from the land of Hel and join the group. Together the gods will remember the knowledge of the high ones, the World Serpent, Fenrir, and Ragnarok. But evil will have left the world."

Third said, "Meanwhile, when the endless winter kills most human beings, one man, Lif (life), and one woman, Lifthrasir (desiring life), will seek safety by hiding among the branches of the great ash tree Yggdrasill. There they will survive by eating and drinking the morning dew. They will escape Surt's flames, and when the earth has revived they will become the parents of the next race of human beings."

High One then announced, "This ends our tale. We have answered all of your questions. Do what you will with all that we have told you."

Suddenly, Gangleri found himself in the midst of a tremendous uproar. When he came to his senses he found that he was alone upon a plain, and Asgard and the hall he had been visiting were nowhere in sight. He assumed his customary shape as King Gylfi and returned to his kingdom. There he told his people what he had learned. And from that day until this, these tales have been passed from one human being to another.

Introducing **The Theft of Idun's Apples**

Historical Background

Snorri Sturluson tells this myth in his *Prose Edda*, written about A.D. 1220. An almost identical version exists in a poem written 300 years earlier. Although Sturluson lists Idun as one of the major Norse goddesses, this is the only existing myth about her. Originally, she was probably a Great Goddess or Mother Goddess like Frigg and Freya. Fruits are associated in my-

thology with life and death, and nuts may represent everlasting life.

Appeal and Value

Like many of the other Norse myths, "The Theft of Idun's Apples" is primarily a good adventure story. It reveals the character of Loki, which becomes progressively more evil as the time of

Ragnarok (doom of the gods) approaches. It also reveals the fragile nature of the Norse gods. Not only will they die at Ragnarok, but without Idun's golden apples to eat, they will lose their youth.

Like the Greek gods, the Norse gods feel, think, act, and speak like human beings. However, unlike the Greek gods, the Norse gods interact primarily with their own kind and leave the world of human beings alone. Because of the distance between the gods and humans, few Norse myths teach people how to behave toward one another and toward the gods.

The Theft of Idun's Apples

One day Odin, Loki, and Hoenir were traveling together as they often chose to do. They had left Asgard without carrying any food with them, and their journey over snow-capped mountains and arid deserts had tired them out. As they descended from the hills into a lush valley, they saw a herd of oxen and suddenly realized that they were very hungry.

"One of those cattle, well-roasted, will provide excellent fare for hungry travelers!" Loki exclaimed. "Look them over, choose a well-built ox, and I will prepare the meat."

The gods slaughtered a fine-looking animal and prepared to roast it upon a fire. They cooked the meat until it looked done, put out the fire, and sat down to eat it. To their great surprise, the meat was completely raw. They built a second fire, put the meat upon a second spit, and roasted it. They cooked the meat until it looked done, put out the fire, and sat down to eat it. Yet, the meat was still completely raw.

"What could possibly be wrong with this meat?" Odin asked his companions.

"Something sitting upon the branches of the oak tree is preventing your meat from cooking!" a voice exclaimed.

The gods immediately looked toward the oak tree and saw the Frost Giant Thjazi in the form of a great eagle sitting upon one of its branches.

"Let me eat as much as I want of your ox," the eagle told them, "and I will permit your meat to cook."

When the gods agreed, the eagle flew down from its perch, landed upon the meat, grabbed the two shoulder pieces and two thighs, and gobbled them up in a flash.

Furious at the eagle's greed, Loki picked up a sturdy stick and with all his might plunged it into the eagle's body. Before Loki could let go of the stick, the eagle flew up into the air, carrying him with it.

Loki found that the stick would not budge from the eagle and that he could not let go of the stick. The eagle dragged him along, flying low enough so that Loki's feet crashed over the surface of the earth, slamming against the stones and bushes in their path. "Let me go," he cried, "before you pull my arms from their sockets!"

"That I will agree to do, Loki," the eagle replied, "if you promise to bring me Idun and her golden apples. You must lure Idun out of Asgard and into the nearby forest so I can capture her. I shall meet you there two days from now. Swear a sacred oath that you will keep your word!"

"I swear that I shall do as you ask!" Loki exclaimed.

With that, the eagle released him and Loki returned to his companions. He did not disclose the promise he had made to the eagle. When the three gods returned to Asgard, Loki approached Idun and said, "I have found some beautiful golden apples in the forest. They look as lovely as yours. Bring your own basket of apples to compare them, and come with me. You will want to add the ones I have found to your collection."

Idun's eyes sparked at the prospect. Smiling with pleasure, the goddess took her basket of apples and set out with Loki for the forest. When they had wandered deep into the woods, the eagle suddenly swooped down upon them. Before Idun was aware of what was happening, the great bird snatched her in his claws and flew away with her.

The gods in Asgard knew that Idun was missing when she did not bring them her golden apples to eat. No matter where they looked, they could find neither her nor the apples, and no one could imagine what had happened to her. Of course, Loki appeared to be as surprised as the other gods.

Idun's disappearance was a very serious matter, for it was only by regularly eating her apples that the gods remained young. As the days passed and still Idun did not return, the gods became older and older. Their hair became gray, their faces and hands became wrinkled, and their walk became slow and hesitating.

Odin called the gods together to discuss the problem. They learned that the last time Idun had been seen, she was walking with Loki away from Asgard. The gods immediately grabbed Loki and bound him. Odin announced, "We will torture you to death unless you tell us what has happened to Idun!"

Loki, realizing that his life was in great danger, replied, "I will see if Idun is in Jotunheim (giants' home). I will search for her there if you, Freya, will lend me your falcon-feathered cloak."

"I will lend you whatever you wish!" Freya exclaimed.

So Loki put Freya's falcon-cloak upon his back and flew north to Jotunheim. When he arrived at Thjazi's house, the giant was out rowing upon the sea and Idun was home alone. Loki immediately changed the goddess and her golden apples into a nut and quickly flew off with her, holding her firmly in his claws.

When Thjazi returned, he looked everywhere but could not find Idun. Expecting that trouble had arrived in his absence, he changed himself into an eagle and flew off to learn what he could. Seeing the falcon, he flew after it.

The gods, who were waiting and watching in Asgard, saw Loki flying toward them bearing a nut in his claws. Approaching him quickly from behind was a huge eagle. The gods immediately gathered bags of wood shavings and set to work placing them around the walls of Asgard. As soon as the falcon flew over the wall into safety, the gods set fire to the shavings, causing roaring flames to rise high into the heavens.

The eagle was pursuing the falcon at too great a speed to change its course. It flew into the flames and its feathers caught fire. In agony, it dropped to the ground by the gates, and the gods killed it.

Skadi, Thjazi's daughter, was obligated to avenge her father's murder. She put on a full coat of armor, grabbed a weapon in each hand, and headed for Asgard.

When she arrived, Odin said, "It is customary to offer the relative of a dead man wergild (man-price) as compensation for his death. Therefore, we offer you the husband of your choice from among us. There is one condition: You must choose him based solely upon his feet."

Skadi agreed. She loved Odin's son Balder because he was so good. "I shall choose Balder as my husband!" she announced. "I am certain that I can find him, for everything about him must be beautiful, even his feet! Therefore, I choose . . . *these* feet!" she exclaimed.

The gods tried to hide their smiles as the owner of the feet appeared, for it was Njord, not Balder, who possessed them.

Odin then said, "Our payment will not be sufficient unless we can make you laugh."

Skadi gave him a dark look and replied, "I would like to see the one among you who can succeed. Given my choice of husband, I do not feel like laughing!"

However, Loki was a god of many talents. He became a trickster and waged a tug-of-war with a billy goat. When the god fell into her lap, Skadi laughed at his silly antics in spite of herself.

Odin then took Thjazi's two eyes and tossed them into the heavens to become bright stars. Skadi was honored by this tribute to her father. Satisfaction replaced her anger, and she made her peace with the gods.

Introducing **The Death of Balder**

Historical Background

"The Death of Balder" and the Norse creation myth are so closely related that the introduction preceding the creation myth applies to this myth as well. The major source of the myth is Icelandic. Snorri Sturluson tells the story in his *Gylfaginning (The Deluding of Gylfi)*.

Balder is one of a number of fertility gods in various mythologies who are killed, go down to the Underworld, and then come back to life. The pattern of life, death, and resurrection reflects the annual, cyclical pattern in nature of birth (spring), maturity (summer), death (autumn and winter), and rebirth (the following spring).

The myth of Balder begins during the period when the Norse gods are alive and well and life moves in an established pattern. However, as Odin knows, Balder's death is the event that initiates the destruction of that world. It ushers in a period in which the world order cracks apart and the gods and giants destroy each other in the last great battle of Ragnarok. Finally the whole world is destroyed, first by fire and then by flood. Balder reappears only when the earth emerges from the flood—fresh, fertile, and ready to support a new race of gods and a new race of human beings.

This myth differs somewhat from the simple scheme of life, death, and rebirth in many other fertility myths. Balder's death has a greater finality than that of the typical fertility god. His funeral is given major prominence, as if he were Beowulf, or any one of the other great Norse kings. The gods are unable to rescue him from the Underworld. In some respects, Balder appears to be a fertility god in name only. His attitudes and actions do not affect the weather, and he does not teach human beings how to plant particular crops. Yet his murder does lead to the disintegration and destruction of society and the entire world.

The emphasis upon the finality of Balder's death may reflect the fact that this is a fairly recent myth that indicates a shift in the interests of the Norse peoples. During the 5th century A.D., Norse society had become less centered on peaceful agricultural pursuits, which depend upon the cyclical aspects of nature. Instead, the Norse were beginning to turn their attention to more aggressive and acquisitive pursuits, in which wealth was provided by the sword instead of by the earth.

That Balder is resurrected at all testifies to the power of the original fertility myth and to the great appeal of the idea of rebirth and regeneration. Balder is the only major Norse god who returns from the dead to live in the new age. However, he reappears as one of a minor cast of divine characters whose function is, at best, undefined. His shadow remains long after his substance has disappeared.

Appeal and Value

The myth of Balder has enduring appeal for many reasons. First, it reflects two universal desires of human beings: to be immortal and to bring back from the dead those loved ones who have died.

Furthermore, the myth of Balder reflects the love of a parent for a child and the parent's anguish over a child's death. This great love is emphasized in the myth by the striking contrast of an equally great hatred, spawned from jealous anger. Our sympathies are with the good child, his loving parents and friends, and his very vulnerable brother.

However, this myth is also fascinating because of the evil god Loki, who is determined to destroy the virtuous Balder. We are drawn to Loki's clever, evil mind as we are drawn to the scene of any catastrophe. We follow him as he searches first for a way to destroy the victor, then for the weakest being to use as his unknowing accomplice, and finally for a way to prevent his own destruction. Although Loki achieves a great victory, we are glad that the fruits of his victory are not sweet and that evil does not triumph in the end.

The Death of Balder

Balder was the son of Odin and Frigg. He was the favorite of everyone among the gods because he was so good. He was the best of the gods, the wisest, kindest, and most gentle of them all. Purity and virtue surrounded him. He was as handsome as he was good, and he shone with a special radiance.

One day Balder the Good approached the assembled gods and said, "Last night I had a dreadful dream! I dreamed I was in Niflheim, the land of the dead, and Hel herself embraced me. She led me through her palace. The rooms were all of gold and the halls were decorated with jewels. My dream terrifies me, for it shows that I shall die very soon!"

The gods were horrified at the thought that their beloved Balder would die. They decided to search the world for whatever could possibly endanger Balder's life and to remove any threat. They were certain they would be able to prevent his death. Frigg, Balder's mother, volunteered to take this great task upon herself.

She traveled from one end of the world to the other. She approached every plant and every animal, every bird and every serpent, every metal and every stone, every illness and every poison, every drop of water, every speck of earth, and every spark of fire. She made each in turn swear a sacred oath that it would do nothing to harm Balder. They were happy to do as Frigg asked, for they too loved Balder.

Once the gods knew that Balder was safe, they enjoyed testing his invulnerability. Some would throw darts at him, some would throw stones, and others would strike him with metal weapons. Balder's eyes would sparkle, and he would grin and announce, "Try again! I did not even feel that!"

Loki watched Balder's invulnerability and hated him for it. He disguised himself as an old woman and visited Frigg. "I have stopped by to talk to you woman to woman," Loki said in a disguised voice. "I hear that you are the queen of the gods, so surely you have great power here. Are you aware that the gods have gathered in assembly to throw things at one who stands among them? I must admit that he seems to enjoy it. But he is such a beautiful god, it would be sad if someone killed him! Maybe you should walk down there and see for yourself. You might want to do something about their foolish sport!"

Frigg replied, "How kind of you to come to me. You must be speaking about Balder. However, there is no reason for you to be concerned because nothing will ever hurt him. I have made everything take a sacred oath not to harm him, so he is quite safe."

"Have you really demanded an oath from everything in the world?" Loki asked.

"Oh, yes!" Frigg replied. "After all, Balder is my son! I have received an oath from everything: every plant and every animal, every bird and every serpent, every metal and every stone, every illness and every poison, every drop of water, every speck of earth, and every spark of fire. Nothing will hurt Balder. I assure you that he really is quite safe!"

"You certainly seem very sure of yourself," Loki said. "If it were my son, I would fear that I had overlooked something. But you must know that you have missed nothing."

"Well, I did miss one thing," Frigg replied, "but that was intentional. A little mistletoe bush grows west of Valhalla. I did not demand that it take a sacred oath because it seemed too young to harm anyone!"

"I am certain you were right about that," Loki replied, and then he left Frigg and casually strolled back in the direction of the assembled gods. As soon as he was out of sight, he resumed his own shape and quickly walked toward the west. He passed the hall of Valhalla and kept walking.

Sure enough, he found the little mistletoe bush exactly where Frigg had said it was. He pulled the plant up by the roots and took it to the palace where the gods had assembled. As he walked, he pulled off the berries, the leaves, and the small twigs. He sharpened the end of the stalk to a point and then tucked the twig into his belt. "No one will notice it," he said to himself. "In fact, I shall see to it that they hardly notice me!"

When Loki reentered the assembly, the game with Balder was still in full swing. The hall resounded with happy laughter as the gods hurled every kind of object at the beautiful god, all with no effect whatsoever. Loki looked around and noticed that Hoder, Balder's blind brother, was standing apart from the other gods. Hoder looked rather forlorn because he had no way to participate in this game. Loki said, "Hoder, why are you the only god who is not throwing things at Balder?"

"Because I cannot see where he is," Hoder replied. "And besides, I have nothing to throw."

"I can take care of that!" Loki exclaimed. "You should be able to honor your brother as the other gods do. My arm will direct your arm to where Balder is standing, and you can throw at him the twig I will give you."

Hoder took the twig of mistletoe that Loki gave him, and letting Loki guide his arm, he threw the twig at his brother. The twig went right through Balder's heart, and he fell to the ground dead.

The gods stared in silent shock at their dead friend. Tears streamed down their cheeks, reflecting the grief that overflowed their hearts. They could not speak. They were so stunned that they did not even try to lift Balder. Some of the gods turned in the direction from which the missile had come. When they saw Loki walking quickly toward the door, they immediately knew who was to blame for the foul deed. However, they knew they would have to be patient. They were assembled in a sacred place and could not take vengeance upon Loki immediately.

Odin was the most upset of all the other gods. Not only had he lost his dear son, but he alone knew that the death of Balder was the first in a series of events that would end in the destruction of their race.

Frigg was the first to speak. "Whoever among you would win my everlasting gratitude and affection will do what I now ask of you. Ride down to Niflheim and see if you can find my son in the kingdom of the dead. If you are successful, approach Hel and see if she will let him return to Asgard. Since she is Loki's daughter, it might be best to offer her a wergild payment in return for Balder's life."

"I am happy to do this for my brother's sake!" Hermod the Bold exclaimed. He took Odin's horse, Sleipnir, and galloped away.

Meanwhile, the gods carried Balder's body down to the sea. They placed it upon a funeral pyre on board his ship and then put his personal treasures next to his body. They even killed his harnessed horse and placed it on the pyre.

All of the gods were present to pay their last respects to the best of the gods. Thor directed the preparations. Odin arrived with Frigg, his Valkyries, and his two ravens, Hugin and Munin. Frey arrived in his boar-driven chariot. Freya arrived in her cat-driven chariot. Heimdall arrived on his horse. Even the Cliff Giants and the Frost Giants came to honor Balder the Good. Each god and guest boarded the funeral ship and added a treasured token of his or her own to the assembled pile of wealth. Finally, Odin added his own great treasure, his wondrous gold arm-ring that created eight more gold rings of equal weight every ninth night.

Balder's wife was so beset with grief that her heart burst and she died of sorrow. The gods placed her body next to that of her husband on the pyre. When the flames of the funeral fire roared toward the heavens, they set the ship afloat upon the sea for the waves to carry as they chose.

Meanwhile, Hermod rode for nine days and nine nights through such dark valleys that he could see nothing in front of him, nothing to the side of him, and nothing behind him. Finally, he reached the last river that divided the land of the living from the land of the dead. Stretching across it was a covered bridge with a roof that gleamed with gold even in the darkness.

As he approached the bridge, the maiden who guarded it asked him, "Who are you, and who is your father? Yesterday five troops of dead men rode across this bridge with less noise than you are making. You must be alive! Why then are you riding this road into Hel?"

Hermod the Bold replied, "I am Hermod, son of Odin the All-Father, and indeed I am very much alive! I must ride this road into Niflheim, for I must search the kingdom of the dead for my beloved brother, Balder the Good. Have you seen him cross your bridge?"

"Yes, Balder has crossed my bridge," the maiden replied. "Follow the road that goes continuously downhill and to the north, for that is the way to Niflheim. However, I warn you that the kingdom of the dead is surrounded by a very high wall. You will have to devise a way to get through its gates."

Hermod thanked her and rode on until he came to the gates of Hel's kingdom. These gates were high and locked to anyone who still had the wind of life within his body. Hermod dug his spurs into Sleipnir and said, "Take me over the gates!"

Sleipnir jumped so high that Hermod could see the gates far below as they cleared them. He rode up to Hel's palace, dismounted, and entered. The hall was crowded with the ghosts of the dead: male and female, old and young, rich and poor, virtuous and evil. Only the great heroes were spared eternal existence in the land of the dead. They were the fortunate ones, for Odin's Valkyries had chosen them when they died in battle and had brought them to the golden-bright Valhalla, where every day they prepared to fight on the side of the gods at Ragnarok in the last great battle.

Hermod walked through the hall, ignoring the hordes of ghosts. Balder was sitting on the high seat, as testimony to the great god that he was, and Hermod had eyes only for his brother.

Hermod spent the night with Balder, and in the morning he said to Hel, "My name is Hermod, and I am the son of Odin and Frigg. I have come from the home of the gods to ask if you will let me take my brother, Balder, back to Asgard. The hearts of all the gods are filled with grief at his death, so great is their love for him. Frigg promises you a fitting wergild in exchange for Balder's life."

Hel replied, "I shall release Balder only if you can meet one condition. You must prove to me that he is so loved that everyone and everything in the world, both alive and dead, will weep for him. If one thing objects to his return or refuses to weep for him, then Balder must remain with me in my kingdom."

"I am certain your condition will be met," Hermod replied. "My mother took an oath from everything in the world to protect Balder's life. Every plant and every animal, every bird and every serpent, every metal and every stone, every illness and every poison, every drop of water, every speck of earth, and every spark of fire promised to value his life. Surely they will weep for him!"

"For your sake, I hope you are right!" Hel exclaimed. "However, no matter how certain you are, I must have proof."

Balder then led Hermod out of the palace. As Hermod prepared to mount Sleipnir, Balder said to him, "Thank you for making this long, fearsome journey on my behalf. The gods call you Hermod the Bold with good reason. Only Father and the great Thor have as much courage as you! Do this favor for me. Return our father's wondrous golden arm-ring to him as a token of my love for him."

"This I shall do, Balder," Hermod replied. "Meanwhile, be of good courage! The gods are determined to free you from this dismal kingdom. I am certain that you will see the world of sunlight once again."

Hermod returned to Asgard and related his tale to the assembled company. The gods immediately sent messengers throughout the entire world requesting that every creature and form in nature, both alive and dead, weep for Balder to achieve his release from Hel. Everything they asked agreed, for Balder the Good was beloved by all that existed. Just as all things weep when they have been covered with frost and then are suddenly exposed to the hot rays of the sun, so every plant and every animal wept, every bird and every serpent wept, every metal and every stone wept, every illness and every poison wept, every drop of water, every speck of earth, and every spark of fire wept.

The messengers were returning to Asgard very pleased with the success of their journey when they came upon a giantess sitting in a dark cave. They greeted her and said, "Every other creature and form in nature, both alive and dead, is weeping for Balder in order to release him from the kingdom of the dead. Please add your tears to theirs, for Hel has demanded that no one must refuse to weep if Balder is to return to Asgard."

To their surprise the giantess replied, "No one will ever see tears flow from my eyes and course down my cheeks. Balder means nothing to me, whether he is alive or dead. If Hel has him in her kingdom, let her keep him there!"

No matter how the messengers pleaded with her, the giantess would not change her mind. They sadly returned to the assembled gods without having met the condition that Hel had set for Balder's release.

When the gods heard their story, tears streamed down their cheeks, reflecting the grief that overflowed their hearts. They knew who was to blame for this foul deed also. The giantess who refused to weep for Balder was none other than Loki in one of his many disguises. With grim determination they silently marched forth from Asgard to take vengeance upon him.

Loki, knowing that he had not fooled them, ran for his life. He hid high upon a mountainside above the sea, where he built a small, inconspicuous house with one door facing in each of the four directions. He hoped to see the gods coming soon enough to assure himself a quick escape. He tried to remain calm and unworried. He tried to take his eyes off the valley below. He tried not to jump at sudden sounds in the night. While he waited for the gods to discover him, Loki often changed himself into the form of a salmon and hid among the waters of a nearby waterfall, where he caught smaller fish for dinner.

At night he would sit in his house by the fire and amuse himself by trying to imagine what device the gods would use in their attempt to capture him. As his mind played with possibilities, he took linen threads and twisted them this way and that until he had created a mesh net. "This would certainly be a fine way to catch a fish!" he exclaimed. Then he shuddered and tossed the net into the heart of the fire as if it already had caught him.

Meanwhile, the gods continued their pursuit. Odin had sat upon his high seat from which he could see everything in the world, and he had watched Loki build his house upon the mountainside. Steadily and surely the gods approached Loki's hideaway. Their rage was implacable. They would capture this devious creature who often seemed to be one of them but whom they never could trust.

When they were near enough for Loki to hear them, he ran out of the back door, transformed himself into a salmon, and jumped into the waterfall.

The first of the gods to enter Loki's house was the wisest of them all. He looked carefully around the room, taking note of every detail as he looked for a clue to Loki's whereabouts. Finally, he spied the white ashes in Loki's fireplace and instantly recognized the pattern of a net. "Loki has taken the form of a fish!" he exclaimed. "Search the mountain stream by the waterfall, and I am sure you will find him there! I shall quickly make you a net like the one that Loki himself designed, and you can catch him with it."

Early the next morning the gods were at the waterfall with this clever device. Together they threw it into the water. Thor grabbed one side of the net and leaped across the mountain stream to the far side of the waterfall. All of the other gods stood on the near side. Together, they dragged the net through the waterfall and downstream toward the sea.

Loki fled deep beneath the cascade of water and hid himself in a crevice between two stones. The gods missed him the first time, but the second time they saw where he was hiding. They put weights into the net so that no fish could swim beneath it. Then they slowly moved the net from the waterfall downstream toward the sea. To avoid being caught, Loki was forced to swim downstream ahead of the moving net.

Finally, Loki saw that he had a difficult choice. He would either have to swim out to sea, which surely would kill him, or jump over the net and swim back upstream to the waterfall. Thor anticipated Loki's decision and waded into the rushing stream. When Loki jumped, Thor was ready to catch him. Salmon are slippery, however. No matter how Thor clutched at the body of the fish, it slid through his fingers. Finally, Thor dug his nails into the salmon's tail. Loki had lost the battle.

The gods took Loki up to a deep, dark cave in the mountain. They took three huge rocks and drilled a hole in each one. Next they captured Loki's two sons. They transformed Fenrir into a wolf, which proceeded to devour his brother. The gods then bound Loki to the three rocks using his dead son's intestines, which hardened into cords of iron. Then they hung a poisonous snake over Loki's head so that it would continuously drip venom on Loki's face. Satisfied with their vengeance, the gods returned to Asgard.

Fenrir found his mother and led her to Loki's side. She could not free her husband, but she tried to make his captivity more bearable by holding a bowl above his face to catch the snake's venom. When the bowl became full and she had to empty it, the venom would sear Loki's skin and he would writhe in excruciating pain, causing the whole earth to shake.

Loki remained imprisoned in this manner until Ragnarok, the time of the last great battle between the gods and the giants. When a violent earthquake caused even the great mountains to crumble, Loki's fetters snapped and he was free once more. He went down to Niflheim and brought his daughter and the fiends of Hel up from the kingdom of the dead to the battlefield. He and his monstrous children fought on the side of the giants. In the end he and Heimdall, the watchman of the gods, killed each other.

The entire world came to an end with Ragnarok. Gods and giants killed each other. Raging flames destroyed anything the earthquakes had left untouched. The earth became a wasteland, and in time a great flood covered it.

At the dawn of the new age, the earth rose forth from the sea, fresh, fertile, and green. Balder left the kingdom of the dead and joined the young gods who had survived the great destruction. The world as they had known it had disappeared, but they hoped to preside over a better world.

Introducing **The Theft of Thor's Hammer**

The first written record of "The Theft of Thor's Hammer" is in the *Elder Edda*, where it is called "The Lay of Thrym." Dating from about A.D. 900, it is one of the oldest Norse poems. As a work of literature, it is the best of the short Norse myths.

"The Theft of Thor's Hammer" is a wonderfully appealing myth because of its great humor. The idea that Thor, the "superman" of Norse myth,

should have to pretend to be a female must have brought smiles to listeners and readers throughout the centuries. Loki's role is also amusing. It is a pleasure to meet Loki, whose mischief is all too often evil, as a good-hearted conspirator, similar to Hermes among the Greek gods. Freya is a beautiful fertility goddess, and her sexual appeal is apparent in other Norse myths also.

The Theft of Thor's Hammer

One morning when Thor the Hammer-Hurler awoke, he could not find Mjollnir, his hammer. His heart flooded with a violent rage. He angrily shook his red hair and tore his fingers through his beard as he looked first in one place and then in another, without success.

Finally, in desperation, he found Loki and said, "Someone has stolen my hammer. The gods in Asgard have not seen him. No one in Midgard has seen him. Whoever the culprit is, he is a crafty one!"

Loki replied, "Come with me to Freya's palace, Thor, and we will see what we can do about it."

Upon finding Freya, Loki said, "Will you lend me your falcon-feathered cloak so I can fly to Jotunheim to search for Thor's sacred hammer? Surely it is there somewhere, for no one but a giant would have taken it!"

"Of course, Loki," Freya replied. "I would give you my cloak even if it were made of pure silver or gold. Take it, and may it bring you what you are looking for!"

The falcon feathers whistled in the wind as Loki flew to Jotunheim. He found the Frost Giant Thrym sitting in the Hall of Giants, twisting strands of gold into collars for the hounds in his pen and combing the manes of the horses that he loved.

Hearing someone enter, Thrym looked up from his work and said, "Hello there, Loki! How are the gods? How are the elves? Why have you come to Jotunheim?"

Loki replied, "The gods and the elves are beset with grave trouble! Have you stolen and hidden the hammer of thunder?"

"Why, yes, indeed I have!" Thrym confessed. "I buried it eight miles deep in the earth. I shall not give it to any god until Freya agrees to be my bride!"

The feathers of Freya's falcon-coat whistled in the wind as Loki flew back to Asgard. Thor was waiting when he landed.

"I hope you have returned with a message and are not up to some mischief!" the Hammer-Hurler exclaimed. "Stay right where you are and tell me what news you bring."

"I do bring news and not mischief," Loki replied. "The giant Thrym has stolen your hammer and hidden it. He will not return it until we bring Freya to become his bride."

"Then let us see Freya immediately!" Thor replied.

Loki said to the goddess, "Place a bridal veil upon your head, Freya, for you must come with me to Jotunheim.

"What do you mean, Loki?" Freya asked angrily. Her palace quivered and quaked with her rage, and her Brising necklace, that glorious dwarf-crafted ring of twisted gold, split into pieces and fell to the floor. "The gods would think me a disloyal wife to Odr if I went to Jotunheim to marry another, and I certainly would never marry a Frost Giant!"

Thor, realizing the justice of Freya's attitude, asked Odin to call the gods and goddesses together in order to consider their next step. The hammer of thunder was a mighty weapon; its theft was no minor matter.

Heimdall, the wisest of the gods, devised the solution. "Thor himself is the answer to the problem!" Heimdall exclaimed. "We must dress him as Thrym's bride. We can repair Freya's Brising necklace and place it upon his neck. We can pin large brooches upon his chest, hide his legs behind a long dress, hang a bunch of women's keys at his waist, put a neat cap upon his red hair, and hide his face behind a bridal veil."

"Seeing me dressed as a bride will give all of you a mighty laugh!" Thor replied. "I am not certain it will accomplish anything else."

Loki replied, "Hold your tongue, Thunderer! We must capture your hammer if we are to defend Asgard against the giants. They would be all too glad to occupy our palaces."

So it came to pass that the gods placed Freya's necklace around Thor's neck, pinned broaches upon his chest, hid his legs behind a long dress, hung a bunch of keys at his waist, covered his hair with a neat cap, and arranged a bridal veil over his face.

When the disguise was complete, Loki announced, "I shall accompany you on your journey, Thor. I shall disguise myself as your handmaid, and together we will go to Jotunheim and make fools of the giants."

Thor drove his goats from their pasture and harnessed them to his chariot. The mountains echoed with the roar of thunder, and fires from mighty lightning bolts scorched the earth as Thor's chariot sped through the sky.

Meanwhile, in Jotunheim, Thrym eagerly prepared to receive his new wife. "Arise, Frost Giants, and place straw upon my benches. The gods may arrive at any time with my bride! I am happy that I have beautiful, gold-horned cattle grazing in my fields. I am happy that I possess a great treasure of gold and many gems. I am happy that I have much to delight my eyes. I lack only Freya for my heart's content!"

Evening arrived, and with it Thrym's beloved. The giants set a feast of food and ale before the bride. She quickly consumed all the sweet dainties that had been reserved for the women, plus a whole ox and eight large salmon. She drank more than three horns of mead.

Thrym could not take his eyes off his beloved, and he could not help but wonder at what he saw. "Has any other bride ever had such a great appetite?" he asked. "Has any other bride ever taken such big mouthfuls of food or drunk as much mead?"

Loki, the handmaid, craftily replied, "Freya has so longed for her wedding day that she has not eaten for eight long days!"

Thrym, overcome with love for his bride, lifted her veil and leaned forward to kiss her. One look at her face sent him leaping backward the full length of his hall. "How fierce my beloved's eyes are!" the giant exclaimed. "Dangerous fires blaze forth beneath her brows!"

Loki craftily replied, "Freya has so longed for her wedding day that she has not slept for eight long nights!"

The unfortunate sister of the unfortunate giant then dared to command the bride, "Give me your golden rings! In return, I will give you my favor, my good-will, and my blessing!"

Then Thrym said, "Bring forth Thor's mighty hammer in order to bless the bride. Lay Mjollnir upon her lap, and wish us joy as we join hands and make our marriage vows."

Thor's heart leapt with joy when his mighty hammer was placed in his lap. Quickly he grabbed Mjollnir and smashed Thrym to the ground. Then, one by one, Thor killed all the Frost Giant's kin. The sister who had dared to demand bridal gifts received a deathly blow on her head instead of gold rings on her fingers. And Thor recovered his hammer of thunder.

Introducing **Sigurd the Volsung**

Historical Background

Many scholars consider the Teutonic epic of *Sigurd the Volsung* to be *The Iliad* of the northern countries. The story exists in Scandinavian, British, and German literature. The earliest existing version appears in the epic of *Beowulf* (written in about A.D. 1000), where a minstrel sings the tale as entertainment for the nobility. Clearly, the story was already famous at that time. *The Volsunga Saga*, written in 1300 by an anonymous author, is the definitive Norse version because it is the most detailed, cohesive, and complete version of the story.

The saga of *Sigurd* reflects the unstable political conditions in northern Europe between A.D. 400 and 600, before the arrival of Christianity in that part of the world. The wars between neighboring kingdoms produced numerous local heroes and villains, and their daring deeds became the subjects of popular songs and poems.

Appeal and Value

For hundreds of years the story of *Sigurd* disappeared from view, because its stark drama and pre-Christian values did not appeal to people living during those centuries. In the 19th century *Sigurd* again became popular when writers recognized the saga's many attractions.

First, *Sigurd* is an outstanding adventure story. It contains magic, a monster, cursed treasure, passionate love, violent hatred, jealousy, treachery, danger, and death. Within its pages are both an early version of the Sleeping Beauty and a major source for the tale of the cursed ring that J. R. R. Tolkien used in the *Lord of the Rings* trilogy and Richard Wagner used in his cycle of four operas, *The Ring of the Nibelung*.

Second, Sigurd is an ideal hero. His wisdom is as great as his courage. He chooses to lead an honorable life by putting the needs of others above his own personal desires.

Third, the story contains numerous complex characters who are loyal to their families and friends until circumstances lead them to act treacherously. They are intelligent but they act foolishly, with tragic consequences. They cannot profit from prophecies because their human frailties doom them. No one in the saga is completely predictable or completely trustworthy, and this creates an atmosphere of suspense, excitement, and danger.

The reader can easily identify with the problems and emotions of the characters in *Sigurd*. They struggle to find happiness and to lead meaningful lives in a world that is uncaring, brutal, and treacherous. Death is inevitable, and the Norse gods offer no solace. The characters cannot control their fates. They can only try to control their values, attitudes, and behavior. Their struggle to create meaning in their lives is viewed on a bare stage under harsh lighting. Life is a tragic experience, and the best the characters can hope for is to live with dignity.

The story of *Sigurd* strikes a sympathetic chord today because we too must create a meaningful life in a world that is often uncaring and dangerous. Ultimately, we must accept the inevitability of death. We must not give in to despair but must concentrate on the aspects of our lives that we can control. Like the characters in *Sigurd*, we cannot determine when we will die, but we can try to determine how we live.

The Norse Hero

In the Norse world, events are controlled by an unalterable fate. Both gods and humans know that their inevitable destiny is death. Since immortality exists only in the memory of the living, achieving honor and fame is the hero's principal goal.

The Norse hero creates his own meaning by living in such a way that others honor him. His greatness is measured by the quality of his life and the courage and dignity with which he faces death. Honor is achieved primarily on the battlefield, where the hero attains glory by reason of whom he kills and the amount of treasure he acquires. The heroic goal is fame after death, the only immortality that a mortal can achieve. The hero aims to accomplish feats worth remembering—the type of great and glorious deeds that inspire poets and singers.

In the Norse world, a person's first loyalty is to his or her king. Family comes second, and friends third. No one else seems to exist. Gold is the greatest treasure. The noble person shares it generously, but the temptation to hoard treasure and let it corrupt one's personal values is very strong. Only the best human beings can withstand the temptation.

Retribution dominates Norse society. Justice is a private affair, between one person and another or between one family and another. In the case of accidental death or murder, each individual takes full responsibility for his or her actions. The killer may choose to offer wergild (man-price), which is a designated payment as restitution for the death, but the recipient is free to reject the offer. As often as not, blood vengeance is the rule. The character accepts his or her punishment—death—without flinching, and the family feud continues to demand one life after another.

Only the fittest survive, but raw courage and strength are not sufficient. The man or woman who is generous and loyal is less likely to have to stand alone against the human and natural world. However, in the Norse world, no one is safe.

Principal Characters*

SIGMUND: son of Volsung; king of Hunland; father of Sigurd

SIGURD: son of Sigmund; performs heroic deeds

HREIDMAR: father of Regin, Fafnir, and Otter; skilled in magic

FAFNIR: son of Hreidmar; brother of Regin and Otter; takes the form of a dragon

REGIN: son of Hreidmar; brother of Fafnir and Otter; tutors Sigurd

OTTER: son of Hreidmar; brother of Fafnir and Regin; often takes the form of an otter

ANDVARI: dwarf; possesses a magic ring and a hoard of gold

BRUNHILD: disobedient Valkyrie; rescued by Sigurd; wife of Gunnar

ATLI: brother of Brunhild; husband of Gudrun after Sigurd's death

GIUKI: king of a land south of the Rhine; husband of Grimhild; father of Gunnar, Hogni, Guttorm, and Gudrun

GRIMHILD: wife of Giuki; mother of Gunnar, Hogni, Guttorm, and Gudrun; skilled in magic

GUNNAR: son of Giuki and Grimhild; brother of Hogni, Guttorm, and Gudrun; husband of Brunhild

HOGNI: son of Giuki and Grimhild; brother of Gunnar, Guttorm, and Gudrun

GUTTORM: youngest child of Giuki and Grimhild; brother of Gunnar, Hogni, and Gudrun

GUDRUN: daughter of Giuki and Grimhild; sister of Gunnar, Hogni, and Guttorm; wife of Sigurd and later of Atli

*For a list of the Norse gods, see pages 207–8.

Sigurd the Volsung

Chapter 1

Sigmund, son of Volsung, pulls the god Odin's sword from the trunk of a tree. On the day that Sigmund is fated to die, Odin smashes the sword. Sigmund tells his wife to save the pieces for their son and then dies.

Listen to this tale from the heart of the north country, a land of snow-capped mountains, icy hills, and cold, grey seas. Hear of Sigurd, hero bright as the sun, and of Brunhild and Gudrun, who loved him. Hear of the treachery and woe that form the dark side of love and joy. Hear of men and women, heroes and villains, love and hate, life and death. Listen!

In days of old, Volsung, the great-grandson of Odin and the king of Hunland, was the greatest of all warriors — the strongest, most skilled, and most daring of all. He built his royal house around a huge oak tree, so the trunk of the tree grew through the center of the great hall and its many branches overshadowed the roof of the building.

The most noble of King Volsung's many children were his youngest, the twins Sigmund and Signy. King Volsung gave his daughter Signy in marriage to the king of Gothland. The Volsung family and their guests gathered in the great hall to enjoy the wedding feast. Suddenly a strange, old, long-bearded man walked, unannounced, into the room. He was barefoot and huge, and something about him seemed to speak of another, ancient time. He wore a blue cloak and a broad-brimmed hat that overshadowed his forehead, and he had only one eye. In his hand he held a shimmering long-bladed sword.

With broad steps, the old man strode up to the great trunk of the oak tree and plunged his sword deep into the wood, so that only the hilt of the sword was visible. While the family and their guests stood in amazed silence, the stranger announced, "Whoever draws this sword from this oak will have the sword as my gift to him, and will find that he never had a better friend in time of need." The old man then turned and left the hall. Everyone present realized that the visitor had been Odin, the All-Father.

Immediately, all of the noblemen rushed toward the sword in the tree. But it would not budge, no matter how hard they tugged. Finally, Sigmund put his hand upon the hilt and withdrew the sword as easily as if it lay loosely in the wood.

Sigmund announced, "I am destined to own this sword, for I have withdrawn it from its place in the tree. I will never give it up, even if a mighty king offers to pay me all the gold that he possesses!"

In time, Sigmund became the noble king of Hunland. So great were his courage and cunning, his skill in warfare, and the treasure he had won with his sword that his name was known throughout the northern lands.

After ruling wisely for many years, one day Sigmund was forced to fight an invading army. In spite of his age, he fought with great strength and skill. The battle raged furiously; the sky became gray with the passage of arrows and spears. Sigmund was covered with the blood of his enemies, yet he himself remained unwounded.

Suddenly, into the midst of the battle came an old, long-bearded man. He wore a blue cloak and a broad-brimmed hat that overshadowed his forehead, and he had only one eye. In his hand he carried a hooked spear. The old man approached King Sigmund and said, "Sigmund the Volsung, your time has come!" With that, he attacked the king.

Sigmund confidently struck the hooked spear with his own marvelous sword. But to his amazement the impact broke his sword into pieces, as if it were an ordinary weapon.

From that moment, Sigmund's success left him. No matter how well he fought, his enemies remained strong, while his men fell to their deaths all around him. Finally Sigmund received his death wound.

That night, the queen came out of hiding and searched among the corpses that littered the battlefield for her husband's body. She found Sigmund still alive.

While she comforted him, he said, "Odin, the All-Father, has brought an end to my days as a warrior. I am dying. Care for our son who is now within you and who is destined to be the most noble and famous of all the Volsungs. Preserve the pieces of my broken sword for him. They can be recast and will make a great sword called Gram, with which our son will accomplish deeds that will make his name live as long as there are bards on earth to tell the tale. Now let me rest here until Death claims me."

The queen sat with her husband throughout the night, and he died with the coming of dawn. The early morning light revealed many ships sailing toward them.

The young king of Denmark landed with his men and took Sigmund's queen and treasure back to his country. He promised the captive queen, "I will make you my wife, and you will live with honor in this kingdom. You will continue to be regarded as the best of women, and your son will be born into a royal home."

Chapter 2

Odin helps Sigurd choose his horse, Grani. His tutor,
Regin, tells Sigurd about the dwarf Andvari's hoard of
gold and the curse that Andvari placed upon it.

Sigurd, the son of Sigmund, was extraordinary from the time of his birth. He was raised in the royal house of Denmark, where he was loved and honored. All who met him marveled at his size, his strength, his courage, his skill, his intelligence, and his good heart. No one in the north lands could match Sigurd's gifts.

Sigurd's tutor was a gifted man by the name of Regin, who had earned fame as a metalsmith. Regin taught Sigurd to speak many languages, understand the ancient letters called runes, use weapons, and master all the other skills a prince was expected to know.

One day Regin said to Sigurd, "I am amazed to see that you are treated like a servant of the Danish king!"

"You are wrong!" Sigurd replied. "I can do whatever I want, and if I ever wish for anything, the king gives me what I desire with a cheerful heart."

"Then," Regin counseled, "I suggest that you ask him to give you a horse."

Sigurd went to the king and said, "I think that I am old enough now to have my own horse. I would like to train it myself."

The king replied, "Choose whatever horse you wish, Sigurd, and whatever else you desire as well."

Sigurd immediately left the great hall and set out to find the royal horses. He was walking through the forest when he came upon an old, long-bearded man whom he had never seen before. The man was wearing a blue cloak and a broad-brimmed hat that overshadowed his forehead, and he had only one eye.

"Where are you going, Sigurd, son of Sigmund the Volsung?" the old man asked him.

"Sir, I am going to find the royal horses," Sigurd replied, "for I intend to choose the best one for myself. You appear to be a very wise man. Would you like to come along and advise me?" he asked.

"That is just what I had in mind," the old man replied. "Let us drive the horses into the fast-flowing river. That should test their courage and strength!"

So the old man and the youth found the royal horses and drove them into the fast-flowing waters. Horse after horse shied away from the turbulent water. Some were so skittish that they would not enter the water at all. Others reared up on their hind legs in fright, turned around, and quickly regained dry land. Only one horse forged across the river. He was beautiful to see: gray in color, unusually large and strong in build, and yet quite young.

"The gray horse is the one I would choose!" Sigurd exclaimed. "I do not remember seeing him among these horses before today, or surely I would have remembered him. What do you think of my choice?"

"You have chosen wisely and well, Sigurd the Volsung!" the old man replied. "That gray horse is related to my horse, Sleipnir. Feed him well, and care for him. He will repay you by being the best of all horses!" And with these words, the old man vanished.

Then Sigurd realized that it was Odin, the All-Father, who had helped him. He called his horse Grani and trained him well.

Regin was still not satisfied. One day he said to Sigurd, "I marvel that you are satisfied to play here upon the royal grounds as if you were a peasant lad. Out in the world you would find treasure for the taking, and you would earn fame and honor by winning it. You are old enough and skilled enough. You have within you the blood of the mighty Volsungs. But tell me, do you have the courage needed for adventure?"

"Of course I do!" the youth replied. "What treasure do you have in mind? Where is it? And why is it available for the taking?"

Regin replied, "I have in mind the treasure that is guarded by the dragon Fafnir, whose den is on the Gnita Heath. He sits upon more gold than you will ever find in one place, and even the most greedy king would be satisfied with such a treasure!"

"Are you trying to help me or kill me?" Sigurd asked. "Young as I am, even I have heard of that treasure and that dragon! The monster is unusually large and evil. He continues to guard that treasure because there is no man alive who has the courage to fight him! How do you expect me to succeed where all others have failed?"

"Clearly you are no Volsung!" Regin replied. "Your father would never let children's tales fill his heart with terror! He had courage in his heart, not mush. Among those whose deeds have earned them lasting fame and honor, Sigmund the Volsung stood tallest. How ashamed he would be to think that his son was afraid of an ordinary dragon!"

"I am still so young that I am certain that I lack my father's strength and skill," Sigurd replied. "But I do not deserve to have you call me a coward! Why are you treating me like this? You must have some reason hiding behind your taunting words!"

"I certainly do!" said Regin. "I have a tale that I have been waiting many a year to tell you. You have come of age, and I have trained you well. You are ready. Listen to my tale, for it is the story of my life."

My father, Hreidmar, was a man of great strength and great wealth, and he taught us his skill in the arts of magic. He had three sons: Fafnir, Otter, and me. Fafnir was most similar to our father, both in physical strength and in greed. He possessed one extraordinary gift. He could change his shape to please himself.

Otter was completely different from Fafnir. He was simple, gentle, and kind. He loved to fish, and he was quite skilled at that pursuit. Like Fafnir, he could change his shape. He particularly enjoyed becoming an otter. In that form he would spend each day, from dawn to dusk, by the side of the river near the base of a waterfall.

Otter loved to plunge into the water to catch a fish, swim back to shore, and place it on the river bank. By the time the sun was setting, he would have stacked a sizable pile of fish. He would gather the fish he had caught into a net and bring them to our father. Otter would eat alone and then go to sleep. Nothing on dry land interested him, so he spent most of his time in the appearance of an otter, and he lived from one day's fishing to the next.

I was different from my brothers. I excelled in a more ordinary way. I loved to work with metals, and I became quite skilled at creating objects in silver and gold, and in working with iron as well.

Behind the waterfall near Otter's favorite fishing place lived a dwarf named Andvari. The waterfall itself was called Andvari's Force. Like Otter, Andvari could change his shape, and he too loved to fish. The dwarf fished in the form of a pike, and he ate the smaller fish that came over the waterfall. So many fish swam over the waterfall that there were always more than enough for both Otter and Andvari.

One day the gods Odin, Loki, and Hoenir were wandering upon the earth disguised as ordinary mortals. They enjoyed leaving Asgard, the home of the gods, to visit the homes of country folk. So it happened that the three gods came upon Andvari's Force. The sun was low in the sky, and it was time for supper. Otter had caught a salmon and was lazily lounging upon the bank of the river, about to eat it.

Loki spied both the otter and the salmon and said, "I think that I can kill that otter with the toss of one stone, and then we will have both otter and salmon to eat! That surely will satisfy our hunger!" He picked up a large stone, tossed it, and killed Otter. The gods then collected the otter and the salmon and walked toward our father's house.

"May we spend the night with you?" Odin asked my father when he opened the door. "We have brought enough food for all of us!"

Hreidmar courteously invited the visitors inside. However, when he noticed the otter hanging from Loki's hand, he became enraged. "What kind of guests are you?" he roared. "You have killed my son! I shall return your kindness in equal measure!"

With these words, my father secretly signaled to Fafnir and me. We quickly grabbed our visitors and placed chains around them.

"Now prepare to die!" Hreidmar exclaimed. "You will pay with your lives for the crime you have committed!"

"You are being unduly harsh, sir!" Odin complained. "Your son's death was an accident! My companion killed what appeared to be an ordinary otter. How could we know that your son had transformed himself into an animal? If you agree to free us, we will pay you as much wergild as you demand. Will you accept treasure instead of our deaths?"

"All right, then," Hreidmar replied. "As payment for slaying my son Otter, I demand that you pay me the value I have set upon his life. Fill the interior of his otter skin with gold, then stand the skin upon its tail and cover the entire exterior with gold. Not one hair on the skin must be visible. If you refuse, I will kill the three of you as you killed my son!"

Hreidmar concluded, "You may discuss among the three of you who will collect the gold, for I intend to keep the other two here as my prisoners until you make this payment."

Odin and Hoenir looked at Loki in dismay. Then Odin said to Loki, "I think it is best that you locate the wergild for us, for you are far more clever than we are and you know where to look for it. As I look upon our host, I can tell that he is a man who will keep his word."

Once we had freed Loki, he went down to the bottom of the sea and borrowed a large net from the sea goddess Ran. He returned with it to Andvari's Force. He swiftly cast his net over the waters with such skill that it enclosed the pike before the fish became aware of the danger and could swim out of reach. Loki then drew the thrashing pike from the water and placed it, still confined in Ran's net, upon the bank next to him.

"Pike," Loki began, "if fish you truly are, how is it that you survive in the waterfall without being crushed, and yet you do not have the good sense to be aware that nets are no friends of yours? Who are you?"

"People call me Andvari," the pike craftily replied, "and in my true form I am a dwarf. The Norns, who determine the destiny of every mortal being, have changed me into the pike you see. They have forced me to spend all the days of my life swimming in rivers. I do not enjoy it, but I have no choice!"

"So you are Andvari!" Loki replied. "You need say no more! Nets are not the only enemies you have! If you intend ever to leave Ran's net alive, you must promise to give me all of the gold that you guard behind Andvari's Force in that cave of yours. Do not try to deny it, for I shall kill you before I believe any other tales you create in order to deceive me!"

Loki convinced Andvari to resume his dwarf shape and bring him the gold that the gods needed in order to free themselves from my father's wrath and make amends for the death of my brother. Andvari soon returned to Loki in his true shape, lugging an enormous bag of gold.

Loki opened the bag and grinned with delight. Then he spied a beautiful gold ring upon Andvari's finger. "I'll take that, too!" he exclaimed.

"Let me keep just this one ring! "Andvari pleaded. "It is of little use to you. However, because I am a dwarf, I can use it to create more gold."

"No," Loki replied, "I intend to take every piece of gold you have, including that ring!"

When Andvari made no effort to remove the ring, Loki grabbed the dwarf from behind and pulled it from his finger. Satisfied that he had acquired every ounce of treasure, Loki then released the dwarf.

Andvari ran to the rocks by the waterfall and shouted, "From this time forth, that gold ring and all of the treasure that accompanies it will be the bane of every being who possesses it! Death and destruction will follow the gold as surely as night follows day, and no one who owns it will remain untouched by its curse. Only when the ring and the gold have returned to the deep waters will the bane end."

Loki ignored the dwarf's curse. He put the beautiful ring on his own finger and walked toward Hreidmar's house, dragging the bag of gold behind him.

Odin admired Andvari's beautiful ring, so Loki gave it to him. Then Loki took the otter skin and stuffed it with gold coins until the skin looked as if it might burst. When not another coin would fit into it, he stood the otter skin upon its tail and began to pile the gold around it. As Hreidmar had anticipated, in order for the fur to be covered it had to be completely buried in gold.

Loki was forced to use every gold coin in Andvari's bag to fulfill the terms of Hreidmar's wergild. Finally, Loki had emptied the bag and had arranged the coins so that even Hreidmar would be satisfied.

Hreidmar examined the pile with great care. "Ah!" he exclaimed. "I see an exposed hair — right there!"

Loki immediately moved a coin to cover the hair, but as soon as he did so, other coins moved also, uncovering more fur. Carefully, Loki set about rearranging them again so that they would completely cover the otter skin. When he had finished, he sat back with a smile of relief upon his face.

Hreidmar examined the pile again with great care. "Ah!" he exclaimed, with a sharp gleam in his eyes. "I see an exposed whisker — right there! If you do not have enough gold to cover that hair, I shall be forced to take your three lives as payment for the life of my son Otter!"

Odin had so far made no attempt to add Andvari's beautiful gold ring to the pile. But when it became clear that the gold pieces were not sufficient, he said to Loki, "Take this ring and place it over the exposed whisker. Then we will have fulfilled the wergild agreement."

Hreidmar was satisfied, so he allowed the three gods to leave his house. Loki turned in the doorway to face Hreidmar and the two of us. Now that he felt safe, he exclaimed, "You have the wergild that you demanded of us, and a wealth of treasure it is! But I must warn you that every last piece of that gold carries with it the curse of the dwarf Andvari. The gold ring and all the treasure that accompanies it will be the bane of every being who possesses it! Death and destruction will follow the gold as surely as night follows day, and no one who owns it will remain untouched by its curse. Only when the ring and the gold have returned to the deep waters will the bane end."

As soon as our visitors had left, our father walked over to the otter skin and placed the beautiful ring on his own finger. Then he shook every last piece of gold out of the otter skin and locked it all away in a heavy wooden chest. He hung the key around his neck and said nothing more about it.

"Do you intend to keep the wergild all for yourself, Father?" I asked. "I think we should divide the treasure among the three of us!"

"You do not deserve a single coin!" Hreidmar replied. "Otter was my son, and the wergild is mine alone. I shall not discuss the matter further!"

Fafnir was furious. Once we were alone, he exclaimed, "Regin, you and I each deserve one-third of that wergild! After all, Otter was our brother! Will you help me steal the key and remove our share of the treasure from the chest?"

"I am afraid that we may have to kill Father in order to get his key!" I objected. "You know how lightly he sleeps. The sound of grass growing is enough to awaken him! I am not certain I have what it takes to murder my father! I shall have to think about it."

As it happened, I did not have long to consider the matter. When I awakened the next morning, the house was strangely quiet and my brother's bed was empty. I found our father stabbed to death in his bed. The key that had hung around his neck was gone. The ring that he had placed on his finger was gone. All of the wergild that he had put into the chest was gone.

I found my brother outside. "Fafnir, you certainly are brave to have had the nerve to kill Father!" I exclaimed. "Now we only need to divide the wergild between the two of us. That is even better!"

"I shall never divide Andvari's treasure hoard with you, Regin!" Fafnir replied. "You were too cowardly to kill our father. Why do you think you deserve any of the gold? The risk was all mine, so the treasure is all mine! If you want it, you will have to fight me for it. I doubt if you have the courage to do that, either! I am much stronger than you are, you know. If you know what is good for you, you will leave here before I kill you as I killed Father!"

Fafnir entered the house and immediately returned wearing our father's helmet upon his head. We called it the Helmet of Terror because it caused the heart of anyone who gazed upon it to flood with great fear.

I took one look at Fafnir in that helmet and, seeing his sword in his hand, I fled. I sought employment with the king of Denmark. My fame as a metalsmith had preceded me, so he welcomed me.

In time, I learned that my brother had taken refuge in a cave on Gnita Heath and had turned himself into a fearsome dragon to protect the wergild he had stolen. He spent every day and night in his lair, with his body draped over Andvari's treasure hoard.

Chapter 3

Sigurd's uncle reveals his fate to him. Regin recasts Sigmund's sword, Gram, for Sigurd. With it, Sigurd kills Fafnir and then Regin. After taking Andvari's treasure hoard, Sigurd sets out to rescue Brunhild, the sleeping Valkyrie.

"Not long thereafter," Regin explained, "the king brought your mother to Denmark. I had bright hopes for my future, for I knew that the child she was carrying within her was a Volsung. I knew it was just a matter of time until I could avenge the death of my father and reclaim the treasure that is lawfully mine.

"I saw to it that your training would be in my hands. I have carefully reared you to reach this day. You have the courage, the strength, and the skill to kill Fafnir. All you need is the desire to help me. May I count on your help?"

Sigurd replied, "My heart is filled with sorrow to hear of your father's and your brother's greed. Surely, Andvari's curse is the bane of your family. Nevertheless, if you wish me to slay the mighty dragon who is your brother, I shall do so. Fashion a sword for me that is equal to such a task. If any smith possesses such skill, surely it is you."

"That I shall indeed do for you, Sigurd," said Regin. "You can put your complete trust in both my intent and my skill. For with that sword, Sigurd the Volsung will become known among all who walk the earth as Sigurd, Fafnir's Bane!"

Sigurd then decided to visit his mother's brother, who understood the lore of the dread Norns and could reveal the destinies of mortal folk. At first his uncle sat in silence. Then he said, "My nephew, it fills my heart with grief to speak of what those who rule men's fate have woven for you, for you are very dear to me.

"The fabric upon the loom of your life is a rich tapestry indeed, with intricate designs woven throughout in silver and gold thread. Truly, your life shines with the brilliance of the noonday sun! The patterns reveal that you will earn everlasting fame by slaying the fearsome Fafnir. You will also kill Regin, the tutor whom you trust, and win the treasure hoard.

"However," Sigurd's uncle added, "Andvari's treasure carries with it the curse of death and destruction to those who possess any part of it. This curse will destroy your love for Brunhild, the Valkyrie. Brunhild's vengeance will set your dearest friends against you, and you will be treacherously slain. You will leave behind a loving widow, who will avenge your death.

"Although you will die young, death is the common lot of all mortal folk," he concluded. "Always remember that it is the deeds you do while the wind of life blows within you that will bring you glory, honor, and lasting fame. You will be the most valiant of heroes: kind, courageous, fair, and skillful. A more noble man will never live beneath the sun!"

As he had promised, Regin fashioned a special sword for Sigurd. When Sigurd took the sword in his hand and struck the anvil with its blade, the blade broke into pieces. "You will have to make a better sword than this, Regin!" Sigurd exclaimed.

So the smith constructed a second sword for Sigurd. Once again, when Sigurd took the sword in his hand and struck the anvil with its blade, the blade broke into pieces. "Can you fashion no better sword than this, Regin?" Sigurd asked. "Or does treachery lurk in your heart as it did in the heart of your father and Fafnir! Do you intend Fafnir to kill me after I have killed him?"

Sigurd then approached his mother and said, "I have heard that my father asked you to save the pieces of his sword for me. If that is true, I wish to have them cast into a new sword. I intend to earn fame for myself by doing great deeds in the world!"

Sigurd's mother replied, "It is indeed true. As he lay dying, your father said to me, 'Carefully keep the pieces of my broken sword for our male child who is about to be born. They can be recast into a great sword called Gram. With it, our son will accomplish the deeds that will make his name live as long as there are bards on earth to tell the tale!'"

Regin was angry that Sigurd would not let him pursue his own craft in his own way. However, the master smith obeyed Sigurd's instructions and recast Sigmund the Volsung's sword. As Regin withdrew the finished blade from the fiery forge, blue flames burned all along its edges. "Here," he said to Sigurd. "Try this! If you are not satisfied I can do nothing more for you, even with all my talent."

Eagerly Sigurd grasped the sword that had been his father's. Raising it aloft, he swiftly brought it down on the anvil, as he had the other two swords. This time, however, the blade remained in one piece. In fact, it sliced straight through the anvil, dividing it in two down to its base.

"I think this sword will do," Sigurd said, "but I must put Gram to a more difficult test. Come with me."

Sigurd went down to the river, where he took a piece of wool and tossed it upstream. As it floated by him, he struck the wool with his sword, slicing it apart as he had split the anvil. "You have indeed served me well, Regin!" Sigurd exclaimed. "Gram will surely defend me against Fafnir!"

Sigurd and Regin set forth to find the mighty dragon. On the Gnita Heath they found the path that Fafnir traveled each day when he left his cave to quench his thirst. The path ended abruptly at the edge of a cliff, and they found themselves staring down at water splashing 180 feet below them.

"If your brother lies upon this path and drinks the water we see below us, then he has transformed himself into the largest dragon that has ever lived upon the earth!" Sigurd exclaimed.

"Fafnir's size should be of little matter to you, Sigurd!" Regin replied. "All you need to do is dig a hole where this path is. Make it deep enough for you to sit in it. Then, when Fafnir comes down the path toward the water, take your sword and thrust it up into his chest until it pierces his heart. What an easy way to earn glory, honor, and lasting fame! Fafnir's fiery breath will not scorch you with its venom. His spiked tail will not lacerate you. His scaly body will not foil Gram's search for blood. Intent on quenching his thirst, Fafnir will have no thought of the peril that awaits him as he glides forth on his vulnerable belly."

"That is all well and good," Sigurd replied. "But what if I should drown in the flood of Fafnir's blood?"

"You are hopeless, Sigurd!" Regin exclaimed. "No matter how well I advise you, your heart still overflows with fear! When your father died, he took the last of the Volsung courage with him! You will never be half the hero Sigmund was, for your heart is soft and weak! If you can find a better way to kill Fafnir, do it. I shall be satisfied as long as you slay him!" With these words, Regin cloaked his own terror and rode off, leaving Sigurd alone upon the heath.

Sigurd set about digging the pit as Regin had advised. While he was working, he suddenly felt as if someone were studying him. He looked up to find standing above him an old, long-bearded man. He wore a blue cloak and a broad-brimmed hat that overshadowed his forehead, and he had only one eye.

"Sigurd, son of Volsung, why are you digging such a pit?" the old man asked. "Whoever gave you that treacherous counsel intends to destroy you! You are digging your own grave, for the flood of dragon's blood will drown you in this hole. It would be far better to dig many pits leading off from this one. Then, while you sit here and let Gram pierce the dragon's heart, Fafnir's blood will drain off into the other pits." The old man abruptly vanished, and Sigurd realized that it was Odin, the All-Father, who had counseled him.

When the tremendous dragon next slithered down the path toward the water, Sigurd was prepared with a network of pits and his trusted sword, Gram. Yet the young hero was unprepared for the terror that faced him. The weight of the monster caused the earth to rumble and shake as he moved along the path. The rhythmic explosions of his fiery venom caused the cliffs to echo with a progressively louder thunder as he approached Sigurd.

But Sigurd courageously remained hidden in his pit. Soon the body of the monster covered the pit like a slab, extinguishing all light. Sigurd plunged Gram up to the hilt into the dragon's vulnerable, exposed chest. Although he quickly withdrew his sword, the blood from Fafnir's gaping wound enveloped him. Fortunately, the side passages drained off the excess blood so that Sigurd did not drown as Regin had hoped.

Fafnir bellowed like an enraged bull as excruciating pain engulfed him. Frantically, he lashed out with his head and his tail, hoping to destroy his invisible enemy. Finally, as he lay dying, his eyes spied Sigurd, who was watching him from a safe distance.

"Who are you that you dared to match your sword against my might?" he asked Sigurd. "Surely my brother, Regin, must have challenged you to perform this deed. For I have terrified all who live in northern lands with my monstrous form and my poisonous breath, and folk for miles around live in dread of arousing my anger. I am comforted by the thought that he who led you to kill me also plans to kill you!"

"I am Sigurd, son of Sigmund the Volsung," Sigurd replied. "My courageous heart, my strength, and my sharp sword enabled me to bring your death upon you, and if Regin has cause to fear them, let him beware!"

"Little good your heart and your sword will be to you, Sigurd, son of Sigmund the Volsung, if you take my treasure," Fafnir replied. "The gold has been cursed by the dwarf Andvari. My beautiful gold ring and all the treasure in my cave are destined to be the bane of every being who possesses them! Death and destruction follow the gold as surely as night follows day, and no one who owns it will remain untouched by its curse. Only when the ring and the gold have returned to the deep waters will the bane end. So beware, lest my bane become yours as well!"

Sigurd replied, "I would fear Andvari's curse and leave your treasure if, by leaving it, I could avoid my death. However, each of us is fated to die sooner or later, so to live in fear of death serves no purpose. It is far better to perform courageous deeds and win treasure, glory, honor, and fame. If, like you, each of us can keep our treasure until the day of our death, we are indeed fortunate!"

When it was apparent that Fafnir was dead, Regin approached Sigurd. "Hail to you, Sigurd, son of Sigmund the Volsung and Fafnir's Bane!" he cried. "You have shown the greatest courage to face Fafnir and kill him. The fame this deed has brought you will endure as long as bards live upon the earth to sing of it!"

"The deed will surely bring you no fame," Sigurd replied, "for you left me alone to fight this mightiest of dragons!"

"Do not forget that I am the one who forged your sharp-edged sword!" Regin exclaimed. "Without it you would not have dared to attack Fafnir, because he surely would have destroyed you!"

"You are wrong, Regin," Sigurd replied. "What deed can a man perform, even with the greatest weapon, if he lacks the heart to do it? A brave man will win because he fights valiantly even if his sword is dull-bladed."

As Sigurd began to cut the dragon's heart out of his body, Regin said, "I have one small request to ask of you, Sigurd. Roast Fafnir's heart upon the fire, and let me eat it. I would like that token of my brother."

Sigurd obediently took the heart to the fire and roasted it upon a wooden spit. When he burned his finger on the bloody juices dripping from it, he put that finger into his mouth. To his amazement, as soon as the heart's blood entered his mouth, Sigurd could understand the language of the birds who sat watching him.

"There sits Sigurd," said one of the birds, "almost completely covered in Fafnir's blood. He cannot see that a linden leaf has stuck to his back between his shoulder blades and is pressed there by the dragon's caked blood."

"Sigurd does not realize that the dragon's blood possesses such protective powers that from this time forth, wherever Fafnir's blood has touched him no weapon of any kind will be able to harm him," added a second bird.

"If Sigurd could understand our words, he would protect his one vulnerable spot," said another bird. "For he can be wounded only where the linden leaf has prevented Fafnir's hot blood from touching his skin."

A fourth bird announced, "Sigurd foolishly is roasting Fafnir's shining heart for Regin. Sigurd should eat that heart himself, for then he, not Regin, would become the wisest of all men!"

"Regin is thinking about the best way to betray Sigurd," the second bird said. "He longs to avenge Fafnir's death. He will try to trick Sigurd with crooked words. Sigurd is foolish to trust him!"

"Sigurd should slice Regin's head from his neck. Then he would have all of Fafnir's treasure for himself!" added the third bird.

"Before Regin beats Sigurd to the deed!" the fourth bird exclaimed. "As the saying goes: 'Where wolf's ears are seen, wolf's teeth are close at hand!' If Sigurd is wise, he will take care of himself. He will ride to Fafnir's den, collect Andvari's hoard, then ride to Hindfell, where Brunhild sleeps. That is the road to wisdom!"

"Sigurd certainly has nothing to lose!" exclaimed the first bird. "He has killed one brother already. That is reason enough for the remaining brother to kill him."

"The birds are right!" Sigurd thought to himself. "Certainly, Regin will soon become my bane. If he shares Fafnir's destiny now, I shall not have to fear him."

Sigurd approached the unsuspecting Regin, quickly drew Gram from its sheath, and sliced off Regin's head. He drank both Regin's and Fafnir's blood. Then he ate most of Fafnir's heart and saved the rest.

The birds chattered in a chorus: "Place Andvari's ring on your finger, Sigurd. You have little to fear. Then ride to Hindfell, where the Valkyrie Brunhild sleeps. High is the shield-hall that stands upon Hindfell, gleaming with gold within a ring of flames. The most beautiful of all maidens lies surrounded by gold, while red flame-shadows dance upon her. Long has the shield-maiden of Odin slept, put to sleep by the All-Father for disobedience in battle. She had pity in her heart and let the wrong warrior live, despite the dread Norns' decree. The sleep-thorn protects her until you come to win her! Place Andvari's ring on your finger, Sigurd. You have little to fear."

Once again, Sigurd obeyed the counsel of the birds. He mounted Grani and rode to Fafnir's den. There he found treasure beyond dreaming. He found Andvari's ring in a special place and placed it on his finger. He placed Hreidmar's Helmet of Terror on his head. Then he put the remaining treasure into two great chests and loaded them upon Grani's back. He thought to walk beside Grani to spare the horse his additional weight, but Grani refused to move. So Sigurd climbed onto his back. As soon as Grani felt the familiar weight of his master, he took off at a gallop as if he were carrying nothing but the wind.

Chapter 4

Sigurd awakens Brunhild and falls in love with her.

As Sigurd rode in search of Brunhild, his fame spread across the northern lands with the speed of the winter wind. Sigurd towered above other men in strength. He carried himself with such confidence that his extraordinary skill in handling the sword, casting the spear, bending the bow, and shooting an arrow were evident to all who gazed upon him. He carried a shield of blazing gold with the image of a red and brown dragon upon it. His suit of armor and his weapons were all of gold, and a similar dragon image decorated his helmet, his saddle, and his armor. Clearly, this was the man who had slain the fearsome dragon Fafnir.

Moreover, Sigurd possessed wisdom beyond that of ordinary humans. Since he could understand the language of birds, few events took him by surprise. He spoke with such eloquence and conviction that he could persuade anyone to his point of view.

He took great pleasure in pursuing challenging adventures, yet he also loved to help the common folk. He was known to take wealth from his enemies and give it to his friends. He was as courteous as he was strong. His courage never failed him, and he was afraid of nothing.

Sigurd rode far to the south, into the land of the Franks. Suddenly he saw before him a great light shining forth from the top of a hill. As he drew nearer, he could see that the source of the glow was a huge fire, whose flames soared toward the heavens. Within the ring of fire was a castle hung round about with shields. A banner floated above the topmost roof.

Knowing no fear, Sigurd rode Grani through the blazing ring of flame. The shield-hall was completely deserted except for a lone figure encased in a golden helmet and golden armor. The person appeared to be dead.

Sigurd removed the helmet. To his amazement, he discovered a maiden beneath the war gear. Her face blushed with the vigor of life, and Sigurd decided to awaken her. He moved her gently, but she remained fast asleep. He then noticed a thorn stuck into the back of her hand, and he removed it.

The maiden's eyes opened. She looked appraisingly at Sigurd, undaunted by the Helmet of Terror on his head. The man who stood before her was fair of face and awesome in stature. His eyes were so piercing that few were comfortable meeting his gaze. A great head of golden red hair tumbled down in heavy locks, and a thick, short beard surrounded his strongly chiseled, high-boned face. His shoulders were as broad as the shoulders of two men. He was so tall that he could wear his sword Gram, which was seven sword-lengths long, upon his waist.

"Who are you," she asked, "who have awakened me from my long sleep? You must be Sigurd, son of Sigmund the Volsung, because you are wearing Hreidmar's Helmet of Terror upon your head, and you are holding Fafnir's Bane in your hand!"

"I am indeed!" Sigurd replied in surprise. "I have heard that you are the daughter of a mighty king and that you are as wise as you are beautiful."

Brunhild replied, "At Odin's command, I have slept for time without measure, helpless to awaken from the prick of his sleep-thorn. I was a Valkyrie, one of the warrior-maidens of Odin who are destined to live forever. I would descend upon the battlefield, bring death to the warrior of Odin's choice, and return with the dead hero to Valhalla in Asgard. There the hero would join other heroes to wait for Ragnarok, when they will help the gods fight the Frost Giants in the great battle that will bring this world to an end.

"In my last battle," Brunhild continued, "two great kings fought against one another. Since the old king was the greatest of warriors, Odin had commanded me to give the victory to him. I, however, decided to strike him down and let the younger king live instead. Odin's fury was implacable.

"'Because you have disobeyed my orders,' he told me, 'never again will I permit you to be a Valkyrie. Instead, you must marry a mortal and live for an ordinary span of years.'

"'If I must marry,' I replied, 'I promise you that I will marry only a man who never lets fear enter his heart!'

"'I will agree to that,' Odin replied. 'In your shield-hall on Hindfell, I will prick you with the sleep-thorn, and you will fall into a long, deep sleep. A ring of flames will rage around the walls of your castle to protect you.'

"He added, 'You will sleep undisturbed until the great hero Sigurd, son of Sigmund the Volsung, rescues you. Only he among mortals has the great courage you desire. He will ride through your blazing fire on his horse, Grani, who is kin to my own Steipnir. He will be carrying Andvari's hoard, for Sigurd, alone of all the men who walk the earth, will have had the heart to slay the fearsome dragon Fafnir and his brother Regin, the master smith.'

"And what Odin revealed to me has, indeed, come to pass," Brunhild concluded. "I have slept until this moment when you awakened me!"

"What knowledge can you teach me?" Sigurd asked. "You have a wisdom that belongs to the gods!"

"Let us drink together," said Brunhild, "and into your ale I will mix knowledge about life. I shall give you knowledge of war to cut upon your sword, knowledge of the sea to cut upon the stern of your ship, knowledge of healing for the wounds of war, and knowledge of helping the simple, good folk.

"I advise you to speak carefully, and always keep your word. Be kind to your family and friends, even when they injure you, so as to win lasting praise. Beware of the presence of evil around you, and remove yourself from it lest it harm you. Be alert to the schemes of your friends so that you will know if one of your wife's relatives hates you and plans to take vengeance upon you. No matter how young he is, never trust the close relative of one you have killed, for even the wolf cub is a wolf.

"May you prosper with this knowledge until the gods bring an end to your days," Brunhild concluded. "May my wisdom bring you success and fame. And may you remember in the future what we have talked about here."

Sigurd embraced and kissed Brunhild. "You are the most beautiful maiden who has ever lived, and surely you are the wisest of all women!" he exclaimed. "I swear that I will have you as my own wife, for I hold you very dear to my heart."

"Then Sigurd, son of Sigmund the Volsung, I choose you above all other mortals!" Brunhild exclaimed. "You will be mine as I will be yours!"

As a token of his love, Sigurd gave to Brunhild Andvari's gold ring. "I shall hold your love in my heart for as long as I live," he promised.

Brunhild looked at the ring that Sigurd had placed on her finger and replied, "We are not destined to live together, Sigurd. I am a shield-maiden. I wear a helmet as kings do in time of war, and I fight in battle. While I am enjoying the battlefield, you will marry Gudrun, the daughter of King Giuki."

"You cannot believe that I shall be tempted by some king's daughter!" Sigurd exclaimed. "You alone have my heart, and I swear by the gods that I shall have you as my wife or have no wife at all!"

Thus Sigurd and Brunhild pledged to love one another faithfully, and then Sigurd went on his way.

Chapter 5

Sigurd forgets Brunhild and marries Gudrun. Then he helps Gunnar win Brunhild as his bride. Gudrun reveals the truth to Brunhild.

After a journey of many days, Sigurd came to the palace of King Giuki, who ruled a kingdom south of the Rhine River. In addition to their beautiful daughter, Gudrun, King Giuki and his fierce-hearted wife, Queen Grimhild, had three sons: Gunnar, Hogni, and young Guttorm. All of their children were extraordinary in both goodness and skill, and the two older sons had earned fame through deeds of war.

When one of the nobles saw Sigurd in their town, he immediately went before King Giuki and said, "I have seen a man, who in form is like a god, riding into our town. Not only does he far surpass any man I have ever seen, but he is wearing gold armor, carrying golden weapons, and riding a horse that is far greater than any other animal of its kind."

King Guiki left the palace to welcome Sigurd and invite him to stay with them. Before long, the King treated Sigurd like his own son, Gunnar and Hogni treated him like the best of brothers, and Queen Grimhild decided that he would be the perfect husband for Gudrun. In addition to being impressed with his great wealth, King Guiki's family loved Sigurd because he was such a good human being. He was kind, loving, loyal, and generous.

Sigurd often spoke of his love for Brunhild. So Grimhild decided that the only way to win Sigurd for her daughter was to make him forget Brunhild. She accomplished this by giving Sigurd a drugged drink. As he drank it, she said, "Consider us to be your family, Sigurd. Giuki, Gunnar, Hogni, and I shall now swear that we are father, brothers, and mother to you." The potion caused Sigurd to forget Brunhild entirely.

Sigurd had spent five seasons with the family when Queen Grimhild said to her husband, "Sigurd has the greatest of all hearts. Moreover, he is trustworthy and helpful. His strength makes our kingdom more powerful. Therefore, give him our daughter in marriage with wealth to spare and the right to rule what he chooses. Then he should be content to live with us forever."

Giuki replied, "Usually a king does not have to offer his daughter in marriage. Suitors apply to him for her hand. Yet I would rather offer her to Sigurd than accept the suit of any other noble."

So it came to pass that Sigurd was offered both power and the beautiful and good Princess Gudrun. He accepted with great pleasure. The older members of the family again swore oaths of brotherhood, and the royal wedding was a time of special joy for all.

With King Giuki's sons, Sigurd pursued the arts of war, returning home victorious and bearing great treasure in addition to glory, honor, and fame. He gave the part of Fafnir's heart that he had saved to Gudrun to eat, and she became even more wise and kind.

Now that her daughter was happily settled in marriage, Queen Grimhild turned her thoughts to her son Gunnar. "Surely Brunhild is the best choice for you," she told him. "I suggest that you set out to win her, and take Sigurd with you." Gunnar knew of Brunhild's beauty and fame, so he immediately agreed.

In high spirits, Gunnar, Hogni, and Sigurd approached Brunhild's father. When Gunnar asked for her hand in marriage, her father replied, "Brunhild will wed only the man whom she freely chooses. In order to win her, you must go to her castle high on Hindfell and ride through the wall of roaring flames around her golden shield-hall."

When the brothers arrived at the castle, Gunnar could not make his horse ride into the flames. No matter how he spurred and struck him, the horse would rear in terror and withdraw. So, Gunnar said to Sigurd, "My horse will never carry me through the fire. Will you lend me Grani?"

Sigurd did so willingly, but Grani would not take one step with Gunnar on his back. "Grani will carry no one but you!" Gunnar exclaimed. "Let us practice the art of shape-changing that my mother has taught us. Make yourself look just like me, and in my name ride Grani through the flames and win Brunhild for me. Meanwhile, I will remain here, looking just like you."

Having no memory of Brunhild and their love, Sigurd agreed to the adventure. He assumed Gunnar's shape, climbed upon Grani, took his sword in his hand, and spurred Grani into the heart of the raging flames. As Grani passed through the fire, the flames roared with an even greater fury and stretched their fiery fingers to the heavens above them, while the earth shook beneath the horse's feet. Nonetheless, Grani carried Sigurd safely through the blaze.

When Sigurd dismounted and entered Brunhild's palace, the warrior-maiden was sitting in the great hall with a helmet upon her head, armor encasing her body, and a sword in her hand. She looked at him and asked, "Who are you?"

"I am Gunnar, son of Giuki," Sigurd replied, "and I have come to claim you as my wife. For I have spoken with your father and have ridden through the flames that surround your hall."

"Do not speak to me of marriage, Gunnar," Brunhild replied, "unless you are the best of all men who walk upon the earth. You will have to combat all who would be suitors of mine, and I am reluctant to give up the life of a warrior, which I so enjoy."

"That may well be so," Sigurd as Gunnar replied, "but you swore a sacred oath that you would marry the man who rode through the ring of flames around your hall, and I have done so."

Brunhild then accepted the man she thought was Gunnar, and they exchanged rings as a sign of their love. Brunhild gave Andvari's ring to Sigurd, and Sigurd gave her a ring of Gunnar's to wear in its place.

Sigurd spent the next three nights with Brunhild. Since he was wooing her for Gunnar, Sigurd neither kissed Brunhild nor embraced her. Although they shared the same bed, each night Sigurd placed his sword between them. He told Brunhild that he could marry in no other way, and she did not question him.

Upon leaving Brunhild's castle, Sigurd had to spur Grani through the wall of flames once again. Then he and Gunnar exchanged shapes and rode to tell Brunhild's family of the news.

Later Brunhild visited her brother-in-law and said, "A king who claimed to be named Gunnar rode through the flames that surround my hall on Hindfell. I have promised to wed the man who possesses Andvari's hoard and who will ride Grani through the ring of flames that surround my shield-hall. But I know that only Sigurd could do this, for only he, of all the men who walk the earth, has the courage in his heart to have slain the fearsome dragon Fafnir."

Brunhild continued, "It is Sigurd whom I love, and Sigurd whom I pledged to marry. Now, what do I do about Gunnar? Rather than marry him, I would far prefer to remain chief over one-third of your army and to spend my time defending your kingdom."

Brunhild's brother-in-law replied, "You must marry Gunnar, for you cannot prove that he did not ride through those flames. Besides, Sigurd has married Gudrun, Gunnar's sister. What is past is dead; you cannot revive it. Only the present and the future are important. If you wish to keep my friendship and avoid my anger, you will forget Sigurd and marry Gunnar!"

So it came to pass that a second great wedding feast was held in the hall of King Giuki, to honor the marriage of Brunhild and Gunnar. The new couple appeared to be very happy. As the celebration ended, Sigurd's memory returned to him. Although he remembered the promises he had made to Brunhild, he never revealed by look, word, or deed that he had ever seen her before. He loved Gudrun and Gunnar, and above all he wanted peace among the members of his adopted family.

All was well until one day when Brunhild and Gudrun went to the Rhine River to bathe. Brunhild immediately walked into the river upstream of Gudrun. "I deserve the fresh water for rinsing my hair because my father is greater than yours, and my husband is more valiant than yours," she said. "Gunnar is known for his many famous deeds, not the least of which was riding through the wall of flames around my castle in order to win my love. Your husband's deeds are certainly no match for that!"

Gudrun waded upstream past Brunhild and angrily replied, "I suggest that you remain silent instead of criticizing my husband. In fact, it is my right to wash my hair upstream of you. You are foolish to demean your first love; all who have tongues to speak acclaim Sigurd as the most courageous man the world has ever known. It was Sigurd who killed Fafnir and Regin. Those valiant deeds gave him the right to Andvari's hoard of treasure."

Brunhild replied, "Well, it was Gunnar, not Sigurd, who rode through the raging fire that surrounds my shield-hall, and that took far more courage than the slaying of Fafnir!"

Gudrun laughed and said, "Brunhild, do you really think it was my brother who rode through those flames? Only Sigurd could have done that! He wooed you in Gunnar's name and shape, because Gunnar could not do it himself! You gave Andvari's ring to the man who shared your bed, and he gave it to me. If you do not believe me, just look at my hand, for I am wearing the ring that my husband originally gave to you!"

Brunhild recognized the ring immediately and became as pale as a corpse. She returned to the palace in silence and remained silent all evening.

Gudrun later asked Sigurd, "Why is Brunhild so silent? Is she not happy being famous, wealthy, and married to the man of her choice? I think I shall ask her about it tomorrow!"

"Do no such thing, Gudrun," Sigurd replied, "for you will be very sorry if you do."

But Gudrun could not let the matter rest. The next day she said, "What is the matter, Brunhild? Did our conversation yesterday bother you, or is something else the matter?"

"You must have a cruel heart to return to that subject," Brunhild replied. "Do not pry into matters that are not good for you to know."

"What can you have against me?" Gudrun asked. "I have done nothing to hurt you!"

"I shall not forgive you for having Sigurd, when he belonged to me! Gunnar may be wealthy and strong, but Sigurd killed the fearsome dragon Fafnir, and that is a greater deed than all of Gunnar's deeds. And Sigurd, not Gunnar, rode through the ring of flames that surround my shield-hall."

Brunhild added, "Your mother is to blame for this entire matter! Sigurd forgot me because she gave him a drugged drink."

"That is a lie!" Gudrun exclaimed angrily.

"Enjoy your husband, Gudrun, knowing that he would not be yours but for the craft of your mother! I wish you only trouble!"

That night as Gunnar lay asleep, Brunhild left the palace. Over the snow-capped mountains and the ice fields she wandered, letting evil thoughts inflame her heart. "Sigurd lies in bed embracing Gudrun, his queen, while I must live without his love and without his treasure," she said to herself. "My only joy will be in revenge!"

Chapter 6

Brunhild persuades Gunnar to slay Sigurd. He
arranges for Guttorm to perform the deed. Gudrun
becomes an unwitting accomplice to the treachery.

When Brunhild returned to the palace, she retired to her room and lay there as if she were close to death. Gunnar was concerned about her health and pressed her to tell him what was wrong. At first Brunhild remained silent. Finally she asked, "Gunnar, what did you do with that ring I gave you? I promised to wed the man who possessed Fafnir's hoard and who rode the horse Grani through my flaming ring of fire. That man could only have been Sigurd, for he alone, of all the men who walk the earth, has the courage in his heart to have slain the fearsome dragon Fafnir.

"You, Gunnar," she added, "have performed no great deeds in your life. What mighty treasure have you won? You may be a king, but you are not a noble leader. You have the courage of a dead man! I promised to marry the most noble man alive, and when I married you I broke that oath. Because Sigurd is not mine, I shall cause your death. And I shall reward Grimhild's treachery with the most evil of gifts, for never has a woman lived who is more vile than your mother!"

Gunnar quietly replied, "You are an evil woman who speaks with a poisoned tongue. You are criticizing a woman who is far superior to you. She has not spent her life killing folk, but has earned the praise of all."

"I have never performed evil deeds in secret, as your mother has," Brunhild replied. "However, my heart overflows with the wish to kill you! Never again will you find me in your hall happy to be your wife. Never again will you see me playing chess or plying my gold embroidery, drinking among friends, speaking kind words, or giving you good advice. My heart is filled with sorrow that Sigurd is not mine, and never again will there be love in my heart for you!"

Brunhild left her bed, tore her needlework to shreds, and opened her doors and windows so her sorrowful wailing would be heard far and wide. For seven days and seven nights she remained alone in her room, refusing food and drink and all offers of companionship. One by one Gunnar, Hogni, and the servants tried to reach her heart, but Brunhild's sorrow and anger were implacable.

Finally Sigurd said to Gudrun, "I fear that evil winds are blowing upon us. As Brunhild remains aloof in her room, in her heart she is plotting dreadful deeds against me!"

"Then please go talk with her!" Gudrun replied, weeping. "Offer her gold. Surely treasure will calm her grief and soothe her anger!"

Sigurd went to Brunhild's room, threw off her bed coverings, and exclaimed, "Awaken, Brunhild! You have slept long enough! The sun is shining, so let happy thoughts push grief from your heart."

"How dare you come before me!" Brunhild replied. "Of all who live upon the earth, I hate you the most, for you have been the most unjust to me."

"What evil spirit possesses you that you blame me for treating you cruelly? I have never had an unkind thought about you. You freely chose the husband that you have!"

"No, Sigurd!" said Brunhild. "I did not choose to wed Gunnar. He did not ride through my ring of flames; you did! I thought I recognized your eyes when I saw Gunnar standing before me in my hall. The Norns blinded me to what was good and what was evil, and so I accepted Gunnar in spite of my doubts. My heart has never loved him, although I have done my best to hide my true feelings. It was you who killed the fearsome dragon Fafnir and rode through the blazing fire for my sake, not Gunnar!"

"Brunhild, it is true that I am not your husband; yet you are wed to a famous man. Gunnar is the noblest of men! He has killed great kings. And he loves you with all his heart. You cannot buy such love with a hoard of treasure. How is it that you cannot love him? Why are you so angry?"

"My heart sorrows that a sword is not yet smeared with your blood!" she replied.

"I fear you do not have long to wait," Sigurd said. "We two are destined to enjoy only a few more days upon the earth."

"It is all the same to me," said Brunhild. "Since you betrayed me, I do not care whether I live or die!"

"I urge you to live, and to love both Gunnar and me!" Sigurd exclaimed. "I shall give you all my treasure if you will but live!"

"You do not understand the feelings in my heart," Brunhild replied. "You, not Gunnar, are the best of all men, and you are the only man I have ever loved!"

"I loved you better than I loved myself," Sigurd replied, "and I love you still. However, I became the victim of Queen Grimhild's craft and lost you. It was not until after Gunnar married you that my memory of you returned, and then my love for you returned as well. My heart sorrowed that you were not my wife, but I made the best of it. After all, I lived in a royal household with a loving wife, and we were all together."

"I have no pity for you, Sigurd! Your tale of love for me and sorrow over our plight comes too late to warm my heart. I swore an oath that I would marry the man who rode though my ring of flames; if I cannot keep that sacred oath, I choose to die!"

"I cannot stand the thought of your death!" Sigurd exclaimed. "If it comes to that, I will leave Gudrun and marry you!"

"No, Sigurd, it is too late. I will not have you or any other man! Without you, power and wealth mean nothing to me, life means nothing to me, and I choose to die."

With no more words to be said, Sigurd left Brunhild. His heart was so heavy with grief that it swelled with the pain and burst the iron rings on his chain-mail shirt. He did not tell Gunnar of Brunhild's anger or of his own grief.

When Gunnar next saw Brunhild, she said to him, "Sigurd betrayed both you and me by sleeping with me when, in your shape, he rode through the ring of fire to win me for you. For this offense Sigurd must die, for he committed it. Or you must die, for you permitted it. Or I will die, for the shame of it. Unless you agree to slay Sigurd, I will cause you to lose your wealth, your land, and your life. I will then return to my family and spend the rest of my days overcome with sorrow."

As Brunhild expected, Gunnar could not see beyond the tale she chose to tell him. All day long he sat with a heavy heart, pondering what he should do. His heart was torn between his love for Sigurd and the oath of friendship they had sworn and his love for his wife and the loyalty he owed her. Finally, he realized that he could not live with the shame of his wife's leaving him. "Brunhild is the best of all women," he thought. "She means more to me than anything on earth, and I would die before I would risk losing her love and her wealth."

Gunnar called his brother Hogni to him and said, "Evil times have come upon us. We must slay Sigurd, for he has been disloyal to us. Then we will divide his rule and his treasure between us."

Hogni replied, "Would you betray Sigurd because you want the treasure that he took from Fafnir? Or are you considering this treachery because you want Brunhild's wealth? We are honor-bound not to break our oaths of friendship with Sigurd. I know that Brunhild has persuaded you to do this, but I urge you to reconsider. If you slay Sigurd, you will bring dishonor and shame upon us all!"

"I am determined to do this deed," Gunnar said. "Let us arrange to have our brother Guttorm slay Sigurd, for he is too young to have sworn the oaths with Sigurd that we two swore, and he will believe whatever we choose to tell him."

"No good will come of this evil deed!" Hogni exclaimed. "Sigurd is an honorable man. If we betray his trust, our foul deed will fall heavily upon our own heads."

"Choose between us, Hogni," Gunnar replied. "Either we slay Sigurd or I shall take my own life!"

Thus Hogni agreed to the treachery. The two brothers called Guttorm before them and offered him great power and wealth if he would slay Sigurd. They used some of the knowledge of witchcraft that their mother possessed. They chopped into paste the flesh of a certain worm together with the meat of a wolf and secretly added it to the wine they gave Guttorm to drink. The drug made Guttorm eager to do whatever they asked of him without thinking about it.

The brothers planned a boar and bear hunt as the occasion on which Guttorm would slay Sigurd. When Gudrun heard that Sigurd was accompanying her brothers on a hunting expedition, her heart filled with foreboding and fear. Knowing the depth of Brunhild's rage, Gudrun feared that Sigurd would be the target of her malice.

"Who can help me protect Sigurd from whatever evil scheme Brunhild devises?" she wondered. "I can no longer trust Gunnar. He will perform whatever deeds his wife asks of him. Hogni, of course, will support Gunnar, for they have always been inseparable. But Guttorm may be able to help me. He is not particularly close to Gunnar and Hogni. Yes, I think I can rely upon him!"

So it came to pass that Gudrun summoned her youngest brother, Guttorm, and said to him, "I fear that Brunhild may have planned some evil to befall Sigurd during the course of your hunting adventure. Sigurd has always been loyal to our family, and I do not want him to suffer for my foolish argument with Brunhild. I have already apologized for my quick tongue."

"I have always been very fond of Sigurd," Guttorm replied. "What would you like me to do, Gudrun?"

"I am afraid of some form of treachery that will appear to be a hunting accident," Gudrun replied. "I would like you to remain at Sigurd's side and guard him for me.

"Therefore," she continued, "I shall confide in you a secret that Sigurd has shared with me alone. When he slew the dragon Fafnir, he became covered with that monster's blood. From that time forth, wherever the blood had touched my husband no weapon could harm him. However, as the blood from Fafnir's gaping wound enveloped Sigurd, the wind blew leaves off a nearby linden tree. One of those leaves stuck between his shoulder blades and warded off the bath of hot dragon's blood. I fear that, in some form of treachery, Sigurd will be shot in his one vulnerable spot and killed."

"If you will sew a design on Sigurd's jacket to mark the place where the leaf lodged, I promise to keep my eyes upon that spot," Guttorm replied.

"Oh, thank you!" said Gudrun. "I will add a leaf of red silk to the design of Sigurd's embroidered hunting jacket. It will stand apart from the rest because of its color, and yet it will blend in with the larger design so that only you and I will know its special meaning."

Gudrun's fears continued to torment her. By the morning of the hunting expedition, she was frantic with worry. "Oh, Sigurd," she cried, "last night I dreamed that as two boars chased you over the meadow, blood from your wound painted the flowers a deep red. Please do not join the hunt. I fear that someone will try to kill you!"

"Nonsense, dear Gudrun," Sigurd replied. "I am going with your kinsmen, and you know how well we love one another. I know of no one who hates me, nor anything I have done to cause such hatred. Be at ease. I shall be back with you in a few days."

"Oh, Sigurd," Gudrun wept, "you are being foolish! Last night I dreamed that two mountains fell upon you and buried you, and I could never see you again. Please do not join the hunt. I know in my heart that someone will try to kill you!"

"Nonsense, dearest wife. You have no cause to fear. Be at ease. I shall be back with you before you have had time to miss me!" And with these words, Sigurd embraced Gudrun tenderly and departed.

With an air of ease and good cheer, the hunting party headed toward the forest. Once they were deep within the woods, they stopped to discuss the best hunting strategy. "Let us divide into two groups to double the chance of success," Sigurd suggested.

"A fine idea," Gunnar replied. "Given your skill, let Hogni come with me while Guttorm accompanies you. Then we will be more evenly matched."

Sigurd and Guttorm hunted easily and well. Together they killed a number of elk and deer. Then they cornered a great wild boar, whose malicious tusks and sharp eyes challenged even the best of hunters. When the animal furiously charged toward Grani, Sigurd slew it with his sword.

They had just spied a bear when a horn blast echoed through the trees, signaling that the time had come to get together for supper. "We have done so well, Guttorm," Sigurd announced, "that I think it is time to have some fun. I intend to capture that bear and bring it back with us alive. That will surprise your brothers, and we will all have a good laugh."

Sigurd took Grani as far as he could. When the forest became too dense, he dismounted and chased the bear on foot. Sigurd was so quick and quiet on his feet that he caught the bear and tied it up without even needing to wound it first. He did not even get a scratch in the process. He dragged the bear back to Grani, tied it to his saddle, and set off with Guttorm to rejoin the other members of their party.

When they came upon a stream, Sigurd realized that he was very thirsty. He had not stopped for food or drink the entire day. Because the live bear was attached to his saddle, he tethered Grani to a sturdy tree. He then placed his hunting weapons near his horse, walked over to the stream, and bent down to take a drink.

Guttorm followed Sigurd's lead, walking behind him to the stream, his sword unsheathed in his hand. As Sigurd splashed the fresh water into his mouth, Guttorm suddenly plunged his sword through the red silk leaf embroidered on Sigurd's hunting jacket. The weapon sank deep into Sigurd's back and came out through his chest.

Blood gushed from Sigurd's back and chest. The stream waters ran red, and the ground was drenched with blood. Furiously, like an enraged, wounded boar, Sigurd turned to kill his murderer — but his weapons lay by the tree, and he was too weak to reach them. Thus, the greatest of heroes fell with his death wound among the wildflowers while Guttorm looked on from a safe distance. The boy gazed at Sigurd with growing horror, as the effects of the drugged drink wore off and his judgment returned.

"Guttorm," Sigurd whispered, "hear my last words and remember them well. Dear boy, you are only the arm of Brunhild's treachery. My uncle told me of my fate long ago, and Brunhild warned me, but I was blind to their words. Few among us can recognize our own destiny, and those who attempt to fight their fate are condemned to lose."

Sigurd added, "I swear to you that I have never harmed Gunnar in any way. I have never been more than a brother to his wife, even though she loved me above all other men. I have always honored our oaths to one another. Return to your kin with these words, for you have killed an honorable man this day."

Sigurd sank back upon the blood-drenched flowers. Death quickly stole upon him, for he had no weapon and no strength to keep it at bay.

Guttorm rode off to fetch Gunnar and Hogni. When they returned, they found Grani standing with his head bent low over Sigurd's body. They placed Sigurd upon his golden shield and prepared to return home. Gunnar said, "Hogni, when we return to the palace, describe how Sigurd went off hunting alone and must have been surprised by robbers as he drank from the stream. Then no one will suspect that we are to blame for this foul deed."

Chapter 7

Guttorm confesses his treachery. Brunhild reveals the future to Gunnar and then commits suicide. Gudrun mourns Sigurd's death. The corpses of Brunhild and Sigurd are burned together.

When her brothers returned to the castle bearing Sigurd's corpse, Gudrun was overcome with grief and anger. "Your tale of robbers may be true," she said, "but let me see you stand before Sigurd's corpse and proclaim your innocence. If you are guilty, his wound will condemn you by gushing forth fresh blood.

"When next you ride off to war," she added, "in vain will you wish that Sigurd were by your side to help you! He was your strength, and without him you will no longer prosper. Now look upon the corpse of your brother and swear that you had no part in his death!"

Guttorm replied, "Enough of false words! As Sigurd bent forward to drink from the stream, his back was toward me, and I struck him through the leaf you had embroidered upon his hunting jacket. I was doing my brothers' deed, dear sister, but Sigurd blamed Brunhild. Sigurd's dying words proclaimed his innocence. He swore that he was never false in any way to you, Gunnar, and that he was never more than a brother to Brunhild."

"Alas that you, my dear brothers, have brought this sorrow upon me!" Gudrun cried. "For breaking your oaths of love and friendship, may your kingdom become a wasteland! May Sigurd's gold drag you to your deaths! It was an evil day when Sigurd rode upon Grani to join you in the courtship of Brunhild. That woman is surely the most hated of all folk! She has destroyed a brave man and has brought nothing but sorrow to his wife!"

Hogni exclaimed, "Our destiny is unrolling before our eyes! Nothing good will come of this foul deed while we are yet alive!"

By now Gunnar had great misgivings about the murder he had instigated. When he heard Brunhild's mad laughter he said, "You laugh like one whose heart is made of stone! You must be evil to the core of your being. How would you feel if you killed your brother, Atli, and then had to look upon his corpse?"

"Atli will not die before my eyes!" Brunhild responded. "He will outlive both you and Hogni and will be a greater king! As for me, I shall take my own life!"

"Choose life, not death!" Gunnar pleaded. "I offer you all of my wealth!"

When his wife would not listen, Gunnar asked Hogni to convince her. But Hogni said, "Let Brunhild die as she has determined. She has brought nothing but evil upon us!"

On the day that the corpse of Sigurd would be given to the fire, Brunhild collected the treasure she possessed and called everyone before her. She picked up her sword, plunged it into her side beneath her armpit, and lay back, calmly waiting for death to claim her. "Come," she said. "Let all who wish some treasure come forth and take my gold!"

Then she said to Gunnar, "While I still have the wind of life within me, I shall tell you of your terrible future. You will ride into the arms of an enemy, and evil times will befall you and all your kin. For you broke your oath to Sigurd when you killed him, and you rewarded his loyalty with evil. Even when Sigurd won me for you, he was loyal to you. For the three nights he slept in my bed, he placed between us his sharp-edged sword, Gram, as a token of his honor.

"You will force Gudrun to marry my brother, Atli, against her will, and she will give him Andvari's ring. Atli will kill you to acquire Andvari's hoard, but in order to prevent the treasure from falling into his greedy hands, you will have buried it at the bottom of the Rhine River. Gudrun will avenge your deaths by murdering Atli and his sons. When she casts herself into the sea, Andvari's ring, like the rest of his treasure, will return to deep waters. Thus, Death will take you and your kin, and with the return of Andvari's hoard to the deep waters, the dwarf's curse will end."

Brunhild concluded, "Carry my corpse to Sigurd's funeral pyre. Place rich tapestries and golden shields around the pyre. Then place me next to Sigurd, with his sword between us as it was when he slept with me in my shield hall. We shall burn as husband and wife and leave this earth together." With these words, Brunhild died.

Meanwhile, Gudrun sat dry-eyed and silent before Sigurd's covered body. Many queens came before her and spoke of their own loneliness when faced with the death of a loved one. They hoped that the warmth of friendship and the sharing of burdens would make it easier for her to accept the common lot of all human folk.

Finally Gudrun's sister pulled back the funeral shroud and said, "Look upon your husband, Gudrun, and kiss him, for I know of no love as true as yours among all who walk the earth. Sigurd was your greatest joy!"

Then Gudrun's heart melted, and her grief flowed from her eyes in a torrent of tears. "My Sigurd," she cried, "towered above all men as a stag stands above all beasts. He shone as gold in the presence of silver. He was the brightest jewel worn on a band, the most precious stone worn by a prince."

Gudrun continued, "As long as Sigurd was alive, I was held in highest regard by all noble warriors. Now that he is dead, I am no more than a lone willow leaf lost among a multitude of others on the tree. Like the leaves stripped from a twig, my joys have been cut off, and with no further nourishment they will wither and die. I miss my husband's sweet words, his love, and his friendship."

When the mighty pyre had been kindled, Gunnar did as Brunhild had wished. The corpse of Sigurd was placed upon it, along with the corpse of Brunhild, and Gram was placed between them. As the flames roared aloft, raising their rosy fingers to the heavens, they consumed wood and flesh alike. Thus, Brunhild burned by the side of Sigurd. She had joined in death the man she was destined never to have in life. As for Sigurd, his fame will last as long as folk live upon the earth.

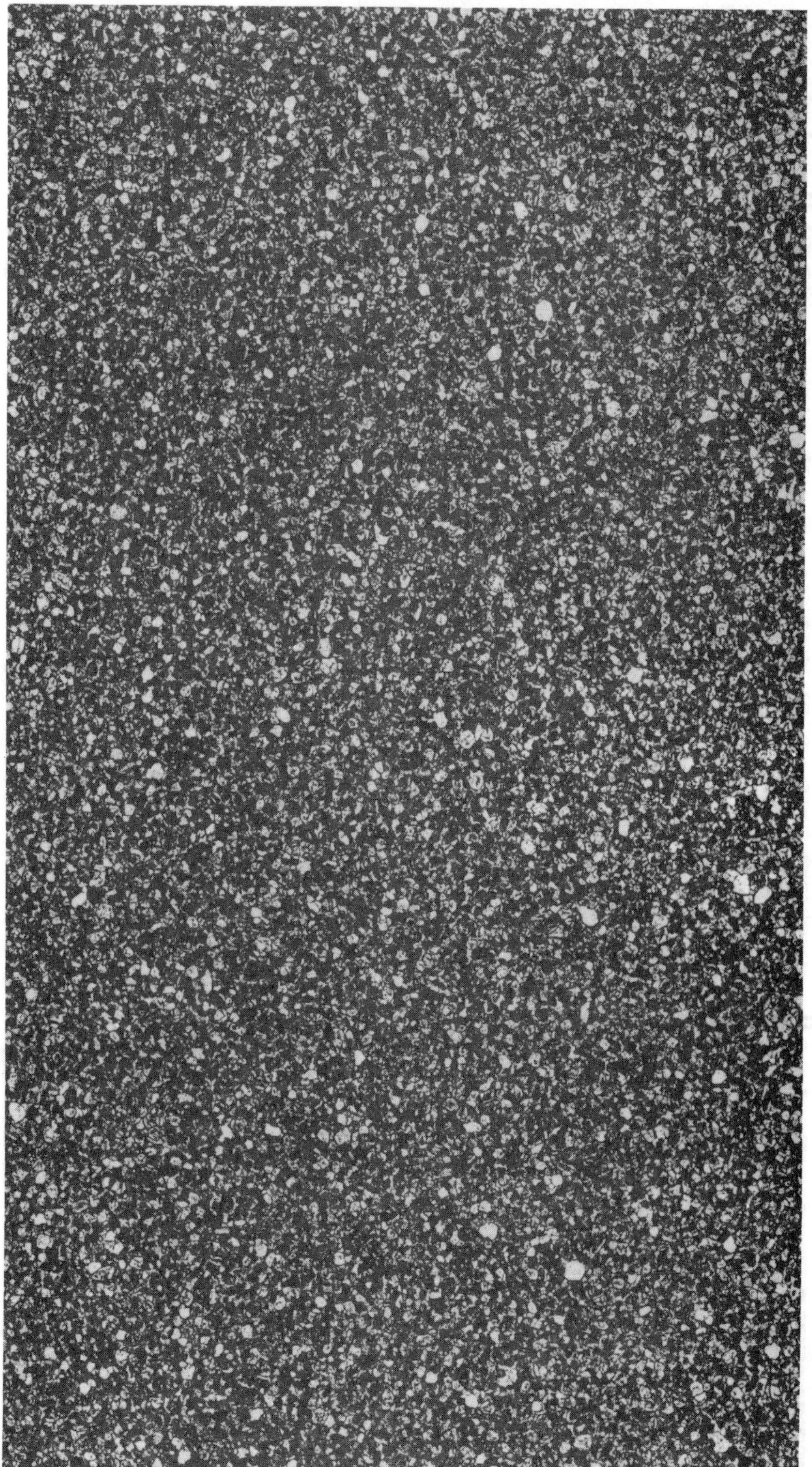

The British Isles

The British Isles were settled by various European cultures, and their myths reflect this diversity. The epic of *Beowulf*, which was written in the early 8th century A.D. by a Christian who loved the pagan tradition, reflects the Norse tradition transplanted to English soil. The Irish myths were recorded by monks between 1100 and 1600. Finally, the story of King Arthur shows a combination of Welsh, English, and French traditions ranging from the early 12th century to the late 15th century.

The Irish myths unite mythology and history by describing the settling of Ireland by successive waves of Celtic peoples. The battles between the race called the Fomorians, who represent the forces of darkness, and the Celts, who represent the forces of light, reflect both the harsh northern environment and the political instability that results when invaders meet the local residents. The use of magic enlivens all the tales, including the creation and fertility myths.

Beowulf is the earliest surviving major work of Germanic literature, and it is a masterpiece. The anonymous writer has created a thematically unified work in which every detail has a role that relates it to the piece as a whole. Moreover, the writer's ability to create psychologically complex characters is unique among the works extant from Northern Europe. However, the epic can be appreciated on a less serious level as well. After all, Beowulf is a hero who resembles Superman, and he combats three memorable monsters. Readers of *Beowulf* in translation understand why students choose to learn Anglo-Saxon in order to read this work in the original language.

The legend of King Arthur is an equally amazing phenomenon for a different reason. The story assigns to King Arthur whatever is great in the Western heroic tradition. His ancestors come from the burning city of Troy. His father and uncle are connected with Stonehenge. Merlin, part prophet and part magician, sprinkles his marvels throughout the early part of the tale. Arthur's many famous knights enliven the story with adventures of their own.

Like Beowulf, Arthur fights a monster. Like Alexander the Great, he is one of the world's great conquerors, becoming the head of the Roman Empire. Finally, from a French tradition comes the tragic love story of Arthur, Guinevere, and Lancelot, in which personal desires overcome the characters' responsibility to society and cause the destruction of a great kingdom. The story of King Arthur has something for every taste, and it continues to inspire readers and writers today.

Introducing **The Ages of the World**

Scholars believe that the first people to settle the British Isles migrated there from northern Africa and Spain. They were the resident population when the Celts arrived from Northern Europe.

The druids were the religious leaders of the Celts. They were the priests, prophets, poets, magicians, scientists, and doctors of their tribes. Experts in human knowledge, the druids also could deal with the gods. They were so highly respected that they ranked next to kings and chieftains in importance. The druids performed particular rituals and sacrifices in the belief that they could persuade the gods who controlled all natural phenomena to grant their people fertility and prosperity.

The Celts worshipped the sun, which represented light, fertility, and life. Their four major holidays focused on the sun's relationship to the earth: the two solstices (summer, when the sun is closest to the earth, and winter,

when it is farthest from the earth) and the two equinoxes (the beginning of spring and of autumn). The Celts may have used the prehistoric monument Stonehenge (which marks the sun's progress through the year) as a religious site.

For the Celts, life was a fragile matter and nature a harsh reality. The powers of darkness brought to the northern countries an early, freezing winter, long months when crops could not grow, and the risk of early death from illness, starvation, or harsh weather. The Celtic year's-end festival on the night before Samain, now celebrated as Halloween, was truly a fearsome holiday because it marked the beginning of winter, when the sun's power would become increasingly weak and the forces of darkness would become increasingly strong. Survival was uncertain.

Halloween was a time of monsters and human sacrifice. As part of the religious festival, residents of villages and towns would appear dressed as the demons of darkness, disorder, destruction, disease, and death so that the other residents could chase them away. Celts would also construct figures representing these demons and burn them in the town square as part of the religious ceremony. They also sacrificed one-third of their healthy children to their gods every year, hoping to motivate the gods to provide the grains and grass that they and their animals needed to survive.

The Celtic myths were preserved by Christian monks in Ireland, Scotland, and Wales between A.D. 1100 and 1600. The Irish and Scottish monks recorded an older and more authentic Celtic tradition in the *Lebor Gahala Erenn (Irish Book of Conquests)* than the Welsh monks did in *The Mabinogion*. The latter collection of myths and tales has the setting and tone of medieval chivalry and often involves the adventures of King Arthur and his knights. Consequently, the Celtic creation and fertility myths are found in manuscripts from Ireland and Scotland rather than from Wales.

According to Irish tradition, ancient history and mythology are the same real event—the settling of Ireland by successive races of divine and human peoples. It was a time when gods walked the earth like human beings, using their supernatural powers to bring fertility, civilization, and peace to Ireland. (It is possible that because of their own Christian bias, the Irish and Scottish monks made the Celtic gods act, and even die, as if they were human warriors.)

The Celtic gods live on Irish soil rather than in the heavens. The male gods are warriors who protect the tribe. The female gods are usually fertility goddesses, but may be warriors as well. When the chieftain marries a fertility goddess, he is increasing the protection and survival of the people.

Whatever race of gods rules Ireland, the force of darkness, in the shape of the Fomorians, opposes it and is often successful in battle. The Fomorians represent the gods worshipped by the native, Mediterranean peoples, while the Túatha Dé Danann (the peoples of the Mother Goddess Danu) represent the gods worshipped by the Celts.

Principal Characters and Gods

LADHRA: leader of the first race in Ireland

PARTHOLON: leader of the second race in Ireland

NEMED: leader of the third race in Ireland

FIR BOLG: fourth race in Ireland; first to survive on Irish soil

TÚATHA DÉ DANANN: fifth and greatest race in Ireland; they conquer the Fir Bolgs and the Fomorians

DANU: Mother Goddess or Great Goddess; Túatha Dé are her people

ERIU: Mother Goddess or Great Goddess; queen of the Túatha Dé

BADB CATHA: great Celtic war goddess

DAGDA: god of fertility; great skill in magic; one of the two greatest Túatha Dé warriors

LUG: god of the sun; one of the two greatest Túatha Dé warriors

NUADA: great king of the Túatha Dé

BRES: son of the king of the Fomorians and a Túatha Dé; replaces Nuada as king of the Túatha Dé

FOMORIANS: race of giants; enemy of all the Irish races

MILESIANS: sixth race in Ireland; conquerors of the Túatha Dé

AMERGIN: great druid and poet of the Milesians

DONN: oldest of the Milesians

The Ages of the World

In the beginning, Ireland existed, and it was the world. In the first age of the world, the first race inhabited Ireland. Ladhra, a great leader, had sixteen wives. He was the first person to die on Irish soil, and after his death Ireland was buried by a great flood. Ladhra's entire race perished by drowning. For the next 268 years, the land of Ireland remained uninhabited.

In the second age of the world, the second race invaded Ireland. This was the race of Partholon, the first of the Irish divine ancestors. The race consisted of forty-eight gods; half were males and half were females. For most of the second age, which lasted for 300 years, the Partholons ruled supreme upon the land. In time, their numbers grew from the original forty-eight to 5,000.

When the race of Partholon arrived, Ireland had no grass or trees, but three lakes and nine rivers already provided fresh water. Partholon created seven additional lakes and made the soil fertile. Then he created three more treeless, grassless plains, and his people began to till the soil. One Partholon merchant imported herds of cattle, which became the prize of farmers. Another merchant introduced gold. Agriculture became the principal activity, and the community flourished.

During Partholon's lifetime, the people built the first houses and guest houses, made the first cauldron, and brewed the first beer from large, wild ferns. They established the beginnings of legal and educational systems and devised formal religious practices involving prophecy and sacrifices.

Although this second age was a time of general prosperity, disagreements sometimes disturbed the peace. The first duel was fought, and adultery first occurred. While Partholon was away, his wife and his servant slept together. When Partholon learned of their crime, he demanded that they pay him a price of honor.

Partholon's wife replied that he was at fault rather than she, and it was she who deserved compensation. She argued that a wife was part of her husband's property, and a husband was responsible for protecting his property. In leaving, Partholon had not properly protected his wife. Therefore, she was entitled to the price of honor. The legal system supported Partholon's wife in the dispute, and the judgment against him became the first legal decision in Ireland.

The Fomorians, a native race of divine, monstrous sea-people who had inhabited the islands off the coast of Ireland for 200 years, envied the Partholons' abundant food supply and attacked. They fought with their one eye, their one hand, and their one foot, and they were adept in the use of magic. A mighty battle raged between the two races for seven days. Finally, the Partholons succeeded in driving the Fomorians off their land. But the victory was only temporary; the Fomorians returned to their islands, where they watched and waited for their chance to conquer the people who had civilized Ireland.

On the first of May, the great feast day of Beltine that marked the beginning of summer, the entire race of Partholon was destroyed by a strange plague. Ireland remained uninhabited for thirty years. Yet the contributions that the Partholons had made to Irish life remained to enrich the lives of races who came after them.

In the third age of the world, the divine race of Nemed (sacred) invaded Ireland. The Nemedians created four more lakes and cleared twelve more plains. They imported sheep, which so thrived upon Irish soil that soon they far outnumbered the cattle of the Partholons. Under Nemedian rule, agriculture became more widespread and the people more prosperous.

To protect themselves against the Fomorians, the Nemedians built two forts. Four times the race of Nemed fought against the Fomorians, and four times they emerged from battle victorious. Then a great disease killed Nemed and 2,000 of his people. The Fomorians took advantage of their vulnerability and attacked again. This time they easily conquered the Nemedians in battle, and then they enslaved them. Thereafter, every year on the first of November, the great feast day of Samain that marked the beginning of winter, the Nemedians had to give the Fomorians two-thirds of their children, two-thirds of their milk, and two-thirds of their corn.

The Nemedians could devise no way to avoid this devastating tribute. In desperation, they made one final attack upon the Fomorians in which 16,000 of the race of Nemed died. Those Nemedians who survived abandoned their homes and farms and left Ireland.

In the fourth age of the world, the race of Fir Bolg invaded Ireland on the first of August, the great feast day of Lugnasad that marked the beginning of autumn. Although the Fir Bolgs consisted of many different tribes, they functioned as one race and lived under one king who held complete power in Ireland. They were the first of the races to survive on Irish soil. Unlike their enemies, the Fomorians, they were not divine.

During the reign of the Fir Bolgs, Ireland became more than an agricultural society. The Fir Bolgs were warrior-aristocrats who introduced the iron spearhead. Their king was the first to establish justice in the land, and under his rule the soil became very fertile. The rains fell as gentle dew, and each year's harvest was a bountiful one. Nevertheless, in spite of their warlike skills, the Fir Bolgs were defeated by a new wave of invaders.

In the fifth age of the world, the divine race of Túatha Dé Danann (peoples of the Mother Goddess Danu) invaded Ireland on the first of May. When they landed, a dense cloud concealed their arrival from the Fir Bolgs. As a sign of their determination to remain on Irish soil, they immediately burned all of their boats; no matter what trials lay before them, they would either have to succeed or die.

Their religious leaders, the druids, blew fog and rain clouds over the entire island. These clouds unleashed a torrent of blood and fire upon the Fir Bolgs, causing them to hide in sheltered places for three days and three nights. The religious leaders of the Fir Bolgs cleared the air by performing their own magic spells. Finally, the two races declared a truce of 105 days in order to give each side time to prepare for war.

The Túatha Dé Danann were divided into two groups, gods and non-gods. The gods were the artisans, artists, and aristocratic warriors, for they possessed the power and talent of the race. The non-gods were farmers and common laborers of the fields.

The Túatha Dé were a very talented and learned race of gods. In the islands of northern Greece they had learned many arts and crafts, along with magic. Their wisdom, their magic, and their four talismans gave them divine power. The three greatest Túatha Dé were Dagda the Good, Lug of the Long Arms, and Nuada of the Silver Arm. Dagda earned his name because he was the god of fertility, and he possessed great skill in magic. Lug, the god of the sun, emitted a great brilliance during the day and reflected the glow of the sun from dusk until dawn. He and Dagda were the greatest of the Túatha Dé warriors. Nuada was the great king of the Túatha Dé.

The first treasure of the Túatha Dé was Dagda's bronze Cauldron of Plenty, which always fed each person the amount of food he or she deserved and yet satisfied the hunger of each person who ate from it. Their second treasure was the Stone of Destiny, which emitted a human cry whenever the lawful king of Ireland stepped upon it.

The third treasure of the Túatha Dé was the Spear of Nuada, which always hit its target and brought death to anyone it wounded. Their fourth and last treasure was the sword of Lug, which flashed and roared with fiery flames and brought certain victory to whoever wielded it. Lug's sword always longed for the taste of blood and searched for a way to appease its hunger. Lug kept its blade stored in a container of juice made from pulverized poppy leaves, for the narcotic put the sword safely to sleep until it was needed. Once Lug unleashed it, his sword would tear into the enemy and tirelessly slay warrior after warrior, feasting upon their warm blood.

By using their great skill in magic, the Túatha Dé won their first battle against the Fir Bolgs. Their warriors killed 1,100 of the enemy, and the few who survived the battle fled to the islands west of the Irish mainland. This became known as the first battle of Mag Tured.

In the course of the war, one of the Fir Bolgs cut off the arm of King Nuada. The Túatha Dé doctor and metalsmith worked together to create a silver arm for Nuada that could move with the life and vitality of the original arm. But even with his wondrous silver arm, Nuada was still considered to be maimed. Since the king had to be in perfect health, Nuada of the Silver Arm had to give up his throne.

The chieftains of the Túatha Dé Danann chose Bres the Beautiful to replace Nuada of the Silver Arm as king of Ireland. Bres was a son of the king of the Fomorians, but his mother was one of the Túatha Dé and he had been reared among them. The Túatha Dé chieftains hoped that their choice of Bres as king would ensure peace between the Fomorians and their race.

However, Bres was a very poor king. He was stingy when he should have been generous. He did not offer beer to his chieftains or grease their knives with fat. He refused to employ musicians, acrobats, clowns, and poets to entertain them, for he wished to keep his wealth for himself. He demanded heavy taxes in the form of jewels and food. He also treated the chieftains of the Túatha Dé as non-gods, forcing them to perform menial chores such as carrying firewood, digging ditches, and constructing forts and castles.

When Bres foolishly mistreated the Túatha Dé poet, who was the god of literature, he brought disaster upon himself and the Fomorians. Bres sheltered the poet in a barren, dark hut without the comfort of a bed or a fire and gave him only three dry biscuits for dinner. In retaliation, the poet used his magical power with words to curse the king. "May it become the fate of Bres to live as he has forced others to live: without food upon his plate, without cow's milk in his cup, and without the comforts of a house to protect him from the dismal night!"

The power of the poet was so great that when the chieftains of the Túatha Dé heard these words they forced Bres to give up the throne of Ireland. Bres asked his father, the king of the Fomorians, to attack the Túatha Dé. His father, hearing the true story, refused to help his son, but the other Fomorians gathered together a fearsome army and prepared for battle. The Túatha Dé also prepared for battle.

Meanwhile, Nuada's shoulder became infected where his silver arm was attached to it. When Nuada heard that the young son of the doctor who had designed his silver arm could perform even more wondrous medical feats than his father, he asked the son to cure his infection. The doctor asked Nuada what had been done with his real arm, and Nuada told him it had been buried. The doctor dug up the arm, placed it next to Nuada's shoulder, and recited the words, "Arm, join Nuada's shoulder, nerve to nerve and sinew to sinew."

After three days and three nights, Nuada's arm returned to life and connected itself to his shoulder once again. So it came to pass that Nuada of the Silver Arm was completely healed of his old injury and resumed his position as king of the Túatha Dé Danann.

The young doctor's father was so jealous of his son's medical skill that he raised his sword and struck his son on the head with it, just cutting the skin. The son easily healed his own surface wound. His father then raised his sword and struck his son on the head again, this time slicing through to the bone. Again, the son easily healed his wound. His father then raised his sword a third time and struck his son on the head, this time slicing through to the brain. Again, the son easily healed his wound. Finally, his father raised his sword a fourth time and struck his son on the head, this time slicing his brain in two. With this stroke, the older doctor killed his son.

Upon the young doctor's grave grew 365 stalks of grass. Each blade could cure an illness in one of the 365 nerves in a person's body. The young doctor's sister carefully collected the stalks and arranged them in proper order upon her cloak so that the Túatha Dé doctors could use them to heal their patients. She knew that with these stalks her brother had produced the cures for all illnesses. Her father, however, was so jealous of his son's contribution to medicine, even in death, that he overturned his daughter's cloak and hopelessly mixed up the stalks. Thereafter they were useless, for no one could determine which stalk could cure which illness.

Lug of the Long Arms arrived at court just after Nuada had returned to the throne. The porter greeted Lug politely but announced, "Although you look as royal as our king, Nuada, you will have to prove that you are master of a particular skill in order to be accepted among the nobility of the Túatha Dé Danann."

Lug replied, "Go before your king and tell him that I am a skilled and strong warrior, an excellent carpenter, a fine metalsmith, a gifted harpist, poet, and teller of tales, a knowledgeable doctor, and a talented magician. I challenge King Nuada to produce another of the Túatha Dé Danann who possesses as many skills as I do!"

When the porter repeated Lug's qualifications to the king, Nuada challenged Lug to a game of chess against the best player of the Túatha Dé. When Lug had won the game, he sat on the Seat of Wisdom and watched as the strongest of the Túatha Dé pushed a huge piece of flagstone across the floor of the palace. The stone was so heavy that it would have taken more than eighty teams of oxen to move it. After the stone had been moved, Lug picked it up, carried it outside, and placed it in its original location.

King Nuada then commanded Lug to play Dagda's harp for them. Lug played a melody that was so sad all the gods cried. Then he played a melody that was so cheerful they all laughed. Finally he played a melody that put all the gods to sleep until the following day.

Seeing that Lug was indeed as talented as he had claimed, Nuada gave him kingship for thirteen days so that he could direct the preparations for war against the Fomorians. Lug called upon each of the Túatha Dé gods to reveal his or her particular skills. The chief magician promised to remove the twelve mountains of Ireland and hurl them as missiles against the Fomorians.

The chief cupbearer promised to hide the waters from Ireland's twelve principal lakes and twelve principal rivers so that the Fomorians would find no water to drink. Yet these lakes and rivers would continue to supply fresh water for the Túatha Dé, even if the war lasted for seven years.

The chief metalsmith promised to create weapons that would not fail those who carried them into battle. His lances would always hit their targets and kill their victims. Moreover, he would continue to supply fresh weapons even if the war were to last for seven years.

The chief doctor promised that, as the battle raged, he would cure the wounded so quickly that they could return to battle the following day. He also advised the Túatha Dé to toss the corpses of their slain warriors into a particular well; his chants would cause the dead to emerge from the well restored to life.

The chief druid of the Túatha Dé promised to cause three streams of fiery rain to wash the faces of the Fomorians. Moreover, he promised to remove two-thirds of each Fomorian's strength and courage, while each of the Túatha Dé would receive renewed strength and courage with every breath. Consequently, even if the war lasted for seven years, the Túatha Dé would be able to wage war without tiring.

Finally, Dagda the Good promised that his great club, which could bring both death and the restoration of life, would crush the bones of the Fomorians as the feet of horses crush hailstones. This eight-pronged war club was so heavy that it would take eight strong men to carry it. In battle, Dagda would pull it behind him on a cart, then lift it and kill nine men with one motion.

The Túatha Dé were now prepared. Soon thereafter, the second battle of Mag Tured was fought upon Irish soil. In this fierce combat, both the Túatha Dé Danann and the Fomorians used every kind of magic they possessed. Although the wondrous magic of the Túatha Dé surpassed that of the Fomorians, the giants were so strong that the Túatha Dé could not win. Consequently, the battle between the gods and the giants raged on and on.

The chieftains of the Túatha Dé had decided that Lug of the Long Arms was so valuable they could not risk his death in battle. They had placed him under the guard of nine mighty warriors, but Lug became increasingly impatient with his captivity. Finally he escaped from the guards, climbed into his chariot, and entered the war. He drove among the Túatha Dé warriors shouting, "Be of good courage! It is far better to face death in battle than to live as a slave and pay taxes to a conqueror!"

The Fomorians saw the brightness of the sun shining forth from among the Túatha Dé warriors and exclaimed, "What dreadful fate is upon us? The sun rises today in the west instead of in the east! Surely that must be Lug of the Long Arms, god of the sun, who will help the Túatha Dé win the war!"

Seeing the fields red with the blood of fallen giants, the surviving Fomorians ran for their lives, with Lug and the other Túatha Dé in relentless pursuit. So many Fomorians died in the battle that it would be easier to count the trampled blades of grass under the feet of many galloping horses, the waves in a stormy sea, the sands upon a beach, the drops of dew upon a broad meadow in the spring, the hailstones in a sudden autumn storm, the flakes of snow in a raging winter blizzard, and the stars in the heavens on a clear night than to count the corpses of the Fomorians.

The decisive Túatha Dé victory put a permanent end to the Fomorian threat in Ireland. As the gods were celebrating their victory over the giants, their great war goddess, Badb Catha, stood before the assembled host and chanted, "We have chased the Fomorians from our land, but all is not well. I see the end of our age and the dawn of a new age.

"I see the race of human beings who will invade our land. They will not honor us, and they will not accept our ways. Under their rule, the summers will bear no flowers, the trees will bear no fruit, the cows will give no milk, and the seas will bear no fish. Women will have no pride, men will have no strength, old men will tell no truths, and rulers will not make just laws. Friends will steal from one another, warriors will betray one another, and all that is good and virtuous will perish from the world."

So it came to pass that in the sixth age of the world, the Children of Mil invaded Ireland on the first of May. They had to sail around the island three times before their 36 ships could set anchor, because the druids of the Túatha Dé Danann had shrouded the land in dense fog.

As soon as the Milesians stepped ashore, they were greeted by the Great Goddess Eriu, a queen of the Túatha Dé Danann. "I am the goddess Eriu," she said, "and this land bears my name. I welcome you to this island. You will find none better between the setting sun and the rising sun. It will belong to you and to those of your race who live after you as long as mortals walk the earth. May you honor me by calling this land the land of Eriu, or Ireland."

The great druid and poet of the Milesians, Amergin of the Fair Knee, responded, "We thank you, Great Goddess, for your welcome and your gift of this land. We are grateful that you honor us. In return, we promise to honor you and to keep your name upon this island forever!" But Donn, the oldest of the Children of Mil, interrupted. "Goddess, the poet Amergin does not know what his mouth speaks! His mind is clouded and his words make no sense. We owe no gratitude to you, for you have done nothing for us. Our own gods brought us to this land. It is they who will sustain us here, and it is they whom we shall honor!"

Eriu replied, "Because you cannot accept us along with your own gods, your gods will sustain your race, but they will not sustain you! You will not live to enjoy this land, and no child of yours will either!"

Eriu's words proved to be true. Donn drowned very soon thereafter. The Milesians buried him on an island off the western coast of Ireland, which they called the House of Donn. Since that time, whenever one of the Children of Mil dies, his or her spirit goes to live in the House of Donn.

Then Amergin said, "Mother Goddess, I ask you to unite your forces with mine and bring prosperity to this land. Bring forth fertility from the mountain, the forest, and the sea. For I, too, have great power. I am the wind that blows upon the sea, the roaring of the surf, the powerful ox, the courageous wild boar, the predatory eagle, the rays of the sun, the most beautiful of plants, the imagination of all art, and the champion wielder of mighty weapons.

"Like one of the gods," Amergin continued, "I can change my shape. I can change the shape of the hills and the valleys. I know the age of the moon. I know where to find springs of fresh water. I can summon the fish from the sea. I see a great battle before us in which we will win victory. We will make our home upon this island, and here we will live in safety and peace."

Amergin and the other leaders of his race then confronted the chieftains of the Túatha Dé Danann and said, "We claim this land as our own. You may submit to our rule, or you may choose to fight us! Know, however, that we possess great power."

So it came to pass that the Túatha Dé Danann fought the Children of Mil. Some chronicles state that the Milesians killed the Great Goddess along with a large number of the Túatha Dé Danann, and that those who survived left Ireland. But the common people know the truth. The great gods of the past continue to live in Ireland and will remain there as long as mortals walk the earth. Their spirits dwell within the hills and beneath the earth.

Introducing **Dagda the Good**

The Irish creation and fertility myths are so closely related that the introduction preceding "The Ages of the World" applies here as well. In the creation myth, several of the races that invade Ireland bring fertility to the land. The Partholons create additional lakes, introduce cattle, cultivate the soil, and turn the island into a successful agricultural society. The race of Nemed continues the work by creating more lakes and fertile plains and introducing sheep. The Túatha Dé Danann are described in the greatest detail; their fertility god is the subject of the myth that follows.

In Irish myth the force of light, fertility, and life must always be on guard against the force of darkness, sterility, and death. These two forces often fight against each other for control of Ireland. Sometimes the force of light — represented by the Partholons, Nemedians, and Túatha Dé Danann — wins, and sometimes the force of darkness — represented by the Fomorians — wins.

What is interesting in the Irish myths is that both forces appear able to assure fertility of the soil, although it is the force of light that civilizes the people. Consequently, the conflict in the Irish fertility myth is quite different from that in most other cultures' fertility myths. The usual pattern of the insulted or deprived fertility god does not exist in this myth. Instead two forces, each possessing powers of fertility, confront each other for control of the land.

Dagda the Good

In the fifth age of the world, the divine race of the Túatha Dé Danann possessed great powers of fertility, and Dagda the Good was one of its major gods. He cared for his people because he was the lord of all knowledge. He nourished them because he was the lord of abundance, and he protected them because he was the lord of life and death.

Dagda could perform great magic. His skill was evident both in the wondrous objects he possessed and in his own activities. He could control the weather and assure a bountiful harvest. He brought forth the seasons, each in its proper order, by playing his harp. He also owned a wondrous bronze Cauldron of Plenty, which fed each person the amount of food he or she deserved yet satisfied the hunger of each. Dagda also owned a grove of fruit trees whose fruit was always ripe. And he had two wondrous pigs; at any time one was cooking in order to be eaten, and the other was living, waiting its turn to be cooked.

Dagda's eight-pronged war club was so heavy it would take eight strong men to carry it. With one end of the club he could kill nine people with a single blow; with the other end he could restore them to life. He took this club into battle against the Formorians, the giant race of monsters who were the enemy of the Túatha Dé Danann.

Dagda was as fertile and vital as the forces in nature that he commanded. He loved to eat, and the Fomorians once challenged his prodigious appetite. Pretending to be very hospitable, they said, "Welcome, Dagda. We know that you must be very hungry, so we are preparing your favorite meal for you: porridge."

Dagda watched with interest as the Fomorians poured into a great cauldron, a pot as large as the fists of five giants, eighty gallons of milk along with flour, fat, and bacon. To this they added whole carcasses of pigs, sheep, and goats. They cooked the mixture over a fire until it boiled and then lifted the pot from its tripod and poured the contents into a hole in the ground.

"Now, Dagda," they informed him, "we insist that you eat your porridge if you wish to remain alive and return to your own people. We certainly do not want you to tell the Túatha Dé Danann that the Fomorians are inhospitable and are sparing with the food they feed their guests. We would kill you before we let you tell such a false tale!"

Dagda was undaunted by this challenge. He picked up a spoon so large that two human beings could recline comfortably in its bowl. With it, he lifted out huge hunks of bacon and salted pork. "It certainly smells delicious!" he exclaimed. Then he proceeded to eat all of his porridge. Using his fingers, he even scraped up and ate the last drops from the bottom of the hole, including some gravel.

As he walked off to find a place to rest, the Fomorians laughed at the sight of him. Dagda's stomach was so distended from his meal that he waddled. It was larger than the largest cauldron a large family would possess, and it puffed out in front of his body like a sail on a ship moving downwind.

But the last laugh was on the Fomorians. Dagda's purpose in visiting the enemy was to distract them from the coming war and give his own people more time to prepare for battle.

Like the Túatha Dé Danann, the Fomorians possessed great power over fertility. When their prince, Bres, was captured by the great warrior Lug of the Long Arms, Bres pleaded with Lug not to kill him.

"What price will you pay me for your life?" Lug asked him.

"I can promise that your cows will always give milk," Bres replied.

"That is not enough," Lug said, "unless you can make the cows live longer."

"I cannot do that," Bres replied. "But I can promise you that year after year the Túatha Dé will have a fine harvest of wheat."

"That is not enough," Lug responded. "We already have the four seasons. We have spring for plowing and planting, summer for growing, autumn for harvesting, and winter for eating our bread. However, if you can tell me *exactly* when to plow, when to plant, and when to harvest, I shall give you your life."

"That I can do," said Bres. "Always perform each of these tasks on a Tuesday."

Lug accepted Bres' advice and let him return to the Fomorians.

Introducing **Beowulf**

Historical Background

The epic poem *Beowulf*, written in Old English, is the earliest existing epic in Germanic literature and one of four surviving Anglo-Saxon manuscripts. Although the *Beowulf* manuscript was written in about A.D. 1000, it was not discovered until the 17th century.

The Germanic tribes, including the Angles, the Saxons, and the Jutes, invaded England from about A.D. 450 to 600. By the time of the *Beowulf* poet, Anglo-Saxon society in England was neither primitive nor uncultured. Christianity had been introduced in about 600, and the Anglo-Saxon monasteries contained large libraries of ancient and contemporary works, both secular and religious. Virgil's *Aeneid* was well known, as was the large body of Germanic myths and legends.

Society was well organized, with a large number of wealthy aristocrats. The Sutton Hoo royal ship burial, dating from between 650 and 660, was discovered in Suffolk, England, in 1939. Its artifacts authenticate the details of court life described in *Beowulf*. Like the epic itself, these articles combine aspects of Anglo-Saxon culture with the contemporary Christian culture.

Scholars do not know whether *Beowulf* is the sole surviving epic from a flourishing Anglo-Saxon literary period that produced other great epics, or whether it was unique even in its own time. Moreover, they disagree as to whether this *Beowulf* is a copy of an earlier manuscript. Many scholars think that the epic was probably written sometime between the late 7th century and the early 9th century. If they are correct, the original manuscript was probably lost during the 9th-century Viking invasions of Anglia, in which the Danes destroyed the Anglo-Saxon monasteries and their great libraries. However, other scholars think that the poet's favorable attitude toward the Danes must place the epic's composition after the Viking invasions, and in the early 11th century when this *Beowulf* manuscript was written.

The identity of the *Beowulf* poet is also uncertain. He apparently was a Christian who loved the pagan heroic tradition of his ancestors and blended the values of the pagan hero with the Christian values of his own country and time. Because he wrote in the Anglian dialect, he probably was either a monk in a monastery or a poet in an Anglo-Saxon court located north of the Thames River.

Although *Beowulf* was written by an Englishman in Old English, the story takes place in the southern part of Sweden and in Denmark — that part of Scandinavia from which the immigrants to England had come. The plots are Germanic in origin.

Appeal and Value

Beowulf interests contemporary readers for many reasons. First, it is an outstanding adventure story. Grendel, Grendel's mother, and the dragon are marvelous monsters, and each fight is unique, action-packed, and exciting.

Second, Beowulf is a very appealing hero. He is the perfect warrior, combining extraordinary strength, skill, courage, and loyalty. Like Heracles, he devotes his life to making the world a safer place. He chooses to risk death in order to help other people, and he faces his inevitable death with heroism and dignity.

Third, the *Beowulf* poet is interested in the psychological aspects of human behavior. For example, the Danish hero's welcoming speech illustrates his jealousy of Beowulf. The behavior of Beowulf's warriors in the dragon fight reveals their cowardice. Beowulf's attitudes toward heroism reflect his maturity and experience, while King Hrothgar's attitudes toward life show the experiences of an aged nobleman.

Finally, the *Beowulf* poet exhibits a mature appreciation of the transitory nature of human life and achievement. In *Beowulf*, as in the major epics of other cultures, the hero must create a meaningful life in a world that is often dangerous and uncaring. He must accept the inevitability of death. He chooses to reject despair; instead, he takes pride in himself and in his accomplishments, and he values human relationships.

Like Beowulf and the other epic heroes, we too are faced with our own mortality. We too must create a meaningful life in a dangerous world. Like them, we must learn to reject despair and adopt a code of behavior that will permit us to take pride in ourselves, our accomplishments, and our relationships with other people. Beowulf kills monsters to protect his society from those life-threatening dangers. Today, it is just as necessary for us to fight against the monsters of famine, sickness, injustice, and war.

The Germanic Hero

The aristocratic society of Beowulf's time involved groups of warriors clustered around particular princes or kings. War was the customary occupation of the Anglo-Saxon nobleman, and he slept with his armor by his side. Under the leadership of the king, warriors spent their time defending their own country from hostile invaders and raiding other countries for wealth. A king was obligated to provide his warriors with food, drink, weapons and armor, land, and jewels. In return, a warrior was obligated to fight to the death to defend his king. In such a society courage, skill in battle, and loyalty were the principal virtues.

The only acceptable justice was retributive justice, usually a death for a death. Wergild (man-price), the specific monetary value placed on the life of an individual, varied according to a person's social status. Retributive justice created an environment in which vengeance and feuds were common and self-perpetuating.

The pagan warriors of the northern lands believed in Wyrd (unalterable fate). Both gods and humans were completely subject to Wyrd, which included their inevitable death. Without an afterlife, immortality could be achieved only through fame that lasted beyond one's death. In an environment where everyone had to face the difficulties of war, severe weather, food shortages, illness, uncomfortable old age, and death, it made sense to take pleasure in whatever good things life offered. So eating, drinking, receiving gifts, and achieving fame and honor were highly valued.

Principal Characters

HROTHGAR: king of the Danes; builder of Heorot

UNFERTH: greatest Danish warrior

GRENDEL: monstrous man; son of a monstrous woman

BEOWULF: great hero of the Geats; later, king of the Geats

HYGELAC: king of the Geats; Beowulf's relative and king

BRECA: Beowulf's friend and competitor when they were boys

WIGLAF: Beowulf's nephew; a young warrior of the Geats

WYRD: the goddess Fate

Beowulf

Chapter 1

Hrothgar, king of the Danes, builds a great hall. But the monster Grendel murders Hrothgar's warriors there, so the hall lies empty. Beowulf arrives from Geatland to fight Grendel.

Hear me! We have listened to many a tale about the Spear-Danes in days of old. We have heard about their mighty kings, whose daring deeds brought them great glory and wealth. They defeated fierce foes, and they ruled with such power that folk across the whale-road paid them tax and tribute. They gave gifts graciously and generously. Then, when war came, their people were loyal and served them well. They were good kings! The Lord of Life, he who gives glory, showered them with fame.

When the time came for such a king to die, his soul made the journey to God, to remain in peace through all etenity. His people honored him. Lovingly they carried his body down to the shore of the sea and placed it aboard a ring-prowed ship that was moored in the icy waters. They set their dead king, their beloved giver of rings, against the mast and surrounded him with a trove of treasure. Gold and jewels from distant lands, chainmail coats, battle armor, and powerful swords all accompanied him on his last, lonely journey.

When all was ready, they cast loose the anchor and launched the ring-prowed ship upon the whale-road to wander where it would. Long after the ship was out of sight, its golden banner waved high above the sea swell. Warriors and wise counselors watched and waited with heavy hearts as the waves carried that wealthy cargo upon the pathless sea.

Hrothgar was one of these mighty kings who ruled the Spear-Danes. Holy God, Lord of Life granted him wisdom, skill, and success in battle. Warriors followed him because he was fierce in war and generous with gifts. Soon he led a mighty army.

Hrothgar decided to build a huge mead-house, a hall so splendid that it would be talked of in lands far and wide. He wanted his warriors to gather in the great hall to feast, drink, and receive treasure as their reward for their deeds of valor. He named the great, gabled hall Heorot, meaning the Hall of the Hart, for the stag was a fitting sign for a king. Hrothgar gave generously all the treasure that God had granted him, awarding his warriors gold rings and shining armbands. He did not give lives of men or land belonging to his people, for these alone were not his to give.

Hrothgar and his noble warriors feasted in their gabled hall, unaware that they were being watched and despised. The gruesome creature Grendel dwelled at night in the darkness of the misty moor. By day, he haunted the marshland with hate in his hard heart. Descended from the race of Cain, Grendel bore the ancient curse, the mark of murder, of his death-dealing ancestor. Like Cain, Grendel had been banished from life among joyful folk. He was condemned to live in a lonely lair, with only his mother and monsters of the deep for company.

Day after day, Grendel heard and hated the harp and sounds of song. One night he waited until the sun, that jewel of heaven, had glided over the earth. Then he stalked out of the shadows and into the towering, timbered mead-hall to spy upon the Spear-Danes. A band of brave warriors met his eye, their bodies relaxed in heavy slumber. Mead had dulled their minds, and for this short time they were free of thoughts of sorrow and woe in the world about them.

Grim and greedy, furious and fierce, the monster grabbed thirty Spear-Danes and pitilessly slew them while they slept. He mangled them with his bloody teeth. A huge bag of dragon's skin hung from his shoulder. Into it he tossed the blameless bodies of the Danes. Then, gloating and gleeful over his plunder, he hurried homeward to his lair with his frightful feast. For the time being, Grendel left the Hall of Heorot to the living. But he would come again.

Not until the bright morning light shone forth over the land did King Hrothgar and his folk hear of the disaster. When they entered that bright hall of brave men, the sight filled them with horror. Sounds of weeping and wailing replaced the songs of joy that had issued forth from the great hall.

The Ring-Danes recognized Grendel's footprints and feared his power, but they did not think that he would return. They were wrong; the monster murdered more men the following night. Thereafter, the Ring-Danes were filled with despair. Each night, they reluctantly deserted the great Hall of Heorot, that best of buildings.

Grendel's ravenous appetite for human flesh drove him to wage war against Hrothgar's entire band. He knew nothing of justice and desired no peace. King Hrothgar could not reward or appease him, for the fearsome fiend valued neither gold nor treasure. So great was his power that he feared no form of retribution, no avenging death.

The people gathered in their heathen temples, offering sacrifices to their idols and prayers to Satan, the slayer of souls. They did not know that they were neglecting the Lord of Heaven, and that their salvation would never come from hell.

For twelve long winters, Grendel haunted Heorot and ruled the Spear-Danes. His ravaging raids filled the hearts of even the bravest warriors with terror. They had neither the strength nor the skill to kill him. The dark death shadow of the dreaded demon stalked the misty moors each night.

The tale of Grendel's terror spread far and wide. Bards sung of his destructive deeds, of the Spear-Danes' hopeless struggle, and of their endless war.

The Storm-Geats, who lived on the southern coast of Sweden, heard about Grendel's dreadful deeds. Beowulf, the strongest of the Geats, great of heart and fearless, determined to sail over the whale-road to help Hrothgar, war king of the Spear-Danes. He chose fourteen brave warriors to accompany him.

When a seaworthy ship had been suitably fitted for the journey, Beowulf's men eagerly boarded it and stowed their gleaming armor and splendid battle gear deep within its hold. They set forth with a spirit of adventure. A brisk wind sent their ship speeding westward across the wavy whale-road like a sea bird, its prow like a foamy beak.

The next day the sun, that bright candle of the world, shone upon their destination, the shining sea-cliffs, high hills, and broad headlands of the Spear-Danes. The Storm-Geats beached their broad-beamed boat and stepped ashore, their chain-mail coats clanking. They thanked God for granting them safe paths for their ocean crossing.

Meanwhile, from the top of the sea-cliff, the watchful warden on horseback saw the group of strange warriors bearing shining shields and gleaming war gear step ashore, ready for battle. He galloped down to the shore, holding his spear poised in his hand.

"What men are you," he challenged, "wearing chain mail and carrying war gear? One among you is the greatest warrior in armor that I have ever seen! Unless his looks and stature lie, he is matchless among noble men!"

Beowulf, the leader of the group, unlocked his hoard of words. "We are Geats, and King Hygelac's hearth companions," he began. "My own father, Ecgtheow, was known among folklands far and wide before Death took him at the end of many winters. Every man of wise mind remembers him well.

"We have come to seek your lord, the protector of your people," he continued. "Our hearts have prompted us to conquer the dread monster who has terrified the Spear-Danes with his deadly deeds."

The warden replied, "Take your weapons and your war gear, and I shall lead you forth to our king. My men will watch your bent-necked ship and protect it from any foe."

As the Geats marched toward the Hall of Heorot, the warlike boars on their gold-gleaming helmets kept watch over their lives. Finally they saw King Hrothgar's gold-trimmed, high-gabled hall, famous beyond all other halls in lands far and wide. There the warden left them to return to his sea watch, and they continued along the cobbled street toward the bright home of brave men.

When they had rested their broad, golden shields and their gray-tipped, ash-wood spears against the wall of the great hall, Hrothgar's herald, Wulfgar, questioned them as the warden had. Wulfgar then returned to his white-haired king and said, "Beowulf, leading a band of Geats, has sailed the whale-road to our land and wishes to speak with you. Grant them your ear, gracious Hrothgar, for their war gear reveals them to be worthy of great respect."

"I knew Beowulf when he was a child," Hrothgar replied. "We are family friends. I have heard from seafaring folk that Beowulf has the strength of thirty men in the grip of his hand! I hope that holy God has sent him to help us fight Grendel! I shall give him glorious gifts for his great heart and valiant spirit. Welcome the Geats, and ask them to come before me."

Standing before Hrothgar in his stern boar's helmet and his shining chain-mail coat, Beowulf said, "Hail to thee, Hrothgar, mighty king of the Spear-Danes! I am Hygelac's kinsman and warrior. In the land of my people I have heard seafaring folk say that Heorot, this best of all buildings, lies deserted and useless once the bright heavens darken with the shadows of dusk.

"From the days of my youth," Beowulf continued, "I have won honor through many daring deeds. I have come bloodstained from battle, having bound a group of five giants and overthrown their tribe. Driven by danger, I have slain perilous sea monsters upon the waves in the dark of night. Now I shall wage war with that giant Grendel, fierce fiend though he is.

"I ask only one favor of you, beloved Hrothgar. Let your folk rest while my brave band of Geats and I cleanse your high-gabled, golden hall of this foul fiend. I have heard that he disdains to use weapons of any kind. I shall do as he does and fight without my sword and my broad, goldrimmed shield. Instead, I shall use my mighty grip and grapple with the fiend hand to hand to the death.

"If Grendel wins the battle," concluded Beowulf, "he will leave you with no bodies to bury. He will munch upon my Storm-Geats in your mead-hall, just as he has devoured your Spear-Danes there. Nor will any part of my mangled corpse remain to trouble you, for Grendel will bear my bloodstained head and body to the moors to chew upon them at his leisure in his lonely lair. Just send my war shirt back to my lord Hygelac, for Wayland, the renowned metalsmith, made it with his own hands. Wyrd always weaves as she must."

The lord of the Ring-Danes replied, "Beowulf, my friend, you are our sole defense in this time of need! Grendel has weakened my brave band and has wasted my mead-hall. So, welcome! join the Spear-Danes in a joyful feast, and speak to my men of your purpose and plan."

Chapter 2

The Danish hero Unferth unjustly criticizes Beowulf.
Beowulf meets Grendel in single combat and kills him.

After the feast, the Danish warrior Unferth, who had earned considerable honor among his own folk, sat at the feet of King Hrothgar. Unferth's heart burned with shame and anger that Beowulf, the bold, brave seafarer, had traveled uninvited to his land in order to slay the monstrous giant that Unferth himself was afraid to meet in battle. Unferth unlocked a hoard of words revealing his hidden anger.

"Are you that Beowulf," he began, "who, foolishly boastful, tempted the waves and risked your life, striving against Breca in a swimming match on the broad billows of winter's swollen sea waters? I heard tell that no man, loved or loathed, could dissuade you from your dangerous desire. You swam in the grip of the waters for seven nights. Breca, being stronger than you are, surpassed you in swimming. The morning tide then carried him near his folk, his home, his walled town, and his treasure.

"If you decide to spend a night in this best of buildings waiting for Grendel," Unferth concluded, "I foresee a harder match and a worse fate for you, strong though you are in the struggle of battle."

Beowulf replied, "Unferth, my friend, your mind is muddled with mead, and it has twisted your tale about Breca and me. The truth is that no man has more strength in the waves and more stamina in the sea than I have.

"Breca and I were still boys when we made that childish boast and decided to risk our lives on the raging whale-road. We swam forth bearing our sharp sword blades in our hands to guard against the assault of fierce seafish. Breca and I swiftly swam side by side on the waves of the flood waters for five nights. Finally the tossing waves, the icy-cold air, the bitter, battle-fierce north wind, and the coming of night drove us apart.

"The rough waves roused the wrath of the fierce sea-fish. I was glad I was wearing my chain-mail battle shirt, hand-linked and hard. A savage sea beast dragged me to the bottom and held me fast in his deadly grip. Yet my golden garment protected my chest. The point of my sword pierced the heart of that mighty monster, and I gladly buried my battle weapon in its breast."

Beowulf continued, "Other loathsome sea creatures, ravenously hungry, pressed close about me and clutched at the chains across my chest. I gladly gave each of them the tip of my sword blade. I robbed them of their meal, for they thought to seize me and feast on my dead flesh.

"Instead, when the bright morning light next shone forth over the land, it found them belly up on the beach, bloody with wounds from my battle blade and slain by my sword strokes. I had killed nine monsters with my bare sword edge. Never again would they harass seafarers crossing the deep waters of the whale-road!

"I have never heard of a harder fight at night, or of a man in worse trouble in the sea streams. When the waves subsided, I could see the headlands and the windy walls of the Finns. The surging sea-flood swept me to their land. So Wyrd, often spares one who is not marked for death if his courage is good.

"I have heard of no daring deeds of yours involving such terror and blood-stained sword blades," Beowulf added. "In fact, if your mind and heart were as fierce as you would have me believe, then Grendel would never have done such horrible deeds in the Hall of Heorot. He slaughters and eats whomever he chooses whenever he chooses, sparing no one, because he has learned that he need not fear the anger of the Spear-Danes.

"However, the spirit, strength, and skill of the Storm-Geats will now bid Grendel to battle. I can assure you that when the morning light next shines forth over the land, the Spear-Danes will be able to return to this mead-hall without fear!" So Beowulf swore.

Hrothgar's Heorot once again echoed with the joy and laughter of heroes. Hearing of Beowulf's great deeds, the lord of the Spear-Danes, giver of treasure and shepherd of his people, was confident that Beowulf would be successful. As was her custom, Hrothgar's gentle-mannered queen, dressed in golden splendor, greeted their guests and offered them the mead cup.

When the sun's light began to fade in the late afternoon sky, the king rose to seek his evening's rest, and all of the Spear-Danes rose with him. They knew that Grendel would soon come forth from the shadows, stalking his prey in the high hall.

Hrothgar said to Beowulf, "Never since my hands could carry a sword and shield have I trusted anyone other than my own people to guard this mighty hall. Keep in your mind your great deeds, and let the fearsome fiend know the strength of your skill. If you succeed, I shall reward you with the greatest of treasure."

To these words, Beowulf replied, "When I boarded my sea craft, I determined that I would either perform daring deeds befitting my birth or face my last day and lay down my life in your mead-hall, mangled by the monster's mighty grip!"

The Storm-Geats prepared to spend the night in the hall where the Spear-Danes feared to dwell. Trusting in his mighty strength, Beowulf removed his golden, chain-mail war shirt, his boar's helmet, and his richly decorated sword, and gave them to one of his men to guard until morning.

Before he lay down, he announced, "I am as strong and courageous as Grendel! I could easily slay him with my sword, for he is not skilled in the use of weapons. But since he fights without sword and shield, so shall I. May God award victory to the one of us he chooses!"

Then Beowulf, brave in battle, lay down but remained awake and alert. His brave, seafaring companions lay down to sleep. Knowing that Grendel took great joy in slaughtering the men he found in this bright hall, each Geat quietly thought of his home. He feared in his heart that never again would he see his family, his home, or the town in which he had been reared. But the Lord gave the Storm-Geats the destiny to overcome their foe through the courage and strength of one man. Mighty God rules mortals forever!

Grendel, the shadow walker, left the misty moor and stalked toward the hall of heroes through the dark night. Everyone in the great-gabled hall slept, except for one man. Beowulf lay awake, watching and waiting. He was anxious for the battle to start, for his anger toward his foe filled his heart to overflowing.

Grendel left the misty moor and quickly strode toward Heorot, the treasure house of men, glittering with gold. He bore God's anger and was a joyless creature. Determined to do dreadful deeds, the fierce fiend angrily placed his hands upon the door and forced it to give way before his furious might, even though its fastenings had been forged in fire.

Quickly he strode inside. A blazing light burned in his eyes like a flame. His heart laughed to see the hall occupied once again by sleeping warriors. He expected to slaughter each and every one of them before returning to his lonesome lair, for the sight of such a full feast filled him with a raging hunger. But it was Wyrd's decree that, after that night, Grendel would never again feed upon human flesh.

Beowulf quietly watched as Grendel set about his beastly business. The monster suddenly seized a sleeping warrior, tore his body to pieces, bit into his flesh and through his bones, drank down his blood, and devoured him piece by bloody piece. Soon he had consumed the entire corpse.

He then stepped toward the reclining figure of Beowulf and clasped the bold-hearted hero with his monstrous claw. Beowulf angrily seized Grendel's arm in his own mighty grip. Grendel had never met a more fearsome foe. Terror flooded the monster's mind and heart. His courage fled. He wanted only to flee into the darkness and return to his lonely lair, but Beowulf held him fast.

Beowulf sprang to his feet and clutched at Grendel's hand with all his strength. The fingers of the giant snapped. The hall clanged and shook with the relentless, savage struggle as the two foes raged. The walls shattered, but the iron bands within and without kept the Hall of Heorot standing in spite of the fierce fight. The Spear-Danes trembled with terror at the sound of Grendel's howling screams of pain and his shrieks of defeat.

Beowulf's brave men tried to help him by using their trusty swords, handed down from their fathers, to slash at Grendel from every side. They did not realize that the sharpest sword blade on earth could not harm his hateful heart, for the dreaded demon had placed a spell on every keen-edged weapon.

So the two fought fiercely on. Through it all, Beowulf gripped Grendel's hand with a vise-like grasp, while Grendel tried to break free. Gradually, a gaping wound opened in Grendel's shoulder. The sinews snapped apart, and the bones split at the joint. Beowulf had ripped Grendel's arm from the rest of his body. He had won the battle, and with it glory and fame.

Close to death, Grendel ran in dreadful pain back to his lonely lair in the misty, marshy moor. He knew that his life was at an end. The breath of life left his body, and his heathen spirit descended to Hell.

Beowulf, who had come from afar and who was bold and brave in battle, had kept his word to Hrothgar, the ring-giving king of the Spear-Danes. The hero had cleansed Heorot of deadly deeds and had saved it from the foul fiend. As token of his great victory, Beowulf mounted Grendel's bloody arm and claw beneath the golden, gabled roof for all to see.

In the morning, many a brave-hearted warrior wandered about the bright hall to marvel at Grendel's giant claw and his great footprints. Neither Spear-Dane nor Storm-Geat sorrowed at the thought of the maimed monster wending his way to the moor with a weary heart, defeated and dying. The warriors fearlessly followed Grendel's bloody track to the marshy moor. There they found the swamp seething with gore, its dread waters bubbling and boiling with hot blood. Seeing no sign of Grendel, they joyfully returned to celebrate Beowulf's victory.

Hrothgar's bard, who knew many ancient sagas, was already skillfully weaving a tale of Beowulf's great victory. He compared Beowulf to Sigurd the Volsung, who had slain a fearsome dragon and won its hoard of treasure.

King Hrothgar, giver of gold rings, entered Heorot and saw the terrifying token of victory. "I thank God for this sight!" he exclaimed, gazing up at Grendel's arm. "Not long ago, while high-gabled Heorot stood bloodstained and gory, I feared that no one in the wide world could help us. From this time forth, Beowulf, I will love you like a son. As long as I live, you will never want for wealth. I have given great treasure to weaker warriors for far less service. Your deeds here have given you fame that will live forever! May God continue to give you a good life!"

Heorot, the best of buildings, was then completely cleansed and decorated for the great celebration. Tapestries gleaming with gold shone from the shattered walls. Many repairs were needed, for by the time the monster had turned to flee with what remained of his life, only the roof of the high-gabled hall was whole.

Hrothgar gave Beowulf a rich array of gifts, including a mighty treasure sword, an embroidered war banner, eight horses with golden bridles, and an ancient saddle that was artfully fashioned and decorated with treasure. Beowulf's band of Geats who had sailed the sea road with him also received gifts, and a payment in gold, wergild, was set aside for the family of the warrior whom Grendel had slain.

When the feasting, drinking, telling of tales, and giving of gifts had come to an end, Hrothgar rose to seek his evening's rest. Most of the Spear-Danes and all of the Storm-Geats followed him, leaving Heorot to the warriors who would sleep there as they had often done in times past.

Those who remained in the high-gabled hall covered the floor with beds and pillows and pushed the benches to the head of their beds. They set their shining shields and their unsheathed swords at their heads and placed their chain-mail coats and their battle spears at their sides. They rested their helmets upon the benches. It was their custom always to be ready for war.

The Spear-Danes were a good people, but they were unaware of what Wyrd had woven for them.

Chapter 3

Grendel's mother invades Heorot and murders Hrothgar's best friend. Beowulf follows the monster to her underwater den and kills her. After praise and celebration, he returns to Geatland.

Hidden away in the misty moor, doomed to dwell deep in Grendel's dark den, his mighty mother lived. She had dearly loved her loathsome son. When Death took his dark spirit, the sorrow in her heart turned her thoughts to vengeance. That night, the mournful mother silently stalked forth from the misty moor, intent on invading high-gabled Heorot, where her son had met his dreadful destiny. Beowulf, that dauntless hero, shield and sword of the Spear-Danes, would have to destroy another demon.

When she broke into the high-gabled hall, the Spear-Danes, usually bold and brave in time of trouble, were frightfully afraid. However, they took some comfort from the fact that this monster was female. Women were, after all, weaker, more afraid, and less fierce in fighting.

The Spear-Danes tried to trust in the bloodstained blades of their shining swords and in their sparkling shields. But in their haste to harm their intruder, they forgot their helmets and their heavy chain-mail coats. Beowulf was not there to cheer their hearts, for he had not slept in Heorot that night.

Fortunately, Grendel's mother felt fear as well. When she discovered danger, she longed to save her own life. She quickly grasped Aeschere, the king's most trusted counselor and comrade, slew him with her bloody teeth, and carried him to her den under the frightful flood waters. The Spear-Danes soon discovered that she had also taken Grendel's gruesome arm.

Hearing heartrending cries, the old king returned to his high-gabled hall. Great sorrow crushed his spirit when he heard of Aeschere's murder, for he was Hrothgar's dearest friend and a warrior of great fame.

When the bright morning light next shone forth, Hrothgar summoned Beowulf and his Storm-Geats to the great, gabled hall. The ring-giving lord unlocked a hoard of words. "I have heard those who dwell in this land say that they have seen two fearful folk prowling in the darkness of the misty moorland and lurking along the borders of their homes. It seemed to them that one of these was a woman and the other a giant of a man. In olden days, these people named the man Grendel. They never saw one who could have been his father.

"These two fearsome fiends claimed the lonely moors as theirs. They chose a land of perilous paths, where the flood of the mountain stream plunges downward to the base of the craggy cliffs and disappears beneath the muddy swampland. That wild, windswept, lonely land is not many miles from here. There, shadowy woods frown upon the frightful flood waters. When the wind stirs up unwelcome weather, those dark waters bubble and boil, and their mist rises to the heavens. At night, those bottomless flood waters burn with flaming fire and become a fearful sight.

"No one knows the depth of that dark, dreaded marshland," Hrothgar continued. "Even the stalwart stag, that roaming heather-stepper who depends upon the strength of his horns for safety, will stop at the brink of that marsh and face death at the hand of a hunter before he will hide in it. The place is haunted by evil spirits!

"Once again, Beowulf, only you can help us. Seek the loathsome lair of this female monster if you dare. Slay the grim and ghastly guardian of the flood's depth. If you return with your life, I shall generously reward you with gracious gifts of ancient treasures and twisted gold."

Beowulf replied, "Put aside your sorrow, my wise king. It is bettter to avenge the death of your friend than to mourn overlong for him. All men must die, sooner or later. The warrior who can, should win glory and fame before death takes his spirit. Then, when his life comes to an end, his good name will live on after him.

"So, my lord, let us quickly seek the tracks of Grendel's companion. I promise that she will not find shelter, either in the heart of the earth, in the depths of mountain forest, or at the bottom of the ocean floor. Have patience just this day."

Then Hrothgar thanked God for Beowulf. The ring-giving king called for his horse and prepared to join Beowulf and his brave band of Geats. He rode in state, accompanied by a foot-band of shield bearers. The path that the fiend had taken was plain to see. Straight over the moor she had traveled, bearing the bloody corpse of the best of Hrothgar's men.

The path became rope-thin and rocky. It led past rugged ravines, over steep stone slopes, by craggy cliffs, and alongside many a sea monster's lair. The courageous king and his company of warriors went forward to where the mountain's trees leaned gloomily out from the rough-hewn rocks of the cliff. Suddenly they saw Aeschere's severed, bloody head lying at the edge of the steep slope. Sorrow overwhelmed their hearts as they saw what had happened to the noble warrior. They approached the head and gazed down at the base of the precipice. Fear joined grief as their eyes scanned the bubbling, turbulent flood waters, boiling with blood and hot gore.

The men sat down in silence at the edge of the cliff. They saw many strange sea serpents swimming in the waves. Other wild sea dragons, which often cause grief on the sail-road by attacking ships, were resting on the flat surfaces of protruding rocks. Startled at the sound of the battle horn, the snake-like monsters sped away.

Beowulf put on his armor. "I have no fear for my life," he announced. "My hand-woven, chain-mail shirt will protect my body from any serpent's battle grip. A cunning smith covered the surface of my ancient helmet with swine shapes so no battle-blade can bite through it."

Unferth, the greatest warrior among the Spear-Danes, extended his own sword, Hrunting, to Beowulf. The Danish hero forgot the taunting words the wine had led him to speak. Unferth knew that he did not possess the courage and skill to risk his life beneath the bloody waves in order to do a warrior's duty.

"Take my sword," he said. "It is one of the most valued of the old treasures. Its iron blade has been dyed with poison twigs and battle-hardened with blood. Although many warriors who wielded it have tread ways of terror, Hrunting has never betrayed in battle anyone who has clasped it in his hand!"

"Thank you," Beowulf replied. "I shall be glad to have such a trusted friend!"

Beowulf was now armed and ready for whatever danger his journey would bring. He said to Hrothgar, "Remember, great king, should I lose my life in this venture, I want you to care for my men. Send the treasure you gave me to Hygelac, my king, so that he will know what a gracious giver of rings you are and how rewarded I was for my deeds while I lived. And let Unferth, your far-famed warrior, keep his ancient, splendid, keen-bladed sword. I shall win fame for myself with Hrunting, or Death shall take me!"

With these words, Beowulf plunged into the seething, swirling, bloody waves. He sank deep beneath the surface all the day long, until finally he reached the bottom. Soon Grendel's mother, who had guarded the flood's depths for fifty winters, saw the warrior who was searching for her secluded sea-cave.

She suddenly appeared before Beowulf in the murky waters and seized him, clutching him in her terrible claws. But she could not even scratch his skin. Her foul fingers could not tear through his mail coat. As she carried him into her lair, strong as he was Beowulf could not wield his weapons. So it happened that many strange sea beasts pressed their treacherous tusks close to his body, breaking through his battle shirt and scratching his skin.

Soon, Beowulf found himself in a high-roofed hall where no water could enter. A brightly shining fire shone upon the walls, illuminating the dreaded demon.

Beowulf immediately raised Hrunting, his blood-hardened battle sword, and smashed the frightful fiend on the head with such strength that the ring-decked blade sang its greedy war song. However, the blade of the mighty weapon could not bite her flesh or break her life. Its brave blade betrayed Beowulf in his time of greatest need. In the past, Hrunting had bitten through many a war helmet and mail coat, dooming the wearer to death. Now for the first time the treasured sword won no glory.

Angrily, the brave warrior threw aside his sword. He trusted instead to his own strength, to the great might of his hand grip. So must any warrior, for if a man wants to win lasting fame in battle, he must put aside all fear of death.

Beowulf eagerly seized Grendel's mother by the shoulders. He was so strong-hearted and swollen with wrath that his strength became great enough to throw her to the ground. Quickly, however, the monster grabbed him. Beowulf's spirits sank as he felt her tremendous strength, and this strongest of warriors staggered and fell.

Grendel's mother hurled herself upon him and drew forth her broad, bright-bladed dagger. She intended to avenge her only child.

Beowulf, the foremost fighter of the War-Geats, would have gone to his death there in the deep sea-cave had not the stout mesh of his woven battle shirt saved him. The chain links withstood the thrust of the demon's dagger point and blade. They shielded his chest and sheltered his life. Holy God, the wise Lord and Ruler of the heavens, granted Beowulf victory in battle. He quickly pushed away the monster and sprang to his feet.

Beowulf then saw an ancient sword, forged by the giants of old, hanging on the wall. This weapon was far greater than any a man, however strong, might bear into battle.

Beowulf seized the giant-sword by its chain-ringed hilt. Raging with fury, he brandished the blade. He struck so angrily and with such savage strength at the monster's throat that the hard-edged blade slashed into her neck, broke her bones, and sliced through her body. The fearsome fiend dropped to her death at his feet.

Beowulf gazed upon the bloody blade of the sword and gloried in his great deed. The fire suddenly flamed forth, bringing light as bright as the candle of the sky when it shines forth from heaven. Beowulf then searched the spacious cave for Grendel. When he finally found the monster's lifeless, broken body, Beowulf swung the giant-sword with such an angry blow that Grendel's head sprang in one direction while his body jumped in another.

Meanwhile, on the edge of the cliff, Hrothgar and the two groups of warriors waited and watched. When they saw the surface of the flood water suddenly swirl in bloody waves, the Danes thought Grendel's mother had slain Beowulf. They waited for nine more hours, and then they returned to Heorot. The Geats, however, still sat staring into the bloody waters. Sick at heart, they hoped but dared not expect to see their leader and lord.

In the sheltered sea-cave, the hot, poisonous blood of the two fallen fiends devoured the broad blade of the giants' shining sword. It began to melt as ice melts when God, who rules the times and the seasons, breaks the bonds of frost and unwinds the floods' fetters. Beowulf saw many treasures in the den, but he took only Grendel's head and the jeweled hilt of the giant-sword.

Beowulf then swam up to the swirling surface of the bloody sea. Carrying a trophy in each hand, he swam to land. His men ran to join him, joyful at his safe return. The pool of water beneath the clouds, previously stained with battle-blood, now grew clean and still. When they left the lake, it took all the strength of four men to carry Grendel's grotesque head on their spear shafts away from the craggy cliffs and back along the perilous paths to the gold-decked hall of Heorot.

Beowulf, bravest in battle and great in glory, came before Hrothgar, bearing Grendel's head by its hair into the high hall. The Danish warriors gazed in amazement and wonder at the strange sight.

Beowulf announced, "With great joy we have brought you this glorious token of triumph. I barely escaped with my life! I would have been killed in that grim battle beneath the waters if God had not shielded me. I could achieve nothing with Hrunting, splendid though that strong-bladed weapon is.

"Holy God, the ruler of men, who often guides the friendless, permitted me to see an ancient and wondrous sword, forged by a giant smith, hanging upon the wall. With that sword, I slew the monstrous guardian of the sea-cave and beheaded the lifeless body of Grendel. The boiling blood and battle gore of those fiends burned the blade to nothing, and I have returned with the hilt as a record of the ruin and death of those dreaded demons, those fiends who were the foes of God.

"I promise," Beowulf concluded, "that you and your warriors can now sleep free from care in high-gabled Heorot.

Beowulf then placed the jeweled sword hilt into the hand of the old king. The hilt revealed the ancient story of the flood. Those rushing waters ravaged and ruined the giant race because they had lived lawlessly. Decorated with dragon shapes, the ancient letters told the tale.

Hrothgar said to Beowulf, "Your fame is echoed among every people throughout the wide world. Maintain your might with a wise heart. Be a comfort to your people and a help to your warriors. Like you, King Heremod of old towered in strength above other men. However, he became bloodgreedy. He killed his companions in anger. He lived for himself alone, without joy, and he suffered for his vengeful deeds. He died alone.

"Mighty God rules all things," Hrothgar counseled. "He permits a noble to think of gaining and keeping power, land, and treasure. Such a man can live luxuriously. The shadows of sickness and age do not bother him. Sorrow does not darken his spirits. Strife does not threaten his kingdom. All the world bends to his will. He does not realize that pride is growing within him. If he is not careful, a poisoned shaft suddenly strikes him in the chest. He decides that he does not possess enough power and wealth. He greedily keeps his gold rings. The blessings of God, the King of Glory, lead him to ignore the future and his inevitable fate. In the end, however, his body dies, and another king acquires his possessions.

"You are a renowned warrior, Beowulf. For a while you will be in the flower of your strength. Later, the sword blade's bite or the spear's flight, the fire's grasp or the flood waters' grip, sickness or sad old age will rob you of your strength. The brightness of your eyes will dim and darken, and Death will overcome you. But enough of an old man's advice," Hrothgar concluded. "Go now, and taste the joy of the feast. I shall give you many treasures in the morning."

When the bright morning light shone forth over the land, the Geats were eager to cross the whale-road and return to their homes. Beowulf said to

Hrothgar, "We seafaring ones from afar are ready to return home. You have treated us well in every way. If ever I may do more to help you, I will be ready. If your neighbors attack you, I shall come to your aid with 1,000 warriors. My king, although he is young, will support me in word and in deed."

Hrothgar replied, "Never have I heard one so young speak so wisely. If the spear, the fierce battle sword, or sickness kills your king, the Geats could have no better king than you. The Spear-Danes and the Storm-Geats will live in peace with one another as long as I am king. We will share treasure and tokens of love."

Hrothgar then gave Beowulf twelve treasures. Tears fell from the white-haired king's eyes as he kissed the youth, whom he loved as a son. Beowulf was so dear to him that his heart hurt. He yearned to keep the young warrior in his own kingdom.

Beowulf, the gold-proud warrior, took his twelve treasures, and he and his brave men walked toward the sea. When they reached the coast, the warden welcomed them. They loaded Hrothgar's hoard, the horses, battle mail, and treasure upon their ship. Beowulf gave the ship's watchman a golden sword, handed down from of old, which brought that warrior great respect among his comrades.

So it came to pass that Beowulf, that safeguard of warriors, and his men set out once again upon the whale-road. A brisk wind sent their ship sailing eastward like a sea bird, its prow a foamy beak. The ship floated forth until they saw the shining sea-cliffs of Geatland. The harbor guard was ready and eager to welcome them home. King Hygelac had their hall prepared for a great celebration, where Beowulf told the assembled warriors of his adventures. He then set Hrothgar's hoard of treasures before his king, for they were royal gifts from one monarch to another.

In return, Hygelac awarded Beowulf a golden sword that was the best of treasures among the Storm-Geats, a hall, a prince's high seat, and a very large estate. Beowulf was now the most highly honored of men.

Chapter 4

Beowulf has been king for fifty years when a dragon ravages his kingdom. With the help of his nephew, Wiglaf, Beowulf kills the monster, but not before it has dealt his own death blow.

Battle swords slew Hygelac, king of the Storm-Geats. Some time thereafter, Beowulf became king of Geatland. He ruled his realm well for fifty winters.

Beowulf was an old, white-haired king when a fearsome fire-dragon suddenly flew over Geatland in the dark of night and burned the buildings with its blazing breath. For 300 winters, this dreadful dragon had kept a silent and secret watch over a hidden hoard of treasure in a towering stone barrow. The barrow was built into the base of a sea-cliff that extended deep beneath the surface of the earth and high within the hollow of the cliff. Below the stone barrow lay a secret path that had remained unknown for 1,000 winters.

How had it happened that such a huge treasure hoard was secretly hidden away in such a structure? Many hundreds of winters ago, a lone warrior who was also a mighty king had been the last living member of his clan. Death had claimed the lives of all his kin long before that, and he had become the guardian of his clan's treasure rings. The king knew that the inevitable fate of all mortals was death and that he would shortly join his clan in the eternal sleep. Before destiny claimed him, he wanted to preserve the wealth of his high-born clan.

A newly built barrow stood empty near the sea waves on the moor, protected from casual entry. The warrior bore the priceless, ancient treasures of his clan within the stone walls of this barrow and hid them there.

Aloud he said, "Earth, hold now this wealth of nobles, for warriors can no longer keep it. It was within your rich body that good men first found the gleaming gold, so I am returning your wealth to you. Death, that dread evil, has destroyed in battle every one of my blood-kin. No one remains to wield the gleaming sword or to shine the gold-decked vessel and the precious drinking cup.

"The hard, gold-plated helmet is tarnished now, for those whose job it was to shine it also sleep the endless sleep. The ring-meshed battle-shirt waits in vain to accompany the warrior into war. Both are decaying into dust. The battle gear that survived such strife, that withstood the crash of shields and the bite of iron sword blades, must crumble as well. No one lives to enjoy the mead hall, to hear the song of the harp, to ride a horse, or to see the hawk. Death has claimed my whole clan, and my heart is filled with sorrow."

As a final protection, the lone warrior placed a deep curse upon his clan's treasure, a spell that would last until Doomsday. Destruction and death would follow whoever disturbed the gold hoard. Soon thereafter, death clutched at the warrior's heart and claimed him, too.

For 700 winters, the treasure hoard remained untouched. Then the fearsome fire-dragon discovered the barrow and made the lonely lair his own.

For 300 winters, the mighty dragon lived undisturbed in that barrow and guarded the ancient, huge treasure hoard. It knew every treasure by sight. Before and after every nap, it counted each precious piece. It passed countless hours enjoying its possessions.

One day, in the fiftieth winter of Beowulf's reign, a slave angered his master and fled in fear from his lashing. Seeking a sheltered, secret hiding place, he stumbled on the ancient trail to the barrow. He discovered the entrance at the base of the barrow and took refuge within its stone walls, not realizing that it was a burial barrow. He was astounded to find within those stone walls a huge, heathen hoard of jewels, woven gold work, and gold-plated objects. The treasure stood heaped on the ground while a sleeping fire-serpent guarded it.

When the slave saw the fire-serpent, terror and panic flooded his heart. Near the dragon's head, he noticed a beautiful goblet of gleaming gold. He stealthily approached the monster, snatched the cup, and sped away from the dreadful demon's den. Wyrd protected him, for his day of destiny was not yet upon him.

The slave offered his master the goblet in hopes of buying forgiveness and peace. His master accepted the gift, for the old goblet was exceptionally fine and rare.

When the fire-dragon awoke, it counted its huge hoard and discovered that its gold goblet was missing. It frantically slithered here and there throughout the barrow. Desperately it searched for the cup, but it could not find it anywhere within those high stone walls.

Finally, in a fury, it smelled the tracks of the thief. Following the scent, the fearsome fire-dragon left its lonely lair. Eagerly it sniffed along the ground around the barrow-mound, anxious to find the thief who had stolen the glorious goblet. As it searched, the dragon's savage thoughts began to turn from rage at the theft to the joy of revenge.

The loathsome creature was determined to avenge the theft of its precious cup. It would punish all the Geats for the crime of one among them. The fire-serpent restlessly waited until evening. When the sun's light began to fade, the dreadful dragon slithered out of its den. It flew low through the night sky like a fiery forge, spewing forth blazing flames and burning the buildings of the Geat-Folk. The glaring fires cast their glow into the high heavens, displaying the detested dragon's might far and wide. Its frightful fury struck horror into every heart.

Before daybreak the demon flew back to its barrow, to its secret stone hall and its treasure hoard of gold. It trusted that its fearful war-craft and the lonely location of its lair would secure its safety. However, the dragon deceived itself. Its life was destined to be as short as the life of their treasure-giving king, for even as an old man, Beowulf protected his people.

Beowulf, that best of kings, learned of the fire-dragon's ravaging raids first-hand, for the dreadful demon burned the Storm-Geats' glorious gift-hall. When Beowulf saw that the fire-serpent's blazing breath had reduced the hall of heroes to a ruin of ashes, his heart filled with deep sorrow. He feared that he might have bitterly angered the ruler of the world, the Eternal Lord, by breaking some ancient law. Beowulf announced to his nobles that he planned to kill the fearsome fiend.

"Oh, beloved Beowulf," they pleaded, "do not face in fight the guardian of this gold! Let the foul fire-serpent lie in its lonely lair. Let it remain buried in its barrow until the world ends!"

But Beowulf's nobles could not dissuade him from the heroic deed. They could not make their lord, the shepherd of their people and the safeguard of warriors, accept their wise counsel. The lord of rings held to his high destiny. He was a good king!

"I am no longer a youth, but I shall always be the shield of my people!" Beowulf exclaimed. "I shall seek the fire-serpent, but not with my large army of warriors. I have no fear of fighting, nor do I fear the detested dragon's great strength and skill in battle. Many times I have survived great peril. I killed Grendel and Grendel's mother, and I have slain many mighty sea serpents. I shall risk only my own death to slay this dragon!"

The old, ring-giving king of the Geats commanded his smiths to create a shining iron shield for him. The linden-wood of their shields would not protect him from the fiery breath of this fearsome fiend.

Beowulf then chose his eleven bravest warriors to accompany him. The lord of rings had learned the cause of the dreaded dragon's wrath, and he ordered the thief to lead them to the loathsome fire-monster's lair. Fear gripped the hearts of most of those men, for the dragon was a fearful foe. Only the bravest of heroes would dare to descend into its barrow and face the beast's blazing fire.

When they arrived, Beowulf, strong in strife and the gold-friend of the Geats, said farewell to his comrades. His spirit was sad and restless within him, ready for death. Wyrd would seek the treasure of his soul and separate his spirit from his flesh.

The bold helmet-bearer announced, "I remember how in my youth I braved countless battles and times of peril. If the fire-dragon will leave its lair and seek me, I shall fight it as Wyrd, the ruler of all, will allow. I shall do daring deeds worthy of great praise. My hand and the blade of my stout sword, Naegling, will wage war for the treasure hoard!

"If I could, I would bear no sword or other weapon against this fire-serpent. I would grip it with my hand as I once grasped Grendel. But since I shall have to face fire, fumes, and fearful poison, I must use my woven mesh war-shirt and a shining iron shield. I shall not retreat from my destiny. Wyrd weaves as she must. I am eager for the fight! I have no need to boast of my bravery or my battle skill.

"Wait here by the barrow," Beowulf told his warriors. "Our fight will be to the death. This is no deed for you; the task is mine alone. By my bold bravery and my battle might, I shall gain the greedy fire-dragon's gold, or I shall die in the battle!"

Then Beowulf, survivor of many grim struggles, carried his shining shield beneath the steep, stone sea-cliffs, sure of his own strength and skill. No coward would choose this way to fight! A stream of flaming fire broke from the barrow. The lord of rings knew that, if he tried to enter the barrow, the flood of fire near the dragon's hoard would burn him to death.

So the good king angrily called his challenge to the fire-demon. His voice resounded in the barrow-hall and roused the fire-serpent's rage.

The dragon's fiery, flaming breath burst forth from the barrow, and the earth rumbled with the roar of its raging blaze. Beowulf, lord of the Geats, raised his shining shield and drew forth Naegling, his ancient, blood-hardened sword, from its sheath.

The ferocious fiend came forth to fight with a joyful heart, eager to find its foe and strike terror into his heart. Beowulf waited in his war gear, steadfast of heart, while the fire-creature coiled for battle.

As the dragon moved to meet its fate, Beowulf approached his own destiny, for Wyrd would not grant the good king victory. His iron shield would not guard his body and his life.

Beowulf raised Naegling and struck the fiery fiend with all of his strength. But his ancient sword, that friend of heroes, won no fame in this fight. Naegling's mighty blade became blunted and could not bite through the hard bone of the dragon.

Beowulf was now beset by evils. His shield was melting under the intense heat. Naegling had lost its strength. The brave king, shield of the Geat-Folk, could not boast of another far-famed victory. He knew that at last he faced death. His long life of great glory and lasting fame were pale now. Life at any age was worth living, and fame came second. Beowulf was unwilling to leave the earth. He did not want to make the last journey to a far dwelling place. Yet all mortals must meet their fate when their days on earth come to an end.

Beowulf's battle-stroke only fanned the hatred in the heart of the savage fire-serpent. It retaliated by blasting forth a blazing torrent of fierce flames that engulfed the old king.

The Storm-Geats who had accompanied Beowulf, the king's close comrades, watched the warfare with increasing terror. They could have rushed to their king's rescue, showing courage in battle and loyalty to their leader. Instead, they thought only of saving their own lives and fled into the forest.

Of the eleven chosen men, only Beowulf's nephew, the young warrior Wiglaf, had a loyal heart and the courage to enter this, his first fight. Wiglaf thought of all the honors his king had bestowed upon him, of his family's wealth and property. He could not, with honor, repay his king's kindness by retreating. To let his king die without aid was an offense beyond pardon.

"Comrades!" he shouted, knowing that they would hear his words. "Remember how, in the mead-hall, we drank to our lord, who gave us these rings. We promised we would repay him for our war gear, our helmets, and our shining swords if he ever needed our help. He chose us to join him on this journey because of our courage, our skill, and our delight in deeds of glory.

"Among all men, he has done the most skillful and daring deeds. He expected to win this mighty battle unaided, but he needs our strength and courage. Let us help him fight the dreadful dragon, that hideous horror with its fiery flames!"

Wiglaf concluded, "God knows that I would rather have the flames enfold my body along with that of my gold-giving king than live as a coward. I, at least, shall share my battle gear, my courage, and my skill with my king!"

Wiglaf resolutely gripped his linden-wood shield, drew forth his sword, and ran toward Beowulf. His shield might scorch. His sword might melt. But Wiglaf's spirit was of the strongest metal. His courage would confront the dragon's blazing breath and the stench of slaughter.

When Wiglaf had fought his way through the fumes, he said, "Beloved Beowulf, remember how in your youth you swore to win glory and fame as long as life was yours? Now you must summon all your strength and guard your life! I shall help you!"

Hearing Wiglaf's words, the dreaded demon launched a second flaming attack, flooding with fire these warriors whom it loathed. Waves of fire scorched the shield of the young spearman, and he took refuge behind Beowulf's shield.

Wiglaf's presence inspired the old king to thoughts of glory. Once again, Beowulf's heart filled with hatred of his fiery foe. With a surge of his great strength, the lord of rings rushed toward the fire-serpent, and drove Naegling deep into the dragon's head. But Naegling broke. The brave blade betrayed the old king in his last battle. It was Beowulf's destiny that no man-made sword, however strong, would bring him victory. His hand was too strong to wield that weapon. In despair, Beowulf withdrew from the wounded beast.

Seeing his retreat, the fierce fire-dragon rushed upon Beowulf for the third time. It gripped him by the throat and sank its savage fangs into his flesh. The old king's lifeblood rushed from his veins in waves.

Chapter 5

Wiglaf becomes king. He punishes the warriors who
deserted Beowulf and directs the preparations for
Beowulf's funeral.

Wiglaf then proved his bravery, strength, and skill. Although the beast's burn-ing breath was scorching his body, he ignored that fountain of fire and struck the dragon deep in its chest with his shining, gold-decked sword. The demon's fire began to fail.

Beowulf revived, drew his sharp dagger, and divided the demon in two. This was his last triumph in this world. His death wound began to burn and swell. The poison began to pulse in his chest. The old warrior slumped down on a seat by the stone wall.

The worthy Wiglaf washed the bloodstained body of his king with water and loosened his helmet. Beowulf knew that his life was ending, and with it his joy. He said to Wiglaf, "The dreadful dragon now lies still and slain, sleeping from its sore wounds and taken from its treasure. Go quickly, dear Wiglaf, and gaze upon the golden treasure hoard that lies buried beneath the lofty stone sea-cliff. Bring forth some of the wealth so that I may see that golden treasure and enjoy the jewels. My winning of it may make it easier for me to give up my life and the realm that I have ruled for so long! "

Within the barrow Wiglaf, the victorious warrior, saw many glittering jewels and gold objects and wondrous wall hangings, all from ancient days. He found drinking goblets and dishes, jars and vessels, all unpolished and stripped of their decorations. Costly swords had been eaten through with rust, for they had rested there for 1,000 winters. Many an old, rusted helmet was there, as was many an arm-ring that had been woven with shrewd skill.

A bright, golden banner hung high over the boundless hoard. It radiated a light that shone upon all the treasures in the barrow. A hoard of such treasure can make mortals overly proud, arrogant, and greedy, try as they will to hide that fact.

Wiglaf quickly filled the inside of his shirt with wine cups and platters and took that golden banner, the brightest of beacons. He wanted his lord to look upon the treasure before death claimed his spirit. When he arrived, Beowulf was bleed-ing and at his life's end. The young man sprinkled water on him to revive him.

Beowulf admired the gold. "I give thanks to the ruler of all, the King of Glory, the Eternal Lord, who has permitted me to see these treasures and to gain this gold for the Geats before my Death. I have paid for this priceless wealth with my life."

The dying king added, "Wiglaf, look now to my people's needs. After they have burned my body, have my battle-famed warriors build me a barrow high on the Whale's Ness. Make the mound rise as a towering memorial to remind my people of me, and call it Beowulf's Barrow. As it stands on the headland, it will serve as a broad beacon for seafarers who drive their deep ships across the whale-road."

Beowulf then gave to Wiglaf his collar-ring of twisted gold, his gold-decorated helmet, and his battle-shirt. "You are the last of my kin. Wyrd has brought them, young and old, to their destiny, and I must now follow them." Those were the old king's last words. His spirit went forth to receive the reward of the good, the loyal, and the just.

Wiglaf looked in sorrow upon the body of his brave king and upon the corpse of the grim and grisly monster that had slain him. The foul dragon, fifty feet long, had fallen to the ground near its treasure house and had died of its wounds. No longer would it sweep through the heavens at midnight, burning for pleasure.

Soon the ten traitorous weaklings left the shelter of the woods. These once valiant warriors were now oath-breakers. With shame on their faces, they wore their battle gear and shouldered their shields to where their old king lay.

Wiglaf faced his cowardly comrades and unloosed an angry hoard of words. "In truth, each of you took the war gear your king gave you and threw it away as soon as you were faced with battle! Now you will pay for your cowardice and lack of loyalty. You and all your kin must give up all your treasure, your gifts of swords, your homes, your land rights, and your birthrights. People far and wide will hear of your cowardly deed. Death is better for a warrior than a dark life of dishonor and disgrace."

Then Wiglaf sent word of the battle and Beowulf's death to the shield-bearing band of nobles who had sat upon the sea-cliff all day long. They were waiting for the news of Beowulf's last day or the victorious homecoming of their dearly loved lord. The news of their king's death brought with it the fear of war, invasion by the Franks and the Frisians, and the renewal of old feuds with the Swedes.

Wiglaf ordered the warriors who owned dwellings to fetch wood for the funeral pyre to be built on the Whale's Ness. The Geat-Folk constructed a huge pyre and hung helmets, shields, and bright battle-shirts around it. A group of honored warriors carried the body of their brave battle-king to the pyre. Sadly, they laid their beloved lord upon it.

Wiglaf said to the assembled group, "Let our beloved Beowulf enjoy the wondrous wealth he won. We shall burn our honored king with all of the dragon's gleaming gold, since Beowulf bought that treasure with his lifeblood.

"Such treasure gives no lasting gladness to anyone," the wise young leader counseled. "Now that our beloved king has left the world of laughter and joy, no Geat will wear these treasures. The dragon's wondrous wealth has delivered only disaster with the death of our beloved Beowulf. Without our valiant king, our shield and shepherd, we will be forced to raise our spears and face terror in battle. Our women, desolate and deprived of gold, will follow their captors into exile to lead a life of shame in captivity. The dark raven will cry with craving over the corpses of our battle-weary warriors, and the wolf will slash away at the slain."

Seven of the most respected nobles then joined Wiglaf and entered the barrow, where the hoard of wealth now rested unguarded. They loaded the precious freight upon the wagon that would carry it to the funeral pyre. Then they thrust the body of the slain fire-serpent over the sea-cliff and let the sea-flood enfold it.

Finally they kindled the death fires at the base of the funeral pyre. As the dark woodsmoke soared above the flames, the sounds of weeping and wailing mixed with the roaring of the fire. In time the blaze consumed Beowulf's bones, and all that was left of the famous lord of rings was a pile of ashes.

Wiglaf announced, "Let us listen to our beloved Beowulf's wishes and upon these ashes let us build, for our most worthy of warriors, a barrow that will be as mighty and memorable as his fame is throughout the wide world."

So it came to pass that, on the sea-cliff around the remains of the funeral fire, the Geat-Folk built a towering burial mound that would be seen from afar by the seafarer. The barrow would be to sea-folk the beacon that Beowulf, their brave battle-king, had been to his people. In the barrow they buried the treasure from the dragon hoard that had not burned with Beowulf, returning it to the earth from whence it had come.

Then the twelve bravest warriors among the Geats rode around the burial barrow. They spoke of their sorrow and told tales of their great king's courage and daring deeds. They gave him praise and honor as is proper when a leader dies. Beowulf's hearth-comrades grieved for their lord of rings, who had been the greatest of all kings, the most gentle, gracious, and kind of men, and the most eager to win praise.

Introducing **King Arthur**

Historical Background

Tales of King Arthur, the great legendary hero of Britain, have been popular for more than 800 years, yet scholars have been able to learn little about the real Arthur, for no contemporary accounts of his deeds exist. Some scholars think the real Arthur was probably a Welsh cavalry general named Artorius, who led twelve successful attacks against the invading Saxons between A.D. 500 and 517.

In 1985, however, the prominent Arthur scholar Geoffrey Ashe published evidence that challenges the traditional view of King Arthur's historical identity. Ashe bases his view upon the writings of Jordanes (6th century), William (11th century), Geoffrey of Monmouth (12th century), and on a letter from a Roman aristocrat to a 5th-century British king called Riothamus (High King) who was then in Gaul (France). Ashe identifies Arthur with Riothamus, thereby placing the reign of King Arthur from 454 to 470 and including in it a British military campaign in Gaul in the late 460s. Geoffrey of Monmouth's description of Arthur's military exploits in Gaul have usually been regarded as fiction, but Riothamus actually led an army of 12,000 men into Gaul, where he fought courageously but unsuccessfully against the Goths in Burgundy. Moreover, like Arthur, he was betrayed by one of his associates, and he probably retreated by way of a French town that is still called Avallon.

Whatever his accomplishments, the real Arthur was such an appealing figure, both in his own day and in the years that followed, that an oral tradition of Welsh folklore became associated with his name. The earlier references to Arthur are found in Nennius' *Historia Brittonum* (c. 800) and William of Malmesbury's *Gesta Regum Anglorum* (c. 1125).

Arthur first appears in literature as Britain's major national hero in Geoffrey of Monmouth's *Historia Regum Britanniae (History of the Kings of Britain)*, written in Latin in 1136. Arthur was already a popular subject in the oral tradition of Wales when Geoffrey recognized the need for a book about the history of Britain. He chose to make Arthur the major figure in his history, which covers the 1,900-year period from 1200 B.C. to A.D. 689.

Although Geoffrey cites sources for his material, scholars believe that he created fictitious sources in order to legitimize his use of folklore and his own imaginatiion. His work must therefore be considered primarily literature rather than history.

To Geoffrey we owe the creation of Arthur as the great British king who conquered all of the British Isles and most of Europe as well. In Geoffrey's version Arthur would have conquered Rome also had he not been called home to fight his nephew, who had taken over the kingdom in his absence. Geoffrey also introduces the world to Arthur's unusual birth and death; Guinevere, his beautiful, unfaithful wife; Merlin, the magician; and the concept of chivalry. Geoffrey was most interested in Arthur as a military leader, but he included just enough about Merlin, Guinevere, magic, and chivalry to inspire other writers to deal with them in greater depth.

Geoffrey's history is so well written that it was popular not only in his own day but with succeeding generations as well. The poet Wace freely translated Geoffrey's history into Norman-French verse in 1155. He concentrated on the Arthurian material, used additional sources, and added a more courtly flavor to the work. It is Wace who mentions the Round Table for the first time.

After the appearance of Wace's poem, Chrétien de Troyes wrote five romances set in King Arthur's court. Being French, Chrétien had little interest in Arthur as the national hero of Britain or as the conquering king. Instead, he wrote of the world of chivalry, where King Arthur reigns over a court of knights who are heroes and lovers. He introduced the idea of courtly love, in which the woman is superior to the man and the lover is completely obedient to the wishes of his lady. In his *Lancelot*, the love between Lancelot and Guinevere appears for the first time. Chrétien was such a good storyteller that his romances were widely read and imitated.

King Arthur finally appeared in the English language when the poet Layamon freely translated Wace's poem into early Middle English in 1205. Layamon added more details to Wace's story and gave it a decidedly English flavor by emphasizing Arthur's courage and his love of adventure. Like Geoffrey of Monmouth, Layamon was patriotic, so he chose to ignore Chrétien's romantic version of the Arthur story.

Still another version of the King Arthur story, *Morte Arthure*, appeared in English in the middle of the 14th century. Again the focus was nationalistic, with the proud warrior-king, Arthur, presented as a great hero in battle. The author had no interest in love, chivalry, or a court of knights. Sir Gawain is Arthur's principal knight, and Lancelot has only a minor role. This presentation resembles the French epic *Chanson de Roland* and the Anglo-Saxon epic *Beowulf*.

Many years later, in 1485, Sir Thomas Malory published what became the definitive story of King Arthur, *Le Morte D'Arthur*. He combined the English tradition of Geoffrey of Monmouth with the French tradition of Chrétien de Troyes. In Malory's version Arthur becomes one of the world's greatest rulers, the equal of Alexander the Great. He does not return to England until he has been crowned emperor in Rome. Malory takes Mordred's treachery and Guinevere's infidelity from Geoffrey, but he combines it with the love affair of Guinevere and Lancelot. In addition, he broadens the picture of Arthur's court by presenting a number of tales about Arthur's principal knights. In this romantic version of English history, the collapse of the Round Table brings tragedy into a number of lives and marks the end of a Golden Age.

Appeal and Value

The story of King Arthur has appealed to writers and readers for hundreds of years because its content is so complex and varied. Something in the story is likely to appeal to almost every taste. Unlike most of the major epics, the story has a broad focus and contains a large cast of important characters. Whether the reader is interested in adventure, magic, chivalry, courtly love, or a great and tragic love story, *Le Morte D'Arthur* is the book to read.

Readers who are familiar with the basic version of the King Arthur legend will find many modern versions of great interest, because the focus of each is different. Enjoyable 19th-century versions include Mark Twain's *A Connecticut Yankee in King Arthur's Court* and Alfred, Lord Tennyson's *Idylls of the King*. The 20th century continues to be fascinated with the Arthurian legend. John Steinbeck, T. H. White, and Mary Stewart are among the writers who have carried on the tradition. Some versions simply retell the tale from the point of view of one of the major characters — such as King Arthur, Lancelot, Guinevere, Mordred, or Merlin. Some of the modern versions have been written with a historical focus, some with a comic focus, and some with a feminist focus.

The theme of the conflict between one's personal desires and one's responsibility to others is common to many ancient epics and as contemporary as the decisions we must make in our own lives. Readers today can still understand and sympathize with the conflicts Arthur, Lancelot, and Guinevere face.

The Arthurian Hero

The principal characters in *Le Morte D'Arthur* are heroic aristocrats. In the age of chivalry, only a man born to the nobility could become a knight. As a young page he learned how to behave at court, and later, as a squire, he learned the necessary martial skills. By his teens, a young man was well on his way to knighthood.

When a man became a knight, he took an oath that obligated him to live according to certain values. He was expected to be loyal to the king, to his relatives and friends, and to the lady he loved. He was also expected to be courteous and gentle, particularly in the presence of ladies. In addition, he was expected to be courageous at all times, whether fighting for his lord in a battle, participating in a contest or tournament, or helping friends or ladies in distress. Finally, he was expected to be a man of honor, to live in such a way that the other members of the nobility held him in high esteem. The challenge was to balance these different values with a minimum of conflict.

It is important to understand that courtly love was often extramarital love. In the society that Chrétien and Malory depicted in literature, and in the real world as well, marriages among the nobility were arranged by the young couple's family or by the ruling lord for political, social, or economic reasons. The participants' feelings were not considered, and divorce did not exist. Therefore, it was not unusual for a married person to find love outside the marriage relationship.

Principal Characters

BRUTUS: great-grandson of Aeneas; leads Trojan exiles to Britain and establishes a kingdom

AURELIUS AMBROSIAS: son of King Constantine; older brother of Uther Pendragon; king of Britain; creates Stonehenge

UTHER PENDRAGON: son of King Constantine; younger brother of Aurelius Ambrosias; king of Britain; husband of Igraine; father of Arthur

IGRAINE: wife of the Duke of Cornwall; later, wife of Uther Pendragon and queen of Britain; mother of Arthur and Margawse

ARTHUR: son of Uther Pendragon and Igraine; husband of Guinevere; father of Mordred; king of Britain; established the knights of the Round Table

ECTOR: foster father of Arthur

KAY: son of Ector; foster brother of Arthur; knight of the Round Table

GUINEVERE: daughter of King Leodegrance; wife of Arthur; queen of Britain

MERLIN: great magician and prophet; adviser to three British kings: Ambrosias Aurelius, Uther Pendragon, and Arthur

LUCIUS HIBERIUS: mythological emperor of the Roman Empire until Arthur defeats and replaces him

MARGAWSE: daughter of Duke of Cornwall and Igraine; half-sister of Arthur; wife of King Lot of Orkney; mother of Mordred by Arthur; mother of Gawain, Agravain, Gaheris, and Gareth by Lot

MORDRED: son of Arthur and his half-sister Margawse; stepbrother of Gawain and Agravain; knight of the Round Table

GAWAIN: nephew of Arthur and one of his two favorite knights; son of Margawse and King Lot of Orkney; brother of Agravain, Gaheris, and Gareth; stepbrother of Mordred; second greatest knight of the Round Table

AGRAVAIN: son of Margawse and King Lot; brother of Gawain, Gaheris, and Gareth; stepbrother and friend of Mordred; knight of the Round Table

GAHERIS: son of Margawse and King Lot; brother of Gawain, Agravain, and Gareth; knight of the Round Table

GARETH: son of Margawse and King Lot; brother of Gawain, Agravain, and Gaheris; knight of the Round Table

LANCELOT: son of King Ban of Benwick; greatest knight of the Round Table; one of Arthur's two favorite knights; champion of Guinevere and her favorite knight

BORS: son of King Bors of Gaul; nephew of Lancelot; knight of the Round Table

PELLINOR: knight of the Round Table

BEDIVERE: knight of the Round Table; last knight to see Arthur alive

---

King Arthur

Prologue

Brutus, great-grandson of Aeneas, leads a group of Trojan exiles to establish a second Troy on an island north of Gaul (France). He names the island Britain, after himself.

At the conclusion of the Trojan War, Aeneas fled from his flaming city with his father, his son Ascanius, and some of his people. His destiny led him by ship to Italy, where he established a new nation. After the death of Aeneas, Ascanius became king. He founded the town of Alba on the Tiber River, and became the father of Silvius. Silvius, in turn, became the father of Brutus. Seers prophesied that Brutus would cause the death of both of his parents, would therefore be banished from Italy, and would wander homeless through many lands, until finally he would settle in Britain, where he would become highly honored.

The prophecy proved correct. Brutus' mother died during his birth. When he was fifteen, he killed his father in a hunting accident, and his relatives banished him from Italian soil.

He first sought refuge in Greece, among people who were descendants of Priam, king of the Trojans. Brutus' courage and wisdom enabled him to free those Trojans from the tyranny of local Greek rule. He surprised the Greeks with a night attack, and the Trojans slaughtered the Greeks like wolves attacking slumbering sheep. Brutus married the daughter of the local king he had conquered and then sailed away with the Trojans for another land.

They came to an island that had been deserted for many years. Investigating an abandoned city, Brutus found a temple of Diana, goddess of the hunt, and offered sacrifices to her. "Oh mighty goddess, both terror and hope of the wild woodlands," he prayed, "tell me where we can safely settle and worship you throughout the years to come."

When he lay down to sleep that night, Diana appeared before him and said, "Brutus, far beyond the setting of the sun, past Gaul, you will find an island in the sea that was once inhabited by a race of giants. This land will suit you and your people for years to come. It will be a second Troy for all those who come after you. There from your blood a race of kings will be born, and the whole earth will kneel before them."

When he awoke, a fair wind was blowing. Brutus took this as another sign from the goddess, and he and his people immediately resumed their journey. They sailed up the coast of Africa, past the pillars of Hercules at the western end of the Mediterranean Sea. There they escaped from the sea monsters known as the Sirens, who almost sank their ships.

Brutus and his companions then came upon another group of Trojan exiles. The two groups decided to join together and share a common future. The Trojans, who were now formidable, fought their way through Gaul acquiring wealth. Finally they returned to the coast and set sail for the island Diana had revealed to Brutus in his dream.

When the Trojans landed, they found that the island was uninhabited except for a few giants, whom they killed. They saw that they would thrive here, for the soil was fertile, wild animals lived in the forests, and numerous fish swam in the many rivers. Under Brutus' direction, the Trojans divided up the land, built houses, and began to farm.

Brutus searched the island for the best location for a capital city. He decided to build it along the Thames River, and he called it Troia Nova (New Troy). He named the island after himself: It became Britain, and Brutus and his companions were called Britons. Brutus gave the city of Troia Nova to his people, and he also gave them a code of laws to help them live in peace with one another.

However, many years of civil wars and invasions followed Brutus' death, including the conquest of Britain by the Romans. After the Romans were called back to defend Rome in about A.D. 400, the Britons had to depend upon their own meager resources for defense against barbarians. Seeking more land, the Teutonic tribes had already moved into Gaul, leaving the Britons isolated on their island. Early in the 5th century the Saxons, along with the Angles and the Jutes, invaded and conquered Britain. King Constantine was the first king of Britain who was able to defeat them. His sons, Aurelius Ambrosias and Uther Pendragon, ruled Britain during the period when the Saxons were their principal adversaries.

Chapter 1

When Arthur is fifteen years old, a sword in a stone miraculously appears in the churchyard in London. Upon the stone is written: "Whoever pulls out this sword is the lawfully born king of Britain." Unaware of its meaning, Arthur pulls out the sword and learns that he will be king.

With the death of Uther Pendragon, the kingdom of Britain fell into a period of great danger, from both without and within. Every noble Briton who had the support of an army of loyal followers wished to become the next king. Meanwhile other nations wished to invade Britain and establish settlements upon its rich soil. Unless a leader could emerge who was strong enough to unite the independent dukes and rally them to defend their land, Britain was certain to be consumed, bite by bite, by foreigners.

The great enchanter Merlin recognized this danger. He advised the Archbishop of Canterbury to summon all of the nobles to London at Christmastime, when the rightful king of Britain would be revealed to the world.

From all parts of the British Isles, nobles and their loyal supporters crowded into the city of London. They all attended the first mass. When they left the cathedral, they were amazed to see that a huge, square, marble stone had miraculously appeared in the churchyard. An iron anvil protruded from this stone, and plunged into the anvil was a beautiful, unsheathed sword. When the nobles excitedly gathered around the sword, they found written in gold letters: "Whoever pulls out this sword from this stone and anvil is the lawfully born king of all Britain."

Many proud knights immediately tried to remove the sword, but none could budge it, so securely lodged was it within the stone and anvil.

"The rightful king of Britain is apparently not with us," announced the archbishop, "but be assured that God will make him known to us at the proper time. Let us gather here on New Year's Day and let all the knights of the kingdom mount their horses and participate in a tournament to reveal their skill with the sword and the spear. Afterwards, whoever wishes may try to withdraw the sword from this stone and anvil."

The archbishop commanded that a tent be placed over the marble block containing the sword. He ordered ten of the most honorable knights to keep a constant watch over the sword, five throughout each day and five throughout each night.

On New Year's Day, Sir Ector, accompanied by his son, Sir Kay, and his foster son, Arthur, prepared to participate in the tournament. Kay had recently become a knight, and Arthur, being only fifteen years old, was his squire.

Arthur watched with admiration as Sir Kay fought courageously and skillfully in the tournament. Suddenly, however, a strong stroke by another knight shattered his sword. "Do me a favor, Arthur!" he cried. "Ride back to the tent and bring me another sword. Hurry, for I do not want to lose my place in the contests!"

Although Arthur searched everywhere in the tent, he could not find another sword. He said to himself, "I know — I will ride into the churchyard and take the sword that is lodged in that stone. Kay will just have to manage with that one!"

When he arrived, the churchyard was deserted, for even those who were supposed to be guarding the sword in the stone had gone off to participate in the tournament. Arthur dismounted, walked up to the stone, grasped the hilt of the sword in his right hand, and easily withdrew it from the anvil.

Thinking little of his accomplishment, Arthur returned to his brother, handed him the sword, and said, "I could not find a sword back at the tent. Use this one!"

Sir Kay immediately recognized the sword as the one that had miraculously appeared in the churchyard. Since he was older and stronger than Arthur, he assumed that he could certainly do whatever his younger brother could do. He said to Arthur, "Tell no one that you found this sword, and I promise that you will become very rich! Now, let us ride over to Father.

"Father!" Kay exclaimed to Sir Ector. "Look! I have drawn this sword from the stone! Therefore, I must be the lawful king of Britain!"

Ector replied, "That may be, Kay, but be certain that your words are more than an empty boast. Let us return to the churchyard. If you are telling the truth, you are indeed the rightful king of this land. But first you will have to prove it by thrusting this sword back into the stone and drawing it free again. If you could do it once, then surely you can do it again. If you cannot, then you will shame yourself before every nobleman in London, for they too will demand proof of your right to kingship!"

Back at the churchyard Sir Kay replaced the sword, but no matter how hard he tried, he could not pull it out again. In the cathedral, Sir Ector commanded Kay, "Place your hand upon this holy Bible and swear that you will tell me truthfully how you came to possess this sword!"

"Sir, the truth is that Arthur brought it to me," Kay replied humbly.

"Yes," Ector responded, "that I can believe. Now, Arthur, how did you acquire this sword?"

Arthur explained, "During one of the contests, Kay's sword broke, so he asked me to get him another one from the tent. When I arrived, I could find no sword, no matter how carefully I searched. Fortunately, I remembered the sword in the stone. I knew how important it was for Kay to have a sword, so I rode over here and took it for him! It was easy — when I put my hand on the hilt and pulled, the sword simply slid from the anvil!"

"Were there no knights here as you did this?" Sir Ector inquired.

"No one was here. They must all have gone to the tournament."

"Arthur," Ector said. "Have you any idea what you have done? You are telling me that you are the rightful king of Britain!"

"Why do you say such a thing?" Arthur asked. "It does not make any sense, and it cannot be true!"

"Sir," Ector respectfully answered his foster son, "you are the rightful king of Britain because God has chosen you for this highest of honors. Only the rightful king of this land could have drawn this sword out of its stone. Now, let me watch you return the sword to its place in the anvil and then withdraw it once again."

"It is a simple task," said Arthur. He replaced the sword in the stone, drew it out, and returned it.

Sir Ector then tried to pull out the sword. But no matter how hard he tried, the sword would not budge. It stuck fast in its marble block.

"Now, you try it again!" Ector commanded Kay.

Sir Kay tried with all his might to pull out the sword, but he could not budge it either.

When Arthur easily withdrew the sword once again, Sir Ector and Sir Kay immediately knelt before him.

"Oh, no!" Arthur cried. "Dear Father and Brother, you have no reason to kneel before me. I am no king of Britain. I am your son!" he said to Ector. "And I am your brother!" he said to Kay.

"No, Arthur, I am not your father. In fact, I am not related to you at all. When you were just an infant, the great enchanter Merlin arrived at our home one night bearing you in his arms. He never told me whose child you were, but he commanded me to rear you as my own son, and so I have."

These words filled Arthur with great sadness. "You have suddenly made me feel all alone," he said to Sir Ector. "I feel as if I have lost my father, and my mother, and my brother! You are the only family I have ever known. You are the ones I love most in the world. I do not know how to be the king of Britain!"

"You have not lost us, Arthur. We will love you as we always have! Think instead about what it is that makes a good king. I am certain Merlin will reappear to advise you."

The next morning Sir Ector gave Arthur armor and weapons and conferred knighthood upon him. Then he sent him off to the tournament. All that day Arthur showed his courage and his skill in many contests, and he earned great honor and praise.

On the following day, Sir Ector went to the archbishop and said, "I know a young knight who is noble, valiant, and well skilled in the use of weapons. He will be king of Britain according to the law, for he can draw the sword forth from the stone in the churchyard."

The archbishop replied, "Bring him here, and I will summon all of the nobles."

When everyone had arrived, all of the nobles in turn tried to pull out the sword, but not one of them could budge it. When they watched Arthur easily accomplish what no mighty effort of theirs could do, they were ashamed and angry. "It is ridiculous that a mere boy should have the right to rule over all of us!" they exclaimed.

The archbishop decided to postpone the decision of kingship until the next holiday, and the knights continued to watch over the sword in the marble stone. At that time, more dukes and barons gathered, and all were given the chance to try to withdraw the sword. Again only Arthur could perform the deed, but the nobles still were not satisfied.

Easter arrived, and the archbishop repeated the contest. Once again only Arthur could remove the sword from the stone, but the nobles still were not satisfied. The archbishop agreed to postpone the decision one more time. The following holiday, everyone was again given the opportunity to pull upon the sword, but no one was able to budge it. Arthur then performed the task as easily as he had before.

This time when Arthur held the sword in his hand, both the common folk and the nobles knelt at his feet and exclaimed, "We will have Arthur as our king, for it is God's will that he rule us!" "And," many added, "we will kill anyone who tries to prevent Arthur's reign!"

Arthur then knelt before the archbishop. Holding one end of the sword in each hand, he raised his arms and offered the sword upon the altar. He took the oath of kingship, promising to be true to both the common people and the nobility and swearing to reign justly all the days of his life. Then he listened to the complaints of his subjects and restored property to those from whom it had unjustly been taken.

As the people left the cathedral, they passed the place where the stone had been and noticed that it was no longer there. It had disappeared as miraculously as it had appeared.

Shortly thereafter, Arthur held a great feast in the city of Caerleon, in Wales. The dukes of northern Britain, Scotland, Ireland, and Wales, accompanied by their attendant knights, were present, but they would accept no gifts of friendship from the new king. Instead they told Arthur's messengers, "We will accept no gifts from a beardless boy! We will give him appropriate gifts of our own choosing — our swords plunged into his heart! It is shameful to see such a noble land as this ruled by an ordinary boy!"

Arthur's barons advised their king that his life was truly in danger. He chose 500 soldiers and retreated to a strong, well-provisioned castle, to which the hostile nobles promptly laid siege. Arthur and his men had been imprisoned there for two weeks when Merlin arrived in Caerleon.

The nobles greeted Merlin warmly and asked him, "Why has that boy been made king of Britain?"

"Sirs," Merlin replied, "his blood is more noble that your own! Arthur is King Uther Pendragon's son, born in wedlock to Igraine, the Duke of Cornwall's wife."

"Then Arthur is a bastard!" they all exclaimed.

"Not so!" Merlin replied. "Arthur was conceived more than three hours after the Duke of Cornwall died, and King Uther married Igraine soon thereafter. This is ample proof that Arthur is not a bastard. Indeed, Arthur shall long be king of Britain, and he will rule many other countries as well!"

Not all of the nobles took Merlin's words seriously. Some laughed derisively, and others called him a witch. However, they did agree to let Arthur come out and speak with them.

Merlin entered the castle and said to Arthur, "Many nobles have gathered outside and would speak with you. Appear before them without fear in your heart. Answer their questions as their chief and their king, for you are destined to overpower all of them, no matter what harm they hope to bring upon you. But let me tell you something about your parents and your country before you face them. Knowledge will fortify your heart."

Chapter 2

Merlin explains to Arthur the circumstances
surrounding his birth. He tells Arthur about his uncle,
Aurelius Ambrosius, and his father, Uther
Pendragon, each of whom reigned as king of Britain.

"Arthur," Merlin began, "I shall start with the tale of your birth."

In the days when Uther Pendragon was king of all Britain, he fought long and hard against the Saxon invaders. The Duke of Cornwall, an old man of great experience in warfare, had aided Uther in these wars. When the king held a great feast in London, he invited the Duke of Cornwall and his wife, Igraine.

Igraine's reputation had preceded her arrival. She was the most beautiful woman in Britain, and she was as good as she was beautiful. It was not surprising that King Uther fell in love with the duke's wife at the banquet. Ignoring his other guests, the king repeatedly sent his servants to her bearing plates of food and golden goblets of wine. Meanwhile, he kept smiling at her and engaging her in conversation. He could not keep his eyes from her, and he showed her as much as he dared of his love.

His attentions did not escape the notice of the Duke of Cornwall, who decided that he owed no allegiance to a king who would tempt his wife. Without a word the duke rose from the table, took Igraine by the hand, and left the hall. No one could convince the duke to return; even the king's orders did not persuade him, so precious to him was his wife.

The duke returned to Cornwall, where he confined his wife under guard in the castle of Tintagel. Uther became determined to make love to Igraine. Since the fortress was surrounded on all sides by the sea, except for a narrow, rocky pathway to its entrance, Uther asked my help to achieve his goal.

When I saw the depths of the king's passion and the intensity of his resolve, I said, "Sir, I shall see to it that you have your wish, for it is destined that Igraine will bear you a son. This son will become the most marvelous king of Britain. He will live to the end of eternity, for people will remember his glory as long as the world exists. All who live in Britain will kneel at his feet. Bards will sing of his adventures, and poets will take inspiration from his deeds. The strongest and bravest will seek his company, for his spirit will live within them as well. Stone walls will crumble before his attack. Dukes and barons will retreat into submission. He and his knights will conquer many peoples in many lands, some far across the sea, and all will live in peace under his laws.

"However, for you to win Igraine, I will have to use magic. Even the strongest of men will never be able to storm the strong, high walls of Tintagel Castle. Enough food is stored within the fortress that a siege will be useless. Moreover, Igraine is so closely guarded that access to her is hopeless. And even if you were able to reach her, you could only despair, for there is no woman more loyal to her husband than Igraine is to the Duke of Cornwall.

"Therefore," I explained, "I shall use my drugs to give you the appearance of the duke in every respect. Your face, your body, your speech, your deeds, your clothing, even your horse will duplicate those of Igraine's husband. I will change my appearance and that of your friend Ulfius to resemble the duke's closest companions. We will all be able to enter the castle without suspicion, for no one will doubt our identity." This was my advice to Uther, your father.

So it came to pass that Uther Pendragon dined with Igraine in Tintagel Castle and spent the night with her. Given his appearance and his conversation, Igraine never knew that her companion was not her husband. The real duke was killed in battle that day, and later that evening you were conceived.

When the duke's men arrived in the morning bearing the news of their lord's death, they found Uther with Igraine. Uther convinced them that he was the duke, and that he was indeed alive and well. He said he intended to leave immediately to summon additional troops, for Tintagel Castle was in danger of attack from King Uther Pendragon. Once the three of us were safely outside, we resumed our proper shapes.

Uther mourned the death of the duke while he rejoiced in Igraine's freedom. He returned to Tintagel, conquered the castle without bloodshed, and married

Igraine. In time Igraine gave birth to you, and two years later Uther died. He and your mother loved each other dearly and were true to one another.

When Igraine was about to give birth to you, Uther asked her whose child she was carrying. "Tell me truthfully," the king said, "and I will love you all the more for it." Igraine explained that she had treated a stranger as if he were her husband because he appeared in all respects to be the Duke of Cornwall. Uther laughed and replied, "All that you say is indeed true, for it was I who came to you in the shape of the duke, and it is I who am the father of your child!" Igraine's heart filled with joy, for she was relieved and happy to know and to love the father of her child.

Shortly before you were born, I said to the king, "It is not safe for your child to live with you; as the heir to the throne of Britain, he will have many enemies. I know a lord who is loyal and good, Sir Ector by name. Let his wife nourish your baby as a foundling. Deliver him to me at the back gate before he is christened."

The elves themselves were present at your birth. They enchanted you with their strongest magic and presented you with special gifts. They gave you the courage and the strength to be the the best of all knights. They gave you the intelligence to become a mighty king, combined with the generosity that would bring you lasting devotion and fame. And finally they gave you the gift of a long life.

The king commanded your mother to wrap you in a golden blanket and have two of her ladies in waiting, accompanied by two knights, bring you out to me. I appeared in the guise of a poor man, so no one recognized me. I brought you to Sir Ector and had you christened by a holy man. And that is how you came to be reared in the home of Sir Ector.

Your father is buried beside his brother, Aurelius Ambrosius, inside the Giants' Ring at Stonehenge. I will tell you of how Aurelius and I came to build that ring. King Aurelius wished to construct a memorial structure that would honor the many noble leaders who had fallen to the Saxons and were buried near Salisbury. Because of my fame as a prophet and as a builder, the Archbishop of Canterbury suggested that he send for me.

I received a royal welcome! Aurelius came forth to meet me, accompanied by many knights. I told him, "If you want to erect a lasting and awesome monument upon the burial site of these patriots, then send for the Giants' Ring in Ireland. That structure is of stone, and there is not another like it throughout the wide world. The stones that form that mighty circle are so enormous and so heavy that no ordinary man, no matter how strong, will ever be able to move them."

Aurelius simply laughed in my face. "Merlin," he asked, "if those stones are beyond the ability of any man to move, then how do you expect my stonemasons to move them? And why would you ever want to move stones from Ireland to Britain? Can't we find large enough stones in our own land?"

"First of all," I replied, "it will take skill and talent, rather than strength, to move those stones, for they are not ordinary stones. Long ago, when the giants lived in Ireland, they brought those stones from Africa because they possessed certain religious and medicinal properties. Whenever a giant became ill, he or she would bathe at the foot of those stones and would become well. No other medicine was needed.

"Knowledge and skill are better than might," I concluded. "So assemble an army and I will accompany them to Ireland. You will honor the burial place with the memorial you wish, and you yourself will be buried there when your life comes to an end."

My explanation convinced Aurelius, so he sent your father and 15,000 knights with me to Ireland to transport those stones to Britain. The Irish met us with an army of their own. Their king could not believe the reason for our invasion. "It is no wonder that the Saxons could invade the island of Britain!" he exclaimed. "The Britons must indeed be fools if they believe that our stones are better than their own! Who in his right mind would cross the sea and invade a country for so poor a treasure? However, they shall not remove one stone from the Giants' Ring! We will teach them how foolish it is to love stones, by causing their blood to flow upon Irish soil!"

We did meet the Irish in armed conflict, but they were a peaceful people and did not wear armor. Their fields welcomed their own blood rather than ours. More than 7,000 Irishmen fell there!

When our men had removed their armor and rested from the battle, I led them to the Giants' Ring. Your father and his knights were awestruck by it. "Only Giants could have arranged these stones and placed them upon one another!" they exclaimed.

"Knights," I said, "you are champions! See if you are strong enough to transport these stones to our ships!"

But 15,000 strong men, using sail ropes and pushing and pulling together, could not budge the stones. I said to them, "Withdraw from the circle, and watch me. I will prove to you that knowledge and skill are far more valuable than physical strength. Do not approach the stones again until I advise you to do so."

I entered the Giants' Ring and walked around the stones. Three times I walked around the ring, both within and without, silently speaking to the stones as I passed them. When I had finished, I said to the men, "Now, enter the ring and move the stones. The rocks will be as pebbles in your hands, and you can transport them to your ships with little effort!" And it was so.

Once we arrived back in Britain, Aurelius summoned clergy and Britons, both rich and poor, from all over the kingdom, to the burial-place near Salisbury. After the Archbishop of Canterbury rededicated the burial-place, I arranged the stones in their proper order so that they formed a circle as they had on Irish soil. The monument became known as Stonehenge.

Not long thereafter, the King was poisoned to death. That night your father, miles away from Aurelius, saw in the heavens a huge star of extraordinary brilliance. A single beam extended from the star, ending in a ball of fire that spread out in the shape of a dragon. Two rays of light shone from the dragon's mouth. One pointed in the direction of Gaul, and the other divided into seven smaller rays and pointed toward the Irish Sea. Three times this wondrous star appeared in the heavens!

Like everyone else, Uther was terrified by this strange sign, and he sent for me. "Merlin, dear friend, prove your wisdom and tell me what I have seen and what it means!"

At first I sat as in a dream. When I awoke and stopped trembling, I said, "Sorrow has befallen our land! Aurelius Ambrosius, the noblest of kings, is dead! Of all your noble family, Uther, you alone remain alive. You will become a good king, but first you must march against the Saxons. The star revealed your brother's death. The fiery dragon beneath it represented you, Uther. You will conquer the Saxon invaders and become king of all Britain.

"The ray of light that pointed toward Gaul represented the son that you will have (you, Arthur!). Your son will become a powerful king and will rule over all of the kingdoms that the beam shone upon. The ray of light that pointed toward the Irish Sea represented the stepdaughter you will have, who will be very dear to you. The seven bands within her ray represent her seven sons and grandsons who will be kings of Britain after your son has died." Thus I prophesied to your father the events of years to come.

After Uther had succeeded in killing many of the barbarous Saxon hordes, he held an elaborate funeral ceremony for Aurelius at Stonehenge. The great king was buried within the Giants' Ring that he had brought to Britain.

Your father was then crowned king of Britain. He was a good king. He upheld good laws and loved his subjects. He became known as Uther Pendragon (head war-leader) because the dragon he had seen with the star signified his kingship. When Uther and his men faced the last of the Saxon leaders, they set upon the Saxons in a surprise night attack and captured their two chieftains. With that victory your father, Uther Pendragon, finally put an end to Saxon terror in Britain.

"And that brings my story back to the point at which I began," Merlin concluded. "Now you know what you need to know in order to feel confident. You come from a family of honored kings, and you yourself will be an even greater king. Go forth and face the dukes of northern Britain, Scotland, Ireland, and Wales with courage in your heart. In time they will kneel before you and will fight at your side."

Chapter 3

Merlin foresees that Arthur's illegitimate son,
Mordred, will kill Arthur. The Lady of the Lake gives
Arthur her sword, Excalibur. Arthur marries
Guinevere, even though Merlin foresees that she and
Sir Lancelot will love each other more than they will
love Arthur.

King Arthur was a born leader. Despite his youth, he possessed the qualities necessary in the best of knights: strength, courage, and skill. He also possessed the qualities necessary in the best of kings. He met arrogance with self-confidence and pride, yet treated the weak and poor with sympathy and understanding. He was a father to the young and a comfort to the old. He was strict with those who acted unwisely or unlawfully, yet he was generous and courteous to all. He used his wisdom, his strength, and his treasure to improve the lives of his people. His subjects loved him. His kingdom brought him fame from the early days of his reign, and he towered above the other kings of his time.

However, many powerful dukes and barons resisted King Arthur's effort to unify Britain. He had to conquer the outlying parts of his kingdom by force of arms. With Merlin to advise him, King Arthur spent the first years of his reign subduing the dukes of northern Britain, Scotland, Ireland, and Wales. He sailed to Iceland and added that island to his kingdom.

During this time, he met and loved Queen Margawse, the wife of King Lot of Orkney. Only later did Merlin reveal that she was Arthur's half-sister. "God is angry with you, for you have slept with your sister, and she has given birth to your son, who will destroy you and all of the knights of your kingdom. It is your destiny to die in battle against him as punishment for your foul deed."

Merlin advised King Arthur to save his life by collecting and secretly killing all the male children of noble blood who had been born on the day Margawse gave birth. Given the penalty of death for withholding such a child, many infants arrived at King Arthur's court. He put them all into a small boat and sent it out to sea. He expected that the infants would drown, or if by chance the boat remained afloat, that they would surely die of exposure or starvation.

The small boat crashed on the rocks by a castle and broke apart. Unknown to Merlin and Arthur, Arthur's son survived the catastrophe and was rescued by a good man, who named him Mordred and reared him to the age of fourteen. Then Mordred returned to the household of his mother and King Lot, where he trained with their four sons to become a knight. Arthur always believed that Mordred was one of his nephews.

When King Arthur's subjects learned of their children's deaths, they were outraged. Many blamed Merlin.

One day soon thereafter, Arthur was riding in the forest when he saw three peasants pursuing Merlin. Arthur forced the peasants to flee and said to Merlin, "You would have been killed if I had not happened to ride by and save you!"

"You are wrong," Merlin replied. "I could have saved myself. You are the one who is riding toward your death, for God is not your friend!"

The two friends came to an armed knight sitting in a chair by a fountain. "I challenge any knight who comes this way to a duel," the knight announced, "and so I challenge you!"

"So be it!" King Arthur replied.

The two men fought fiercely on horseback, breaking their spears to splinters upon one another's shields. When King Arthur reached for his sword, the knight said, "It is better if we continue to fight with spears. My squire will supply us with two good ones."

The two fought on with the new spears until they too shattered. Again King Arthur reached for his sword. "Let your sword rest," the knight said, "for you are the best spearman I have ever encountered. Let us do battle with spears once more for the love of knighthood! "

The squire brought two good spears, and the two men resumed their contest. This time, however, King Arthur's spear shattered while the knight's spear remained whole. The knight gave Arthur such a mighty blow upon his shield that he knocked both Arthur and his horse to the ground. Arthur drew forth his sword and said, "I will fight you on foot, Sir Knight, since I can no longer fight on horseback."

Thus began a new contest, sword to sword, with each knight on foot. They charged one another like two rams until the earth ran red with their blood. Finally the knight's sword sliced King Arthur's sword into two pieces, and the king was at the knight's mercy. But Arthur quickly leaped upon the knight, threw him to the ground, and removed his helmet.

The knight, realizing how vulnerable he now was, summoned all of his strength and overturned Arthur. He removed Arthur's helmet and raised his sword.

Before the knight could behead the king, Merlin cast a spell upon him, causing the knight to fall into a deep sleep. Merlin then picked up King Arthur and rode off with him on the knight's horse.

"What have you done, Merlin?" Arthur cried. "Have you killed that knight with your enchantments? He is one of the best knights I have ever fought!"

"I advise you not to worry about him, Arthur," Merlin replied, "for he is far healthier than you are! I have simply put him to sleep for a short time. He is indeed a great knight, and from this time forth he will serve you well, as will his two sons. His name is Sir Pellinor."

Merlin took King Arthur to a hermit skilled in the art of medicine, who healed the king. When they were leaving, Arthur said to Merlin, "I no longer have a sword."

"Do not be concerned," replied Merlin. "Not far from here you will find a suitable sword."

As they rode together, they came upon a lovely, wide lake. A woman's arm protruded from the middle of the water. It was clothed in a white embroidered silk fabric, and its hand held a beautiful sword. "There!" exclaimed Merlin. "Now you can see the sword I had in mind."

Then they noticed a lady in a boat upon the lake. "Who is that lady?" Arthur asked.

"She is the Lady of the Lake," Merlin replied. "She is coming to speak with you. Treat her well so that she will give you that sword."

When the lady arrived, King Arthur said to her, "Lady, what sword is being held above the water by that arm? I wish that it were mine, for I have no sword."

The lady replied, "King Arthur, that is my sword, Excalibur, but I will give it to you if you will give me a gift when I ask for it."

"I will give you whatever gift you wish," Arthur replied.

"Then take my boat and row out to the sword. Take both the sword and its sheath, and I will request a gift of you when I am ready to do so." Once Arthur took the sword and its sheath, the hand and arm withdrew beneath the water.

"Which do you prefer," Merlin asked, "the sword Excalibur or its scabbard?"

"I prefer Excalibur of course!" Arthur replied.

"Then you are not wise," Merlin responded, "for the sheath is worth ten of the swords! As long as you wear the scabbard upon your body, no matter how wounded you are, you will not lose a drop of blood. So take care of that sheath, and always keep it with you!"

When King Arthur returned to Caerleon, his knights were amazed to hear of his adventure with Sir Pellinor. They were disturbed that he would risk his life in such a way, and yet they were glad to serve a king who would take the same risks they themselves did.

The time came when King Arthur said to Merlin, "My nobles want me to marry so that I will not leave the throne of Britain without an heir. Whom do you advise?"

"Whom do you love above all others?" Merlin asked.

"Guinevere, the daughter of Sir Leodegrance, who has in his possession the Round Table. She is the most beautiful lady alive!"

"If you did not love her as you do," Merlin replied, "I would find you another lady whose beauty and goodness would please you. But I can see that your mind is set on Guinevere, and I cannot hope to change it."

"You are right," Arthur responded. "But why would you want to change my mind?"

Merlin counseled: "As beautiful as she is, Guinevere will not be a good wife for you. In days to come, she and the great knight Sir Lancelot will love each other more than they will love you."

This prophecy did not deter King Arthur. He sent Merlin and a group of knights to Sir Leodegrance to request the hand of Guinevere in marriage.

Sir Leodegrance was delighted to have Guinevere marry the king of Britain. Since a dowry of land would be no gift for Arthur, Leodegrance decided to give him 100 knights and the Round Table, which Uther Pendragon had given him. "This is a most fitting gift for King Arthur," Sir Leodegrance said. "It will bring peace among all of his knights, since the table has neither a head nor a foot. Whenever the knights meet, their thrones, their services, and their relationship to one another will be equal."

King Arthur marrried Guinevere at Camelot in a solemn ceremony that was followed by a great feast. He appreciated the gift of the Round Table, which seated 150 knights. When the knights went to sit around the table, each found his name magically inscribed upon the throne that would be his.

Chapter 4

Lucius Hiberius, Emperor of Rome, demands tribute
from Britain; King Arthur declares war upon Rome.
Arthur fights and kills a giant in northern Gaul. He
and his knights then defeat the Roman army, and
King Arthur becomes the ruler of the Roman Empire.

King Arthur conquered Norway and Denmark. Then he conquered Gaul, which was a province of Rome. One day King Arthur was seated with his knights when twelve old men, their white hair encircled with gold bands, entered the hall two by two. Each man grasped the hand of his companion with one hand and held an olive branch in his other hand as he approached King Arthur's throne. They greeted the king and announced that they were ambassadors from Emperor Lucius Hiberius of Rome.

King Arthur read aloud to the assembled group from the parchment scroll they handed him. "From Lucius Hiberius, Emperor of Rome, to King Arthur, his enemy.

Who are you that you can steal Roman land? Who are you to teach law to Rome, the father of justice? How dare you refuse to pay the tribute you owe to Rome?

"Why do you refuse to render unto Caesar that which is Caesar's?" the document continued. "Do you expect the lion to run from the calf? The wolf to fear the lamb? The leopard to quake before the hare? Such miracles do not occur in this world! Julius Caesar, our valiant ancestor, conquered Britain, and since that time, Britons have paid tribute to Rome."

King Arthur continued reading. "If you do not appear before the Roman Senate and pay what you owe, then I will come with a mighty army and take Gaul from you. I will burn all of Britain and crush your knights. Should you attempt to flee, I will pursue you and give you no rest until I have destroyed you. Even if you were to dig a hole in the earth and hide yourself there, you could not escape the might of Rome!"

The Roman emperor's words were greeted with such a hostile uproar that King Arthur physically had to restrain his knights from harming the Roman ambassadors. Then he met with his private council in the Giant's Tower. King Arthur said, "Friends and companions, your skill has enabled me to acquire treasure and gold and to subject many neighboring kingdoms to British rule. A nation is entitled to keep whatever land it can conquer and defend. However, Rome is a mighty nation. We must decide what action is in our own best interest."

The council decided to go to war against Rome. King Arthur said to the ambassadors, "Tell your emperor that I intend to travel to Rome, but I will demand tribute, not pay it. I will bind and hang Lucius Hiberius. I will destroy your land and kill any knights who fight against me."

The Roman ambassadors returned to their homeland and reported King Arthur's decision. Emperor Lucius decided to fight King Arthur in the mountains of Gaul. Arthur and his noblemen also prepared for war.

On board the ship that was transporting him across the English Channel, King Arthur had a dream. He saw a dreadful bear flying through the air from the east. Its appearance was huge, hideous, and black as storm clouds. Lightning and thunder accompanied its flight, and the seacoasts trembled from its horrible roars. A fearsome dragon flew toward the bear from the west. The glare from the dragon's eyes illuminated the sea and the countryside. The bear fought valiantly, but it could not withstand the dragon's repeated attacks. The dragon's fiery breath burned the bear until its scorched body fell lifeless to the earth below.

When Arthur described his dream to his companions, they said, "The dragon signifies you. The bear represents a terrifying giant that you will have to fight. Just as the dragon overcomes the bear, so you will emerge victorious over the giant."

Arthur replied, "I disagree with your interpretation. To me, my dream represents my coming conflict with Emperor Lucius Hiberius. In time, God will reveal its true meaning."

Soon after the Britons arrived in northern Gaul, a knight came in search of King Arthur. "Lord king," he began, "for seven years a monstrous giant has been tormenting us. The fiend destroys the farmers' houses, tears up their crops, and devours their cattle, horses, sheep, goats, and pigs.

"We have even seen him seize and eat men alive! He carries off women and children to his den on Mont-Saint-Michel. So far he has eaten more than 500 people, including infants. On the cliff where he lurks, you will find more dead than you can count and more treasure than the Greeks found in Troy when they captured that ancient walled city.

"Now," the knight continued, "the fiend has captured the noble niece of the Duke of Brittany. He has been holding her on the crest of Mont-Saint-Michel for the past two weeks. By now she may even be dead. No one has been willing to risk death in order to save her. No one in this land, neither knight nor commoner, possesses the courage and strength to confront the giant. We no longer dare to attack him on land, for that means certain death. When we tried to attack him from the sea, he hurled huge boulders upon our ships and sank them, drowning those who were aboard. He roams wherever he wishes and does whatever he pleases.

"You must have noticed, that our countryside lacks any sign of human life. To escape the giant's wrath, many people have hidden deep in the forests. Others are dying of starvation in their own secret hiding places. The fields have become a barren wasteland.

"We desperately need your help," the knight concluded. "The monstrous giant will destroy this entire land and all of its people unless you come to our aid!"

"Alas!" King Arthur replied. "Had I known about this giant, I would have offered him my life before I let him ravage this land. I shall seek this fiend upon his crag. If it is treasure or land that he wants, I shall appease his anger. If his hatred is implacable, I shall fight him to the death! I doubt that he surpasses me in skill and strength!"

That evening Arthur took his foster brother, Sir Kay, aside and said, "At midnight tonight, without a word to anyone except our squires, I want you to come with me to find this giant. I intend to kill him myself—it is important for a king to set a fine example for his knights. I think my own strength and skill will be all that I need. However, if it looks as if I need help, come to my aid."

At midnight the two were riding toward Mont-Saint-Michel when they noticed a great fire blazing above the cliffs upon its crest. Reaching the inlet, they tethered their horses to a tree. They had to make the middle part of their journey in a small rowboat that was kept tied far up the beach, for whenever the tide was high, the hill rose straight out of the sea.

As they climbed toward the crest of the high cliffs, they heard the sound of a woman's cry echoing through the trees above them. King Arthur withdrew Excalibur from its sheath and bravely continued on his way. "I shall walk on ahead of you, but follow me," he said to Sir Kay. "When we reach the crest of the hill, place yourself where you can observe what is happening. For your own safety, remain deep within the shadows. No matter what blows I may suffer, remain in hiding unless the giant pins me to the ground and has me at his mercy. It is not appropriate for anyone but me to fight the giant."

Upon the crest of the hill, King Arthur found the huge, blazing fire. Human bones lay scattered upon the ground, more or less picked clean of flesh. But there was no sign of the giant. Instead, the flames flickered upon the body of an old woman in torn clothing who was sitting by the side of a fresh grave mound. Her long hair fell over her face, and she was weeping and wailing with grief.

As King Arthur entered the lighted area with Excalibur ready in his hand, the woman stopped her wailing and turned in his direction. "Who are you, and what evil fate has brought you here?" she asked. "Are you an angel, or a knight? If heaven is your home, you may wander upon this mountain in safety. But if you are a knight and the earth is your home, then you are indeed an unfortunate man!

"I pity you, for you are about to be tortured to death by a giant, who will then tear your limbs to pieces. Even if you were made of the strongest metal, he would destroy you. Even if you had come with fifty knights as strong as you are, he would destroy you all! May his name be cursed!

"I have just buried the Duke of Brittany's niece," the woman continued, "and the giant will not hesitate to kill you as well! He attacked the best of all castles in Brittany. The gates fell to pieces in his hands. He pulled down the wall of the great hall. He tore the door to my lady's room into five pieces. He grabbed us and carried us into this wild, wooded area. My poor child was only fifteen years old. I was her nurse and had cared for her ever since the day of her birth. She died of terror in the monster's arms! I watched as the light of my life flickered and went out!

"Take my advice, fair lord, and flee while you can. To remain here is to seek your death. If the giant finds you, he will tear you to pieces and eat your flesh. Do not try to win him with words. He cannot be bought with lands, or with treaties, or even with chests of gold. He will rage where he chooses, regardless of the law, for he is his own master, and he answers to no one."

Then the woman's face filled with terror. King Arthur turned to follow her gaze and found himself staring at the monstrous giant.

The horrible appearance of the fiend was matched only by the terrible nature of his deeds. His face was darkly splotched like the skin of a frog. His eyebrows hung low over his eyes, which burned with fire. His ears were enormous, and his nose was hooked like a hawk's beak. His mouth was as flat as a flounder's, and his fat, loose, fleshy lips spread apart to display his swollen gums. His bristly black beard fell over his chest, concealing part of his fat body. He had the broad neck and shoulders of a bull. His arms and legs stretched out like the limbs of a mighty oak tree. From the top of his head to the tip of his shovel-shaped feet, he was thirty feet tall.

The giant wore a tunic made from human hair, fringed with the beards of men. He carried the corpses of twelve peasants tied together on his back. In his hand, he carried a club so mighty that the two strongest farmers in the land could not have lifted it off the ground.

The giant dropped the corpses by the fire and approached Arthur with broad strides. As Arthur fingered Excalibur, he saw that the giant's mouth was still smeared with the clotted blood and scraps of flesh from his last meal. Even his beard and his hair were strewn with gore.

Arthur said to him, "May great God in heaven, who rules the world, give you a short life and a shameful death! Surely you are the most foul fiend that was ever formed! Guard yourself, you dog, and prepare to die, for this day my hands will kill you!"

The giant responded by raising his fearsome club. He grinned like a ferocious boar, confident of its menacing tusks. Then he growled, and foam spilled from his gaping mouth.

King Arthur raised his shield and prayed to God that it would protect him against the fiend's mighty club. The giant's first blow fell upon Arthur's shield, making the cliffs clang like an anvil and shattering his source of protection. The shock of the impact almost knocked Arthur to the ground, but he quickly recovered.

The blow ignited King Arthur's rage, and he furiously struck the giant on the forehead with his sword. Blood gushed into the giant's eyes and down his cheeks, blinding him.

Just as an enraged boar, its flesh torn from the attacks of hunting hounds, turns and charges upon a hunter, so the giant, maddened with the pain of his wound, rushed with a roar upon King Arthur. Groping blindly with his hands, the giant grabbed the king by the shoulders and clasped him to his chest, trying to crush Arthur's ribs and burst his heart. King Arthur summoned all of his strength and twisted his body out from under the giant's grasp.

"Peace to you, my lord!" the giant exclaimed. "Who are you that fights so skillfully with me? Only Arthur, the most noble of all kings, could defeat me in combat!"

"I am that Arthur of whom you speak," the king replied. Then, quick as lightning, Arthur struck the giant repeatedly with his sword. Unable to see through the blood in his eyes, the giant never knew where the next blow would fall. Arthur's sword thrusts rained upon him relentlessly until one finally entered his ear and plunged into his skull.

The giant gave a dreadful roar and crashed to the ground like a mighty oak tree torn up by a furious storm wind. Arthur gazed upon his fallen prey and laughed with relief.

Sir Kay stepped into the firelight and said, "That was an impressive death blow! The fiend should have worn a helmet!"

"Take your sword, Kay, and slice off his head," Arthur commanded. "I want to take it back to our companions for everyone to admire. If we place our swords through his ears, we can carry the head between us all the way back to our tents. If you want any treasure, take whatever pleases you. I want nothing more than the fiend's tunic and his club."

The first glow of dawn was streaking the sky with shades of rose when King Arthur and Sir Kay entered their camp. Word had already traveled from tent to tent, so an enthusiastic group of knights greeted their return. They stared at the giant's huge, hideous head in awe, for its size and ugliness were beyond compare.

The Duke of Brittany built a chapel over his niece's grave on top of Mont-Saint-Michel, so that she would not be forgotten. By the time it was finished, the allies of King Arthur had arrived from Ireland and Scotland, and they all set forth to meet the Roman legions.

The two knights without equal in King Arthur's court were Sir Lancelot of the Lake and Sir Gawain, the king's nephew. Both showed their prowess in the war against Rome.

In the first battle, Sir Gawain received serious wounds but fought on. When the battle ended, Arthur's knights had killed more than 10,000 Roman soldiers, had taken many prisoners, and had sent the rest fleeing.

King Arthur put Sir Lancelot in command of the prisoners, who were to be taken to Paris. Emperor Lucius Hiberius sent 60,000 Roman soldiers to ambush Lancelot.

Lancelot's scouts warned him of the ambush. Even though the Romans outnumbered the Britons six to one, he met them in deadly combat. He was so strong and skillful that his soldiers won the battle, killing many Roman soldiers and forcing the rest to run from them as sheep run from a lion or a wolf.

But when he returned to the king, Arthur said, "Your courage nearly destroyed you, Lancelot! It is foolish to fight under circumstances where you are badly outnumbered."

Sir Lancelot replied, "No, it is not foolish, for once a person acts shamefully, he can never recover his honor."

The decisive battle followed. King Arthur met Emperor Lucius Hiberius in a long, mighty contest. Arthur received a serious wound, but ultimately he took Excalibur and sliced off the Roman emperor's head. That day, King Arthur and his men also killed sixty Roman senators and twenty kings of countries that were Roman allies.

"Bring these corpses before your Senate with this message," King Arthur commanded the three senators who remained alive. "Tell them this is the tribute they have demanded of me. Tell them also that if this is not sufficient, I will pay an additional tribute when I arrive in Rome. Make it clear to them that this is the only kind of tribute I will pay. Finally, tell them that they may never again demand a tribute or a tax of any kind from Britain."

Shortly after the funeral procession started, Arthur and his knights began their own march toward Rome. City after city in the provinces yielded to them. The cities of Italy — including Rome — also yielded. When the leading Roman officials asked for peace, Arthur agreed to hold his Round Table in Rome that Christmas and to be crowned Emperor of Rome at that time.

Thus it came to pass that King Arthur ruled all the lands of the Roman Empire. After his coronation, Arthur rewarded his knights and servants generously with land. Each knight now longed to return home to his wife.

King Arthur himself had no desire to acquire more power. "We have achieved great glory and honor," he announced. "It is not wise to tempt God."

So Arthur and his army returned to Britain and received a royal welcome throughout the kingdom.

Chapter 5

Sir Lancelot has many adventures and performs many heroic deeds. He then returns to the Round Table and resumes his love affair with Queen Guinevere. He defends her against a charge of treason. In tournaments, he fights in disguise on the side against the king.

After King Arthur and his knights returned to Britain, Sir Lancelot became the leading knight of the Round Table. Not only had he performed outstanding feats upon the field of battle in Gaul, but at home he surpassed all other knights in tournament skills and in noble deeds. Queen Guinevere loved him above all other men, and he loved her above all other women.

Sir Lancelot loved to earn glory, honor, and praise. He soon tired of the routine of tournaments and other such contests of skill with arms. He decided to increase his honor by seeking adventures in which he could excel in other, equally noble ways.

One noble way in which Lancelot proved himself was in his loyalty to Queen Guinevere. After falling asleep under a tree, he awoke to find himself imprisoned by four queens. They said to him, "We know Queen Guinevere is the only lady you love, but she is lost to you forever. You must choose one of us or die in this prison."

Lancelot replied, "You have given me a difficult choice, but I will die rather than choose one of you. If I were free, I would prove to you that Queen Guinevere is true to her lord, King Arthur."

Sir Lancelot also proved himself by defending ladies in distress. Not long after his adventure with the four queens, he came upon a maiden in the forest who complained of a knight who assaulted any woman who passed his way.

"Are you telling me that a knight is a thief and a rapist?" Lancelot asked. "He brings shame upon the order of knighthood! He has broken his sacred oath, and he should die for it. Ride ahead of me, slowly, through the forest. If that knight bothers you, I will come to your rescue."

When the knight appeared and forced the maiden from her horse, Sir Lancelot challenged him to a duel and killed him. "Now, lady," he said, "what other service can I perform for you?"

"Nothing at this time, sir," the maiden replied. "But you need a wife. You are the most courteous of knights to all ladies, yet you love none of them. I have heard that Queen Guinevere has placed an enchantment upon you so that you will never love anyone but her."

"Fair lady," replied Lancelot, "I have no interest in marriage, for then I would have to remain with my wife and give up the tournaments, battles, and adventures that I love. To love a woman and not marry her would be even worse! God punishes such immoral behavior. Such knights are unfortunate in their contests and wars."

Sir Lancelot then left the maiden. After riding through the forest for two days, he found himself at the castle of Tintagel, where King Arthur had been born. Two giants approached him, each armed with a huge club.

Lancelot immediately raised his shield, fended off the blow of the first giant's club, and sliced off his head with his sword. Seeing this, the other giant ran for his life. Lancelot caught him and sliced through his body from the shoulder to the stomach.

Sir Lancelot then returned to the castle. When he entered the great hall, sixty ladies came and knelt before him in thanks.

"Most of us have been imprisoned here for seven years," they told him, "earning our food by embroidering silk. Who are you that you were able to deliver us from these giants? Many knights have tried, but their courage brought them only death. We thought that only Sir Lancelot of the Lake could save us, for these giants feared him alone."

"Fair ladies," Lancelot replied, "I am the very knight you hoped to see!" Then he left them to their freedom and went on his way.

Sir Lancelot had many more adventures. Word of his triumphs reached King Arthur and Queen Guinevere in various ways. Sir Lancelot asked some of the people he helped to go to Arthur's court and relate their stories to the queen and the knights assembled there. He also sent knights he had defeated to Queen Guinevere to become her prisoners. Other tales of Lancelot's heroic deeds were told by those of King Arthur's knights who met him in the course of their own adventures.

By the time Sir Lancelot returned to the Round Table, he had already earned the greatest name of any knight in the world and was honored by both the common folk and the nobility.

Lancelot's love affair with Guinevere resumed on his return. Their relationship was common knowledge at court. Lancelot was embarrassed by the gossip and began to spend his time helping the numerous maidens and ladies who asked for his assistance.

Queen Guinevere finally called Sir Lancelot to her and said, "Lancelot, your love for me must be dying, for you no longer seem to enjoy my company. Instead, you spend your time helping other women with their problems."

Lancelot replied, "Since I was last a part of the Round Table, I have given up all the pleasures of this world except my love for you. I might have chosen to become a holy man if I did not love you as I do. You are my earthly joy, and I love you too much to give you up for anyone — even Arthur, my lord and king.

"However, our continued boldness will bring great slander and shame upon us, and I do not want to see you dishonored. Surely you are aware, Guinevere, that many knights already speak openly of our love. I fear them more for your sake than mine, since if I must I can return to my own country across the sea. But you must remain here and face whatever is said about you.

"Therefore," Lancelot concluded, "I am making an effort to help various ladies so that the members of the court will think that I love attending all women, and not just you."

Queen Guinevere said, "I see from your words that you are a false knight. You love other women and have only scorn for me! Therefore, I shall no longer love you. Leave this court and never return, for I never want to see you again!"

To prove that she loved other knights as much as she loved Sir Lancelot, Queen Guinevere gave a dinner for them. One of the knights ate a poisoned apple and immediately died. Because Queen Guinevere had prepared the feast, she was blamed for his death. Another knight came before King Arthur and the knights of the Round Table and accused the queen of treason, which was punishable by death.

King Arthur said, "Fair lords, my heart is heavily troubled. I must be the judge in this matter, so I cannot also defend my wife. I ask that one of you come to her aid so that she will not be burned for a crime she did not commit."

"Forgive me, my gracious lord," said the knight, "but not one of the twenty-four knights who attended the dinner is willing to defend the queen's innocence in this matter."

Arthur replied, "Be armed and ready for a contest in fifteen days. When that day comes, if no knight has come forward to defend the queen, then that will indicate her guilt, and she will be burned."

King Arthur then went to Queen Guinevere and asked, "Where is Sir Lancelot? He would defend you!"

"His relatives tell me that he has left Britain," she responded.

The king advised, "Ask his nephew, Sir Bors, to fight for you for Lancelot's sake!"

But Bors was unwilling to honor Queen Guinevere's request. "Madam," he replied, "how can I defend you when I attended that dinner? If I take your part, the other knights will suspect that I poisoned the apple!

"Sir Lancelot would have defended you even if you were guilty, but you drove him out of Britain although he worshipped you! How can you ask me to defend you when you have treated my uncle in such a cruel manner?"

King Arthur found Queen Guinevere pleading with Lancelot's nephew. "Gentle knight," he said, "have mercy upon the queen, for I am certain that she is innocent. Defend her for the love of Sir Lancelot!"

"My lord," replied Bors, "you are asking me to incur the wrath of my fellow knights. Nevertheless, I will defend the queen for Lancelot's sake and your sake, unless a better knight is willing to be her champion."

When Guinevere banished Lancelot from court, he went to stay with a hermit in the countryside. He received the news of Guinevere's distress with great joy, for now he had an opportunity to win back her favor.

The day of the contest arrived. The two knights were prepared to begin, when suddenly another knight, riding a white horse and bearing a shield with a strange coat of arms, galloped out of the woods and talked with Sir Lancelot's nephew. Sir Bors then announced that this stranger would defend the queen in his place. The strange knight defended Guinevere against her accuser and proved her innocent of treason.

After the contest King Arthur asked the strange knight to remove his helmet and reveal his identity. It was, of course, Sir Lancelot. Queen Guinevere rejoiced at his return and regretted her harsh treatment of him.

Arthur and the knights of the Round Table then prepared to participate in a great tournament at Camelot. The king asked Queen Guinevere to accompany him, but she said she was too ill to ride. Sir Lancelot also refused to attend the tournament because his wounds from his combat in defense of Guinevere had not yet healed. The coincidence provided those who loved scandal with much to discuss, and King Arthur left for Camelot with sadness and anger in his heart.

After the king departed, Queen Guinevere said to Sir Lancelot, "You were wrong to stay behind! Our enemies will accuse us of remaining here to make love!"

Lancelot decided to attend the tournament in disguise and fight on the side against the king. Guinevere could not convince him to appear in a more honest manner. But King Arthur recognized Lancelot when they lodged in the same town en route to Camelot and was pleased to see him.

All was not well, however. Since Lancelot never wore the token of any woman, he agreed to wear one as part of his disguise. During the course of the tournament, he was seriously wounded by his own nephew, Sir Bors. In time, Sir Gawain discovered Sir Lancelot's identity. Queen Guinevere was furious that her knight had worn the token of another woman, when he had always refused to wear her own token.

As a result, when the next great tournament was announced, Guinevere said to Lancelot, "I understand why you wore a maiden's token at the last tournament. However, from now on, I want you to wear my golden token upon your helmet as a sign of your love for me. And make certain that your relatives are well informed of your disguise so they do not injure you."

Sir Lancelot agreed, and at the next tournament he again rode against the knights of the Round Table, wearing Queen Guinevere's token. His relatives, who were also in disguise, fought on his side. Sir Gawain recognized them, and he counseled King Arthur that it would be better to let Sir Lancelot and his relatives win the day rather than to contest heavily against their own knights.

Chapter 6

Two of King Arthur's nephews reveal to him the love affair between Sir Lancelot and Guinevere. The queen is condemned to die, but Lancelot rescues her and takes her to his castle.

Sir Agravain and Sir Mordred, brothers of Sir Gawain, had long concealed their hatred of Queen Guinevere and Sir Lancelot. Finally Agravain's emotion conquered his good judgment, and he announced in a voice that many knights could hear, "What false men we are! I am amazed that we are all not ashamed to see how Sir Lancelot openly loves Queen Guinevere. Yet, day after day, we endure this shame and permit King Arthur to suffer this embarrassment without making any effort to punish the offenders! How long are we going to conceal Lancelot's treason? It is time to tell the king!"

Sir Gawain replied, "Do not speak of such matters within my hearing, for I will have nothing to do with that subject!"

"I will!" exclaimed Sir Mordred.

"You would do us all a service to leave the matter alone, my brother," Gawain replied, "and tend to your own affairs, for I know what will come of your mischief."

"Come of it what may," Sir Agravain answered, "I intend to disclose the affair to King Arthur."

"Not with my approval," said Sir Gawain. "If you proceed with this, you will cause a war between Lancelot and us. And as you well know, many dukes and barons will side with Lancelot. As for me, I will never take a stand against Sir Lancelot. He is my friend!"

"Do as you wish," replied Agravain. "I will keep silent no longer!"

"Your action will destroy the noble fellowship of the Round Table and bring ruin upon us!" Gawain exclaimed. "I urge you both to reconsider!"

But Agravain and Mordred could not be dissuaded. They told King Arthur of the relationship between Sir Lancelot and Queen Guinevere. "We will prove that Lancelot is a traitor to you," they concluded.

"You will need to prove it," Arthur replied, "for Sir Lancelot is the mightiest of knights, and he will kill the knight who insults his honor."

King Arthur had long been aware of the love between his wife and Lancelot. He had pretended ignorance because Lancelot had helped both him and the queen on many occasions, and King Arthur loved him. If their relationship became public, Arthur knew that, as king, he would have to consider his honor and his position and would be compelled to take action.

Yet Agravain was determined to make a public issue of the matter, so Arthur reluctantly consented to his plan. King Arthur would go hunting and send back word to Queen Guinevere that he would be away for the night. If Sir Agravain, Sir Mordred, and twelve knights found Sir Lancelot with the queen in his absence, they would bring Lancelot before him.

Lancelot was indeed with Guinevere when Agravain and his party of knights knocked on the queen's door. They called, "Sir Lancelot of the Lake, you are a traitor knight! Come out of the queen's bedroom! We intend to bring you before King Arthur."

"Alas!" Queen Guinevere cried. "Our love has destroyed us! Since you do not have armor and weapons, surely these men will kill you, and I shall be burned!"

Lancelot put his arms around Guinevere and said, "Most noble queen, you have always been my lady, and I have at all times been your true knight. I have never failed you since King Arthur first made me a knight. Pray for my soul if I am killed here. My relatives will rescue you from the fire. Take comfort in that and return with them to my lands, for there you will live like a queen."

"No, Lancelot," Guinevere replied. "I shall not choose to live once you are dead!"

"Know that I will do my best to stay alive," Lancelot said, "although I am more concerned for you than for myself. Nevertheless, I would rather have my armor upon me right now than be lord of all Christendom! I would choose to die performing deeds that bring fame rather than to die a shameful death!"

With that, Sir Lancelot opened Queen Guinevere's door just wide enough for one knight to enter the room. Lancelot killed him, took his armor and weapons, and attacked those who had chosen to destroy him. Only Sir Mordred escaped.

Lancelot then said to Guinevere, "Because I have killed these knights, King Arthur will always be my enemy. I must leave Britain. Come with me! I will save you from the dangers that await you."

Guinevere replied, "No, Lancelot. I will not do more harm to the kingdom by fleeing. But if I am condemned to burn, please rescue me!"

"Have no doubt of that!" Sir Lancelot exclaimed. He kissed Queen Guinevere, and they exchanged rings.

Sir Lancelot returned to his lodgings, where he gathered his family and the knights who were loyal to him. "You all know," he explained, "that ever since I came to Britain, I have been loyal to my lord, King Arthur, and to my lady, Queen Guinevere. Tonight the queen sent for me to speak with her. King Arthur commanded Sir Agravain, Sir Mordred, and twelve knights to betray me while I was in her room.

"Now that I have killed these knights," he continued, "war is certain to follow. The king, in his anger and malice, will order the queen to be burned. I will fight for her and declare that she has been true to her lord."

Meanwhile, Sir Mordred returned to King Arthur and his knights with the terrible tale of his encounter with Sir Lancelot.

Arthur exclaimed, "The fellowship of the Round Table is broken forever, for many a noble knight will side with Sir Lancelot! Alas, that I wear this crown upon my head! Now I must lose the fairest fellowship of noble knights that a king has ever had!

"It must break with Sir Lancelot in order to keep my honor," King Arthur continued. "And the queen must suffer the penalty of death, for under the law, she is guilty of treason. She is responsible for the deaths of thirteen knights of the Round Table. Therefore, I command that she be put into the fire and burned!"

Sir Gawain said, "My lord, I counsel you not to judge the queen too hastily. Even though Sir Lancelot was found in her room, he may have been there for no evil purpose. You know that the queen owes more to Lancelot than to any other knight, for he has often saved her life and has fought for her when the entire court refused to do so. Perhaps she sent for him with good reason.

"Maybe," Gawain continued, "the queen asked Lancelot to come secretly to her room in order to avoid slander. Many times we choose what we think is the best course of action, only to learn that it is the worst! I say to you that Queen Guinevere is both good and true to you. As for Sir Lancelot, he will defend the queen's honor against any knight living, and he will take the crime and the shame upon himself in order to save her."

"I have no doubt that he will!" Arthur replied. "Sir Lancelot trusts so in his courage and his skill with arms that he fears nothing, neither man nor law. But this time I will not permit him to fight for the queen. She will suffer the consequences of her actions, for we all are subject to the law. And, if I can, I will bring a shameful death upon Lancelot."

Then Arthur asked Gawain, "Why are you defending Lancelot? He has killed two of your sons, and last night he killed one of your brothers and severely wounded another."

"They brought their deaths upon themselves!" Gawain answered. "I warned them of the perils of their action, but they refused to heed my counsel."

"Dear Nephew," the king commanded Sir Gawain, "put on your best armor, and with your brothers, Sir Gareth and Sir Gaheris, bring my queen to the fire. There she will receive her judgment and her death."

"No, my most noble lord," said Gawain. "That I will never do. My heart will not permit me to witness the shameful death of such a noble lady! And let no one ever say that I supported you in judging the queen guilty and condemning her to death!"

"Then," replied King Arthur, "permit your brothers to be there."

Gawain replied, "They feel as I do! However, they are too young to reject your command."

"Indeed, you may command us and we will obey you," Gareth and Gaheris said, "even though we are much opposed to the deed. But we will wear no armor and will carry no weapons."

Thus it came to pass that Queen Guinevere was led from the castle of Carlisle in a simple smock to face her death. Most of the lords and ladies wept with sympathy, and few would bear arms to support her execution.

Just as Guinevere reached the fire, a group of knights led by Sir Lancelot galloped forth to save her. Everyone who fought against the invading knights was killed, for Sir Lancelot had no equal on the field of combat.

A sword thrust intended to pierce some knight's armor struck the unprotected heads of Gaheris and Gareth, who were unarmed and unprepared for battle. It was Lancelot who cut them down, though he did not even see them in the heat of battle.

Once Sir Lancelot had killed or scattered anyone who would deter him, he placed a robe upon Queen Guinevere, sat her behind him on his horse, and rode off with her to the castle of Joyous Gard. There he kept her as a noble knight keeps a lady.

Sir Gawain had remained in his room, where he learned of Guinevere's rescue. He exclaimed, "I knew that Sir Lancelot would save the queen or die in the attempt! He would not have been a man of honor otherwise, since she was being burned because of his deed. I would have done the same thing myself in his place."

Then Gawain was told of his brothers' deaths. He could not believe that Lancelot had killed them. "Gareth loved Lancelot better than he loved any of his brothers or the king!" he exclaimed. "If Lancelot had wished it, Gareth would have stood with him against all of us!"

Sir Gawain was overwhelmed with grief and anger. "How did Sir Lancelot slay my brothers?" he asked King Arthur. "Neither bore arms against him!"

"I can only tell you what I have been told," Arthur replied. "They were standing among a great group of armed knights, and he did not see them there. He did not know that he killed them. However, let us plan how to avenge their deaths."

"My king, my lord, and my uncle," Sir Gawain replied, "I now make you a promise that I shall hold as sacred as my knighthood. From this day forth, no man on earth will convince me to make peace with Sir Lancelot of the Lake! I shall not rest until I have met him in battle and one of us has killed the other! If necessary, I shall seek Sir Lancelot throughout seven kings' kingdoms, but I shall find him and avenge the deaths of my brothers!"

Thus the war between King Arthur and Sir Lancelot began.

Chapter 7

The siege of Lancelot's castle in Britain is unsuccessful. He returns Guinevere to King Arthur, but Sir Gawain compels Arthur to follow Lancelot across the sea in order to continue the war. Mordred seizes the throne, and Arthur returns to fight him. Sir Gawain is mortally wounded. Before he dies, he asks Lancelot to come to Arthur's aid in the war against Mordred.

Sir Lancelot and his knights prepared the castle Joyous Gard for a siege, and soon King Arthur and Sir Gawain arrived with a huge army. Although great fighting occurred, Lancelot and his best knights remained within the castle for almost four months and would not take part in the battle.

Finally Sir Lancelot spoke with King Arthur and Sir Gawain over the castle wall. "You win no honor here with this siege, since I refuse to do battle with you. I will never fight the noble king who made me a knight!"

Arthur replied, "Spare me your honeyed words! I am your mortal enemy until I die! You have killed my good knights and relatives. You have slept with my queen for many years. And now, like a traitor, you have taken her from me by force!"

"Most noble lord and king," said Lancelot, "say whatever you wish to me, but I will not fight against you. I am sorry that I killed your knights, but I did so only to save my own life. And as for Queen Guinevere, of all the knights under heaven, only you or Gawain could charge me with being a traitor and yet live! I will defend the queen's honor against any other knight alive, for she is as true to you as any lady living is to her lord.

"It is true that the queen has treated me kindly and has cherished me more than any other knight, but then I have deserved her favor. In your anger, more than once you would have had her burned, and I have saved her from the judgment and the flames. Then you loved me, and thanked me, and were loyal to me."

Lancelot continued, "I would have lost my honor if I had let the queen burn for my deeds. I have always taken her part in quarrels with others. How then could I leave her undefended when this quarrel concerned me? So, my good and gracious lord, take your queen and honor her, for she is both true and good!"

"You are a false knight!" Sir Gawain exclaimed. "I shall never think shameful thoughts of the queen. But what cause did you have to kill my brothers? They were not even armed!"

"I know that you will not accept my excuse," Sir Lancelot replied, "but by the faith I owe to the high order of knighthood, I did not mean to kill them!"

"You lie, cowardly knight!" cried Gawain. "I will fight you as long as I live, until one of us kills the other!"

"From the moment I learned of their deaths," said Lancelot, "I knew that I would never again have your friendship and that you would cause my noble lord, King Arthur, ever to be my mortal foe. If it were not for your abiding anger, I believe that I would again be in my king's good graces."

Sir Lancelot was indeed correct. The noble King Arthur would have welcomed his queen and made his peace with that valiant knight if Sir Gawain had permitted it. But Gawain's anger was implacable, and he led many of Arthur's knights to call Lancelot a false, cowardly knight.

To preserve his honor, Sir Lancelot was forced to leave the castle and fight for his good name. He pleaded with King Arthur and Sir Gawain to leave the field, but Gawain said that they had come to fight. Lancelot instructed his knights to fight everyone except those two.

Lancelot himself rescued Arthur from the sword of Sir Bors. "As dearly as I love you," Lancelot said to his nephew, "I will kill you before I see the noble king who made me knight either shamed or killed!"

As Lancelot put Arthur back on his horse, tears flowed from the king's eyes, for he knew that Sir Lancelot was more noble than any other man. "Alas, that this war ever began!" he moaned.

Finally news of the war reached the Pope in Rome. He sent King Arthur a papal order commanding him to accept his queen and make peace with Sir Lancelot. Gawain agreed that Guinevere should return to Arthur, but he would not permit the king to make peace with Lancelot.

Sir Lancelot rode with Queen Guinevere to King Arthur's castle in Carlisle. An escort of 100 knights, each clothed in green velvet and carrying an olive branch as a token of peace, accompanied Lancelot and the queen, who were dressed in white and gold. When they arrived at Carlisle Castle, Lancelot and Guinevere knelt before Arthur in the presence of Gawain and many great lords.

"My most honored king," Lancelot said, "It was never my thought to withhold your queen from you. My only desire was to save her from danger. I am a thousandfold happier bringing her here than I was taking her away."

He continued, "If any knight, except for you, my lord, dares to say that Queen Guinevere is other than true to you, I, Sir Lancelot of the Lake, will defend her good name. You have listened to liars, and they have caused this argument between us. Without the might of God on my side, unarmed and surprised as I was, I could never have killed thirteen armed knights who were determined to kill me. Remember how well I have always served you, and favor me with your goodwill."

"The king may make his peace with you if he chooses," said Gawain, "but I shall never forgive you for killing my brothers! If you were not here under the Pope's command, I would fight you right now to prove that you have been false to both my uncle and me. Know that I shall prove it once you have left Britain, wherever I find you! You must leave this land within two weeks."

Lancelot then said to Guinevere, so that everyone could hear him, "Madam, I must now depart from you and this noble fellowship forever. However, if any false tongues slander you, send me word and I will defend you." He kissed the queen and said, "Now let us see who will dare to speak against the queen and say that she is not true to my lord, Arthur."

With these words, Sir Lancelot handed Queen Guinevere to King Arthur and left the court. Neither king nor duke nor earl nor knight nor maiden nor lady could hold back a flood of tears. Only Sir Gawain remained unmoved, for his hatred of Lancelot was implacable.

King Arthur's heart ached with sorrow for his country. He knew that from this time forth, his kingdom would be torn with debate and strife. The fellowship of the Round Table had brought responsible leadership to Britain. Without that fellowship to sustain them, duke would fight duke, baron would fight baron, and knight would fight knight.

Sir Lancelot returned to his lands across the sea. King Arthur and Sir Gawain prepared to follow him with a huge army. Arthur decided to leave Britain in the care of his nephew, Sir Mordred. Mordred had virtues, but loyalty was not among them. He schemed to reign in King Arthur's place and marry Queen Guinevere, whom he loved.

Arthur was unaware of Mordred's evil plans. He left Mordred in control of all he possessed—his queen, his land, and his people. Then he left to fight Sir Lancelot, for he would remain loyal to Sir Gawain, and Gawain's heart was set on vengeance.

For six months Gawain fought Lancelot's knights, but Lancelot refused to appear and contest with him. Many knights were slaughtered on both sides. Finally Gawain appeared before the castle gates and shouted, "Where are you, Lancelot, you false traitor? Why do you hide within the walls of your castle like a coward?"

Then Sir Lancelot realized that he would have to fight the knight who had once been his dear friend. His own sense of honor could not let Sir Gawain publicly shame him. They agreed to do battle and told their knights that no man should come near to help until one of them died or yielded to the other.

Gawain possessed a gift that a holy man had given him: Every day of the year, from nine o'clock in the morning until noon, his might increased to three times its normal strength. Only King Arthur knew of this gift, and he always set the contests to resolve quarrels at that time of day.

Sir Lancelot was amazed to see Sir Gawain's strength gradually double and then triple. He fought more and more carefully, preserving his own strength. As noon passed and Gawain's strength began to diminish, Lancelot gave his helmet such a blow that it knocked him off his horse. Gawain lay defenseless on the ground, but Lancelot walked off and left him there.

"Turn around, traitor," Sir Gawain called after him, "and slay me! If you leave me as I am, when I am well I will fight you once again!"

Sir Lancelot replied, "You know very well, Gawain, that I will never strike a knight who is down!"

For the next three weeks, Gawain lay sick in his tent. When he felt well enough to resume the battle, he approached the castle and taunted Lancelot until he had to come out and fight. Again the contest between the two knights began at nine o'clock in the morning, and Lancelot carefully bided his time until after noon. Again Lancelot struck Gawain upon the helmet, reopening his wound, and again he walked away from the sorely injured knight.

As soon as Sir Gawain had recovered enough to speak, he called to Sir Lancelot. "Traitor knight, you know that I am still alive! Come and kill me, or I will live to do battle with you again! I will not give up until one of us lies dead!"

"I will do no more than I have done," Lancelot replied. "As long as you can stand on your feet, I will fight you. But I will not shame myself by striking a wounded man who cannot stand!"

This time Gawain lay sick in his tent for a month. He was preparing to resume the contest when King Arthur received news that Sir Mordred had formally been crowned king of Britain and that he intended to marry Queen Guinevere.

Fake letters claiming that Lancelot had killed Arthur had convinced the House of Lords of the need to crown a successor. Since Guinevere found the idea of marrying Mordred both shameful and distasteful, she told him she was going to London to prepare her trousseau. Then she stocked the Tower of London with food and knights and took refuge within it.

Try as he might, Sir Mordred could not win Queen Guinevere, who publicly announced that she would die rather than marry him. Then he received word that King Arthur had withdrawn the siege from Sir Lancelot and was returning home with his army.

Quickly Mordred wrote to barons throughout Britain asking for their support. Most of them sided with him, forgetting what a good king Arthur had been. They foolishly believed that King Arthur's reign had caused strife and war. With Sir Mordred, they thought that they would be able to live in joy and in peace.

The two armies met at Dover, and even the water ran red with blood. King Arthur was such a courageous leader that his knights followed him ashore with great spirit in their hearts. After a deadly battle, Sir Mordred and his forces retreated. Arthur returned to find Sir Gawain dying in one of the boats.

"Now all my earthly joy has left me!" the king cried. "I loved you and Lancelot above all other knights, and now I have lost you both!"

"Dear uncle, my lord and king," Gawain said, "I am dying because of my own rash judgment! Lancelot's wound is killing me. If he were still at your side this unhappy war would never have begun! When I set you against him, I caused the destruction of your kingdom. I beg you, give me paper, pen, and ink that I may write to Lancelot in my own hand."

Gawain wrote to Lancelot of Mordred's treachery, Guinevere's seclusion, Arthur's need for help, and his own impending death. He publicly cleared Sir Lancelot of blame and asked him to return to Britain to help Arthur and to visit Gawain's own tomb.

When his letter was finished, Sir Gawain told King Arthur to send for Sir Lancelot and to cherish him above all other knights. Gawain was given the last rites, and then he died.

Chapter 8

Arthur kills Mordred, but Mordred fatally wounds Arthur, as Merlin had predicted. Excalibur returns to the Lady of the Lake, and four queens take Arthur away with them. Guinevere and Lancelot recognize the destruction that their love has caused; she becomes a nun, and he a priest. Guinevere dies, and Lancelot dies shortly thereafter.

King Arthur had a dream in which he was sitting on a chair that was attached to a wheel. He was wearing his crown and a robe of rich, gold cloth, and all his knights were bowing before him. Far below him he could see deep, black water in which dragons, serpents, and wild beasts were fighting. The sight was terrible to behold! Suddenly his chair turned upside down, and he fell into the deep, black water. All of the monsters immediately swam toward him and began to attack him. Arthur cried out in his sleep.

Then in his sleep he saw Sir Gawain approach him. "My lord and uncle," Gawain said, "If you fight Mordred tomorrow, you and most of your knights will be killed. I advise you to offer Mordred a great reward if he will agree to postpone tomorrow's battle for one month. By that time Sir Lancelot will have arrived with his noble knights. They will kill Sir Mordred and those who support him." With these words, Sir Gawain disappeared.

Arthur revealed his second dream to his knights and sent two of them to Sir Mordred to bargain for the month's delay. Mordred had gathered 100,000 men and was prepared for battle. But he agreed to the postponement in return for the regions of Cornwall and Kent during King Arthur's lifetime and all of Britain after his death.

Arthur and Mordred each chose fourteen knights and met between the two armies to sign the treaty. The two leaders had so little trust in one another that each directed his men to watch for any drawn sword. At the first sign of an exposed blade, the knights were to kill every enemy in sight.

During the signing, a poisonous snake slithered out from a heath bush and stung one of the knights on the foot. The knight instinctively drew his sword to slay the snake. Seeing his drawn sword, both armies immediately clashed in warfare.

King Arthur sadly rode into battle, encouraging his knights and fighting his best. "Would that great God in heaven had destined me to die for all of you!" he exclaimed. "I would rather save your lives than rule all that Alexander possessed while he lived upon this earth!"

By dusk, 200,000 men had fallen upon the earth, their bodies as cold as the ground they lay upon. When the king looked about him, only one of his knights, Sir Bedivere, remained alive. "Alas, that I have seen this saddest of days!" Arthur exclaimed.

Then Arthur noticed Mordred standing among a great heap of dead men. The king said to his knight, "Give me my spear, for I see the traitor who caused all this woe! I will repay him for his treachery and treason!"

"My lord," Bedivere replied, "remember your dream and let him be. If you leave Mordred alone, your day of destiny will pass."

"Come death or come life," King Arthur replied, "I will kill him now." He took his spear in both hands and ran toward Mordred, shouting, "False knight and traitor! Dark death now comes upon you, and no man on earth will rescue you!"

Mordred ran toward Arthur with his sword drawn. The king struck Mordred beneath his shield with a mortal blow, but Mordred summoned his last strength and struck King Arthur on the side of the head, piercing through his helmet to his brain. Then Mordred's body crumpled to the earth.

King Arthur cried, "Ah, Lancelot, I sorely missed your help this day! The rich blood of my Round Table soaks this muddy earth. My loyal knights, who by the might of their hands made me master of the earth, have been struck down by treachery. This day's bloody deeds have drowned all my joy. I weep for the glory, the honor, and the fellowship that are no more. Even I have received my death blow."

Arthur then said to his knight, "Take my sword, Excalibur, to the lake that is nearby and throw it into the water. Then return and tell me what you saw there."

Sir Bedivere went off as King Arthur had directed, but when he saw that the hilt of the sword was covered with precious stones, he thought, "Nothing good can come from throwing such a valuable sword into the lake! Why waste all this wealth?" So he hid Excalibur under a tree.

When he returned and said that he had tossed the sword into the lake, Arthur asked, "What did you see?"

"Only the deep waters, the dark waves, and the wind," Bedivere replied.

"Then you have not done what I asked you to do. Return to the lake, and throw the sword into it!"

Bedivere went back to the lake, but again could not bear the thought of tossing away an object of such great value. He left Excalibur under the tree.

When he said that he had tossed the sword into the lake, Arthur asked, "What did you see?"

"Nothing but the water lapping upon the shore and the dark waves," Bedivere replied.

"Now you have twice betrayed me!" King Arthur exclaimed. "Go quickly and do as I have asked you, for your delay is endangering my life. Already I feel cold. If you disobey my command this time, I shall kill you with my own hands!"

When Sir Bedivere approached the lake for the third time, he took Excalibur and threw it as far out into the water as he could. To his amazement, an arm rose out of the water and caught the sword in its hand. Three times the arm waved the gleaming sword aloft in the air; then, sword in hand, the arm withdrew into the water.

When the knight returned with this tale, King Arthur said, "Help me reach the lake, for I fear that I have stayed here too long."

So Bedivere carried the king to the edge of the lake. A rich ship, containing the Lady of the Lake and three fair queens, was waiting where the waves met the shore. The four women wore black hoods of mourning, and they wept and wailed as Bedivere brought Arthur aboard.

Bedivere watched as the queens rowed the ship out into the lake. "Farewell," King Arthur called. "I am going to Avalon, where I will be healed of my wound. Some day I will return to my kingdom and live among the Britons with great joy."

The last sounds the knight heard were the mournful sobbing and wailing of the queens on board the ship.

Sir Bedivere spent the night walking through the forest. The next morning he came upon a chapel near Glastonbury, where he saw a holy hermit praying beside a newly dug grave.

When he asked for whom the hermit was praying, the holy man replied, "Last night, at midnight, a number of ladies came here bearing a corpse, and they asked me to bury it. They gave me 100 candles and 100 gold coins."

"Alas!" exclaimed Bedivere. "That was my lord, King Arthur, whom you buried in this chapel. We have lost the best king who ever ruled Britain!"

When Queen Guinevere learned of the deaths of King Arthur, Sir Mordred, and their armies, she entered a convent and became a nun. She spent her days fasting, praying, and performing deeds for the poor. People marveled at how virtuous she had become.

By the time Sir Lancelot arrived in Britain to fight on the side of the king, Arthur and Mordred were both dead, and Queen Guinevere was in the convent at Almesbury. Lancelot visited the tomb of Sir Gawain, and then he set out to find Guinevere.

When he came to the convent, Guinevere said to the other nuns, "This man and I caused this terrible war and the deaths of the most noble knights in the world. Our love for each other caused my most noble lord, King Arthur, to be killed by Sir Mordred. "

Then Guinevere said to Lancelot, "I am determined to heal my soul of its sins. In the name of all the love we two shared, I ask you never to look upon my face again. Leave me now. Return to your kingdom across the sea, and work to keep war from destroying it. Take a wife, and live with her in joy and contentment. As much as I love you, I may not see you, for our love for each other has destroyed the flower of kings and knights. Pray for me, that I may be able to atone for my past life."

Lancelot replied, "My lady, you and you alone have been my earthly joy. If you were willing, I would now take you back to my kingdom to be my wife. But I will never marry anyone else. I have promised always to be true to you. I will turn away from the world as you have done, and I will always pray especially for you. I ask you to kiss me for the last time."

"No," Guinevere replied. "That I will not do."

Thus Sir Lancelot and Queen Guinevere parted. Even the hardest heart would have wept to see such pain in the noble knight and his noble lady.

Lancelot became a priest at the chapel where King Arthur was buried. There he served God by praying and fasting. One night a vision came to him and said, "Come to the convent at Almesbury, where you will find Queen Guinevere dead. Bury her beside her husband, the noble King Arthur."

Lancelot journeyed to the convent, where he found that Guinevere had died a few minutes earlier. He buried her next to her lord, the king. As Guinevere's body was lowered into the earth, Sir Lancelot wept. The holy hermit, feeling that it was inappropriate for a priest to lament the loss of his beloved lady, criticized his behavior.

Lancelot replied, "I trust that I do not displease God with the nature of my sorrow, for it is not sinful. When I saw King Arthur and Queen Guinevere lying together in their final earthly resting place, my heart overflowed with sorrow. I remembered her great beauty, and the nobility that she and her king both possessed. I remembered their kindness and my unkindness. I remembered how my pride and my fault destroyed both the king and his queen, who were without equal."

Thereafter, Lancelot took so little nourishment that he wasted away. Day and night he lay by the tomb of King Arthur and Queen Guinevere and prayed, and no one could comfort him. Finally, he died.

The body of Sir Lancelot was carried to his castle at Joyous Gard for burial. His brother gazed at his corpse and said, "Ah, Lancelot! You were the most courteous man who ever carried a shield. You were the kindest man who ever struck with a sword. You were the most courageous man who ever fought with the spear. You were the most loyal friend and truest lover who ever rode a horse. Truly, you were the greatest of all knights!"

So ends the story of King Arthur and his noble knights of the Round Table. Many people believe that King Arthur is still alive in Avalon and that, when Britain is in great peril, he will return and rescue his country.

The Far East and the Pacific Islands

The myths of the Far East and the Pacific Islands represent a number of different cultures and were recorded over a wide range of time. The earliest myths from India reflect the culture of the Aryan peoples who invaded the country in about 1500 B.C. Later the Hindus adopted and adapted some of these myths, among them the creation myth and the myth of Rama.

Most of the Chinese myths were recorded during the Han Dynasty (206 B.C.–A.D. 220). They are the earliest Chinese myths still in existence because in 213 B.C. the first emperor of China burned all books that were not about medicine or farming.

The Japanese crossed the Korea Strait into Japan during the early period of the Han dynasty. Much later, in the 8th century A.D., they recorded their myths. The epic *Kotan Utunnai* is a modern transcription of a myth of the aboriginal Ainu people, who were living in Japan when the Japanese arrived.

The Polynesian peoples migrated from Asia to Tahiti, and then from Tahiti to New Zealand, Hawaii, and other Pacific islands. The fate of Polynesian mythology was determined, island by island, by the interaction between a particular group of Polynesian people and particular Christian missionaries, many of whom arrived during the first quarter of the 19th century. Maori mythology shows little Western influence. However, many Hawaiian myths were changed or lost due to the missionaries' intervention in the native peoples' culture. The first collection of Polynesian (Maori) myths was published in the middle of the 19th century.

The creation myths of the Far East and Pacific Islands are quite distinct. Both the Indian and the Chinese creation myths begin with an egg, involve creating the universe from the body of a divinity, and explain the creation of human beings. However, the Indian myth, which is Hindu, involves regeneration and the cyclical nature of time. It sets forth four ages of man. The Japanese creation myth explains the creation of the Japanese islands. Its treatment of the relationship between men and women and its depiction of death give it special interest. The Maori creation myth emphasizes the development from nonbeing to thought to creation. In this myth the creation of the natural world reflects human nature, and New Zealand is created by a trickster-hero.

The four fertility myths are traditional in feeling. The Indian myth, which is pre-Hindu, the Chinese myth, and the Hawaiian myth all relate how a god, demigod, or mortal saves the world from a great threat. The Japanese myth involves a god of fertility who is insulted and must be appeased for fertility to be restored.

Each hero myth has its own special appeal. The Hindu *Ramayana* is one of the world's great epics. Not only is it a superb adventure story, but its emphasis upon responsibility and righteous behavior make us think about our own values. The Chinese myth is a delightful hero story, with appealing characters and a good plot. The Ainu epic from Japan is unusual in that its ancient, pristine quality gives it a primeval power.

Introducing **The Creation, Death, and Rebirth of the Universe**

Just as the Hindu religion accommodates a number of different religious views, it accepts a number of different creation myths. Vishnu, who was associated with the sun, and Rudra, who was associated with storms, existed as divinities before the Hindus elevated Vishnu to major importance and incorporated Rudra into Vishnu's destructive aspect. The following myth was probably written down sometime between A.D. 300 and 500, and it contains a number of elements that are distinctively Hindu.

First, the idea of reincarnation is a Hindu concept. The Hindu creation myth reveals Vishnu in three forms: as Brahma, the creator of life on earth; as Vishnu, the preserver of life on earth; and as Shiva-Rudra, the destroyer of life on earth. The myth also explains how Vishnu often descends to earth and becomes reincarnated as a human hero to protect gods and mortals against the forces of evil beings (demons).

The duty of each person to live according to his or her *dharma*, a definite pattern of righteous behavior dictated by that person's position in society, is also a Hindu concept. Vishnu establishes dharma as a way of preserving civilization. Without it society disintegrates, war results, and civilization brings destruction upon itself.

Finally, the unending cyclical nature of time and life is a Hindu concept. Creation is always re-creation, part of a cycle that has no beginning and no end. The universe progresses from birth to maturity to death to rebirth, over and over again. The four stages of life on earth progress from the ideal golden age to the dark age and back to the golden age, over and over again. Vishnu, in his three forms, directs the life cycle of the universe from creation to disintegration to dissolution to re-creation, over and over again.

Thus, in Hindu thought, a sense of unity and pattern remains at the foundation of all apparent differences. Vishnu creates, preserves, and destroys. His names change, and his roles change, but the great god remains the same. The golden age will inevitably disintegrate into the dark age, which in turn will inevitably lead back to the golden age.

Like the four ages of the Greeks, the Indian ages reveal the moral disintegration of society and show how people bring suffering upon themselves through their selfish and unjust treatment of one another. In each case, the ages become progressively worse. The last age is always a time of cruelty, pain, grief, and unnecessary death, and it is always the age in which the reader is living.

The Creation, Death, and Rebirth of the Universe

The world is created, destroyed, and re-created in an eternally repetitive series of cycles. It continuously moves from one Maha Yuga (great age) to the next, with each lasting for 4,320,000 years. Each Maha Yuga consists of a series of four shorter yugas, or ages, each of which is morally worse and of shorter duration than the age that preceded it.

The beginning of each Maha Yuga is the Krita Yuga, the age of virtue and moral perfection, a bright, golden age on earth. The great god Vishnu, in his form of Brahma, the grandfather and creator of the world, is the presiding god, and dharma (ideal, righteous behavior or moral duty) walks steadily and securely upon all four feet. The Krita Yuga lasts for 1,728,000 years. During this period, human beings need no shelters, whether they live in the mountains or by the sea. Gift-giving trees provide them with an abundant supply of food, clothing, and decorative objects. Everyone is born good and lives a happy, contented, unselfish, and beautiful life. People are devoted to meditation, the highest virtue, and spend their lives being loyal to dharma. They work for the pleasure of it, rather than from necessity. Sorrow does not exist.

The second age in each Maha Yuga is the Treta Yuga. *Treta* means three and refers to the fact that dharma now walks less steadily, on three of its four feet. Virtue and moral perfection still exist, but they have declined by one-fourth. The duration of the age has similarly declined by one-fourth. Vishnu, lord of heavenly light and the preserver of life on earth, is the presiding god. People are now devoted to the pursuit of knowledge, which they consider the highest virtue.

In the Treta Yuga the gift-giving trees supply food and clothing to everyone in abundance until greedy people try to make them their private property. Then the special trees disappear, and life on earth becomes difficult for the first time. Heavy rainfall creates rivers, and the mixture of earth and water makes the soil fertile for the growth of many new kinds of trees. Although the new trees bear fruit and are useful to human beings, they are ordinary trees rather than gift-giving trees. Therefore, people must work hard to acquire food and clothing. Because of the rain and severe changes in the weather, they also need to construct houses for shelter.

In the Treta Yuga people are more passionate and greedy. They are no longer happy with what they have. Dissatisfaction, resentment, and anger replace satisfaction, peace, and contentment in their hearts. They covet their neighbors' possessions. The strong take land from the weak in order to possess more food and greater wealth. Many men take the wives of others.

The third age in each Maha Yuga is called the Dvapara Yuga. *Dva* means two, and eternal dharma now totters unsteadily on two of its four feet, creating a precarious and shifting balance between good and evil. Virtue and moral perfection still exist, but they have declined to one-half what they were in the Krita Yuga. Correspondingly, the duration of this age is half that of the Krita Yuga. Vishnu, the preserver of life on earth, is still the presiding god, and people devote themselves to sacrifice, which they consider the highest virtue.

In the Dvapara Yuga, disease, misfortune, suffering, and death are part of everyone's existence; people have become more passionate and greedy, and war is commonplace. Religious doctrines are developed in an attempt to guide human behavior toward dharma, but the gradual process of moral deterioration continues.

The fourth age in each Maha Yuga is the Kali Yuga. This is the dark age, *kali* meaning quarrel and war. Dharma drags along on only one of its four feet, and virtue barely exists. This age is one-fourth the length of the golden Krita Yuga. The great god Vishnu is the presiding god, in his form of Shiva-Rudra, the destroyer of life on earth.

In the Kali Yuga people achieve noble rank in society based on the amount of money and property they own rather than their moral virtue. The quality of virtue is measured only in terms of material wealth. Sexual passion alone binds husband and wife together in marriage. People become successful in life through a succession of lies, and their only source of enjoyment is sex. They live with continuous fear of hunger, disease, and death.

In the Kali Yuga only the poor are honest, and the only remaining virtue is charity. To escape the oppression of greedy kings, a few people retreat to isolated mountain valleys. They clothe themselves with rough-hewn garments made from the leaves and bark of trees, and they live by gathering wild fruits and edible roots. Harsh weather and primitive living conditions make them prey to devastating illnesses. One who attains the age of twenty-three is considered very old.

Vishnu as Shiva-Rudra, Destroyer of Life on Earth

At the end of 1,000 Maha Yugas, which is one day of the life of the world, the great god Vishnu will adopt the form of Shiva-Rudra and will destroy all life on earth. He will usher in one night in the life of the world, a period lasting as long as the day. First he will enter the sun's rays and intensify them for 100 years, causing great heat to evaporate all water on the face of the earth. All three worlds — heaven, earth, and the Underworld — will burn up from this intense heat. The great drought and scorching fire will create a wasteland. Famine will stalk the universe, and by the time the 100-year period ends, no living creature will remain.

When the fires have consumed all life on the three worlds, Shiva-Rudra, the destructive form of Vishnu, will exhale dreadful storm clouds. Accompanied by terrifying thunder and lightning, these clouds will move across the face of the earth, obscuring the sun and cloaking the world in darkness. Day and night, for 100 years, a deluge of rain will pour forth until everything in the world has been buried beneath the deep waters of a devastating flood. Besides the desolate sea, only the great god Vishnu will continue to exist, for the fire and flood will have destroyed all of the other gods along with the rest of all life.

Just as the great flood begins to bury all life, a large golden egg will appear. This egg will contain the seeds of all forms of life that existed in the world before the flood. As the world drowns, the egg will float safely upon the waters of the boundless ocean.

When the ocean completely covers all three worlds, Vishnu will exhale a drying wind. For 100 years this wind will course across the world, dispersing the storm clouds. For the remainder of the 1,000 Maha Yugas, that night in the life of the world, Vishnu will sleep and the world will lie asleep also.

Vishnu as Brahma, Creator of Life on Earth

At the end of the long night of 1,000 Maha Yugas, Vishnu will awaken. A marvelous lotus flower will emerge from his navel, and Vishnu will emerge from the lotus flower in his creative form of Brahma, creator of life on earth. The lotus will become the foundation of the three worlds. Once he has emerged from the blossom, Brahma will rest upon it. Realizing that the flood has killed all life, Brahma will break open the egg to initiate the process of rebirth. Thus, as the god Brahma, Vishnu will usher in the next day in the life of the world, a new period of 1,000 Maha Yugas.

The image of all three worlds, complete with gods, demons, and human beings, exists within Brahma. First Brahma the creator will bring forth water, fire, air, wind, sky, and earth, with mountains and trees upon the earth. Then he will create the forms of time, as a way of organizing the universe.

Soon thereafter, Brahma will concentrate upon creating gods, demons, and human beings. First he will bring forth the demons from his buttocks. He will then cast off his body, creating the darkness we call night, which belongs to the enemies of the gods. Taking a second body, Brahma will bring forth the gods from his face. He will cast off this body as well, creating the lightness we call day, which belongs to the gods. From successive bodies, Brahma's powers of concentration will bring forth human beings and Rakshasas, snakes and birds. Then Brahma will bring forth goats from his mouth, sheep from his chest, cows from his stomach, antelope, buffalo, camels, donkeys, elephants, and other animals from his arms and legs, horses from his feet, and plant life from the hair on his body.

Thus the great god Vishnu exists eternally in his three forms. First he is Brahma, the grandfather and creator of the world. Then he is Vishnu, the preserver of life on earth. As Vishnu, he protects human beings with dharma, a code of civilized behavior, and often defends them from their greatest enemies by descending to earth and being born as a human being in order to help them. Finally he is Shiva-Rudra, the destroyer of life on earth.

Introducing **Indra and the Dragon**

When the Aryans invaded India from the northwest in about 1500 B.C., they brought their religious ideas into the land they conquered. This included a group of gods who personified the forces of nature—among them fire, rain, and wind. The conquest of India produced heroic leaders, such as Indra, whose accomplishments gave rise to a body of oral legend that was based partly on fact. Indra gradually became one of the great gods of ancient India, acquiring both the divine attributes of older gods and the heroic exploits of mythic characters.

Indra was the king of the gods and the defender of gods and humans before the Brahmans and the later Hindus elevated Vishnu to his supreme position. He was also associated with rain and the fertility of the soil. With his great weapon, the thunderbolt,

he destroyed demons who lived in darkness and created drought. Such heroic feats were necessary because India's soil was often very dry. Indra's role as a fertility god is evident in this myth, where he successfully fights the dragon and releases the seven rivers that make the earth fertile.

The earliest heroic exploits of Indra are celebrated in the Rig Veda, a collection of more than 1,000 mythic hymns, rituals, and treatises dedicated to the pre-Hindu group of gods. For hundreds of years following the period from 1500–1200 B.C., the Vedas were preserved through an oral tradition. Finally the myths were written down in Sanskrit, an Indo-European language that is closely related to Greek and Latin.

The Hindus revered the Vedas, but they also changed the roles of the gods to reflect their own developing religious tradition. They created the idea of reincarnation in about 700 B.C., and as their myths reveal, any god or hero could be an incarnation of any other god or hero. This concept united their new gods with the older tradition by making the later gods reincarnations of the earlier ones.

Centuries after the Rig Veda, the god Indra still exists in Hindu myth but as a shadow of his earlier self. In the Hindu epic *The Mahabharata* (written sometime between 300 B.C. and A.D. 300), Indra shows fear where once he showed courage, and the dragon he conquered in the earlier myth conquers him in the later myth. In the Hindu *Ramayana* (written between 200 B.C. and A.D. 200), Indra is still the king of the gods, but the demon, Ravana, has conquered him, and Vishnu, rather than Indra, is the defender of gods and humans. Indra's connection with rain is still evident, although he showers flower blossoms rather than raindrops.

Soma, the intoxicating beverage that gives Indra his great strength in the Rig Veda, had a very important role in later Hindu religious ritual. Priests sacrificed soma to preserve the strength of the gods. Hindus came to believe that without soma their gods would not have the strength to direct the cyclical progress of the world from one age to the next.

Indra and the Dragon

Indra, who carries the mighty thunderbolt in his hand, rules all that moves and all that rests, all that is aggressive and all that is peaceful. He alone rules the people of the earth as their king, enclosing them as the rim of a wheel encloses the spokes. Whenever they need him, he comes to their aid. I will speak of the god Indra's first heroic deed.

Long ago, a mighty dragon named Vritra lived upon the earth. This demon was the enemy of gods and humans alike. One day he swallowed the seven rivers of the earth and imprisoned them within his great mountain. Then he lay down on the mountaintop to guard the waters he had captured. Day and night he lay awake, prepared to defend his conquest against any being who challenged him.

The fiery sun rose each day as always. It burned the earth with its blazing rays. Trees, grass, and all forms of plant life gradually shriveled and died, for river water no longer supplied the moisture necessary for them to thrive upon the earth.

People prayed to the gods for help, but not one of the gods was strong enough to combat the great dragon-demon. As days passed, the gaunt and greedy figure of Famine began to stalk the land. More and more people were starving. At first they tried to buy food. Then they begged for food. Finally, in desperation, they cried for food. Their cries fell upon a great silence, for even the storehouses of the rich were empty, and scarcely a trace of food remained upon the earth.

Weak with hunger, the people fell upon the dry and barren earth and pleaded with the gods to heed their prayers. The gods gazed upon the earth with sorrow in their hearts, knowing that they were powerless against such a deadly foe as Vritra. But Indra was determined to help the dying humans. He was the youngest of the gods, but he intended to prove himself the bravest and strongest.

One by one, he picked up three bowls of soma, a sweet, intoxicating drink, and he drank them down. With each drink he became stronger and stronger. Finally Indra knew that he had become the mightiest of the gods. He took his great weapon, the deadly thunderbolt, in his right hand and set out to fight Vritra. He knew that he would find the dragon-demon reclining upon his mountaintop, watching and waiting for a god who would be courageous enough to attack him.

As Indra approached, the mighty dragon prepared for battle. Unlike the gods, Vritra had neither hands nor feet to defend himself, but his mouth terrified gods and humans alike. Inflamed with anger, the demon exhaled a foggy mist, shutting out the rays of the sun and shrouding the earth in blackness. Then he spewed forth blinding lightning, deafening thunder, and a cutting storm of hailstones.

To Vritra's surprise, Indra showed no fear of the dark. The lightning did not blind his eyes, the thunder did not threaten his ears, and the hailstones did not slash his skin. The young god calmly raised his deadly weapon, and when the dragon's next bolt of lightning illuminated the scene, Indra hurled his great thunderbolt at Vitra. The missile flew straight as an arrow and lodged firmly in the dragon's flesh.

The mighty blow crushed the demon's spirit and shattered his body with one stroke. The dragon tottered upon the mountain peak and then fell to the base far below, where he lay like the severed branches of a tree chopped from the trunk.

Vritra's mother came forth to avenge her son, but Indra was undaunted by the sight of another fearsome demon. He summoned his strength and hurled his mighty thunderbolt at her also, killing her as he had killed Vritra. She fell to the ground near her son, lying near him in death as a cow rests near her calf.

Indra now freed the imprisoned waters. With his deadly weapon he split apart the mountainside, opening the sealed outlet and releasing the seven rivers. The waters rushed straight down the mountainside and swept across the land to the sea, roaring as noisily as a herd of cows.

When the seven rivers once again flowed across the earth, moisture soaked through the parched soil of every land. Parched roots drank their fill and sent renewed life coursing through the trunks of dying trees. Greedy seeds sprouted, quickly growing into nourishing grasses. Thirsty humans drank their fill and lived to eat a new crop of life-sustaining plants. Famine retreated from the sight of plenty as a lion backs away from a pack of hungry wolves.

Indra, the brave god, confronted the great dragon Vritra in battle and won. Indra, the mighty bringer of rain, relieved the drought and restored the fertility of the earth. Indra, the supreme god, rescued those who walk the earth from certain death. Indra, who carries the mighty thunderbolt in his hand, rules all that moves and all that rests, all that is aggressive and all that is peaceful. He alone rules the people of the earth as their king, enclosing them as the rim of a wheel encloses the spokes. Whenever they need him, he comes to their aid.

Introducing **The Ramayana**

Historical Background

The Ramayana reflects the traditions of two politically powerful peoples, represented by Rama's family and Sita's family, who lived in northern India between 1200 and 1000 B.C. They were the most cultured of many cultured peoples who lived in India at that time. Their kings were as famous for their great learning as for their military skills. Their religious leaders founded universities of such high academic excellence that students came from other countries to attend them.

Scholars believe that *The Ramayana* was composed sometime between 200 B.C. and A.D. 200, with the last chapter added later, possibly as late as A.D. 400. The poet Valmiki, to whom this epic poem is attributed, is almost as vague a figure as Homer. He was probably born a Brahman and probably had some close association with the kings of Ayodhya. He collected the myths, songs, and legends about Rama and shaped them into a connected poetic narrative using meter and style of his own invention. The epic itself states that Valmiki is a contemporary of Rama's and contains an explanation of how Valmiki created *The Ramayana*.

Valmiki provides a window onto the ancient past. Through him we see the culture of the ancient Hindus. We see something of their political, social, and religious life, and we are introduced to their values. Valmiki viewed the period in which the poem is set as the Golden Age of India. Dasa-ratha is the ideal king of the ideal city. Rama is the ideal prince, and Sita is the ideal wife.

A direct relationship exists between *The Ramayana*, which is a moral epic, and the life and values of the ancient Hindus. Just as Rama spends fourteen years living as a hermit in the forest, so in ancient times, every Hindu boy from a religious home left his parents when he was very young in order to live with his teacher. For a period of twelve, twenty-four, or even thirty-six years, the young man lived a hard, simple life. He wore a garment made of rough cloth, went from door to door begging for food, and served his teacher as a menial servant. Endurance and suffering were as important a part of his training as traditional learning, for devotion to duty was the foundation of a righteous and successful life.

An interesting aspect of *The Ramayana* is the close relationship between human beings and animals. The monkey Hanuman is a great hero without whose help Rama would not have succeeded. Their partnership reflects the respect that the creators of the Rama myths and legends felt for other living creatures.

Appeal and Value

Like *The Iliad*, *The Ramayana* tells of the rescue of an abducted queen. Like *The Odyssey*, it tells of the adventures of a hero in the course of a long journey. As Odysseus is blown from one land to another during his journey from Troy to Ithaca, so Rama travels from northern to southern India and finally to Ceylon.

Certainly one reason for the lasting appeal of *The Ramayana* is that it is a superb adventure story. Its focus is the battle between the forces of good and the forces of evil. Heroes combat villains, magic adds interest, and humane, intelligent animals lend a very special flavor.

The Ramayana has had a phenomenal impact on its culture. It has molded the values of Indian society by presenting a variety of models for heroic human behavior to countless generations of people. For many centuries *The Ramayana* was a required part of every Indian child's education, since it provided moral instruction as part of an adventure story. The characters in *The Ramayana* have long served as models of proper behavior among Hindus. The person who based his or her actions under stress on what Rama or Sita would do in that situation could be sure of doing the right thing.

The Ramayana is still a living tradition and, for many, it is part of a living religious faith. Indian children are raised with stories from the epic. *The Ramayana*, whole or in part, is celebrated and dramatized in religious festivals and is the subject of books and movies.

Despite the fact that Rama, Sita, Lakshmana, and Bharata are ideal figures, they are still very appealing human beings. The ordeals that Rama and Sita endure so virtuously are exaggerated versions of the trials that ordinary men and women must face. Each serves as a role model for his or her sex and teaches the satisfaction to be found in devotion to one's duty and righteous behavior.

Contemporary readers can identify with Sita, Rama, and Rama's brothers. We all enjoy seeing people behave at their best under very difficult circumstances, for righteous behavior elevates the person and thus the human race. Like the ancient Hindus, we value love, friendship, loyalty, dedication, and perseverance. We too know how it feels to be jealous, envious, and greedy; we too experience grief and suffering. We are often called upon to act our best in difficult situations.

However, contemporary Western codes of behavior sometimes differ from those portrayed in *The Ramayana*. For example, some readers may find it incomprehensible that Rama renounces Sita because of her abduction by Ravana and that he banishes her for the same reason many years later.

The Ramayana centers on the love between husband and wife, with parental relationships and society's values operating as complicating factors. At the root of almost every incident are the affection and responsibility between two people: husband and wife, parent and child, two brothers, two friends, or, on a larger scale, the king and his subjects.

Because *The Ramayana* is a very personal story about people's emotions as they face their tasks and trials, its appeal is universal. Noble or peasant, ancient Indian or modern American, we all have the same basic needs and emotional responses.

The Hindu Hero

According to ancient Hindu tradition, each person should be loyal to dharma, or righteous behavior. A prescribed code of behavior exists for each role in life — king, queen, father, mother, son, daughter, brother, sister, friend. Therefore, each person knows what he or she ought to do in each situation that occurs. Conflicts between loyalties present problems, as always. However, suffering and sorrow are part of the righteous life, and each person must endure whatever life brings.

In ancient Hindu society, a wife's obligation is to dedicate her life to her husband. Her love must be pure and faithful, her devotion complete. The extent to which she can meet the ideal standard despite all trials and temptations determines her self-worth and the worth society accords her. The greater the challenge, the greater the success. If she meets the standards of her society despite a host of adverse circumstances, she is a great heroine.

To the ancient Hindus, a woman should not think of herself or function as an independent human being. Thus, in terms of her own tradition, Sita is one of the greatest females in literature. She represents the highest ideal of female love, devotion, and faithfulness, and Hindu society has loved her throughout the ages.

The obligation of the husband is more complex. He functions in a male-dominated culture and therefore has more responsibilities to fulfill, in society as well as at home. He is expected to remain devoted to duty while enduring trials and deprivation. Lakshmana is a great hero because he is a loyal brother and friend and an exceptional warrior. Reflecting his primary loyalty, he does not take his wife with him when he goes into exile with Rama. Similarly, Bharata feels a greater obligation to Rama, his brother, than to his father, his mother, or himself.

As the king, Rama has a special obligation to society. Kingship involves putting his responsibilities to his subjects ahead of his personal life. Because he is the model for proper behavior among his subjects, Rama's personal behavior must be beyond criticism. Therefore, to his dismay and grief, he must honor the attitudes of his subjects and obey their wishes — even when they are wrong.

The Rakshasas are the enemy, but they are not evil within their own society. While they feel free to indulge in violence and deception with outsiders, among themselves they have the same values as Rama's people do. They exhibit love and loyalty and are courageous and skillful in battle. Ravana is not a good king, because he puts his personal wishes before the needs of his subjects. Yet he is a great hero. His brother, Vibhishana, will be a good king.

The Role of the Gods

The gods in *The Ramayana* are immortal and powerful, but they are not omnipotent. The Hindu gods can be conquered by a skillful enough adversary. Thus, Ravana is able to wield great power.

Like the Greek and Sumerian gods, the Hindu gods come down to earth and interact with heroes but do not determine their behavior. Human beings bring their misfortunes upon themselves. In *The Ramayana* it is Sita's attitude that makes her abduction possible.

The heroes of *The Ramayana* are free to choose between proper and improper behavior, between good and evil. Their human natures often lead them to react with the passion of emotion rather than with cool reason, and that always brings unnecessary suffering. The Rakshasas are to be feared because they are evil and devious, and they can transform themselves into creatures of rare beauty. As such, they conquer good people through deception and temptation. Evil often comes disguised as good, and its temptation is always difficult to resist, whether a Rakshasa is at the root of it or not.

The Ramayana expresses the Hindu idea that a person's behavior in one life determines what happens to him or her in the next life. Thus, Sita wonders what evil she committed in a previous life to reap such suffering and sorrow in this life. The scene in which Rama and his brothers renounce life on earth and ascend to heaven reflects Hindu beliefs about the death of the righteous.

Principal Characters

DASA-RATHA: king of Kosala; father of Rama, Bharata, Lakshmana, and Satrughna

RAMA: one earthly form of Vishnu; eldest and favorite son of Dasa-ratha; brother of Bharata, Lakshmana, and Satrughna; husband of Sita

BHARATA: second earthly form of Vishnu; second son of Dasa-ratha; brother of Rama, Lakshmana, and Satrughna

LAKSHMANA: third earthly form of Vishnu; third son of Dasa-ratha; brother and companion of Rama; brother of Bharata and Satrughna

SATRUGHNA: fourth earthly form of Vishnu; youngest son of Dasa-ratha; brother and companion of Bharata; brother of Rama and Lakshmana

JANAKA: king of the Videhas; husband of Mother Earth; father of Sita

SITA: earthly form of Lakshmi, Vishnu's wife; daughter of Mother Earth and Janaka; wife of Rama

RAVANA: demon king of Lanka and the Rakshasas; enemy of both gods and mortals

MARICHA: Ravana's adviser; a Rakshasa demon

KUMBHA-KARNA: giant brother of Ravana; greatest Rakshasa warrior

VIBHISHANA: youngest and good brother of Ravana; king of Lanka and the Rakshasas after Ravana's death

SUGRIVA: monkey king who helps Rama fight Ravana

HANUMAN: son of the wind; great monkey hero who helps Rama

NARADA: great wise man who tells Valmiki the story of Rama's life

VALMIKI: hermit; poet who composes *The Ramayana*; teacher of Rama's twin sons

Principal Gods

INDRA: king of the gods; god of rain

VISHNU: preserver of life on earth

BRAHMA: Vishnu in the form of creator of life on earth

SHIVA: Vishnu in the form of destroyer of life on earth

LAKSHMI: goddess of beauty and good fortune; wife of Vishnu

MOTHER EARTH: mother of Sita

YAMA: lord of the dead

AGNI: god of fire

The Ramayana

Chapter 1

The god Vishnu, preserver of life on earth, descends to earth in order to kill Ravana, a monster who is an enemy of both gods and humans. Vishnu is reborn as the four sons of King Dasa-ratha: Rama, Bharata, Lakshmana, and Satrughna. Rama wins the hand of Sita, daughter of Mother Earth.

We sing of the way of Rama, the great hero. We sing of kings and queens, of humans and animals, of heroes and monsters who lived long ago. One wanted power and would do anything to acquire it. Others, when power was given to them, chose to reject it. We sing of love and loyalty and of courage and kindness in the face of jealousy, greed, and violence. We sing of trials and temptations and of sorrow and suffering, for these are part of devotion to duty and righteous behavior. Listen to our words and become wise, for this tale will reveal what is good, what is true, and what is beautiful.

In time of old a great king, Dasa-ratha, ruled his kingdom of Kosala from the capital city of Ayodhya. He had been born into the ancient Solar Race. As a human being and as a leader of his people, King Dasa-ratha outshone other men as the full moon outshines the stars. His city was known far and wide for the intelligence, righteousness, loyalty, generosity, self-restraint, piety, and happiness of its citizens. Dasa-ratha lacked only one thing: a son to rule the kingdom after his death.

The king had made many sacrifices, hoping that the gods would hear his fervent prayers and grant him a son. But all his prayers had been in vain. Finally he told his priests, "Sacrifice a horse to the gods above. Perhaps they will accept this greatest of all offerings and give me the son I long for."

So the priests set free for one year a magnificent horse, one that was lithe, graceful, and strong. When the horse returned, the wise men announced that King Dasa-ratha would become the father of four sons. These words fell sweetly upon the king's ears. His three wives beamed with delight, their faces shining like lotus flowers when they first open to the warmth of the sun's rays after many months of winter cold.

Meanwhile, the gods above were complaining to Brahma. "Ravana, the wicked Rakshasa king, is destroying us with his tyranny!" they exclaimed. "He wields unlimited power. You are to blame for our troubles, for you made Ravana immune to attack by either the gods or his own people. If you do not want this monster to control both heaven and earth, you had better devise some way to destroy him. Unless you act quickly, evil will triumph over good, and we will be ruined!"

Brahma, the grandfather and creator, replied, "It is true that Ravana asked me for protection from his own people and from every creature who lives above and below the earth, and that I gave him that gift. However, he very foolishly did not ask for protection from either humans or animals because he saw no threat from them. Therefore, by human and animal he will be killed. Just be patient, and you will see for yourselves!"

No sooner had Brahma spoken than the great god Vishnu, preserver of life on earth, joined the assembly. The gods honored and respected Vishnu as their great defense in time of need, so they pleaded with him for help. "Ravana, king of the Rakshasas, is terrorizing both heaven and earth!" they cried. "His evil ways know no end. Yet we are powerless to stop him. Only you can help us! Descend to the kingdom of Kosala and accept birth as King Dasa-ratha's four sons. As one man, you can destroy Ravana."

"This I will do," Vishnu replied. "My goddess-wife, Lakshmi, will accompany me and become my mortal wife on earth."

Vishnu changed himself into the form of a tiger and appeared to Dasa-ratha in the midst of the king's sacrificial fire. "King Dasa-ratha, tiger among men," Vishnu called from within the flames. "Brahma, the grandfather and creator, has sent me to you with this sacred rice and milk. Give it to your wives, and they will bear you sons."

So it came to pass that King Dasa-ratha's three wives gave birth to four sons, each of whom embodied Vishnu, preserver of life on earth. Rama was born first, Bharata second, then Lakshmana and Satrughna. The gods also created a band of monkeys whose courage, strength, and wisdom would help Vishnu destroy the wicked Ravana and the Rakshasas who supported him.

Rama and his three brothers became known for their virtue and their courage. Lakshmana was Rama's constant companion, while Satrughna always accompanied Bharata. In their sixteenth year, one of the great wise men said to King Dasa-ratha, "Most honored king, I request a gift from you."

"Ask whatever you wish, and it will be yours!" the king replied.

"Most honored king," the wise man replied, "I need your son Rama's help to fight Ravana and the Rakshasas. Without his aid, we cannot make our sacrifices. We have no hope of stopping the destructive acts of this monstrous creature and his demons!"

"Why do you ask for my Rama, when the gods can help you?" King Dasa-ratha asked.

"Unfortunately for all of us," the wise man exclaimed, "the gods are powerless against Ravana! He has already subdued all who live above and below the earth.

Only the best of men can destroy him, and Rama is that man. Do not worry. Your son will be successful!"

So Rama and Lakshmana set out to accompany the wise man with their father's blessing. Indra, king of the gods, smiled upon the young men as they set out with their bows in one hand and their swords at their sides. He poured down upon them a shower of blossoms, a great rain of flowers from the heavens.

When Rama had easily destroyed the troublesome Rakshasas, the wise man said to him, "Now accompany me, lion among men, to the sacrifice to be held by King Janaka. This great king is married to Mother Earth, and he possesses a marvelous bow, which the god Shiva, destroyer of life on earth, gave to his ancestor long ago. None of the gods above, none of the Rakshasas, and none of the kings and princes of the earth has been able to string it. I would like you to try it!"

When the king had told Rama and Lakshmana the history of the bow, he announced, "Whoever can bend and string my mighty bow of war, long prized by kings of this land, will win my daughter Sita, child of Mother Earth. This child, the light of my life, arose from the soil one day as I plowed and blessed my field. Many men of fame have tried to conquer the bow and win my daughter, but in vain. Rama, I now offer that trial to you. If you succeed, Sita, the most fair and virtuous of women, will become your wife."

"Most honored king," Rama replied, "it is my pleasure to accept your invitation and to try my hands upon your mighty bow. To win your glorious daughter would be the greatest of honors! "

Word quickly spread far and wide that the great prince Rama had agreed to test himself against King Janaka's mighty bow. Kings, chiefs, famous warriors, noble suitors, and ordinary people from many nations gathered at Janaka's palace to witness the event.

Janaka's mighty bow was indeed great. It took the king's strongest lords and warriors, working together, to pull the weapon slowly forth on an eight-wheeled iron chariot.

Rama lifted the cover of the bow case and admired the awesome weapon of war. "With your permission," he said to the wise man, "I will place my hands upon this bow. Then I will lift and bend this greatest of weapons."

The wise man and King Janaka replied, "May it be so!"

Rama lifted the great bow from its case with ease and grace. He bent and strung it as if it were as supple as a leaf. Then he took the stance of the archer and drew the bow, but the strain was more than the wood could bear. It snapped in two with a clap like the roar of thunder. The earth quaked, and the hills resounded. So terrifying was this sudden sound that kings, and warriors — everyone except Rama, Lakshmana, Janaka, and the wise man — fell cowering to the ground.

King Janaka said to the wise man, "My old eyes have seen Rama perform this marvelous deed. It brings me special pleasure to know that my peerless daughter will wed the godlike son of King Dasa-ratha. I will be true to my promise, for Sita has been fairly won by a man whom no one can surpass in valor and in worth."

As Rama and Sita stood together to take the sacred marriage vows, King Janaka said, "Rama, this is my child, Sita, who is dearer than life to me. From this moment on she will be your faithful wife. She will share your virtue, your prosperity, and your sorrow. Cherish her in joy and in grief. No matter where life takes you, she will follow like your shadow, and she will be with you in death as in life." The king, tearful in his joy, sprinkled holy water upon the bridal couple.

Then King Janaka married Lakshmana to Sita's sister and Bharata and Satrughna to two other beautiful maidens. Indra, king of the gods, smiled as the four couples walked around the sacred fire celebrating their weddings. He poured down upon them a shower of blossoms, a great rain of flowers from the heavens.

So Rama married Sita, queen of beauty, who was as faithful and devoted as she was beautiful.

Chapter 2

King Dasa-ratha plans to give his kingdom to Rama,
but Bharata's mother forces him to give it to her son
instead. Rama is banished from Ayodhya for fourteen
years. Sita and Lakshmana accompany him on his
journey.

Of King Dasa-Ratha's four sons, Rama was the dearest to his father and to all the people of Ayodhya. He was the ideal male figure: loyal, devoted, even-tempered, trained in all the arts of peace and war, and kind to all. When the king sent his gentle second son, Bharata, to live with his grandfather for a year, Satrughna, the king's youngest son, accompanied him.

During their absence, Dasa-ratha thought, "I will give up my throne to Rama, for I am old and no longer possess the strength I had in my younger days. What is best for me is surely best for my subjects as well. I will end my days in ease, and since Rama is unmatched in virtue and valor, Ayodhya and the kingdom of Kosala will prosper under his rule."

The king then called the leaders of his country to council: chiefs, princes, and leaders of the ariny. His voice pealed like thunder as he announced, "I have cared for my people as a father cares for his children, without excessive pride and without anger. Now, in the evening of my life, I am very tired. Honoring royal obligations and carrying out the laws of our land require more strength and skill than I now possess. I hope that you will accept my son Rama in my place. Rama combines the courage of Indra, king of the gods, with the knowledge of sacred lore of a wise priest. Among those who walk the earth, he has no equal!"

The king's subjects applauded his announcement with such enthusiasm that the sky above and the ground below trembled with their joyous acclaim. "We would see Rama seated on your revered throne, for his heart is blessed with valor, his words and deeds show virtue, his love of truth and loyalty to dharma are un-surpassed. He is our father in time of peace and our protector in time of war. He towers above those who walk the earth as Indra towers above the gods in the heavens. He is as forgiving as Mother Earth."

So the city of Ayodhya prepared to celebrate Rama's coronation. Flags and banners proclaimed the event. Actors, dancers, and musicians entertained the gathered throngs of citizens from all parts of the kingdom.

Rama entered the assembly as beautiful as a full moon in the autumn sky. King Dasa-ratha seated him on his throne and counseled, "Rama, dearest and most honored of my sons, tomorrow you will be crowned king. You must be even more dedicated and virtuous than you already are. You must practice restraint in all things. You must be just to everyone. You must maintain the military might and the wealth of our nation. My heart is content knowing that I am leaving my subjects and my kingdom in your hands."

Rama returned to Sita and Lakshmana. To Sita he said, "We must prepare for our sacred fast." To Lakshmana he said, "Prepare to rule Mother Earth with me, for my good fortune is always yours as well. I value my life and my kingdom only because of you."

Not everyone, however, was happy with King Dasa-ratha's decision. Bharata's mother was watching the festivities with a mother's joy when her nursemaid placed deep and deadly thoughts in her heart.

"Why are you so happy when this is your time of greatest sorrow?" the nurse-maid asked. "Another queen's son has won the throne, not your son. Yet your son is the better of the two, being unmatched in merit and in fame. Because Rama fears Bharata's virtue and valor, he will spring upon his brother like a wolf and tear him to pieces! And Rama's mother and his wife will treat you and Bharata's wife as bond-slaves!"

Bharata's mother replied, "You speak wicked words, woman! Rama is as dear as Bharata to me. He loves his brothers as he loves himself, and he will protect them as a father protects his sons. King Dasa-ratha is obligated by ancient custom and the law of the land to leave his throne to the oldest and best of his sons, and that son is Rama. My Bharata will rule after Rama because he is younger."

"You must be blinded by madness, my fair queen!" the nursemaid responded. "Rama's son, not Bharata, will inherit the throne. Brothers do not divide their reign. In fact, once Rama is king, he will force your son to wander from land to land, alone and friendless. Bharata will be a man without a home and without a country!

"Trust your old nurse!" she continued. "I have lived long years, and I have seen many dark deeds performed in the most noble of palaces. Rama's allegiance is to Lakshmana, not to Bharata. Your son has already been ordered to leave the kingdom. You must save his life! Speak to your husband before it is too late. Otherwise, Rama will force Bharata to serve him and will hate Bharata if he refuses."

The nursemaid's words seeped into Bharata's mother's heart like a serpent's deadly poison, awakening her jealousy and her fears for her child. She entered the room reserved for mourning the death of loved ones, and there she lay upon the cold ground and wept. The old king found her lying there like a blossoming vine that has been uprooted. The sight of such sadness sorely distressed him, for he loved his young wife more than his own life.

"Why do you lie here in tears?" he asked. "Are you suffering from some sickness? Has someone insulted you? Speak, and your words will dissolve your anger as the sun's rays melt the winter snows. My great love for you gives you great power. I promise you that my court and I will obey your wishes, whatever they may be!"

The love-blinded king thus gave his sacred oath to the jealous queen. The sun, moon, and stars, the earth, and the household gods heard King Dasa-ratha's words. As he was an honorable man, his promise was unbreakable.

His wife began, "Years ago, when the Rakshasas sorely wounded you, I cared for you and saved your life. In gratitude, you granted me two rewards. I did not ask for them then, but I do now. If you will not honor them, I will die! First, let Bharata be crowned king in place of Rama. Second, make Rama live as a hermit in the wild forestlands for fourteen years. These are the rewards I now claim from you. I will be satisfied with nothing less!"

The aged king could not believe his ears. "This must be a monstrous dream!" he exclaimed. Then anger dried his tears, and he said to his young wife, "You are a traitor to me and to your family! What cause can you possibly have to hate a son who loves you as a mother? I feel as if I have been harboring a poisonous snake in my palace!

"Banish my wives, if you will," the old king continued. "Take my kingdom and my life from me, if you insist. But do not make me part with my son Rama! The world can continue to turn without the light of the sun. The harvests can survive without the moisture the rains bring. But I cannot survive without Rama! I am an old man, and I am weak. I do not have long to live. Be kind to me, dear wife! Ask for cities; ask for land; ask for treasure. But do not ask for Rama. Do not force me to break my sacred word to my son and to my people. That would be the greatest of crimes!"

The queen replied, "If you, who have always been known for your honesty and your virtue, break your sacred word to me, the world will know how poorly you rewarded the loyal, loving wife who saved your life. The world will know that you caused me to die of a broken heart. I demand kingship for Bharata and banishment for Rama. I will accept nothing less!"

On the following morning — the day of the coronation — Rama, accompanied as always by Lakshmana, approached his father. He found Bharata's mother sitting at the king's side. King Dasa-ratha was so sad of heart that he could speak nothing more than Rama's name. Rama asked, "Mother, what have I done to cause my father such distress? Why do tears glisten upon his cheeks? Is Bharata all right?"

Bharata's mother calmly replied, "The only pain grieving your father is that he cannot bring himself to tell you the bad tidings. Many years ago, he gave me his royal promise. Now, because of his great love for you, he would break it if he could. Yet you know that King Dasa-ratha cannot break his sacred word. If you are a true and righteous son, you will be loyal to dharma. Prove your virtue by holding your father to the vow that, in time long past, he made to me."

Rama exclaimed, "Tell me what I must do. I will obey my father even if he wishes me to drink poison and die!"

"If you would save your father's honor, act upon your words. Leave here immediately and live in the wild forestlands as a hermit for the next fourteen years. Wear your hair matted and clothe your body with the skins of animals and the bark of trees. My son, Bharata, will return to Ayodhya and rule your father's kingdom in your place."

Rama accepted these words with a calm heart. He was neither sad nor angry. "I hope that my journey will bring peace to your heart, Father," he replied. "Send for Bharata; I will leave as soon as I have seen Sita and my mother."

As the two brothers left the hall, the young and loyal Lakshmana gave vent to his rage. "Why should you let Bharata's mother destroy your life? Our father surely suffers the illness of old age to let her rule him in matters of state! Fight for your rightful title, and I will stand at your side!"

"No, Lakshmana," Rama replied. "I have no wish to rule our father's kingdom under these circumstances. Other men in our family have had difficult tasks placed before them. Surely this time in the forest is part of my destiny. I will live my life with honor, obeying my father as a good son is expected to do. That is the way of dharma."

Rama then told his mother and Sita, "Remain here in peace while I am in the wild forest. Mother, no matter how unhappy you are, your place is with my father. If you leave him to accompany me, he will die. Sita, I want you to watch over my mother. Love Bharata and Satrughna as your brothers, for they are dearer to me than my life."

The gentle and devoted Sita replied, "Just as your mother's place is with your father, so my place is with you! What is the moon without its light? A flower without its blossom? A lute without its strings? A chariot without its wheels? Without you I am nothing! Fine clothes, rich food, and palace comforts are nothing! Your banishment will be mine as well. The berries and roots that will sustain you, will nourish me. The beauty of the forest will bring joy to our eyes, and I will fear neither fierce wild animals nor the hard life of a hermit. As long as I am by your side, I will not count the years!"

"I too will accompany you!" Lakshmana exclaimed. "I am happy and content if I can be wherever you are. It will be my pleasure to find the forest paths and to gather food. How bad can exile be when we are together?"

So Rama, Lakshmana, and Sita went into exile. King Dasa-ratha angrily left Bharata's mother to herself and took comfort in Rama's mother. On the evening of the fifth day of Rama's journey, the old king's heart could no longer bear its burden of grief, and he died. Then sorrow flowed over the land, for without a king a kingdom is like a river without water, a meadow without grass, or a herd of cattle with no one to herd them. The people feared for their safety and their well-being, so the palace officials sent for Bharata.

Chapter 3

Bharata learns of his mother's treachery and tries to convince Rama to return, but Rama refuses. A wise man gives Rama weapons of the gods. Ravana's sister becomes infatuated with Rama, and when he rejects her, a Rakshasa army attacks him. Rama manages to kill the entire army.

On the seventh day Bharata, accompanied as always by Satrughna, arrived in the city of Ayodhya and immediately went to see his mother. He grieved to hear of his father's death. "Where is Rama?" he asked his mother. "To me Rama is father, brother, and friend. It brings me joy to serve him."

Bharata's mother told her son the truth about Rama's departure, for she expected him to be pleased with his good fortune. To her surprise and dismay, Bharata was furious.

"If it were not for Rama's love for you, I would renounce you as my mother!" he exclaimed. "In spite of your treacherous designs, I will not rule my father's kingdom! It is too great a task for me, and the kingdom is Rama's to rule. I will search the broad forestlands for Rama. And once I have found him, I will bring him home to rule as is his right.

"As for you," Bharata continued, "your fate will bring you misery both in this life and in your life to come. You deserve to be banished, or hanged, or burned for your dreadful deed!"

Bharata refused the throne when it was formally offered to him. Instead, he and Satrughna gathered together a huge host of nobles, cavalry, learned men, and traders and led them through the wild forestlands in search of Rama. In the course of the journey, they encountered a wise man who said to Bharata, "Each man's destiny takes him along strange and unforeseen paths. Do not blame your mother for Rama's banishment. His exile is destined to benefit both humans and gods alike. Be patient, and remain true to dharma."

Finally Bharata and his companions found Rama. Bharata wept when he found his brother living with Sita and Lakshmana in a leaf-thatched hut and dressed in clothing made of deerskin and bark. Yet in spite of his simple manner of living, with his mighty arms and lion-like shoulders, Rama seemed like Brahma, the grandfather and creator of the wide earth.

"Are you that Rama, prince among men, whose people placed him on the throne of Ayodyha to rule the kingdom of Kosala?" Bharata asked him. "You have exchanged your luxurious robes for forest leaves and animal skins, and you have left your palace for the solitary life of a hermit. The very sight of you fills my heart with sadness!"

Rama embraced Bharata and Satrughna and lovingly welcomed them into his simple home. Then he asked, "Bharata, why have you sought me in my forest dwelling? Tell me, did our father ask you to come? Is he well? Do our warriors guard our kingdom as they should? Do the king's counselors serve him as they should? Surely some serious matter has moved you to undertake this long and difficult journey into the wilderness to find me!"

Bharata tearfully replied, "Rama, our father is dead! He walks the paths of heaven now instead of earth. His death has brought my mother to her senses and made her ashamed of her treacherous deed. I have come to ask you to return with me to Ayodhya and rule the kingdom of Kosala as the eldest son of King Dasa-ratha should. It is your duty according to the ancient law of our land. Besides, I need you! You are not only my brother; you are my father and my teacher."

Rama replied, "Bharata, I cannot return with you to Ayodhya, no matter how you plead with me to do so. I cannot claim the throne of our kingdom, for I cannot disobey the command of my father and king. Even though he is dead, I cannot break the promise that I made to him.

"And, Bharata, have kindness in your heart for your mother. She is not to blame for my exile. As for you, you must rule our kingdom and protect our people during my years in these wild forestlands. That is the way of dharma. As a dutiful son, you also must obey our father's wishes."

Rama concluded, "You must remember to care for the ordinary people in our country. Think of the herders who tend their cattle and the farmers who work their land. Make certain our soldiers guard our borders. Guard our nation's great treasure. Give gifts of food and wealth to all who are worthy, not just to the nobles. Always rule with justice, defending those who are innocent, no matter who they happen to be."

Bharata replied, "Rama, in truth, I cannot rule your kingdom. Our people look to you, not me, as their leader."

"Nonsense!" Rama exclaimed. "You possess the virtue and the strength to rule an empire that is as great as the world. Surely, then, you can rule the kingdom of Kosala. Our father's trusted counselors will advise and guide you.

"As for me," Rama concluded, "I am as firm in my resolve as a great rock. Your pleas, no matter how eloquent, cannot move me. The pleas of your entire company cannot move me. The moon may lose its glow and the mountains may lose their snow, but I cannot forget my promise to our father."

"So be it, then," Bharata replied. "Give me your golden sandals. I will place them upon the throne of Ayodhya to rule in your absence. They will give me the courage and the will to keep our kingdom for you. As for me, I will spend the next fourteen years as a hermit, even though I live in the royal palace. I will dress and eat as you do. If you do not return at the end of that period, I intend to die in the flames of a funeral pyre."

"So be it," Rama replied. "Take my sandals, then, and return to Ayodhya with Satrughna and your companions. We will meet again in fourteen years. You have my respect, my love, and my friendship."

So the ever-true Bharata and the righteous Rama parted. At first Rama wandered from place to place in the pathless forest, accompanied by his faithful Sita and his loyal Lakshmana. He met many of the holy hermits who lived within its dark shelter. To many people, the endless forest seemed nothing more than a dark, gloomy, and fearsome wilderness. But within its trackless depths Rama and his companions, like the holy hermits, found purity and peace. Ripe, wild fruits hung from broad, bending trees. The fragrant lotus and the lily rested on quiet inland waters. Drops of sunlight glittered upon lush, green leaves that sheltered grazing deer. Both day and night, the air was alive with the songs of birds.

In the course of their wanderings, Rama and his family came upon a mighty wise man, one of the holy hermits who also made the wild forestlands his home. "Rama," he said, "you are a hero, but even in this forest you will need weapons of war. Here is Vishnu's bow. Take it with you, for it is truly a wondrous weapon that was shaped in the heavens. Here is Brahma's shining arrow. In the hands of a good bowman, it will never miss its target. Here is Indra's large quiver filled with sharp-tipped arrows. They will never fail you in battle. Finally, take this case of burnished gold. Within it rests a sword with a golden hilt that should belong to a valiant warrior and a king.

"The enemies of the gods," the hermit continued, "know and fear these great weapons. So make them your constant companions because you will need them often. Here in the peaceful forest you will meet Rakshasas, those evil hunters who haunt the forest ways at night. Only you can defend us from those who disturb our prayers and defile our holy shrines. Even here, a hero will find deeds of honor to perform."

"Thank you, respected sage," Rama replied. "You have blessed my exile with your kindness and your friendship."

Rama, Sita, and Lakshmana lived in the forest for ten years, defending the hermits against the attacks of the Rakshasas who hunted in the night. The young and valiant Lakshmana built a comfortable house of bamboo and leaves for them in an area where food was plentiful. Their clearing was surrounded by date palms and mango trees. Nearby, a river teemed with fish and the forest with deer. Both fragrant lotus flowers and ducks made their home upon a beautiful, small lake.

All was well until the sister of Ravana, king of the Rakshasas, came upon Rama's forest home, observed Rama, and fell in love with him. "Who are you," she asked Rama, "dressed like a hermit, yet armed with a mighty bow? Why do you live in a lonely house in this dark forest where the Rakshasas are accustomed to having their way?"

When Rama had explained the nature of his stay in the forest, he asked the maiden about herself. She replied, "Ravana, king of Lanka, is one of my brothers. I usually wander through this forest with my brothers, but my love for you has caused me to leave them to their own pursuits. My kingdom is broad and boundless, so you should feel honored that I have chosen you to be my husband and my lord. Put your human wife aside; she is not as worthy a companion for you as I am! Rakshasas feed on human flesh. With no effort at all, I can kill your wife and your brother. Compared to the Rakshasas, humans are weak, fragile, puny beings."

Rama repressed a smile, but he could not resist teasing the brash maiden. "You do not want a married man for your husband," he replied. "Instead, you should consider my brother, Lakshmana. You see no wife of his in this forest home of ours!"

When Ravana's sister approached Lakshmana, he smiled and rejected her advances. "You certainly would not be satisfied with me!" he exclaimed. "I am Rama's slave. Given your royal birth, you would not become the wife of a slave, would you?"

These words caused unrequited passion to unite with wounded pride, igniting a blazing rage in the maiden's heart. "You insult me, Rama, by not treating my feelings seriously," she announced. "That is very foolish of you! Apparently you have not felt the fury and wrath of an injured Rakshasa. No female will live as my rival!" Like a demon of destruction, she moved to attack Sita, who fell to the ground shuddering with terror.

Rama placed himself between his wife and the savage maiden. "I was wrong to treat any Rakshasa lightly," he said to Lakshmana. "My humor provoked this danger, and now we must deal with this shameless female as best we can."

Lakshmana wasted no time with words. The threats of the Rakshasa struck like lightning in his heart. He quickly raised his sword and sliced off the maiden's ears and nose before she could defend herself. Her cries of anguish tore through the forest as she fled to her brothers.

With only one glance at their sister's bloody face, they sent a group of fourteen Rakshasas to avenge her. Rama raised his mighty bow and killed them all with his arrows. With mounting fury, the maiden's brothers then assembled a force of 14,000 Rakshasas, each as cruel as he was courageous.

Rama ordered Lakshmana and Sita to take refuge in a well-concealed cave. He was determined to protect them and to fight the enemy alone, so he put on his armor and waited for the Rakshasas to arrive. Many of the gods in heaven came down to earth to watch the battle.

Like the waves of the ocean, the 14,000 Rakshasas attacked Rama. The gods fled at the sight of them. Rama, however, stood firm, without fear in his heart. Like stinging raindrops in a raging storm, his arrows fell upon the Rakshasa warriors. In return, the Rakshasas dislodged mature trees and mighty boulders and hurled them upon Rama. But even these missiles could not stop the defender of the earth. He killed all 14,000 demons, leaving alive only their leader, one of Ravana's brothers.

Rama and the Rakshasa leader then faced one another in a fight to the death. They fought long and hard, like a lion against an elephant. Finally Rama triumphed and the Rakshasa leader lay lifeless upon the bloody earth. The forest floor was strewn with the bodies of the enemy host.

Indra, king of the gods, smiled upon Rama. He poured down upon him a shower of blossoms, a great rain of flowers from the heavens.

Chapter 4

Ravana is determined to capture Sita. His adviser, Maricha, devises the deception that makes it possible. After Sita is captured, Rama seeks the help of the monkeys to find her. When the monkey Hanuman learns where she is, Rama and the monkeys set out to kill Ravana and rescue Sita.

When Ravana heard of the death of his brother and the total destruction of his army, he became determined to destroy Rama by capturing Sita. His adviser, Maricha, objected to his plan. "If you provoke Rama, you will destroy your city of Lanka and every Rakshasa in your kingdom!"

"You speak of an empty threat," Ravana replied. "Rama is but a man, and all men are easy prey for a Rakshasa. You must either help me or forfeit your life. I have no use for cowards in my kingdom!"

So Maricha devised a plan to capture Sita by deceptive means. He transformed himself into a beautiful golden and silver deer, with antlers of sapphire and skin as soft as the petals of a flower. He wandered in the forest near Rama's house until Sita noticed him.

When the gentle Sita saw the beautiful creature, she was as enthralled as Maricha had hoped. "Please, Rama," Sita begged. "Follow that deer and capture it for me. I long to have it for my companion, or if you must kill it, I will cherish its shining hide as a golden and silver carpet. I have seen many graceful creatures roaming the forest ways, beautiful antelope and frolicsome monkeys, but never have I seen such a one as this deer! Its beauty illuminates the forest as the moon lights up the sky."

"Beware, Rama!" Lakshmana warned. "No real deer possesses such beauty. This creature must be a Rakshasa in disguise! Their ability to change their shape makes them a treacherous foe. Remember how quick they are to slaughter unwary victims." Thus he prevailed upon Sita to view the animal in its true light.

"On the contrary, Lakshmana," Rama replied, "if this creature is really a Rakshasa, then I feel obligated to kill it before it threatens us. Guard Sita in my absence. I will not be gone long, and I will bring Sita that star-studded deerskin."

Maricha led Rama on a long, tiresome chase through the deep forest. Finally he came within bowshot and killed the creature with an arrow. As Maricha lay dying, he resumed his own shape. Making one last attempt to help Ravana, he disguised his voice as Rama's and called out, "Lakshmana! Help me! I am dying, helpless, in this forest!"

Rama heard these words with a sense of terror and impending doom. He immediately set out for home, painfully aware of the long distance he had to travel.

"Lakshmana," Sita asked, "did you hear Rama's cry? You must go, right now, to help him. What a fool I was to send my dear lord after that deer! If blood-thirsty Rakshasas have found him, they will slaughter him as raging lions slaughter even a fearsome bull."

"It must be some clever Rakshasa trick," Lakshmana protested. "No one in heaven or earth or the netherworld can conquer Rama! Besides, I gave my word that I would guard you from all danger."

"You must be a wicked monster of a man!" Sita replied angrily. "You only pretend to be compassionate. Your heart is as callous as a stone! You cannot love Rama as much as you claim if you will not go to his aid when he needs you."

"All right, Sita. I will do as you wish, although I fear the outcome. A clever trick has clouded your mind. I do not deserve the dishonor you cast upon me. May the guardian spirits of the forest protect you in my absence, and may I soon see Rama by your side!"

Ravana, who was secretly watching nearby, bided his time. Changing himself into a holy hermit, he appeared before Sita with a staff in one hand and a beggar's bowl in the other. As leafy trees conceal a deep, dark cave, so Ravana's disguise artfully concealed his evil purpose. However, all of nature knew what Sita could not sense. Aware of Ravana's dark plans, the fragrant forest breeze ceased to blow, and the trees stood like silent sentinels. No sound of any kind could be heard.

Beneath his pious exterior, Ravana gazed upon Sita with illicit passion. Even in her simple clothing, Rama's queen illuminated her forest home as the moon's silver rays illuminate a starless sky. He spoke of her great beauty with flattering eloquence. Then he said, "Why do you live in this lonesome forest, where dangerous beasts wander and terrifying Rakshasas haunt the gloomy woodland? Your beauty deserves silken robes instead of leafy garments, a palace instead of the trackless forest, and thousands of servants instead of none.

"Choose a royal suitor," Ravana concluded, "a king and a mighty hero, who will treat you with the attention you deserve! I am not the pious hermit that I appear to be. I am Ravana, king of Lanka and the fearsome Rakshasas. My courage and skill have made me ruler of both the heavens and the wide earth. I have many lovely wives, but your beauty has so won my heart that I offer to share my glory and my empire with you alone!"

The faithful Sita angrily replied, "My husband is Rama, a lion among men! Why should the woman who has his love desire yours? In valor and virtue, in word and deed, Rama shines with the brightness of the full moon. You could sooner tear a tooth from the mouth of a hungry lion as it feeds upon a calf, touch the fang of a deadly serpent as it reaches for its victim, uproot a majestic mountain as it stands rooted in rock, than you could win the wife of the righteous and mighty Rama!"

Sita's words did not deter Ravana. Resuming his monstrous shape, he grabbed her hair in one hand and her body in the other. He carried his prisoner to his golden chariot and away through the sky to his distant kingdom.

"Rama! Rama!" Sita cried to the dark forest below. "Save me! Attack the evil Ravana who assaults your faithful wife! Lakshmana, save me from Ravana! Your warning was true, and my charge against you was false. Forgive me! Oh you towering mountains and wooded hills, tell Rama of my abduction."

While all of nature grieved for Sita, Brahma, in the heavens above, was delighted. "Now Ravana surely will die!" the grandfather and creator exclaimed.

Gentle Sita, scanning the land below for some sign of life, spied a group of monkeys sitting on a mountain peak. Secretly, she threw down to them her jewels and her golden veil in the hope that Rama would somehow find her tokens and learn of her fate.

When Rama returned to his house with Lakshmana, whom he had met along the way, his worst fears were realized. Tirelessly the two brothers searched the forests, the mountains, and the plains for Rama's beloved wife without success. In the course of their journey, they mortally wounded a Rakshasa who said, "You will find Sita if you enlist the aid of Sugriva, the great monkey king, and his band. They too can change their shapes, and they know where to locate every demon."

So Rama sought Sugriva, king of the monkeys. "Rama," the monkey king said, "We do not know where Ravana lives, but we do know that he has captured Sita. We were sitting on a mountaintop when Ravana's chariot passed overhead, and Sita dropped these tokens down to us." Sugriva handed Rama Sita's golden veil and her jewels.

Once Rama held Sita's possessions in his hands, joy brightened his face as the light of the full moon illuminates the midnight sky. "Can you and your people help me find her, Sugriva?" he asked.

"We can certainly try!" the monkey king replied. "I will summon the monkeys from all over the earth. We will divide the earth into four quarters and send one-fourth of the monkeys searching in each direction. I place my greatest hope in the ability of Hanuman, son of the wind. He is strong enough to leap into the heavens and to reach every place on earth, and his courage and intelligence are as great as his strength."

Hanuman, who was standing next to Sugriva, grinned with delight at the praise. "If anyone can find Sita, I can!" he assured Rama. "As a child, I leaped 9,000 miles into the heavens because I hoped to pull down the sun as if it were a ripe fruit swinging on the branch of a tree. Brahma, the grandfather and creator, has made me invincible. Indra, king of the gods, has given me the power to choose my own death. Surely I am the one to perform this heroic deed!"

Hanuman's words caused hope to shine in Rama's eyes as the evening journey of the sun causes the stars to glow in the heavens. "I too feel certain that, if Sita is still alive, you will be able to find her," Rama said. "If your search is successful, Hanuman, show Sita this signet ring of mine. It will make her trust you, and it will remind her of my great love for her."

The monkey band divided into four groups and set out to search the earth for Sita. Hanuman's band was in charge of the southern quarter. They learned that Ravana lived in Lanka, an island that lay on the other side of an ocean 300 miles wide. The broad sea stopped all of the monkeys except Hanuman himself.

Using his extraordinary strength, Hanuman leaped over the great body of water. He glided gracefully across the heavens as a duck moves smoothly upon the water, landing safely and energetically upon the far shore. He rested until the evening journey of the sun brought darkness upon the land.

Then, in order to perform his secret mission, the monkey transformed himself into a cat. In this inconspicuous form, Hanuman entered the golden-walled city and prowled the streets until he learned that Ravana's palace was located on a mountaintop. Again, protective walls were no deterrent. However, no matter where he looked, Hanuman could find no sign of the gentle Sita. He finally returned to the wall of the city and sat down to consider what he should do.

"I hope the Rakshasas have not killed and eaten Sita!" the monkey king thought. "I cannot leave here until I know what has happened to her. If I return without any news, Rama will die of grief!"

Hanuman decided to search the wooded area that lay beyond the city wall. He sprang down from the wall like an arrow leaving a bow and set off among the trees with renewed hope in his heart.

He found Sita deep within the forest, guarded by a number of female Rakshasas. She looked pale, thin, and careworn, but her beauty shone through her grief as moonlight shines through a covering layer of clouds. Hanuman hid among the leafy branches of a tree and waited in silence.

He watched Ravana approach Sita and offer her power, wealth, and comfort if she would accept him. He watched Rama's devoted wife hide her face from her captor and sob. He heard her exclaim to Ravana, "One of these days, Rama will arrive and kill you!" He heard Ravana reply, "My patience with you is fast coming to an end! If you have not given yourself to me by two months from this day, it is you who will be tortured and slain."

Once Ravana departed, Sita took refuge at the base of the tree in which Hanuman was hiding. He wished to attract her attention without frightening her or alerting her guards. So he softly spoke about Rama's life in Ayodhya and the major events that had followed, concluding with the search for Sita and his own discovery of her.

At first Sita feared that Hanuman was simply a Rakshasa in another disguise. But when he gave her Rama's signet ring, she plied him with questions. "Does Rama live in safety, and does Lakshmana still serve him faithfully? Does he miss me? Does he still love me? Is he planning to kill Ravana and the Rakshasas for this insult to my honor?"

"Be at ease, gentle Sita," Hanuman replied. "Rama remains as loyal and courageous as ever. He thinks of you day and night. Without you, he takes no pleasure in eating and finds no joy in the beauties of nature. His only goal is to destroy Ravana and rescue you."

Devoted Sita's face brightened as the sky glows once dark clouds move away and reveal a full moon. "Give Rama this jeweled token from my hair," she said, "and tell him to rescue me soon. It has been ten months since I last saw him, and each day of each month creeps to an end. Good luck, heroic monkey! In coming here, you have done what no human could have done, and you have brought the light of hope into my life again."

Rama too revived when he learned that Sita was still alive. "Hanuman, your heroic deed has made you as dear as a brother to me!" he exclaimed. "Tell me again how Sita looked and what she said to you. Your words are like water to a thirsty man, like food to a starving man. Speak to me of my gentle wife, who weeps in sorrow, surrounded by wicked Rakshasas. Then let us arm at once and prepare to cross the ocean. My heart longs to invade Ravana's kingdom and avenge my faithful Sita's honor!"

So it came to pass that Sugriva and Rama led the huge host of monkeys south to the great sea.

Chapter 5

Rama and the monkeys invade Lanka, Ravana's kingdom. After many difficult battles, they defeat the Rakshasas, and Rama kills Ravana. Rama makes Sita prove her purity in an ordeal by fire. Rama, Sita, and Lakshmana then return to Ayodhya, where Rama rules for 10,000 years.

Hanuman had burned a large part of the city of Lanka before returning across the sea. Therefore, Ravana gathered his leaders together to discuss retaliation. Most of them told Ravana what they thought he wanted to hear and advocated total war against Rama and the monkeys. However, two of Ravana's brothers were more thoughtful in their comments.

Kumbha-karna, the mightiest warrior of all the Rakshasas, awoke from his usual slumber and said, "Ravana, stealing Sita was a foolish thing to do, and it has brought needless strife to our land. However, I will continue to support you, for you are my brother and my king. I will slay Rama and tear his limbs apart! Then you can marry Sita."

Vibhishana, Ravana's youngest brother, was more critical. "Ravana, who can fight a war against Rama and win? Rama has a righteous cause behind him, and you are the offender. The warrior who fights with right on his side is doubly armed. Sita has brought evil omens into our land. The cows give no milk, serpents sleep in our kitchens, and wild beasts howl all night long. Like a falcon diving upon its victim, Rama and the monkeys will swoop upon our land with bow and with fire. If you value virtuous behavior and peace, you will save the lives of your people. I advise you to return Sita to Rama and cleanse yourself of your foul deed. Then we can avoid the war that would surely destroy us."

Ravana angrily replied, "Sita is mine, and she will remain mine no matter whom I must fight in order to keep her! I would have taken her by force long ago if Brahma, the grandfather and creator, had not warned me that I would die for such an action."

Ravana concluded, "Either you are jealous and want my kingdom and my queen for yourself, or else you are a traitor. If you were not my brother, I would kill you for what you have said. Because you are of my blood, I order you to leave the kingdom at once. Join Rama, since your heart is already with him!"

"I will leave you, Ravana," Vibhishana replied, "but I pity you, for you cannot see the wisdom of my words. You cannot see the danger and the destruction that will follow if you listen to those who misguide you with their self-serving, honeyed speech. You have lost the ability to save yourself!"

So it came to pass that Vibhishana flew across the sea and joined Rama and the monkeys as an important adviser. In return for his help, Rama promised him the kingship of Lanka once they had killed Ravana. The monkeys collected rocks and trees and placed them in the sea to create a bridge across the broad expanse. Ravana's enemies crossed the bridge, and the war began.

Battle raged both day and night, for the Rakshasas always were most aggressive at night. Rama was the greatest fighter on the field, but Ravana was second only to him in might, and each had a brother who was also a great warrior to support him. The forces were thus closely matched. Clouds of dust from charging elephants obscured friend and foe alike. Arrows fell like hissing serpents upon all warriors. The best on both sides were strong enough to hurl mountaintops upon their enemies. Streams of blood from hundreds of slain Rakshasas and monkeys flooded the earth like summer rains.

Ravana was so certain of victory that he let his great warrior-brother Kumbha-karna sleep through most of the war; he himself did not enter the battle until the monkeys had killed all of his strongest warriors. Ravana seemed invincible as he fought his way across the battlefield in his chariot. But the balance tipped in favor of Rama when that mighty son of Dasa-ratha climbed upon Hanuman's back and fought a fierce battle with Ravana. He demolished Ravana's chariot, broke the Rakshasa's crown in two, and severely wounded him with an arrow.

Then, instead of killing Ravana while the advantage was his, Rama said, "You are too weak to fight, so return to Lanka and rest. When you have recovered your strength, we two will fight again. Then I will show you how strong I really am!"

Ravana decided that the time had come to seek the aid of his great warrior-brother Kumbha-karna, who was fast asleep as usual. Kumbha-karna often slept for as long as ten months at a time and awoke only to gorge himself with food. So the Rakshasas first prepared for the huge creature a mountain of food: heaps of buffalo and deer meat, rice, and jars of blood.

Once they could feed him, they tried to awaken him. They shouted and beat their drums so loudly that the birds in the sky died of fright, but Kumbha-karna did not wake up. In unison, 10,000 Rakshasas yelled at him, beat 1,000 kettle-drums, and struck his body with huge log clubs, but Kumbha-karna still did not wake up. Then they bit his ears, poured pots full of water upon him, drove 1,000 elephants against him, and wounded him with spears and maces. At long last, Kumbha-karna woke up.

The monstrous Rakshasa ate the mountain of food and drank 2,000 flasks of wine. Then he put on his golden armor and marched upon the monkeys. They fled from this moving mountain in terror — with good reason, for whomever Kumbha-karna caught, he devoured.

Rama, Hanuman, and the monkeys gathered around him as clouds cling to a mountain peak. Although they hurled massive rocks and huge trees upon him, their weapons splintered against the giant Rakshasa's metal coat. Meanwhile, Kumbha-karna killed hundreds of monkeys with each thrust of his mighty spear, and he ate twenty or thirty monkeys at a time, the excess blood and fat dribbling from his mighty mouth.

Having wounded the best of the monkey leaders, he came face to face with Lakshmana. "You are the finest of warriors, Lakshmana," Kumbha-karna said. "You have shown great skill and have won great glory. I have no desire to fight you because I intend to pit my might and skill against the only human who is greater than you are, your brother. I shall fight Rama to the death."

Kumbha-karna's fortune turned when he fought Rama, for Dasa-ratha's son sent deadly flaming arrows against him. Rama severed the giant's two arms with two of his arrows. He sliced away the giant's two legs by hurling two sharp-edged discs at him. Finally Rama aimed Indra's great arrow at the giant's neck. It pierced his armor and severed his head from his shoulders. His headless body crashed upon the bloody earth and tumbled into the sea, where it created such violent waves that it seemed as if a tempest were stirring them.

Lakshmana killed Ravana's son. Soon thereafter, he was severely wounded by a flaming arrow that he intercepted in order to save the life of Vibhishana, Ravana's brother who had become their ally. These two incidents brought Ravana and Rama against one another in their final battle.

From the heavens the gods were watching the great battle. When Ravana entered the battle in a new chariot drawn by fresh horses, Indra, king of the gods, announced, "We gods always help those who are righteous and brave. The time has now come to help Rama in his fight against Ravana. Rama already has my quiver filled with sharp-tipped arrows. I will now give him golden armor that was fashioned in the heavens and my own golden, horse-drawn chariot, driven by my own driver."

Now Rama's war gear was superior to Ravana's. Nevertheless, Ravana was such a great warrior that the battle raged long and furiously. Some of Ravana's arrows wore fiery, flame-spewing faces that turned into hissing poisonous snakes. Against these, Rama used Vishnu's bow, and arrows belonging to Vishnu's golden-winged bird, for these arrows turned into birds and consumed the snakes on Ravana's arrows. Still the battle raged. In terror, the brilliant sun turned pale, the winds ceased blowing, and the mountains and the sea shook. With Indra's mighty arrows, Rama sliced off Ravana's ten heads one by one, but each time he severed a head another grew in its place. Finally Rama lifted Brahms's shining arrow, which blazed like the fire of the sun and had wings like Indra's lightning bolt. It shattered Ravana's heart, killing him.

Indra smiled upon Rama. He poured down upon the bloody earth a shower of blossoms, a great rain of flowers from the heavens. The sun shone forth in its full brilliance. Gentle, cool breezes rustled the leaves on the trees, perfuming the air with their fragrance. Heavenly harps played celestial music, and Rama heard a heavenly voice exclaim, "Rama, champion of the righteous and doer of virtuous deeds, now you have completed your noble task. Peace reigns in the heavens and on the earth. We shower our blessings upon you!"

Rama unstrung his bow and joyfully put aside his weapons. When Vibhishana mourned Ravana's death, Rama said to him, "Ravana was one of the earth's great warriors and heroes. Even Indra, king of the gods, could not stand against him. Such heroes should not be mourned when they die in battle, for they have died with honor, and none of us can escape death."

After giving Ravana a hero's funeral, Rama sent Hanuman to Sita with news of the victory. She returned freshly bathed and dressed. At the sight of her husband, her face shone with the radiance of the full moon in the midnight sky.

Rama said, "Dear Sita, with the help of Hanuman, Sugriva, and Vibhishana, I have kept my promise to you and have performed the obligation of a man on whose honor a stain has been placed. I have cleansed my family and myself of dishonor by killing Ravana.

"However," Rama continued, "you bear the stain of a woman who has lived with a man other than her husband. Ravana gazed upon you and touched you. No man of honor can accept such behavior in his wife. Therefore, I must publicly renounce you. You may live with whomever you choose—Lakshmana or Bharata, Sugriva or Vibhishana—but you may not live with me!"

Sita trembled like a leaf in the wind and sobbed as she heard these words. Then she dried her tears and said, "If you doubted my faithful devotion to you, my purity of heart, why did you cross the broad ocean and risk your life for me? Have you forgotten that I am the daughter of Mother Earth and that I followed you into the wild forestlands with a woman's deep devotion? At no point in my life have I ever been unfaithful. If Ravana gazed upon me and touched me, you must realize that I had no power to stop him.

"However," she continued, "when the shadow of dishonor casts its shade upon an innocent woman's life, death by fire is the only way to restore the honor she deserves. So, Lakshmana, if you love me, build a funeral pyre for me and light it. I would rather die than live with a stain upon my name."

Rama showed no sign of weakness or anguish at these words. So Lakshmana, with an aching heart, did as Sita had asked him.

As she stood before the roaring flames, Sita announced, "If in thought and in deed I have been faithful and true, if in my lifelong devotion to dharma I have lived without a stain, may this fire defend my name!" Then, showing courage and faith and no sign of fear, the gentle Sita entered the flames and disappeared. All who watched her wept with grief and awe.

The gods descended from the heavens in their golden chariots and said to Rama, "Preserver of life on earth, how can you act like a common man and treat Sita in this way? Do you not remember that you are the first of all the gods, the grandfather and creator of all? As you were in the beginning, so will you be in the end."

Rama replied, "I believe that I am Rama, eldest son of Dasa-ratha. If I am wrong, then let the grandfather tell me who I am."

Brahma said, "Rama is an earthly form of the great god Vishnu, who lives forever. In your heavenly form, you are both creation and destruction, the savior of all gods and holy hermits, the conqueror of all enemies. You live in every creature and in every part of nature. Day comes when you open your eyes, and night comes when you close them. I am your heart. Sita is the earthly form of your heavenly wife, Lakshmi.

"Now that you have killed Ravana," Brahma concluded, "you can assume your divine form and return to heaven, for you have accomplished the task for which you adopted human form. Those who love you and who tell your story will be rewarded."

The flames parted and Agni, the god of fire, appeared with faithful Sita. The flames had not touched her. Her face, her hair, and her clothing were as fresh as the grass in the morning. Agni said to Rama, "Son of Dasa-ratha, reclaim your devoted wife. She resisted all the temptations Ravana put before her and has remained pure in both thought and deed."

Rama's eyes glowed with the radiance of the sun as he announced, "In all the years that I have known her, I have never doubted my Sita's virtue. Now the whole world knows what I know, for Agni has attested to her pure and shining name. I reclaim her with delight in my heart, now that my people know that the eldest son of Dasa-ratha puts the law of his country above his own personal desires." Rama then embraced his loving wife, who understood the reason for her trial and forgave him.

The gods then revealed the presence of King Dasa-ratha in their midst. "Rama," his father said, "not only have you helped the gods and the holy hermits, but you have saved my honor. Your exile is now at an end. Return as a victorious hero to Ayodhya, and rule there with your brothers. May you live a long life!"

King Dasa-ratha turned to Lakshmana and said, "My son, you are ever true to deeds of virtue. Continue to take care of Rama, and may you have a good life."

Finally the king turned to Sita and said, "Forgive Rama. It was for your own good that he spoke against you in public. You have earned glory that few women can ever achieve."

Then Indra, king of the gods, appeared before Rama and said: "Righteous Rama, lion among men, in return for what you have done for us, ask whatever you wish, and the gift will be yours!"

Rama replied, "Lord of heaven, please grant renewed life to all those who fought on my behalf against the Rakshasas, and provide them with food and fresh water wherever they may go."

"So be it," Indra replied.

When it was time for Hanuman to leave Rama, he said, "Rama, I ask you to grant me one special gift. As you may remember, Indra, king of the gods, gave me the power to choose my own death. I ask you to permit me to live on earth as long as people tell the tale of your glorious deeds."

"So be it, Hanuman," Rama replied, "and as a token of my gift to you, I also give you this jeweled chain from around my neck and place it, with love and respect and gratitude, around yours."

So Rama, Lakshmana, and Sita returned to Ayodhya after an absence of fourteen years. Bharata had remained true to his word. His face now glowed with the radiance of a great wise man, for he had been loyal to dharma. He had faithfully honored Rama's sandals as the token of Rama's kingship and had lived the life of a holy hermit within the palace walls.

Rama and Sita became the king and queen of Ayodhya and ruled their kingdom of Kosala for 10,000 years. During all of that time, neither terrible diseases nor untimely death visited their land. Yama, lord of the dead, let infants grow to maturity and husbands live to old age. Farmers rejoiced, for rains came reliably and winds were friendly. In gratitude Mother Earth provided bountiful harvests, fruitful trees, and rich pastureland. The people were loyal to dharma and loved their neighbors and their king. Those who lived in towns and cities worked at their customary tasks on the loom or the anvil without fearing liars and robbers. It was truly a time of happiness and peace for all.

Chapter 6

The people of Kosala again question Sita's virtue, and Rama banishes her. In exile she gives birth to Rama's twin sons. Valmiki teaches them The Ramayana. *When Rama hears his story and meets his sons, he brings Sita back and asks that her purity be tested again. Instead, Sita returns to Mother Earth, her mother. After 1,000 years of additional rule, Rama and his brothers return to heaven as Vishnu.*

When Rama had reigned for 10,000 years, Sita became pregnant and decided to visit the hermitage of the wise men along the holy Ganges River. The night before the start of her journey, Rama asked his friends and advisers, "What do my subjects say about my brothers, Sita, and me?"

One replied, "They speak admiringly of your alliance with the monkeys and your conquest of the Rakshasas and Ravana."

"Surely that cannot be all they speak of," Rama said. "Do they not say more?"

Another replied, "Since you press us, you should know that your subjects criticize you for taking Sita back after she had lived with Ravana in Lanka. They feel they must accept improper behavior from their own wives because their king has done so."

Rama's heart flooded with dismay. He dismissed his companions and sent for his brothers. Tearfully, he told them what he had just heard. "My heart knows that Sita is pure, and she has proven her purity by fire. Yet my subjects force me to renounce my devoted wife for a second time. A king cannot reign with disgrace upon his name.

"Therefore," Rama continued, "I want you, Lakshmana, to take Sita to Valmiki's hermitage along the Ganges River as if you are simply honoring her request. Then, however, you must leave her there."

When Lakshmana had brought Sita to Valmiki and had told her of Rama's position, she said, "In some past life I must have committed grave sins to be punished this way twice in spite of my purity! I would drown myself in the Ganges if I were not carrying within me Rama's child.

"Return to Rama with this message," Sita concluded. "Tell him that, as always, I will be loyal to dharma. I will continue to serve my husband with a woman's deep devotion no matter what the circumstances. I accept my exile but grieve over my false reputation."

Lakshmana gave Rama Sita's message. Then he said to his brother, "Do not grieve over what you have had to do. Each of us must accept whatever life brings. Wherever there is growth, there is decay. Wherever there is birth, there is death. Wherever there is prosperity, there is poverty. Wherever there are friendship and love, there is separation."

In time, Sita gave birth to twin sons, who grew up with their mother and the holy hermits in the forest. The hermit Valmiki taught them wisdom and the skill of recitation. Then he taught them to sing *The Ramayana*.

Valmiki knew the story of Rama because one day, years earlier, he had asked the great wise man Narada, "Is there any man alive who possesses perfect righteousness and courage?" Narada had replied, "Rama is such a man. I will tell you about him."

Soon after that, Brahma, grandfather and creator of the world, appeared before Valmiki. "I have watched how you live your life. Your thoughts and your deeds have shown me that you are a wise and compassionate man. Therefore, I have chosen you to fashion the story of Rama into beautiful verses that will reveal truth from beginning to end."

Brahma continued, "Be confident that you already possess the understanding of human nature and the gift of poetry. Whatever more you need to know about Rama's story I will see that you discover. Your *Ramayana* will be told from one generation to another as long as snow-covered mountains rise from Mother Earth and sparkling seas wash her shores." With these words, Brahma disappeared.

As Valmiki sat in deep thought, the people in Rama's life came alive in his mind and revealed their tale. The holy hermit shaped their words and deeds into verses. Thus he was able to teach *The Ramayana* to the sons of Rama and Sita.

After many lonely and joyless years had passed, Rama decided to hold the sacred sacrifice of the horse. During the year that the horse wandered in freedom, the king gave many gifts to the poor: clothing to the needy, food and drink to the hungry, shelters to the weak and aged, and gold and homes to orphans. He invited all of his subjects as well as the monkeys and Vibhishana, king of the Rakshasas, to the final ceremony.

When the time came, Valmiki arrived with Rama's sons. He instructed them to sing *The Ramayana* from beginning to end, reciting twenty of the 500 cantos each day from morning until night. "Do not speak of your own misfortunes," he advised them. "If Rama asks who your parents are, tell him that I am your teacher and your father here on earth."

The children captivated everyone who heard their song. The people whispered to one another how much like Rama they looked. As the days passed and the boys continued their performance, Rama realized that these were his own sons. He called Valmiki to him and said, "I long to have Sita at my side again, for I have never forgotten our love. Let her prove her purity before the assembled guests once more. Then she can again share my throne and my kingdom with me."

When Sita arrived in Ayodhya, Rama said, "Gentle, devoted, faithful Sita. Let the world once again know of your virtue. I have never questioned your purity. Forgive me for banishing you in order to please my subjects. It was a shameful deed and an error, but I knew no other way to stifle the voice of rumor."

Sita looked upon the assembled throng. She saw her husband and king, as bright as a star. She saw her sons performing as hermit-minstrels, as radiant as two moons. She saw kings from many lands and the gods from heaven. "How many times should I have to prove my purity?" she asked herself. "I am Rama's queen and the daughter of Mother Earth and a great king. Surely it is time to put this life behind me and leave the earth."

So Sita sadly announced, "If my thoughts and deeds have been pure from the day of my birth, and I have been loyal to dharma in my devotion and duty to my husband, I call upon you, Mother Earth, to receive your child. Put an end to the pain and shame of my life, and claim me as your own!"

Before the astonished eyes of the crowd, the earth opened, and a golden throne rose from its depths, supported by serpents from the netherworld as a rosebud is enfolded by leaves. Mother Earth stretched forth her loving arms to embrace her virtuous daughter and to place her upon her own throne. Then mother, daughter, and throne descended into the earth, which closed above them.

Rama watched the spectacle with grief and anger. Brahma, the grandfather and creator, then appeared before him and said, "Rama, do not grieve for Sita or for yourself. Sita is pure and innocent, and her reward is to join her mother. Remember that you are the great god Vishnu. You will be with Sita once again in heaven, where she is your wife, Lakshmi. The end of Valmiki's story will reveal your future to you."

Rama reigned for another 1,000 years without joy. He had his craftspeople fashion a golden statue of Sita, which he kept by his side. His kingdom prospered.

One day the figure of Time entered Rama's palace and said to him, "As Rama, you have reigned on earth for 11,000 years. The grandfather has sent me to ask you: Do you wish to reign longer over mortals, or are you ready to reign once again over all of the gods?"

Rama replied, "I am ready to return to my place among the gods in heaven."

When Rama announced that he was going to leave the earth and return to heaven, his brothers left their thrones to their children and joined him. Sugriva, king of the monkeys, also joined him. "Wherever you go," he said, "I will follow!"

Rama permitted any monkey who chose to follow him to do so — except Hanuman. "Do you remember the gift you asked of me long ago?" he asked Hanuman. "You asked to live on earth for as long as people spoke of my great deeds. Therefore, you will live here forever. May you be happy!"

Vibhishana, king of the Rakshasas, prepared the departure rites. When Rama's brothers and their wives, his counselors and servants, all the people of Ayodhya, the Rakshasas, monkeys, bears, and birds had assembled, Brahma arrived on earth with 100,000 chariots. Indra, king of the gods, smiled upon the loyal host. He poured down upon them a shower of blossoms, a great rain of flowers from the heavens.

Brahma exclamed, "Hail, Vishnu, preserver of life on earth! Enter heaven in whatever form pleases you."

Rama and his brothers entered heaven in the form of Vishnu, and all of the gods rejoiced and bowed before him. Then Vishnu said, "Brahma, all of those who assembled wish to follow because they love me. In order to remain with me, they are renouncing their lives on earth. Therefore, give each his or her place in heaven."

So it came to pass that those who followed Rama assumed their godly forms, and now they live in heaven.

So ends *The Ramayana*, created by Valmiki and honored by Brahma, the grandfather and creator. Those who recite it will eam rich gifts of cows and gold. Those who hear it or read it will become cleansed of all sin. They will have a long and honored life. They will enjoy the blessing of children and grandchildren, both on earth and in heaven.

Introducing **The Creation of the Universe**

Scholars believe that the Chinese myths that have come down to us are not as old and authentic as the myths from other ancient cultures. The principal reason is that in 213 B.C., the first emperor of China burned all books that were not about medicine, prophecy, or farming.

During the great Han dynasty (206 B.C.–A.D. 220), the emperors instituted the teachings of Confucius as the state religion and banned religions that involved nature worship. Many of the old myths that had been passed down orally were recorded anew during this period, but Han scholars revised them to reflect their own attitudes and the political and religious climate of their times.

The creation myth of Pangu is the most detailed Chinese creation myth

in existence. It is found in texts written between A.D. 200 and 500. This myth focuses on the creation of order out of chaos and the preservation of that order. Pangu first brings order into the universe by separating heaven from earth. His body provides additional structure by differentiating the surface of the earth into a variety of natural forms, such as mountains, oceans, and forests, and by differentiating the heavens as well. Later, after the monster Gong-gong inadvertently destroys the natural environment, the Mother Goddess Nugua restores order to the world.

Unlike other ancient cultures, the Chinese divide the universe into two complementary essences, *yin* (shaded) and *yang* (sunlit), which, taken together, comprise the whole. Yin is the female principle in nature—dark, earthy, passive, submissive, and cool. Yang is the male principle—bright, celestial, active, aggressive, and warm. Just as male and female unite among humans, so the sun, a god represent-ing the qualities of yang, marries the moon, a goddess representing the qualities of yin. Even heaven and earth represent complementary aspects of the whole.

The Creation of the Universe

In the beginning an egg contained the entire universe. Within the egg was one chaotic mass. Heaven and earth were identical, and all was eternally dark, for neither the sun nor the moon existed. From within this dark mass, Pangu, the first being, was formed. Finding himself alive in darkness, encased within an egg, and surrounded by chaos, Pangu decided to bring order into the universe.

First he broke open the world egg. The lighter part (yang) rose and became the heavens, while the heavier part (yin) sank and became the earth. Pangu tried to stand upon the earth, but the heavens pressed heavily upon his head. He realized that no life would ever be able to exist on earth if the heavens were not high in the sky, so he sat down and thought about how to solve this problem. Finally, Pangu decided that the only way living objects and creatures would form and survive upon the earth would be if he held up the sky.

For the next 18,000 years, Pangu worked constantly to keep the heavens from crushing the surface of the earth. He ate only the mists that blew into his mouth. He never slept. At first he could only rest on his knees with his elbows bent, as, summoning all of his great strength, he pushed his hands upward against the sky. Then the time came when he could rise to his feet with his elbows bent as he pushed his hands upward against the sky. At last Pangu could stand at his full height and stretch his arms upward to their full length as he pushed his hands upward against the sky.

Day after day and night after night, month after month and year after year, Pangu stood as firmly as a rock column and continuously pushed the heavens upward with his hands. Little by little, the sky rose higher and higher above the earth, moving an additional ten feet each day. The higher the heavens rose, the taller Pangu became.

Finally the heavens rested high above the earth, and Pangu realized that he was very, very tired. He looked up at the sky above his hands and then he looked far, far down to the earth beneath his feet. He felt certain that the distance between heaven and earth was so great that he could lie down and rest without fearing that the sky would collapse and crush the earth.

So Pangu lay down and fell asleep. He died in his sleep, and his body gave shape and substance to the universe.

Pangu's head formed the mountain of the East while his feet formed the mountain of the West. His torso formed the mountain of the Center, his left arm the mountain of the South, and his right arm the mountain of the North. These five sacred mountains defined the four corners of the square earth and its center. Each stood firmly upon the earth like a giant stone column and did its part to hold up the heavens.

The hair on Pangu's head and his eyebrows formed the planets and the stars. His left eye formed the sun and his right eye the moon. His flesh formed the soil of the earth and his blood the oceans and rivers. His teeth and his bones formed rocks, minerals, and gems. His breath formed the clouds and the wind, while his voice became lightning and thunder. His perspiration formed rain and the dew. The hair on his body formed trees, plants, and flowers, while parasites living on his skin became animals and fish.

The Mother Goddess Nugua created the first people. She herself was formed like a human being, except that instead of legs she had the tail of a dragon. Nugua glided over the earth, admiring the beautiful forms that had emerged from Pangu's body. She loved the trees, plants, and flowers, but she was particularly fascinated by the animals and fish, for they were more active, living creatures. After studying them for a while, however, Nugua decided that creation was not yet complete. Animals and fish simply were not intelligent enough to satisfy her. She would create creatures who would be superior to all other living things.

As Nugua glided along the Yellow River, she decided to use the substance of this riverbed to form human beings. Sitting down along the shore of the river, she took handfuls of wet clay from the riverbed and formed them into little people. She made them look almost like her, except that instead of dragon tails, she gave them two legs to match their two arms. Once they were prepared to walk, Nugua breathed life into them. Some she impregnated with yang, the masculine, aggressive principle in nature, and they became men. Others she impregnated with yin, the female, submissive principle in nature, and they became women.

After a while, Nugua became tired of fashioning people one at a time, so she thought of a faster way. She placed a rope in the wet clay of the riverbed and rolled it around until the upper end of it was completely covered. Then she picked up the rope and shook it over the shore. Each drop of mud that fell off became a human being. The two methods did not create exactly the same kind of people, however. The ones Nugua had made by hand were richer and more intelligent than those who had fallen in drops from her rope.

Some time thereafter, when all of Nugua's children had built homes and had settled into villages and farms in order to provide for their daily needs, the monster Gong-gong became very angry. He rammed his head into one of the mountains that supported the sky. The mountain came tumbling to the ground, tearing a great hole in the part of the heavens it had supported and causing the earth to crack open in many places. Flames blazed from some of the crevasses, burning homes and crops. Rivers overflowed their banks and torrents of underground water gushed from other fissures, flooding the land and creating a vast ocean where once there had been villages and farms.

The Great Goddess watched in horror as hundreds of human beings starved to death or drowned. She knew that she had to act quickly if she hoped to save any of the children she had created. First she set fire to the reeds that grew beside the river and stuffed their ashes into the burning cracks in the earth to smother the flames. Then she forced the floods to seep into the earth and to flow in controlled river channels by piling up more of the reed ashes as dikes.

Once human beings could return to their farms and villages and resume their daily occupations, Nugua glided over to the Yellow River and chose a number of stones in five different colors. She melted them in a forge and covered the hole in the heavens with them. Then she removed the four legs from a giant tortoise and used one at each corner of the earth as an additional pillar to support the sky. In this way, the Mother Goddess repaired the devastation that Gong-gong had so thoughtlessly created.

But Nugua knew of no way to raise the northeast corner of the earth on which the fifth pillar had fallen. To this day that land is lower than the rest of China, and rivers flow eastward across that low land into the sea.

Introducing **Yi the Archer and the Ten Suns**

The myth of Yi the Archer and the Chinese creation myth are so closely related that the introduction to the creation myth applies here as well.

Just as the Mother Goddess Nugua restores order in the world in the creation myth, so Yi the Archer restores order in this nature myth. He kills the suns that are destroying the environment. Like many other heroes, Yi is both human and divine. He uses his skill to save the world from forces beyond the control of ordinary humans.

During the Shang dynasty (1500–1000 B.C.), people may have believed that ten suns actually existed. Later, people connected the king with the sun. They believed that, just as only one king ruled them, only one sun existed. Some people believed that ten suns would appear in the sky as a sign that a dynasty was about to collapse.

Yi the Archer and the Ten Suns

Once, when the world was young, ten suns rode across the sky rather than just one. Their mother was the wife of Di Jun, the god of the east. She would bathe her ten children in a pool of hot water located in the Tang Valley, at the far end of the eastern part of the world. Then the suns would rest, like birds, in a huge mulberry tree, for the core of each sun was a bird. Nine suns would perch among the lower branches of the tree, while one — a different sun each night — settled on the topmost branch.

When the time came for dawn to usher in the morning light, the sun that sat at the top of the tree would venture across the heavens in its chariot. Sometimes the chariot would be drawn by horses, sometimes by dragons. Each week had ten days, and a new sun crossed the sky each day of the week.

Since the ten suns looked alike and only one rode across the sky at a time, the people who walked the earth did not know that more than one sun existed. At this time, humans and animals lived together as neighbors and friends. Animals could leave their young in their nests without fearing that humans would harm them. Farmers could leave their harvest stacked in piles in their fields without fearing that animals would rob them. A person could accidentally step on a serpent without being bitten. A child could pull the tail of a leopard or a tiger in play without being mauled to death. The time was one of plenty, with more than enough food for all. Humans and animals found it easy to think well of one another and to respect each other's property.

One day, however, the ten suns decided that it would be fun to travel across the heavens together instead of one at a time. So when dawn arrived, all ten suns climbed aboard the chariot and set forth across the sky. Their blazing heat scorched the earth. Forests caught fire and burned to ash, killing many animals. Those who had not perished in the flames roamed among humans, vicious now in their desperate search for food.

Rivers and even seas dried up; all the fish died, and water monsters scrounged for food upon the land. Many humans and animals died of thirst. Crops and orchards withered, putting an immediate end to the food supply of humans and domesticated animals. Some people burned to death because they left the shelter of their homes and caught fire from the heat of the sun. Others became the prey of wild animals, now that no other source of food existed.

The people pleaded with their emperor, Yao, to help them. Yao quickly sought the aid of the only person he knew who could save the universe, a great archer named Yi. The archer had begged the queen mother of the west for the elixir of immortality and had drunk some of it before his wife had stolen the rest. The emperor commanded Yi to rescue civilization from the devastation by shooting his arrows at nine of the suns.

Yi the Archer's aim was true. One by one he shot his arrows at the suns, and one by one they hit their marks. The nine suns could not survive the thrust of an arrow, and one by one they died. One by one their feathers fell to the earth, and one by one their light burned out. The earth became darker and darker until finally it was illuminated by the light of only one sun. Everywhere, the people gazed into the sky and rejoiced. Now they could begin again.

Introducing **The Quest for the Sun**

"The Quest for the Sun" is one of approximately 400 myths and folktales collected from the area of West Lake (located on the west side of Hangzhou, the capital of Zhejiang Province, which is south of Shanghai). The material was collected principally by Xu Fei, Chen Weijun, and Shen Tuqi in 1959. However, the collection, *The Folk Tales of West Lake*, was first published by the Zhejiang People's Publishing House in 1978.

West Lake is the most famous lake in China, both because of its ancient history and because of the beauty of its setting. Since olden times, the Chinese have built beautiful structures in the area. This folktale explains the origin of Bao Chu Pagoda, one such building.

The hero, Bao Chu, is similar to the heroes of myths throughout the world. His birth and growth are unusual. His task is to restore order to the natural world by recovering the sun and, with it, the fertility of the earth. He is prepared to sacrifice his life for the good of society.

Like other heroes, Bao Chu endures a number of trials in the course of his great accomplishment. These tests exhibit his remarkable strength and his creative intelligence, and they win him great fame. Being mortal, he dies — but not until after he has saved the world.

Bao Chu's mother is also a heroine. Hui Niang is presented as the ideal wife and mother. She is creative, intelligent, and self-sacrificing, consciously choosing a life of loneliness and hardship when she encourages her husband and then her son to set off on a heroic pursuit.

Principal Characters

LIU CHUN: husband of Hui Niang; young farmer; first to search for the sun

HUI NIANG: wife of Liu Chun; mother of Bao Chu; weaver

BAO CHU: son of Hui Niang; hero who finds the sun

KING OF EVIL: demon king who has captured the sun

The Quest for the Sun

Long ago, a small village sat at the base of Precious Stone Mountain along the shore of West Lake. In this village lived the young farmer Liu Chun and his wife, the weaver Hui Niang. Since they were a hard-working, prudent couple, the other villagers admired them.

One morning, soon after the rising sun glowed red upon the eastern horizon, black clouds blew across West Lake and brought with them a violent rainstorm.

The sun immediately sank below the horizon, and even after the storm had blown past it did not reappear.

The world became dark and cold. The trees withered and turned from green to brown. The flowers shriveled and turned from red to brown. The crops dried upon the fields and turned from gold to brown. Demons, ghosts, and other evil creatures of the night ventured forth with great delight, for an endless night shrouded the world in blackness. Their wicked deeds caused much suffering.

"What are we going to do?" the people asked one another. "Where has the sun gone? How can we survive if we cannot grow food?"

Liu Chun went to see the oldest person in the neighborhood, an elder who was 180 years old. "Can you tell me what has happened to the sun?" he asked.

"I think I can," the elder replied. "A demon king lives beneath the Eastern Sea. It is he who rules over all of the wicked ghosts, demons, and other evil creatures. To these creatures the sun is a great enemy. They fear and hate it, for it exposes their terrible deeds. Therefore, I think that the demon king has stolen the sun."

Liu Chun thanked the elder and returned home. He said to his wife, "Hui Niang, I must go forth and try to find the sun. The people are freezing and starving to death! I feel their pain burning in my heart."

"It is a good deed that you would do," his wife replied. "Go with a happy heart. I will send you on your way with special clothing."

Hui Niang made her husband a thickly padded cotton jacket. She then combined a lock of her long hair with strands of hemp and fashioned a pair of sandals from them.

As Liu Chun was leaving, the couple saw a bright golden light moving through the sky toward them. When it landed on Liu Chun's shoulder, they recognized it as a golden phoenix. Liu Chun asked it to accompany him on his journey, and the bird nodded.

Liu Chun then addressed his parting words to his wife. "Hui Niang, I will not return until I have found the sun. If I die first, I will become a bright star. In that form I will guide anyone who would find the sun." He and the phoenix began their journey.

Each day thereafter, Hui Niang climbed to the top of Precious Stone Mountain and scanned the horizon for the sun. Each day she was disappointed. The world remained shrouded in endless night.

One day as she watched, however, a brightly shining star rose from earth to the heavens. Then the golden phoenix came to rest at Hui Niang's feet with its head downcast. Hui Niang knew that her husband had died. Her heart was so filled with grief that she fainted.

When Hui Niang awoke, she found that she had given birth to an infant son. She named him Bao Chu. With the touch of the first gust of wind, the infant could talk; with the second gust of wind, he could walk; and with the third gust of wind, he grew to be eighteen feet tall. Hui Niang was delighted to be the mother of such a great son but sad that the boy would never know his father.

Seeing his mother's tears, Bao Chu questioned her, and she told him the story of his father's fatal quest. "Mother, with your permission, I will go and find the sun!" he exclaimed. "It will give me great pleasure to complete my father's task."

Hui Niang's heart was torn in two. One half thought of the honor to her husband; the other half worried over the danger to her young son. She felt obliged to do her part to save the people of the earth, so she gave her consent. Once more she made a thickly padded cotton jacket and a pair of sandals woven from a lock of her hair and strands of hemp. Once more the golden phoenix arrived at their gate. It alighted upon Bao Chu's shoulder when he was ready to depart.

Hui Niang said to her son, "Notice the brightest star in the heavens, there in the east. Your father transformed himself into that star when he died. Follow it, and it will lead you to the sun. The golden phoenix is a friend. Just as it accompanied your father on his journey, it has come to accompany you on yours."

"I will do just as you wish, Mother," Bao Chu replied. "No matter how long I am away, do not let your heart grieve for me. Any tears you shed would break my heart, and I would not have the strength to complete my task." With these words, Bao Chu and the phoenix began their journey.

They headed east, in the direction of the brightest star. On and on Bao Chu walked, over eighteen cliffs and nineteen precipices. The bushes on the mountainsides tore his jacket to shreds and his body to a mass of bloody wounds. He looked worn, haggard, and very cold as he limped into a mountain village. When the villagers heard of his quest, each tore a piece of cloth from his or her own jacket and had it sewn into a new jacket for Bao Chu, which they called the "100-family coat."

Feeling warm in body and refreshed in spirit, Bao Chu and the golden phoenix went on their way again. They walked on and on, over many more mountains, and they swam across many rivers.

One day they reached a river so wide that even an eagle could not fly across it. A mighty current swept boulders as large as houses downstream. With no fear in his heart, Bao Chu stepped right into the turbulent water and set out for the far, invisible shore. Huge waves dashed over him and fiercely swirling whirlpools captured him, but Bao Chu mustered his strength and swam boldly on. When he could see the farther shore, his heart flooded with pleasure.

Suddenly, however, a frigid wind blew upon the river, transforming the fierce current into a river of ice that imprisoned Bao Chu and froze the phoenix. Miraculously, the 100-family coat kept the ice from freezing Bao Chu. In fact, the magic coat kept him so warm that his body heat melted the ice that encased him. He warned the phoenix against his own body with one arm while he pounded the ice into chunks with the fist of his other hand, making the water dance. The surging waves lifted him upon one of the floating pieces, and he made his way to shore by leaping from one piece of ice to the next.

Bao Chu walked on and on with the phoenix until they came to another village. When the villagers heard of his quest and the dangers he had encountered, the elder of the village announced, "Without the sun, we are poor people. The best thing we can give you is our soil, for it has been watered by the sweat of our labor since the time of our ancestors. Maybe you will find our gift useful as you pursue your journey." One by one, the villagers each put a handful of soil into a large bag.

When the bag was full, Bao Chu placed it on one shoulder. With the phoenix on his other shoulder, he continued to walk toward the brightly shining star in the eastern sky. He climbed ninety-nine mountains and swam across ninety-nine rivers. Finally he came to a place where two roads met.

As he stood there wondering which road to take, an old woman approached and asked, "Young man, where are you going?" When he told her the object of his journey, she said, "The distance is far too great! I advise you to return to your home before it is too late."

"I will not return home until I have found the sun!" Bao Chu replied. "No matter how long the road or how difficult the journey, I will do what I have set out to do!"

"If you are so determined," she counseled, "follow the road to the right and you will find the sun. When you come to the next village, you would be wise to rest there."

While the woman was speaking, the golden phoenix repeatedly attacked her. It struck her eyes with its beak, scratched her face with its claws, and beat her body with its wings. Bao Chu was embarrassed, so he chased it away.

He took the path the woman had advised, even though the phoenix continually flew in front of him and tried to block his way. Given how difficult his journey had been until then, Bao Chu was surprised that the road was so smooth and easy. Before long he reached the village that the old woman had mentioned. To his amazement, it was a thriving town. The men were prosperous and fat, and the women were well dressed and beautiful. The villagers welcomed him warmly. They praised him as a hero and held a bountiful feast in his honor.

Bao Chu raised his wine bowl as the villagers prepared to drink a toast to him. "I wonder why these people are so prosperous when those in every other village are cold and starving?" he thought. The golden phoenix suddenly hovered above his head and dropped an object into his wine bowl. As Bao Chu stared in wonder, the wine caught fire and began to burn the object. Bao Chu noticed that it was a sandal just like his own, made of hemp and hair.

"This must be one of my father's sandals!" he exclaimed to himself. "My father must have died here!" He dropped the wine bowl to the ground and screamed at the villagers. At the sound of his voice, the entire village and all its inhabitants disappeared in a puff of smoke. In their place ran hundreds of frightened ghosts, demons, and other wicked creatures.

With the golden phoenix once more upon his shoulder, Bao Chu returned to the fork in the road and took the road to the left. Meanwhile, the evil creatures decided to try to harm Bao Chu in another way. They had been unable to freeze him in the river. They had been unable to kill him in the Village of Lost Souls. Now they turned themselves into high mountains and blocked his way, but one by one, Bao Chu climbed over each mountain. Next they turned themselves into wide rivers, but one by one, Bao Chu swam across each river.

Finally the demons turned themselves into the wind and blew themselves to Bao Chu's village at the base of Precious Stone Mountain. They found Hui Niang and told her that Bao Chu had slipped while climbing up a cliff and had fallen to his death in the river below. They hoped that the news would fill her heart with grief and that her tears would weaken Bao Chu.

However, Hui Niang remembered her son's parting words. She tried not to believe their tale. Instead, she clenched her teeth and held back her tears.

Each morning since the day of Bao Chu's departure, Hiu Niang and the other villagers had picked up a flat rock and walked to the top of Precious Stone Mountain. When they reached the crest, they would stand on the stone that they had carried and gaze intently into the east, hoping for a glimpse of the sun. Each day they stood higher than they had the day before, hoping for a better view of the sun. But day after day, month after month, and year after year, the sky remained black. The stones had become a high stone terrace, but the sun still had not returned.

Meanwhile, Bao Chu climbed mountain after mountain and crossed river after river until his journey seemed endless. Finally, from the peak of a mountain, he heard the sound of the sea far in the distance. He continued to travel eastward until he came to the shore of the Eastern Sea. "Now what do I do?" he asked himself. "How do I find the sun from here? How can I cross the sea?"

Bao Chu opened the bag on his back and poured the soil into the sea. As the soil hit the surface of the water, a great wind arose and transformed it into a chain of islands that stretched to the middle of the sea. Bao Chu swam from island to island. When he reached the last island, it suddenly sank to the bottom of the sea, carrying Bao Chu along with it.

On the ocean floor Bao Chu found a huge cave, with a giant boulder sealing its entrance. "Ah!" he exclaimed. "This must be where the demon king has imprisoned the sun!"

The King of Evil had gathered a large army of hideous demons at the cave entrance, all armed and ready for battle. "If I can kill the demon king, I will survive," Bao Chu thought, "for once their king is dead, the army will flee in panic."

So Bao Chu and the King of Evil fought one another to the death. Their battle raged from the bottom of the sea to its surface, and from the surface back down to the bottom. It created tempestuous waves over 100 feet high.

Finally the demon king retreated to the ocean floor. Bao Chu punched him in the nose, causing him to stumble and fall backward. Then the golden phoenix tore out his eyes with its beak. Screaming in pain, the wicked creature lunged blindly back and forth. Then he crashed into a huge boulder and died. The army of demons vanished immediately.

Bao Chu moved aside the boulder that was blocking the cave and found the sun within. Summoning the last of his strength, he held the sun in his hands and slowly swam up to the surface of the sea. He managed to push the sun to the top of the water before his strength gave out, and he died of exhaustion.

The golden phoenix dived beneath the sun, spread its wings, and rose from the water with the sun upon its back. Once the sun was free of the water, it rose into the sky under its own power.

Hui Niang and the villagers were watching from their stone terrace on the top of Precious Stone Mountain when the sun at long last began to rise into the sky. First clouds of purple appeared on the horizon, followed by clouds of rose and gold. Then 10,000 golden rays appeared, followed by the golden disk itself. Its light turned all the demons to stone.

As the villagers shouted with joy, the golden phoenix came to rest at Hui Niang's feet with its head downcast. Then Hui Niang knew that her son had died. Her heart filled with grief, but she felt joy as well, for Bao Chu had completed his father's task and had become a great hero.

From that day until this, the star of Liu Chun shines brightly in the eastern heavens before dawn breaks across the sky. The people call it the morning star. As the phoenix rises with the sun upon its back, its wings shine upon the clouds and paint them purple, red, and gold. A pagoda now stands upon the stone terrace where the golden phoenix landed. The people named it Bao Chu Pagoda in tribute to the young man who rescued the sun and made it possible for plants to grow upon the earth again.

Introducing The Creation of the Universe and Japan

The Japanese were not the original occupants of the islands that now comprise Japan. Mongoloid peoples crossed the Korea Strait and invaded these islands during the 2nd and 1st centuries B.C. and brought their Shinto religion with them. This religion included the worship of nature, ancestors, and heroes. It assumed that every aspect of nature had a divine spirit within it.

The Japanese did not record their religious beliefs for hundreds of years; by then, the influence of China on Japanese culture was widespread. The year A.D. 552 marks the beginning of the great Chinese influence on Japan in the areas of religion, literature, and art. But it was not until the early 8th century that the Japanese recorded anything of their religion.

The Kojiki (Record of Ancient Matters), written in A.D. 712, and the Nihon Shoki (Chronicles of Japan), written in 720, are the two major sources of Japanese mythology. They were written at a time when the Japanese accepted their traditional myths as fact. The authors of these books made an effort to minimize the Chinese and Indian influences on their earliest religious beliefs.

The creation myth is particularly Japanese in that it quickly moves from the creation of the earth to an explanation of how the islands that comprise Japan were created. The fact that the creators are a pair of male and female gods may be a Chinese influence.

As is the case with most cultures, the Japanese gods are anthropomorphic. They are human in appearance, thought, speech, and deed. In the course of explaining the origin of local natural phenomena — such as islands, mountains, forests, and streams — the creation myth also presents a pattern of birth, marriage, and death in the lives of the two major gods that reflects that pattern in the lives of human beings.

A provocative aspect of this myth is the subservient role of the female. Every one of the many versions of the myth states that it is proper for the male to speak first. If the female speaks first, her behavior is worse than socially unacceptable; dreadful consequences, in the form of abnormal children, result. Yet the principal Japanese deity is female. The sun goddess Amaterasu Omikami rules all of the gods and the entire universe. She is also a

Great Goddess or Mother Goddess figure, for she is responsible for fertility.

The subservient role of the female in this myth is also unusual in terms of early Japanese society. The oral tradition of the Ainu, who were among the earliest peoples living on Japanese soil, reveals that women were very powerful figures in their society. They were the shamans, or seers. They fought side by side with the greatest of noblemen on the battlefield, where they displayed equal courage, strength, and skill.

Until late in the 8th century, women often ruled the small political states in Japan. They did not become completely subservient to men until the 16th century. Therefore, it is particularly interesting that a myth recorded early in the 8th century should have such a masculine bias.

The Creation of the Universe and Japan

In the beginning, heaven and earth were one unformed mass, similar to a shapeless egg. The lighter, clearer part remained above and, in time, became heaven. More slowly, the heavier, denser part sank below and became earth. At first, pieces of land floated about in the void as a fish floats on the surface of the sea. A detached object, shaped like a reed-shoot when it first emerges from the mud, floated in the void between heaven and earth as a cloud floats over the sea. This became the first god. Other gods followed, the two youngest being Izanagi no Mikoto and Izanami no Mikoto.

Izanagi and Izanami stood side by side upon the floating bridge of heaven, which we call the rainbow, and looked down from the heights. "Can you see anything below us?" Isanagi asked.

"Nothing but water," Izanami replied. "I wonder if there is any land."

"That is something we can determine!" Izanagi replied. "Let us take the jewel-spear of heaven and thrust it into the depths. If land exists, this spear will surely reveal it."

The two gods moved the jewel-spear around in the depths and then pulled it up to see if any material had collected on its tip. Salty water dripped from the point of their spear and fell as a salty mass into the sea below, forming an island.

"Now we can live on the waters below us!" Izanami exclaimed. "We have land to rest on."

So Izanagi and Izanami left heaven and went to live upon the island they had created in the middle of sea. They built a large palace there and placed the jewel-spear in its center as a supporting pillar. Then they married. They hoped to have many island-children, who would join together to become a country.

Once they had established their home, Izanagi said to Izanami, "Let us sepa-rate and investigate our island. You go in one direction and I will go in the other, and we will meet."

Izanagi turned to the left of the palace, Izanami turned to the right, and they walked around the island. When they came together again, Izanami exclaimed, "How wonderful! I have met a handsome young man!"

In time, Izanami gave birth to their first child. Instead of being an island, it was a disgusting leech-child, who could not stand up even at the age of three years. They had no desire to keep such a child, so they sent it floating upon the sea in a reed boat and let the winds determine its destiny.

The two gods then returned to heaven and asked the older gods, "Why did Izanami give birth to an abnormal child? Is there anything we can do to prevent her from having another one?"

The gods replied, "Izanami gave birth to a useless child because she does not appear to know her proper place. A woman should let the man be the first to speak, for that is his right. When a woman speaks first, she brings bad luck. If you wish to have proper children, then you must begin all over again. Return to your is-land, walk your separate ways, and try meeting and greeting each other once more."

Izanagi and Izanami obeyed the advice of the gods, and this time when they met, Izanami let Izanagi speak first. "How wonderful!" he exclaimed. "I have met a lovely young woman!"

Izanami smiled and replied, "How wonderful! I have met a handsome young man!"

In the course of time, Izanami gave birth to eight lovely children, each of whom became an island. Together the eight islands formed one country.

Izanagi then said to his wife, "The country we have created is covered with sweet morning mists, but what good are islands if no one can see them? I shall solve the problem by creating a child who will be the god of the wind."

He took a deep breath and exhaled their next child. The newborn god cloaked himself in a great blast of air. Then he flew over his sisters and brothers, scattering the mists that concealed them.

Izamani said to her husband, "Now that you have revealed the country we created, we must make our islands beautiful. We must create lofty mountains and peaceful valleys, cool forests and lush meadows, sparkling waterfalls and bubbling streams." So Izanagi and Izanami created the gods of the sea, the gods of the mountains, the gods of the rivers, and the gods of the trees.

When they saw that their country was truly beautiful, Izanagi said, "Now let us create the god who will rule the universe."

Together they produced the goddess of the sun, Amaterasu Omikami. From the time of her birth, Amaterasu shone with a brilliance that illumined the entire world. Izanagi and Izanami were delighted with their youngest child. "We have many children," Izanagi said, "but not one of them can compare with our beauti-ful Amaterasu! Clearly our country is no place for such a great goddess. She belongs in heaven where she can shine down upon the earth! As soon as she can, let her climb the ladder of heaven."

Amaterasu was in heaven when Izanami gave birth to the god of the moon. His beauty and brilliance were almost as great as Amaterasu's. He too climbed the ladder of heaven, for in time he would become Amaterasu's husband and would rule the universe with her.

Izanagi and Izanami's next child, Susano-o-no-Mikoto, had a disposition that brought no joy to anyone. Whenever he was not creating havoc with his temper tantrums, he was crying. His parents gave him the power to rule the earth, but he misused that power. He caused the forests to wither, and he brought early deaths to many people.

Finally Izanagi and Izanami said to him, "Your love of destruction gives us no choice but to banish you. You are so cruel that it is unfair to let you rule the earth! We are sending you down to rule the netherland, where you can do less damage."

Izanagi and Izanami's next child was the god of fire. In the process of being born, he burned his mother, and Izanami died. As she was dying, she gave birth to the earth goddess and the water goddess. The god of fire married the goddess of the earth, and their daughter produced the mulberry tree and the silkworm from the hair on her head, and five kinds of grain from her navel.

Meanwhile, as Izanami lay dying, Izanagi cried, "How grieved I am!" In anger and resentment, he drew his sword and sliced the god of fire into three pieces, each of which became a god.

Overcome with sorrow and loneliness, Izanagi then followed Izanami, traveling the long path into Yomi, the dark land of death. When he found her he said, "I have come to you here in this dreadful place, Izanami, because I love you, and I cannot bear to live without you!"

To his surprise, Izanami did not welcome his words. "Izanagi, my husband and my lord, why did you take so long in coming?" she complained. "I have already eaten Yomi's food! Now I cannot go with you. If you love me, please let the darkness be a blessing, and do not look upon me. Instead, you must return the way you came, for my death has put an end to our marriage."

But Izanagi truly loved Izanami. He could not leave his beloved wife so easily, nor could he refrain from looking at her one last time. Secretly, he broke off an end tooth from the many-toothed comb that he wore in his hair and created a torch by igniting it. Then he confidently held the blazing torch toward his beautiful wife.

As the glow illuminated her figure, Izanagi recoiled with shock and revulsion. Izanami's body was now in a state of decay, and a host of maggots were voraciously feeding upon her rotting flesh. "The land of the dead is indeed a dreadful place!" he exclaimed in a whisper.

Izanami heard him and rose in a fury. "Why did you not leave as I wished?" she asked. "Now you have shamed me, and I will punish you for it!" Izanami called forth the eight ugly females of Yomi, who relentlessly pursued Izanagi.

To delay them, Izanagi removed his black headdress and tossed it on the ground. It immediately turned into a large bunch of grapes, which the pursuing females stopped and ate. When they had finished eating, they resumed their chase.

Izanagi removed his many-toothed comb from his hair and tossed it on the ground. It immediately turned into bamboo shoots, which the pursuing females stopped and ate. When they had finished eating, they resumed their chase.

By the time they caught up with Izanagi, he had reached Yomi Pass, the border between the dark land of the dead and the bright land of the living. There he blocked the path with a huge rock that it would take 1,000 men to move. From his safe position behind the rock, Izanagi remained to talk with his wife.

"Izanagi!" she exclaimed. "You have so shamed me that I am prepared to kill every one of your subjects! I can strangle 1,000 each day. In no time at all, you will rule over an empty kingdom."

"If you do so, Izanami," Izanagi replied, "I will see to it that 1,500 people are born each day!"

"Izanagi, my husband and my lord, you must accept my death," Izanami said soothingly. "We have loved one another long and well. Together we have created a beautiful country and many gods. Is this not enough? My time on earth has come to an end, and it is too late for me to return. So let us come to peaceful terms with each other."

"All right, Izanami," Izanagi replied. "I know that it was weak of me to follow you into the land of death. I know that bad luck follows those who visit the land of Yomi while the wind of life blows through their bodies. Our marriage is hereby severed. As you wish, I will leave you to your life with Yomi in his dreadful land. I will return to the land of the living and will not bother you again."

True to his word, Izanagi never did.

Introducing **Amaterasu**

The myth of Amaterasu and the Japanese creation myth are so closely related that the introduction to the creation myth applies here as well. Like the Japanese creation myth, the myth of Amaterasu is told in the *Kojiki (Record of Ancient Matters)* and in the *Nihon Shoki (Chronicles of Japan)*.

The Amaterasu myth is also part of the Shinto religious tradition, which assumes that every aspect of nature contains a divine spirit. Amaterasu Omikami is the principal Japanese deity. She is the sun goddess, the Great Goddess or Mother Goddess who is responsible for fertility, and she is the ruler of the gods and the universe. Moreover, she has the personality and skill to remain in power. In her multiple divine roles, Amaterasu reflects the important role of women in early Japanese life, where they were warriors, rulers, and seers.

The myth of Amaterasu reflects the Shinto interest in fertility and rituals associated with it. The myth explains the separation between the sun and the moon, the origin of food on earth, and the beginning of agriculture and the silkworm industry.

Although in many other cultures, two different deities are responsible for the shining of the sun and for fertility, a logical connection exists between the two. Without the sun no plants would grow, and without plants human beings would starve for lack of food. The gods would also starve, for they eat the same food that humans do, either directly or in the form of sacrifices offered to them. Thus, when Amaterasu locks herself in the cave,

her action brings the ultimate catastrophe upon both gods and humans.

Presumably, as long as Amaterasu
was treated with respect, the sun
would continue to shine and human

beings would prosper. This optimistic
view of nature was supported by the
abundance of plant life, wild animals,
and fish in Japan at the time the myth
was created.

Amaterasu

Amaterasu Omikami, goddess of the sun and of the universe, was reigning in
heaven when she sent her brother and husband, the god of the moon, down to
the reed plains to serve the goddess of food. As soon as the goddess saw him, she
turned toward the land and spit boiled rice from her mouth. Next she turned
toward the sea and spit all kinds of fish from her mouth. Finally, she turned
toward the mountains and spit a variety of fur-coated animals from her mouth.
She then prepared all of these as food and placed them upon 100 tables for the
moon god to eat.

When the moon god saw what she had done, he was furious. "How dare you
feed me with food that you have spit from your mouth!" he exclaimed, "You
have made the food filthy and disgusting!" He drew his sword and killed the goddess. Then he returned to Amaterasu and told her of his deed.

To his surprise, Amaterasu exclaimed, "You are an evil god! I can no longer
stand the sight of your face. Take yourself from my presence, and see to it that
we do not meet face to face again!" So the sun and the moon lived apart from
one another, separated by day and by night.

Amaterasu sent her messenger, the cloud spirit, down to the goddess of food.
He found that the goddess was indeed dead. However, he also found that the ox
and the horse had issued forth from her head, grain had grown from her
forehead, silkworms had come forth from her eyebrows, cereal had emerged from
her eyes, rice had grown from her stomach, and wheat and beans had grown from
her abdomen. The cloud spirit collected all of these and returned to Amaterasu
with them.

The goddess of the sun was delighted with the variety of foods. "You have
given me great cause for rejoicing!" she exclaimed to her messenger. "Human
beings will be able to eat these foods and survive."

Amaterasu extracted the seeds from the various grains and beans and planted
them in the dry fields. She took the rice seed and planted it in the water fields.
She then appointed a heavenly village chief and let him supervise the sowing of
these seeds. The first harvest that autumn was a pleasure to behold. Meanwhile,
Amaterasu placed the silkworms in her mouth and collected silken thread from
them. Thus, the sun goddess initiated the art of raising silkworms.

Not long thereafter, Izanagi and Izanami gave their son Susano-o-no-Mikoto the netherland to rule and banished him there. Before he took his place in the netherland, he decided to visit his shining sister. He was such a violent god that the mountains and hills groaned aloud and the sea frothed in tempestuous tumult as he made his way up to heaven.

When she saw him coming, Amaterasu thought, "Surely my wicked brother is coming to visit me with no good purpose in mind. He must want my kingdom, the plain of heaven. Yet our parents assigned a particular realm to each of us. Susano-o-no-Mikoto should be satisfied with the kingdom they have given him. I had better prepare for the worst!"

The goddess bound up her hair in knots and tied her skirts into trousers as if she were a male. She placed two quivers upon her back, one containing 1,000 arrows and one containing 500. At her side she placed three long swords. In one hand, she carried her bow upright in shooting position, with an arrow ready on the bowstring; in her other hand, she firmly grasped one of her swords.

When the two gods came face to face, Amaterasu felt confident that her appearance would intimidate her brother. "Why have you come to me?" she calmly asked him.

"You look as if you are expecting trouble!" Susano-o-no-Mikoto replied. "Certainly you should have no fear of me. I have never had a black heart, although our parents dislike me and have condemned me to rule the netherland. I simply wanted to see you before I left the world of light. I do not intend to stay long."

Amaterasu, wishing to believe the best of her brother, put away her weapons. She welcomed him among the heavenly gods and hoped that his visit would be as brief as he had said.

But Susano-o-no-Mikoto stayed longer than he was wanted, and his behavior was very rude. He and Amaterasu each had three rice fields of their own. Whereas Amaterasu's fields thrived in spite of excessive rains or prolonged drought, Susano-o-no-Mikoto's rice fields were always barren. In times of drought, the soil was parched and cracked; in heavy rainfall, the soil washed away. Finally Susano-o-no-Mikoto became possessed by jealous anger. When the rice seeds were sown in the spring, he removed the divisions between the fields, filled up the channels, and destroyed the troughs and pipes. Amaterasu, wishing to believe the best of her brother, remained calm and tolerant.

In the autumn, when the grain was mature, Susano-o-no-Mikoto freed the heavenly colts and caused them to lie down in the middle of the rice fields. Again Amaterasu remained calm and tolerant.

Then Susano-o-no-Mikoto spoiled the harvest feast of first-fruits by defiling the purity of the palace with disgusting filth. Again Amaterasu remained calm and tolerant.

Finally, while Amaterasu sat weaving cloth for the clothing of the gods in her sacred weaving hall, her evil brother silently removed some roof tiles in order to create a hole in the ceiling. Then he threw a colt of heaven into the room. Amaterasu was so startled that she pricked herself with her shuttle.

This time the sun goddess could not forgive Susano-o-no-Mikoto. In great rage, she left the palace and entered the rock cave of heaven. She locked the door and remained there in isolation. Now that her brilliance no longer illuminated heaven and earth, day became as black as night. The universe was forced to exist in total, continuous darkness. Without the sun, plants could not grow. People everywhere stopped their activities, watching and waiting to see how long the deprivation would last.

All of the gods gathered along the banks of the Peaceful River of Heaven and discussed how to placate Amaterasu's wrath. They placed a statue of the sun goddess outside the rock cave and offered prayers to it. They also made many special offerings — including fine cloth, rich jewels, combs, and a mirror — which they hung upon a sakaki tree — and goddesses danced and chanted by the door.

Amaterasu heard the music and said to herself, "I hear both beautiful prayers of supplication addressed to me and the sounds of music and dance. Why are the gods so happy when my seclusion in this rock cave has brought constant darkness to the central land of fertile reed plains?" Her curiosity overcame her anger, and she opened the door a crack to look outside.

This was just what the gods had hoped Amaterasu would do. Rejoicing in the return of the sun's brilliant rays, they took Amaterasu by the hand, had her among them, and convinced her to rejoin them.

The gods punished Susano-o-no-Mikoto by demanding from him 1,000 tables of offerings. They also plucked out his hair and the nails on his fingers and toes. Finally they said to him, "Your behavior has been intolerably rude and improper. From this time forth, you are banished from heaven and from the central reed plains as well. Go forth with all speed to the netherland. We have had enough of your wicked ways!"

So Susano-o-no-Mikoto left heaven forever and began his journey to the netherland.

Introducing **Kotan Utunnai**

Historical Background

The Ainu people are the remnant of a Stone Age Asiatic people who lived in Japan before the islands were invaded by the Mongoloid people who became the Japanese. The Ainu remained unaffected by civilization for hundreds of years, because they lived in isolated river valleys and an abundant food supply was always available to feed their small population. The Ainu had no system of writing, no political organization beyond the small village, no domesticated farm animals or system of agriculture, and no bronze or iron metalwork of their own.

Ainu life remained as it had in ancient times until about 1670, when the Ainu began to have much closer contact with the Japanese. About 200 years later the Japanese began a concerted effort to settle the island of Hokkaido, on which most of the Ainu were living. The Japanese cleared the land of forests and wild animals and set up permanent fishing nets, in the process destroying the Ainu's traditional way of living. The Ainu men became migrant farm workers, and alcoholism and disease ravaged their society.

In the early 20th century, 15,000 to 16,000 Ainu were still living on Hokkaido. Because of the great value their society placed upon oral recitation, it was easy to find an Ainu who had a superb command of his oral tradition, and most of the literature we have today was collected and recorded in the 1920s and 1930s. By the 1940s, Ainu adults spoke both Japanese and their native language, but Ainu children spoke only Japanese. By 1955, fewer than twenty Ainu in all of Hokkaido could speak their native language fluently. The plight of the Ainu had become a public issue by the 1970s, and an interest developed in trying to preserve the Ainu heritage.

The epic of *Kotan Utunnai* is particularly important among the literary works acquired from the Ainu. John Batchelor, an English missionary, recorded it between 1880 and 1888, at a time when the ancient Ainu traditions were still vital. *Kotan Utunnai* was first published, in both Ainu and English, in an 1890 volume of the *Transactions of the Asiatic Society of Japan*.

Aspects of this epic are so old that they were unfamiliar to those who recited it. The Ainu of the 1880s and later did not know who the Repunkur (people of the sea) were. Many years later, archaeologists discovered that the term refers to the Okhotsk, a people who lived on the northern coast of Hokkaido. The Ainu, who were the Yaunkur (people of the land), defeated the Okhotsk (the Repunkur) in a series of wars between the 10th and the 16th centuries. *Kotan Utunnai*, like a number of other Ainu heroic epics, reflects these wars.

Appeal and Value

The epic of *Kotan Utunnai* is appealing because it is an unusual adventure story. The hero fights against strange adversaries. The blending of the divine with the human throughout the story provides a magical setting. In the characters themselves, this blend creates surprise, magic, and mystery. The hero is a human being, but he possesses such godlike qualities that even those who are supposed to be gods are not certain he is human. Similarly, the hero is not certain whether those who battle against him are divine or human.

The epic is also appealing because it reminds us of how similar human beings are to one another, even when separated by hundreds of years and by very different cultures. We understand and identify with the heroic characters because they have the same need to prove their excellence and to acquire fame that the characters in other major epics have — and that we ourselves have.

As in other epics, the best of human beings on both sides in *Kotan Utunnai* are heroic figures. The major characters possess courage, affection, loyalty, and perseverance, whether they are friend or foe. For example, the hero's "older sister" is not really his sister at all — she is a member of one of the enemy communities. She rescues the hero when his parents die and then rears him. She fights side by side with him, and he repays her loyalty. The ruler of Shipish is as much a hero as the narrator is. He fights only because the hero insists upon fighting him. When the sister of the ruler of Shipish leaves her brother and joins the hero, the author provides her with credible motivation for her decision.

The epic of *Kotan Utunnai* is also appealing because of its simplicity. The characters live in a world that they do not question. They know their strengths and their limitations, and they accept themselves and their destiny. They accept death as an integral part of life, and they know the rules for proper living. Those who lead good lives will be reborn after death; those who do not, will remain dead.

The world of the gods is an ever-present part of the world of *Kotan Utunnai*. The spirits of the gods rumble, and human ears hear their presence. Each human being possesses divine qualities just as each god possesses human qualities. Thus, a sense of unity and order exists in the universe of which *Kotan Utunnai* is a part.

These special qualities are transmitted by the epic's style. Like the other Ainu epics, *Kotan Utunnai* was recorded as it was sung, in the form of a first-person narrative. The first-person narrative is the most immediate kind of narration. The narrator is the hero of the epic, and he describes his own experiences as they unfold. We see what he sees as he sees it, and we hear what he hears as he hears it. We know only what he knows, and nothing more. We must depend upon what he tells us, and we learn as he learns from what others say or do to him. Because we as readers participate in the thoughts and actions of the hero as we do in no other form of narration, we become completely immersed in his world.

All the major characters of *Kotan Utunnai* are members of the nobility, as they are in the major epics from every other culture as well. The subject matter reflects the values and concerns of its noble audience. Thus, the major subject is war and the major values are courage, strength, and skill. The marriages of the hero and his brother to princesses of the enemy may have been used by the Yaunkur to justify and popularize their rule over the Repunkur.

One interesting feature of *Kotan Utunnai* is that the female characters possess great power and skill and are considered the equals of men. Aristocratic women fight side by side with their fathers, husbands, and brothers. The hero's mother dies in battle with her husband, and we are told that she has been a warrior all her life. The hero appreciates both his older sister and Shipish-un-mat because their courage, strength, and skill on the battlefield equal their great beauty.

Principal Characters

NAMELESS NARRATOR: Yaunkur heroic youth; son of the king of Shinutapka

OLDER SISTER: Repunkur maiden who rescues and rears the narrator when his parents are killed in battle against her people

KAMUI-OTOPUSH: narrator's older brother; great Yaunkur warrior

DANGLING NOSE: famous Repunkur warrior; an evil being

SHIPISH-UN-KUR: heroic ruler of Shipish; older brother of Shipish-un-mat; famous and respected Repunkur warrior

SHIPISH-UN-MAT: heroic sister of Shipish-un-kur; ally of narrator

Kotan Utunnai

Chapter 1

*The hero, who is the narrator, learns that the Repunkur
killed his parents. Taking his father's war gear, he sets
out to avenge their deaths. In Repunkur country, he
finds his older brother a prisoner. With his sister's
help, the hero frees his brother and kills his captors.*

I was reared by my older sister in the land of the Repunkur. For many years, we lived in a little grass hut. I would often hear a rumbling sound throughout our land. My sister told me that this was the sound of gods fighting. When many gods were dying, the sound would go on and on without interruption.

When I grew older, I would often hear similar sounds made by the spirits of the Yaunkur upon the roof of our grass hut. I could not understand this, so I said, "Older Sister, you have reared me well. Now it is time to tell me how this has come to be."

As my sister looked at me, her eyes trembled with fear and shining tears coursed down her cheeks. She replied, "I intended to tell you the story when you were older. I shall tell you now, since you wish it, but I must warn you not to act rashly when you have heard it.

"Although I have reared you, you and I belong to different people," she began. "Mine are the Repunkur, people of the sea. Yours are the Yaunkur, people of the land. Long ago your father ruled the upper and lower regions of Shinutapka. He was a great warrior and hero. One day he decided to go across the sea on a trading expedition. He invited his second son, Kamui-otopush, and your mother to join him on his journey. Since you were just a baby, she strapped you to her back and took you along.

"When they sailed by the coast of the island of Karapto, the people invited them ashore. Although they were Repunkur, they offered a sign of peace and wine to drink. Day and night, the people of the island encouraged your family to drink that poison. Your father became drunk with the wine, and his mind became clouded. He announced that he and his family intended to buy the major treasure of the people of Karapto and take it away.

"Your father's announcement caused fighting to break out, which spread to neighboring lands, including my own. My country is a land of many great warriors, and in one of his battles against the Repunkur, your father was killed.

"I was there when he died," my sister continued. "I took your father's war helmet and his clothes from his dead body. To help your mother, I took you from her back and tied you securely to me with my baby-carrying cords. With my sword, I did my best to protect your mother's life, but she had been a warrior all her life, so she insisted on fighting. Like your father, she was killed in that battle.

"Seeing that both your mother and your father were dead and that you were far too young to help your brother or survive on your own, I carried you to this land where we have been living all these years. It is a safe and isolated place; neither gods nor humans ever visit it.

"Since the time of your parents' death," my sister concluded, "your older brother, Kamui-otopush, has been fighting all alone against the Repunkur to avenge them. I must tell you this, for you asked to hear the whole story. However, remember that it would be unwise for you to act rashly."

I listened to the words of my older sister with complete surprise. My heart overflowed with rage. Was she not my enemy? Her own people had killed my parents. It took a great effort to calm myself and refrain from killing her!

I did not feel like thanking her for saving my life, but I forced myself to be polite. "You have reared me well, Older Sister," I said. "Now I would like you to find my father's clothes and give them to me."

She immediately entered the hut, untied the cord of her treasure bag, and brought forth six magnificent robes, a belt with a metal buckle, a small metal helmet, and a wondrous sword. All of these she held out to me.

With great pride and pleasure I put on my father's robes, placed his belt around my waist, tied his helmet on my head, and thrust his sword beneath his belt. My father's heroic spirit infused my body through his war gear. I strode up and back in front of the fireplace, flexing my shoulders and stamping my feet. Soon I felt my body go up the smoke hole of our little hut. Then I found myself being pushed through the air by a strong wind.

The mighty breeze blew me into a country formed of majestic mountains. I landed on the shore of the sea, not far from the mountains. My older sister dropped down at my side with the roaring of the wind. We traveled over a series of metal spruce forests, which clinked and clanked as the wind struck their branches. Certainly only great gods would live in a land such as this!

Suddenly I smelled smoke. When I descended into the lower regions of the forest, I found its source — a great bonfire. Along one side of the fire sat six men wearing stone armor. Next to them sat six women. Across the fire from them sat six men wearing metal armor, and next to them sat six women.

At the far end of the fire, between the two groups of warriors, stood a very strange-looking being I had never seen before. I wondered whether he could possibly be human, for he looked more like a small mountain that had arms and legs sprouting from it. His face looked like a cliff sheared off by a landslide. His huge nose looked like an overhanging rock. Strapped to his side he wore a sword as large as the oar of a boat. I knew that he must be the evil human demon called Dangling Nose, a famous Repunkur warrior.

While I stood gazing upon this strange group, the earth beneath my feet moved this way and that, and the metal branches of the spruce trees clinked and clanked as they struck each other. When my eyes left the group by the fire and searched the trees, I saw the most surprising sight. A gravely wounded man was tied to the top of a large spruce tree. Now and then he would rearrange his bound limbs, and it was his movements that were causing the earth beneath my feet to move this way and that. Even though I had never seen him before, I knew that he must be Kamui-otopush, my older brother.

My older sister said, "Younger Brother, this man is too sorely wounded to accompany us to battle. His presence will only hurt us. Let me carry off his body while you fight these people alone."

As soon as my ears had heard her words, the six warriors in metal armor announced together, "We are the people of Metal River, six brothers and six sisters. We were hunting in the mountains today when we came upon Kamui-otopush. He was returning to his country, for he had finished fighting. He was moving slowly, for his many battles had sorely wounded him. We would have killed him then and there if we did not fear the anger of Shipish-un-kur, our mighty uncle and ruler. So we tied him to a large spruce tree."

They added, "Soon these six warriors of Stone River came by with their sisters, and they stopped here with us. And now you also have come along. Are you a god, or are you human? Together, let us take Kamui-otopush as a gift to Shipish-un-kur. He surely will praise us when he sees this trophy!"

The man standing at the head of the fire proclaimed, "The famous warrior Dangling Nose adds his deep voice in agreement."

While he was speaking, my older sister went to the top of the spruce tree and freed my older brother. The sound of his loosened ropes falling on the metal branches drew the eyes of all the demons in that direction.

I did my best to prevent them from seeing me in my human form. Like a light breeze I flew with my sword into their midst. Beginning on one side of the fire, I raised my father's wondrous sword and sliced into the flesh of three of the warriors in stone armor with a single stroke, slashing three of their women as well. Turning to the other side of the fire, I sliced into the flesh of three of the warriors in metal armor with a single stroke, slashing three of their women as well.

Swinging my sword back, I aimed to kill Dangling Nose. However, he flew over my blade like a light breeze and said, "I thought that Kamui-otopush was bound to the top of the spruce tree, but he has strength enough to kill our people. I doubt that we would be able to kill such a man in battle. Let us take him to the battle-chasm, for it will be easier to kill him there."

Meanwhile, our sword blades gleamed as he and I fought fiercely against one another. In the midst of our battle, my older sister dropped down at my side with the roaring of the wind. "I have taken the body of your older brother back to your country," she announced. "There I found your oldest brother, now the ruler of your land, and your oldest sister. It is fortunate that your parents left them behind when they set off on that trading expedition across the sea so many years ago. Before I left, we restored Kamui-otopush to life, so do not let concern for him distract your fighting."

While my older sister was speaking, the remaining six women attacked her with their swords. Wicked women can be brave and strong fighters! My sister raised her sword, her blade shining against theirs. She was a match for them, but she would not be able to kill them easily.

As their battle carried the women toward the distant mountains, an attack by the six remaining warriors and Dangling Nose directed my attention back to the men. I raised my sword, my blade shining against theirs. I was a match for them, but I would not be able to kill them easily. I did my best to prevent them from seeing me in my human form. Like a light breeze, I flew with my sword over their blades.

As we fought, I noticed a river flowing from one group of mountains to the next. Between them, it descended into a deep ravine. When I saw many sharp sword-blades and spear-blades of stone rising from the poisonous water, I knew that this must be the battle-chasm Dangling Nose had mentioned.

The warriors banded together and forced me toward the chasm. Time and again they almost killed me, but I did my best to prevent them from seeing me in my human form. Like a light breeze, I flew with my sword over their blades.

Meanwhile, I chanted, "Hear me, gods of the chasm, gods of the deep ravine! I am one Yaunkur against many Repunkur. If I die here, my blood will give you little wine to drink. Take my side against these warriors, and you can gorge yourselves upon their blood!"

With these words, my heart flooded with renewed spirit and strength. With my father's wondrous sword, I drove the Repunkur toward the battle-chasm. The oldest of the warriors in stone armor was the first to fall to the bottom of the ravine and be sliced into chunks of human meat. His spirit left his body with a loud roar and rumbled as it flew off to the west.

Next, the largest of the warriors in metal armor fell to the bottom of the ravine and was sliced into chunks of human meat. His spirit left his body with a loud roar and rumbled as it flew off to the west.

In time I killed all but Dangling Nose. One by one, their spirits left their bodies with a loud roar and rumbled as they flew off to the west. Not one among the dead would be restored to life.

Dangling Nose and I then fought to the death. Time and again he almost killed me, but each time I returned his sword thrust with one of my own. Finally he said, "Great warriors fight in more than one way. I now challenge you to a contest of strength!"

He did not wait for my response but quickly rushed toward me. As we wrestled together, he enclosed me between his mighty hands and began to press the breath out of me. My heart fluttered with pain, but I made a quick twist and escaped from his hands as running water rushes through open fingers.

Finally I was able to hurl Dangling Nose down into the deep ravine. When his body hit bottom, the sharp blades of the stone swords and stone spears sliced him into chunks of human meat. His spirit left his body with a loud roar and rumbled as it flew off to the west. He would not be restored to life either.

Chapter 2

The hero travels to Shipish to fight the fearsome Repunkur ruler. The ruler's sister helps the hero. Together, they rescue the hero's older sister and kill her Repunkur enemies. Then they fight two storm demons. Victorious, they return to the hero's homeland, where they are reunited with the hero's older brother and older sister. The two Yaunkur men marry the two Repunkur women and live in peace.

In the quiet time that followed, I walked along the river and said to myself, "Who is this fearsome ruler who would have received my older brother as a trophy? If I were to return to my country without seeing Shipish-un-kur, my people would look upon me as a coward. He may kill me, but I must see how we two warriors compare with one another."

A light breeze carried me above the river as it flowed down to the sea. At its mouth I found the large village of Shipish surrounding a lone, majestic mountain. Its peak soared so far into the heavens that it was wrapped in clouds of mist. I followed the winding trail to the stockade at the top. Fearsome spirits rumbled their warnings from the top of the stockade, but I entered in spite of them.

Peering through the windows of the large house, I saw the fearsome ruler of this country. The sight of Shipish-un-kur filled my heart with awe, for he wore magnificent robes and carried wondrous swords. However, he was only a young man. Whiskers had just begun to grow upon his chin.

As he sat by the side of the glowing hearth, the most beautiful young woman I had ever seen sat next to him. Even my older sister was not this beautiful! I could tell from her face that she possessed the magical powers of a prophet, and their conversation soon proved my judgment correct.

"Shipish-un-mat, dear younger sister," I heard him say, "ever since you were a child, you could tell the future. Tell me, then, why do I have the feeling that danger is approaching?"

Shipish-un-mat tied her hair with the band of a prophet and picked up her magical wand. A prophecy immediately streamed forth from her mouth. "By the battle-chasm of our river," she began, "I can see that people have joined together to fight a Yaunkur. At times the blood and gore conceal my view of the scene. At other times, I see the tangle of their swords in battle. Then I see the broken swords of the Repunkur disappear into the west. Meanwhile, the sword of the Yaunkur is brightly shining in the east.

"Then," the prophetess continued, "I see the Yaunkur, in the form of a marvelous little bird with speckled feathers, flying downstream above our river. Fierce fighting suddenly breaks out in our land, completely destroying our villages. I see your sword entangled with the sword of the Yaunkur. At times the blood and gore conceal my view of the scene. At other times, I see the tangle of swords in battle. Then I see a terrible sight — your broken sword disappearing under blood and gore. Meanwhile, the sword of the Yaunkur is brightly shining in the east. Then the entire vision disappears."

"You have spoken dreadful, wicked words!" Shipish-un-kur exclaimed, with rage blazing forth in his eyes and in his voice. "The gods may be speaking through you, but their words infuriate me. I fight only against the gods; I keep peace with human beings. The evil Repunkur may have fought against the young Yaunkur all his life, but I will not fight him! Should he ever come here, I will greet him with kindness and peace in my heart."

I flew through the window and up to the rafters of their large house. I walked this way and that on the beams, stamping my feet so that the rafters creaked and the household gods rumbled with fright. Then I dropped down beside the young ruler with the roaring of the wind. I caught him by his hair and twisted his head this way and that.

As I tossed him about, I said, "Tell me, Shipish-un-kur, why was Kamui-otopush taken prisoner and bound at the top of a spruce tree? I avenged him by fighting the Repunkur. They spoke of you as a fearsome ruler who would have received my older brother as a trophy. I knew that if I were to return to my country without seeing you, my people would look upon me as a coward. So I have come. If you greet me with kindness and peace in your heart, I cannot accept that. I must see how we two warriors compare with one another. Even if we kill each other, our hearts will be content. Show me your courage, strength, and skill."

With these words, I grabbed the great warrior's younger sister and carried her toward the smoke hole, while she screamed for help. Shipish-un-kur quickly drew his sword and prevented me from leaving through the smoke hole. I then dashed to the window, but again I could not get past his sword. The two of us flew from side to side beneath the ceiling like a pair of birds. Angry at her prophecy, the great warrior became determined to kill his sister.

I carried Shipish-un-mat before me as a shield, believing that her brother would spare us both because of his loyalty to her. I was wrong. Shipish-un-kur's repeated sword-thrusts finally turned Shipish-un-mat against him, and she became determined to kill him. As soon as I released her, she drew a dagger from her robes and began to attack him, gaining strength from the wrath in her heart.

Hearing the commotion, throngs of armed men rushed in and attacked us. My companion spirits joined the local spirits on top of the stockade, and they rumbled together like one great spirit. The gods sent a fearsome wind rushing into the house, fanning the flames in the hearth until they left their bounds and began to consume the house itself. We escaped just before the building collapsed.

When I saw armies of spearmen coming toward me, I chased them toward Shipish-un-mat. Somewhat to my surprise, she proved to be as courageous and as skilled as she was beautiful. She stood her ground and fought them off, slashing as if she were facing only a few warriors rather than hundreds of them. The flashing of her sword concealed all other swords. She cut down the warriors like blades of grass, and corpses soon covered the earth like a blanket.

Strong as we were, we could not have killed hundreds if a mass of clouds had not blown toward us as swiftly as an arrow in flight. While a mighty god rumbled a warning, my older brother dropped down beside me with the roaring of the wind. We saluted one another with our swords, and then Kamui-otopush began his attack.

Although I swung my father's wondrous sword against the warriors, my skill was small compared to that of Kamui-otopush. The flashing of his sword concealed all other swords. He cut down the warriors like blades of grass, and corpses soon covered the earth like a blanket.

Suddenly Shipish-un-mat screamed, "Valiant Yaunkur warrior, your older sister is fighting mighty demons in a far land. Unless we hurry to her aid, they may kill her, and you will never see her again! Kamui-otopush has the strength and skill to stand alone against all the warriors here. Let us quickly depart!"

Shipish-un-mat flew into the heavens. I sheathed my sword and quickly flew behind her. When we came to the land Shipish-un-mat had seen in her vision, we heard the loud rumbling crashes that told of many dying gods. Below us, battle-mists concealed the earth. Through the clamor we could hear the sad rumblings of my older sister's companion spirits.

The rumbling of my sister's spirits led me to her rescue. I saw with dismay that she was gravely wounded. She would swing her sword once or twice but then faint from the effort. When she regained consciousness, she would swing her sword again. I dropped down at her side with the roaring of the wind.

I unsheathed my father's wondrous sword and swung it against the warriors, but my skill was small compared to that of Shipish-un-mat. Once she began her attack, the flashing of her sword concealed all other swords. She cut down the warriors like blades of grass, and corpses soon covered the earth like a blanket.

Then my older sister collapsed to the ground while a host of spears fell upon her. I pulled her into my arms and held her body up toward the heavens. "Oh gods," I said, "you to whom my father prayed, my older sister reared me lovingly and well. Reward her for the care she gave me. Even though she is the child of my enemy, I pray you to restore her to life!"

The gods heard my words, and their hearts were kind. My sister's spirit left the body in my hands as a new, living spirit. It flew up with a loud roar and rumbled all along its eastward journey to our land, the land of the Yaunkur.

Shipish-un-mat and I continued the fight with renewed spirit. We did not stop until we had avenged my older sister by completely destroying those who had fought against her. When we had finished and all was quiet, Shipish-un-mat's eyes suddenly filled with tears. She said to me, "I can see that to the west of this land, the storm demon and his younger sister are preparing to attack us, man to man and woman to woman!"

Before long a mass of clouds rose in the west, bringing stormy weather upon us. I watched as two creatures walked toward us. First came a very strange-looking being whom I had never seen before. I wondered whether he could possibly be human, for he looked more like a small mountain that had arms and legs sprouting from it. His face looked like a cliff sheared off by a landslide. Strapped to his side he wore a sword as large as the oar of a boat. Behind him came a woman dressed in leather armor sewn from the skins of both land and sea animals. She walked toward Shipish-un-mat with a red knife poised in her hand. As Shipish-un-mat had foretold, the storm demon fiercely attacked me, and his younger sister fiercely attacked her.

I did my best to hold onto my life. I flew here and there like a light breeze, avoiding the storm demon's sword-thrusts. Then I discovered how his armor was tied together. Holding my father's wondrous sword like a spear, I stabbed the storm god through those ties. Good fortune smiled upon my blade, for the tip went right into his flesh, and he fell flat upon the earth. "He must be human after all!" I thought.

To my surprise, a handsome young boy jumped out from beneath the storm god's armor! He looked at me and said, "You amaze me, young Yaunkur! Even the greatest gods cannot destroy my armor, and yet you have succeeded. But great warriors should fight without armor. I must see how we compare with one another. Even if we kill each other, our hearts will be content, for everyone will speak of our fame. Now show me your courage, strength, and skill!"

He drew his sword and thrust it at me. Again I flew here and there like a light breeze, avoiding his sword-thrusts. Finally good fortune smiled upon my blade, for the tip of my father's wondrous sword slashed right into his flesh, and I heard his spirit leave his body and fly up with a loud roar.

Meanwhile, Shipish-un-mat and the storm demon's younger sister were also fighting fiercely. I discovered how the demon's armor was tied together. Holding my father's wondrous sword like a spear, I stabbed the goddess through those ties. Good fortune smiled upon my blade, for the tip went right into her flesh, and she fell flat upon the earth. "She must be human after all!" I thought.

To my surprise, a beautiful young woman jumped out from beneath the leather armor! She looked at me and said, "You amaze me, young Yaunkur! Even the greatest gods cannot destroy my armor, and yet you have succeeded. But do not let Shipish-un-mat hurt me!"

Shipish-un-mat angrily replied, "I must see how we compare with one another. Even if we kill each other, our hearts will be content, for everyone will speak of our fame. Now show me your courage, strength, and skill!"

Shipish-un-mat drew her sword and thrust it at the demon. Good fortune smiled upon her blade, for the tip of her sword slashed right into the goddess' flesh, and I heard her spirit leave her body and fly up with a loud roar. Her living spirit rumbled as it traveled to the east.

Shipish-un-mat said to me, "I know that after we left them, Kamui-otopush and my brother fought one another until your older brother killed mine. Because my brother was your enemy, perhaps you think of me as your enemy also. If you choose to kill me right now, my heart will be content. Or you may choose to pity me and take me to your country. Either way, it is time to stop fighting."

I chose to take Shipish-un-mat with me, for I knew that no other woman could ever compare with her. We traveled to my country, the land of the Yaunkur, which I had never seen. When we dropped down at the majestic house of my father, I called out to the herald, "Have my older brother and my sister who reared me arrived? If not, I will leave right now to fight the Repunkur."

The herald replied, "Kamui-otopush has finished fighting and has returned. The gods have restored your older sister to life, and she is here also."

It was as he said. My older sister had indeed been restored to life, and she was now more beautiful than ever. In gratitude for saving my life, my oldest brother gave my older sister to Kamui-otopush in marriage. In gratitude for saving my life, he gave Shipish-un-mat to me in marriage.

From that time until this, we have lived in peace.

Introducing **The Creation Cycle**

The ancestors of the Polynesian peoples originated in Asia. Conflict over land and available food probably led them to cross the Pacific and settle on Tahiti and other nearby islands. When conditions on Tahiti could no longer sustain their population, groups once again took to the sea in search of a new home.

One group of Polynesians traveled southwest and became the first inhabitants of New Zealand. They called their land *Aotearoa* (long white cloud) and themselves *Maori* (a person of this place). In their myths, they refer to their land of origin as *Hawaiki* (homeland). Although another group of Polynesians traveled east to the islands of Hawaii, whose name is derived from Hawaiki, scholars have concluded that the Polynesian land of origin was not the Hawaiian Islands.

Although the first Christian missionary, Samuel Marsden, arrived in New Zealand in 1814, Maori mythology shows little Christian influence. The earliest written collection of myths from the Maori oral tradition is Sir George Grey's *Polynesian Mythology and Ancient Traditional History*, published in 1855.

The Maori creation myth is unusual in its emphasis on the development from nonbeing to thought to the creation of the universe and human beings. The myth focuses on the relationship between nature and human beings. The behavior of Father Rangi and Mother Papa's six sons explains physical aspects of the environment while reflecting important characteristics of human nature.

Maui is the trickster-hero of Polynesia. Like many of the great heroes in mythology, he is a demigod, the son of a goddess and a mortal father. Maui can be compared with other trickster-heroes in mythology, such as Hermes, Loki, and Raven.

The cycle of myths that depicts Maui's exploits traveled with the Polynesian people to their new lands, including Tahiti and Little Tahiti, New Zealand, Samoa, and the Hawaiian Islands. The cycle includes Maui's mysterious birth, his theft (in another version, his capture) of fire, his taming of the sun, his fishing for New Zealand (in other versions, Tahiti and Little Tahiti or the Hawaiian Islands), and his quest for immortality (in another version, his introduction of death). These episodes may be very similar, or they may vary considerably from one island to another. Their broad distribution is an indication of their great age.

The Creation Cycle

The Creation of the Universe and the Gods

In the beginning, there was nothing but an idea. The idea was remembered. It then became conscious. Finally, it became a wish to create. So it came to pass that out of nothing came the power to live and to grow, even in emptiness.

And it came to pass that out of this power to live and to grow came the deep, dark, long, and gloomy Night, a presence felt, but unseen, in the sightless, empty universe.

And it came to pass that out of this power that was the Night came life, in the form of the sky, far-reaching Father Rangi. Father Rangi lived with rosy dawn's pale light and created the moon. He lived with golden morn's warmer rays and created the sun. Then he tossed both the moon and the sun into the deep, dark, and gloomy Night so that they would illuminate the universe and be its eyes. Now there were both Night and Day.

Father Rangi then lived with Mother Papa, the Earth. In love, he lay upon her, and they created land.

Father Rangi and Mother Papa produced many children, who lived in the darkness of the small space that existed between their parents. Mother Papa's body was covered with low plants, and the sea was as black as Father Rangi.

Father Rangi loved Mother Papa and clung to her. No light could come between them. Their first children became tired of living in everlasting darkness, and their six sons met together to discuss what they could do to improve their situation.

"We can kill Father Rangi and Mother Papa, or we can force them apart. For only then will we be able to escape this darkness. Which will it be?"

Tu, the fierce father and god of war-spirited human beings, finally exclaimed, "We must kill them!"

To these words, Tane, father and god of trees, birds, and insects, replied, "No, it would be better to push Father Rangi away from Mother Papa, to live like a stranger far above us. Meanwhile, we could let Mother Papa remain where she is under our feet, so that she can continue to nourish us with the foods that she grows for us."

Tane's words were so wise that even the warrior Tu was quick to agree with his brother's advice. But one brother, Tawhiri, father and god of all winds and storms, stood alone against the others. Now and forever, he separated himself from his brothers, fearing the loss of his own power and regretting his parents' separation. In defiance he held his breath and would do nothing. So it came to pass that five of Father Rangi and Mother Papa's six sons made an effort to try to separate their parents.

First came Rongo, father and god of the sweet potato and other edible cultivated plants. He lacked the necessary strength to separate Father Rangi and Mother Papa. Next came Tangaroa, father and god of all fish and sea reptiles. Tangaroa was stronger than Rongo, but no matter how hard he pushed, he could not separate Father Rangi and Mother Papa either. Third came Haumia, father and god of the fern root and other edible wild plants. However he, too, was unsuccessful. Then, confident in his own strength, Tu, the fierce father and god of war-spirited human beings, grabbed an axe-like tool and chopped away at the tendons that bound his parents together. The blood from these tendons created sacred red clay. However, Father Rangi and Mother Papa remained bound together.

Finally, Tane, father and god of forests, birds, and insects, took his turn. Just as a young tree pushes up from the earth, increasing in strength as it grows, so Tane slowly used his body to force his parents apart. First he tried to use his arms and his hands, but all their might could not move Father Rangi up and away from Mother Papa. Then, he decided to rest his head and shoulders against Mother

Papa and to use his feet to push up against Father Rangi. Very, very slowly, Tane's continuous pressure stretched and then tore the tendons that bound his parents together. Despite their anguished cries, he pushed Mother Papa far under him and thrust Father Rangi far above him. So it came to pass that Tane freed all of Father Rangi and Mother Papa's other children from their dark world.

Tawhiri, father and god of winds and storms, had sympathized with his parents' love for each other and had considered their attachment to be appropriate. Living in darkness was also compatible with the nature of his power, whereas living in a lovely, bright world was not. Tawhiri greeted Tane's success with jealousy and anger. Tane had created exactly what Tawhiri dreaded — Day, with its power to push away the gloomy darkness of Night and light up and beautify the universe. The father and god of winds and storms feared that there would no longer be a place for him in this new world.

So it came to pass that Tawhiri hurried to join Father Rangi. The god of the sky and weather was pleased to have this son's companionship and help. Together, they worked to create many great winds and storms that flew north, south, east, and west, battering those on Mother Papa with their blows. Tawhiri sent winds that delivered fiery blows, winds that delivered freezing blows, winds that dumped rain, and winds that dumped sleet. Finally, Tawhiri came down to his mother's realm as a hurricane. He surprised Tane by tearing apart his forests and leaving his mighty trees to rot away, broken and useless upon the earth.

Having felled Tane's forests, Tawhiri then attacked Tangaroa's seas. Tangaroa loved to live along the seashore, but now he found himself battered by great tides, churning whirlpools, and mountainous waves. Terrified, he ran and hid in the deepest part of the ocean, where Tawhiri would not be able to find him.

Meanwhile, Tangaroa's two grandchildren, the father of fish and the father of reptiles, together with their own children, argued about whether they would be safer on land or in the sea. Shark tried to persuade Lizard and the other members of his family to seek refuge in the sea with the fish. "If you are captured on land," he warned, "you will have to endure death by fire before being eaten!"

"That may be," Lizard replied, "but all of you will be caught and eaten as well!"

And so it came to pass that the children of Tangaroa separated forever. Tangaroa became furious with Tane for sheltering Lizard and his children in the forests, and from that time to this, the god of the sea has been at war with his brother Tane. Tangaroa continues to nibble away at the forests that grow along the seashore, causing Tane's trees to fall prey to his waves. And Tangaroa enjoys chewing the wood from houses and trees that floods bring him. Meanwhile, Tane provides his brother Tu's children with the means to capture Tangaroa's sea-bound children by supplying human beings with wood for their canoes, fishing spears, and fish-hooks, and with flax and other plant fibers for their fishing nets. In response, Tangaroa attacks Tu's children with his waves and tides, capsizing their canoes and claiming their lives.

During the war between Tangaroa and Tane, revenge continued to occupy Tawhiri's thoughts and actions. After he was satisfied with his punishment of Tangaroa, he attacked Rongo and Haumia, the gods of planted and wild food. However, Mother Papa came to their rescue. Knowing that her other children needed the sweet potato and the fern root in order to survive, she hid Rongo and Haumia where Tawhiri could not find them.

Finally, Tawhiri attacked his last brother, Tu, the father and god of war-spirited human beings, and the one brother who originally had suggested that the gods kill Father Rangi and Mother Papa. However, Tu was ready for the assault. He placed his feet upon Mother Papa's chest, where they took their strength from their mother. Thus Tu survived Tawhiri's strongest storm-winds. Tu's victory caused Tawhiri to give up his battle.

Peace had little opportunity to reign on earth, however. Once Tu, the eternal warrior, had proved himself against Tawhiri, he became angry with his four other brothers. Not one of the gods of the earth and the sea had shown the courage and strength against Tawhiri that he had. Tane had been surprised by Tawhiri's attack and had made no effort to stop the father and god of winds and storms from destroying his forests. Tangaroa had avoided any confrontation with Tawhiri and, instead, had taken refuge in the depths of the sea. Rongo and Haumia had let Mother Papa protect them from Tawhiri by hiding them.

Tu was most angered by the fact that not one of his brothers had had the courage and the sense of loyalty to help him in his own fight against Tawhiri. The eternal warrior, therefore, set out to punish the four of them by taking control of their kingdoms.

The fierce father and god of war-spirited human beings decided to attack Tane's children first, before they became numerous enough to outnumber and overwhelm his own children. He fashioned leaves into nooses and hung them cleverly to trap Tane's birds. Once caught, he defiled them by cooking them, and then he ate them.

Next, Tu attacked Tangaroa's children. He wove the flax from Tane's plants into nets and dragged them through the sea to catch Tangaroa's fish. These, too, he defiled by cooking them, and then he ate them.

Finally, Tu attacked the children of Rongo and Haumia. He fashioned a digging stick from one of Tane's trees and wove a flaxen basket from one of Tane's plants. With these, he dug up and collected the sweet potato and the fern root. Once again, he defiled them by cooking them, and then he ate them.

So it has come to pass that, from the time that Tu conquered Tane, Tangaroa, Rongo, and Haumia, the warrior god and his human children have dominated and eaten the children of these gods of earth and sea. To this day, the human family continues to eat Tane's birds, Tangaroa's fish, Rongo's sweet potatoes, and Haumia's fern roots. Tu has never been able to gain power over Tawhiri, but, to this day, he continues to fight him, for Tawhiri's winds and storms remain a destructive force on both earth and sea.

The Creation of Human Beings

Before there was man, there was woman, and it was Tane who created the first woman. He molded her from the sacred red clay that had received the blood from the tendons that had bound Father Rangi and Mother Papa together. When he had finished, he blew the breath of life into her nostrils and called her Hine Ahu One, the Earth-Maiden.

Tane loved the woman he had made, and from their love, a daughter called Hine Titama, the Dawn-Maiden, was born. Tane loved Hine Titama as well, and from their love, children were born who became the first men and women.

All was well until Hine Titama asked Tane, "Who is my father?"

When she learned that Tane was her father as well as her husband, she exclaimed, "Because I am so ashamed, Tane, I must now leave you, and our children, and this world of light that I love! I will find my grandmother, Mother Papa, deep in the Underworld, and I will remain there with her from this time forth and forever. I will make a path as I walk, for I know that, in time, our children, their children, and all who come after them will know death and will follow me into the lower world."

In order to be certain that no one attempted to prevent her going, Hine Titama cast a spell of weakness upon Tane and a sleeping spell upon her children. Down, down, down, she traveled from the world of light into the eternal darkness of the lower world.

At the entrance to the Underworld, a guard confronted her. "Return to the upper world, Dawn-Maiden," he advised, "while you still can. Our spirit world is not for one like you! Here it is always black and grim. You would never choose to be here, for this is truly a joyless place!"

"I know that what you say is true," Hine Titama replied. "But it is here that I intend to live, and it is here that I will watch over my children who will be coming to me from the world above."

As Hine Titama turned from the guard to walk through the gates, her eyes fell upon Tane. Despite the deep gloom, she could see that he was tearfully following her.

"Poor Tane!" she cried. "Return to the upper world, and be a father to our children while they live in the world of light. Know that, in time, all of our children, and their children, and their children's children, from this time forth and forever, will follow this path that I have made.

"For death should come to all men and women," she explained, "and then, they should return to the dark world from which they came. That is why I intend to remain here. I want to be a mother to them when it is time for them to join me."

With these words, Hine Titama turned and walked into the Underworld, where she became known as the Night-Maiden and the goddess of Death. From that day to this, the sun begins its morning journey in the east and returns to its home in the west, while Tane follows it on its journey. And men, women, and children follow Hine Titama's path down into the Underworld when Death claims their spirits.

Meanwhile, despite their forced separation, Father Rangi and Mother Papa have continued to feel a great love for each other. In the beginning, Father Rangi cried so long and hard that his tears caused the sea to flood and swallow up most of the land and its people. Most of these people continue to live beneath the sea. Many of them have become so accustomed to living in their murky world that if the sun's rays ever were to touch them, they would die.

Some of Father Rangi and Mother Papa's sons began to fear that the upper world would entirely disappear into the sea unless they could find a way to stop Father Rangi's tears. They decided to ease their parents' grief by turning Mother Papa's face down upon the earth so that she and Father Rangi would not be able to see each other's tears. Their plan succeeded. The flood-waters that lay upon the upper world subsided, and from that time until this, Father Rangi's tears form the morning dew, while Mother Papa's tears form the morning mist.

Her sons turned Mother Papa's body while her infant son, young Ruaumoko, was drinking at her breast. At first Ruaumoko continued to cling to his mother. Then he fell into the Underworld. In time he grew up. Now whenever he walks around the Underworld, he creates earthquakes in the upper world. Some say that he has become Hine Titama's husband.

The Creation of New Zealand

Maui, the son of the goddess Taranga and the mortal Makea, was a hero, a trickster, and an inventor. It was he who tamed the sun so that those who live on the earth would have an easier life. However, it was also he who, for a prank, stole fire from those who live on the earth, thereby making life more difficult. And, it was he who first thought of using a barbed spear-point to capture birds and a barbed fish-hook to catch fish.

Maui's success in acquiring food for his wives and children far surpassed the success that his brothers had using traditional fishing methods, and since he never revealed the secrets of his success, his brothers preferred to hunt and fish without him.

One day, Maui overheard his wife complaining that she needed more fish than Maui caught for her. "If you want more fish," he announced, "why don't you simply ask me! You forget my magic powers. If it's fish that you want, I'll catch a fish that is so large that it will spoil before you can finish eating it! And then, I'm sure you will complain about the food that you had to throw away!"

So it came to pass that Maui used a piece of his grandmother's jawbone to create a magic fish-hook. Once he had recited the proper chants over it, he was determined to accompany his brothers on their next fishing trip. He expected that they would set out in their canoe just as the sun set out on its morning journey. He knew that his brothers would be watching out for him, even in one of his transformations, so he decided to hide beneath the planking in the canoe.

The canoe was safely out to sea before Maui decided to reveal his presence. Even then, his brothers were determined to take him home. So it came to pass that Maui resorted to magic. While his brothers were turning the canoe around, Maui so extended the distance between their canoe and land that they decided that it was more trouble to return Maui to shore than to keep him with them.

All was well until the brothers stopped at their usual fishing spot. Then, Maui suddenly spoke up and exclaimed, "Don't anchor here today! There's better fishing farther out!"

So the brothers resumed their paddling and continued toward their second fishing spot. By this time, they were very tired, but Maui was undaunted. "You don't want to anchor here, either!" he told them. "If you really want to catch a boatload of fish, let me take you to the place that I like best!"

Lured by the promise of fine fish, Maui's brothers agreed to paddle further out to sea. Finally, when they no longer could see the land they had left, Maui announced, "Here we are! Throw in the anchor and prepare your lines!"

Just as Maui had promised, fish continually bit their bait and were caught. Soon the canoe was weighted down with a huge load of fish, and the brothers prepared to return home.

"Wait a minute!" Maui cried. "You can't leave just yet! I have to try my own hook!"

"Your own hook!" his brothers exclaimed. "You don't own a hook, and if you mean to use one of our hooks, you can't have it!"

"Don't worry! I don't want one of your hooks," Maui replied. "I have my own right here."

Maui's brothers gaped in astonishment as he reached under his loincloth and pulled out a marvelous fish-hook. At one end of the sparkling, shell shank, a tuft of dog hair waved in the sea breeze. At the other end, Maui had fastened a hook that he had made from his grandmother's jawbone.

Maui found a fishing line in the bottom of the canoe, but his brothers refused to let him use their bait. Therefore, he gave himself a nosebleed and used his blood instead.

"All right now," he told them. "I am ready to fish. Do not say anything, no matter what I say or do! One word from you could make me lose my catch!"

He then threw out his line and recited this spell: "Blow kindly, winds, both you from the northeast and you from the southeast. I have come for my great land. Line, be strong and straight, and lead me to my catch!"

The line suddenly caught, and Maui pulled on it, causing the heavy canoe to tip and take in water. Maui's magic fish-hook had grabbed onto the house of Tangaroa's grandson.

"Let go, Maui!" his brothers screamed, as they frantically bailed out the seawater. They were sure that they would drown, but Maui refused to obey. He was busily using his fishing skill and his magic chants, and he impatiently replied, "What Maui has caught, he cannot set free! He is catching what he has come to catch!"

Meanwhile, Maui's brothers sat in silent terror in their quaking canoe, fearing the tumultuous waves that Maui's fishing had caused. Just when they could endure their fears no longer, they saw a group of thatched, pointed roofs, followed by the houses themselves, and, finally, the great piece of flat land on which the community stood, all slowly emerge from the waves. Maui's "fish" was no creature of the deep. It was a huge island filled with living people who were busily occupied with village life.

Maui tied his fishing line onto a paddle that lay securely in the canoe, and then he told his brothers, "I am going to the sacred place in this village so that I can perform the ritual offering to the gods. Until I have returned to you, you must not eat any food, and you must leave my fish just as it is. If you do not listen to me, you will anger Tangaroa and bring great trouble upon us!"

Despite Maui's warning, his brothers only waited until he was out of sight before they began to eat the sweet fruits of the land. The gods were quick to retaliate. Maui's fish began to thrash about, just as if it were an ordinary fish. Its movements caused the land to become mountainous and, therefore, difficult for human life. When the sun ended its day's journey, the fish finally became quiet. However, the surface of the land had permanently settled into the shape that it has had from that time until this.

Meanwhile, Maui and his brothers paddled back to their home on Hawaiki, where their father greeted them with a song of praise for Maui. "Maui Tikitiki, you are my pride and joy!" he exclaimed. "You have rescued our ancient land from its burial place at the bottom of the sea. This land disappeared long ago when Father Rangi, being angry over his separation from Mother Papa, helped Tawhiri take vengeance on his brothers by flooding the earth with his rain of tears.

"In times to come," Maui's father continued, "you will become the father of human beings like myself, and not gods like your mother. Some of your children and your children's children will continue to live here in our homeland of Hawaiki, but others will live on the islands that you have rescued from the sea. Therefore, your catching of your great fish will be as important an event to them as the separation of Father Rangi and Mother Papa!

"Your wonderful catch has made you a great hero!" Maui's father concluded. "And for this, you will have everlasting fame! From this time forth and forever, the Maori people will call their fish-shaped north island, 'The Fish of Maui,' their south island, 'Maui's Canoe,' and the cape at Heretaunga, 'Maui's Fish-Hook.'

"In fact," he laughed, "your deed is so great, Maui, that Hawaiki peoples of other lands will also claim that you rescued their islands from the bottom of the sea. And they will call their lands "The Fish of Maui" as well!"

Introducing **The Taming of the Sun**

Historical Background

Since the Hawaiians and the Maori of New Zealand share the same Polynesian origins, the introduction to the Maori creation myths includes a discussion of historical background that also applies to the following Hawaiian fertility myth.

Polynesian society in the Hawaiian Islands was divided into social classes that consisted of chiefs and royalty at the top, then priests, then the common people, and finally, slaves at the bottom. Each ruling chief claimed a divine ancestor through whom he had inherited his land.

Because Hawaii is a fertile land and fish are plentiful, life for the Polynesians was easy, and leisure time existed for the development and enjoyment of oral tales. Some bards were part of the chief's court, while others traveled from one court to another.

Both types of bard performed only for the aristocracy.

The Polynesians worshipped nature gods who are important in their legendary history. In the Polynesian myths, the gods are often depicted as chiefs who live in distant lands or in the heavens. Like the Hawaiian chiefs, who claimed divine ancestors, the heroes of Hawaiian myth are also related to the gods, either by birth or by adoption. Consequently, in Hawaiian mythology, divine power flows from the gods to their human relatives.

Captain James Cook, the British navigator and explorer, discovered the Hawaiian Islands in 1778, nine years after he had reached New Zealand. The first missionaries arrived in 1820, and they had a profound effect upon the native Hawaiians and their mythology. Under their direction, the Hawaiian chiefs discarded their native religion and adopted Christianity. The Polynesian creation myth disappeared from the culture and was replaced by one that is consistent with the account in the Bible.

During this period, the native oral language was given a written form, and by the 1860s, Hawaiian newspapers included Western literature. As a result, native Hawaiian literature became heavily influenced by foreign ideas.

Moreover, the first people who collected native Hawaiian literature chose to ignore the tales that collectors on other Polynesian islands had chosen to preserve. Consequently, the literature that survives from the Polynesian culture on Hawaii is later than the literature obtained from the Maori of New Zealand and from the native peoples of Tahiti and Samoa.

Two collections of Hawaiian mythology are particularly interesting. The *Legends and Myths of Hawaii*, by His Hawaiian Majesty King David Kalakaua, published in New York in 1888, presents a selected group of Hawaiian legends and folklore in a form designed to promote Hawaiian nationalism and cultural pride. The author rescues his subject from being viewed as mere children's tales by writing in a grandiose style and treating his Hawaiian material as if it were similar to the Bible, *The Iliad*, and the heroic myths and legends of medieval Europe.

The second collection is a series of books and articles written by William Drake Westervelt, an ordained minister who settled permanently in Hawaii in 1899 and became an authority on the customs and legends of the islands. His first book, *Legends of Ma-ui* (1910), tells the myth of Maui's capture of the sun and also includes Polynesian sources of the tale from such islands as Samoa and New Zealand.

Appeal and Value

The Hawaiian version of "The Taming of the Sun" is very similar to the Maori version of the same myth. Like "The Creation of New Zealand" (and its counterpart, "The Creation of Hawaii"), "The Taming of the Sun" is another of the demigod Maui's great deeds, and it provides an accurate depiction of this trickster-hero at work. Like the Hawaiian chiefs, Maui also has both divine and human relatives, being related to the gods through his mother, who is the patron goddess of kapa-beating (bark cloth–making) and other women's tasks.

A common theme in fertility myths involves a hero saving the world from a great threat. Sometimes the hero is a god, like Indra and Raven; sometimes, he is a demigod, like Ahaiyuta; and sometimes he is simply an ordinary mortal, like Bao Chu. Maui's deeds compare with those of other trickster-heroes in mythology, such as Hermes and Loki.

The Taming of the Sun

Life was easier for those on earth after Maui had raised and fastened the sky high above. However, life was still very difficult because the sun god now traveled quickly across the sky and made each day much too short.

In fact, it was impossible for trees and plants to produce enough food for the human family because it took them so long to grow. And it was impossible for men and women to finish any one task within the few hours of available light. Farmers did not have time to plant or to harvest a crop. Hunters did not have time to set their traps or to empty them. Fishermen did not have time to reach their fishing grounds or to return from them. And women did not have time both to prepare and to cook the day's food, or to make the bark cloth that they used. Even prayers to the gods were completed after the sun had returned to his home. For most of each day, the world was damp, dreary, and dark.

From the time that he could remember, Maui would watch his mother, Hina-of-the-Fire, as she tried to make the bark cloth, called kapa, during the brief time that the sun was traveling across the sky. It was a long and complex task at best.

First, Hina-of-the-Fire had to take branches from the mulberry trees and soak them in seawater until their bark was soft enough for her to remove it. Once she had removed the bark, she had to separate the inner layer from the outer layer, since she would only be able to use the inner bark to make kapa. She would stack the wet pieces of inner bark in bundles and lay them upon the kapa board where, beginning at one end of the board and moving to the other end, she would pound them with a four-sided wooden beater until the bark had become soft, thin sheets of pulp. Finally, she would paste these thin sheets together into large cloths that would make fine clothes to wear and mats on which to sleep.

Since the sun traveled so quickly across the sky, the process of collecting the bark took one month. The process of soaking it took a second month. The process of separating it took a third month. And the process of pounding it into thin sheets took six more months. In the early stages of this process, it was difficult to keep the bark wet. After the sheets had been pasted together, it was difficult for the kapa to dry. The entire process could take as long as a year, and making kapa was only one of a woman's daily tasks!

Maui watched his mother hard at work day after day, rushing to prepare her materials for one task, working faster at another task, sighing in despair as the sun entered his home before she had completed anything, and his heart ached for her. And the more Maui's heart ached for his mother, the more his heart filled with anger at the sun. So it came to pass that Maui turned his attention away from his mother and toward the sun. In order to observe the sun more carefully, he climbed the extinct volcano that can be found on the northwest side of the island. From there, he noticed that each morning as the sun began his journey, the sun would travel up and over the eastern side of the great mountain called Haleakala (the House of the Sun).

Then one day Maui asked his mother, "Why does the sun have to travel so quickly? Why doesn't he care about those who live on the earth? Is there a way to stop him from behaving so selfishly? I am going to tame him! What if I cut off his legs? That should keep him from running so fast!"

"The sun does what he has always done and what he will always do," his mother replied. "No ordinary person can confront him and live to tell about it. If you are going to try to change his behavior, you have set yourself a great task, and you will need to prepare yourself well. The sun is very large and powerful, and his rays are fiery hot. Once you come face to face with him, your courage will dry up in his heat as if you were no more than a dead plant!

"I think that you had better visit your grandmother and ask her to help you," Hina-of-the-Fire suggested. "She can give you good advice, and she has just the weapon that might bring you success.

"Your grandmother lives on the side of Mount Haleakala, not far from where the sun always begins his morning journey. You will know that you have found the place when you come upon a large wiliwili tree. Your grandmother prepares breakfast for the sun every morning, and he stops there to eat before he begins his journey.

"Your grandmother cooks bananas for the sun to eat," Hina-of-the-Fire explained. "You must be at the wiliwili tree as the sun makes the sky rosy-red with his first rays. A rooster stands watch by the tree, and he announces the sun's arrival by crowing three times. It is then that your grandmother will come out with a bunch of bananas and put them on the ground while she makes a fire in order to cook them for the sun to eat. You must take these bananas.

"Your grandmother will then come out with a second bunch of bananas and put them on the ground in order to cook them for the sun to eat. You must take these bananas as well."

Maui's mother concluded, "Your grandmother will then come out with a third bunch of bananas and put them on the ground in order to cook them for the sun to eat. She will notice that someone has taken the first two bunches of bananas and will begin searching for the thief. It is then that you must present yourself to her. You must tell her that you are Maui, and that you are the son of Hina-of-the-Fire."

So it came to pass that, while the sun was asleep, Maui set out to climb Mount Haleakala. Just as the sun made the sky rosy-red with his first rays, Maui saw the great wiliwili tree painted in black against the pale-colored sky. The rest happened just as his mother had told him it would. The rooster crowed three times. The old woman, who was his grandmother, appeared two times with a bunch of bananas that Maui took. When she discovered that these two bunches were missing, she cried, "Where are the sun's bananas?" and began to search for the thief.

Maui's grandmother was so old that she was almost totally blind. As she searched for the thief, she came close enough to Maui to smell the scent of a man. She then approached him, peered into his face with her clouded eyes, and asked, "Who are you? And what do you want with the sun's bananas?"

"I am Maui, the son of Hina-of-the-Fire," Maui replied, "and I have come for your help. I want to tame the sun! I need to find a way to stop him from behaving so selfishly. He travels much too quickly! He makes each day so short that even my mother cannot finish any of her tasks. It can take her a full year to make kapa! Those who are not gods must have an even more difficult time!"

Maui's grandmother listened carefully to his words. And as she listened, the things of the earth and sky praised Maui. In his honor, thunder roared and the rainbow bridge appeared. In his honor, pebbles chattered and ants sang. In his honor, dogs without fur walked the land. Surely, Maui was born to be a hero among men!

So it came to pass that Maui's grandmother decided to help him. "Listen carefully to my words, my grandson," she said, "and I will help you tame the sun. First, you must make sixteen ropes that you must twist from the strongest coconut fiber. Then, you must ask your sister, Hina-of-the-Sea, to give you enough of her hair to enable you to make a noose for the end of each of them.

"When these are ready," she concluded, "return to me, and I will tell you how to arrange the ropes so as to catch the sun. I will also give you a magic axe of stone so that you will have a great weapon to use against the sun."

Given the short days, it took many months for Maui to make the ropes and nooses, but finally he was ready to return to his grandmother's home. While the sun slept, she showed him how to set the nooses as traps and how to tie the ropes to the great wiliwili tree. Then Maui dug a hole for himself by the roots of the great tree and hid inside the hole so that the sun would not be able to see him when he began his morning journey.

When the sun made the sky rosy-red with his first rays, Maui was ready for him. Soon, the sun's first ray appeared over the top of Mount Haleakala and became caught in one of Maui's nooses. Then the sun's second ray appeared over the top of Mount Haleakala and became caught in one of Maui's nooses. One by one, the fourteen other rays of the sun came over the top of Mount Haleakala, and, one by one, each ray became caught in one of Maui's nooses. Finally, the sun, dressed in his bright crimson robe, stood on top of Mount Haleakala. He was ready to begin his morning journey, but he was unable to move even one of his rays.

At first, the sun violently thrashed this way and that, desperately trying to pull his rays out of the nooses and to retreat down the back of Mount Haleakala into the sea-home from which he had come. But he could not pull the ropes off the wiliwili tree, and the roots of that great tree held the tree fast.

"Who has trapped me in these snares? And what do you hope to gain by it?" the sun roared.

"I am Maui, the son of Hina-of-the-Fire," Maui replied, "and I have come for your help. You must stop behaving so selfishly. You travel much too quickly! You make each day so short that my mother cannot finish any of her tasks. It can take her a full year to make kapa! Those who are not gods must have an even more difficult time!"

"I don't care about your mother and her kapa!" the sun exclaimed. "And I certainly don't care about those who are not gods! The faster I travel each day, the longer I can sleep each night. This is what I have always done, and this is what I will always do! As for you, if you don't release me from these snares right now, you will not live to see your mother again!"

Maui immediately bent down, but he did not intend to release the sun's rays. Instead, he picked up his grandmother's magic axe and waved it threateningly at the sun.

The sun responded by turning his blazing face upon Maui. He seared Maui with his fiery breath, hoping to burn him quickly to ashes.

Maui retaliated by attacking the sun. Despite the intensity of the sun's heat, Maui mercilessly struck the sun, again and again, with the stone axe.

Finally, the sun screamed, "Stop it! I can't stand the pain any longer! If you keep beating me like this, you're going to kill me! And if I die, you and everything that lives will die as well! As it is, I'm going to hobble all the way home!"

"I will stop," Maui replied, "if you promise me that you will travel slowly across the sky each day."

"Do I have to travel slowly every day from this day forth and forever?" the sun wailed.

"No," Maui replied, relenting. "It will be good enough if you travel slowly for just half of the year. Your light and your heat will enable plants to grow faster and produce more fruit, and they will permit men and women to get their work done faster and more easily. Then, for the other half of the year, you can travel as fast as you wish."

The sun was quick to agree to this compromise. So it came to pass that Maui released the sun's sixteen rays from the nooses. However, as a daily reminder of their agreement, he left the ropes and nooses next to the great wiliwili tree on the side of Mount Haleakala, where the sun would be sure to see them as he climbed over the top of the mountain.

So it came to pass that, because of Maui's efforts, life became much easier for human beings. Each day during the long season that came to be known as summer, the sun traveled across the sky so slowly that the days were very long.

Now it was possible for trees and plants to produce enough food for the human family because they grew fast and well. And now it was possible for men and women to finish a difficult task within the long hours of available light. Farmers now had time to plant or to harvest a crop. Hunters now had time to set their traps or to empty them. Fishermen now had time to reach their fishing grounds or to return from them. And women now had time to prepare their food and to cook it, or to make the bark cloth that they used.

In honor of Maui's taming of the sun, the people celebrated and sang, "How good it is that the sun's journey is long and that he now gives us the light we need for our daily work!"

Africa

No one "African" culture exists. Instead, many different cultural groups live side by side on the same continent. Many of these cultures have existed for hundreds and even thousands of years.

The creation myth in this section comes from the Yoruba nation. Part of its appeal lies in the nature of the Yoruba gods, for they are caring and intelligent beings. It is also interesting to recognize the common ties that this myth shares with the numerous other tales of people who suffer the ravages of a great flood.

The fertility myth belongs to the Fon nation, the people of Benin (formerly Dahomey). It describes a family argument that results in an extensive drought. The myth is similar to two universal kinds of fertility myths: one in which a god saves the world from devastation, and one in which a god is insulted and must be appeased for fertility to be restored.

Gassire's Lute, the Fasa (Soninke) epic from Ghana, is a fascinating study of the conflict between an individual's personal desires and his or her responsibility to society. Gassire wants what almost every hero wants, everlasting fame. He is as courageous, determined, and skillful as the greatest of heroes. What is unique about this epic is that Gassire must choose between fame and his responsibility to his community.

Sunjata, the epic of the Mande-speaking peoples, describes the physical and spiritual journey of a hero from his childhood to his creation of the empire of

Mali. Sunjata lives in a world in which prophecy and magic are part of life. Like Odysseus and Rama, his period of exile strengthens his character and skills. He fights formidable enemies for the good of his society. The many loving human relationships and the role of the griot (bard) as the adult Sunjata's counselor give this epic an additional dimension.

Mwindo, the hero of the Nyanga epic by that name, is a traditional hero. Like many other heroes, he must travel to the Underworld, and like them, he makes the world a safer place because of his adventures. Mwindo is concerned with ethical behavior: life must be more than a series of heroic deeds. The most impressive quality of this myth is its reverence for all life.

Introducing **The Creation of the Universe and Ife**

The Yoruba people represent a major African culture that has roots extending back as far as 300 B.C., when a technologically and artistically advanced people lived just north of the Niger River. Today, more than ten million Yoruba people live in the southwest corner of Nigeria, from the Benin border north to the Niger River.

Like the ancient Greeks, the ancient Yoruba identified with the city-state in which they lived rather than with their larger culture. One Yoruba city-state was as likely to fight against another Yoruba city-state as against a neighboring culture.

Historically, Ife was the principal Yoruba city and was considered a sacred city. Religious ideas developed there and spread to other Yoruba city-states. The Yoruba religious system of prophecy even spread to other cultures in western Africa.

The mythology of the Yoruba people contains hundreds of gods, from major gods — the subjects of the following creation myth — to minor gods who protect local villages and regions. The Yoruba gods are human in form, thought, and way of life. They relate to one another as members of a large,

human family, and they experience love, jealousy, anger, and sympathy. They enjoy human beings and like to spend time with them on earth. It is not surprising, therefore, that the Yoruba gods are sensitive to human problems and receptive to human prayers.

The Yoruba creation myth shares many characteristics in common with the creation myths of other cultures. For example, the creation of land is similar to the Japanese myth, the creation of human beings is similar to the Chinese myth, and the occurrence of a great flood is similar to the myths of the Greeks, the Sumerians and Babylonians, and the Scandinavians. The gods in the Yoruba myth are likable because they exhibit many of the best characteristics of the human personality, most notably creative intelligence and the ability to care about others.

The Yoruba creation myth is recorded in *The Treasury of African Folklore* (1975), edited by Harold Courlander, a noted scholar of the Yoruba. Courlander relates other Yoruba myths in *Tales of Yoruba Gods and Heroes* (1973).

Principal Gods

OLORUN: ruler of the sky; creator of the sun; most powerful and wisest god

ORUNMILA: oldest son of Olorun; god of prophecy; advisor to Obatala

OBATALA: favorite of Olorun; creator of land and human beings

OLOKUN: ruler of the sea

ESHU: messenger god

The Creation of the Universe and Ife

In the beginning the universe consisted only of the sky above and the water and wild marshland below. Olorun, the god who possessed the most power and the greatest knowledge, ruled the sky, while the goddess Olokun ruled the endless waters and wild marshes. Olokun was content with her kingdom, even though it contained neither vegetation nor animals nor human beings.

However, the young god Obatala was not satisfied. As he looked down from the sky, he said to himself, "The world below needs something of interest! Everything is water-soaked, and not one living thing enlivens the area! I must talk with Olorun and see what can be done to improve the situation."

Obatala said to Olorun, "Poor Olokun rules nothing but marshland, mist, and water! What she needs in her kingdom are mountains and valleys, forests and fields. All kinds of creatures and plants could live on that solid land."

Olorun replied, "Of course, solid land would be far better than this endless expanse of water. But who can create it? And how?"

"With your permission," Obatala replied, "I will create solid land."

"It is always my pleasure to give you whatever you wish, Obatala," Olorun replied. "You know that I love you as my son!"

So Obatala went to the house of Orunmila, the oldest son of Olorun, who had the gift of prophecy. Orunmila understood the secrets of existence, including fate and the future.

Obatala said to Orunmila, "Your father has given me permission to create solid land where now nothing exists except endless water and wild marshland. With your superior knowledge, you can teach me how to begin my project. I want to populate the earth with living beings who will be able to raise crops and build villages."

Orunmila replied, "First, Obatala, you must acquire a chain of gold long enough to reach from the sky above to the waters below. Then you must fill a snail's shell with sand. Finally you must place that shell, a white hen, a black cat, and a palm nut in a bag and carry them with you as you climb down the chain to the wild marshland. That is how I advise you to begin your project."

"Thank you, Orunmila," Obatala replied. "I will find the goldsmith and begin at once."

The goldsmith said, "I will make you a chain of the length you need if you will bring me the gold I need to fashion it. I do not think you will find enough gold in the sky. But ask each of the gods for whatever gold he or she possesses, and you may succeed. I wish you well!"

Obatala approached the gods one by one. To each god he said, "I plan to create solid land where now there is nothing but water and wild marshland. Then I will create all sorts of plants and creatures to live on that land. Before I can begin, I need the goldsmith to make me a chain that will stretch from the sky above to the waters below. Will you contribute whatever gold you possess?"

The gods were sympathetic to Obatala's cause. They gave him their gold: necklaces, bracelets, rings, and even gold dust.

The goldsmith examined the gold Obatala had collected and said, "Can you not find more gold? This will not be enough!"

"It is the best I can do," Obatala replied. "I have asked every god in the sky, and each has given me whatever he or she owned. Make as long a chain as you can, with a hook at one end."

When the chain was ready, Orunmila accompanied Obatala while he hooked one end of the chain to the edge of the sky and lowered the rest of it toward the waters far below. Orunmila gave Obatala the sand-filled snail's shell, the white hen, the black cat, and the palm nut. One by one, Obatala put them into a bag, which he slung over his shoulder. Then he said farewell to Orunmila and began to climb down the golden chain.

Obatala climbed lower and lower and lower. When he was only halfway down, he saw that he was leaving the world of light and entering the world of twilight.

Again he climbed lower and lower and lower. As he reached the end of the chain, he could feel the mist rising cool and wet upon him and hear the splashing of the waves as they crashed upon the sea. But he could see that he was still far above the ocean.

"I cannot jump from here," he thought. "The distance is so great that I will drown!"

Then, from the sky far above, Orunmila called out, "Obatala! Use the sand in your snail shell!"

Obatala reached into the bag at his side, withdrew the snail's shell, and poured the sand on the waters below him.

No sooner had he finished when Orunmila called out, "Obatala! Free the white hen!"

Obatala reached into the bag at his side, withdrew the white hen, and dropped it on the waters where he had poured the sand.

The hen fluttered down, landed upon the sandy waters, and immediately began to scatter the sand by scratching at it. Wherever the sand fell, it formed dry land. The larger piles of sand became hills, while the smaller piles became valleys.

Obatala let go of the golden chain and jumped to the earth. He named the place where he landed Ife. He walked with pleasure upon the solid land that he had created. The earth now extended farther in all directions than his eyes could see. It was still completely devoid of life, but it was a beginning.

Obatala dug a hole in the dry land and buried his palm nut in the soil. Immediately, a palm tree emerged and grew to its full height. The mature tree dropped its nuts upon the land, and they also quickly grew to maturity. Obatala built himself a house of bark and thatched the roof with palm leaves. He then settled down in Ife with his black cat for company.

Olorun wished to know how Obatala was progressing with his plan, so he sent his servant, the chameleon, down the golden chain to find out.

When the lizard arrived, Obatala said to him, "Tell Olorun, ruler of the sky, that I am pleased with the land I have created and the vegetation I have planted. But it is always twilight here. I miss the brightness of the sky!"

When the chameleon gave Obatala's message to Olorun, the ruler of the sky smiled and said, "For you, Obatala, I will create the sun!" Once Olorun tossed the sun into the sky, it shed light and warmth upon Ife as it moved across the sky on its daily journey.

Days passed. Months passed. Obatala continued to live on the earth that he had created with only his black cat for company. Then one day he said to himself, "I love my cat, but its companionship does not satisfy me. I would be happier if creatures more like myself could live in Ife with me. Let me see what I can do."

Obatala began to dig in the soil. He found that the particles held together in his hand, for the substance he dug up was clay. He laughed as he shaped little figures just like himself. One by one he finished them and set them aside to dry. Obatala worked on and on so enthusiastically that he was not aware of how tired and thirsty he was.

Finally his fatigue overcame him. "What I need is some wine to drink!" he thought. Obatala placed his last clay figure upon the ground and went off to make palm wine from the juice of the palm tree. Obatala drank bowl after bowl of the fermented palm juice, for he was very thirsty. He did not realize it, but the wine made him drunk.

Obatala returned to his task of making clay figures, but his fingers were clumsy now. The figures he created were no longer perfect. Some had arms that were too short, some had legs of uneven length, and some had backs that were curved. Obatala was too drunk to notice the difference. He continued to fashion one figure after another. In time, he was satisifed with the number of clay figures that he had created.

Obatala then called out to the ruler of the sky, "Hear me, Olorun, you who are like a father to me. I have created figures out of clay, but only you can breathe life into them and make them into living people. I ask you to do this for me so that I can have human companions in Ife."

So it came to pass that Olorun breathed life into the figures Obatala had created, and they became active, thinking human beings. When they noticed Obatala's house, they fashioned houses for themselves and placed them nearby. Thus they created the first Yoruba village in Ife where there had been only one solitary house.

When the effects of the palm wine wore off, Obatala realized that the creatures he had fashioned while he was drunk were imperfect. With a sad heart he announced, "I promise that I will never drink palm wine again! Moreover, I will devote myself to protecting all the people who have suffered from my drunkenness." And Obatala became the protector of all those who are born deformed.

The people prospered, and the Yoruba village of Ife grew into a city. Iron did not yet exist, so Obatala gave his people a copper knife and a wooden hoe to use as tools. The Yoruba cleared the land and began to raise grain and yams.

Obatala eventually tired of ruling his city of Ife, so he climbed up the golden chain and returned to his home in the sky. Thereafter, he divided his time between his home in the sky and his home in the Yoruba city.

The gods never tired of hearing Obatala describe the city that he had created on earth. Many of them were so fascinated with what they heard about Ife that they decided to leave their sky homes and live among the human beings on earth. As they prepared to leave, the ruler of the sky counseled them. "Remember," Olorun said, "that you will have obligations to the humans among whom you live in Ife. You must listen to their prayers and protect them. I will give each of you a specific task to fulfill while you are living there."

Not every god, however, was pleased with Obatala's success on Ife. Obatala had not consulted the goddess Olokun, ruler of the sea, when he had created solid earth and a Yoruba city in her kingdom. As the ruler of the sea watched one of the great sky gods usurp her power and rule a large part of her kingdom, she became angrier and angrier. Finally she conceived a plan that would avenge Obatala's insult to her honor.

Olokun waited until Obatala had returned to his home in the sky. Then she summoned the great waves of her vast ocean and sent them surging across the land that Obatala had created. One after another, the waves flooded the earth until water once again flowed as far as the eye could see, and only marshland existed amidst the waves of the ocean. Whole groves of palm trees became uprooted and floated away. Yams rotted and washed like dead fish upon the surface of the sea. People drowned in their fields, in their groves, and in their homes.

Those who still remained alive fled into the hills and cried out to Obatala for help, but he could not hear them over the roaring of the waves so far below him. So they sought the god Eshu, who was living among them. They knew that he could carry messages to Obatala and to Olorun. "Please return to the kingdom of the sky," they pleaded, "and tell the great gods of the disastrous flood that is destroying us!"

Eshu replied, "You must send a sacrifice along with your message if you want one of the great sky gods to listen to you."

The people sacrificed a goat to Obatala and said, "We send this goat as food for Obatala."

"That is not enough," Eshu replied. "I too deserve a gift for the service I am performing for you."

When the people had sacrificed accordingly, Eshu climbed the golden chain and told Obatala about how Olokun had flooded Ife and the rest of the earth.

Obatala did not know how to deal with Olokun, so he asked Orunmila for advice. Orunmila replied, "You rest here in the sky while I go down to Ife. I can make the waters withdraw and the land come forth once again. "

So it came to pass that Orunmila climbed down the golden chain to the waters that covered Ife and the earth. Using his special knowledge, he caused the power of the waves to wane and the waters to retreat. Once the waves had subsided, he dried up the marshland and put an end to Olokun's attempt to recover the area that she had lost to Obatala.

The people who had survived greeted Orunmila as their hero and pleaded with him to stay and protect them. Orunmila had no desire to remain in Ife, but he agreed to stay long enough to teach the gods and humans who lived there how to tell the future so that they could begin to control the forces they could not see. When he had done so, Orunmila returned to his home in the sky but, like Obatala, he often climbed down the golden chain to see how life was progressing in Ife.

The ruler of the sea made one final attempt to remain the equal of the ruler of the sky. Olokun was an excellent weaver of cloth, and she possessed equal skill in dyeing the fabrics she had woven. So the ruler of the sea sent a message to Olorun, ruler of the sky, challenging him to a weaving contest.

Olorun said to himself, "Olokun is a far better weaver than I am. However, I cannot give her the satisfaction of knowing that she is superior to me in anything. If I do, she will exert her powers in other ways as well, and that will disrupt the order that now exists throughout the universe. Somehow I must appear to accept her challenge and yet avoid participating in her contest. Now, how can I do this?"

Olorun thought and thought. Suddenly his eyes sparkled. With a smile, he summoned his messenger, the chameleon, to his side. "Go before Olokun, ruler of the sea," he ordered, "with this message: 'The ruler of the sky greets the ruler of the sea. He asks you to display samples of the cloth that you have woven to his messenger. Let the chameleon judge your skill. If your cloth is as beautiful as you say it is, then the ruler of the sky will compete with you in the contest you have suggested.'"

The chameleon climbed down the golden chain and gave the goddess Olorun's message.

Olokun was happy to obey Olorun's request. She put on a bright green skirt, and to her amazement the chameleon turned a beautiful shade of bright green. She next put on a bright orange skirt, and to her amazement the chameleon turned a beautiful shade of bright orange. She then put on a bright red skirt, and to her amazement the chameleon turned a beautiful shade of bright red. One by one, the goddess Olokun put on skirts of various bright colors, and each time the chameleon turned into the particular color that she was wearing. Finally Olokun gave up.

The goddess said to herself, "If someone as ordinary as Olorun's messenger can duplicate the bright colors of my finest fabrics, how can I hope to compete against the greatest of the gods?"

She said to the chameleon, "Tell your master that the ruler of the sea sends her greetings to the ruler of the sky. Tell him that I acknowledge his superiority in weaving and in all other pursuits as well. Olorun is indeed the greatest of the gods!"

So it came to pass that peace returned between the ruler of the sky and the ruler of the sea, and that peace restored order in the universe.

Introducing **The Quarrel Between Sagbata and Sogbo**

The following myth belongs to the Fon, the people of Benin (formerly Dahomey), a culture known since the early 1600s for their skill in battle. In the 1700s the Fon established a female army, which became a fixed part of their society.

The traditional enemies of the Fon were their neighbors, the Yoruba. Frequent warfare resulted in extensive cultural contact. Consequently, the two peoples developed very similar religions, sharing the same complex system of prophecy and gods who possessed the same personalities, roles, and sometimes even the same names.

Like many other peoples, the Fon believed that the forces of nature were controlled by individual gods. In their

location, the sun was a reliable force in daily life. Rain was less reliable, yet necessary if the Fon were to have enough to eat. The following myth explains why a particular drought occurred and why it will not happen again.

This myth combines two thematic strains that are common in fertility myths. As in the myths of the Greeks, the Hittites, and the Japanese, a god is insulted and must be appeased for fertility to be restored. As in the myths of the Indians, the Chinese, and the Zuñi, a god saves the world from a great threat.

The myths of the Fon people were collected by Melville and Frances Herskovits and published under the title *Dahomean Narrative* in 1958.

The Quarrel Between Sagbata and Sogbo

When the Great Goddess Mawu had created the universe, she stepped aside and told her two sons, Sagbata and Sogbo, to rule the world together. However, Sagbata and Sogbo could not work well together. Each brother was always making decisions that annoyed the other.

Finally they had a great argument and Sagbata, the older of the two, said, "Sogbo, I cannot put up with you any longer! I am your older brother, and yet you do not think I am wise and you do not respect my decisions. Therefore, I am going to collect everything that is mine, and I am going to go down to the earth to live! I warn you that I am taking all of our mother's wealth with me. It is my rightful inheritance since I am the older son."

"Go then, if that is your wish," Sogbo replied. "I shall not miss you!"

When Mawu heard of her sons' quarrel, she called them before her. "I disapprove of your quarrel, and I will not support one of you against the other," she announced. "You two must fit together like a closed calabash (a round gourd), and together you must rule the universe that exists within that calabash."

Mawu continued, "You, Sagbata, being my older son, should be as the lower part of the calabash and rule the lower part of the universe, which is the earth. To you will belong all my wealth. You, Sogbo, being my younger son, should be as the upper part of the calabash and rule the upper part of the universe. Sogbo, you too will possess great power, for you will rule with the thunder and fire of the lightning bolt. Now go, both of you, and rule your kingdoms in peace!"

Sagbata collected his possessions, including everything that belonged to his mother. As he put the treasures into a large bag, he thought, "If I put water into my bag, it will soak every treasure and then leak out. If I put fire into my bag, it will burn everything. Therefore, I have no choice but to leave water and fire behind."

Sagbata then finished packing and went down to live on the earth. The journey was so long and difficult that he realized he would never be able to return to his home in the sky.

Meanwhile, Sogbo remained near his mother in the sky. In time he won her great affection and her complete confidence. Once he had Mawu's support, it was easy to win the confidence of the other sky gods as well.

Sogbo then said to himself, "Now I have achieved just what I wanted, unlimited power. I can do whatever I choose, and no god can stop me! I will prove to my brother that I even have power over his kingdom. I will see to it that from now on, no rain will ever fall upon the earth! I will enjoy watching what my brother tries to do about that!" He laughed at the thought of it, rejoicing in his power.

When rains stopped nourishing the earth with their life-giving moisture, the people came to Sagbata and cried, "Now that you live among us and are our king, the rain no longer falls upon our land and our villages. Our food has withered and died. We too are withering and dying!"

"Do not worry," Sagbata replied calmly. "It will rain in a few days!"

But it did not rain in a few days. A year passed, and it did not rain. A second year passed, and it did not rain. A third year passed, and still it did not rain.

Then two sky-beings came down to earth in order to tell the people of the earth about destiny. They had brought with them seeds of prophecy. When someone needed the answer to an important question, the sky-beings would toss their seeds upon the ground and read the answer in the pattern formed by the fallen seeds.

Sagbata sent for the two sky-beings because he wanted to learn why it did not rain. When they came before him, he could tell that they spoke the truth. He watched as they tossed and studied the pattern of their seeds of prophecy.

Finally the sky-beings said to Sagbata, "It is clear from the arrangement of these seeds that you and your younger brother have argued because both of you want the same thing. It is also clear that if you are to live peacefully with your brother, you will have to meet his demands."

"I do not see how that will be possible," Sagbata replied. "The sky is too far above the earth, and I have never had the strength to climb back up there. Before I left the sky, my mother permitted me to take all of her wealth with me, since that was my right as her older son. I took everything but water and fire, leaving them behind only because I had no way to carry them. As soon as I arrived on earth, I realized that water is necessary here, but I have not been able to find a way to get it. Do you have a suggestion?"

"Yes, we do," the sky-beings replied. "We advise you to summon Sogbo's messenger, the bird Wututu, and tell him to fly up to your brother with an important message. Tell Wututu to tell Sogbo that you are offering him part of all of the riches on the earth in return for water. The bird will find a way to Sogbo's heart. He always does!"

Sagbata summoned Wututu and sent him to Sogbo. "Tell my brother," he said, "that I will let him rule my part of the universe as well as his own. From now on he, not I, will protect fathers, mothers, and their children. From now on he, not I, will rule over the villages and the countryside."

Sogbo directed Wututu, "Return to my brother with this message. Tell him that when he took all of our mother's wealth, which was his rightful inheritance, he was unwise to leave water and fire behind. Water and fire are so powerful that whoever controls them controls the universe. Therefore, I control Sagbata and all of his wealth whether he wishes it or not. However, tell him that I accept his offer and I will send nourishing rains down upon the earth!"

Wututu was halfway between the sky and the earth when suddenly a flash of lightning illuminated the universe, and the world resounded with the rumble of thunder. Streams of water began to pour forth from the sky. It rained and it rained. By the time Wututu arrived, Sagbata knew that his brother had accepted his terms, and he was delighted. He told his people that Wututu was a sacred bird and should never be killed.

From that day until this, Sagbata and Sogbo have remained friends, and nourishing thunderstorms visit the earth year after year. Rain falls on the grass, causing it to put forth new blades. Rain falls on the people, causing them to become fertile. Rain showers glory upon Sogbo, god of the thunderstorm!

Introducing **Gassire's Lute**

Historical Background

The African people called the Soninke possess a history that is over 2,000 years old. Their ancestors were an aristocratic nation called the Fasa, who moved inland from the seacoast in about the 3rd century B.C. They settled in the fertile land of Faraka, an area that is bordered by the Sahara Desert on the north, the Senegal River on the west, the Sudan on the south, and the Nile River on the east.

The Fasa were an aristocratic people who fought on horseback with spears and swords for pleasure, as well as for conquest. Their goal was to achieve honor by displaying courage and skill in combat. They would fight in single combat only against those who were their social equals.

Wagadu was the legendary city of the Fasa. The four other cities mentioned in *Gassire's Lute* also have ancient roots. Dierra may have been located near Mursuk, where the ruins of Djerma are located; Agada may refer to Agadez, which is located north of the Hausa states in the central Sudan; Ganna and Silla may have been located on the upper Niger River.

The Soninke created the first empire in West Africa, Ancient Ghana, in the 4th or 5th century A.D. At its peak, their empire extended into the Sahara Desert and controlled all the land and peoples between the Senegal River and the upper Niger River. Trade in gold was the basis of its power. Mined in the south, gold was valued by the Berber Muslims of Morocco and Algeria in the north.

Wagadu became the cosmopolitan capital of Ghana. It was a city known for its artisans, traders, and Muslim teachers of the Koran. Agricultural produce, cloth, and the products of leatherworkers, blacksmiths, and goldsmiths, as well as items from many other nations, could be found in its great markets. Many languages, such as Mande, Hausa, and Arabic, were commonly heard on its streets.

Berber attacks that were designed to gain control of important trade routes, combined with politically motivated revolts by peoples who were subjects of the empire, led to Ghana's decline and fall during the 12th to mid-13th centuries.

Today the Soninke are a small group, mostly Muslim, who live in the desert oases of Tichit and Walatu, areas watered by the Niger River and its tributary, the Bani, in what is now Mali.

Cassire's Lute is an important part of the existing fragment of the Soninke epic *Dausi*, which was created as a group of songs between A.D. 300 and 1100. The influence of Islam on Soninke culture, combined with a long emphasis upon peaceful, agricultural pursuits, has contributed to the loss of much of the original Soninke epic. The epic reflects the Soninke heroic period of 500 B.C.

Cassire's Lute was recorded in the 1920s by the German anthropologist, Leo Frobenius. His study of Stone Age rock drawings led him to search for a common, prehistoric, European-African culture. His African expeditions, in turn, led him to investigate the mythology behind the pictures. He recorded numerous African folktales, legends, and myths, including *Gassire's Lute*, and published them as part of a series entitled *African Folktales and Folk Poetry*. In 1938 *Gassire's Lute* was published by Frobenius and Douglas C. Fox in a collection called *African Genesis*.

Appeal and Value

Like many other epics, *Gassire's Lute* focuses on the conflict between what an individual hero wants for himself and what is best for his family and the society in which he lives. Like many other heroes, what Gassire wants most of all is everlasting fame. Once he learns how to acquire such immortality, he pursues his goal with great courage, skill, and determination.

In most myths, the hero's great deeds help his or her people and achieve for the hero the immortality that comes from fame. What is unique about this myth is that Gassire's heroic deeds will harm his family and his community. He knows this, but his desire for immortality is so great that he does not care. It is interesting to consider how heroes from other cultures would have acted if they had been forced to choose between actions that would make them famous and immortal and actions that would help their family and their community.

Gassire's Lute

Four times beautiful Wagadu has existed. And four times Wagadu has disappeared from sight: the first time because her children were vain, the second because they were deceptive, the third because they were greedy, and the fourth because they were quarrelsome. Four times Wagadu has changed her name: first to Dierra, next to Agada, then to Ganna, and finally to Silla. Four times Wagadu has changed the direction she faces: first to the north, next to the west, then to the east, and finally to the south.

Wagadu receives the strength to endure from the four directions, which is why she has had four gates to her city: first to the north, next to the west, then to the east, and finally to the south. She has endured when her children have built her of earth, of wood, or of stone, or when she has existed only as a vision in the imaginations and desires of her children.

Wagadu actually is the strength that exists in the hearts of her children. She is visible in times of war, when the air resounds with the clash and clamor of battle as sword meets sword or shield. She is invisible when the errors in the hearts of her children tire her and make her fall asleep. Wagadu has fallen asleep four times: the first time because her children were vain, the second because they were deceptive, the third because they were greedy, and the fourth because they were quarrelsome.

If her children ever find Wagadu a fifth time, the vision of her beauty will shine so radiantly within their minds that they will never again lose her. Then, even if her children suffer from vanity, deception, greed, and dissension, these will never be able to harm her.

Hoooh! Dierra, Agada, Ganna, Silla! Hoooh! Fasa!

Each time the errors in the hearts of her children have caused Wagadu to disappear, she has reappeared possessing an even greater beauty. Her children's vanity created the great songs of heroes that bards sang in the second Wagadu and have continued to sing for countless generations, songs that all peoples of the Sudan still value today. Her children's deception brought forth showers of gold and pearls in the third Wagadu. Her children's greed created the need for writing in the fourth Wagadu, writing that the Burdama still use today.

Her children's quarrels will produce a fifth Wagadu that will continue as long as it rains in the south and rocks jut forth from the Sahara Desert. Then every man will carry a vision of Wagadu within his heart, and every woman will carry a vision of Wagadu within her womb.

Hoooh! Dierra, Agada, Ganna, Silla! Hoooh! Fasa!

Her children's vanity led Wagadu to disappear for the first time. Then she was called Dierra, and she faced north. The last king of Dierra was Nganamba Fasa. The Fasa were strong warriors and great heroes, but they were growing old. Every day of every month they had to fight their enemies. Day after day, month after month, without ceasing, they had to fight their enemies. Yet the Fasa remained strong. Each man was a hero in his own right, and each woman was proud of the heroic strength of each man.

King Nganamba was old enough to have a son, Gassire, who was the father of eight grown sons. Even these sons were the fathers of sons, making King Nganamba a great-grandfather among men. It was at the end of King Nganamba's rule that Wagadu disappeared for the first time. Would this have happened if Nganamba had died, and Gassire had ruled in his place?

Hoooh! Dierra, Agada, Ganna, Silla! Hoooh! Fasa!

Yet Gassire never had the opportunity to rule in his father's place. Gassire longed for his father's death and his own kingship. He listened for some sign of weakness in his father, and he searched for a sign of impending death as a lover searches the sky at dusk for the evening star, the first sign of night. Day after day and month after month passed, and still Nganamba did not die.

Each day Gassire raised his sword and shield and rode into battle against the Burdama, fighting like the great hero that he was. Each night, when evening shrouded the land in shadow, Gassire rode into Dierra and took his place in the circle among the men of the city and his eight grown sons. His ears listened to the praises the other heroes sang of his great deeds upon the battlefield, but his heart was jealous of his father's power.

Deep within, night after night and month after month, Gassire wept with longing for his father's death and his own kingship. He longed to carry his father's sword and shield, but they belonged to the king alone. His anger grew into wrath, his wrath grew into rage, and he could no longer sleep at night. So late one night Gassire quietly arose, dressed, left his house, and visited the oldest wise man in the city.

"Can you tell me when I shall become king of the Fasa?" Gassire asked.

"Ah, Gassire," the old wise man replied, "your father, King Nganamba, will die — but you will not inherit his shield and sword. That is for others, not for you. You will carry a lute, and your lute will cause the disappearance of Wagadu! Ah, Gassire!"

Gassire said, "You lie, old man! It is clear that you are not wise at all. As long as her heroes can defend her, we shall not lose Wagadu!"

"Although you do not believe me, Gassire," the old wise man answered, "your path is not that of the warrior and hero. You will find the partridges in the fields, and when they speak to you, you will understand them. They will reveal your path and the path of Wagadu."

Hoooh! Dierra, Agada, Ganna, Silla! Hoooh! Fasa!

The next morning Gassire set out to prove that his path was indeed that of the warrior and hero. He said to the other Fasa heroes, "Today there is no need for you to fight the Burdama. I shall take them upon my spear and my sword without your help."

So it came to pass that Gassire fought against the Burdama, one against many. As a farmer's sickle cuts down the wheat in the field, so Gassire's sword cut down the Burdama.

The Burdama felt terror enter their hearts. "We are fighting more than a hero, and more than a Fasa!" they cried. "Against such a being, we have no strength and no skill." So each Burdama tossed away his two spears, turned his horse in retreat, and fled in fear.

As the Fasa heroes entered the field to gather the spears of their enemies, they sang, "Gassire has always performed the greatest deeds of any Fasa. He has always been the greatest of our heroes. Yet by winning so many swords, as one against many, Gassire has outdone himself today! Wagadu smiles with pride."

That night, when evening shrouded the land in shadow and the men gathered into their circle, Gassire wandered into the fields. He heard a partridge that was resting beneath a bush sing, "Hear the song of my deeds!" And then the partridge sang of its battle against a snake. "In time, all who live will die, will be buried, and will decay," the partridge sang. "Like all creatures, I too will die, will be buried, and will decay. But the song of my battles will live! Bards will sing my battle song again and again, long after heroes and kings have died and decayed. Wagadu will disappear, but my battle song will live on and on. Hoooh, that my deeds will become such a song! Hoooh, that I will sing such battle songs!"

Hoooh! Dierra, Agada, Ganna, Silla! Hoooh! Fasa!

Gassire returned to the old wise man. "I heard a partridge in the field brag that the songs of its deeds will live long after Wagadu has disappeared. Do humans also know great battle songs? And do these battle songs live long after heroes and kings have died and decayed?"

"Yes, they do, Gassire," the old wise man replied. "Your path is to be a singer of great battle songs rather than a great king of the Fasa. Ah, Gassire! Long ago the Fasa lived by the sea. They were great heroes then, too. They fought against men who played the lute and sang great battle songs. And those men were heroes also. Often they caused terror to enter the hearts of the Fasa. You too will play battle songs on the lute, but Wagadu will disappear because of it."

"Then let Wagadu disappear!" Gassire exclaimed.

Hoooh! Dierra, Agada, Ganna, Silla! Hoooh! Fasa!

The next morning Gassire visited the Fasa smith and said, "Master Smith, I want you to make a lute for me."

The smith replied, "Make a lute I will, but it will not sing!"

Gassire responded, "Master Smith, just make the lute. I will make it sing!"

When the smith had finished the lute, Gassire immediately tried to play it, but he found that it would not sing.

"Master Smith, what good is this lute to me? I cannot make it sing," Gassire complained. "Tell me what I should do."

The smith answered, "Gassire, until it develops a heart, a lute is only a piece of wood. If you wish to make it sing, you must help it develop a heart. When you next go into battle, carry your lute upon your back. Let it feel the thrust of your sword, and let it absorb the blood of your wounds. Right now, your lute is still part of the tree from which it was made. It must become a part of you, your sons, and your people. It must share your pain as well as your fame. It must absorb the lifeblood of your sons. Then the feelings of your heart will enter the lute and develop its heart. Your sons will die and decay, but they will continue to live in your lute. However, I must warn you. You will play battle songs on the lute, but Wagadu will disappear because of it."

"Then let Wagadu disappear!" Gassire exclaimed.

Hoooh! Dierra, Agada, Ganna, Silla! Hoooh! Fasa!

The next morning Gassire called his eight sons together and said, "Today, when we fight the Burdama, our sword thrusts will live forever in my lute. May we fight with such courage, strength, and skill that our deeds will create a battle song that surpasses the battle songs of all other heroes! You, my eldest son, will lead the charge with me today."

So it came to pass that Gassire hung his lute upon his shoulder and rode into battle with his eldest son at his side. They fought against the Burdama as more than heroes and more than Fasa. Together they fought against eight Burdama. As a farmer's sickle cuts down the wheat in the field, so Gassire's sword and the sword of his eldest son cut down four of the Burdama heroes.

Then a Burdama thrust his sword into the heart of Gassire's eldest son. He fell from his horse, his lifeblood pouring from him. Gassire sadly dismounted, lifted the corpse of his son upon his back, and returned to the other heroes and the city of Dierra. As he rode, the blood of his eldest son poured over the lute and was absorbed into the wood.

Hoooh! Dierra, Agada, Ganna, Silla! Hoooh! Fasa!

Gassire's eldest son was buried, and the city was solemn with morning. That night Gassire tried to play his lute, but no matter how hard he tried, it would not sing. He called his seven sons together and said, "Tomorrow we again ride into battle against the Burdama. "

Each of the next six days passed as the first day had passed. Each day, in the order of their birth, a different one of Gassire's sons joined his father in leading the charge against the Burdama. Each day, one of the enemy thrust his sword into the heart of that son and he fell from his horse, his lifeblood pouring from him. Each day, Gassire sadly dismounted, lifted the corpse of his son upon his back, and returned to the other heroes and the city of Dierra. Each day, as he rode, the blood of his son poured over the lute and was absorbed into the wood.

By the end of the seventh day of fighting, the men of Dierra were angry, the women were weeping with fear and grief, and everyone was mourning the dead. That night, when evening shrouded the land in shadow and the heroes had gathered into their circle, they said, "Gassire, enough is enough! You are fighting out of anger, and without good reason. Gather your servants and your cattle, take those who would join you, and leave our city. Let the rest of us live here in peace. We too want fame, but we choose life over fame when the cost of fame is death."

The old wise man exclaimed, "Ah, Gassire! Today, for the first time, Wagadu will disappear."

Hoooh! Dierra, Agada, Ganna, Silla! Hoooh! Fasa!

So Gassire gathered his wives, his youngest son, his friends, and his servants and rode off into the Sahara Desert. Only a few of the Fasa heroes accompanied Gassire on his journey.

Gassire and his companions rode far into the lonely wilderness. They rode day and night, sleeping only when they could ride no farther.

One night Gassire sat awake and alone by the fire. The world around him was lonely and silent, for everyone else was asleep: his youngest son, the heroes, the women, and the servants. Gassire had just dozed off himself when a sudden sound awakened him. Next to him, as though he were singing himself, Gassire heard a voice singing. It was his lute, and it was singing his great battle song.

When the lute finished singing his great battle song for the first time, back in Dierra, King Nganamba died, and Wagadu disappeared for the first time. When the lute finished singing his great battle song for the second time, Gassire's anger disappeared and he wept. He wept with grief and with joy: grief over the death of his seven sons and the disappearance of Wagadu, and joy over the great battle song that would bring everlasting fame to him and his sons.

Hoooh! Dierra, Agada, Ganna, Silla! Hoooh! Fasa!

Four times beautiful Wagadu has existed. And four times Wagadu has disappeared from sight: the first time because her children were vain, the second because they were deceptive, the third because they were greedy, and the fourth because they were quarrelsome. Her children's quarrels will produce a fifth Wagadu that will continue as long as it rains in the south and rocks jut forth from the Sahara Desert. Then every man will carry a vision of Wagadu within his heart, and every woman will carry a vision of Wagadu within her womb.

Hoooh! Dierra, Agada, Ganna, Silla! Hoooh! Fasa!

Introducing **Sunjata**

Historical Background

The Mande-speaking African peoples, also called the Mandingo, have a distinguished place in the history of West Africa. The principal group began as a small, unimportant kingdom in the southern part of West Africa. In time, they became the Mandingo nation of Manding or Kangaba, later known as Old Mali. During the decline and fall of the first West African em-pire of Ghana (from the 12th to the mid-13th centuries), Mali gradually grew to become an even larger empire in the Sudan. At the height of its power, it extended into the Sahara Desert on the north, to the Atlantic Ocean on the west, and past the northern bend of the Niger River on the east.

In the Sudan, wars periodically occurred in order to further political or economic goals, such as the control of neighbors or important trade routes, or to provide opportunities for heroism and fame. The same forces that, 300 years earlier, had caused the decline and fall of the empire of Ghana — attacks from the peoples of the Sahara, combined with the revolt of peoples who were part of the empire — caused the decline and fall of the empire of Mali during the 15th to the mid-16th centuries.

Mande society was composed of social castes. At the top were the nobles, the hereditary caste that produced the kings and the heroes. Beneath the nobility were the castes of professional people, such as the blacksmiths, the leatherworkers, and the bards, all of whom inherited their vocations from their fathers. At the bottom of the social system were the slaves.

Blacksmiths had exceptional stature both in war and in matters of religion. Working in iron, gold, and wood, they created weapons and tools as well as ceremonial and decorative objects. Mande society believed that the best blacksmiths had the power to imbue the objects they fashioned with their own special, mystical powers, thereby providing a hero with the ability to be invincible.

In contrast, slaves were treated as property, and were bought, sold, and even given away. The fortune of a slave depended upon his or her situation; the luckiest slave belonged to a wealthy or powerful family.

The oral tradition provided the professional bard, called a *griot*, with a repertoire of narratives about the deeds of kings and famous heroes that he recited to his own musical accompaniment, often before a large audience. These narrative songs taught the Mandingo peoples their values as well as their history. Great events were attached to the names of heroic leaders, who were models of ideal heroic and human behavior.

Like the Soninke of Ghana, the Mande became Islamized, and therefore were familiar with Arabic script and literature. This knowledge influenced the form of many West African songs. By the 14th century, the griots had a good understanding of written history from their knowledge of the Koran and other Arabic writings. Thus the stage was set for the development of the West African epic.

Scholars debate whether the griot was close to the nobility, and therefore near the top of the social system, or close to the slave, and therefore near the bottom. Because the griot put himself into his songs, it is possible that he gave himself greater influence and prestige than he actually had. However, it may have been within the griot's power to mediate arguments within the royal family, to arrange marriages, and to serve as the voice of the king in certain political situations. Certainly, from the perspective of members of the royal family, it was in their own best interest to treat their nation's historian well, so that, through his songs, he would immortalize their honor and glory rather than their less desirable traits.

According to the epic of *Sunjata*, a griot was not only the historian of his nation, but the teacher and adviser to the king. His profession was passed down from father to son, and the griots in his family served successive generations of the royal family of the Keita and Manding.

The epic of *Sunjata* is known not only in Mali, but in Guinea, Senegal, the Ivory Coast, the Upper Volta,

Ghana, and the Gambia. D. T. Niane's version, published first in French in 1960, is considered to be the classic rendition of the epic. Niane translated the work as he heard it from Djeli Mamudu Kuyate, a griot from the village of Djeliba Koro (Siguiri), in Guinea.

The epic probably includes earlier hunter epics. Sunjata is called the "son of the lion and the buffalo." The lion was the ancestor and emblem of his father and all other members of the Keita nation, whereas the buffalo was the ancestor and emblem of his mother, the Buffalo Woman, and her family. From the Stone Age, the buffalo was considered to be the king and father of all game animals and, consequently, was regarded as the god of the hunter.

The historical Sunjata lived in the early part of the 13th century and ruled the empire of Mali a century before it reached the height of its power. The action of the epic occurs between 1217 and 1237.

Appeal and Value

The principal appeal of the epic of Sunjata is its ability to entertain the reader. Sunjata lives in an exciting world that contains complex family relationships, unstable political conditions, magic, and prophecy.

The heroic code by which Sunjata lives reveals the values of his society. Intelligence, strength, skill, and courage in battle are only part of what is important in a warrior's life. Honor, respect, thoughtfulness, loyalty, and generosity in interpersonal relationships are equally important. Supernatural forces in the universe affect everyone's life and need to be placated. Fate or destiny is predetermined

and unalterable, based at least in part on the fact that a predictable relationship exists between each person's particular personality and the situations that he or she encounters. These factors influence the life of every character and the outcome of every battle.

The epic of Sunjata contains many themes that are found in other epics from around the world. Like many other heroes, Sunjata has an unusual youth, is able to perform magical feats, endures a period of exile, kills a monster, does his best to protect his community from destructive forces, is a fierce warrior, and becomes a great ruler of an enlarged kingdom. His life and the lives of other characters in the epic are governed by prophecies.

Moreover, like the great epics from every culture, the epic of Sunjata was designed to have a profound effect upon the lives of the Mandingo people and all others who would be exposed to it. Everyone needs goals to which to aspire and models who lead the way. Everyone needs to be encouraged to tackle the tasks and problems that are part of the experience of living. The hero always serves these functions, and Sunjata is such a hero.

Principal Characters

NARE MAGHAN KON FATTA: chief of the Keita and king of the larger nation of Manding (Old Mali) and the Mandingo people; husband of Sogolon Kedju, Sasuma Berete, and Namandje; father of Sunjata, Kolonkan, Dankarantuma, Nana Triban, and Manding Bory

SASUMA BERETE: first wife of Nare Maghan; mother of Dankarantuma and Nana Triban

DANKARANTUMA: son of Sasuma Berete and first son of Nare Maghan; brother of Nana Triban; older stepbrother of Sunjata; king of Manding following death of Nare Maghan

NANA TRIBAN: daughter of Nare Maghan and Sasuma Berete; sister of Dankarantuma; stepsister of Sunjata

SOGOLON KEDJU: the Buffalo Woman; second wife of Nare Maghan; mother of Sunjata and Kolonkan

SUNJATA: popular name of Mari Djata; son of Sogolon Kedju and second son of Nare Maghan; brother of Kolonkan; stepbrother of Dankarantuma, Nana Triban, and Manding Bory; later, chief of the Keita and king of Manding; emperor of Mali and the Mandingo peoples

KOLONKAN: daughter of Sogolon Kedju and Nare Maghan; younger sister of Sunjata

NAMANDJE: third wife of Nare Maghan; mother of Manding Bory

MANDING BORY: son of Namandje and third son of Nare Maghan; Sunjata's stepbrother and best friend

GNANKUMAN DUA: Nare Maghan's griot, historian, and counselor; teacher of Keita princes

BALLA FASSEKE: Sunjata's griot, teacher, counselor, and recorder of his heroic deeds

FRAN KAMARA: prince and later king of Tabon; Sunjata's closest childhood friend and later ally

KAMANDJAN: prince and later king of Sibi; Sunjata's other close childhood friend and later ally

TUNKARA: warrior-king of Mema, who befriends Sunjata as a father

SUMANGURU KANTE: sorcerer-king or demon-king of Sosso; Sunjata's enemy

FAKOLI KOROMA: Sumanguru's nephew; king of Koroma; Sumanguru's chief general until Sumanguru takes his wife; then, Sunjata's ally

---

Sunjata

Prologue

You would call me a bard. To my own people, I am a royal griot, the historian of my village in Mali, the teacher and adviser of my king. I am the living memory of our nation's past and a master of my ancient art. Just as my father has taught me what, in his time, he learned from his father, so I will teach these time-honored tales of the Keita people to my son in the form that I have learned them. It is speaking of the past, and not reading about it in books, that enables you, my listeners, to feel its life. However, I know more than I will tell you.

Learning is a well of deep and secret waters. A griot dips into that well and gives you what you should drink.

The words I speak give new birth to the ancient ones, the kings of old, enabling them to inspire those who lead us today and those who will lead us in times yet to be. I am not a seer, for I cannot see what is surely to come. Yet, what I know of the past has made me wise about what may indeed come to be.

Therefore, you who would learn the history of Mali, listen to my song! I will take you back to the kingdom of Manding, the land that the songs of some griots say is Old Mali, and I will tell you the tale of Sunjata, the son of the Lion and the Buffalo, and the father of Mali and the Mandingo peoples. Greater than the famous Alexander, Sunjata moved like the sun from east to west, lighting the world with his deeds. Beloved of Allah, even sorcery proved powerless against him! Sunjata was a giant among men, a king of kings, the emperor of emperors!

Chapter 1

*King Nare Maghan Kon Fatta learns that if he
marries Sogolon Kedju, their son will become a great
ruler. In time, he meets and marries her, and she
becomes pregnant with his child. Sasuma Berete,
Nare Maghan's first wife, then curses Sogolon.*

My tale begins with Nare Maghan Kon Fatta, the handsome Keita king of Manding, who, in time, would become Sunjata's father. One day, this good king was sitting in his favorite place, beneath the large silk-cotton tree that shaded his royal compound. As he was talking with his young son, Dankarantuma, with his kinsmen and nobles, and with his griot, Gnankuman Dua, a strange hunter suddenly appeared.

The hunter approached the royal group and, as was the custom, proceeded to share a portion of an animal that he had killed. However, he declined the request to speak of his travels. Instead, he boasted that he was able to see what is surely to come. He then removed twelve bright cowrie shells from his bag, and mumbling some words, shook them out upon the ground and studied them.

"King of Manding," he said, "the world is a mysterious place. The great silk-cotton tree was once no larger than a grain of rice. Every great king was once a small child. Even great kingdoms grow from small villages like this one."

The hunter shook the cowries upon the ground again. "King of Manding," he continued, "your kingdom is moving from night to day. Your capital, Niani, shines in a light that comes from the east, like the sun. Your male child who now sits beside you will not become your heir. That honor belongs to another son of another wife, a son who is as yet unborn to a wife whom you have yet to meet.

"Another hunter will come to your village, bringing with him a woman who is an ugly hunchback," he continued. "Even though you are handsome and she will be hideous, you must choose to marry her. For only then will you become the father of the king whose great deeds will make the name of Mali live forever. If you are willing to do this, then you must now sacrifice a red bull and soak the ground with its blood."

With these words, the hunter took his leave and returned to his own people.

King Nare Maghan performed the sacrifice, and then time passed. He did not forget the hunter's prophecy because he knew that what will be, will come!

One day, the king was again sitting under his favorite tree with his kinsmen, his nobles, and his griot, when a young hunter and a young girl suddenly appeared. The girl had concealed her face behind a scarf, and she walked with her head lowered. However, she could not conceal the ugly hump that rested upon her shoulders and her back.

The hunter approached the assembled group and addressed the king. "King Nare Maghan Kon Fatta, I give you my greetings!" he began. "I live in another Mandingo village, but I happen to be returning from the far land of Do. I traveled there in search of game and adventure, and there I found this young maiden. She is worthy of becoming your queen, so I have brought her to you as a gift!"

King Nare Maghan studied his gift, looked at his griot, and then turned his handsome face aside in embarrassment.

Gnankuman Dua immediately understood the situation. Quickly speaking for his master, he announced, "Son of Manding, you are our welcome guest! When you have quenched your thirst, please tell the king how it has come to pass that you have brought this young girl from Do."

The hunter accepted the drink and then proceeded to relate the following tale:

Once the great harvest had ended in our village, I set out on a hunt. However, game was so scarce that I found myself tracking it all the way to the great land of Do. I was not far from there when I came upon two hunters. They told me that, if I continued on my way, I might not live to see the sun begin its morning journey. All the hearts of Do were now shaking like leaves in the wind, for a great buffalo was ravaging the land, and it killed anyone who crossed its path. Once the sun returned to its home, no one would dare to leave the village. The king promised a great reward to the hunter who killed this buffalo, but the greatest courage and skill were powerless against it. The beast possessed a magic that would turn away any weapon.

I decided to try my own luck, so I continued on my way. The land looked as if both hunters and animals had deserted it. In time, I came to a river, and I was surprised to see an old woman crying on its bank.

"What can I do for you, old woman?" I asked.

"Would you please give me something to eat?" she replied. "My belly hurts with hunger! The few hunters who have passed by here have had hearts of stone and have hurried on their way."

I had a large portion of red meat with me, and I gave her as much as she wanted.

When her belly was satisfied, she said to me, "You are a good man, hunter, for giving so generously. May it come to pass that you reap as fine a harvest from these seeds of kindness as you have sown.

"I know that you are searching for the Buffalo of Do," she continued, "but are you aware of your great danger? The sharpest arrow sent forth by the most skillful hunter will not make its mark, and those who would bring death, find death instead!

"However, if you would still pursue this beast, your kindness to me will bring you good fortune. The Buffalo of Do has killed 107 hunters and has wounded seventy-seven others. Every day, it finds someone in Do to destroy. Yet, you will do what the most powerful and skillful hunters have been unable to do. You will conquer the buffalo, and it will spare your life.

"But in order to succeed," she added, "you must listen carefully to my directions and follow them without fail. Take my spinning rod and my darning egg with you. When you find the royal garden, the Buffalo of Do will be eating the king's vegetables. However, the beast will be quick to notice you, and then you will be in great danger! When it lowers its head with its great horns, it will rush toward you. You must be prepared for its attack, and you must resist the urge to run.

"Instead, you must stand your ground and point my spinning rod at its head three times. Then, draw your bow and shoot. Your arrow will pierce the buffalo's hide and cause the beast to fall to its knees.

"However," she continued, "you will still be in great danger, for the buffalo will manage to pull itself to its feet and rush toward you again. This time, you should run from it, but, now, you must toss my darning egg behind you as you run.

"The land on which the egg falls will become a great marsh that the buffalo cannot cross. This will save your life and enable you to kill the beast. Once the buffalo is dead, take its golden tail for your trophy. When you present it to the king of Do, he will give you your reward.

"If you remember my advice," she concluded, "all will go well with you. I know, because I am the Buffalo of Do. The king is my brother, and I am now satisfied that I have punished him enough for taking my share of our family's wealth."

Anxious to be on my way, I grabbed the spinning rod and the darning egg from the old woman and started off. Suddenly, I felt a surprisingly strong hand upon my arm.

"Not so fast, young man!" she exclaimed. "If you intend to be successful, you will have to agree to one condition. The king of Do has announced that the man who kills the buffalo will receive the most beautiful maiden in the kingdom for his wife. However, you are not free to accept this reward. All of the maidens of Do will gather around you, their beauty reflected in their ornaments of silver and gold. But do not be tempted by them.

"Instead, search for the ugliest maiden present, for you must choose her as your prize. Her name is Sogolon Kedju because she has a humpback. She is my other self, and she will be a wonderful wife for you if you are able to capture her spirit. You will find her sitting alone, watching the scene from a distance.

"Of course, once you make your choice known, the king and all the people of Do will laugh at you and treat you like a fool. But, be that as it will," she concluded, "you must promise me that you will choose Sogolon Kedju, or else give me back my spinning rod and my darning egg right now!

I took the old woman's hands between my own and gave her my sacred word. Each event came to pass just as the old woman had said it would. The buffalo charged angrily; her darning egg worked its magic; and the beast had a golden tail. The maidens of Do were especially beautiful, and Sogolon Kedju was unusually ugly. In fact, once I chose her, I wondered if I were not really the fool that everyone thought I was! We had no reason to remain, so we left as quickly as we could, and here we are! So the hunter concluded.

Fortunately, neither King Nare Maghan Kon Fatta nor his griot, Gnankuman Dua, thought to question the hunter about why he had not kept Sogolon Kedju for himself. The hunter paused briefly at the end of his tale, possibly wondering whether to relate the incident that had terrified him, for he knew more about this young woman than he apparently was willing to tell. As it happens, he had, in fact, tried to win Sogolon Kedju's spirit, but he had failed. The Buffalo Woman defeated his efforts by causing a great trunk of light to spring forth from her body, and the hunter was afraid to have a wife who knew the ways of magic.

As for King Nare Maghan, he was pleased that this hunter's tale agreed with the other hunter's prophecy that he had received long ago. He immediately began to prepare to wed his second wife. The twelve villages of Manding and their allies were invited, and the great day was filled with singing, dancing, and the distribution of clothing, grain, and gold.

King Nare Maghan could not win Sogolon Kedju's spirit on their wedding night, nor was he successful at any time during the next week. Whenever he tried to get close to her, she grew long hair all over her body. Then one night he dreamed that the protective spirit of the kings of Manding told him to sacrifice Sogolon Kedju because it was necessary to spill her blood. Nare Maghan immediately awoke. Sword in hand, he grabbed Sogolon by her hair, awakened her, and told her his dream. In terror, Sogolon fainted, and while her spirit slept, Nare Maghan made her his wife. By the time Sogolon Kedju awakened, she was carrying the king's child within her womb.

As soon as King Nare Maghan knew that Sogolon Kedju was going to become the mother of his child, he announced that if she gave birth to a male child, her son would inherit the kingdom of Manding. Sasuma Berete, the king's first wife, was overwhelmed with jealousy. The king's words confirmed the hunter's prophecy that her son, Dankarantuma, had repeated to her long ago. She secretly tried to get a sorcerer to help her kill Sogolon Kedju, but not one would agree to do it.

Finally, in fury, she secretly called upon the nine great witches of Manding, the ancient ones who rule the night and who weave the tapestry of life and death in their dark kingdom. "May Sogolon Kedju be thrice cursed!" she exclaimed. "May her pregnancy be long and labored! If she gives birth to a male child, may he be deformed and helpless! And may this son bring nothing but trial and trouble on both his mother and himself!"

Poor Sasuma Berete! People are so impatient and blind about life! They cannot understand God's mysterious ways, nor do they realize that one's destiny cannot be changed. Each event adds its thread to the tapestry of one's life, and those who try to separate themselves from their destiny only succeed in furthering that which they would destroy!

Chapter 2

*After a long pregnancy, Sogolon Kedju gives birth to
Sunjata, who is lame. King Nare Maghan dies, and
Dankarantuma becomes king of Manding. Sunjata
finally walks. Fran Kamara and Kamandjan become
his friends.*

So it came to pass that Sogolon Kedju carried her child within her womb for
eight years. King Nare Maghan became concerned about his wife's health and
consulted the sorcerers of Niani. They assured him that Sogolon was quite well,
but that she was carrying a child who would become a great king. They also told
the king that the unborn child left his mother's womb each night while the sun
slept, and that he returned when the sun awakened.

"When you want the birth to occur, have Sogolon Kedju sleep in your own
house, instead of in hers," they advised. "Meanwhile, place her grinding jar on
her own bed and cover it with a cloth. Then, when the unborn child returns, he
will think that the jar is his mother's womb, and he will enter the jar. It is in this
way that the greatest king of Manding will be born!"

King Nare Maghan followed this advice, and it came to pass that the unborn
child entered the jar just as the sun began its morning journey. The forces of
nature immediately proclaimed his birth. Suddenly, clouds covered the clear sky
with a black robe. Winds began to bend the strongest trees, and rain fell in sheets
despite the fact that it was the dry season. Brilliant flashes of lightning suddenly
illuminated all the buildings in the king's compound so brightly that one would
think that the sun had completed half its journey. Angry peals of thunder followed, shaking the houses and the earth beneath them. Then, just as suddenly as
it had come, the storm blew away, and the sun resumed its morning journey.

King Nare Maghan called his people together and joyfully announced, "Let us
welcome my new son, the Lion of Manding!"

Gnankuman Dua, the king's griot, announced that this child of the Lion and
the Buffalo would have two names. He would be called Maghan Djata, after his
father, as well as by his own name, Mari Djata. However, it came to pass that the
boy was usually called Sogolon Djata, or Sunjata, after his mother, although the
songs of some griots say that King Nare Maghan named the infant Sunjata because it means "our lion."

Despite his handsome father, Sunjata was an unattractive child. His head was
much too large for his body; he was too young to have such large eyes and an
unsmiling mouth; and he seldom talked. His favorite activity was eating. He
would spend each day crawling from one gourd bowl to another, stuffing whatever food he found in these calabashes into his mouth.

As Sunjata grew, his legs remained too weak to support his body, so that long
after children his own age were running about, he still crawled on all fours like an
infant. Children's games appeared to bore him, but he enjoyed frightening the
other children by beating them up whenever they dared to ridicule him. And he
was fond of warning hunters that if they came upon a lion with a white spot, they

should let it pass. "That lion is also Sunjata," he would tell them. "Your arrows will not pierce its skin, but it will kill any hunter who shoots at it!"

Sasuma Berete loved to taunt Sogolon Kedju by saying, "I'm glad that I have an ordinary son who can walk instead of a lion cub who crawls!" And, given the hunter's prophecy that he had heard, her son, Dankarantuma, had no love for the Buffalo Woman and her crippled child either. Only Sasuma's daughter, Nana Triban, who had a kind heart, felt sorry for them and did her best to treat them well.

Despite her gifts as a sorceress, Sogolon Kedju could not strengthen her son's legs, and the king lost faith in the hunter's prophecy of long ago that had marked Sunjata as his heir. No one had ever heard of a crippled king! Gnankuman Dua's reminder that "the great silk-cotton tree grows from the smallest seed" brought Nare Maghan no consolation.

Poor Sogolon Kedju! People are so impatient and blind about life! They cannot understand God's mysterious ways, nor do they realize that one's destiny cannot be changed. Each event adds its thread to the tapestry of one's life, and those who try to separate themselves from their destiny only succeed in furthering that which they would destroy!

Sogolon Kedju gave birth to a second child, a girl named Kolonkan, who looked like her mother. Then the king took a third, very beautiful wife, who presented him with a third son. Upon this infant's birth, those in Niani who could see what is to come said, "Namandje's son, Manding Bory, will be a great king's right hand!"

When Sunjata reached the age of seven, his father continued the tradition of the royal family of Manding and gave his son a griot of his own. This was Balla Fasseke, who was the son of Nare Maghan's griot, Gnankuman Dua.

King Nare Maghan told Sunjata, "Although Balla is three times your age, he will be your great friend. He will also teach you the history of our people and how to be a good king. When I die, you will inherit a larger kingdom than I received from my father and many good allies as well. No matter how great you become, always remember that Manding is the home of your ancestors."

Both the king and his griot died shortly thereafter. Despite the old king's intentions, Sasuma Berete was able to make her own son, Dankarantuma, the king of Manding, and, therefore, take great power into her own hands. No one had ever heard of a crippled king, and the people of Niani were not about to take that risk.

Sasuma Berete relegated Sogolon Kedju and her children to an old hut and let them have a small garden outside the village wall. Meanwhile, she continued to take every opportunity to taunt Sogolon about her lion cub who could not help her, as other sons helped their mothers, since he could not walk.

One day, Sasuma Berete's customary insults were more than the Buffalo Woman could bear. Sogolon Kedju returned home to find Sunjata inside the hut as usual, happily eating scraps of food from a calabash. She immediately thought about how the other children his age were either outside playing or were helping their mothers by performing the necessary tasks of collecting wood for the cooking fire, picking vegetables, or hunting game animals. Sogolon became enraged that she had given birth to a lame child whom she could not heal, and, in frustration, she tearfully beat Sunjata with a stick.

Sunjata stopped eating, calmly looked up at his mother, and asked her for an explanation.

"For over four years Sasuma Berete has been taunting me about you, and I simply cannot bear it any longer!" Sogolon Kedju exclaimed. "Every day she brags about her own son, who has taken the place that is truly yours as the king of Manding. Every day she forces me to realize that you cannot do what every other child your age in Niani does so well."

She continued, "It is not your fault that you cannot walk! And I have tried every skill that I possess to make you well! But, because of your weak legs, you cannot go with the other boys to pick baobab leaves when I need them! And I must go to this cruel woman and beg baobab leaves from her so that we can have tasty food to eat. I love you very much, Sunjata. I just wish that you could walk!"

When Sogolon Kedju had finished, Sunjata calmly looked up at her and said, "Mother, I do not want you to cry any more over baobab leaves and my weak legs. I will stand before the sun sleeps! And, if you wish, I will bring you the whole baobab tree as soon as the sun begins its morning journey. Then all of the women and children in Niani will have to come to you when they want to season their food! But first, you must ask our blacksmith to forge a very strong metal staff for me."

When Balla Fasseke approached the blacksmith and ordered the staff, the smith, who could see what is surely to come, exclaimed, "So this is to be the great day!"

"Yes, it is!" Balla replied. "What has begun in the most ordinary way will be extraordinary before it ends!"

The blacksmith fashioned a great iron staff that was so heavy that six apprentices had to drag it to Sogolon Kedju's hut. Balla Fasseke then said to Sunjata, "Come, Mari Djata, it is time for the lion cub to rise and roar! The waters of the Niger can wash a stain off one's body, but an insult to one's honor cannot be washed off as easily!"

Sunjata rose to his knees and leaned upon the staff, but, great as it was, the staff could not bear his weight, and it broke in two.

The blacksmith then fashioned a new iron staff that was twice as heavy as the first. This time, it took twelve apprentices to lug it to Sogolon Kedju's hut. Again Sunjata put his weight upon it, and again it broke in two.

"Iron clearly will not do for Sunjata!" exclaimed the blacksmith. "A great man needs a great staff. And if the Lion of Manding is going to walk, he must have a staff of gold!"

So it came to pass that Sunjata finally leaned upon a great golden staff and slowly rose to his feet. In the process, his weight twisted the staff into a wondrous golden bow. The sun returned to its home as usual, and while it slept, Sunjata walked about Niani, using his wondrous bow as a staff.

When the sun began its morning journey, Sunjata set his staff aside and walked to the baobab tree that provided the village children with its leaves, tore it out by its roots, and carried it home to his mother's hut. "Now, Mother," he exclaimed, "the people of Niani will have to come to you for their baobab leaves!"

Sogolon Kedju had begun to teach her son the arts of medicine and the ways of the wild animals. Now that he could walk into the forest and collect wood for his mother's fire, as all the other boys did, Sunjata announced, "Let no one ridi-cule my mother by saying that I cannot provide her with wood for our fire!"

He then asked the forest animals to bring enough wood to fill the huts of his mother and of all the women who had helped her during the many years that he had been lame. Acting out of both respect and fear, the animals honored Sunjata's request.

So it came to pass that the Buffalo Woman and her son suddenly became ac-cepted and respected by the people of Niani. The villagers now looked upon Sogolon Kedju as a model wife and mother. She was properly humble and mod-est, and she treated the members of her larger family with respect and, wherever possible, with love. Moreover, since a son always takes his spirit from the mother who gave him life, every mother in Niani who had a son close to Sunjata's age now wanted him to play and hunt with the Buffalo Woman's son.

For both social and political reasons, it was the custom at that time to send the prince of one kingdom to be reared in the court of a different kingdom. This arrangement assured a period of peace between the two kingdoms, and, years later, the kings who had been childhood friends usually became allies. Once Sunjata could walk, the kings who were allies of Manding and who had sons who were close to Sunjata's age sent these children to the court in Niani.

Two of these young princes, Fran Kamara, who was the son of the king of Tabon, and Kamandjan, who was the son of the king of Sibi, became Sunjata's close friends. Whatever they did, whether it was playing games, hunting game animals, or sitting at Sogolon Kedju's feet while she told them tales about the animals, they were always together.

By the time Sunjata had reached the age of ten, he was as strong as ten men and had become unusually skillful at hunting game, his favorite activity. He spoke to the other princes as their leader. His younger brother, Manding Bory, already was his constant companion and his best friend.

Chapter 3

Sunjata kills the beast that is ravaging Niani and becomes a hero.

It came to pass at this time that a strange animal began to ravage the crops that grew in Niani. The kingdom of Manding was known for its hunters, and they were quick to take this opportunity to show off their courage and skill. Coming from far and wide in the kingdom, one group of hunters after another arrived in Niani and set out to kill the beast.

One week passed, and they had no success. Two weeks passed, and they had no success. Three weeks passed, and they had no success. Four weeks passed, and still they had no success.

Group after group showed the greatest courage and skill, but they were all powerless against this beast. It possessed a magic that would turn away any weapon and a strength that would kill any man. The most skillful hunter who sent forth the sharpest arrow would find himself charged and mortally wounded by the beast that he had attempted to kill. Therefore, by the end of a month, the greatest hunters had decided that they could do nothing more and had returned to their own villages.

Sunjata was much younger than they, but he knew that he was not only a skillful hunter but a sorcerer as well. He said to his mother, "If I am able to kill the beast that is too powerful for all the hunters of Manding, maybe it will prove to the people of Niani that the Lion of Manding is their true king and the one who should be ruling our kingdom!"

"This is, indeed, just the task for you, my son!" Sogolon Kedju replied. "I know that your father found it necessary to kill a young man who attempted to take over our kingdom. I also know that the mother of that youth is as powerful a sorceress as I am, and that she turns herself into this beast and destroys our crops in order to punish our people for her son's death. If you wish to kill the beast, you will first have to conquer it in its human form.

"Therefore, Sunjata," she continued, "in addition to your food, I will give you a gold coin that I have been saving for you and two white kola nuts. Put them into your hunter's bag, and gather twenty-five cows from the royal herd. When the sun begins its morning journey, take these with you into the forest, and what will be, will come!"

So it came to pass that Sunjata set out on his first heroic adventure. He had traveled far enough into the forest for the sun to have completed half its journey, when he realized that he was hungry enough to stop and have something to eat. Just then, he saw a blind man at the side of the path.

"Can I do anything for you, old man?" he asked.

"Would you please give me something to chew?" he replied. "My teeth hurt with hunger! The few hunters who have passed by here have had hearts of stone and have hurried on their way."

"I just have enough food for my lunch, but I also have two white kola nuts, a gold coin that my mother saved for me, and this herd of twenty-five cows," Sunjata replied. "You are welcome to take whatever you need. Some will satisfy you now; some will satisfy you later."

"I do not want the only food that you have with you, and I do not want the gold coin that your mother saved for you," the old man replied. "But I would be pleased to have your two kola nuts to chew."

Sunjata took the nuts from his hunter's bag and handed them to the old man, who immediately put them into his pocket.

Then, the old man said, "You are a good prince, Sunjata, for offering me what you have. And because you have been so generous, may it come to pass that you reap as fine a harvest from these seeds of kindness as you have sown.

"I know that you are searching for the strange beast that is ravaging Niani. But are you aware of your great danger? The sharpest arrow sent forth by the most skillful hunter will not make its mark, and those who would bring death, find death instead!

"However, if you would still pursue this beast," he continued, "your kindness to me will bring you good fortune. You will do what the most powerful and skillful hunters in your kingdom have been unable to do. You will conquer the beast, and it will spare your life."

He then concluded by saying, "In order to succeed, you must follow this path to the next village. It is not near, but it is not too far, either! When the sun begins to return to its home, you will come upon its walls. Then, you must look for an old woman. She will be working in the field, using a broken calabash to remove the chaff from her grain, and on the ground beside her will be a stack of wood. You must give her the gold coin that your mother saved for you, and you must manage to get her to let you stay in her house with her. If you succeed, what will be, will come!"

Sunjata continued on his way. As the old man had said, he came to the walled village and the old woman just as the sun was beginning to return to its home.

When Sunjata approached her, the woman saw him and stopped working. She then bent down to pick up her wood and appeared to be ready to return to her home. Sunjata took the gold coin from his hunter's bag, dropped it into her calabash, and said, "Here, old woman, take this coin, and may it make your life a little easier!"

The old woman stared at him and asked, "Who are you, and why are you here?"

Sunjata decided that it was best to conceal his identity, so he created both a name and a task. "I have come to sell my cows at your village market," he replied, "but I have arrived so late that I need a place to spend the night. May I stay with you?"

"My hut is too small, and I have no one to wait on you," she replied. "It is all I can do, at my age, to take care of myself!"

"Do not worry, old woman," Sunjata replied. "No hut is too small for my needs, and it is I who will take care of you!"

So it came to pass that Sunjata stayed the night with the old woman. When the sun began its morning journey, he killed one of his cows and gave the old woman its meat. He then spent the day at the village market, where he sold the cows that he could sell. At the end of the first day, he had sold three cows, and he spent the night with the old woman. At the end of the second day, he had sold three more cows, and he spent the night with the old woman. At the end of the third day, he had sold three more cows, and he spent the night with the old woman. So it came to pass for five more days and four more nights that each day he sold three more cows, and each night he spent with the old woman.

When Sunjata returned from the village market at the end of the eighth day, he had sold the last of his cows. The old woman met him at the entrance to her hut, and, again, asked him his name. Sunjata repeated the name that he had first given her.

"You are not giving me your real name because you want to kill me!" the old woman exclaimed. "I know who you are! You are Mari Djata, the son of the Lion, King Nare Maghan Kon Fatta, and the Buffalo Woman, Sogolon Kedju.

"I also know that you are here because you want to kill the strange beast that is ravaging Niani's crops," she continued. "Because you have been kind and generous to me, you will do what the most powerful and skillful hunters have been unable to do. You will conquer the beast, and it will spare your life.

"But in order to succeed," she added, "you must listen carefully to my directions and follow them without fail. Take this rice, this charcoal, and this egg, and return to your village. When the sun has returned to its home for the second time, take your bow and a good supply of arrows, take the hunters of Niani who have the courage to accompany you, and go into the forest until you reach the three lakes of Manding. Tell the hunters to climb into the trees, for, when I arrive, I will kill any hunter I find.

"While you are waiting for me, the sun will be asleep," the old woman continued. "But you will see a beast with six horns approach the lakes from the east in order to drink its fill. Do not lift your bow, for I will not be that beast. You have nothing to fear. After it roars three times, it will wander away.

"The sun will still be asleep, but you will then see a beast with twelve horns approach the lakes from the east in order to drink its fill. Do not lift your bow, for I will not be that beast. Again, you will have nothing to fear. After it roars six times, it will wander away."

She continued, "Just as the sun is about to begin its morning journey, you will feel the earth shake under your feet, and you will hear the forest rustle as if an army of warriors is marching through it. Then, you will see a great beast with eighteen horns, and with an eye in the middle of its forehead, approach the lakes from the east in order to drink its fill.

"After it roars nine times, you must lift your bow, for I will be that beast! You must send forth your arrows while I drink from the first lake, but you have nothing to fear. You must send forth your arrows while I drink from the second lake, but, still, you have nothing to fear. However, if you do not stop me from drinking from the third lake, I will kill you!" she exclaimed.

"I will confront you between the second lake and the third lake. You will now be in great danger! When I lower my head with my great horns, I will rush toward you. You must be prepared for my attack, and you must resist the urge to run. Instead, you must stand your ground and throw my rice on the earth between us. The land on which it falls will become a thick web of bamboo.

"Once I have struggled through this patch of bamboo, you will again be in great danger!" she exclaimed. "I will again lower my head with my great horns and rush toward you. Again, you must be prepared for my attack, and again you must resist the urge to run. Instead, you must stand your ground and, now, you must throw my charcoal on the earth between us. The land on which it falls will burn with a raging fire. I will walk into this fire, take its flames into my mouth, and blow them toward you. But, once again, you must stand your ground and resist the urge to run.

"Once I have struggled through this patch of fire, you will again be in great danger!" she exclaimed. "I will again lower my head with my great horns and rush toward you. Again, you must be prepared for my attack, and again you must resist the urge to run. Instead, you must stand your ground and, now, you must throw my egg on the earth between us. The land on which it falls will become a great river. I will walk into this river, but I will be unable to struggle through its strong currents. It is here that I will die, and once I am dead, the river waters will disappear. Command the hunters of Manding to descend from their trees and bury me in a secret place.

"If you remember my advice," she concluded, "all will go well with you. I know, because I am the strange beast that is ravaging the crops that grow in

Niani! Your father is responsible for the death of my son. However, I am now satisfied that I have punished the people of Niani enough for his deed."

Each event came to pass just as the old women had said it would. The rice, the charcoal, and the egg worked their magic; the beast charged angrily through the bamboo and the raging fire; it died in the strong currents of the river; and the hunters of Niani buried it in a hollow tree.

Chapter 4

Sasuma fears Sunjata and unsuccessfully plots his death. Sogolon then decides to take her family into what will become a seven-year exile. They travel first to Djedeba and then to Tabon and Wagadu. Finally, they arrive in Mema, where they remain.

When Sunjata led the hunters of Manding back from this expedition, the people of Niani and other Mandingo villages gathered to give him a hero's welcome. They now held Sogolon Kedju and her son, whom they called the Lion of Manding, in such high regard that Sasuma Berete feared the loss of her son's position and, with it, the loss of her own power.

"The court at Niani will surely remember the hunter's prophecy of long ago, and Mari Djata will take his place as the true king of Manding," she thought to herself. "Then what will become of my son, Dankarantuma? And what will become of me? Unless I act quickly, the Buffalo Woman and not I, will be the mother of the king. And she, not I, will have that power!"

So it came to pass that, like the spider who spends its life spinning webs in which to trap and kill its prey, Sasuma Berete again called upon the nine great witches of Manding, the Ancient Ones, who rule the night and who weave the tapestry of life and death in their dark kingdom.

"Mari Djata deserves to die!" Sasuma told them when they appeared before her. "If you permit him to live, he will only bring endless troubles upon the people of Niani."

To these words, the eldest and most powerful Ancient One replied, "It is true, Sasuma Berete, that life and death are one thin thread in the tapestry of each person's life, but every event has a cause. The snake strikes only the foot that approaches it, and we cannot cause Mari Djata to die before his time unless he offends us in some way."

"Arranging that will not be difficult," Sasuma replied. "Mari Djata thinks only of himself and his mother's family. Appear in Sogolon Kedju's vegetable garden as if you are a group of poor old women, and pick a few choice leaves. Her son defends that patch from all who are in need! You will discover for yourselves the moldy threads that form the tapestry of his life. You will find none of silver and gold in his spirit! Take what you need from him, and he will be quick to whip you despite your age and your need!"

So it came to pass that, as the sun was returning to its home, Sunjata returned from the hunt to find nine poor old women stealing his mother's vegetables. As soon as they saw him, they ran from him in terror.

"Welcome, old folk!" Sunjata cried. "You have no need to run away! Our garden supplies all who need its vegetables. Come, and I myself will fill your calabashes. And remember to return whenever you need what we grow here." Sogolon's son then acted upon his words.

When their calabashes were full, the oldest and most powerful of the nine witches addressed Sunjata. "Mari Djata, Lion of Manding and Child of Justice, we Ancient Ones do not need your mother's vegetables," she explained. "The king's mother persuaded us to test the threads of which you are made. If they had been moldy, as she assured us they were, you would have turned our powers against you. However, you have shown us that your spirit is woven with threads of silver and gold. Therefore, from this time forward, it will be our pleasure to protect you!"

Sogolon Kedju was a wise woman. Soon after Sunjata's meeting with the Ancient Ones, she gathered her children together and said, "We have no choice but to leave Manding. Realizing that she cannot hurt Sunjata, Sasuma will try her power over Manding Bory. Unlike Kolonkan and myself, he cannot see what is surely to come, and he has yet to be welcomed by the Ancient Ones who rule the night.

"Meanwhile," she concluded, "let your spirit be at ease, Sunjata. You will return to Niani when the time has come for you to rule its people, for your destiny is here in Manding, and what will be, will come!"

Sunjata agreed that, for the present, it was best for him to permit Dankarantuma to rule in his place. So it came to pass that Sogolon Kedju took her family into exile. Only Balla Fasseke did not accompany them. King Dankarantuma had sent Balla on a special mission to King Sumanguru Kante of Sosso, even though he had no right to order Sunjata's griot to perform any service for him.

Poor Dankarantuma! People are so impatient and blind about life! They cannot understand God's mysterious ways, nor do they realize that one's destiny cannot be changed. Each event adds its thread to the tapestry of one's life, and those who try to separate themselves from their destiny only succeed in furthering that which they would destroy!

Once Sogolon Kedju left Niani with her family, the visiting princes returned to their own kingdoms. However, distance and time do not make the heart forget those it has loved. Fran Kamara, Kamandjan, and Sunjata would remember their years together in Niani and would remain loyal friends.

For seven years, Sogolon Kedju and her family knew the life of wanderers, who must depend on the kindness and generosity of others for their own well-being. At that time, strangers were considered to be sacred, and therefore the Buffalo Woman and her children were entitled to hospitality. However, the time inevitably came when they had to move on.

The family first sought refuge in Djedeba, a capital village along the Niger River that was two days' journey from Niani. The family had been the king's guests for two months when, as was his custom with most strangers, the king suddenly called Sunjata before him and challenged him to be his adversary in a popular game called wori. The king was known to be a great sorcerer, and he took his power from this game.

"Mari Djata," he said, "I want to be certain that you understand the rules by which I play. If I win, and I always win, I will kill you! That is why I am known as the King of Death!"

"And what do I get if I win?" Sunjata asked. His courage surprised the king, but Sunjata knew that a great destiny lay before him, and that therefore he had nothing to fear from the king of Djedeba.

"You would get whatever you want," the king replied. "But don't expect it, because no one can beat me at this game!"

"Then I will ask for that wondrous sword that hangs on your wall," Sunjata responded, undaunted.

So it came to pass that the king and Sunjata played the king's game and that Sunjata won. The winner always needed to possess secret knowledge that was known only to the king, and the king was unaware that Sunjata had learned the secret clue to this particular game from Manding Bory.

Sasuma Berete was still busily spinning the webs in which she hoped to trap Sogolon Kedju's son. She had recently offered the king of Djedeba a great supply of gold if he would kill Sunjata, whom she knew was his guest. The king loved wealth far more than honor. He decided to play the game of wori with Sunjata because it was an easy way to bring about Sunjata's death and acquire the gold. It never occurred to him that his daughter liked Sunjata's brother, and that she would reveal her father's treacherous plan to Manding Bory.

The king was furious with Sunjata for knowing his secret and winning the game, and he refused to give Sunjata the promised sword. Moreover, the king told Sogolon Kedju and her family that they must leave his country immediately.

In parting, Sunjata said to him: "We appreciate your hospitality for as long as we received it. You have chosen to make us leave Djedeba. However, know that I will return on my terms when I choose to do so!"

Sogolon Kedju and her family then left the Niger River and traveled west, into the mountains, to the fortified capital of the kingdom of Tabon. This was the home of Fran Kamara, one of Sunjata's best friends during their recent years together in Niani. However, despite his son's friendship with Sunjata, the old king was afraid that his hospitality to Sogolon Kedju and her children would antagonize King Dankarantuma and his mother, whose alliance he needed. Therefore, the king of Tabon advised the family to join a caravan of merchants that was about to leave for the capital of the kingdom of Wagadu, the land of the Soninke.

Tabon was much larger and more impressive than the small village of Niani, so before the caravan left, Fran Kamara showed Sunjata its famous sights, including its great iron gates, its fortresses, and its royal armories.

"I will miss you, Fran Kamara," Sunjata told his friend. "But some day, when you and I are grown men, I will return to claim my kingdom. And on my way back to Manding, I will stop at Tabon so that you can join me. You will be my chief general as well as my friend, and together we will conquer many kingdoms!"

The long days spent in travel to Wagadu passed quickly because the merchants told Sunjata all about the greatest king of that time, Sumanguru Kante, the sorcerer-king of Sosso. He was known to be a man of great wealth, extraordinary power, and unbelievable cruelty. Sunjata was particularly interested because it was to Sumanguru's court that Dankarantuma had sent Balla Fasseke, his griot.

Sunjata had spent all his life in the village of Niani, and he found Wagadu to be even more remarkable than Tabon. This city had once been ruled by the descendants of Alexander the Great. Now it was protected by great walls which, as tall as they were, still permitted a view of the many mosques within. Inside the walls, the narrow streets teemed with camels and their traders, many of whom were Moors from the Sahara region. Sunjata was not surprised to find that the king of Wagadu lived in an impressive palace.

This king greeted Sogolon Kedju and her family with great warmth. "Consider Wagadu to be your new home," he told them. "The kingdoms of Manding and Wagadu have been friends from time of old. Once all of us even spoke your beautiful language. Today, few remain who can speak the Mande language, but many will still be able to understand it."

The king was as good as his word. He treated Sogolon Kedju and her children as if they were part of the royal family. During this time, Sunjata's unusual social and political skills led the king to remark, "It is clear that, one day, Mari Djata will be a great king! He remembers everyone, and he commands in a way that leads others to obey!"

Unfortunately, however, Sunjata and his family were only able to remain in Wagadu for a year, because Sogolon Kedju became very ill. Thinking that she would recover if she returned to a town on the Niger River, the king sent the family to his cousin, King Tunkara, in Mema, the capital of that great kingdom.

When Sogolon Kedju and her family arrived, they were first warmly welcomed by King Tunkara's sister, who immediately became Sogolon's friend. Here, many people spoke the Mande language, and Sogolon, as well as her children, thrived.

When King Tunkara returned from his military campaign, it was obvious that he was a great warrior. Sunjata was invited to participate in one of these campaigns as soon as he became fifteen. The warrior-king and his cavalry were amazed at the youth's great courage, self-confidence, and strength in battle. Despite the fact that he lacked skill, Sunjata had caused the enemy to retreat in panic.

Many a warrior said to his companions, "That youth will be a fine king!"

As for King Tunkara, he embraced Sunjata and joyfully exclaimed, "Mari Djata, surely Destiny has sent you to me! It will be my pleasure to train you to be a great warrior!"

Thereafter, King Tunkara, who had no heir, kept Sunjata at his side and instructed him as if he were his own son. Sunjata repaid his efforts by earning an extraordinary reputation, first among the king's warriors, then among the people of Mema, and finally among Mema's enemies.

The warrior-king and his people were overjoyed, because now they could look forward to a future in which Sunjata would be their king. Peace would replace war, and their kingdom would enlarge to include the kingdom of Manding. Their old enemies were already choosing to threaten weaker kingdoms.

When Sunjata became eighteen, King Tunkara appointed him to rule in his place whenever he was away. The lion cub of Manding had matured into a lion! He had grown as tall as a tree. He was so strong that only he could bend his wondrous, golden bow. His trials and troubles had made him skillful and wise. He was loved and honored by the people of Mema and feared by its enemies. Those in the kingdom of Mema who could see what is surely to come, proclaimed that Sunjata's deeds would surpass those of the great Alexander.

So it came to pass that Sogolon Kedju said to her son, "Mari Djata, the time has come for you to fulfill your destiny in your own kingdom of Manding. You must have patience as well as skill, but what will be, will come!"

By this time, King Sumanguru Kante of Sosso had conquered so many kingdoms that it was clear to Sunjata that he would eventually have to confront the great sorcerer-king in order to reclaim Manding.

Chapter 5

Meanwhile, Sumanguru Kante has his way in the western kingdoms, and both Balla Fasseke and Nana Triban prepare to help Sunjata conquer the sorcerer-king.

Sumanguru Kante was the son of a Soninke warrior and was a member of the caste of blacksmiths that had been the first to tame fire and teach others how to forge iron into weapons. Long ago, the sorcerer-king had consulted a Muslim who was known for his knowledge of supernatural events. This is what he had been told:

"Sumanguru Kante," the prophet had begun, "for forty days, I left the world of human life. I lived in the spirit world, where I saw the seven layers that form the sky and the seven layers that form the earth. In the darkness of the night, a black creature came forth from the depths of its home in the bottomless pond. It stood beside me in its human form and told me many things.

"Sumanguru Kante, you will become the most powerful ruler among the kingdoms of the evening sun!" the prophet had revealed. "However, you will also come to believe that you alone are invincible, and you will have only contempt for everyone else. You will be like a great tree that, being unable to see the storm that will uproot it, proudly withstands the violent winds until it suddenly falls. With the Sosso spearmen behind you, you will defeat and kill nine kings. You will rule the kingdom of Wagadu and the kingdom of Manding as well. These things you will accomplish, and you should enjoy them while it is within your power to enjoy them!"

The prophet had then said, "Allah be praised! God plans to fashion a king in his own image whom nothing will be able to harm. Sumanguru Kante, you should enjoy whatever you wish to enjoy before this child is born, because it will come to pass that your power will be like a droplet of water in the fiery heat of his sun!

"Sumanguru Kante, doubt my words if you will," the prophet had concluded. "But you can put them to the test. Return to your palace, gather two white roosters, and mark them. Name one of them after yourself, and fasten a band of pure gold around one of its legs. Then, take the rooster of the child-king who is to be born, whose name you do not know, and fasten a band of pure silver around one of its legs. When you have done as I have advised, set these two roosters against each other in contest somewhere within your palace grounds, and see which of them is the winner!"

Sumanguru Kante had returned to his palace, gathered and marked the two roosters, and set them in contest against each other. Although the rooster with the silver band had killed the rooster with the gold band, the sorcerer-king dismissed the words of the prophet as pure foolishness.

However, it came to pass that, given their great skill in the making and use of weapons as well as their natural talents as sorcerers, it was easy for Sumanguru Kante's great army of blacksmiths to conquer their enemies. The spearmen of Sosso came to be feared far and wide. And Sumanguru Kante became the most powerful ruler among the kingdoms of the evening sun.

The community of villages that combined to form Sumanguru Kante's capital of Sosso was now encircled by a triple wall that protected no less than 188 fortified palaces within, including the palace of the king, which had a tower that rose seven stories to meet the sun. One huge iron gate controlled the only entrance to the town. It is, therefore, not surprising that the capital was called Sosso the Magnificent. Sosso was the stronghold of fetishism and the enemy of Allah.

Sumanguru Kante was often called Sumanguru the Untouchable because he lived surrounded by his collection of fetishes in his secret room on the top floor of his tower. The sorcerer-king could transform himself into sixty-nine different shapes, and his fetishes contained such great supernatural power that they terrified every king and brought those who dared to fight Sumanguru to their knees. Therefore, no one could measure Sumanguru Kante's power, and no one could find a way to conquer him.

So it had come to pass that Sumanguru Kante now had cause to believe that he alone was invincible, and, therefore, he had come to have contempt for everyone else. He was, indeed, like a great tree that, being unable to see the storm that will uproot it, proudly withstands the violent winds until it suddenly falls. With the Sosso spearmen behind him, he had already defeated and killed nine kings. He now ruled the kingdom of Wagadu, and, for the past three years, the kingdom of Manding as well. He was considered to be a demon-king, one who was known to steal maidens without marrying them and to flog old men in the streets of Sosso. And he had brought nothing but war to his people.

In the years before Sasuma Berete's son, Dankarantuma, surrendered the kingdom of Manding to Sumanguru Kante, Dankarantuma had tried to please the sorcerer-king and establish a political alliance with this ruler who terrified him. Therefore, he sent his sister, Nana Triban, to Sosso against her will to become Sumanguru's wife. Fortunately for the unhappy maiden, Balla Fasseke, Sunjata's griot, was there to befriend her. Together they devised a plan whereby Nana Triban could do her part to discover the source of Sumanguru Kante's great magical powers and thereby help to bring about the eventual destruction of the demon-king.

First, Nana succeeded in becoming Sumanguru's favorite, and then she became his best friend. However, she would not become his wife before he agreed to give her what she wanted.

Pretending to hate Sunjata as much as her mother, Sasuma Berete, did, Nana told Sumanguru, "I have come to you because I want to be your wife. Mari Djata knows this, because I told him when I refused to marry your nephew, Fakoli Koroma, the man he had chosen for me. I told him that I would only marry the man whom I chose for myself, and that you are worth more than a thousand Fakolis! This is the real reason why Mari Djata is your enemy.

"It is because I want to be your wife," Nana Triban continued, "that I am willing to reveal my brother's secrets to you. And what I can tell you will help you win the war that is bound to occur between the two of you."

"I am ready to marry you today!" Sumanguru Kante exclaimed. "I have never met a woman like you! You are truly magnificent!"

"But you have only heard what I am willing to do for you," Nana Triban replied. "Now you must hear what you must be willing to do for me. You and I have come to one another because we have freely chosen to do so. No one has made this decision for us. Therefore, before we marry, it is only proper that we know each other's secrets, and that we reveal our taboos.

"Your power makes all other kings weak in their knees, so that they fall before you!" she exclaimed. "The look in your eyes causes the eyes of others to turn away in fear. Your arm is stronger than the arms of ten warriors. I must know what gives you your great strength, so that I can help keep you strong. And I must know what it is that can hurt you, so that I can protect you from harm."

"I am yours!" Sumanguru Kante exclaimed. "I will tell you what I have told no one. Arrows and spears have no power to kill me. Even witchcraft has no power to kill me! The true source of my power comes from my ancestors through the fetishes that live in my secret, sacred room. I worship these fetishes, since it is they who give me the strength of ten warriors and who protect me from harm.

"My ancestors have decreed that their power is mine as long as the one thing that can kill me does not touch me. I fear only the sharp spur on the leg of a one-year-old white rooster, if that spur has been removed and has been filled with the pure dust of gold and silver. Should such a spur ever touch my body, my ancestors will remove their power and their protection. My fetishes will no longer make me invincible, and I will surely die!

"Now, Nana Triban, will you be mine?" asked the demon-king.

"Of course!" Nana Triban exclaimed. She smiled, secretly waiting for the time when she could reveal this information to Balla Fasseke and then to Sunjata.

Meanwhile, the clouds of war sprouted like poisonous mushrooms in the damp soil of a forest. Sumanguru Kante's love for Nana Triban did not deter him from taking the wife of his nephew and chief general, Fakoli Koroma. Outraged, Fakoli declared war on his uncle, thereby giving many other kings the courage to support him.

King Dankarantuma of Manding was among them. He now gave up trying to please Sumanguru Kante and, instead, gathered his warriors and marched to join Fakoli Koroma. However, Sumanguru attacked him before he reached Fakoli, and Dankarantuma, never a lion at heart, panicked and ran like a hare from the sorcerer-king—and from his kingdom as well. He sought refuge in the forests of Guinea, where he established a village called Kisidugu, the "place of safety."

Clearly, a king who had possessed power had lacked courage. Other kings possessed courage but lacked power. And the king who would possess both courage and power was still in the kingdom of Mema. So it came to pass that, with no one to stop him, Sumanguru Kante burned Niani to the ground and proclaimed himself to be the king of Manding.

Those who can see what is surely to come, told the people of Niani that their kingdom would be restored by its true king, "he who possesses a double name." Clearly, this was the son of the Lion, King Nare Maghan Kon Fatta, and the Buffalo Woman, Sogolon Kedju, but no one had heard anything about Sogolon's family for seven years. Therefore, the seers of Manding advised members of King Nare Maghan's old court to conduct a search by dressing as merchants and selling their local wares in the major towns along the Niger River. One of these towns was Mema.

Meanwhile, even after Dankarantuma's flight and his own conquest of the kingdom of Manding, Sumanguru Kante kept Balla Fasseke in his palace in Sosso. So it came to pass that one day, when Sumanguru was away, Balla decided that it was time to do his part to discover the source of Sumanguru's great magical powers and thereby help to bring about the eventual destruction of the sorcerer-king. For him, this involved investigating the secret room on the seventh floor of the king's tower. Being a sorcerer himself, he felt that he had the courage to confront whatever fetishes were giving the demon-king his power. And he was confident that he could calm their spirits if such action proved to be necessary.

However, Balla Fasseke was completely unprepared for the view that greeted him once he stood at the entrance to this room. As he looked around, he could see that, here, Sumanguru Kante wore a robe and slippers that were made from human skin. He apparently was accustomed to sitting in the center of the room upon still another human skin. Other human skins draped the walls.

In another part of the room, Balla Fasseke saw nine human heads, which he thought were probably the skulls of the kings that Sumanguru Kante had killed. Like fetishes, they surrounded a water-filled pottery jar that contained a dancing snake. Three owls were presently sleeping on a perch above what appeared to be Sumanguru's bed. Wondrous weapons, including knives that had three edges, decorated the wall across from the entrance.

Finally, just to the right of the entrance, Balla Fasseke noticed an unusually large balafon. Having the griot's love of music, he immediately sat down and skillfully made the instrument sing. What magic properties it possessed when he played it! The heads of the three owls rocked to his rhythms. The snake became quiet and listened from its place in the jar. And the nine skulls acquired their former flesh and blood so that they appeared to have come alive. As the griot played Sumanguru's balafon, he discovered that he could control the behavior of the demon-king's fetishes by the type of music that he chose to play.

Balla Fasseke did not know that Sumanguru Kante could hear his musical instrument wherever he happened to be. And so it came to pass that as soon as Balla began to play, the sorcerer-king knew that someone had invaded his sacred space. He quickly returned to his palace and, wild with anger, entered his special room. Balla Fasseke was still creating music. Without a pause, the griot looked up at the king, changed melodies, and began to create a song in his honor, one in which he praised King Sumanguru Kante's many talents and accomplishments.

The demon-king's anger wafted away with Balla's music. When the song was over, Sumanguru Kante exclaimed, "Balla Fasseke, nothing brings me as much pleasure as to hear you praise me in song! Therefore, from this day forward, you will remain in Sosso and be my griot. You will never see Niani again!"

So it happened that for this reason, if for no other, it was destined that Sumanguru Kante and Mari Djata would become great enemies. However, Balla Fasseke smiled to himself as he heard Sumanguru's words, for now he knew that it was not his destiny to remain in Sosso. The griot had discovered that he had the power to control the sorcerer-king's fetishes. "What will be, will come!" he exclaimed to himself. "And when it is time for Nana Triban and me to leave Sosso, I now know how to manage our escape!"

Chapter 6

Sunjata leaves Mema to become king of Manding. His journey takes him to Wagadu and then to Tabon, the site of the first battle against Sumanguru. Sunjata's victory brings Balla Fasseke and Nana Triban to join the armies at Sibi.

Meanwhile, the Niani nobles had been searching for Sogolon Kedju and her family for two months without success when Sunjata's sister, Kolonkan, saw them in the marketplace of Mema selling vegetables that grew in Niani. It was their wares that drew her to them, and her conversation led them to Sunjata.

Sunjata, at eighteen, possessed the bearing of the lion and the strength of the buffalo. His eyes blazed, his voice commanded, and his arm accomplished. The nobles from Niani were impressed and delighted to discover that the kingdom of Manding would have such a great ruler.

"Mari Djata, king of Manding," began the leader of the search party, "your father's kingdom longs for your return! We have suffered destruction and death at the hands of Sumanguru Kante, and although many brave men continue to fight, they fight a losing battle. Those who can see what is surely to come, have told us that, of all the men who walk the earth, only you can destroy Sumanguru Kante! We know that you have found a good life here in the kingdom of Mema, but your destiny is in your own kingdom of Manding. Will you come?"

"I am ready," Mari Djata, the Lion of Manding, replied. "When the sun begins its morning journey, we, too, will be on our way."

Sunjata then went before King Tunkara and said, "My king, like a father you have watched over me and trained me to fight and to rule. Now the time has come for me to leave you, for I must return to Niani and rule my father's kingdom. I will never forget all that you have done for me and my family!"

King Tunkara listened to Sunjata's words, but he was slow to give up his adopted son and the heir to his own throne. Sogolon Kedju had suddenly developed a great fever and had died, and the warrior-king selfishly tried to tie her burial to Sunjata's remaining in Mema with him. He found it hard to accept the fact that no matter what a king gives of his heart and his kingdom, another king's son is never his own.

Poor Tunkara! People are so impatient and blind about life! They cannot understand God's mysterious ways, nor do they realize that one's destiny cannot be changed. Each event adds its thread to the tapestry of one's life, and those who try to separate themselves from their destiny only succeed in furthering that which they would destroy!

However, Tunkara had a wise adviser, who said to him, "My king, what will be, will come! So it is best that you endure the pain in your heart and think about the time that will surely come. The king of Manding would be a powerful ally of the king of Mema!"

So it came to pass that King Tunkara relented and sent Sunjata off with half the royal army. With his brother, Manding Bory, at his side, Sunjata first traveled by way of Wagadu, where that king gave him half his cavalry, including warriors who were renowned bowmen.

Then, remembering his promise to Fran Kamara, who was now the king of Tabon, Sunjata journeyed toward that mountain fortress. As they traveled, he listened to the tales of the great Alexander, who had also crossed the world from west to east. The Lion of Manding hoped that he, too, would gain such power, wealth, and fame.

Sumanguru Kante, the sorcerer-king, had it within his power to know Sunjata's location, and he decided to prevent the Lion-King from reaching Tabon. He commanded his son to take an army and block the one possible entrance, which was the valley road.

However, an army of Sosso spearmen did not daunt Sunjata! Faster than lightning, more frightening than thunder, and more unpredictable than a flood, the Lion-King pounced on his enemy like a lion among sheep. The earth soon ran red with Sosso blood. Many warriors found death beneath the hooves of Sunjata's horse. Others dropped their heads beneath his sword as a tree drops its ripe fruit. Sumanguru Kante's son and his spearmen panicked and fled in terror toward Sosso.

Fran Kamara, now called the Feared One of Tabon, arrived in time to celebrate his friend's victory. He had become a great warrior-king, who led an army of skilled and fearless blacksmiths, many of whom were known for their use of the bow. It was common knowledge that Fran Kamara himself could split the heads of ten warriors with just one swipe of his iron sword.

"Mari Djata, dear friend!" the king of Tabon exclaimed. "I put myself and my army at your command. Together we will conquer Sumanguru Kante or die!"

So it came to pass that the Lion of Manding became the commander of three great armies, those of Mema, Wagadu, and Tabon.

When Sumanguru's son returned to Sosso, he told his father, "Sunjata is greater than a lion! No one can conquer him!"

These words suddenly reminded Sumanguru Kante of an old prophecy that had implied that he would remain in power until a great, young king killed him and conquered his kingdom. He remembered how he had laughed at such foolishness! However, now he realized that many of the events that the prophet had revealed had indeed come to pass. Therefore, he thought that it would be wise, at this time, to consult another Muslim who was known for his knowledge of supernatural events. This is what he was told:

"Sumanguru Kante," the second prophet began, "you have become the most powerful ruler among the kingdoms of the evening sun! However, believing that you alone are invincible, you have only contempt for everyone else. You are like a great tree that, being unable to see the storm that will uproot it, proudly withstands the violent winds until it suddenly falls. With the Sosso spearmen behind you, you have already defeated and killed nine kings. You now rule the kingdom of Wagadu and, for the past three years, the kingdom of Manding as well. These things that you have accomplished, enjoy them now, Sumanguru Kante, while it is still within your power to enjoy them!

"For forty days I left the world of human life," the prophet continued. "I lived in the spirit world, where I saw the seven layers that form the sky and the seven layers that form the earth. In the darkness of the night, a familiar spirit came forth and stood beside me in its human form. It told me that a king lives who does not recognize the power of God, and that — praise Allah! — God has fashioned another king in his own image, whom nothing can hurt. Nothing can alter God's plan. Compared to you, Sumanguru Kante, this other king is but a child, and yet your power will be like a drop of water in the fiery heat of his sun!

"Sumanguru Kante, doubt my words, if you will," the prophet concluded. "But you can put them to the test. Return to your palace, gather two white rams, and mark them. Name one of them after yourself, and place a band of pure gold upon one of its legs. Then, take the ram of the one whom you fear, the child-king whose name you do not know, and place a band of pure silver upon one of its legs. When you have done as I have advised, set these two rams against each other in contest somewhere within your palace grounds, and watch carefully to see what happens. For if you touch this child-king, whatever the other ram has done to your ram, the child-king will do to you!"

Sumanguru returned to his palace, gathered and marked the two rams, and set them in contest against each other. When the ram with the silver band killed the ram with the gold band, the sorcerer-king knew that Sunjata was the child-king of these prophecies and his great enemy. So it came to pass that Sumanguru Kante gathered his great army of Sosso spearmen and decided to conquer the Lion of Manding at Tabon.

From the top of one of the hills, the sorcerer-king studied Sunjata's battle strategies. He watched as the Lion-King, wearing the Muslim attire of Mema, would surprise the enemy by charging prematurely with Tunkara's well-trained cavalry. Meanwhile, the bowmen of Wagadu and Tabon, under the command of Fran Kamara, would defend the rear and respond to surprise attacks.

Keeping his eyes on Sunjata's white Muslim turban, Sumanguru Kante entered the battle. As soon as Sunjata saw him, the Lion-King came within range and hurled his spear at his enemy's chest. However, like a rock, it bounced off. Sunjata then sent forth an arrow, but Sumanguru caught it and waved it triumphantly at him. Spear in hand, the Lion-King was charging forth once again when, suddenly, the sorcerer disappeared. It was Manding Bory who noticed that Sumanguru Kante was again observing the battle from the top of one of the hills.

Later, while the sun slept, Sumanguru Kante gathered his warriors and initiated a surprise attack on Sunjata's forces. At first, it looked as if the sorcerer-king would be successful, but the combined armies soon rallied and retaliated. Once again, the army of Sosso spearmen did not daunt Sunjata! Faster than lightning, more frightening than thunder, and more unpredictable than a flood, the Lion-King pounced on his enemy like a lion among sheep. The earth soon ran red with Sosso blood. Many warriors found death beneath the hooves of Sunjata's horse. Others dropped their heads beneath his sword as a tree drops its ripe fruit. The sorcerer-king and his spearmen panicked and fled in terror toward Sosso.

Sunjata had found it hard to believe the stories he had heard about Sumanguru Kante, but he now knew that he faced an enemy who could not be killed and who could appear and disappear as he chose.

"What weapons can I use against such a man?" Sunjata asked himself. "In order to conquer him, I must destroy the power that protects him. And, somehow, I must discover what that power is!"

Just as the sun spreads forth its light before it begins its morning journey, so Sunjata's fame scaled the mountains and spread across the Niger plains. When the Lion of Manding reached the kingdom of Sibi, he was greeted by Kamandjan, the other close friend from his childhood, who was Fran Kamara's cousin and now Sibi's king.

"Mari Djata, dear friend!" the king of Sibi exclaimed. "I put myself and my army at your command. Together we will conquer Sumanguru Kante or die!"

So it came to pass that the Lion of Manding became the commander of four great armies, those of Mema, Wagadu, Tabon, and Sibi.

Being allies of Manding, armies from all of the other Mandingo kingdoms had gathered at Sibi to welcome home their king and prepare for the great war against Sumanguru Kante for the control of their lands.

"The sons of the Mandingo nations cheer the son of the Lion and the Buffalo, our true king!" they sang.

"Sons of the Mandingo nations, I return your cheer!" Mari Djata replied. "I have returned to restore the freedom that our Mandingo ancestors bequeathed to us! I will punish Sumanguru Kante for bringing destruction and death to the kingdom of Manding and its allies! And as long as the wind of life courses through my mouth, I will defend our great lands against any who would try to enslave us!"

In preparation for the next battle, those who can see what is surely to come, advised Sunjata to sacrifice 100 white rams, 100 white bulls, and 100 white roosters. These sacrifices were occurring when Nana Triban and Balla Fasseke arrived in Sibi. Once Sumanguru Kante had returned to Sosso, Balla and Nana had learned that Sunjata would be in Sibi. They had already prepared their plan of escape and were successful in leaving Sosso.

Upon hearing of their arrival, Sunjata told Fran Kamara, "If Nana and Balla have acquired power that can master Sumanguru Kante's power, then we will conquer him after all!"

After a joyful reunion, Nana Triban told Sunjata the tale of her time in Sosso, revealing that the secret source of Sumanguru Kante's power was his collection of fetishes, and that the secret source of his protection was his taboo against the touch of the sharp spur on the leg of a one-year-old white rooster, if that spur has been removed and has been filled with the pure dust of gold and silver.

When she had finished, Balla Fasseke told Sunjata what he had discovered about the fetishes in the sorcerer-king's secret room. He concluded by saying,

"While in that room, I learned that my powers as a sorcerer with Sumanguru Kante's balafon could control the fetishes that gave the demon-king his power. Then I knew that all I needed to do to escape from Sosso was to wait until the sorcerer-king had left his palace, put his fetishes to sleep, and meet Nana Triban. We carried out this plan as soon as we learned that you had won the battle at Tabon, for then I knew that the Lion of Manding had become strong enough to break his fetters.

"Together," Balla Fasseke continued, "you and I will now begin to fulfill your destiny. You will act, and I will sing of your great deeds! For without the songs of the griot, heroic deeds and those who performed them are forgotten! Your heroic spirit will continue to live through my song, so that all who live now, and all who will live in times still to come, will remember you and admire you!"

Word now arrived that Sumanguru Kante had returned with his great army in order to prevent Sunjata from entering the kingdom of Manding.

"Good!" Balla Fasseke exclaimed. "We are ready to leave Sibi, and what will be, will come! Now, it is time to gather the armies together so that Fran Kamara and Kamandjan can light a fire in each warrior's heart!"

The armies had formed a circle around Balla Fasseke and Sunjata, when the griot challenged Fran Kamara. "I hear that you are now called the Feared One of Tabon!" he exclaimed. "But is it really true, Fran Kamara, that you can split the heads of ten warriors with just one swipe of your iron sword? Do something now, if you can, to prove your strength and your skill!"

The king of Tabon, who was sitting upon his charger at the head of his army, was quick to accept Balla Fasseke's challenge. He galloped into the center of the circle, drew forth his sword, and proclaimed, "Mari Djata, in the presence of all the warriors assembled here, I give you my sacred word that I will lead my men to victory at your side, or we warriors of Tabon will die fighting!"

The Feared One of Tabon then charged through the mass of warriors toward a mighty mahogany tree. Brandishing his great sword, he sliced through the trunk, splitting it in two from top to bottom. He then galloped back to Balla Fasseke and Sunjata and proclaimed, "Mari Djata, Lion of Manding, just as I have divided the trunk of that great mahogany tree, so on the Niger plain at Krina, my warriors and I will divide and conquer the army of the sorcerer-king, Sumanguru Kante!"

When Fran Kamara had taken his place on Sunjata's right, Balla Fasseke then challenged Fran Kamara's cousin, Kamandjan, who was also a great warrior.

"Kamandjan, king of Sibi, I hear that you are a good match for your cousin, the Feared One of Tabon!" Balla Fasseke exclaimed. "Do something now, if you can, to prove your own strength and skill!"

The king of Sibi, who was sitting upon his charger at the head of his army, was quick to accept Balla Fasseke's challenge. He galloped into the center of the circle, drew forth his sword, and proclaimed, "Mari Djata, in the presence of all the warriors assembled here, I give you my sacred word that I will lead my men to victory at your side, or we warriors of Sibi will die fighting!"

Kamandjan then charged through the mass of warriors toward the mighty mountain that watches over Sibi. Brandishing his great sword, he sliced through its red rock, causing the earth to shake and the air to become red with dust. As the air cleared, the warriors could see that Kamandjan's sword had opened a path into the mighty mountain, revealing a tunnel inside.

He then galloped back to Balla Fasseke, Sunjata, and Fran Kamara and proclaimed, "Mari Djata, Lion of Manding, just as I have divided the rock of Sibi's great mountain, so on the Niger plain at Krina, my warriors and I will divide and conquer the army of the sorcerer-king, Sumanguru Kante!"

Hearing these words, Balla Fasseke moved aside and permitted Kamandjan to take his place on Sunjata's left.

Chapter 7

The armies under Sunjata's command move to Krina,
where Sunjata and Sumanguru Kante declare war.
Fakoli Koroma joins Sunjata, and together they defeat
Sumanguru. Sunjata's forces then destroy Sosso,
making their victory complete.

So it came to pass that the combined Mandingo armies, under the command of the Lion of Manding, left Sibi and traveled to the village of Dayala, in the Niger River valley. Sunjata knew that Sumanguru Kante was camped with his army in nearby Krina. A great battle between the two kings was now inevitable, since the sorcerer-king needed to march through Dayala if he were going to try to prevent Sunjata from entering the kingdom of Manding.

It was the custom at that time that before taking action, one must state a cause for that action. Until now, the two kings had fought without a specific declaration of war, but now that they were fighting for the kingdom of Manding, formal communication would have to occur. Because Sumanguru and Sunjata were both sorcerers, it was possible for them to avoid speaking directly to each other by sending their owls to do it for them. So it came to pass that two owls spoke the following thoughts, each speaking for his own king:

Sumanguru's owl flew to Sunjata's tent, perched there, and said, "Mari Djata, you are threatening the king of Manding! If you are wise, you will return to the kingdom of Mema in peace."

Sunjata's owl then flew to Sumanguru Kante's tent, perched there, and replied, "The true king of Manding will never kneel to you, Sumanguru Kante! One cannot restore the dead to life, but if you are wise, you will return to your own kingdom of Sosso, and from there you will do what you can to heal the injuries that you have brought upon the Mandingo peoples."

"Not you, but I am the true king of Manding!" Sumanguru's owl exclaimed. "My army has given me the right to rule."

Sunjata's owl replied, "Then my army will conquer your army and restore my right to rule."

To these words, Sumanguru's owl exclaimed, "Just as the wild yam clings to the rocks, so will I cling to the kingdom of Manding!"

"Then let fear enter your heart, Sumanguru Kante," replied Sunjata's owl, "for my seven great blacksmiths will shatter those rocks to which you cling, and, when they have dislodged you, I will eat you!"

"You will not succeed, Mari Djata," replied Sumanguru's owl, "for I will become a poisonous mushroom in your mouth, and despite your great courage, you will be compelled to spit me out!"

"Your magic will not save you, Sumanguru Kante," Sunjata's owl responded, "for I will become such a hungry rooster that your poison will have no power over me!"

"Then, Mari Djata, I will become a fiery cinder that will roast your foot!" Sumanguru's owl exclaimed.

"And I will become the rain that will quench your fire!" Sunjata's owl replied. "I will become the raging torrent that will sweep you away!"

"Then I will become the great silk-cotton tree that rules all other trees!" said Sumanguru's owl.

"And I will become the creeping vine that lives off the silk-cotton tree and strangles it!" Sunjata's owl exclaimed.

Sumanguru's owl then replied, "You may or may not win this war with words, but know that I will not let you have the kingdom of Manding!"

"But you will do just that," Sunjata's owl responded, "for two kings cannot rule one kingdom!"

"You are correct about the two kings," Sumanguru's owl replied. "So if you are wise, you will prepare to have your own head join those of the nine other kings whom I have already killed!"

"Enough of this war of words!" Sunjata's owl concluded. "Our swords will defend the thoughts our words have expressed, and what will be, will come! So if you are wise, Sumanguru Kante, you will prepare to meet a king who may have greater power than you possess!"

It was at Krina that Sumanguru Kante's nephew, Fakoli Koroma, joined Sunjata in his fight against the sorcerer-king.

"Greetings, Mari Djata, king of Manding!" Fakoli began. "I am Fakoli Koroma, king of the fearless Koroma blacksmiths. Since you are at war with my uncle, we have a common enemy! Therefore, I put myself and my army at your command. Together we will conquer Sumanguru Kante or die!"

To these words, Sunjata replied, "If my generals agree, I will be pleased to have you join us. I defend all those who need my strength to avenge injustice!"

So it came to pass that the Lion of Manding became the commander of five great armies, those of Mema, Wagadu, Tabon, Sibi, and Koroma.

The night before any great battle, it was the custom at that time for a griot to appear before the assembled forces and light a fire in each warrior's heart. Therefore, once the sun had returned to its home, Balla Fasseke spoke to all the armies that had gathered under Sunjata's command.

The griot began, "I will direct my thoughts to you, Mari Djata, king of Manding. What will be, will come! But, as you approach your destiny, I would give you a wise heart. First, I would have you know that kingdoms are like people, in that they are born, they grow, and they die. Each king lives during one part of the life of his kingdom.

"I would have you remember that the kingdom of Wagadu once included many, many lands, and it possessed great glory, fame, and fortune," he continued.

"But now Wagadu is but a tiny kingdom, and its great glory, fame, and fortune live only in the songs the griots sing.

"Today it is Sumanguru Kante who rules, not only his kingdom of Sosso, but the kingdoms of other kings as well. Are this sorcerer-king's arrogance and cruelty going to continue to torment us?" Balla Fasseke asked. Then, after a brief pause, he replied, "I think that this is not to be. Sumanguru Kante has pushed his kingdom beyond its limits, and like a horse that has been driven by its rider without mercy, the kingdom of Sosso is doomed to collapse."

Balla Fasseke continued, "Mari Djata, you are returning to Manding at a time when another king already rules your kingdom. I would have you realize that, just as two roosters cannot live peacefully together in a chicken coop, so two kings cannot eat from the same calabash. Yet you are the sixteenth king of Manding, and just as the silk-cotton tree is deeply rooted in the earth, so you have deep roots in the history of your Mandingo people.

"Son of Nare Maghan and Sogolon Kedju, listen to your griot while he sings about your ancestors. Through his song, he would have the old kings of Manding teach you how to handle your destiny. Remember the good king who first conquered Manding. Remember the good king who made Manding grow. Remember the good king who went to Mecca and brought the blessing of Allah upon Manding. Remember the good king who transformed the hunters of Manding into warriors. And remember his evil son who brought a time of terror to Manding. Remember your father, the good king who brought the blessing of peace to Manding. Remember the majestic lion to whom you owe your majesty and the buffalo to whom you owe your might, for it is your father, Nare Maghan Kon Fatta, and your mother, Sogolon Kedju, to whom you owe your life and your destiny."

Balla Fasseke then concluded by asking, "Mari Djata, what great deeds will you perform tomorrow that will become part of my songs? What will your actions teach all those who come after you? What will you leave the Mandingo peoples to remember about you? I would have these questions give you a wise heart. My power is small compared to your own. I am able to sing songs that will give you lasting life. But my songs are only the shadows of a life well-lived. You have the greater power, for you are able to create the song that you would have me sing."

The sun had long returned to its home when the warriors returned to their tents for a good rest. But although the sun and the warriors slept, Fakoli Koroma remained awake, listening to the night sounds and anticipating the battle in which he would finally avenge the theft of his wife. So it came to pass that, just as the sun was about to begin its morning journey, it was Fakoli Koroma who heard the sounds of his uncle's army on the move and immediately alerted Sunjata.

For this great battle for his kingdom, Sunjata exchanged the Muslim attire of Mema, with its white turban, for that of the hunter-king of Manding. He took down his wondrous golden bow and chose an arrow that had been specially prepared for this occasion. The arrows that he always used in battle were made of iron, but this arrow had a wooden shaft that was tipped with the sharp spur from the leg of a one-year-old white rooster that had been filled with the pure dust of gold and silver.

Sunjata knew, from Nana Triban's tale, that if he could touch the demon-king with this arrowhead, it would break Sumanguru Kante's taboo and destroy his power! The Lion of Manding was delighted when Balla Fasseke told him that a renowned seer had dreamed that Sumanguru Kante had died in battle.

The battle of Krina occurred on the Niger plain. Sumanguru Kante's great army stretched all the way from the river to the hills. With Kamandjan of Sibi and Fakoli Koroma at his sides, Sunjata led the forces with Tunkara's cavalry. As usual, the bowmen of Wagadu and Tabon, under the command of Fran Kamara, fought in the rear.

It came to pass in the course of the battle that Sumanguru Kante came down from the hills and attacked his nephew's army. Sunjata then slashed his way through the warriors of Sosso in order to support Fakoli Koroma and confront the demon-king. Once again, the army of Sosso spearmen did not daunt Sunjata! Faster than lightning, more frightening than thunder, and more unpredictable than a flood, the Lion-King pounced on his enemy like a lion among sheep. The earth soon ran red with Sosso blood. Many warriors found death beneath the hooves of Sunjata's horse. Others dropped their heads beneath his sword as a tree drops its ripe fruit.

Sunjata was determined to capture Sumanguru Kante alive, but the songs the griots sing reveal that this was not to be. Some songs relate how Sumanguru Kante was too involved in his fight with Fakoli Koroma to think of Mari Djata. Therefore, the Lion of Manding was able to gallop within range of Sumanguru's tall head-piece, raise his wondrous golden bow, and send forth the fatal arrow. The point barely touched Sumanguru's shoulder, but the touch of the rooster's sharp spur was enough to destroy the sorcerer-king's power. Sumanguru Kante suddenly disappeared and was never seen again.

However, other songs tell a different tale. They say that Sumanguru Kante saw a large black bird cross the sun and knew that his end had come. He fled in terror toward the north, accompanied only by his son, while his warriors scattered in panic. Here, too, the earth ran red with Sosso blood.

These songs say that the sun had completed half its journey, when it looked down and saw that Sunjata and Fakoli Koroma were pursuing Sumanguru Kante and his son. The sun continued its journey, and they continued their pursuit. In time, the cavalry of Mema joined them. Fortunately, Fakoli Koroma was no stranger to this country, for while the sun slept, they continued their pursuit.

When the sun began its morning journey, it looked down and saw that they continued their pursuit. They were still far behind Sumanguru Kante and his son. The sun continued its journey, and they continued their pursuit. However, now they were beginning to close the distance between them and the demon-king. The sun was once again returning to its home, and they continued their pursuit. However, now they were close enough for Sumanguru Kante and his son to hear them.

The songs of some griots say that the sorcerer-king's ancestors protected him one last time, and that his protective spirit transformed him into a rocky part of the mountain before Sunjata could capture him. However, the songs of other griots say that Sumanguru Kante entered a large, black cave in the mountain and was never seen again.

Meanwhile, Sumanguru Kante's army retreated to Sosso, now the only kingdom to take a stand against the Lion-King. Well fortified with food and water, and well armed, the people of Sosso could survive a year's siege. However, Sunjata planned to capture this last stronghold in the time that it took the sun to complete the first half of its journey.

The Mandingo warriors were expert at capturing a walled town. While those in the front line used ladders to climb the wall, these ladders were held in place by warriors in a second line, while spearmen in a third line used their shields to protect those who were holding the ladders. Meanwhile, Sosso warriors stood upon the wall and threw huge boulders down on their invaders, and the bowmen from Wagadu and Tabon directed their arrows at the Sosso warriors. The best bowmen of all, those from Bobo, had joined Sunjata's forces in time for the Krina battle, and they now shot flaming arrows over the wall, igniting the thatched roofs of the village houses and causing the town to become a mass of flames and smoke.

Sosso immediately surrendered and opened its great gate to the invaders. Sunjata's armies massacred the Sosso warriors on the spot, while the women and children of Sosso begged for mercy.

Led by Balla Fasseke, Sunjata entered Sumanguru Kante's palace and went up to the sorcerer-king's sacred room. Since Sunjata's arrow had broken Sumanguru's power, the owls were wandering about on the floor, and the snake was dying in the jar. While he was in the demon-king's palace, Sunjata gathered Sumanguru's wives together and prepared to return them to their royal families. When everything of value had been removed, the Lion-King commanded his armies to burn whatever fire could destroy and to demolish the rest. The sun was completing the first half of its journey as the flames of Sosso climbed toward the sky.

So it has come to pass that, from that day to this, the land that once was the famous kingdom of Sosso has remained barren and deserted. Nothing remains of Sumanguru Kante's wondrous town of fortified palaces, with its triple walls and the demon-king's tall tower. Today, Sosso lives only in the songs the griots sing.

Chapter 8

Sunjata expands Manding into the empire of Mali and becomes its emperor. He then returns to Niani, where he reigns in peace as the king of kings.

Following the destruction of Sumanguru Kante's capital, the Lion of Manding divided his Mandingo army into three parts and continued his conquests. Fakoli Koroma led one division and Fran Kamara led another, while Sunjata led the largest division himself. By the time Sunjata was ready to return to the kingdom of Manding, he and his Mandingo allies controlled all the land from Wagadu in the north, to Manding in the south, and from the mountains of the Fouta in the west, to Mema in the east. Moreover, it was a time of peace!

In the process, Sunjata had visited his mother's land, where he sacrificed a white rooster on the huge mound that marked the death of the Buffalo of Do. He also had sent messengers to King Tunkara, bearing fine gifts and proclaiming eternal friendship between Mali and Mema.

It came to pass that Sunjata gathered all of the Mandingo armies together again at the village of Kaba (Kangaba), in the kingdom of Sibi, in order to celebrate the birth of the empire of Mali. There, Mari Djata, the Lion of Manding, appeared before his peoples in the robes of a Muslim king. He was accompanied on the platform by Balla Fasseke, Manding Bory, Fran Kamara, Kamandjan, and Fakoli Koroma. Kamandjan, being the king of Sibi and therefore the host, was the first to speak in Sunjata's honor.

"Praise Allah!" Kamandjan exclaimed. "What will be, will come, and we are finally at peace! May we never see it end! This day we are happy in our hearts and in our homes because one man among us had the courage, the strength, and the skill to confront Sumanguru Kante and destroy him."

The king of Sibi continued. "It had come to pass that Sumanguru Kante was the most powerful ruler among the kingdoms of the evening sun. Believing that he alone was invincible, he had only contempt for everyone else! He was a great tree that, being unable to see the storm that will uproot it, proudly withstands the violent winds until it suddenly falls.

"With the Sosso spearmen behind him, Sumanguru Kante had already defeated and killed nine kings. But he was not satisfied, and we were powerless against him! Again and again, he would steal our silver and our gold. But he was not satisfied, and we were powerless against him! Again and again, he would steal our wives and our daughters. But he was not satisfied, and we were powerless against him! Again and again, he would steal our kingdoms. But he was not satisfied, and we were powerless against him! Kings who possessed power, lacked courage. Kings who possessed courage, lacked power. When would the forces of nature combine to produce the storm that would uproot this great tree?

"Meanwhile," Kamandjan continued, "one king, a courageous and strong lion cub, was gaining skill in the kingdom of Mema in the East. And it came to pass that this lion cub grew to be a great Lion-King in this kingdom that was not his own. Sunjata was loved and honored by the people of Mema. Sunjata was admired and respected by the great warriors of Mema. And Sunjata was feared by the enemies of Mema.

"Just as the sun spreads forth its light before it begins its morning journey, so the Lion-King's fame brought a new light from the east that scaled the mountains and shone upon the kingdoms of the western sun. With the love of a father for his children, the Lion of Manding came to our rescue. Mari Djata possessed both the courage and the power to combine the forces of nature to produce the storm that would uproot this great tree!" Kamandjan exclaimed.

He continued, "At Tabon, Sumanguru Kante's army of Sosso spearmen did not daunt Mari Djata! Faster than lightning, more frightening than thunder, and more unpredictable than a flood, the Lion-King pounced on the enemy like a lion among sheep. The earth soon ran red with Sosso blood. Many warriors found death beneath the hooves of Sunjata's horse. Others dropped their heads beneath his sword as a tree drops its ripe fruit. The sorcerer-king and his spearmen panicked and fled in terror toward Sosso. We had feared Sumanguru Kante as if he were a demon, but when we saw him run, we knew that he was but a man. We could conquer him after all!"

Kamandjan continued, "And so it came to pass that the forces of nature combined to produce the storm that uprooted this great tree, for with Mari Djata in command, we Mandingo combined our armies to fight the war that destroyed the great sorcerer-king. No longer will Sumanguru Kante steal our silver and gold! No longer will Sumanguru Kante steal our wives and daughters! And no longer will Sumanguru Kante steal our kingdoms!

"Mari Djata," Kamandjan concluded, "I proclaim you to be my king, the king of my nation, the king of kings, and my emperor!" And with these words, he plunged his spear into the ground and exclaimed, "I give you my spear. From this time forth, it is yours!"

Fran Kamara then took his spear in his hand, stood up, and proclaimed, "Mari Djata, I proclaim you to be my king, the king of my nation, the king of kings, and my emperor!" And with these words, he plunged his spear into the ground and exclaimed, "I give you my spear. From this time forth, it is yours!"

Fakoli Koroma then took his spear in his hand, stood up, and proclaimed, "Mari Djata, I proclaim you to be my king, the king of my nation, the king of kings, and my emperor!" And with these words, he plunged his spear into the ground and exclaimed, "I give you my spear. From this time forth, it is yours!"

So it came to pass that Kamandjan's words and deed were repeated by each of the twelve kings of the Mandingo empire, until twelve spears proclaimed Mari Djata to be emperor of Mali. Then the festivities began in honor of the new empire and its emperor, including spectacular war dances by various groups among the empire's armies, a parade of prisoners, and the display of war trophies.

Finally, Mari Djata stood before the assembly and greeted the armies from each of the twelve Mandingo kingdoms by name. He then pulled up Kamandjan's spear and said, "Take back your spear, honored friend of my childhood, and with it, take back your kingdom. From this day forward, your people and mine will be brothers."

Mari Djata then pulled up Fran Kamara's spear and said, "Dear friend, I return your spear, and with it, your kingdom. Tabon and all the lands that you conquered are yours. Just as you grew up at the court of Niani with me, so your children and your children's children will grow up in Niani, and we will treat your children and their children as we treat our own."

In this way Sunjata returned to each king his kingdom and gave to each king his power. To Fakoli Koroma he gave the kingdom of Sosso and additional lands. And to his griot, Balla Fasseke, he gave the honor of having all future griots in the kingdom of Manding chosen from among the members of the Keita nation. Finally, after many more days of celebrating peace and friendship, each of the Mandingo armies returned to its homeland.

It came to pass that Sunjata and his Mandingo army crossed the Niger River into the kingdom of Manding in honor, stepping from one dug-out canoe to the next, as the personal gesture of gratitude from the nation that controlled the Niger. As soon as he stepped on home soil, Mari Djata sacrificed 100 rams and 100 oxen in gratitude to Allah for his safe and victorious return. So many people had gathered to welcome home their hero and king that the journey to Niani took three days instead of two. However, Sunjata found Niani in ruins, its wall still charred from the ravages of fire.

"Do not be disheartened," Balla Fasseke told him. "Niani, the village of your ancestors, is yours to rebuild into a great city, whereas Sumanguru Kante's Sosso has disappeared forever!"

It came to pass that Mari Djata did rebuild Niani, which became much larger than before, being the capital city of the empire of Mali. He appointed his brother, Manding Bory, to be his governor and put him in charge of all parts of the empire.

Sunjata, Lion of Manding and emperor of Mali, became an impartial and just king. He defended the weak, rewarded the good, and punished the wicked. Workers could enjoy the fruits of their labors. Thieves lost their right hands and, if they did not reform, lost their lives. Sunjata ushered in a time of peace, justice, order, and prosperity.

A bad king can gain power through his army. Then his people fear him, and when he dies, no one speaks well of him. A weak king can accomplish so little in his time that, when he dies, no one remembers him. A great king can be loved by his people because he uses his power to create justice. Sunjata was the greatest of kings!

The songs the griots sing say, "If you wish to see the center of the world, then Niani is the place for you! If you wish to find salt and the best fish and meat, then Niani is the place for you! If you wish to find the finest cloth and gold, then Niani is the place for you! If you wish to find the greatest army, then Niani is the place for you! But best of all, if you wish to find the king of kings, then Niani is the place for you, for it is there that you will find Sunjata, son of the Lion, Nare Maghan Kon Fatta, and the Buffalo Woman, Sogolon Kedju!"

Epilogue

Today, Mali's secrets remain buried with the griots who keep them. Many things you will never know.

Sunjata is buried near Niani, but his spirit continues to live. Of course, many kings ruled Mali after Sunjata. They expanded Mali's borders, and they built new towns. But not one was Sunjata's equal!

Today, many great towns exist only as ruins, and their wealth is buried or gone. But Mali lives on! Today, you can still see the forest that Sunjata loved. You can still see Sumanguru Kante's balafon. You can still see the bird that revealed Sumanguru Kante's destiny to him. You can still see where the people assembled in the kingdom of Sibi to make Sunjata their emperor. And you can still see the stone that marks the place where the body of Sunjata, the father of Mali and the Mandingo peoples, sleeps in peace.

You must accept the mysteries that remain in my song. Do not be so foolish as to disturb the spirits of the dead, for they would never forgive you. And do not ask me, for I have given my sacred word to my masters that, as a griot, I will keep the secrets of the past.

Introducing **Mwindo**

The epic of *Mwindo* was recorded by Daniel Biebuyck in 1956 from the people of the Nyanga nation in Zaire. It was performed over a twelve-day period, and the performance was believed to protect the bard or griot from disease and death. Later, in 1971, *Mwindo* was published under the title *The Mwindo Epic, from the Banyanga,* edited and translated by Daniel Biebuyck and Kohombo C. Mateene.

At the time the epic was recorded, the Nyanga community consisted of only 27,000 people, who lived by trapping, gathering, and cultivating food. Like all epics, *Mwindo* reflects cultural values and beliefs.

A major appeal of the myth lies in strands within it that are similar to major myths from around the world. The hero is born into royalty, the son of the tribal chief, and is banished by one of his parents. In this myth, the parent even tries to kill him. However, even as an infant, Mwindo can outwit the most powerful and clever adults.

Like many heroes, Mwindo possesses at least one special, magic object that can save his life. He risks his life to save members of his community from forces of evil. Again, the hero has the friendship and help of powers that are greater than he is. Finally, Mwindo makes a journey that takes him across the earth, into the Underworld, and into the heavens. He learns from his experiences and returns to educate his people.

The most unusual aspect of the *Mwindo* epic is that the hero presents a code of proper behavior to his people. The message is that interpersonal relationships are at least as im-portant as heroic deeds. Courage, skill in battle, and pride have their place, but not at the expense of kind and thoughtful behavior. Human beings cannot afford to lose sight of the fact that they are only one part of a multifaceted universe. While humans are superior to some forms of nature, gods and supernatural beings are superior to them.

At the root of the myth is the concept that all forms of life are good and deserve respect. Males and females, the young and the old, the handicapped and the healthy should be given equal consideration.

Principal Characters

SHEMWINDO: chief of the village of Tubondo; father of Mwindo

NYAMWINDO: favorite wife of Shemwindo; mother of Mwindo

MWINDO: heroic son of Shemwindo and Nyamwindo

IYANGURA: sister of Shemwindo; aunt of Mwindo

MUKITI: husband of Iyangura

KASIYEMBE: village elder; protector of Iyangura

Principal Gods

ONFO: god of creation

MASTER MUISA: ruler of the Underworld; lord of the dead

SPIRIT OF GOOD FORTUNE: spirit who advises Mwindo in the Underworld

MASTER LIGHTNING: guardian and friend of Mwindo

Mwindo

Chapter 1

*Chief Shemwindo, having forbidden his wives to give
birth to a male child, becomes the father of the boy
Mwindo. He unsuccessfully tries to kill his son.
Mwindo overcomes all obstacles and finds Iyangura,
his father's sister, in a different village. There too
Mwindo overcomes those who would harm him.*

Long, long ago, a chief named Shemwindo had seven wives. He announced
before his people, "My wives may give birth to female children only. I will kill any
male child and despise the wife who bears him."

Shemwindo's seven wives became pregnant at the same time and expected to
give birth to their children at the same time. When their time came, six wives
gave birth to female children.

The seventh wife, Nyamwindo, was called the Preferred One because she was
Shemwindo's favorite wife. Days passed, and the child within her showed no sign
of beginning the birth process. Nyamwindo became very frustrated at the delay,
for she was large with child, and the burden was very great. "How terrible to remain in my condition!" she exclaimed to herself. "Every one of Shemwindo's
wives has given birth except for me! I wonder what kind of child I am carrying
that it so stubbornly remains within my belly!"

As the days passed, strange events began to occur. One day Nyamwindo
noticed a bundle of firewood stacked neatly by the door to her house. She knew
of no one who would have put it there. Another day she noticed a jar of fresh
water in her house. Yet another day, raw vegetables appeared in her house.
Nyamwindo was amazed and could not explain these marvelous occurrences. She
did not suspect that the child within her womb was helping with her chores.

The child also determined the time and manner of its own birth. It refused to
be born in the customary way, as the ordinary child of an ordinary woman. It
refused to be born from its mother's mouth, as bats are born. It chose to travel up
its mother's body and down her arm, in order to be born from the middle finger
of her right hand.

The child was a male, and from the time of his birth, he spoke and laughed as
if he were already mature. He was born holding a sceptre in his right hand and an
axe in his left hand. He carried a little bag of good fortune, containing a long,
marvelous rope, slung over his shoulder. So great was his beauty that he shone
with the brightness of the sun and the moon.

The midwives, who were of no use in helping with this birth, named him
Mwindo — "first-born male" — because the children who had been born earlier
were all female. They attempted to protect the infant and his mother from
Shemwindo by refusing to announce his birth.

However, a cricket had been present at Mwindo's birth. The insect went to
Shemwindo and chirped in its loud voice, "Chief Shemwindo, the Preferred One

has given birth, and you are the father of a male child! No one else wishes to tell you, so I have made myself the bearer of this news."

Shemwindo immediately rose to his feet, sharpened his spear, and strode toward the birth hut. "This cannot happen to me!" he exclaimed to himself. "I will not permit it! I will kill my son. As punishment for giving birth to a male, my Preferred One will now become my Despised One. I will not raise my eyes above the soles of her feet."

As Shemwindo stood outside the birth hut with his spear arm raised, he heard his child's voice cry out from within the building. "May my father's spear strike the ground at the bottom of the house pole, missing the midwives, my mother, and me!"

Six times Shemwindo carefully aimed and thrust his spear, and six times the spear struck the ground at the bottom of the house pole. Finally Shemwindo gave up, in frustration, anger, and exhaustion. "Counselors and nobles," he announced, "dig a grave, throw this newborn male into it, and bury him alive! I refuse to look upon a male child!"

The counselors and nobles carried out their chief's orders without any argument. They had buried Mwindo and were about to throw banana trees and dirt upon the grave when everyone heard the child's voice. "Oh, my father!" he called. "After you have suffered great sorrow, it is you who will die like this!"

Shemwindo heard the curse and called, "Hurry up and cover the grave!" To himself he said, "It is very clear that my son possesses such great powers, even as an infant, that he will only cause trouble for me in this village! I must kill him, or he will force me from my royal chair."

That night, after the burial ceremony, a great light, as bright and as hot as the fiery sun, emanated from the grave. Once everyone was asleep, Mwindo left his grave and entered his mother's house, where even Shemwindo could hear his crying.

Shemwindo shivered with fear of his child's great powers. Like a snake, he slithered silently to Nyamwindo's house to see whether it was really Mwindo who was crying. Then he gathered his counselors and nobles together and announced, "Tomorrow, I want you to cut a piece of a tree trunk and hollow it out to form a drum. Place Mwindo inside the drum and cover it with softened antelope hide. Choose two expert divers and command them to swim with the drum to the center of the river and drop it where it will sink to the deepest depths."

Again the counselors and nobles carried out their chief's orders without any argument. Shemwindo rewarded the divers by giving them wives. However, seven days of heavy rains brought famine to Shemwindo's village.

Meanwhile, Mwindo lay within the drum, which rested on the sandy base far below the surface of the river. "I must not float downstream before I warn my father and the people of his village of their punishment for treating me in this way! If I am Mwindo, they will hear my voice," he said to himself. With these words, the drum floated up to the surface of the river, where it remained without moving.

When a group of maidens came down to the river with their water jars, they saw the drum floating and heard Mwindo singing, "Farewell to my father,

Shemwindo. Because his counselors and nobles have failed him in their advice, they will become as dead as dried leaves."

The maidens left their jars and ran back to the village with the news of Mwindo's return. Their words brought Shemwindo down to the river, where Mwindo again sang his farewell to his father. Then, as the chief and the villagers watched, the drum returned to the bottom of the river.

Mwindo decided to visit Iyangura, his aunt, who lived upstream. He left the drum and swam through the river waters, using his power to frighten all the fish and crabs away. Over and over again he announced, "I am Mwindo, the little one just born he walked. You are helpless against me, so get out of my way!"

Finally, Mwindo came upon a guard posted by Mukiti, Iyangura's husband, "No one is permitted to pass this barrier," the guard announced.

"I can go wherever I wish," Mwindo replied. "Even Mukiti is powerless against me, for I am Mwindo, the little one just born he walked!" He dived to the bottom of the river, dug into the sand, and traveled beneath the dam that blocked his passage.

Mukiti himself shook the heavens and the earth, but he could not frighten Mwindo, who continued his journey. Iyangura's protector, Kasiyembe, who was an elder of her village and carried hatred in his heart, did not give up so easily. Kasiyembe hoped to kill Mwindo by constructing traps in the ground with sharp, pointed sticks emerging from the floor of each pit.

However, Mwindo had friends as well as enemies. Master Hedgehog said to him, "As I burrowed in the ground, I found pits with spikes set up to trap you. Beware! I shall build an underground road to your aunt's house."

Master Spider built bridges over the spiked pits. "No one can defeat Mwindo as long as we are here to help him!" he exclaimed.

Mwindo soon reached his aunt's house. "I am glad to see you, Mwindo!" she said. "But before you eat, you must dance! The drum will inspire you. Kasiyembe has commanded it, for he wishes to tire you."

So Mwindo danced and danced. He danced into every pit that had been dug to kill him. He danced right over the sharp spikes, shaking his sceptre and singing. He danced and danced, and nothing injured him.

Kasiyembe, who carried hatred in his heart, still wished to kill Mwindo. "Why should I fear the power of a small boy?" he asked. "I will get Master Lightning to come down to earth and slice Mwindo in two with his lightning bolts!"

Mwindo said, "Master Lightning, you are my friend too! If you insist on attacking this house, then you must avoid the side where I am sitting! As for you, Kasiyembe, it is you who will die by fire. He who lives in a grass hut should take care with flame!"

Seven times Master Lightning struck Mwindo's side of the houses, and seven times the bolt avoided Mwindo and burned the opposite side of the house. Mwindo remained uninjured, while the other side of the house was reduced to a pile of ashes.

Mwindo then walked out of the house and announced, "I am Mwindo, the little one just born he walked. I have power even over lightning! Watch while the hair on Kasiyembe's head is consumed by fire!"

Before the eyes of the entire village, the elder's hair caught fire and burned. They watched in horror as flames greedily leaped into the air.

Fearing that their elder would die, the villagers ran for their water jars. But the jars were completely dry; not a drop of liquid remained in them. The villagers then ran to gather their juicy plants, but these too had completely dried up; not a drop of liquid remained in them. The villagers then ran to Mukiti's pool, but it too was completely dry. Butterflies and flies flew here and there, but not a drop of liquid remained in it. In desperation, the villagers tried to spit on Kasiyembe's hair, hoping their saliva would extinguish the raging flames. But their mouths were completely dry; not a drop of liquid remained in them.

Mwindo's aunt said to him, "Let kindness enter your heart, my boy. Forgive Mukiti and my protector and let them live in peace."

Mwindo waved his sceptre and replied, "I am Mwindo, the little one just born he walked. I will show my power over Mukiti and Kasiyembe. They will return to their former state."

Suddenly the flames retired from Kasiyembe's head. The water jars became filled with water; the juicy plants became filled with liquid; Mukiti's pool became full of water; and saliva filled each villager's mouth.

The villagers cried, "Hail, Mwindo! You are indeed a great man!" And Kasiyembe, who carried hatred in his heart, added his cheers to those of his companions.

Mwindo announced, "Tomorrow I go to take vengeance upon my father, for three times — by spear, burial, and drowning — he has tried to kill me."

"I urge you to reconsider!" Iyangura exclaimed. "You may possess great power, but you are too young to conquer your father, and you are too young to rule his great village of seven gates. Nevertheless, if you are determined to do this, I will accompany you and watch your father cut you to pieces."

Mwindo blocked the power of Iyangura's words by humming to himself.

Chapter 2

*Mwindo sets out to take vengeance. He destroys his
father's village and the people who live there, but
Shemwindo, his father, escapes. Mwindo follows his
father into the Underworld. After performing many
tasks for its ruler, he finally captures Shemwindo.
Together they return to the surface of the earth.*

Mwindo, Iyangura, and her companions then traveled to see his uncles, who were great metalsmiths. "I am going to fight my father, Shemwindo," he announced. "You are known for your large, light spears. Heat your forges and make me whatever I shall need for this great battle. I need both strength and protection."

Mwindo's uncles provided him with an iron shirt, iron pants, iron shoes, and an iron hat. "These iron clothes will protect you from your father's unceasing spear-thrusts," they said. "We will come with you and watch the battle."

When they reached Shemwindo's village, Iyangura exclaimed, "I am afraid, Mwindo! Your father and his people will surely destroy us! We have arrived in a great rainstorm, and we have no shelter. We have arrived in a large group, and we have no food."

Mwindo replied, "I am Mwindo, the little one just born he walked. My heart knows no fear! My father has too much pride in his heart. I must fight him to teach him his proper place! We will escape the rain, the lightning bolts, and the thunder. We will have plenty of food to eat!

"May two rows of houses surround the house of Mwindo, the little one just born he walked!" Mwindo then exclaimed. Two rows of houses assembled themselves in the clearing around a lone house.

Mwindo raised his eyes to the heavens and sang, "May the wood, fire, water, and palm trees that Shemwindo's village possesses come to Mwindo, the little one just born he walked. May there be nobody left to use them! May the animals, banana groves, tobacco, and salt that Shemwindo's village possesses come to Mwindo, the little one just born he walked. May there be nobody left to use them! May the jars, baskets, pots, bags, and wooden dishes that Shemwindo's village possesses come to Mwindo, the little one just born he walked. May there be nobody left to use them! May the clothes, necklaces, rings, drums, and beds that Shemwindo's village possesses come to Mwindo, the little one just born he walked. May there be nobody left to use them! May the spears, knives, needles, fire drill, and tools that Shemwindo's village possesses come to Mwindo, the little one just born he walked. May there be nobody left to use them! For Mwindo is going to fight his father, Shemwindo, and he will conquer him!"

Whatever Mwindo wanted came to him. His companions said in astonishment, "Mwindo is our leader and great hero! Anyone who attempts to overpower him will surely die!"

Mwindo sent his uncles into battle against the people of his father's village. They fought on land and in the air, but they could not overpower Shemwindo's villagers. Their strength dried up as water leaves the soil under the sun's light, and they died bloody deaths.

Mwindo said to his aunt, "I will enter my father's village and learn how my uncles were defeated. Then I will fight my father face to face. I will carry my sceptre with me, but I want you to remain here with my axe and my little bag of good fortune. The bag contains a long, magic rope."

"You are very foolish, Mwindo!" Iyangura exclaimed. "You will bring death upon all of us!" However, she took his axe and his bag before he went on his way.

Shemwindo was not afraid when he saw his son enter his village. "Why should I fear the power of a small boy who comes alone to fight against all of us!" he exclaimed. "If he comes any farther, we will cut his throat and send his life rushing forth from his body!"

"You are wrong!" the villagers said. "Small though he is, Mwindo is more powerful than we are. He will force us to run from our own village! Do not stand against your own son!" In spite of their fears, they hurled taunts at Mwindo because he was so young and so small.

Mwindo shouted up to the sky, "I am Mwindo, the little one just born he walked. Hatred fills my heart! I have come to take vengeance upon my father, for three times — by spear, burial, and drowning — he has tried to kill me. May he become as dead as dry leaves! My father's counselors and nobles failed to advise him well. May they become as dead as dry leaves! My father's villagers supported him when he tried to kill me. May they become as dead as dry leaves!"

Mwindo then raised his sceptre to the heavens and called, "Master Lightning, my friend, take my side and bring me victory! Send seven of your lightning bolts to close the seven gates to my father's village."

Master Lightning, hearing Mwindo's plea, struck Shemwindo's village seven times. Flames engulfed the houses, turning them and all their inhabitants to dust. Only Shemwindo escaped. The chief ran from his village until he came to a fern plant. He quickly tore the plant out by its roots and entered the earth through the opening he had created.

Mwindo prepared to follow Shemwindo. He brought his aunt and her companions to the ruined village. All of their possessions arrived by themselves. Mwindo then touched his uncles, one by one, with his sceptre and brought them back to life. To Iyangura he said, "I go now to seek my father in the depths of the earth, in the land of Master Muisa, where all is dark and cold. Take one end of this rope from my bag of good fortune. As long as the rope moves, I am alive, so wait here for me. If the rope does not move, you will know that I am dead."

Master Sparrow flew down and said, "Mwindo, I will show you the path your father took into the Underworld, for I watched him from the sky as he left the light of earth."

Mwindo followed his father's trail into the Underworld. There he was greeted by the spirit of good fortune, who advised him how to proceed. "You will recognize Master Muisa, the ruler of this dark and dismal land, when you find a large man resting in the ashes near the hearth in the meeting place," she counseled. "You must take great care if you hope to leave his village, for he will do everything in his power to trick you into remaining with him. Address him as 'my leader' and 'my father,' and when he blesses you, bless him in return. When he offers you something to sit on, politely refuse it. When he offers you a small gourd of banana beer to drink and a paste of ashes to eat, politely refuse them also."

Mwindo thanked the spirit for her wise counsel and went on his way. He found Master Muisa in the ashes, greeted him appropriately, and refused to sit, drink, or eat.

Master Muisa said to Mwindo, "Tomorrow you must prepare a new banana grove for me. My servant will watch you to be sure you perform each task correctly. When you bring me the bananas, I will return your father to you."

The following day, Mwindo and Master Muisa's servant set out together. The servant watched as Mwindo's iron tools performed each task without any help from Mwindo. Some created new paths, some cut down trees and weeds, some mowed the grass, and some cut supporting poles for the banana trees. Once the tools had prepared the ground, the banana trees planted themselves, matured, and produced ripe bananas.

When Mwindo had passed every test, Master Muisa said to his magic belt, "Find Mwindo, strike him so that he breaks in two, and see that he smashes his mouth on the ground when he falls."

The magic belt did as its master commanded. Mwindo fell to the ground, and his rope stopped moving. But Mwindo's sceptre quickly raised itself and touched him, restoring its master to life as it had earlier restored Mwindo's uncles.

When Mwindo returned to Master Muisa's village, the ruler said, "Tomorrow you must gather honey from a particular tree. When you return to me with the basket of honey, I will return your father to you."

However, as soon as it appeared that Mwindo would succeed with this task also, Master Muisa again sent his magic belt to kill Mwindo. Again Mwindo's rope lay still, and his sceptre rushed to restore its master to life. When Master Sparrow flew down from the sky and told Mwindo that his father had fled, Mwindo beat Master Muisa to death and then set out in search of Shemwindo. With the sparrow's help, he found his father hiding nearby. Before leaving the Underworld, Mwindo used his sceptre to return Master Muisa to life so that he could rule his people.

Having captured his father, Mwindo now treated him with appropriate respect. "You were wrong, Father," Mwindo began, "not to accept a son. It was not your place to change what Onfo, god of creation, provided. But you have suffered enough for your pride."

As Mwindo carried Shemwindo up to the surface of the earth, he sang, "Mwindo, the little one just born he walked, returns with Shemwindo, the dearest one, who fathered a son who is a hero!"

Chapter 3

Mwindo restores the lives of his father's people. Peace is formally restores between father and son in an assembly. Shemwindo divides his kingdom with Mwindo and makes him a chief. When Mwindo kills a dragon, Master Lightning takes him up to the sky in order to teach him about his place in the universe. When Mwindo returns, he teaches his people how to lead a good life.

Mwindo and Shemwindo emerged upon the earth's surface at just the place they had left it, the root of the fern plant. When they had rejoined their people, Mwindo sang of his great adventures in the Underworld.

Iyangura then said, "Mwindo, this village is desolate without the people who lived here. Prove your power by returning to life all who died in Master Lightning's great fire. Then I can tell everyone of your father's injustice and your own heroic deeds."

So Mwindo brought new life to all who had perished. One by one, he touched them with his sceptre, awakening them to life. Each who had died pregnant awakened pregnant. Each who had died preparing a particular food awakened preparing that food. Each who had died setting traps awakened setting those traps. Each who had died cultivating a crop awakened cultivating that crop. Each who had died making jars and pots awakened making those jars and pots. Each who had died quarreling with another awakened quarreling with that person. Each who had died loving another awakened loving that person.

It took Mwindo three long, tiring days to revive all of the villagers, for Shemwindo's village had been a large one. Finally the village was just as it had been before Master Lightning had struck it. Old folk and young, noble folk and common, wandered the village paths, along with a variety of domesticated animals. Each person again possessed whatever he or she had possessed before death. Shemwindo announced that a great feast and an assembly of the people would be held eight days hence.

When the day of the assembly arrived and the people had gathered together, Shemwindo, Mwindo, and Iyangura dressed in their finest clothes and appeared before the villagers. Mwindo called upon Shemwindo to explain why he had treated his son so badly.

Shemwindo immediately acknowledged his guilt. He explained his attitude toward a male child and described how he had tried to kill Mwindo. "My foul treatment of my son brought me only pain and suffering," he concluded. "As long as I had evil thoughts and committed evil deeds, my spirit was dry and withered, like an old banana. Mwindo rescued my spirit and restored it to life when he captured me and brought me back to our village. Indeed, Mwindo has brought joy to my heart. He has taught me to appreciate the beauty of each sunrise and the friendship of our people. Because of what my son has done for me, I now honor and respect all male children!"

Iyangura spoke next. "Mwindo rescued his father, so that he would not die, like an animal, among the leaves. That was good. But the way Shemwindo acted and the way his counselors and nobles supported him was bad. Whatever Onfo, god of creation, gives us is good. All children are good. Shemwindo was wrong to feel that some children are bad. If any other man in this village had treated a child as Shemwindo treated his son, Shemwindo would have ordered that man's throat cut. Shemwindo was responsible for the deaths of everyone in this village. But since Mwindo has restored life and order, all is well."

Finally Mwindo spoke. "I, Mwindo, man of many feats and the little one just born he walked, feel no anger toward my father," he said. "What my father did to me and what I did to him are past. Instead, let us look ahead. Let us live together in peace and care well for our people. That is what is important."

Shemwindo then said, "A chief should not feel shame before his son and his people. Yet I am ashamed of my behavior toward my son. Therefore, I wish to make Mwindo chief of this country."

Mwindo replied, "Father, sit down in your royal chair. As long as you are alive, only you can be chief of this country. If I were to take your place, I would die."

The counselors and nobles agreed. "Mwindo is right. If you were to give him all your power, in time you would become jealous, and then you would cause trouble for all of us. Instead, you should divide the country into two parts so that you and Mwindo have equal power."

So Shemwindo divided his country with Mwindo. Mwindo became chief of his father's village, and Shemwindo moved to another village. With great ceremony, the chief conferred kingship upon his son. He dressed Mwindo in the clothing of a chief, handed him the symbols of power and the royal weapons, and ordered his counselors and nobles to support him.

Mwindo's first act as chief was to announce, "I, Mwindo, the little one just born he walked, am now a famous chief. I will rule with a more open mind and a more kind heart than my father ruled before me. I will acknowledge and respect many different family groups, not just my own. I will welcome the birth of many children, males as well as females, and the deaf and lame as well as the healthy. No country is uniform and perfect."

Many days later, Mwindo decided that he wanted to eat the meat of the wild pig. His Pygmy hunters set out for the deep forest, where they found and killed this animal. They were cutting the carcass into pieces when their noise aroused a great and monstrous dragon. The beast was as large as the sky, and it possessed seven heads, seven horns, and seven eyes. Like a giant snake, the dragon quietly slithered toward those who had invaded its forest and swallowed three of the four Pygmy hunters. The fourth hunter ran back to the village with his tale of terror.

Mwindo immediately said to his father, who was visiting the village, "Remain here while I go fight this dragon."

"My son," Shemwindo urged, "let the dragon remain in peace. If you provoke it, you will destroy yourself and your country. The monster will eat you, bones and all!"

"That may be," Mwindo replied. "But I will not let it have its way with my hunters in the forest."

The next morning Mwindo picked up his sceptre and said to it, "Bring victory to me this day!" Then he set out for the deep forest with the fourth Pygmy as his guide.

They came to the dragon, which had remained by the slaughtered pig. Mwindo whispered to the Pygmy, "Stay here. If the dragon swallows me, you must be able to return to the village with the news."

Raising his sceptre, Mwindo slithered toward the dragon as if he were also a serpent. He came face to face with the monster before it noticed him. "Dragon," Mwindo announced, "I am the hero Mwindo, the little one just born he walked. You have swallowed my men, but you are powerless against me!"

The dragon opened its gigantic mouth and prepared to swallow Mwindo. However, Mwindo quickly raised his scepter and beat the monster with it until it died. Then he said to the Pygmy, "I will send my sceptre to the village to bring men who can help us carry this dragon home. I want my father to see the great feats I can perform."

Mwindo's sceptre came to Shemwindo and shook itself at him. "Either Mwindo is dead, or the dragon is dead!" Shemwindo exclaimed. "I think Mwindo wants help with the dragon. Shemwindo is the father of a hero!"

Although the dragon was very heavy, the people eventually carried it into the village, where everyone was awed by the sight of it. When Mwindo ordered the men to carve up the monster, their first stroke brought forth an amazing sight. From the slash in its belly, one of the Pygmies climbed out alive. The other two Pygmies followed. "Eat this monster, bones and all!" Mwindo commanded.

They roasted the pieces of flesh over a large fire in the center of the village. As its eyes cooked, they burst open and splattered juices upon the ground. From each drop, a human being appeared. By the time all seven eyes had been roasted, 1,000 people had emerged from the splattered juices. "These are my people!" Mwindo exclaimed proudly.

However, all was not well. Master Lightning was a friend of the dragon as well as of Mwindo, and he was obligated to avenge the dragon's death. He came down to Mwindo's village and said, "Because you have dared to kill my friend the dragon, I must take you from your village and teach you some lessons."

Mwindo replied, "I will go with you. But remember, you are powerless against Mwindo, the little one just born he walked and the heroic son of Shemwindo."

When they arrived above the clouds, Master Lightning said to Mwindo, "Many times I have rescued you from great dangers. Yet you say that you possess more power than I do. Show me that is true!"

So Mwindo began to live in the sky as Master Lightning did — wandering from place to place without shelter of any kind, freezing with cold and shivering from the attacks of the icy wind.

When Mwindo had survived this trial, Master Lightning brought him up to Master Rain. Master Rain said, "We have heard of your heroic deeds. Let us see how well you fare here in the sky, where your heroism cannot help you."

So Mwindo suffered Master Rain to fall upon him in fourteen storms, which completely soaked him with their cold moisture. Master Rain sent hail upon him in stones that bruised his skin.

When Mwindo had survived these trials, Master Lightning brought him up to Master Moon. Master Moon said, "We have heard how proud you are. No one can criticize you and survive. Let us see how well you fare here in the sky, where your pride cannot help you."

So Mwindo suffered as Master Moon burned his hair. The flames were so painful that he cried, "Oh, Father, bless me, and keep my hands on my sceptre! "

When Mwindo had survived this trial, Master Lightning brought him up to Master Sun. Master Sun said, "We have heard how tough you are. Let us see how well you fare here in the sky, where your strength cannot help you."

So Mwindo suffered as Master Sun directed his blazing rays against him. Mwindo could summon no defense against the excruciating heat. His throat became parched; his thirst was intolerable. But when he begged for water, Master Sun and Master Lightning replied, "Here in the sky there is never any water, so you will have to get along without it!"

When Mwindo had survived this trial, Master Lightning brought him up to Master Star. Master Star said, "As you can see, here in the sky your heroism cannot help you. If we did not respect you, we would have killed you. Listen well to the words we speak, and remember them. We forbid you to kill any animal or insect, whether in your village, in the forest, or in the rivers. Master Lightning is your guardian. He will watch your deeds. If you do wrong, he will seize you at once, and we will kill you." Master Star pulled Mwindo's ears fourteen times and said, "Remember."

Mwindo spent a full year in the sky with Master Lightning, seeing all that is good there and all that is bad. Then Master Lightning took Mwindo down to his village.

Mwindo assembled his people and told them, "I, Mwindo, the little one just born he walked and the performer of great feats, return from the sky to be your chief. From this time forth, on penalty of death, I am forbidden to kill animals and insects. In the past year I have seen much that is hidden, but the masters of the sky have forbidden me to reveal these things to you. I have learned that it is good to be a hero, but it is just as important to be forgiving and kind. The greatest of all heroes one day will meet a greater hero who has the power to destroy him."

Chief Mwindo passed wise laws, telling his people, "Grow many crops of many foods. Live in good houses, and make your village beautiful. Agree with one another, for argument is the path to anger and hatred. Do not pursue another's spouse, for the man who seduces another man's wife will be killed. Onfo, the god of creation, gives only what is good to you. Accept all of your children, whether they are male or female, tall or short, healthy or disabled. Be considerate of the sick person who walks along your village paths. Accept, fear, and protect your chief as he should accept, fear, and protect you."

Mwindo became a famous chief, known in countries far from his own. Not only did his own people support and admire him, but people from other countries came to pay him allegiance as well.

The Americas

The New World has always been populated by many different cultural groups. The Native American peoples represented in this book include those who were living in Central and South America when the Spanish invaded and conquered them in the 1500s, those who were living in North America when the French and the English invaded and conquered them from the 1500s to the 1800s, and those who remain living cultures today.

The American creation myths fall into two patterns: some describe the creation of the universe and human beings, and others describe the origin of the particular peoples to whom the myths belong. Like the creation myths of many other cultures, those of the Maya, the Aztecs, and the Aymara/Tiahuanaco, who preceded the Incas, describe the creation of the world. In unusually poetic language, the Mayan myth describes the great efforts of their creators to fashion a race of human beings who please them. It is interesting to follow the process and see what kind of people these gods desire and why.

The first part of the Aztec creation myth describes a series of worlds, inviting comparison with the Greek ages of man and the Indian four ages of man. It emphasizes the idea of blood sacrifice, a practice that permeated the Aztec culture. The final section of the myth is remarkable because it reveals the Aztecs' great love of the arts. A beautiful poem, rendered in prose in this chapter, describes the creation of music.

The creation myth of the ancient Tiahuanaco culture (the ancestors of the Aymaras in the Bolivian highlands) presents a god who is both creator and benefactor. An interesting description of the creation of human beings is followed by a journey in which the god and his companions teach people how to lead civilized lives, with an emphasis on the humane treatment of other human beings.

In contrast, the creation myths of the Incas, the Navajo, and the Iroquois focus on the origin of their particular peoples. The Inca myth reveals the arrogance and prejudice of a conqueror toward the peoples it has conquered. The myth describes how the Incas arrived in Peru and civilized the local people, such as the Aymaras of Bolivia, whom they present as living like wild animals. The Navajo myth describes how their people moved upward through four worlds into our fifth world, developing from insects into human beings in the course of this journey. Two aspects of the Navajo myth give it a distinctive flavor: the use of the sacred number, four, and the depiction of the close relationship between human beings and the animal kingdom.

In the Iroquois creation myth, a matrilineal society envisions the earth as having been created by a female divinity. Good and evil are divided between twin brothers, who represent two sides of one personality. Unlike the myth of Quetzalcoatl, in the Iroquois myth the good brother destroys his evil brother. The Inuit myth of Sedna explains the creation of sea animals in a manner that reflects the harsh environment in which the Inuit peoples have always lived.

The fertility myths from the Americas fall into three patterns: those in which a god or a supernatural figure teaches the people how to raise crops and thus achieve a higher standard of living; those in which a god or a godlike hero protects the fertility of the earth from some threat; and those in which an angered and vengeful god must be appeased in order for fertility to be restored. The Trio and Inca myths follow the first pattern. They form an interesting comparison because they both tell the same type of story, but from different points of view.

The Haida/Tsimshian/Tlingit and Zuñi myths follow the second pattern. They tell the same type of story about a god who protects the earth, and in the process they reveal much about their own particular cultures. The Micmac myth, which is tangentially related to these myths, reveals the need of this Algonquian people for control over its natural environment. However, the Inuit myth focuses on a deity whose anger must be placated by the gods or by mortals.

Four of the hero myths resemble the traditional heroic pattern in that a hero performs a great task or tasks for the benefit of society. The Haida/Tsimshian/Tlingit, Micmac, and Zuñi myths are both hero and fertility myths because of the double focus of their subject. The Crow myth involves twins who perform a number of heroic feats, while always behaving like the children they are.

The Aztec myth "Quetzalcoatl" is one of the most fascinating of all hero stories, and it is truly remarkable given when it was written. In the Aztec creation myth, Quetzalcoatl and Tezcatlipoca are depicted as divine creators and benefactors, but here Quetzalcoatl is a traditional hero, a godlike mortal, and Tezcatlipoca is his enemy. With a focus that is completely modern, the myth describes how Quetzalcoatl is conquered by his alter ego or double.

Introducing The Creation

Historical Background

The following creation myth comes from the Tiahuanaco culture, an important highland civilization that flourished in the region of Lake Titicaca before the Incas invaded. Since the 1960s, archaeologists have been investigating sites in the area of the famous ruins of Tiahuanaco. Monumental stone figures, located near the southern shore of Lake Titicaca in the Andean highlands of Bolivia, were built in approximately A.D. 500, and testify to the importance of the Tiahuanaco culture.

Archaeologists have discovered that the city Tiahuanaco began as a rural village in about 1000 B.C. and that it was occupied for over 2,000 years, becoming important enough to influence the culture of the Andean peoples from about A.D. 500 to 1200. By 1200, Tiahuanaco had become the capital of the great Tiahuanaco empire, which may have included much of Chile and Peru, as well as the Andean highlands of Bolivia and Argentina. The reason for the empire's collapse remains a mystery, but the area it encompassed did not become unified again until the Incas conquered it sometime during the late 14th and early 15th centuries.

Scholars are mystified by the fact that the Spaniards could learn nothing about the culture from the Aymaras who were living in the area. The local population had no idea who the people were that had constructed the huge structures. One theory is that the Incas shifted populations from one area to another, so tribes could have been living in areas that were relatively new to them. Another theory is that the residents of the area, the Aymaras of that time, refused to communicate with the Spaniards about their ancestors.

The following myth was recorded in the early 1550s by Juan de Betanzos, the official interpreter for the Spanish governor of Peru. He took it from a Peruvian narrative song. Such songs were a customary way for Inca historians to preserve their nation's history.

Lake Titicaca, which extends from Peru to Bolivia, plays a major role in the mythology of both the Inca of Peru and the Aymara of Bolivia. When the Incas extended their rule to the Bolivian shores of Lake Titicaca, they adopted and transformed the myths of the native Aymara people and the Tiahuanaco culture to reflect their own nationalistic point of view. The Incas' political values also led them to establish their Quechua language as the official language of their empire, even though Aymara was the most widespread native language at that time. However, although the Inca emperors demanded that the Aymara people accept their authority and their religion, they did not require the Aymaras to give up their own, older religion. Thus, the two religions coexisted.

Today, more than five million people continue to speak the Quechua language. However, the Aymara language is also a living language. Many of the Aymara people continue to live in the Andean highlands of Bolivia, where most of them are still involved in herding and agriculture.

Appeal and Value

Inca mythology and sun worship are directly related to the religion of the Tiahuanaco culture. It is interesting to compare this creation myth with the Inca creation myth that follows it, to see how the Incas built their myths upon those of older civilizations. The Incas adopted Con Ticci Viracocha (creator emerging with thunder) as their creator-god.

The creator who is also a benefactor of the human race is common in American cultures, such as the Aztec and the Haida/Tsimshian/Tlingit. Other cultures also Tlingit have a divine creator who teaches moral values and punishes those who ignore them. Like many other creators, Viracocha uses a flood to destroy a race of human beings who have acted immorally.

The role played by stone in this creation myth reflects the abundance of rock and the presence of ancient, rock-shaped figures in the area. The religious practice of worshiping natural phenomena is reflected in the birth of human beings from caves, rivers, mountains, and rocks.

The Creation

In the beginning, Lord Con Ticci Viracocha, prince and creator of all things, emerged from the void and created the earth and the heavens. Next he created animals and a race of gigantic human beings who lived upon the earth in the darkness of an eternal night, for he had not yet created any form of light. When the behavior of this race angered Viracocha, he emerged again, this time from Lake Titicaca, and he punished these first human beings by turning them into stone. Then he created a great flood. Soon even the peaks of the highest mountains were under water.

When Viracocha was satisfied that the flood had destroyed all forms of life, he caused the flood waters to subside until the face of the earth stood revealed once again. So great was his creative power that he then created day by causing the sun to emerge from the island of Titicaca and rise into the heavens. In the same way, he created the moon and the stars, setting each brilliant light upon its proper path. With a wave of his hand and a command from his mouth, some hills and mountains sank to become valleys, while some valleys rose to become hills and mountains. With another wave and command, streams and rivers of fresh water sprang from the rocky cliffs, cascaded down the mountainsides, and flowed through the valleys.

Viracocha then turned his attention to creating new animals and a new race of human beings. First he created birds to fly in the air and fill the silence with song. He gave each type of bird a different melody to sing, sending some to live deep in the forested valleys and others to live in the high plains and mountains. Then he created the animals that walk the earth on four legs and the creatures that crawl on their stomachs. These too he divided between the lowlands and the highlands.

Once he had created all the animals, Viracocha was ready to create human beings. He decided to model them in stone, so he fashioned and painted stone men, stone women, and stone children.

He created some of the women in the condition of pregnancy. He created others in the process of caring for their young children, who were in cradles just as they would be once he brought them to life. He painted long hair on some figures and short hair on others. On each figure he painted the kind of clothing that that person would continue to wear. In this way Viracocha gave each human being the appearance that he or she would have in life. Then he fashioned a stone community in Tiahuanaco as a home for some of these stone people.

Finally Viracocha divided his stone figures into groups. He gave each group the food it would grow, the language it would speak, and the songs it would sing. Then he commanded all of the stone figures to sink beneath the earth and remain there until he or one of his helpers summoned them.

Viracocha explained their duties to the companions who had emerged with him from Lake Titicaca. "I want some of you to walk to the north, some to the south, and the rest toward the early morning sun. Divide among you the regions that I intend to populate with human beings. When you arrive in your region, go to the fountains, or the caves, or the rivers, or the high mountain plateaus. Summon from these places the groups of stone figures that I have assigned to your region."

So it came to pass that each of Viracocha's companions became a helper in the process of creation, and the land was populated with many groups of people. As each "viracocha" called forth his group of stone figures, Viracocha shouted, "Con Ticci Viracocha, who created the universe, commands his human beings to emerge from the stone figures he has created and occupy this empty land! Live in your area, and increase in number."

Viracocha himself walked the Royal Road across the Andes Mountains toward what would become the city of Cuzco. As he traveled, he called forth group after group of human beings and taught each group how to live on the land. He told them the name of each tree, each plant, each fruit, and each flower. He showed them which were good sources of food, which could heal sickness and injuries, and which would bring certain death. He also taught the people to treat one another with kindness and respect so they could live with one another in peace. Meanwhile, Viracocha's helpers were teaching the same knowledge to the groups of human beings who had emerged in their regions.

Viracocha continued this process until one group of people emerged armed with rocks. They did not recognize Viracocha, and they attacked him. Viracocha punished them by causing fire to fall from the heavens. The people immediately threw their stones to the ground and fell at Viracocha's feet in surrender. Viracocha extinguished the flames with three blows from his staff and explained that he was their creator.

These people constructed a great stone figure of Viracocha. They established a place of worship where Viracocha had brought down the fire and set the statue within it. Their descendants continue to present offerings of gold and silver in that sacred place.

Finally Viracocha reached the site of Cuzco, which he named. He created a ruler for the area and then returned to the seacoast. His companions rejoined him, and they set forth over the ocean toward the setting sun. Those who saw them last watched in fascination as Viracocha and his companions walked upon the waves as if the sea were solid land. The people called their creator Viracocha, which means "foam of the sea," in honor of this event.

Viracocha and his companions were never seen again.

Introducing **The House of Origin**

Historical Background

Civilized peoples had lived in Peru for almost 4,000 years when, in the 13th century A.D., the Incas settled in the Cuzco Valley, high in the Andes Mountains. In the beginning, the Incas were simply one small group living among many others. Nothing distinguished them from their neighbors. Manco Capac became their first ruler, and at first other peoples willingly came under Inca rule.

By the early 1400s, the Incas had become more aggressive and had established themselves as conquerors. They had pushed outward from the Cuzco Valley and now dominated all of the land west to the coast of Peru, north to Quito, Ecuador, and southeast to Lake Titicaca.

By 1438, the Incas had created a great empire, which extended south from southern Colombia through Ecuador and Peru into southern Chile, and west across the highlands of Bolivia into the northwestern part of Argentina. The Inca emperor Pachacuti, who reigned from 1438 to 1471, transformed Viracocha from the god of the Aymara people to one of the great gods of the Inca. After Pachacuti dreamed that Viracocha helped him win a major military victory, the emperor had a solid gold statue of Viracocha created that was as large as a ten-year-old child. He then placed the golden image of the god in a great temple that he had had constructed and dedicated to Viracocha in Cuzco.

The Inca empire was the largest empire in the New World until the Spanish arrived, and it contained six million people. The empire thrived for the next 100 years, but fell to the Spaniard Francisco Pizarro and his conquistadores in 1532. Today, Quechua, the language of the Inca, remains the language of approximately five million people, called the Quechua, who live in Peru, Ecuador, and the highland regions of the Andes in Bolivia, Argentina, and Chile.

In many ways the Incas resembled the Romans. They conquered many civilized peoples and ruled them successfully by tolerating their cultural ways. As long as their subjects paid their taxes and worshipped the Inca gods, particularly the sun, they could live and worship in whatever other ways they chose. The Incas were skilled administrators, builders, and technicians. Their system of roads was one of the best in the world. They successfully farmed the mountainous regions of their empire by creating an elaborate system of terraces and a network of irrigation canals. Large surpluses of food supported the non-agricultural members of their society, including the nobles, priests, warriors, craftspeople, and artists.

Since they had no written language, the Incas were completely dependent on their oral tradition to record their past and preserve their fame for the future. A group of professional historians and performers was responsible for preserving and reciting Inca "history," a blend of fact, myth, legend, and self-serving propaganda. All of the Inca myths are part of this "history" and exhibit a double bias, both Inca and Christian. The Incas first adapted the myths of other peoples in order to glorify their own accomplishments. After the Spanish conquest, the recorders of the myths shaped them to reflect a Christian point of view.

The following myth was recorded by Pedro de Cieza de León, a Spanish chronicler who was writing fifteen years after his nation's conquest of the Inca. Cieza de León is known for his two-volume study of the Inca: *The Travels of Pedro de Cieza de León, Contained in the First Part of His Chronicle of Peru*, A.D. *1532–1550* and its sequel, *The Second Part of the Chronicle of the Inca*, which contains "The House of Origin." Harold Osborne, in his *South American Mythology*, includes English translations of material from both of Cieza de León's books.

Appeal and Value

When the Incas conquered Lake Titicaca and the region that surrounds it, they built this myth on the Tiahuanaco myth of Viracocha. Since the sun was the supreme god of the Inca nation, the sun takes the place of Viracocha. The Incas believed their rulers were all children of the sun god, and thus gods themselves. The characters in the following myth are actually the sun's children.

The Inca creation myth explains the importance of the Inca capital city of Cuzco and the supremacy of the Incas over their neighbors, rather than providing an explanation for the creation of the universe and human beings. The treatment that Ayar Cachi receives from his brothers is similar to the treatment other mythological brothers receive from their jealous siblings. It is interesting to consider the role that wealth plays in this myth.

The House of Origin

Long ago, the races who lived in this area were aggressive and selfish, causing much unnecessary hardship and death among the peoples of our land. Then three strange and powerful men and three women, children of the mighty Sun, suddenly appeared in a place called the House of Origin. All six came forth dressed like royalty, in clothing made of fine, patterned wool. Each man carried a stone within a golden sling, and each woman wore much gold. They intended to become the rulers of our land and to create a new settlement. They brought with them great quantities of jewels, gold, and other precious things, which Pizarro found when he conquered our people.

The man named Ayar Cachi was so powerful that the stones shot from his sling divided the hills and created valleys between them. His two brothers, seeing him perform deeds that they could not do, were overcome with envy. They plotted against him.

"Ayar Cachi, dear brother," Ayar Ucho began, "please return to the cave where we keep our treasure and bring out that beautiful, large, golden vase. We forgot to bring it with us."

"And while you are there," Ayar Manco added, "please pray to our father, the Sun, and ask him to look favorably upon our journey and help us become rulers of this land."

Ayar Cachi, suspecting no evil, immediately returned to the cave for the golden vase they had requested. His two brothers followed stealthily behind him. As soon as he entered the cave, they quickly gathered rocks that were lying nearby and blocked up the entrance. They heard no sign of protest from Ayar Cachi, but they trembled with fear as the earth suddenly shook with such a mighty force that many mountains came tumbling into the valleys, creating heaps of rubble where once green trees had flourished and rivers flowed.

The two brothers, the three women, and other people who joined them formed a settlement nearby. When Ayar Manco and Ayar Ucho had all but forgotten about Ayar Cachi, he flew toward them one day in the form of a magnificent bird, the brightly colored feathers of his powerful wings shimmering in the sunlight.

As they turned to flee, Ayar Cachi said, "Have no fear of me, my brothers! I come to you only with advice about establishing the great Inca Empire. I ask you to leave this settlement and travel down into the valley, where you must establish the community of Cuzco. Build a great city there, with a temple to honor and worship the Sun."

He continued, "I will use my favor with our father to help you become powerful rulers. In return, I ask you to honor me and to worship me as a god. If you are faithful with your sacrifices, I will help you in time of war. Put the crown of empire upon your heads. Take the young men of this land, make nobles of them, and arm them for battle. As a sign of our new relationship, I will pierce your ears as mine are pierced and decorate them accordingly."

Ayar Cachi's brothers were speechless. They agreed to his wishes and made the hill into a sacred place for his worship. As the three brothers stood together upon that hill, Ayar Cachi said to Ayar Manco, "Take our three women into the valley and establish the city of Cuzco there. Do not forget me, however. I will wait for your sacrifices."

Then, right before Ayar Manco's eyes, both Ayar Cachi and Ayar Ucho were transformed into stone statues.

Ayar Manco obeyed the counsel of Ayar Cachi and founded the city of Cuzco. He changed his name to Manco Capac and became a humble ruler. In the name of Con Ticci Viracocha and his father, the Sun, he laid the foundations of the new city. The first structure he built was a simple stone house with a roof of straw. He called it the Place of Gold, and his gods were worshipped there. The great Temple of the Sun was eventually built where that simple house had stood.

Introducing **The Children of the Sun**

Historical Background

Because this fertility myth is closely related to the preceding Tiahuanaco/ Aymara and Inca creation myths, the historical background of those myths applies here as well.

The Incas took credit for all the achievements of prior cultures, giving the Spaniards a revisionist version of history in which their great nation conquered and instructed local savages in the ways of civilization. Similarly, the Incas adapted myths from the oral traditions of the local peoples to fit their own attitudes, values, and cultural traditions.

When the Spaniards, under Francisco Pizarro, conquered the Incas in 1532, they learned the Inca language and began to convert the Incas to Christianity. They sent reports back to Spain explaining in great detail the nature of the people they had conquered, including their pagan beliefs. These reports reflected the Spaniards' own Christian attitudes, values, and beliefs.

The few writers who were Inca were new converts to Christianity. Their writings also reveal the influence of Christian doctrine, for it was all too easy in an oral tradition for new ideas to blend with the older ones.

The following myth was recorded by Inca Garcilaso de la Vega (1539– 1616?) in Volume 1 of his masterpiece, *The Royal Commentaries of the Inca*, published in Spain in 1609. The author was born in Cuzco, Peru, the son of a Spanish conquistador and an Inca princess. Because he was illegitimate, he was given the name of Gomez Suarez de Figueroa instead of receiving his father's name. Garcilaso converted to Catholicism, and, in 1558, after his father's death, he moved to Spain in order to complete his education and attempt (unsuccessfully) to gain title to his father's estate. He took his voluminous notes on the Inca along with him.

In 1590, Garcilaso was living in Cordoba under his father's name, to which he had appended Inca in honor of his mother's people. His first book was published in that year. His third and last book, the second volume of his masterpiece, was published in 1617, close to the time of his death.

Garcilaso has long been regarded as one of the finest prose stylists who wrote during Spain's Golden Age. Today, he is also valued as the first great South American author and the father of Spanish-American literature.

Appeal and Value

"The Children of the Sun," like the Trio fertility myth, involves a supernatural being who leads humans to a more civilized life. It illustrates how the Incas took this common mythical theme and shaped it to suit their own purposes.

The Incas' goal was to glorify their heritage and their people. They disparaged the people who preceded them by describing them as living like wild animals. The myth shows the Incas improving the lives of the local inhabitants, changing them from a people who lived as migrant hunters and food gatherers, with no surplus of food and no leisure time, to a people who settled down as farmers and reaped the benefits of division of labor. (In reality, the local populations were as civilized as the Incas were.) The Incas who rescue and teach these "uncivilized" peoples are the children of the sun, who is the kindly benefactor of all living creatures. Viracocha, the divine creator, is not mentioned in the myth.

The rod of gold reveals an awareness of the scarcity of good farmland in the Andean highlands and explains how Cuzco, the capital city of the Incas, came to be built. The end of the myth paves the way for creation of the Inca Empire.

The Children of the Sun

In times of old, our land was one of shrubs and small trees and tall mountains. The people were unmannered and untaught. They lived as wild animals live, without clothes made from woven cloth, without houses, and without cultivated food. They lived apart from other human beings in small family groups, finding lodging as nature provided it, within mountain caves and in hollow places beneath the great rocks. They covered their bodies with animal skins, leaves, and the bark of trees, or they wore no clothes at all. They gathered whatever food they could find to eat, such as grass, wild berries, and the roots of plants, and sometimes they ate human flesh.

Father Sun looked down from the heavens and pitied these humans who lived like wild creatures. He decided to send one of his sons, Manco Capac, and one of his daughters, Mama Ocllo Huaco, down to earth at Lake Titicaca to teach them how to improve their lives.

When his children were ready to leave, the Sun said to them, "I devote myself to the well-being of the universe. Each day, I travel across the sky so that I can look down upon the earth and see what I can do for the human beings who live there. My heat provides them with the comfort of warmth. My light provides them with the knowledge that comes from sight. It is through my efforts that fields and forests provide food for them, for I bring sunshine and rain, each in its proper season.

"Yet all this, good as it is, is not enough. The people live like wild animals. They know nothing of living in houses, wearing clothing, or raising food. They have no villages, they use no tools or utensils, and they have no laws.

"Therefore," Father Sun continued, "I am making you the rulers of all the races in the region of Lake Titicaca; I want you to rule those peoples as a father rules his children. Treat them as I have treated you, with tenderness and affection, with devotion and justice. Teach them as I have taught you, for the races of human beings are my children also. I am their provider and their protector, and it is time they stopped living like animals.

"Take this golden rod with you," the Sun concluded. "It is only two fingers thick and shorter than the arm of a man, yet it will tell you how good the soil is for cultivating crops. As you travel, whenever you stop to eat or to sleep, see if you can bury it in the land. When you come to the place where the rod sinks into the earth with one thrust, establish my sacred city, Cuzco, city of the sun. Soft soil as deep as this golden rod will be fertile soil."

So Manco Capac and Mama Ocllo Huaco went down to Lake Titicaca and set out on foot to examine the land. Wherever they stopped they tried to bury the golden rod, but they could not do it. The soil was too rocky.

Finally they descended into a valley. The land was wild and without people, but the plant growth was lush and green. They climbed to the crest of a hill (the hill where Ayar Cachi and Ayar Ucho had turned to stone) and pressed the golden rod into the soil. To their great pleasure, it sank into the earth and disappeared.

Manco Capac smiled at Mama Ocllo Huaco and said, "Our father, the Sun, intends us to rule this valley. Here we will build his sacred city, Cuzco. Let us now go separate ways, you to the south and I to the north. Let us gather together the peoples we find and bring them into this fertile valley. Here we will instruct them in the ways of human beings, and we will care for them as our father has commanded us."

Manco Capac and Mama Ocllo Huaco set out for the mountain plateaus to collect the peoples of the land. The men and women they found in the barren regions were impressed with their clothing and pierced ears, their regal bearing, and their message. "Let us teach you how to lead a better life," the children of the Sun announced. "Let us teach you how to build houses, make clothes, and raise cattle and crops. Right now you live like wild animals. Let us teach you how to live like human beings. Our father, the Sun, has taught us and has sent us here to teach you."

The peoples of the land placed their confidence in these children of the Sun and followed as they led the way toward a new and better way of living. When many people had gathered together, Manco Capac and Mama Occlo Huaco divided the group into those who would be responsible for gathering food and those who would learn how to build houses. Their new life had begun.

Manco Capac taught the males which foods were nourishing so their diet would include both grains and vegetables, how to choose the best seeds, and how to plant and cultivate each kind of plant. In the process, he taught them how to make the tools and equipment necessary for farming and how to channel water from the streams in the valley for irrigation. He even taught them how to make shoes. Meanwhile, Mama Ocllo Huaco taught the women how to weave wool and cotton into cloth and how to sew that cloth into clothing.

So it came to pass that the Incas became an educated people. In honor of their great provider and protector, the Sun, the people built a temple on the crest of the hill where Manco Capac and Mama Ocllo Huaco had plunged the golden rod into the earth and from which they had set out to gather the Inca people together and teach them. Their prosperity drew other peoples to join them and learn their ways. Manco Capac finally taught the men how to make weapons — such as bows and arrows, clubs, and lances — so that they could defend themselves and extend their kingdom. The Incas were on their way to becoming a great people.

Introducing **Paraparawa and Waraku**

Historical Background

This fertility myth comes from the Trio people, who inhabit the tropical rain forests of Surinam and Brazil. Like many other people who live in that area, the Trios live in thatched houses in large, semipermanent villages. They are primarily hunters and gatherers. They live without domesticated animals, so they have no wool. However, they weave cloth made of bark using primitive looms. They also weave baskets and make pottery from clay. They have neither metal nor stone, so their tools are made from parts of plants.

Few of these forest peoples have patron gods or buildings in which to worship them. They believe in nature spirits — beings who personify aspects of nature such as the sun, moon, stars, thunder, and rain. Beings and animals often merge into and out of one another, as if each spirit has a double identity. The Trio myths are concerned with explaining what exists in the universe and how it came to exist — for example, the creation of farming.

Appeal and Value

"Paraparawa and Waraku" follows a pattern common to the myths of Central and South America. The fisherman Paraparawa lives by gathering the food he eats. His diet usually includes grasses, wild berries, wild fruits, and roots. He also catches fish and hunts small game. As long as an abundant supply of simple foods exists to provide for the needs of his relatively small community, he may relocate only occasionally. However, his survival is very vulnerable to changes in weather patterns and to the invasion of other forest people into his hunting and gathering area.

A supernatural being arrives to teach Paraparawa how to improve the quality of his life. The change from food gathering to food cultivation is a major step in the process of civilization, and it brings with it far-reaching changes in the community's way of life. Planting food requires remaining in that location to cultivate and harvest that food. Consequently, people can construct more comfortable, permanent housing. With a predictable crop, a community can grow enough food to have a surplus. Once the whole community does not have to spend all its time gathering food, some people are free to specialize in other occupa-

tions: building and repairing structures; weaving cloth; making weapons, implements, and pottery; and developing artistic talents.

One common idea reflected in the myths of cultures such as the Trio is that women are a different kind of creature who originally emerged from water in the form of fish. In some myths the male fisherman fishes the woman out of a deep hole or pool, and in others out of a river. The women in such myths are more knowledgeable than men. It is they who teach men how to develop a better way of life by becoming an agricultural people.

The following myth has been recorded by Peter Riviere in *Marriage Among the Trio: A Principle of Social Organization*, published in 1969.

Paraparawa and Waraku

Paraparawa was fishing along the bank of the river when he caught in his hands a small fish called a *waraku*. It slipped out of his grasp, flopped about upon the ground, and then disappeared. No matter where Paraparawa looked for it, he could not find it. He shrugged his shoulders in resignation and set about preparing to catch another fish.

Suddenly, from behind him, Paraparawa heard a woman's voice say, "Here I am!"

Paraparawa turned around and saw that a strange woman was talking to him. "Who are you?" he asked.

"I am Waraku, the spirit of the fish you just caught," the woman replied. "Please take me to your village. I would like to see where you live."

"It is a simple village, set deep among the reeds," Paraparawa said. "There is nothing special about it."

"Take me there anyway," Waraku said.

When they arrived at Paraparawa's village, Waraku said, "Now show me your house. Show me what you drink and what you eat. I want to see just how you live."

"My life is very simple," Paraparawa replied. "I told you there was nothing special here. I have no house; I sleep outside among the reeds. For food, I eat the soft center of the reeds that you see all about you. The pulp is juicy. It is enough for my simple needs."

"All right, then. You have satisfied my curiosity," Waraku said.

When they had returned to the river, she said, "Do not leave me just yet. My father is coming with food: yams, sweet potatoes, yucca, and bananas. I want you to see what he is bringing."

As Paraparawa stood on the bank of the river, he suddenly saw the head of a giant alligator rise to the surface with a mouthful of plants. As the creature glided toward them, its fiery red eyes caused Paraparawa's heart to fill with terror, and he ran away.

From a safe distance, Paraparawa turned toward the river again. He watched as the alligator slithered upon the shore, dropped a number of green plants at the feet of Waraku, and returned to the depths of the river.

"That giant beast must be Waraku's father!" Paraparawa exclaimed to himself. "I am glad I did not catch him as I was fishing!"

"Come back, now!" Waraku called, motioning with her arms. "My father has brought the food I told you about."

When Paraparawa returned to the river bank, Waraku said, "These plants are for you. From now on, they will be your food. You will find them far tastier than the center of the reed plant. Here are the yams and the sweet potatoes. These are bananas, and this plant with the thick, edible root is the yucca. It will provide you with drink as well as food."

"Thank you," Paraparawa replied. "But how do I eat these plants? And what do I do when I have eaten all of them?"

"Oh, these are not for you to eat!" Waraku exclaimed. "At least, not just yet. You must plant them in the ground so they can grow and produce more plants just like them. Then you will be able to eat them and still have more of the same plants to eat. Remember, you should never eat all of the food you have. Always save some of each plant so you can place it in the ground and let it grow into more plants. Now, let me show you how to prepare a field and plant them."

Paraparawa followed Waraku among the reeds and learned from her how to clear a field and plant each of the plants that she had given him. He planted the yams in one row, the sweet potatoes in a second row, the yucca in a third row, and the bananas in a fourth row.

When they had finished, Waraku said to Paraparawa, "All you need to do is keep the reeds from growing in this field. These new plants will have enough sunlight and rain to grow very quickly. When they are ripe, I will return and show you how to eat them. Meanwhile, work in this field each morning, and one day I will find you here."

Paraparawa accompanied Waraku back to the river. He watched as she dived into the water and was again transformed into the small fish. When he could no longer see her in the water, he returned to his field, sat down on the ground, and thought about all that had happened to him.

Paraparawa's plants grew quickly. Every morning when he came to examine his field, he could see new growth. With a smile in his heart, Paraparawa pulled all other plants from his field. He worked carefully, trying to do just what Waraku had told him.

Many weeks passed. Paraparawa's plants now had large leaves. "I see green bananas growing on the banana plants," he said to himself, "but where are the yams and the sweet potatoes? Does Waraku expect me to eat leaves? Maybe they are roots like the yucca. I will have to wait for her and see."

Every morning when Paraparawa arrived at his field, he expected to find Waraku there. Every morning he was disappointed. But finally the morning arrived when she was there.

Waraku now taught Paraparawa how to make the tools and utensils that he would need to prepare and cook the foods he had raised. Then she showed him how to make bread from the yucca plant.

Paraparawa had to learn how to eat and enjoy all of his new foods. At first the new foods were so different from what he was accustomed to eating that it was very difficult for him to swallow them. But he kept trying, because Waraku had convinced him that he would come to prefer the new foods. She was right. As the new tastes and textures became more familiar to Paraparawa, the inside of the reed became less and less appealing. Finally Paraparawa no longer ate the reed plant.

And that is how our people came to eat the foods we eat.

Introducing **The Creation**

Historical Background

The Maya were one of the major cultures in the New World. Located in what are now Guatemala and the Yucatán Peninsula, they were farmers of a soil so rich that it was easy for them to acquire a surplus of food. Corn was their major and revered crop. Their surplus enabled them to devote as much as half their time to other pursuits, and they became well-known for their knowledge of astronomy, their construction of major pyramid-shaped temples and limestone palaces, and their works of art. The Maya were expert mathematicians, and they also possessed a written hieroglyphic language that they used in writing books.

The Spaniards conquered the Maya in A.D. 1524 and burned their principal city, including all of their books, to ashes. Spanish missionaries converted the Mayan population to Roman Catholicism and taught many of the

Maya to write their own language in the Latin, phonetic alphabet. They encouraged the Maya to record their traditions and history in the Western form of writing. Today, more than 300,000 people continue to speak the Maya language.

The Mayan creation myth is part of an ancient epic known as *The Popol Vuh*, which is the greatest surviving Mayan document. It was written anonymously in the Mayan language using the Latin alphabet between 1554 and 1558. Scholars believe this document is either a translation of a manuscript in the ancient Mayan hieroglyphic language or a collection of stories and songs recorded directly from the Mayan oral tradition.

In about 1700, a Catholic missionary translated *The Popol Vuh* into Spanish. He spoke the Mayan language fluently, and he persuaded the Maya to show him this manuscript of their ancient history. There is no record that any other Spaniard ever saw the Mayan document.

The Spanish manuscript disappeared for 150 years. In the 1850s, it was discovered in the library of the University of San Carlos in Guatemala City; it was first published in Vienna in 1857.

Appeal and Value

The Popol Vuh is an ancient document of striking literary beauty. It reveals more than the talent of the anonymous recorder. It reflects the thoughts and values of this ancient people and the ability of their language to express them.

The part of the epic that tells the Mayan creation myth shows a Christian influence. The language and some of the ideas are similar to the opening chapters of the Old Testament. This is not surprising, given the fact that Spanish missionaries were already teaching the Maya about Christianity when the anonymous author recorded *The Popol Vuh*.

It is interesting to compare the type of human beings the Maya gods wished to create and the relationship between these gods and their people with those of other creation myths.

The Creation

In the beginning, only the sky above and the sea below existed in the eternal darkness, and they were calm and silent, for nothing existed that could move or make noise. The surface of the earth had yet to rise forth from the waters. Grass and trees, stones, caves and ravines, birds and fish, crabs, animals, and human beings had yet to be created. Nothing could roar or rumble; nothing could sing or squeak; nothing could run or shake, for there was nothing but the vacant sky above and the tranquil sea below.

Hidden in the water under green and blue feathers were the Creators. These great thinkers talked quietly together in the water, alone in the universe, alone in the darkness of the eternal night. Together they decided what would be. Together they decided when the earth would rise from the waters, when the first human beings and all other forms of life would be born, what these living things would eat in order to survive, and when dawn would first flood the world with pale light.

"Let creation begin!" the Creators exclaimed. "Let the void be filled! Let the sea recede, revealing the surface of the earth! Earth, arise! Let it be done!"

And so they created it. The Creators made it. Out of the mist, out of a cloud of dust, mountains and valleys rose from the sea, and pine and cypress trees took root in the rich soil. Fresh water ran in streams down the mountainsides and between the hills.

And the Creators were satisfied. "We have thought about it and planned it," they said, "and what we have created is perfect!"

Then the Creators asked, "Do we want only silence beneath the trees we have created? Let us create wild animals, birds, and snakes. Let it be done! "

And so they created them. The Creators made them.

"You, deer, will walk on four feet through the thicket and the pasture. You will multiply in the forest, where you will sleep in the cool shade of the ravines and in the fields along the banks of rivers. You, birds, will live in the branches of the trees and in the vines. There you will build your nests, and there you will multiply." This the deer and the birds were told, and this they did.

And the Creators were satisfied. "We have thought about it and planned it," they said, "and what we have created is perfect!"

Then the Creators asked for more from the living creatures they had created. "Speak, call, cry, as each of you can. Call us by name, praise us and love us."

But all this the birds and animals could not do. They could scream, hiss, and cackle, but they could not name their creators.

The Creators were disappointed with the living creatures that they had made. They said to them, "We will not take from you that which we have given you. However, because you cannot praise us and love us, we will make other beings who will. These new creatures will be superior to you and will rule you. It is your destiny that they will tear apart and eat your flesh. Let it be done!"

And so they created them. The Creators made them. They decided to fashion an obedient and respectful creature who would praise and love them. First they tried to model him out of muddy earth, but the material was too soft. He was limp and weak. He could speak, but no mind gave meaning to the words he spoke.

"Creatures fashioned from mud will never be able to live and multiply!" the Creators exclaimed. So they destroyed this creature.

Next the Creators tried to carve their new creature out of wood. "This material seems to be just right! It is firm and strong," they said. "These creatures look and speak like human beings. Let us make many more of them. Let it be done!"

The wooden creatures lived and multiplied, but no mind gave meaning to the words they spoke, and no soul existed within them. Their faces lacked all spirit, their hands and feet all strength. Their flesh was yellow and dry, without a bloody moisture pulsing beneath the surface to nourish it. They wandered aimlessly on all four limbs and did not think of their creators.

"Creatures fashioned from wood are not good enough to be able to live and multiply!" the Creators exclaimed. So they determined to destroy these wooden creatures.

The Creators caused a great flood of sap to form in the sky and fall to earth, striking the heads of the wooden creatures and felling them like trees. Then an eagle descended upon them and tore out their eyes. A bat descended upon them and cut off their heads. A jaguar leaped upon them and broke and mangled their bones. The face of the earth became covered in darkness, and a black rain fell without ceasing.

Once they were powerless, these wooden creatures were beset by enemies. Animals, both large and small, attacked them. Sticks and stones, plates and pots attacked them. Dogs they had starved and taunted now tore into their faces with their teeth. Stones they had used for grinding now ground them. Pots and griddles they had burned upon the cooking fire now burned their faces.

Desperately fighting for their lives, the wooden creatures tried to climb to the roofs of their houses, but the houses collapsed and tossed them back to the ground. They tried to climb the trunks of trees and find safety in their branches, but the trees shook them off and threw them to the ground. They tried to enter caves, but the caves closed and refused to shelter them.

All but a few of the wooden creatures were destroyed. The others survived with mangled faces and jaws, and their descendants became known as monkeys.

The Creators then took counsel together in the darkness of the night. The sun, the moon, and the stars had yet to appear in the sky above them. "Let us try again to create creatures who will praise us and love us. Let it be done! Let noble creatures live on the surface of the earth. Let us search for the substance we can use to fashion them."

Four animals — the mountain cat, the coyote, the crow, and a small parrot — came before the Creators and told them of yellow ears and white ears of corn that grew abundantly nearby. The Creators took the road the animals showed them. They found the corn, ground it up, and fashioned their noble creatures from this food. "Let it be done!" they exclaimed.

And so they created them. The Creators made them.

So it came to pass that the four First Fathers were created. The Creators fashioned their bodies from cornmeal dough. They made corn drinks from ground yellow and white corn and fed them to their new creatures to give them muscles and flesh, and with these strength.

And the Creators were satisfied. "We have thought about it and planned it," they said, "and what we have created is perfect!"

These four First Fathers looked and talked like human beings. They were attractive, intelligent, and wise. They could see far into the distance. Mountains and valleys, forests and meadows, oceans and lakes, the earth beneath their feet, and the sky above their heads all revealed their natures to them.

When the four First Fathers saw all there was to see in the world, they appreciated what they saw, and they thanked their creators. "We thank you for having created and formed us," they said. "We thank you for giving us the ability to see, hear, speak, think, and walk. We can see what is large and what is small, what is near and what is far. We know everything, and we thank you!"

The Creators were no longer pleased. "Have we created creatures who are better than we intended? Are they too perfect?" they asked each other. "Have we made them so knowledgeable and wise that they will be gods like ourselves? Should we limit their sight so that they will see less and know less? Let it be done!"

So the Creators spoke, and they changed the beings they had created. They blew fog into their eyes so they could see only that which was close to them. In this way, the Creators destroyed the original knowledge and wisdom that the four First Fathers had possessed.

After the Creators had created and formed our grandfathers in this way, they said, "Now let us carefully create and form wives for the First Fathers. Let their wives come to them while they are asleep and be there to bring them joy when they awaken. Let it be done!"

And so they created them. The Creators made them.

And the Creators were satisfied. "We have thought about it and planned it," they said, "and what we have created is perfect!"

So it came to pass that the Creators made many more human beings like the First Fathers and the First Mothers. They lived and multiplied in darkness, for the Creators had not yet created light of any kind, neither sun, nor moon, nor stars. These human beings lived together in the east in great numbers, both light-skinned and dark-skinned, rich and poor, speaking different languages.

They made no images of their gods, yet they remembered their creators and were loving and obedient. They raised their faces to the sky and prayed, "Oh, Creators! Stay with us and listen to us! Let there be light! Let there be dawn! Let there be day! Let dawn flood the world with pale light, and let the sun follow. As long as the sun shines from the sky, brightening each day, grant us daughters and sons to continue our race. Give us good, useful, happy lives, and give us peace!"

With these words the people entreated the sun to rise and to illuminate with its golden rays the steps of those whom the Creators had made.

"So let it be!" the Creators said. "Let there be light! In the dawn of the universe, let the light of early morning shine upon all that we have created! For we have thought about it and planned it, and what we have created is perfect!"

And so they created it. The Creators made it. The sun rose from the waters and cast its golden rays upon the surface of the earth. And the animals and the people were joyful because of it. Large and small animals rose to their feet in the cool shade of ravines and along the banks of rivers and turned to face the rising sun. The jaguar and the puma roared, and the snake hissed. The birds stretched their wings and broke into song. The people danced around their priests, who were burning incense and making sacrifices. For the Creators had illuminated the earth with light, and it was perfect.

Introducing **The Creation Cycle**

Historical Background

Archaeological studies of the Mexican plateau reveal that human beings have been living in that region since 6000 B.C. From A.D. 900 to 1200, the Toltec people dominated the northern part of Central America, and their capital city of Tula was located just north of what is now Mexico City. The Toltecs captured the Maya who lived in the Yucatán Peninsula. Like the Maya, the Toltecs possessed a rich heritage of myths and legends. Their spoken language, Nahuatl, also had a rich cultural tradition. Toltec power was destroyed from within by civil war, which left Tula in ruins in 1200 and left the area without a dominant power for more than a century.

According to Aztec tradition, the Azteca (people of Aztlan) obeyed the command of their god and left Aztlan (located far north of the Colorado River) sometime in the 12th century. They wandered from place to place until, in 1325, they finally settled the area that has become Mexico City. The Aztecs held the Toltecs in high regard both politically and culturally. The first Aztec ruler, who came to power in 1376, claimed to be a descendant of Quetzalcoatl, the founder of the Toltec people. Thereafter, Toltec culture became an integral part of Aztec culture.

The Aztecs adopted the Toltec language and their myths and legends, blending them with their own and recording them. Under Aztec rule, architecture, the arts, and literature flourished. Their largest cities were much larger than any Spanish city of that time, and they contained elaborate palaces, temples, and waterways. The Aztecs took pride in creating works of metal and of feathers, in carving wood and huge sculptures of stone, and in forming mosaics of gems. They had a great interest in history, in the form of myths and legends, and in poetry. Today, more than a million people continue to speak Nahuatl, the Aztec language.

When the Spaniards invaded Central America and conquered the Aztecs in 1519, Hernán Cortés was helped both by neighboring peoples and by the Aztec emperor himself. The bloody practices of the Aztecs had created many enemies, who mistakenly thought the invaders would be better. The Aztec emperor welcomed Cortés because he believed that the Spaniard was Quetzalcoatl, returning as their tradition said he had promised.

The Spaniards burned most of the literature of the pagan peoples whom they conquered. As with the Maya, whom they conquered five years later, they burned entire libraries because they feared the pagan materials were harmful to Christians.

The Spaniards preserved certain aspects of the Aztec culture by learning the language and recording the literature in Spanish. Their point of view is clear from the nature of their accounts. They were both fascinated and repelled by the non-Christian myths and legends.

In the process of converting the more educated Aztecs to Christianity, the Spanish friars taught them to write their own language in the Roman alphabet and to record their myths and legends in this more Westernized version of the Nahuatl language. The Aztecs often blended newly acquired Christian concepts and literary style into their own, older oral tradition. These transcriptions, made by both Spaniards and Aztecs in the 1500s, reflect the Spanish influence and so are not entirely authentic.

"The Five Worlds and Their Suns" and "The Creation of Human Beings" were recorded in the 16th-century Nahuatl manuscript, the *Chimalpopoca Codex: Annals of Cuauhtitlan and Legend of the Suns*. "The Creation of the Earth" was recorded in a 16th-century French manuscript, *The History of Mexico*. The myths that relate how Quetzalcoatl is tricked and driven from the Toltec capital by Tezcatlipoca appear in two major, primary sources: the *Chimalpopoca Codex* and the *Florentine Codex: General History of the Things of New Spain*, a collection of Nahuatl texts made in the 16th century by the Spanish priest Fray Bernardino de Sahagun.

Appeal and Value

Like the Greeks, the Irish, and certain other cultures from the Americas, the Aztecs describe the creation of a succession of worlds, with their world being the current one. Like many other cultures, the Aztecs also describe a great flood.

The Aztecs did not create their myths; instead, they adopted existing Toltec myths to conform to their own beliefs. They identified the major Toltec god, Quetzalcoatl, with Huitzilopochtli, who was the Aztec god of the sun and of war. Aztec/Toltec myths are unusual in that both gods and human beings are required to make sacrifices in order to preserve the life of the universe and the lives of people. In "The Five Worlds and Their Suns," human beings who live in the first four worlds are unwilling to do this, so the gods punish them.

The need to sacrifice human beings to the sun was an important religious concept among the Aztecs. The Aztecs knew that the fiery rays of a motionless sun would destroy the earth, and they lived in fear that the sun would halt in the midst of its daily journey. They believed that the heart and blood, divine or human, would quench the hot sun's thirst and renew its strength so it could continue its journey. The Aztecs were known to go to war to obtain these human sacrifices, evoking hatred from neighboring cultures.

The fifth world acquires light because two gods are willing to sacrifice their lives for the sun. According to another myth, Quetzalcoatl later makes the same sacrifice that Nanautzin does in this myth.

As part of their religious tradition, each year the Aztecs chose a boy to live like a god for the coming year and then, on the anniversary of his selection, to die in order to revitalize the sun. During that year, this boy was honored as the earthly form of the god Tezcatlipoca. He was dressed in fine clothing, given eight servants to accompany him constantly, and trained in music and religious practices.

Twenty days before his day of sacrifice, the boy put on the clothes he would wear at his death and married four virgins, to whom the Aztecs gave the names of goddesses. The five days preceding his death were filled with feasting and dancing.

On the day of his sacrifice, the boy was transported in a canopy-covered canoe to the temple. As he climbed the temple steps, he played and broke a succession of flutes. When he reached the top, waiting priests bound him to an altar, cut out his heart, and offered it to the sun. Then a new boy was chosen to perform this role for the following year.

The remaining myths in the Creation Cycle explain other aspects of Aztec life. "The Creation of the Earth" explains why the earth also needs to feast upon human blood. In "The Creation of Human Beings," Quetzalcoatl injures himself to provide the blood that will bring life to a new race of people. "The Creation of Music" reveals the importance of music in the Aztec/Toltec culture. The language is unusually beautiful because the source of the myth is a poem.

The Creation Cycle

The Five Worlds and Their Suns

Five worlds were created, each with its own sun, each following upon the death of the preceding one. The first world was illuminated by the sun of earth. The people of this first world acted improperly, so the gods punished them by causing jaguars to feast upon their flesh. No one survived, and their sun died along with them.

The second world was illuminated by the sun of air. Its people acted without wisdom, so hurricane winds descended upon the earth, and the people were punished by being turned into apes. Their sun died when they became animals.

The third world was illuminated by the sun of the rain of fire. Its people acted without respect and reverence for the gods, refusing to sacrifice to them, so they were punished by earthquakes, volcanic eruptions of fiery ash, and other forms of flaming death. Their sun burned along with them.

The fourth world was illuminated by the sun of water. The great god Quetzalcoatl created a race of human beings from ash. The people were very greedy, so they were punished by a great flood. Their sun drowned when most of the people were transformed into fish.

The Supreme Being tried to save one human couple from the deluge. His voice came to them and said, "Find a mighty tree, make a hole in the trunk large enough to hide in, and take refuge there until the flood waters recede. You will survive if you master your greed and eat only one corncob each."

The husband and wife eagerly obeyed the instructions of the Supreme Being. They found a great tree, took refuge in it, and survived the flood.

When the waters had receded, they looked upon a strange world. Fish lay twitching on the ground where animals once had roamed. "Why should we gnaw on a corncob when fish are so plentiful?" they asked one another.

They proceeded to break off dry twigs from their tree, make a fire, and roast one of the fish. The gods smelled the savory smoke and became enraged at the greed and disobedience of this couple. They descended upon them in wrath and cut off part of their heads, giving them brains the size of animals'. Then they transformed them into dogs.

Before the gods created the fifth world, our own world, they gathered together in the darkness to choose who would illuminate it by creating the fifth sun, the sun of four movements. This sun would combine within it the earlier four elements of earth, air, fire, and water. One wealthy god, lavishly dressed in shining feathers of the hummingbird and in jewels of turquoise and gold, volunteered — thinking more about the praise he would receive than about what the deed would entail.

"One will not be enough for this great deed," the gods said. "We need a second volunteer." Each god remained silent. Finally the gods asked, "Will you help us, Nanautzin?"

Nanautzin looked up in surprise. Never before had he been worthy of their attention. He knew that the other gods despised him because he was misshapen, ugly, covered with disgusting-looking sores, and dressed in plain clothing made from woven reeds.

"If you will help us bring forth a fifth world, we will truly value you!" they said.

"If you wish it, I will do it," Nanautzin replied.

The two gods spent the next four days purifying themselves for the sacrifice. Then they approached the blazing fire upon the stone altar with their best gifts. The customary offerings were hay, dead branches, cactus needles, and bloody thorns. However, the wealthy god made a mighty show as he offered nuggets of gold, rich feathers, and gems. Nanautzin's offering seemed scanty as he placed in the fire three bundles of three green reeds, hay, the scabs from his sores, and thorns covered with his own blood.

All of the gods then built a towering pyramid of stone, made a bonfire on top of it, and let it burn for four nights while they too purified themselves. Finally they said to the wealthy god, "We are ready. Now perform the deed that you said you would do. Light up the world."

"How do you expect me to do this?" the wealthy god asked.

"You must leap into the center of the flames!" the gods replied.

The wealthy god's heart filled with terror, but he was ashamed to go back on his word. Four times he gingerly approached the flaming bonfire, and four times he retreated in the face of the terrifying flames and the great heat. "I know I volunteered, but I just cannot do this," he admitted in shame.

"Then, Nanautzin, it is your turn to perform this great deed," the gods said.

So Nanautzin forced courage into his heart and jumped into the flames. As the fire burned away his life, his blazing clothing lighted up the sky and gave life to the sun. The wealthy, cowardly god felt that he had no choice but to follow Nanautzin's brave example, so he too gathered the courage to sacrifice his life and he cast himself into the flames. But because Nanautzin had courageously led the way, from that time forth it was he who was honored among the gods. Many even say that Nanautzin was a form of the great god Quetzalcoatl.

The Creation of the Earth

Quetzalcoatl, the light one, and Tezcatlipoca, the dark one, looked down from the sky and saw only water below. A monstrous goddess floated upon the water, eating whatever she could find with her many mouths, for every joint in her body contained eyes sharp enough to spot any source of food and mouths that bit like wild animals.

"We must find some way to stop that goddess from devouring whatever we create," the two gods said to one another.

So it came to pass that the two great gods transformed themselves into two huge serpents. One of them quickly grabbed the goddess by her arms, while the other quickly grabbed her by the feet. Then, before she could resist, they pulled until she broke apart in the middle. Her head and shoulders became the earth, while the lower part of her body rose into the sky and became the heavens.

The other gods were angry at what Quetzalcoatl and Tezcatlipoca had done to the goddess. They came down to earth and decided to give her gifts that would compensate for her mutilation. They decreed that whatever human beings needed for survival, she would provide. They created trees, tall grass, and flowers from her hair, fine grasses and tiny flowers from her skin, small caves, fountains, and wells from her eyes, large caves and rivers from her mouth, hills and valleys from her nose, and mountains from her shoulders.

The goddess is often unhappy. Sometimes in the night, people can hear her crying. Then they know that she is filled with a ravenous thirst for human blood. Whenever this thirst comes upon her, the goddess will not provide the fruits of the soil and will not stop crying until the blood from human hearts has quenched her thirst. She who provides sustenance for human lives demands human lives in return for her own sustenance. So it has always been; so it will ever be.

The Creation of Human Beings

In the fifth world, our own world, the great god Quetzalcoatl prepared to create a new race of human beings. First he decided that his creations must have nourishing food to eat. He set forth across the face of the earth, stopping to examine every plant and animal to see if that particular food would be best for his people.

When the ants showed him the grains of corn they ate, Quetzalcoatl decided that this was the food for which he had been searching. But he knew the ants would never give him their corn. He would have to steal it from them.

So Quetzalcoatl transformed himself into a black ant. Along with the other black ants, he laboriously transported the corn from the field to a place of storage, grain by precious grain. But Quetzalcoatl only pretended to store the corn for the ant community. He was really building an enormous pile of grains for the people he was about to create. Finally he collected enough corn in his secret hoard to enable him to teach his people to plant it and produce a crop for themselves. He resumed his normal shape, put the corn into a huge bag, and returned to the heavens with it.

Quetzalcoatl was now ready to turn his attention to the second part of his plan, the creation of our present race of human beings. Each day he flew across the heavens from east to west, following the path of the sun. Each night he traveled through the Underworld from west to east, emerging at dawn. During one of his night journeys through the Underworld, Quetzalcoatl decided to find the Lord of the Dead Land and take the first step toward creating the new race of human beings.

"I would like you to give me the bones of my father that are buried in this land," he said to the Lord of the Dead Land.

"Why should I do you this favor, Quetzalcoatl?" the Lord of the Dead Land asked. "Whatever is buried belongs to me. What do you intend to do with these bones?"

Quetzalcoatl replied, "These bones are very dear to me, since they are all that remains of my father. The gods want another race of human beings to live upon the earth, and I intend to create them from my father's bones."

"Here they are, then," the Lord of the Dead Land replied. "The bones will be yours once you perform the deed I require of you. Take this conch shell in one hand and carry the bones in your other hand. Blow into the shell, making a great sound, as you walk four times around that circle of jade."

Quetzalcoatl took the bones and the conch shell from the Lord of the Dead Land and began to walk around the jade circle. When he tried to blow into the shell, it made no sound, for something was blocking its interior.

Quetzalcoatl called on the worms and the bees who lived in the Underworld to help him. First the worms entered the shell and pushed through the substance that was blocking it. Then the bees entered the twisting passages and cleared out any material that the worms had left behind.

Once Quetzalcoatl had successfully blown on the conch as he walked around the circle, the Lord of the Dead Land had said, he could take the bones. However, the lord secretly told his servants to examine Quetzalcoatl before he left and make certain that the god left the bones behind.

When the servants commanded Quetzalcoatl to leave the bones behind, the great god did not know how to evade the order. He called on his *nahual*, his animal double, for advice.

"Pretend to leave the bones, Quetzalcoatl," his nahual replied. "Then, once the servants have returned to their master, pack up the bones and take them with you."

So Quetzalcoatl pretended to obey the order to leave the bones, but he carefully wrapped them up and returned to the upper world.

The Lord of the Dead Land was not deceived by Quetzalcoatl's actions. He said to his servants, "Quetzalcoatl has disobeyed my orders and has taken the bones with him. Dig a pit that will trap him and cause him to drop the bones."

The servants of the Lord of the Dead Land dug a pit in the earth and concealed it well with leafy branches and dirt. As they had planned, Quetzalcoatl tripped and fell into the trap. Birds threatened him so menacingly that the great god fainted from terror, dropping his precious package. The birds then pecked apart the wrappings and the bones within them.

When Quetzalcoatl awakened, he wept with grief at his plight. "Oh, my nahual," he cried. "What should I do now?"

"Do not despair," his nahual replied. "Make the best of it, and continue your journey."

Quetzalcoatl gathered up the bones that the birds had pecked into tiny pieces, wrapped them as best he could, and returned with them as he had intended.

The goddess Woman Snake ground the bits of his father's bones into bone meal and placed it in a jade bowl. Then Quetzalcoatl pierced his body and moistened the meal with his own blood. From this mixture he molded the new race of human beings, both male and female.

The Creation of Music

One day Tezcatlipoca, God of the Heavens, came down to earth and wandered from place to place, observing all the beauties of nature. As he walked, he said to himself, "Earth Monster has brought forth mountains and valleys, rivers and streams, forests and meadows. In the light of Sun's rays, her flowers sparkle like brilliant jewels among her blades of grass. Clearly, there is much on Earth to please the hearts of human beings. Yet creation is not complete. Something is missing. Animals roar and people talk, but I hear no music! My heart is heavy with sadness, for music delights the soul as nothing else can."

So Tezcatlipoca summoned Quetzalcoatl, in his form as Wind. "Wind, hear my voice and come to me!" he called to each of the four corners of the world.

Wind groaned complainingly and reluctantly gathered himself together from where he lay scattered over Earth's surface. He rose higher than the tallest tree and the mightiest mountain, and in the form of a great black bird, he came forth to meet the god of the heavens.

Tezcatlipoca heard the waves rise in tumult from the ocean depths and crash with a roar upon the sandy shore. He heard the branches of the trees creak and moan as their leaves tossed and touched. He smiled. Quetzalcoatl had heard his voice, and he was coming.

Quetzalcoatl arrived quickly. As usual, his tempestuous disposition gave him an angry look even when he was quiet. He rested at Tezcatlipoca's feet without complaint.

"Quetzalcoatl," Tezcatlipoca began, "I find that ripe fruits, colorful flowers, and the brightness of Sun's rays make the whole earth beautiful. Yet, in spite of such beauty, Earth is sick with sadness! Not one beautiful sound fills the silence. Not one animal, bird, or human being can sing! Even you know only how to whine and howl, or moan and groan!

"Life must contain music! Music must accompany the awakening dawn. It must inspire the dreaming man. It must comfort the waiting mother. One must be able to hear it in the wings of the bird overhead and in the waters of the nearby brook.

"You must travel high above to the roof of the universe, find the house of Sun, Father of All Life, and ask him to give you musicians to live on Earth and add their beauty to the world. Surely Sun can do this, for he houses many musicians and a flaming choir whose brilliance sheds light upon the earth. Choose the best among both and return to Earth with them.

"When you reach the shore of the ocean," Tezcatlipoca concluded, you will find my three servants, Water Monster, Water Woman, and Cane and Conch. Command them to unite their bodies and create a bridge on which you can travel up to Sun."

Quetzalcoatl agreed. As he traveled across the face of Earth, he heard what Tezcatlipoca had described, either sad silence or harsh, raucous chatter. When he reached the seashore he found Tezcatlipoca's three servants, who created the bridge for him. Even with the bridge, it took all of his mighty breath to bring him to the house of Sun.

Sun's musicians strode about the halls in colors appropriate to the music they played. Those who played cradle songs and melodies for children wore gleaming white. Those who played songs accompanying the epics of love or war wore brilliant red. Those who wandered with their music as minstrels among the clouds wore bright blue, and those who sat in the golden rays of Sun playing their flutes wore radiant yellow. Quetzalcoatl could not find a musician dressed in a dark, sad color, for there were no sad songs.

As soon as the Father of All Life saw Quetzalcoatl, he exclaimed, "Musicians! I see Wind, that turbulent pest who annoys Earth, approaching our peaceful kingdom. Be silent! I want to hear no singing! I want to hear no playing of instruments! Whoever makes a sound when Wind speaks will have to return to Earth with him, and you will find no music there."

Wind climbed the stairways to the halls of Sun. As soon as he saw the musicians, he raised his deep voice and shouted, "Musicians! Singers! Come with me!"

Not one musician or singer replied to his call.

Wind shouted again, more harshly, "Come, musicians! Come, singers! The Supreme Lord of the Universe summons you to join him!"

Again, not one musician or singer replied to his call. They remained in frozen silence in obedience to the wishes of flaming Sun, like a colorful array of dancers suspended in the midst of their dance.

Then Tezcatlipoca, God of the Heavens, expressed his rage. From the four corners of the sky, flocks of black storm clouds rumbled ominously toward the house of Sun, lashed forward by the whip of their lord's lightning bolts. Mighty roars of thunder poured from the great god's throat, engulfing the house of Sun in torrential sound.

The storm clouds swallowed Sun, Father of All Life, who drowned like a flaming beast. Shivering with terror, the musicians and singers flew into the lap of Wind, who lifted them gently — so as not to crush their music — and happily carried them down to Earth, who was waiting far below.

Meanwhile, Earth scanned the heavens with her dark eyes, watching for the first appearance of Wind. Her face shone with a special radiance and she smiled with delight upon seeing that Quetzalcoatl's quest had been successful. All life welcomed the wanderers. Trees lifted their leafy branches, birds fluttered their wings, people and animals raised their voices, and flowers and fruits lifted their faces in greeting.

Sun's musicians and singers landed happily upon Earth and wandered off in small groups. One could not travel to the most distant corners of the world without meeting singers and musicians all along the way. Even Wind was now happy. No longer did he sadly sigh, moan, and groan as he had in former days. He now sang along with the rest of all life, refreshing the trees of the forest, the meadows, and the ocean waters with his gentle breezes.

So it came to pass that Tezcatlipoca and Quetzalcoatl helped one another to create music upon Earth. Music accompanied the awakening dawn. It inspired the dreaming man. It comforted the waiting mother. One could hear it in the wings of the bird overhead and in the waters of the nearby brook. From that time forth, every living thing could create its own kind of music.

Introducing **Quetzalcoatl**

Historical Background

The myth of Quetzalcoatl and the Aztec creation myths are closely related, and the historical background preceding the creation myths applies here as well.

Scholars believe that the hero Quetzalcoatl is a combination of fact and myth. They may argue about whether Quetzalcoatl was one man or many, whether he was native to the Americas or a foreigner, whether he lived in one century or another. However, they all agree that his myth left a powerful, lasting impression on the major cultures of Central America.

An analysis of Quetzalcoatl's name reveals that he was a part of both the Toltec and the Mayan cultures. The quetzal is a rare, green-feathered bird found in the land of the Maya, particularly in Guatemala. *Co* is the Maya word for serpent, and *atl* is the Nahuatl word for water. *Coatl* is the Nahuatl word for snake. Consequently, Quetzalcoatl was a mythic being who combined earth (in the form of the snake), water, and air (in the form of a

bird). He was identified with the wind, with the planet Venus, and, as a creator, with the sun. As the plumed serpent-god, he dominates the ancient monuments of Central America.

On the historical level, Quetzalcoatl was probably Topiltzin (Our Prince), the great leader of the Toltecs, a 10th-century-A.D. Nahuatl-speaking culture. Topiltzin had become a high priest of Quetzalcoatl, the great god of the Toltecs. He knew that other priests and kings had adopted Quetzalcoatl's name as the symbol of their own virtue. Consequently, once Topiltzin became king of the Toltecs, he changed his name to Quetzalcoatl. In 950, Topiltzin-Quetzalcoatl moved the capital of the Toltec nation to Tula, located fifty miles north of what is now Mexico City. There, he gave his people laws and ethical principles by which to live and taught them how to improve their standard of living. However, the historic Quetzalcoatl would not have had to teach his people to raise corn as food, because the peoples who inhabited Central America thousands of years before the Toltecs arrived already knew how to cultivate corn.

Appeal and Value

On the symbolic level, the myth of Quetzalcoatl may represent the conflict between those who supported Topiltzin in his desire to establish the benign, civilized Quetzalcoatl as the principal god of Tula and those who preferred to establish Quetzalcoatl's rival, the fierce warrior-god Tezcatlipoca, who exacted human hearts that were still beating and human blood that was freshly warm as part of his worship. Given the distinction between the two gods, the conflict had a political as well as a religious dimension, and the warlike Toltecs won.

The myth of Quetzalcoatl may also symbolize the conquest of the Toltec empire by the Aztecs. Tezcatlipoca was the god of the principal Aztec tribe, the Mexica. In the following myth, he destroys the Toltec people of Tula and succeeds in driving their ruler, Topiltzin-Quetzalcoatl, from power.

Two versions of the Quetzalcoatl myth exist. In one version, after Quetzalcoatl becomes drunk and has sexual relations with his sister, he builds a funeral pyre and jumps into it just as Nanautzin does in the creation myth.

In the version that follows, Tezcatlipoca successfully tempts both Quetzalcoatl and his people, first causing the king to become drunk and commit his immoral act, and then causing his people to bring their destruction upon themselves.

Tezcatlipoca is an unusually interesting figure. In the series of creation myths, he is a creator-god and a gift-giving god along with Quetzalcoatl. However, in the Quetzalcoatl myth, Tezcatlipoca is more than Quetzalcoatl's enemy. He is the dark side of Quetzalcoatl himself, his alter ego or double.

According to the Aztec tradition, Tezcatlipoca is invisible and intangible, which is most appropriate because his temptations represent all the evils that test the moral fiber of human beings. Whatever gifts he and Quetzalcoatl have given to human beings — food, wine, music, pride in self and country — Tezcatlipoca supplies in irresistible excess, and the gifts destroy the creatures they were designed to help. Even Quetzalcoatl himself, who personifies moral and ethical virtue, is unable to recognize his own weakness and his own potential for evil, thereby making it possible for Tezcatlipoca to destroy him. Everyone Tezcatlipoca destroys is ruled by emotion rather than by reason.

Quetzalcoatl

Quetzalcoatl was a large man. He often wore a conical cap made from the skin of the jaguar and a cloak made from the feathers of the quetzal bird. He wore a chain of seashells around his neck and a chain of rattles around his ankles. His voice was so strong that it could be heard for thirty miles. While he was alive, every cob of corn was as strong as a human being, pumpkins were as tall as human beings, and corn grew in many colors.

Quetzalcoatl was the son of Sun and the goddess Coatlicue. Coatlicue would sweep the heavens twice each day: once to usher in the night and the arrival of her children, the stars, and once to usher in the day and the arrival of her husband, Sun.

One day at twilight, after Sun had left the sky and Coatlicue's hundreds of children had yet to appear, a lone, multicolored feather floated down from the heavens. It was so lovely that Coatlicue picked it up and placed it in the neckline of her dress.

Later that night, when she had finished sweeping, Coatlicue sat down on the surface of the earth and rested. She reached for her feather, but she could not find it. She called to it, but it did not answer. In tears over her loss, she was heartbroken until she realized that she was pregnant.

When the stars heard that their mother was pregnant, they were determined to kill the father of the fetus. When they found that Sun was the father, they were not surprised. He was their father too, and they hated him. They were always attempting to kill him. As yet, they could not kill him for more than one night. In spite of their best efforts, every dawn he climbed into the eastern sky as usual.

It was not long before Quetzalcoatl was born, and in an even shorter time he grew to be the size of a nine-year-old. Soon thereafter, the stars killed Sun and buried his body in sand. Vultures saw the event as they flew through the sky. They quickly found Quetzalcoatl and told him of the murder. Quetzalcoatl sought the help of an eagle, a coyote, a wolf, and hundreds of moles, and together they followed the vultures to the burial site. The animals helped Quetzalcoatl dig up his father's body. Once again, the stars had been successful only temporarily.

When he had grown to be a man, Quetzalcoatl arrived as a stranger in the Toltec city of Tula. He taught the people how to raise corn and cotton, weave cloth, work with gold, jade, feathers, wood, and stone, and write, paint, and dance. Quetzalcoatl became famous for his moral principles. He had a great respect for all forms of life. He did not believe in killing flowers by picking them, or killing any of the animals of the forest. He became the ruler of the Toltec people, and even evil magicians could not tempt him to perform human sacrifices.

A powerful man, even when he is good, is never without enemies. Tezcatlipoca, who had worked with Quetzalcoatl to create the earth and to bring music to human beings, now wished to destroy his rival's power.

Tezcatlipoca was a formidable enemy. The Dark One had originally emerged from a cloud and descended to earth by means of a twisted spider's web. He was capable of performing deeds of virtue as well as deeds of evil. So great was his intelligence that he could create whatever his mind imagined. He could see into the depths of trees and rocks and into the minds and hearts of human beings. He had given human beings the gift of intelligence, and he was known to reward people who were good and to punish with disease those who were evil.

Once Tezcatlipoca set his mind to conquering Quetzalcoatl, he was clever enough to succeed where all others had failed. First, in the course of playing a game with Quetzalcoatl, Tezcatlipoca transformed himself into a jaguar and chased Quetzalcoatl from one community to another for the cruel enjoyment of it.

Next Tezcatlipoca held a mirror up to the ruler's face. "Oh," Quetzalcoatl groaned. "My skin is wrinkled like that of an ancient creature. My eyes look sunken like valleys in my face, and my eyelids are all puffed up. I am truly hideous to behold! I cannot walk the face of the earth if this is the way I look. I am so ugly that my people will be tempted to destroy me. I must leave the world of human beings!"

"Nonsense," Tezcatlipoca replied. "I can make you look handsome. Then you will be proud of yourself!"

Tezcatlipoca dressed Quetzalcoatl in splendid clothes. He covered his body with a robe made of feathers from the quetzal bird, he colored his face with red and yellow dye, and he placed a turquoise mask over his eyes. Finally he added a wig and a feathered beard. When his decoration was complete, he again held a mirror up to Quetzalcoatl's face. This time Quetzalcoatl was delighted. He looked so young and handsome that he gave up the idea of living a secluded life.

However, Tezcatlipoca had planted the seeds of fear in Quetzalcoatl's mind. His vision in the mirror had convinced him that he was an old man, and he began to have a great fear of death. Tezcatlipoca catered to this fear by offering Quetzalcoatl an intoxicating beverage. "Drink this, my friend," he said. "It will bring joy to your heart, peace to your mind, and youth to your body. It will chase away all thoughts of death as the rays of Sun scatter dark clouds."

"I have no interest in your drink, no matter what properties you say it possesses," Quetzalcoatl replied.

"Oh, come now!" Tezcatlipoca said. "You act like a man who is afraid of his own shadow! Dip the tip of your finger into the bowl and taste the wine. Surely you can have no fear of just a lick! How foolish you are being!"

Once Quetzalcoatl tasted the wine, he could not resist it. He drank bowl after bowl, until he had consumed five containers of wine and was very drunk. Quetzalcoatl's sister and his servants followed his lead, and soon they too had become very drunk. In this state, Quetzalcoatl no longer thought about living an honorable life. He forgot his religious practices and did whatever his senses enjoyed, without caring about the consequences.

When the effects of the wine eventually wore off, Quetzalcoatl realized that, among other immoral deeds, he had had sexual relations with his sister. He felt terribly ashamed. "Knowing what I have learned about myself, how can I walk among the Toltecs as a proud man?" he asked himself. "My people are weak. They need a strong man to lead them, a man they can admire and follow. However, if I leave them, they will only follow Tezcatlipoca. Surely they are better off if I remain their king."

So Quetzalcoatl remained king of the Toltecs. Tezcatlipoca also remained among them. "I have done all I need to do to destroy Quetzalcoatl," he said to himself. "Now it is time to destroy his people! I shall begin by making them sing themselves to death!"

Tezcatlipoca came before the Toltecs as a great entertainer, leading them in song after song. The people cheered as they sang along with him. They sang as the sun sank in the western sky. They sang as the stars appeared in the heavens. They sang throughout the night. The music Tezcatlipoca created pulsed within their hearts, faster and faster, stronger and stronger. One by one, their hearts cracked from the strain, and many collapsed and died.

Tezcatlipoca next transformed himself into a warrior and called the remaining Toltec men to join him in battle against a great enemy. Once they had assembled, he assumed his natural form and killed many more Toltecs.

Tezcatlipoca then transformed himself into a puppeteer. He appeared in the marketplace with a puppet of Quetzalcoatl and entertained the Toltecs by making the figure dance in the palm of his hand. The people gathered eagerly about him, captivated by his performance.

When he was satisfied with the size of his audience, Tezcatlipoca said, "Why are you watching us, you fools! Are we not trying to make you dance as, not long ago, we made you sing? Surely we deserve to be stoned to death! Who among you is sensible enough to throw the first stone?"

Tezcatlipoca goaded the Toltecs into stoning him. His body fell to earth as if rocks had killed him, and dreadful fumes began to issue from the fallen figure. Whoever smelled the fumes died. The wind blew the fumes throughout the city.

Finally Tezcatlipoca gave the Toltecs the courage to approach the figure and attempt to get rid of it. But the corpse turned out to be so heavy that it could not be budged.

In the meantime, the food the Toltecs raised began to have such a bitter taste that it was inedible. Before long the people began to starve to death. When they were desperate for food, Tezcatlipoca appeared in the marketplace in the guise of an old woman. He built a bonfire and began to roast kernels of corn.

The Toltec people could not resist the tantalizing aroma. It had been so long since they had eaten a tasty morsel that word spread like a summer storm, and they quickly gathered from all parts of the city, hoping to appease their hunger. When the last person had arrived, Tezcatlipoca assumed his natural form and killed them all.

So it came to pass that Tezcatlipoca destroyed Quetzalcoatl's people and forced their king to leave the city of Tula. Quetzalcoatl hid his wealth and his treasures deep within the mountains and canyons. He burned his rich palaces, turned cacao trees into desert brush, and ordered the birds to leave the area. Then he went on his way, traveling in a southeastern direction toward the sea.

At one point in his journey, Quetzalcoatl stopped, looked at his image in a mirror, and saw that he was as old as he had feared. In anger, he threw stones at a huge tree that was standing nearby; those stones have remained embedded in the trunk to this day.

At another point, Quetzalcoatl sat down to rest on a large rock. While he was sitting there, he wept tears the size and weight of hailstones. His body and his tears have left their impression upon that rock to this day.

Finally Quetzalcoatl came upon a group of demons who said, "Quetzalcoatl, stop and turn back! Where do you think you are going?"

"Sun has called me, and that is where I am going!" Quetzalcoatl replied.

"You may proceed, but only if you will agree to our conditions," the demons said. "You must toss away all your jewels and all your wealth. You must leave every skill that you possess with us: your ability to write, to cut gems and jade, to cast gold, to create objects from feathers, and to carve objects from wood and stone."

"If that is what I must do," Quetzalcoatl replied, "then I will do it. For I must go where Sun calls me."

Before he reached the end of his journey, Quetzalcoatl planted fiber-producing plants, built a ball court, built a house in the land of the dead, and proved that, even as an old man, he was strong enough to push a rock with his little finger that no other man could move at all.

Finally Quetzalcoatl reached the shore of the eastern sea. He wept with joy as he put on his feathered cloak and his turquoise mask. He climbed on a raft woven of snakes and set off toward Sun, who was beginning his morning journey across the heavens.

Some observers heard Quetzalcoatl exclaim, "Someday I will return to my people and my land!"

Others watched Quetzalcoatl's body burn up from the heat of Sun's rays. They say that his ashes became transformed into a colorful array of birds. The birds rose high into the air and carried his heart into the heavens, where it became the morning star that we call Venus.

Introducing **The Emergence**

Historical Background

Sometime between A.D. 1000 and 1500, the people who became known as the Navajo left the northern woodlands, bringing with them the bow and arrow. They were accustomed to hunting and fishing, but they settled among the agriculturally oriented Pueblo peoples in northern New Mexico and northeastern Arizona.

The Navajo adapted the ideas of the peoples they met. When the Pueblo people fled from the Spanish invaders in the late 1500s, they took refuge among their Navajo neighbors. They introduced the Navajo to farming and weaving, and to their heritage of myths and religious ceremonies. With these new skills, the Navajo became known for their poetic, elaborate myths, their striking sandpaintings, and their beautiful blankets.

After the first Spanish colonists brought sheep, goats, and horses into New Mexico in 1598, the Navajo became a nation of shepherds. They also began to use Spanish silver and United States coins to fashion beautiful jewelry.

The Navajo nation, the largest group of Native Americans in the United States, presently comprises between 110,000 and 150,000 people. Most Navajos live on or near the Navajo reservation, a 24,000-square-mile area in northeastern Arizona, northwestern New Mexico, and southeastern Utah. This reservation is the largest in the United States and is comparable to the size of West Virginia.

The Navajos are organized into matrilineal clans and, both on and off the reservation, often live in groups of extended families that are related through the women in the family. Women have social, political, economic, and religious importance in their society.

Agriculture is the basis of the Navajo economy. It includes the dryfarming of corn, beans, and squash and the herding of sheep. Many Navajo men continue to be known for their beautiful work in silver jewelry, while Navajo women have long been admired for their beautifully designed and woven wool rugs.

Appeal and Value

Every people has an explanation of how it came into existence. In the Navajo creation myth, the Navajo progress from world to world and become more civilized as they move upward. Like other peoples, the first Navajo are created from a plentiful local material — in this case, two ears of corn. Like other peoples, the Navajo are the victims of a great flood — but the Navajo survive.

Four is a sacred number throughout the creation myth. There are four seasons, four directions, and four winds. The Navajo tradition also speaks of four sacred mountains (one in each of the four directions), four sacred colors (black, white, yellow, and blue), four sacred plants (corn, squash, beans, and tobacco), and a progression upward through four worlds. Moreover, four important human beings are created in the image of the gods (First Man, First Woman, First Boy, and First Girl).

One of the interesting aspects of this myth is the close relationship among insects, animals, and human beings. A distinctive feature of Native American mythology is the idea that all living creatures deserve respect, since they are all creations of the same Supreme Being.

The primary source for the following myth is Washington Matthews' *Navajo Legends*, published in 1897. Matthews continues to be respected for his pioneering research in Navajo religious ceremonies and texts during the last twenty years of the 19th century. He preserved the integrity of the material he transcribed by presenting it as it was believed and practiced and by preserving the inherent interrelationships that exist among the text, the songs, the prayers, and the sandpaintings.

The Emergence

In the beginning was the First World, or Black World. It consisted of a small area of solid land surrounded by burning resin, which provided the only available light. Most of the inhabitants were wingless insects and crawling creatures accustomed to living in holes in the ground, among them red ants, yellow beetles, black beetles, and white locusts. One day the insects gathered together and said, "This place is too small, too dark, and too unpleasant! We must find a new world that will be larger and lighter."

"How can we do that?" asked the ants. "You can see that we are surrounded by fire!"

Dragonfly replied, "We will all make wings for ourselves and fly toward the roof of our world."

The dragonflies, bees, flies, locusts, and ants tied wings to their bodies and flew upward. Locust noticed a crack in the roof through which a blue light came, and he led the insects through that crack into the next world.

The Second World, or Blue World, was larger and lighter than the First World. Each group of insects went off among the grasses and bushes to find a home. They had not gone far before four great birds, White Crane, Blue Heron, Yellow Loon, and Black Loon, flew from the four corners of the world and swooped down upon them. "This is our land!" the birds exclaimed. "You may not remain here! Besides, you will starve here for lack of food. We have to fly far away to the sea in order to find food, and your wings will never carry you that far."

"Have no concern for us," the insects replied. "We have no interest in your food. Here we have leaves, seeds, pollen, and honey. That is more than enough!"

"Then you may stay," the birds replied, "but see to it that you stay far away from us!"

So the insects remained in the Blue World. As time passed, they increased in number until there was not enough food to feed them all. In search of more food, they set out to find where the great birds lived. When the birds spied the swarms of insects flying toward them like great clouds of dust, they summoned all of their own kind to fight the invaders. Led by White Crane, Blue Heron, Yellow Loon, and Black Loon, the birds won the battle.

Locust gathered the surviving insects and announced, "We must move to another world. Follow me!"

With many birds flying in close pursuit, the insects followed Locust to the roof of the Blue World, where Blue Wind led them into the Third World, or Yellow World. This world was larger and brighter than the Blue World, and it was populated with animals and human beings. Together, these became known as First People.

Here there was food for all. Grass and bushes grew along springs and rivers, and the mountains that stood to the north, south, east, and west were covered with trees. All living creatures spoke the same language, and they all had the teeth, claws, feet, and wings of insects.

Human beings, however, wore their wings as part of their furry or feathered coats, which they could remove. They lived in caves, and they ate only what food they could gather and eat raw, such as nuts, seeds, roots, and berries.

One autumn four gods — White Body, Blue Body, Yellow Body, and Black Body — appeared before First People for four days in succession. Each day they silently made signs and then departed. On the fourth day Black Body remained behind and said to First People, "The gods want to create people who look like them. Many of you have bodies like the gods, but you have the teeth, claws, and feet of insects and animals. Be clean and ready when we return to you in twelve days."

On the morning of the twelfth day, Black Body and Blue Body returned with two sacred buckskins. White Body returned carrying two perfect ears of corn, a white ear and a yellow ear. They placed the ears of corn on one of the buckskins, with the head of the buckskin facing west and the tips of the corn facing east. They placed an eagle's feather under each ear of corn, one from the white eagle under the white ear and one from the yellow eagle under the yellow ear. Then they covered both ears of corn with the second buckskin.

The White Wind entered from the east and the Yellow Wind from the west, and they blew on the ears of corn that lay between the two buckskins. When the gods lifted the upper buckskin, First People saw that the white ear of corn had become First Man and the yellow ear of corn had become First Woman. The winds had blown life into them just as they blow life into each of us.

For many years First People lived together peacefully in the Yellow World. Eventually, though, they increased in number until there was not enough food to feed them all. Those who were strong and fleet found food; those who were clever and stronger stole it. First People sent messengers to the four corners of the Yellow World to call all the people to assembly in order to choose one who would rule them all.

From the west came the Mountain People, who suggested that Mountain Lion should lead First People because he was both strong and wise. From the east came the Plains and Mesa Peoples, who suggested that Wolf should lead First People because he was both strong and clever. From the south came the Valley People, who suggested that Bluebird should lead First People because he was both wise and kind. From the north came the Forest People, who suggested that Hummingbird should lead First People because he was both swift and just.

When no group would accept the animal that another group suggested, Owl announced, "Let Lion return to his home in the west, Wolf to his home in the east, Bluebird to his home in the south, and Hummingbird to his home in the north. Let each of them bring back something that will help us. When we see what they can do for us, we can choose our leader."

Everyone agreed, and the four animals set forth. When eight days and nights had come and gone, Wolf returned. He was dressed all in white, from the cloud on his head and the robe on his body to the stalk of white corn and the white gourd rain-rattle in his hands. "Far to the east," he said, "I found these gifts for you: springtime rain, the light of morning, and young corn.

Wolf had hardly finished speaking when Bluebird arrived. He was dressed all in blue, from the cloud on his head and the robe on his body to the stalk of blue corn and the blue turquoise rattle in his hands. "Far to the south," he said, "I found these gifts for you: summer rain, blue sky, and soft corn."

Then, from the west, Lion arrived. He was dressed all in yellow, from the cloud on his head and the robe on his body to the stalk of yellow corn and the jasper rattle in his hands. "Far to the west," he said, "I found these gifts for you: autumn rain, evening light, and ripe corn."

Finally Hummingbird arrived from the north. He was dressed in the bright colors of the northern lights, from the cloud on his head and the robe on his body to the stalk of multicolored corn and the abalone-shell bowl of colored beans in his hands. "Far to the north," he said, "I found these gifts for you: northern lights for winter nights, dried corn and beans for winter food, and an abalone storage bowl that will always be full."

First People realized that they needed the gifts of all four leaders. They decided to be ruled by a council of wise people rather than by a single chief. From that day until this, in order to remind the Navajo people of the gifts they brought them, Wolf wears a silvery white coat, Bluebird a blue-feathered coat, Lion a coat of yellow fur, and Hummingbird a coat of many colors.

But solving the question of leadership did not solve the problem of food. First People did not know the proper way to plant the seeds they had, and they did not think to pray and bless the seeds before they planted them. Consequently, it was not long before First People knew that the time had come when they must move to another world or starve. They all flew up to the roof of the Yellow World, but they could find no cracks in it. They flew around and around, becoming more and more tired, but still they could see no way to enter the Fourth World.

Suddenly four voices called to them from the next world — one from the east, one from the south, one from the west, and one from the north. Four faces, each wearing a blue mask, were looking down from the four edges of the roof. First People divided into four groups, and each flew toward a different face. Those who became the first Navajo flew to the east and let First Woman direct them into the next world. The Bird People flew to the south and let First Girl direct them toward the warm part of the next world, where they spent each winter thereafter. The Animal People flew to the west and let First Man direct them toward the mountainous part of the next world, where they made their homes among the trees. The Insect People flew to the north and let First Boy direct them toward the cold part of the next world, where they immediately burrowed into the ground and waited for warmer weather.

To the surprise of First People, the Fourth World, or Black and White World, was already populated with other human beings. Their neighbors were the Hopi, Zuñi, Acoma, and other Indians who lived in pueblos. They also met Comanche, Apache, and Ute nearby. First Man and First Woman taught their people how to live in the Fourth World, where the days were white and the nights were black. They added corn and beans to their diet of roots, seeds, nuts, and berries. "Learn from your neighbors who live in pueblos how to cultivate beans and corn," they advised.

First Man and First Woman had hardly finished talking when two dust columns blew upon them, one from the south and one from the north. The two columns met with a crash, deposited two bundles upon the land, rose into the air, and disappeared.

"Oh, dear!" First Man exclaimed. "The North Wind has given us Coyote, who thinks only of being lazy and playing tricks!"

"Do not worry!" First Woman responded. "The South Wind has brought us Badger, who has the industry and determination that Coyote lacks!"

One day Coyote went to the Pueblo People and challenged Water Monster to a game of chance. Since Coyote cheated, he won everything Water Monster had, even his fur coat. When Coyote returned home, he noticed Water Monster's two babies sleeping inside the pocket of their father's fur coat. "Oh, well! I will keep these along with the coat," he said. "And I will be very careful not to say one word about them."

When Water Monster found that Coyote had taken his babies along with his coat, his heart filled with rage. "I will destroy the land in the Fourth World and all the people who live on it!" he cried. He dived to the bottom of the sea and opened up all the dams that confined the waters beneath the earth. As these waters poured into the ocean, the sea rose and began to cover the dry land. As more and more water filled the ocean bed, more and more water washed upon the land in angry black waves. Higher and higher the waves stretched, until they formed a wall of water as tall as the highest mountains.

Turkey, who was a pet of First Man and First Woman, was the first to discover the invading flood. When people heard his story, they prepared to leave their homes and head for the high mountains to the west. The people were sad to leave their rich crops, but they had no choice.

Most of the Navajo, the Hopi, the Zuñi, the Acoma, the Apache, the Ute, and the Plains Indians gathered a supply of food and necessary items and headed for the mountains. At the head of the procession was Coyote, who had Water Monster's children, along with many other possessions, in a great bag. By the time the last people reached the mountaintop, the land below them had completely disappeared under a great flood. Those who remained behind turned into water people, such as fish and seals.

Once the people had gathered on the mountain peak, one wise man from each of the thirty-two clans of the Navajo stood in a circle, and each of them planted a bamboo seed. For four days and nights the medicine men prayed for a quick, strong growth of bamboo. When the dawn of the fifth day arrived, the bamboo plants had joined together to form one huge, high, hollow, stalk-like tree. The people carved a door in the eastern side of the tree, and one by one went inside, using ladders they and Spider had made to climb higher and higher.

Turkey was the very last to reach the mountaintop. He had stopped to gather some of each kind of seed, which he buried in his feathers. White, blue, yellow, red, and multicolored corn, black and white beans, squash, melon, pumpkin, tobacco, and sunflower seeds were among them. As Turkey waddled up the trail, the black waters were angrily rushing upon him. Their foam brushed the tip of his tail as First Boy grabbed his head and pulled him inside the bamboo tree, and the marks of that foam remain on Turkey's tail feathers to this day.

Inside the tree, the people remained safe and dry. They showed First Woman the treasures they had brought from their homes in the Fourth World. Together they had collected everything they would need to begin life anew once the flood waters had receded. Only Turkey had remembered to bring the seeds of all the foods they ate, although these were the most important of all. The people honored Turkey for his good sense, and they honor him still.

As the black waters continued to swirl angrily around the great bamboo tree, rising higher and higher, the people climbed higher and higher inside the reed. Locust was the first to leave the bamboo stalk. He made a hole in the sky and won the island he found in the Fifth World for the peoples of the Fourth World. One by one the small animals entered the upper world, each using the treasures he or she had brought to make that world a better place. Badger, with a little help from Coyote, enlarged the tunnel so the creatures who were larger in size could also climb into the upper world.

So it came to pass that the last of the peoples of the Fourth World traveled up the tunnel into the Fifth World. The large animals were followed by the Hopi, the Zuñi, and the other Pueblo people. The Apaches and the Plains Indians followed them. Finally the thirty-two Navajo clans emerged from the tunnel. First Woman was the last to leave. She brought Spider's ladder and the sacred eagle feathers. "From this time forth," she announced to her people, "we women will wear eagle feathers on our sacred headdresses, and we shall do the weaving for our people."

Even in the new land, the flood was still a threat. The angry waters continued to rise, and a lake began to form at the top of the tunnel. "Water Monster must be angry with us for some reason. Only he could create a flood as great as this!" First Woman exclaimed. "We had better find out what is wrong, or we shall all drown!"

"I am certain Coyote is to blame for our problem," First Man said. "Everywhere he goes, he wears a fur coat that is not even his. Let us search his possessions."

First Woman and First Man discovered Water Monster's babies in the fur coat Coyote had won. "Look here!" First Woman exclaimed. "Coyote has Water Monster's two babies. No wonder Water Monster is punishing us with a great flood! We must return his children to him at once!"

First Man and First Woman placed Water Monster's coat, with his babies in the pocket, into a boat and sent the boat out into the lake. When the boat came near a large blue bubble floating in the middle of the lake, the bubble suddenly burst and the boat, coat, and babies disappeared. Water Monster never troubled the people again.

Introducing **Ahaiyuta and the Cloud-Eater**

Historical Background

The Zuñi nation has lived in the New Mexico desert for 800 years. Francisco de Coronado discovered the first of the Zuñi's seven pueblo communities in 1540 while searching for the fabled Seven Cities of Cíbola and their gold. However, he found that their only gold was corn.

Today, Zuñi is the largest Pueblo nation, with a population of 7,000. A huge five-story pueblo near Gallup,

New Mexico, houses approximately 2,500 of the Zuñi people.

The Zuñi have a long, peaceful history and live today much as they have lived for centuries. By having little contact with outsiders, they have remained a closely knit society in which traditions continue to be very important. They are a nation of farmers, raising corn without irrigation as their ancestors did before them. Their religious ceremonies follow the agricultural year, with planting and harvesting being major occasions. They are known for beautiful jewelry, pottery, and kachina dolls, which were originally created to teach their children to recognize the numerous national spirits.

Appeal and Value

The Zuñi myth is similar to the fertility myths of many other cultures, in that a godlike being performs the heroic task of restoring fertility to the land of his people. The myth reflects the constant threat of drought in the southwestern part of the United States. Like many other Native American peoples, the Zuñi depend on their corn crop for survival. Since sunshine is more frequent than rain, rain is the subject of both myth and ritual dances.

Many Native American peoples recognize a kinship among all living creatures and treat animals with great respect. The relationship between Ahaiyuta and the gopher reflects this attitude. Often those aspects of nature that are feared are personified as monsters or as giants. Thus, in this myth, the lack of rain is caused by a gigantic monster.

In other versions of this myth, in-stead of being one boy, the Ahaiyuta are a pair of twin brothers who participate in adventures together as if they are one person. Like other traditional heroes, these twins had an unusual birth. Two Zuñi warrior gods asked their father, the sun, for two more warrior-gods to help them. The sun obliged by causing a great rainstorm, which transformed a mountain waterfall into a larger, joyful cascade. When the Sun Father embraced the cascade, called Laughing Water, the twin boys emerged from their mother's foam.

In Zuñi mythology, the boys are called by alternate titles, depending on the nature of their adventures. In times of war, they are known as the "diminutive gods of war." In times of peace, they are called the Ahaiyuta. This myth is part of a peace-time cycle in which the Ahaiyuta destroy a series of monsters who create problems for their people.

The major Zuñi myths, including those of the Ahaiyuta, are recorded in Matilda Coxe Stevenson's The Zuni Indians, published in 1904, and in Ruth Benedict's Zuni Mythology, published in 1935. Benedict includes every Zuñi myth recorded from 1884 to her date of publication.

Ahaiyuta and the Cloud-Eater

Long, long ago, the monster Cloud-Eater lived in a great mountain in the east. He had an endless appetite for clouds, so each morning he stood on the peak of his mountain, opened his gigantic mouth, and swallowed each cloud that appeared upon the horizon. Without clouds rain did not fall, and soon the land suffered from a severe drought.

Day after day the sun shone in a cloudless sky, baking the land with its intense heat. The corn in the fields shriveled and died, and the animals and people began to suffer from lack of food. Even those who had stored food soon ate what they had saved. When months passed and still the rains did not come, the people knew that they would survive only if someone could kill Cloud-Eater.

Ahaiyuta lived with his grandmother far to the west on Corn Mountain. He was as strong as his father, the sun, and as fast as a deer. When Ahaiyuta heard his grandmother complain about the drought that Cloud-Eater was causing, he said to her, "I shall go to that great mountain in the east and slay Cloud-Eater. Then the nourishing rains will come, and our people will be well and happy."

"Be careful!" his grandmother advised. "Cloud-Eater is a dangerous enemy. Even the bravest and strongest warriors have been powerless against him."

Ahaiyuta chose his largest bow and his longest arrows. As he said farewell to his grandmother, she said, "Take these four feathers and guard them well, for they are great treasures. The red feather will lead you along the right path. The blue feather will let you talk with all the animals. The yellow feather will let you make yourself as small as the tiniest creature. The black feather will give you the strength you need to do the tasks you have set out to do."

Ahaiyuta put three of the feathers into his pocket and placed the red feather in his hair. Then he thanked his grandmother and set out toward the east. He walked and walked and walked. The land was as parched as his grandmother had said. Where once corn had stood straight, tall, and green in the fields, now only brown, curled stems lay collapsed and shriveled upon the cracked earth. The land was silent. The birds were too hungry to chirp, and the animals were too weak to run about in a futile search for food.

As the sun beat relentlessly down upon his head, Ahaiyuta grew thirsty, hungry, and tired. After a long period of emptiness and silence, he was surprised to come upon a gopher standing beside its hole. He immediately put both the blue feather and the yellow feather into his hair and shrank down to the size of the gopher.

"You are strong and brave to be wandering about in this great heat! And you certainly possess marvelous powers!" the gopher exclaimed. "Where are you going?"

When Ahaiyuta explained his mission, the gopher said, "Come into my hole, and you can take my underground passageways to Cloud-Eater's mountain. You will find food and water along the way, and I will lead you to the monster."

The gopher tunneled his way first through the earth and then through Cloud-Eater's mountain until they could hear the sleeping monster breathing deeply below them. The gopher broke through the dirt and began to gnaw the fur away from the monster's heart.

Cloud-Eater opened his eyes, saw the little gopher, and sleepily growled, "What do you think you are doing here?"

"Peace, peace, Grandfather," the gopher replied. "I have just taken a few hairs for my nest. You will hardly miss them!" Then, quick as a deer, he scampered back up his tunnel.

Once he had rejoined Ahaiyuta, the gopher whispered, "Quickly, before the monster wakes fully, take your bow down my tunnel and shoot your arrows into his heart! The tunnel leads directly to his heart, and I have gnawed away the fur that covers it. You should be able to kill him with your first arrow."

Ahaiyuta placed his black feather in his hair, walked to the end of the tunnel, raised his bow, set an arrow on the string, and carefully aimed at the monster's heart. The bowstring was still humming when Cloud-Eater gave a roar that echoed throughout the mountain and made the earth tremble. Dirt and rocks crashed around them as the monster thrashed this way and that. Finally all was silent. "Cloud-Eater has eaten his last cloud!" Ahaiyuta exclaimed. "Now the rains will surely come!"

When the monster's body lay lifeless and still, Ahaiyuta retrieved his arrow and let the gopher lead him back toward the tunnel entrance. As Ahaiyuta emerged, he saw that a heavy layer of dark clouds now obscured the sun.

He had barely begun his journey back toward Corn Mountain and his grandmother when great drops of rain began to splatter upon him. Faster and faster they fell, until the path Ahaiyuta trod became a stream of rushing water. Everywhere about him the hungry earth was gurgling with delight as the moisture quenched its great thirst.

Ahaiyuta grinned with delight. He had accomplished what he had set out to do. He had saved his people, and he would be known as a great hero.

Introducing **Lodge-Boy and Thrown-Away**

Historical Background

The Native Americans known as the Crow are related to the Sioux. They traveled northwest into the Plains States sometime between A.D. 1200 and 1600. Originally they lived in small villages and farmed the land. The buffalo was not a major source of food at that time because it was so large and fast. However, after 1598, when the first Spanish colonists brought horses to New Mexico, the Crow way of life changed. The Spaniards traded their horses in exchange for peace with the Plains peoples, and a man on horseback could kill a buffalo. Native Americans measured wealth by their supply of food, and the buffalo made those who lived on the Northern Plains among the wealthiest native peoples in North America. Today, many of the Crow continue to live in southern Montana and to speak their native language.

Appeal and Value

Lodge-Boy and Thrown-Away are traditional heroes in that they perform many tasks to make their community safer. Like all other heroes, they possess courage and skill. They also use their creative intelligence to compensate for their small size. They fit the heroic pattern of an unusual birth.

What is most unusual and appealing about this myth is the fact that the heroes are young boys. Like ordinary boys their age, they cannot resist attempting anything their father tells them not to do.

The nature of these heroes and their adventures has probably contrib- uted to the popularity of this myth, which exists in various but similar versions among the Native Americans who inhabited the Northern Plains. Stephen Chapman Simms included the following version in *Traditions of the Crows*, which was published in 1903.

Lodge-Boy and Thrown-Away

One day while her husband was away on a hunt, a pregnant woman was murdered. The murderer cut open the victim, removed twin sons, and disposed of them separately. The murderer threw one behind the curtain in the tepee and the other into the spring.

The husband of the murdered woman returned home. As he sat eating dinner alone, his son Lodge-Boy, who had grown into a young boy, came out from be- hind the curtain and joined him. Thereafter, each day the father went out hunt- ing, and each evening he returned to have dinner with his son.

One night Lodge-Boy said, "Father, I would like you to make me two bows and two sets of arrows."

His father made them and then hid to see how his son used the weapons. When he found Lodge-Boy playing with another boy of the same age, the father said, "Have your friend come and live with us!"

Lodge-Boy replied, "I will try to do that if you will make me a rawhide set of clothing. My friend lives in the spring and has the sharp teeth of an otter. Catch- ing him will be difficult!"

The first day Lodge-Boy wore the rawhide suit, he enticed his brother, Thrown-Away, out of the spring by suggesting a game with the bows and arrows. In the course of an argument over the score, Lodge-Boy captured Thrown-Away and held him until their father arrived. Thrown-Away tried to bite Lodge-Boy, and the water in the spring flooded the land to aid him, but Lodge-Boy and their father were too strong. They carried Thrown-Away to the crest of a nearby hill, burned incense under his nose, and turned him into a human being. From that time on, both sons lived in the tepee with their father.

One day the boys decided to go to their mother's burial place and revive her. When they said, "Mother, your hide chest and your stone pot are both falling!" she sat up. When they said, "Mother, your bone crusher is falling!" she began to fix her hair. Then, she exclaimed, "I have been sleeping a long time!" She stood up and returned home with her sons.

Another day the father said to his sons, "You may play wherever you wish, but do not go near the old woman who lives at the bend in the river. Whenever she sees a living creature, she tips her pot of boiling liquid in its direction. The creature is then pulled into her pot and boiled for her dinner."

The boys immediately went to the bend in the river, found the old woman asleep by her boiling pot, tilted the pot toward her, and watched as she was pulled into her own pot and boiled to death. They brought the pot home as a gift for their mother.

One day the father said to his sons, "You may play wherever you wish, but do not go over the hill."

The boys immediately went over the hill, where they found a huge serpent that resembled an alligator. The serpent opened its enormous mouth and swallowed the boys, and they found many other people inside. Some were dying, and some were already dead. The boys killed the serpent by cutting out its heart. Then they sliced open a passageway between its ribs, helped those who were still alive to escape, took a piece of the serpent's heart for their father, and returned home.

Another day the father said to his sons, "You may play wherever you wish, but do not go near the three trees that stand in the form of a triangle. They bend their branches to the ground and kill whatever comes beneath them!"

The boys immediately found the three trees. They ran toward them as if seeking the shade beneath their branches, but then they stopped short. The trees, expecting two victims, sent their branches crashing to the ground. The boys jumped on the bent branches and broke them so that they could never again rise and kill anyone.

One day the father said to his sons, "You may play wherever you wish, but do not go near the man who lives on top of the cliff with deep water at its base. He pushes anyone who comes near him over the cliff to become a meal for his father, who lives in the deep water!"

The boys immediately headed for the clifftop. As the man rushed toward them, the boys suddenly fell to the ground. The man could not stop running in time and fell off the cliff to become a meal for his father.

Another day the father said to his sons, "You may play wherever you wish, but do not go near the man who wears fiery moccasins. Whenever he wants anything, he walks upon it and burns it!"

The boys found the man and waited until he was asleep. They quietly stole his moccasins, and each boy put on one of them. Then they jumped on him, burned him to ashes, and carried the moccasins home.

One day as the brothers were walking, they felt themselves being lifted up and transported to the high peak of a mountain that rose out of a large lake. There they found themselves face to face with Thunder-Bird, who said, "I need your help. A great otter who lives in the lake below us eats all the young I produce. Please kill it for me!"

The boys prepared to kill the otter. First they made many arrows. Then they went down to the shore, built a fire, and heated many rocks. When the otter approached they shot their arrows into its open mouth, but the animal kept coming. They waited until it was within close range and then threw their hot rocks into its open mouth, killing it. Thunder-Bird thanked them and transported them back to their tepee, where they continued to live happily for many more years.

Introducing **The Woman Who Fell from the Sky**

Historical Background

The five Iroquois-speaking nations were, from east to west, the Mohawk (on the Atlantic coast), the Oneida, the Onondaga, the Cayuga (in central New York), and the Seneca (in the Lake Erie area). The Iroquois earned lasting fame by creating a great political organization, called the League of the Iroquois or the Confederacy of the Five Nations, in 1452. In its time, the League was more democratic than any other form of government, and it existed for more than 300 years. In fact, the League was such an impressive political structure that it influenced the formulation of the United States Constitution.

The fathers of the Iroquois League were Hiawatha, an Onondaga chief, and Deganawida, a Huron, each of whom had been adopted by the Mohawk nation. Organizing the League took political talent. The Onondaga joined on the condition that they would chair the council. Deganawida persuaded the fifth nation, the Seneca, to join by telling them to watch the sun when their corn became knee-high. They joined when, following his advice, they witnessed a total solar eclipse. The League enlarged to six nations in 1722, when the Tuscarora, an Iroquois nation that was then living in North Carolina, was admitted.

The Iroquois League was designed to facilitate equality, peace, and prosperity among its member nations. It was only concerned with the issue of war. The members decided that war could not occur without a unanimous vote, and that all the member nations would fight together on the same side. This agreement was a particularly great accomplishment since the major way to achieve honor, fame, and glory was through war.

The League was run by fifty sachems or clan leaders, who had been nominated by women of noble rank in their nation and had been approved by their own nation's council. Each nation had proportional representation in the council. A second group of representatives, leaders who were called Pine Trees, could speak but not vote.

The Iroquois lived in stockaded villages that were organized according to matrilineal lines. All property was inherited through the mother. The women owned the houses in which they lived, taking their husbands in to live with them as visitors. The male head of the family was the brother of the oldest sister. Sisters and daughters lived in the same longhouse, which was large enough to house eight to ten families.

The women also owned the land and farmed their family's fields. They grew corn, squash, and beans. The Iroquois called the three crops the Three Sisters, believing that the crops were guarded by three spirit sisters.

In 1614, the Dutch navigated the Hudson River and built Fort Orange where Albany, New York, is located. The Iroquois traded beaver furs for Dutch guns and became wealthy and powerful. However, by the mid-1600s, they had exhausted the local beaver supply. In order to acquire the furs they needed to continue their trade, the Iroquois moved west and, in 1648, conquered the Huron, who also spoke the Iroquois language.

The Revolutionary War destroyed the Iroquois League by dividing the nations. The Mohawk, Seneca, Cayuga, and Onondaga peoples supported the British, while the Oneida and Tuscarora peoples supported the Americans. Consequently, in January 1777, the League's great council fire was extinguished in a formal ceremony.

In the years after the war, many of the Iroquois were given the land near Brantford, Ontario, that is known as the Six Nations Reserve. Today, more than 7,000 Iroquois live in that area. In the United States, most of the Oneida moved to Wisconsin in 1832, and most of the Seneca moved to Oklahoma.

The Iroquois council fire was rekindled in the l960s. As of 1971, the six nations were located on six reservations and had formed a modern republic. Many Iroquois continue to live within the Iroquois tradition, adhering to the values of their people and participating in longhouse ceremonies under the leadership of one of their chiefs.

The Huron, who call themselves the Wendat, were originally a confederation of four nations, numbering between 45,000 and 60,000 people when the Europeans first encountered them. The Huron lived in Ontario in large villages of from 4,000 to 6,000 people until the Iroquois destroyed most of them in 1648. The Huron took the side of the British in the Revolutionary War. Since 1867, many of them have lived in Oklahoma.

Appeal and Value

The special relationship between a divine grandparent and grandchild and the adventures of twin brothers are both common themes in mythology. When one twin is good and the other is evil, the twins can be viewed as representing the capability of any one human being to be both kind and cruel.

The Iroquois creation myth is remarkably similar from one Iroquois-speaking nation to another. One of the oldest versions was recorded by David Cusick, a Tuscarora Iroquois historian, whose *Sketches of Ancient History of the Six Nations* was first published in 1827. The oldest Huron version was related, in 1874, by a seventy-five-year-old Huron sub-chief, who had heard it as a child from those who had been alive in the mid-18th century. It appears as part of Horatio Hale's "Huron Folklore," published in 1888. J. N. B. Hewitt, an important mythographer of Tuscarora descent, specialized in the Iroquois creation myth and collected detailed Mohawk, Seneca, and Onondaga versions for the Bureau of American Ethnology.

The Woman Who Fell from the Sky

When time was young, there were two worlds, the upper world and the lower world. Divine Sky People lived in the upper world. Great Water covered the earth in the lower world, and there the only living beings were the animals who knew how to swim. Great Darkness covered everything between Great Water and the upper world.

In the upper world, the Sky People had a great chief, who had a lovely daughter named Atahensic. It came to pass that the goddess Atahensic became very ill with a strange disease. The medicine man tried one remedy after another, but nothing would make her well.

A great corn tree stood near the chief's lodge and provided the Sky People with their principal food. It came to pass that a Sky Person dreamed that the goddess would be cured if the chief placed her on the ground by this tree and then dug up the great tree by its roots.

To the chief, the welfare of his daughter was more important than the welfare of his nation. Consequently, as soon as the chief heard the Sky Person's dream, he decided to follow its prescription without delay. He placed Atahensic beside the great corn tree and directed other Sky People to dig the earth away from its roots. The great tree soon toppled to the ground with a thunderous crash.

Alarmed by the terrifying sound, another Sky Person — a young man — ran toward the great corn tree and was horrified to see that it had been uprooted. It was clear that the chief had committed an outrageous act! The young man turned to his chief and unleashed his fury. "You have no right to destroy this tree!" he exclaimed. "Without its fruit, we will all die of starvation! Even the life of a chief's daughter is not that important!"

The removal of the corn tree's roots had left a large hole in the ground. The young man was so enraged that, before the chief could stop him, he kicked Atahensic into that hole.

Down, down, down the goddess fell, through the hole that formed a tunnel from the world above into the dark world below.

Loon was the first to see the glow that marked the fall of the goddess, and he decided to rescue her. He called out to the other water animals, "Look! Sky Woman is falling into our world! She needs our help, or she will drown!"

Loon caught Atahensic on his wings and then slowly descended with her to the Great Water on which he lived. Meanwhile, many of the animals wished to do their part to save Sky Woman's life, so they gathered together and made a raft of their bodies on which she could rest.

Sky Woman landed safely, and the animal raft was able to support her. However, the animals could not live forever in the form of a raft, and Sky Woman could not live forever upon their backs. The animals needed to rest, and the goddess needed to move about. So it came to pass that the water animals who were forming the raft said, "We must come up with a better plan to care for Sky Woman! We are all tired out! Do any of you have a good idea?"

Great Turtle was the first to volunteer. "Place her upon my back," he directed. "Mine is larger and stronger than all of yours put together!"

Once they had done this, Muskrat said, "That's all well and good, for now! But Sky Woman will surely die unless we can create a bed of earth upon which she can live. It will have to be large enough for her to be able to walk happily during the day and to sleep comfortably at night."

"I agree," Great Turtle said. "Those of you who think that you can do it should dive down to the bottom of Great Water, bite off a piece of the earth that you find there, and carry it back up here in your mouth."

It came to pass that Muskrat was the first to muster the courage necessary to make the deep dive. He was followed by Beaver, and then by Otter.

Beaver was the first to return alive. He was very tired and very short of breath, but when Great Turtle looked inside his mouth, he could find no earth. Otter returned quite a while after Beaver. He was more tired and more short of breath, but when Great Turtle looked inside his mouth, he could find no earth.

By this time, all of the water animals had become very worried about Muskrat, who had not yet returned from the deep. While they were discussing what to do, Muskrat's body suddenly reappeared on the surface of the water. He was dead. However, Muskrat had been as skillful as he was courageous, for clutched in his claws and lodged inside his mouth was earth from the bottom of the sea.

Great Turtle gave the earth to Sky Woman, who spread it carefully around the edges of Great Turtle's shell and the more earth she spread, the larger grew Great Turtle's shell and the more earth there was to spread. In fact, the earth continued to grow broader and deeper until it formed an enormous expanse of dry land, called Great Island. And from that day to this, Great Island has rested upon Great Turtle's shell.

It came to pass that on Great Island the goddess Atahensic recovered from her strange disease, just as the dreamer had dreamed she would. Sky Woman now built herself an earth lodge and, despite the eternal darkness, she lived happily with the water animals for neighbors. In time, she gave birth to a baby girl, who became known as Earth Woman.

It came to pass that one day, as Earth Woman was digging the wild potatoes that grew in the dirt of Great Island, she inadvertently forgot to face the west and, instead, faced the east. Not long after that, Earth Woman found that she had become pregnant. West Wind had blown into her body and had impregnated her.

Just as her birth pangs were beginning, Earth Woman heard the twin sons within her body angrily arguing about when and how to be born. Evil Twin, who was bold and selfish, was determined to emerge first, from his mother's armpit. Good Twin, who was gentle and unselfish, was content to emerge second, in the usual way. So it came to pass that, while Good Twin was being born, Evil Twin impatiently burst forth from their mother's side, thereby causing her death.

Sky Woman buried Earth Woman on Great Island and reared her twin grandchildren by herself. Good Twin was her favorite. She had no love for Evil Twin, whom she blamed for the death of her daughter. Every day, she would sit by Earth Woman's grave and weep over her.

It came to pass that, in time, Good Twin became tired of living in eternal darkness. He told his brother, "I want to create a great light that will illuminate our world."

"Don't be absurd!" Evil Twin replied. "Our world is good enough as it is! Leave it alone!"

Despite his brother's opinion, Good Twin was determined to live in a bright world. Therefore, from his dead mother's face, he fashioned a brilliant sphere, which he tossed high into Great Darkness to shine upon Great Island each day. From the back of his mother's head, Good Twin then fashioned a smaller sphere and many tiny spheres, which he also tossed high into Great Darkness to shine upon Great Island each night. So it came to pass that Great Island and Great Water enjoyed Sun, Moon, and Stars, and with them, Day and Night.

It then came to pass that, nourished both by Sky Woman's tears and by Sun, the Three Sisters began to push through the earth that covered Earth Woman's body — the squash vine from what remained of Earth Woman's head, corn plants from her chest, and bean plants from her arms and legs. Good Twin loved these plants, and so he asked Thunder to provide the rain that they would need in order to flourish.

In their own time, the twin boys grew to become young men. They continued to have different personalities and different opinions. However, they agreed that the time had come to prepare Great Island for the Eagwehoewe people, who would soon live on it. They planned to start out together, to spend the day apart from each other, and to meet at their lodge, as usual, that night. When they separated, Evil Twin would walk toward the west, while Good Twin would walk toward the east. And, as they walked, each would create such things as lakes, forests, plants, and animals. Then, during the next two days, each brother would take the other to see what he had created.

So it came to pass that as Good Twin walked toward the east, he would reach down to the earth at his feet, pick up a handful of dirt, and toss it. Sometimes he tossed it in front of him; other times he tossed it behind him. Sometimes he tossed it to the right of him; other times he tossed it to the left of him. Sometimes he tossed it on the ground; other times he tossed it into the air. However, no matter where Good Twin tossed his handful of dirt, living plants or animals came into being. Meanwhile, wherever Good Twin had placed his feet, maple trees began to grow.

Still determined to be the first in everything, Evil Twin, whose Iroquois name means "like flint," was the first to show off his creations. Unlike Good Twin, he possessed an evil imagination and enjoyed creating mischief. Consequently, he had created a range of mountains on his part of Great Island. It was difficult to walk there because of all the rocks underfoot and the many treacherous ledges.

As they traveled, Good Twin was annoyed by the company of Mosquito, who was as large as Turkey. Finally, Good Twin told him to run away. Mosquito then ran toward a young tree, stuck his sharp, pointed nose into the slender trunk, and caused the tree to fall to the ground.

"You can't do that, Mosquito!" Good Twin exclaimed. "The Eagwehoewe people are soon going to live on Great Island, and if this is what you do to a tree,

I can see what you will do to them! They are much weaker than a tree, and they will surely die from the thrust of your nose!"

With these words, Good Twin grabbed Mosquito and rubbed him between his hands until he had become very small. Then he opened his hands and blew Mosquito away. From that day to this, Mosquito has remained just as Good Twin changed him.

In the course of their walk, Evil Twin also showed Good Twin the fierce animals that he had made: Bear, Wolf, and Panther, as well as Fox, Porcupine, Raccoon, and Snake. These animals were all much larger than they are today.

Good Twin looked at these huge predators and exclaimed, "What have you done, Brother? The Eagwehoewe people are soon going to live on Great Island, and these fierce animals will surely kill them!"

Good Twin did not have the power to undo what his brother had created, but he was able to make each animal smaller, so that the Eagwehoewe people could hunt and trap them for their skin and their meat. It was then that Good Twin spied Partridge, whom he had created, but who was now on Evil Twin's land.

"What are you doing here, Partridge?" Good Twin asked him.

"Toad came onto our land and drank up all the water," Partridge replied. "I have heard that if there is any water left, I will only find it here in the land of Flint!"

"Where is Toad?" Good Twin asked his brother.

"I was just about to show him to you," Evil Twin replied. "Of all the animals that I have created, I love him the best! I have fashioned him to be so thirsty that he will drink every drop of fresh water on Great Island."

When Good Twin found Toad, he took one look at his bulging body and shot an arrow into his neck. Suddenly all of Great Island's fresh waters poured forth in a great waterfall that ran off in different directions as the first rivers.

Good Twin was quick to divide each river down the middle so that half the water flowed in one direction and half flowed in the other. "I want one side of every river always to flow downstream," he explained to his brother. "Then the Eagwehoewe people will not have to work at paddling their canoes. Instead, they can float with the current!"

"I can't let you do this!" Evil Twin exclaimed. "The Eagwehoewe people will have to work for whatever they get!" And, with these words, Evil Twin changed all of his brother's rivers so that their waters flowed in only one direction. Moreover, he was not satisfied until he had placed waterfalls, whirlpools, and rapids in many places on each of them. From that day to this, the rivers have remained just as Evil Twin changed them.

Evil Twin was very angry that Good Twin had changed the animals, reptiles, and insects that he had created, but he did not say anything aloud. However, to himself he said, "Just wait until tomorrow, Brother, when you show me what you have created! You have seen what I have done to your rivers. Tomorrow, you will see what I will do to everything else that you have made to please the Eagwehoewe people!"

The following day, the twins walked toward the east so that Good Twin could show Evil Twin the fine animals and the beautiful trees that he had created. Evil Twin was annoyed to see that the animals his brother had created—Buffalo,

Elk, Deer, Dog, Rabbit, Squirrel, and Bird—would be useful to the Eagwehoewe people. They were so fat that they would be easy to catch and good to eat.

Later, Evil Twin returned to the area. Despite their cumbersome size, he quietly gathered together all of the animals that Good Twin had created and herded them toward a great cave. Using Good Twin's food as bait, he then imprisoned them inside the cave, blocking the entrance with a huge boulder. He smiled with satisfaction as he imagined how they would all die of starvation.

However, Bird had followed Evil Twin and watched him from above. Bird then flew to Good Twin and told him what Evil Twin had done. Good Twin followed Bird as he flew through the trees in the forest until, in time, Bird led him to discover the huge boulder that blocked the entrance to the cave. Good Twin gathered all his strength and pushed aside the boulder, permitting his animals to regain their freedom.

Evil Twin also noticed that his brother had created sycamore trees that produced sweet fruits and sugar-maple trees whose syrup dripped from the branches.

Of course, Evil Twin was not at all happy with what Good Twin had done. "Brother, I see that you and I can never agree on anything!" he exclaimed. "If I let you have your way, the Eagwehoewe people will have too happy a time! However, as you are beginning to see, I don't intend to let you have your way!"

So it came to pass that Evil Twin later went about from animal to animal, shaking each one until it became smaller and thinner. From that day to this, these animals have remained just as Evil Twin changed them.

Evil Twin then turned his attention to the sycamore tree and caused its fruit to become small and of no use. He changed the sugar-maple tree's syrup to a sweet water. And from that day to this, these trees have remained just as Evil Twin changed them.

It came to pass that one night not long thereafter, Earth Woman appeared to Good Twin in a dream. "Beware of your evil brother, my son!" she exclaimed. "He will try to kill you by any means. So, meet his treachery with your own!" And with these words, she disappeared.

The next morning, Evil Twin said to his brother, "It is clear that we will never be able to get along! I am furious with you for changing my creations, and you are furious with me for changing yours. So I suggest that we fight each other for the control of Great Island. Do you agree?"

"I agree to the idea of a contest, and I agree to the prize," Good Twin replied, "but I would like to avoid violence. We should just have a race."

"I agree to that," Evil Twin replied, "but I insist that the victor will then have the right to do whatever he wishes to the loser! And you may as well know that if I win—and, of course, I will win—I will take the wind of life from you!

"So tell me," Evil Twin concluded, "what is it that can hurt you? If you will confide in me, I will confide in you!"

"I fear the wild rose," Good Twin revealed.

"And I fear Buck's horns," Evil Twin confessed.

So it came to pass that once the twins had chosen their racing path, Evil Twin collected large quantities of the wild rose bush from their grandmother, the goddess Atahensic, who had created it. He placed its branches on the trees that grew along Good Twin's side of the path, and he scattered its flowers on the path itself. Meanwhile, Good Twin wandered through the forest collecting many of Buck's horns, which he then scattered upon Evil Twin's side of the path.

Just as the sun began its morning journey, the twins began their race. Evil Twin, who was always determined to be the first in everything, was so certain that he could outrun his brother that he permitted Good Twin to start first.

Evil Twin chased Good Twin all that day, tearing up mountains and trees like a great whirlwind as he raced after him. However, whenever Good Twin became tired, he would snatch some of the wild rose and eat it, thereby recovering his energy. Evil Twin found no such respite from his own fatigue because Buck's horns were constant thorns in his feet. Therefore, Evil Twin could not catch up to his brother that day. And no matter how Evil Twin pleaded, Good Twin would not stop and permit him to rest.

The sun began its journey on the second day while Evil Twin continued to chase Good Twin, tearing up mountains and trees like a great whirlwind as he raced after him. However, whenever Good Twin became tired, he would snatch some of the wild rose and eat it, thereby recovering his energy. Evil Twin found no such respite from his own fatigue because Buck's horns were constant thorns in his feet. Therefore, Evil Twin could not catch up to his brother that day. And no matter how Evil Twin pleaded, Good Twin would not stop and permit him to rest.

The sun was ending its journey on the second day when Good Twin became the first to reach the finish line. By this time, Evil Twin felt defeated by exhaustion as well as by the constant thrust of Buck's horns. He pleaded with Good Twin to let him stop where he was and rest, but Good Twin had the right of the victor to insist that his brother finish the race. Finally, Evil Twin dragged himself to the end of the path and collapsed at Good Twin's feet.

"Don't kill me, Brother!" he pleaded.

"But, according to our agreement, that is exactly what I must do!" Good Twin exclaimed. "The idea of the contest was yours. The idea of the prize was yours. And, despite my objections, the idea of violence was yours. As the winner, I must treat you as you would have treated me if you had won!" And with these words, Good Twin picked up a branch of Buck's horns and beat his brother until the last wind of life had escaped from his body.

That night, the soul of Evil Twin came to Good Twin and said, "I would like to join you in our lodge."

"That I cannot permit you to do," Good Twin replied.

"Then, I bid you farewell, for you will never see me again!" Evil Twin exclaimed. "I shall travel far to the northwest, to the Land of the Great Silence, and there I shall wait for all among the Eagwehoewe people who die to join me. Know that, from this time forth and forever, it is I who will have power over the soul once the last wind of life leaves the body. The souls of the dead will leave Great Island and will live in my land forever." And with these words, Evil Twin left on his journey and became Evil Spirit.

Good Twin repaired the damage to the mountains and the trees that their chase had caused. Then he created the Eagwehoewe people, who would inhabit Great Island. From the dirt at his feet, he formed a male and a female figure that resembled himself and his mother. He then bent down and breathed the wind of life into their nostrils, making their souls come alive. Then Good Twin disappeared from Great Island.

First Man and First Woman loved each other, and from their union the first six pairs of the Eagwehoewe people came forth from the heart of Great Island. They all spoke the Iroquois language, and they became the ancestors of all the Eagwehoewe people.

The first pair traveled toward where the sun begins its morning journey, and they settled beside a great river. They became the parents of the Mohawk people and the keepers of the eastern door. For two and a half days, the second pair traveled toward where the sun ends its journey, and they settled beside an enormous boulder. They became the parents of the Oneida, the "upright-stone people." The third pair continued to travel toward where the sun ends its journey, and they settled on Mount Onondaga. They became the parents of the Onondaga people and the keepers of the central council fire.

The fourth pair continued to travel toward where the sun ends its journey, and they settled by a long lake from which a mountain rises like a great pipe. They became the parents of the Cayuga, the "long-pipe people." The fifth pair continued to travel toward where the sun ends its journey, and they settled along the western border of the land of the Eagwehoewe people. They became the parents of the Seneca, the "great-hill people," and the keepers of the western door. The last pair traveled toward where the sun begins its morning journey and settled on the shore of Great Water. They became the parents of the Tuscarora people.

In the beginning, the first five families resolved that from that time forth and forever, despite differences in language and in location, they, their children, and their children's children would always understand each other and would remain united. It was they who established the great Iroquois nation. In time, the sixth family joined the Iroquois League.

So it came to pass that the Eagwehoewe people inhabited Great Island just as Good Twin had known they would. And their Confederacy of the Six Nations has brought everlasting renown to their nation.

Introducing **Raven and the Sources of Light**

Historical Background

The Native American peoples known as the Haida, the Tsimshian, and the Tlingit settled along the Pacific Northwest Coast of Canada and the United States; the Haida in the Queen Charlotte Islands; the Tsimshian east of the Haida, along the coast of British Co- lumbia; and the Tlingit from the southern part of the Alaska Panhandle north to Prince William Sound, near Anchorage, Alaska. They have traditionally been among the wealthiest of all Native American peoples because they have had the most abundant food supply. This, combined with the relatively moderate climate brought by the Japanese Current, gave them the time to develop a rich cultural heritage.

These peoples are known for their striking arts and crafts, their mythological dramas, performed in masks and costumes, and their potlatch feasts, in which the host would give an incredible array of valuable gifts to his or her guests (and would receive them in turn as a guest at another potlatch). The Haida, Tsimshian, and Tlingit peoples began to carve the totem poles that have made them famous some time between 1774 and 1779, when many American and European ships sailed up the Pacific Coast, bringing them their first iron tools and great wealth from the trade in sea-otter pelts. The golden age of totem poles was between approximately 1830 and 1880.

Appeal and Value

The Haida, Tsimshian, and Tlingit peoples lived among animals of the forest, sea, and sky, and these animals provided them with both food and spiritual nourishment. The raven, the eagle, the crane, the whale, the salmon, and the bear are all familiar faces on their masks, totem poles, and carved wooden chests. In these cultures, animals are benefactors.

The role of Raven in this myth is that of animal hero and helper of human beings. In his study of the peoples of the Pacific Northwest, the anthropologist Franz Boas found forty-five principal myths about Raven. In Haida and Tlingit mythology, Raven is the bird called the raven. However, in Tsimshian mythology, Raven is the bird form of a supernatural being who often changes his shape. Raven is called Nankilslas (He Whose Voice Is Obeyed) in Haida mythology, Txamsem (Giant) in Tsimshian mythology, and Yetl (Raven) in Tlingit mythology. Moreover, depending on the particular myth, Raven may be a creator, a fertility-hero, or a trickster-hero.

The following myth combines Haida, Tsimshian, and Tlingit versions of the same myth. Although Raven is a creator, he is not a creator figure here. He brings light to the universe by taking what has already been created and placing it where it can benefit human beings. The Pacific Northwest is known for its heavy rainfall, so it is not surprising that the local Native American peoples have a myth about placing the sun in the heavens.

The major Raven myths are found in John Reed Swanton's *Haida Texts and Myths* (1905) and *Tlingit Myths and Texts* (1909), and in Franz Boas' *Tsimshian Mythology* (1916).

Raven and the Sources of Light

Long ago when the world was young, the earth and all living creatures were shrouded in the darkness of an eternal night, for neither the sun nor the moon shone in the sky. It was said that a great chief who lived at the headwaters of the Nass River was keeping all this light for himself, but no one was certain, for the light was so carefully hidden that no one had ever actually seen it. The chief knew that his people were suffering, but he was a selfish man and did not care.

Raven was sad for his people, for he knew that without the sun the earth would not bring forth the food the Haida needed to survive, and without the moon his people could not see to catch fish at night. Raven decided to rescue the light. He knew that the way from the Queen Charlotte Islands to the source of the Nass River was very long, so he collected a group of pebbles. As he flew, whenever he became tired he dropped a pebble into the sea. It immediately formed an island where Raven could alight on solid land and rest for a while.

When Raven arrived at the chief's village, he said to himself, "I must find a way to live in the chief's house and capture the light." Raven thought and thought. Finally he exclaimed, "I know just the way! I will change myself into something very small and wait in the stream to be caught."

So Raven transformed himself into a seed and floated on the surface of the nearby stream. When the chief's daughter came to draw water, Raven was ready. No matter how she tried to drink some of the water, the seed was always in her way. Finally she tired of trying to remove it, and she drank it along with the water.

The woman became pregnant, and in time she gave birth to a son, who was Raven in disguise. The chief loved his grandson, and whatever the child wanted, his grandfather gave him.

As the boy crawled, he noticed many bags hanging on the walls of the lodge. One by one he pointed to them, and one by one his grandfather gave them to him. Finally his grandfather gave him the bag that was filled with stars. The child rolled the bag around on the floor of the lodge, then suddenly let go of it. The bag immediately rose to the ceiling, drifted through the smoke hole, and flew up into the heavens. There it burst open, spilling the stars into the sky.

As the days passed, the boy still wanted to play with toys. He pointed to this bag and that box, stored here and there in his grandfather's lodge. His grandfather gave him whatever he chose.

Finally the child cried, "Mae! Mae!" His grandfather took down a bag containing the moon and gave it to his grandson as a toy. The boy chuckled with delight as he rolled it around and around upon the floor of the lodge. Suddenly he let go of that bag just as he had let go of the bag of stars. The bag immediately rose to the ceiling, drifted through the smoke hole, and flew up into the heavens. There it burst open, spilling the moon into the sky.

The boy continued to play with bag after bag and box after box until one day he pointed to the last box left in the lodge. His grandfather took him upon his lap and said, "When I open this box, I am giving you the last and dearest of my possessions, the sun. Please take care of it!"

Then the chief closed the smoke hole and picked up the large wooden box he had kept hidden among other boxes in the shadows of one corner of the lodge. Inside the large box a second wooden box nestled in the wrappings of a spider's web, and inside that box, a third wooden box nestled. The chief opened box after box until he came to the eighth and smallest of the wooden boxes. As soon as the chief removed the sun from this box, his lodging was flooded with a brilliant light.

The child laughed with delight as his grandfather gave him the fiery ball to play with. He rolled the sun around the floor of the lodging until he tired of the game and pushed it aside. His grandfather then replaced the sun in its box and replaced the box inside the other seven boxes.

Day after day Raven and his grandfather repeated this process. Raven would point to the sun's box, play with it until he tired of it, and then watch as his grandfather put the fiery ball away into its series of boxes.

Finally the day came when the chief was not as careful as usual. He forgot to close the smoke hole, and he no longer watched Raven play with the fiery ball. The child resumed his Raven shape, grasped the ball of light in his claws, and flew up through the smoke hole into the sky, traveling in the direction of the river.

When he spied people fishing in the dark, he alighted on a tree and said to them, "If you will give me some fish, I will give you some light."

At first they did not believe him. They knew that the light was well hidden and that Raven was often a lazy trickster. However, when Raven raised his wing and showed enough light for them to fish with ease, they gave him part of their catch. Day after day they repeated this procedure, until Raven tired of eating fish.

Finally he lifted his wing, grabbed the sun with both claws and tossed it high into the sky. "Now my people will have light both day and night!" he exclaimed. And from that day until this, the sun, moon, and stars have remained in the sky.

Introducing **Sedna**

Historical Background

Ten thousand years ago, the ancestors of the Arctic peoples crossed the land bridge from Siberia to Alaska that today is known as the Bering Strait. Calling themselves the *Inuit* (the human beings), they remained in Alaska for about 5,000 years and then began to move east across the Arctic, finally establishing themselves across a 12,000-mile area that extends from eastern Siberia to lands east of Greenland. It was the neighboring Abnaki people who first called the Inuit by the name of *Eskimo*, an Algonquian term that means "eater of raw meat."

Although the Inuit have lived in Alaska for thousands of years, the Thule culture that identifies them is only about 1,000 years old. It includes the use of dogsleds and boats made of animal skins. The Thule culture offered such great advantages over the previous way of life that, in less than 400 years, it spread to all the Inuit communities from Alaska to Greenland.

The Inuit, now numbering about 100,000, continue to live along the coasts of harsh lands, where the waterways are solid ice for all but the two summer months of each year. Those who live in small, isolated communities continue to live a traditional Inuit life as a society of hunters, and their life continues to focus on the annual cycle of procuring food. They hunt land animals, such as the caribou, and sea animals, such as the seal, and continue to rely upon these animals for food, clothing, and materials for their tents. However, today, supply boats bring modern food, clothing, building mate-rials, rifles, outboard motors, and videotapes to large and small Inuit communities in the Canadian Arctic and Greenland. Many Inuit families use motor boats and snowmobiles, although dogsleds continue to be of major inportance in Greenland because of its mountainous terrain.

Some Inuit peoples no longer live in the traditional manner. In Alaska, members of the Inuit community have taken leading roles in the state's economic and political organizations. In Greenland, good Inuit students may choose to pursue higher education in Denmark. Many Inuit work in the radar warning stations and air bases that span the Arctic from Alaska to Greenland.

Appeal and Value

The myth of Sedna (She Down There) has been found among Inuit peoples across the Arctic. It is part of the oral tradition of a hunting people and thus reveals values that are important in the traditional Inuit culture. The Sedna myth reveals Inuit attitudes toward the relationship between men and women and reflects the harsh world in which the Inuit live. It also reflects the Inuit peoples' intense focus on the need to acquire food, the importance of land and sea animals to this hardy people, and their preoccupation with the need

for balance and harmony as they interact with the natural world.

Sedna is one of the most powerful deities in mythology. She is the sole focus of Inuit myth and religious ritual and the supreme ruler of the Inuit supernatural world. She functions as the divine intermediary between the Inuit people and the animals (Sedna's children) that the Inuit need in order to survive.

Because she has been mistreated, Sedna is a hostile goddess, and she needs to be ritually appeased in order for the society to thrive. Sedna punishes her people by withholding their food supply whenever she feels that she has been insulted. Consequently, the Sedna myth reflects the Inuit need for taboos and, equally important, it sets forth rituals designed to appease Sedna and restore order whenever those taboos have been violated. These taboos and rituals enabled the traditional Inuit society to operate in an orderly and productive manner.

The Sedna myth also reveals the importance of the shaman, or medicine man, in Inuit society. In the eastern Arctic regions, the shaman must go into a trance that permits him, symbolically, to visit the goddess in her home beneath the sea in order to convince her to release her children — the animals on which the Inuit depend for food — for the well-being of the Inuit community. This ritual reflects the confidence of the Inuit people in their shaman's ability to increase their food supply when land and sea animals are scarce.

Today, some Inuit peoples continue to perform their traditional winter dances in which masked dancers enact their society's major myths. One such dance involves a woman named

Ooyalu (the flinty-hearted, or the contrary woman), who rejects the many men who attempt to court her and is punished by being carried off by a monster.

Inuit myths were recorded by Franz Boas in the late 1800s and early 1900s, and by Knud Rasmussen in the early 1920s. The most famous version of the Sedna myth was originally told to Franz Boas in 1884–1885 by the Oqomiut and the Akudnirmiut people of southern Baffin Island, in Canada, shortly before Anglican missionaries converted those communities to Christianity. Franz Boas recorded this material in *The Central Eskimo*, published in 1888.

Sedna

Long ago, an Inuit man lived alone with his daughter, Sedna, in a skin-covered tent on the shore of their lonely land. Sedna grew to be a beautiful maiden whom many young men wished to marry. However, no matter who approached her father and asked for her hand, he was not appealing to Sedna, and she refused to marry him.

Meanwhile, in another land across the water, a proud seabird — a stormy petrel or a fulmar — looked upon the female birds in his community with disdain and decided, instead, to choose a human wife from among the Inuit people. He flew over one Inuit household after another until he found the woman of his choice. Then, he set about preparing for his conquest. He fashioned a striking sealskin parka to adorn his human form, and he built a swift kayak for his long journey.

Once the warm winds of spring caused the ice to break up, the bird-man kayaked to Sedna's homeland. He wore his magnificent parka because he was going to woo the most beautiful Inuit maiden to become his wife.

As he expected, the bird-man found Sedna by the shore of the sea, busily working at her tasks. Without beaching his kayak, he attracted Sedna's interest by calling to her from the water. Then, once her eyes rested upon him, he sang, "Come with me, my dear, to the land of my people, the land of the birds. There, you will live in a beautiful skin tent, and you will sleep on the softest bearskin mat. My people will bring you whatever you wish. With the feathers they bring you, you can make your clothes. With the oil they bring you, you can light your lamp, and with the meat they bring you, you can cook your food. For my part, I will make you a necklace of ivory as a token of my love. Marry me, and put an end to cold, put an end to darkness, and put an end to hunger!"

Sedna was immediately impressed by such a handsome man. She loved the stranger's beautifully dark and intelligent eyes. She admired his magnificent sealskin parka. And she longed for the luxury that he promised her in his song. Finally, a suitor had come whom she could not resist.

Sedna ran to the tent, collected her few belongings in a sealskin bag, and announced to her father that she was leaving to marry the man of her choice. She did not care that the stranger was a bird-man, and no argument of her father's could dissuade her. Sedna returned to the stranger in the kayak, who had now beached his craft on the shore, climbed into the bow of his boat, and went off with him.

So it came to pass that Sedna became the wife of the well-dressed, promising stranger. The sea journey was difficult and tiring. When the couple finally reached the land of the seabird people, Sedna found that the bird-man's song had been nothing but a ruse to win her. Instead of having a tent made from beautiful skins, she had to live in a tent fashioned from smelly fish-skins that made so poor a cover that every blast of wind and flake of snow found its way inside. Instead of sleeping on a mat of the softest bearskin, she spent sleepless nights on the hard hide of the walrus. And instead of having tasty meat to eat, she had to eat whatever raw fish the seabirds brought her.

Sedna did not care that her husband loved her. She spent her long days and longer nights remembering all the suitors whom she had rejected with her proud heart. She would sing longingly to her father, saying, "Oh, Father! If you only knew how miserable I am, you would put your kayak into the water, paddle to this dreadful land, and rescue me from this terrible people! My tent does not shelter me; my bed does not comfort me; and my food does not nourish me! Oh, how I want to go home to my own people!"

In this way it came to pass that, once again, it was spring. Once the warm winds caused the ice to break up, Sedna's father paddled off in the direction that he had seen the stranger take his daughter, for he wanted to visit Sedna in her husband's homeland. He arrived to find that the bird-man was away fishing and that Sedna was home alone.

When Sedna's father saw how she was living, and when he heard Sedna's tales of her life among the arctic seabirds, his heart filled with rage. As soon as her husband returned, Sedna's father killed the deceitful bird-man who had enticed his daughter to come to this dreadful place. Then he took Sedna away with him in his kayak and paddled as quickly as he could toward their homeland.

It soon came to pass that the other seabirds returned to find that their friend had been murdered and that his wife had disappeared. Crying mournfully over their friend's death, they set out to sea in order to find and punish Sedna.

The seabirds did not have to fly far over the sea before they spied Sedna and her father in their kayak. Immediately, they swooped down upon the water, stirring up a terrible windstorm as they violently flapped their wings. Their bodies darkened the sky, and the winds caused the waters of the sea to rise above the kayak in mountainous waves. The small boat was doomed to swamp and sink in such a sea!

Sedna's father knew that he was about to die unless he could think of a way to save himself. "This is no fault of mine!" he exclaimed to himself. "If Sedna had accepted a husband from one of our own people, this never would have happened! If I get rid of her, the seabirds may take pity on me and call off the storm-winds that are threatening my life!"

Sedna's father then grabbed his daughter and threw her overboard into the icy waters of the sea. "Take her, seabirds, if you really want her!" he shouted. "And let me return safely home!"

Having no wish to die an early death, Sedna swam to the surface and grabbed onto the edge of the kayak with her freezing fingers. Despite the tumult of the waves, she desperately hung on for her life!

Sedna's father, crazed by his own fears, took his sharp fishing-knife and cut off Sedna's fingers from her nails down to the first joint. As her fingertips fell into the waves, her nails became whalebone, and her flesh became whales. They quickly swam away, very much at home in the tumultuous sea.

Sedna still had no wish to die an early death. So she once again grabbed onto the edge of the kayak, this time with what was left of her freezing fingers. Despite the tumult of the waves, she desperately hung on for her life!

Sedna's father, now more determined, took his sharp fishing-knife and cut off Sedna's fingers from her first joint to the middle joint. As her bones and flesh fell into the waves, these pieces of her fingers became ringed seals. Like the whales, they quickly swam away, very much at home in the tumultuous sea.

Sedna still had no wish to die an early death. So she grabbed onto the edge of the kayak with what was left of her freezing fingers. Despite the tumult of the waves, she desperately hung on for her life!

Sedna's father, now even more determined, took his sharp fishing-knife and, with two blows, first cut off the last of Sedna's fingers and then cut off her thumbs. As her bones and flesh fell into the waves, these pieces of her fingers became bearded ground-seals, while her thumbs became walruses. Like the whales and the ringed seals, the walruses quickly swam out to sea. However, the bearded seals swam in search of the nearest shore on which to make their home.

Watching the scene from above, the arctic seabirds flew away once Sedna's father had chopped off the last of her fingers and her thumbs. They knew that Sedna could no longer hang onto the kayak and, therefore, they were satisfied that she would drown. Their departure caused the winds to subside and calm waters to return.

Sedna's father then helped his daughter climb back into the kayak, and he paddled her back to their home. All the way home Sedna's heart pounded with rage against her father, and she thought and thought of how best to punish him for what he had done to her.

As soon as they arrived, they were greeted by her huskies. "That's the way!" Sedna exclaimed to herself. That night, when her father was asleep, she called her dogs into their tent and encouraged them to feed upon her father's hands and feet.

Her father awakened in agony and hurled a curse upon himself, his daughter, and her dogs. To his surprise, the earth began to rumble with a low roar. And as it rumbled, it began to shake, at first so that one might hardly feel it, but then more and more violently. Suddenly, the earth gave way beneath their home, engulfing daughter, father, dogs, and tent. Down, down, down they fell into the land of Adlivun, the Underworld. There, Sedna became its ruler and the supreme power in the universe.

From that day to this, Sedna lives at the bottom of the sea, where she rules over the living and the dead. Her hair remains in two fat braids, just as she wore it in her earlier life, although she no longer has the fingers that are necessary in order to comb it. The animals that she created respond to her commands, giving themselves to those who are good, and hiding from everyone else.

Sedna insists that the Inuit people cook sea animals and land animals separately. To disobey this taboo angers her, and whenever Sedna becomes angry, her braided hair becomes tangled. She then withholds her animals from the Inuit hunters and creates the storms that swamp their kayaks and claim their lives.

Whenever this happens, the Inuit people must perform special, solemn ceremonies to win back Sedna's affection. Their shaman must make a spirit pilgrimage to her home beneath the sea, where he combs the tangles from her braided hair and pleads with her to forgive his people for breaking her taboos and to provide them with meat once again. On these occasions, Sedna is so happy to have the shaman's help that she generously rewards him and his people. Then, once again, the Inuit hunters find the animals that they desperately need in order to have food, clothing, and shelter in their harsh world.

Introducing **Caught by a Hair-String**

Historical Background

The Micmacs were an Algonquian people who, for 2,000 years, lived in the forested areas of Canada's maritime provinces, particularly in Nova Scotia and Prince Edward Island.

The name *Micmac* was given to these people by the French fur traders in the 16th century. The Micmacs called the French *nikmaq* (my kin-friends), and the French came to call the Micmacs by the same name. However, the Micmacs actually called themselves *Lnu'k* (the People).

Like the other Algonquian peoples, the Micmacs were involved in the fur trade with the French. The European demand for beaver pelts caused many wars between the Algonquian and the Iroquois peoples, who competed to barter their furs for European guns and metal implements. In time, the Micmacs were decimated by wars and disease, and, finally, the surviving remnant ethnically disappeared through intermarriage with the non-native communities.

The Micmacs lived in villages or camps, each composed of approximately 100 families. Their society was patrilineal, with inheritance occurring from father to son. Their homes were long structures with rounded tops that were covered with birchbark. In small groups, the men hunted deer, elk, and beaver, which was the principal focus of the fur trade. They also used birchbark canoes to fish the waters of lakes, rivers, and streams.

Like the other Algonquian peoples, the Micmacs were known for their *wampumpeag*, or *wampum*, long strands or belts of strung beads made of seashell or bone. Long before the arrival of the French, men used wampum as money, as a memory device, and as a guarantee of an agreement. Women used strings of wampum as hair-ties, necklaces, bracelets, and belts, and as decoration for their head-coverings and their buckskin shirts. Strings of wampum played a role in marriages, where it was the custom for the groom's family to present the brides's family with wampum.

Appeal and Value

Like the other Algonquian peoples, the Micmacs viewed life as filled with dangers, and they felt the need to protect themselves against strangers, the animals that were their prey, and their enemies in war. Their myths reveal that they treated strangers with a blend of respect, caution, and self-assertion.

The Micmac both respected and feared the wildlife that they needed for their food, clothing, shelter, and trade. Possessing neither claws, wings, nor fins, the Micmac felt they were dependent upon the goodwill of their prey. Micmac society attributed supernatural qualities to the creatures of land, sea, and air, believing that they once had possessed human form and that they still had the power to adopt it if they chose to do so. Consequently, the Micmacs lived in a world that was infused with spirits, and they valued spiritual power in matters of marriage, hunting, and war.

The bones of animals had religious importance in Micmac society. The Micmac believed that, after a creature's death, its spirit watched the hunter to be certain that he treated its bones with proper respect. The bones

of water creatures had to be tossed back into the water, whereas the skulls of land creatures had to be hung up to the accompaniment of prayers and other rituals.

Some among the Micmac people developed the ability to surpass others in their perceptions and their talents. Such power usually came to a person who was already different from everyone else in some way and, therefore, already socially isolated from the group. This person acquired power privately, at some time when he or she was alone. This often occurred, either literally or symbolically, when the person was deep in the forest, through an encounter with a supernatural being who possessed the power and could confer it upon others.

However, Micmac myths reveal how society exacted a toll from those who gained such power. The unusually successful husband, hunter, or warrior separated himself from his more ordinary neighbors, and they retaliated by treating him with a hostility that reflected their jealousy, resentment, hatred, and fear. In extreme situations, the villagers ostracized and even banished from their community those who had spiritual power.

The medicine man held an important position in the Micmac world. Part of a medicine man's training involved a ritualistic form of death, which symbolized his leaving his old life behind and entering a new life in which he now possessed greater perception and comprehension.

Like the myths of all peoples, Micmac myths both preserve a particular way of viewing the world and enhance our own perception of the world in which we live. This is particularly true when the mythographer has the ability to communicate the spiritual nature of one people to those of a different culture. Silas T. Rand's *Legends of the Micmacs*, published in 1894, is an early source of Micmac mythology.

Caught by a Hair-String

Deep in the woods, on the outer edge of a large camp of the People, lived an old man and his wife. They had two daughters who were very beautiful but were so shy that they hid from anyone who wished to see them. One suitor after another wished to marry them, but neither daughter would consider any of these young men.

Now the chief of the People had a son who wished to marry one of these daughters. So, as was the custom, the chief accompanied his son to the wigwam of the old couple one evening when the sun had gone to its rest. They had a fine time together, eating, playing games, and telling stories. Meanwhile, the maidens hid behind a screen in the wigwam so that they could listen to the chief and his son without being seen by them.

When it came time to leave, the chief announced, "My son is a fine hunter. He will be a fine husband. He wishes to marry one of your daughters, and it is time that he had sons of his own."

To these words, the maidens' father replied, "Thank you. I will have some word for you when the sun begins its morning journey."

After the chief and his son had gone, the father asked his daughters how they felt about this opportunity. The older daughter replied for both of them, "We do not choose to marry, even the son of the chief."

When the sun began its morning journey, the father kept his word and passed his daughters' words onto the chief, who repeated them to his son. Those words put great sadness into his son's heart.

Meanwhile, another young man lived among the People. He was very lazy and unattractive-looking, and he liked to joke about serious matters. The People wondered what maiden would ever want him for a husband!

When this young man heard that the beautiful maidens had rejected even the son of the chief, he laughed and bragged to his friends, "Those young women may have rejected everyone else, but they would not reject me!"

His friends could not resist such a challenge. "Is that so!" they exclaimed. "As soon as the sun has gone to its rest, let us go together to the wigwam of these young women. We should be clever and plan to arrive while the family is eating. We will surprise the maidens and get a good look at them before they have a chance to hide! Then we will see what comes of our visit!"

So it came to pass that the group of young men, the lazy and unattractive-looking fellow among them, appeared at the wigwam. They were in time to surprise the old couples' beautiful, shy daughters, and they were invited inside for a visit.

The young men spent the evening with the old couple and their daughters who, having been discovered, did not retreat from view. They had a fine time together, eating, playing games, and telling stories. The wigwam was filled with the joyous sounds of youthful laughter. Then, when it came time to leave, the young men all returned to their wigwams.

Not once during the evening had the lazy and unattractive-looking young man mentioned the idea of marriage, and, of course, none of his friends had mentioned it either. Before they went their separate ways, his friends laughingly said to him, "You have shown that you are one for big words and small deeds! We all had a fine visit, but it did not get you a wife for all that!"

Many moons came and went. One day, the lazy and unattractive-looking young man was hunting deep in the woods when he came upon a very old woman. She was sitting upon the trunk of a large tree, and she was so old that her weathered face was as wrinkled as a dried apple. She had pulled and twisted her gray hair into a bun at the back of her neck, and she had fastened it with many long and beautifully designed beaded hair-strings. These hair-strings hung over her rounded shoulders and draped over her clothing like a beaded robe that, in her seated position, reached down to touch her moccasins.

Upon seeing the lazy and unattractive-looking young man, the old woman looked up at him, her youthful eyes shining between strands of her hair-strings, and asked, "Where are you going, my grandson?"

"Oh, I'm just walking through the woods," he replied. "But what about you, Grandmother? What brings you to this solitary part of the woods, so far from your wigwam?"

"Oh, I have not come as far as all that!" the old woman exclaimed. "I hear, my grandchild, that you would like to marry one of the two beautiful but shy daughters of the old ones who live on the outer edge of your camp."

"That is not correct," the lazy and unattractive-looking young man replied. "I was just bragging about that to my friends in order to give them a good laugh."

"You must tell me the truth in your heart, my grandson," the old woman replied, "because, if you wish it, I am able to help you win the love of one of those daughters and become her husband. Would you like that?"

"Oh, yes, Grandmother!" the lazy and unattractive-looking young man replied. "Just tell me what to do, and I will do whatever you advise."

"Then take this beaded hair-string that I am giving you," the old woman responded, "and put it into your medicine pouch. Do not tell anyone about my gift or our meeting. Just keep my hair-string with you until you happen to see the young woman whom you would choose to marry. Then approach her and, without making her aware of what you are doing, lay my hair-string upon her back." And with these words, the old woman disappeared.

So it came to pass that the lazy and unattractive-looking young man gathered his friends together and suggested to them, "As soon as the sun has gone to its rest, let us once again go together to the wigwam of the two beautiful, shy young women, and let us see what comes of our visit! Once again, we should be clever and plan to arrive while the family is eating. And, once again, we should surprise the maidens so that we get to spend the evening with them before they have a chance to hide!"

They readily agreed. So it came to pass that, once again, the group of young men, the lazy and unattractive-looking fellow among them, appeared at the wigwam. They were in time to surprise the old couples' beautiful, shy daughters, and they were invited inside for a visit.

The young men spent the evening with the old couple and their beautiful daughters who, once again, having been discovered, did not retreat from view. They had a fine time together, eating, playing games, and telling stories. The wigwam was filled with the joyous sounds of youthful laughter. Then, when it came time to leave, the young men all returned to their wigwams.

Not once during the evening had the lazy and unattractive-looking young man mentioned the idea of marriage, and, of course, none of his friends had mentioned it either. Before they went their separate ways, his friends laughingly said to him, "Once again, you have shown that you are one for big words and small deeds! We all had a fine visit, but it did not get you a wife for all that!"

However, during one of the games, the lazy and unattractive-looking young man had found an opportunity to approach the younger sister. Without making her or anyone else aware of what he was doing, he had placed the old grandmother's beaded hair-string upon the back of the maiden of his choice.

When the sun began its morning journey, the lazy and unattractive-looking young man decided to take another walk deep into the woods. This time, he was not hunting animals, and he was not hunting beaded hair-strings. He was hunting the maiden whom he would marry!

The lazy and unattractive-looking young man was not surprised when he suddenly came upon the younger of the two beautiful, shy sisters walking all alone in the woods. The power of the hair-string had brought her to where the two of them would be able to speak to one another without the companionship of relatives or friends.

"What are you doing here in the woods?" the shy younger sister asked the lazy and unattractive-looking young man.

"That is an easy question," he replied. "I always hunt in these woods. But I have never found one such as you so far from our camp! Tell me, why is it that I have found you here alone? Have you lost your way?"

To his words, the shy younger sister only replied, "No, I have not lost my way."

"Then, if you are willing to have me accompany you, I will take you home to your mother and father," the lazy and unattractive-looking young man responded. "And if you are willing, I will tell them that I found you lost deep in the woods."

To his words, the shy younger sister replied, "I will accompany you, and you may tell my mother and father that you found me lost deep in the woods."

When the lazy and unattractive-looking young man brought the old couple's younger daughter back to them and told them how he had found her, her father said to him, "If you wish to marry my younger daughter, she is yours!"

The lazy and unattractive-looking young man was delighted, and the marriage was celebrated by a feast that all the People attended. Not long after that, a day came when the young husband found that his wife was wearing the beaded hair-string.

Taking his wife's beautiful face in his hands, he looked lovingly upon her and asked, "Where did you ever get this handsome hair-string?"

"Oh, one night I found it where I sleep," she replied.

The young husband thought of the old grandmother, her power, and his good fortune, and he smiled.

Once the lazy and unattractive-looking young man had acquired his beautiful wife, his thoughts turned to the chief's son, who had not been as fortunate as he in his attempt to win one of the two shy sisters. He liked the thought that, through marriage, they might become brothers, and he decided to see what he could do about it.

So it came to pass that the lazy and unattractive-looking husband went to visit the chief's son and said to him, "Now that I have married one of the two beautiful, shy maidens, the sister of my wife must be very lonely. Surely, now she would like to share her nights with one who would be as dear to her as her sister."

"I think that your words speak the truth," the chief's son replied. "I know, because I am also alone."

"You may not have noticed, but my wife now wears a very beautiful, beaded hair-string that someone found in the woods. It seems to me that her sister might also like to be able to wear a beautiful, beaded hair-string like that," the lazy and unattractive-looking husband suggested.

"Let me know when you plan to go hunting again in the woods, and I may go with you," the chief's son replied.

So it came to pass that when the sun began its morning journey, it looked down upon two young men who were walking deep into the woods. They were hunting, but they were not hunting animals. They were hunting beaded hair-strings!

Suddenly, the two young men came upon a very old woman. She was sitting upon the trunk of a large tree, and she was so old that her weathered face was as wrinkled as a dried apple. She had pulled and twisted her gray hair into a bun at the back of her neck, and she had fastened it with many long and beautifully designed beaded hair-strings. These hair-strings hung over her rounded shoulders and draped over her clothing like a beaded robe that, in her seated position, reached down to touch her moccasins.

Upon seeing the chief's son, the old woman looked up at him, her youthful eyes shining between strands of her hair-strings, and asked, "Where are you going, my grandson?"

"Oh, I'm just walking through the woods," he replied. "But what about you, Grandmother? What brings you to this solitary part of the woods, so far from your wigwam?"

"Oh, I have not come as far as all that!" the old woman exclaimed. "I hear, my grandchild, that you would like to marry the elder of the two beautiful but shy daughters of the old ones who live on the outer edge of your camp."

"Well, yes, Grandmother!" the chief's son replied. "I have thought about that maiden now and then."

"Then this is what I would have you do," the old woman responded. "Take this beaded hair-string that I am giving you, and put it into your medicine pouch. Your brother will tell you what to do with it. Do not tell anyone about my gift or about our meeting. Just have many sons!" And with these words, the old woman disappeared.

So it came to pass that the chief and his son appeared at the wigwam once again. This time, they were in time to surprise the old couples' beautiful, shy elder daughter, and they were invited inside for a visit.

The chief and his son spent the evening with the old couple and their beautiful daughter who, having been discovered, did not retreat from view. They had a fine time together, eating, playing games, and telling stories. And during one of the games, the chief's son found an opportunity to approach the elder daughter. Without making her or anyone else aware of what he was doing, he placed the old grandmother's beaded hair-string upon her back.

When the sun began its morning journey, the chief's son decided to take another walk deep into the woods. This time, he was not hunting animals, and he was not hunting beaded hair-strings. He was hunting the maiden whom he would marry!

The chief's son was not surprised when he suddenly came upon the elder of the two beautiful, shy sisters walking all alone in the woods. The power of the hair-string had brought her to where the two of them would be able to speak to one another without the companionship of relatives or friends.

"What are you doing here in the woods?" the shy elder sister asked the chief's son.

"That is an easy question," he replied. "I always hunt in these woods. But I have never found one such as you so far from our camp! Tell me, why is it that I have found you here alone? Have you lost your way?"

To his words, the shy elder sister only replied, "No, I have not lost my way."

"Then, if you are willing to have me accompany you, I will take you home to your mother and father," he responded. "And if you are willing, I will tell them that I found you lost deep in the woods."

To his words, the shy elder sister replied, "I will accompany you, and you may tell my mother and father that you found me lost deep in the woods."

When the chief's son brought the old couple's elder daughter back to them and told them how he had found her, her father said to him, "If you wish to marry my elder daughter, she is yours!"

The chief's son was delighted, and the marriage was celebrated by a great feast that all the People attended. It pleased the new husband to see that his wife was wearing the beautiful beaded hair-string on this special occasion.

So it came to pass that the lazy and unattractive-looking husband and the chief's son became brothers. Like brothers, they always hunted together, and like brothers, they always talked together.

One day, the chief's son said to his brother, "If a person wanted to learn how to become a fast runner, it would be possible, although not many know how to teach this skill."

"That would, indeed, be a useful thing to know!" exclaimed the lazy and unattractive-looking husband. "Such a person could find more animals, and he could escape from his enemies. A person who knows how to teach this can find someone who wants to learn it!"

"Then," the chief's son advised his brother, "you must capture feathers from the birds in the woods, and you must save them for a day when the wind loves to whistle. On that day, free the feathers so that you and the wind can chase them. Let the wind chase you as you chase the feathers, and you will find that the power will grow in you and enable you to run faster than the feathers, faster than the wind, and, of course, faster than any other man. And once you can do this, you will always be able to do it!"

So it came to pass that the lazy and unattractive-looking husband became the fastest of runners.

Another day, the chief's son said to his brother, "If a person wanted to learn how to escape from a great danger, it would be possible, although not many know how to teach this skill."

"That would, indeed, be a useful thing to know!" exclaimed the lazy and unattractive-looking husband. "Such a person might find an animal that he cannot kill, or he might find an animal that can run even faster than he can. Then he would have to have the skill to save his life. A person who knows how to teach this can find someone who wants to learn it!"

"First," the chief's son advised his brother, "you must find some very old clothes, and wear them over your own. Then you must find someone and make him angry enough to grab you. As soon as he grabs you, you must pull yourself out of the old clothes, and run from him. You will find that the power will grow in you and enable you to do this. This man, like any man or animal, will believe that you are still inside the old clothes, and long after you have escaped to a safe distance, he will remain behind with those clothes, attacking and killing what he believes to be you. In this way, you can escape from any animal and, of course, from any man. And once you can do this, you will always be able to do it!"

So it came to pass that the lazy and unattractive-looking husband became the fastest at escaping danger.

Another time, the two young men were paddling a canoe down the river when the chief's son said to his brother, "If a person wanted to learn to see where all the moose in the woods are hiding, it would be possible, although not many know how to teach this skill."

"That would, indeed, be a useful thing to know!" exclaimed the lazy and unattractive-looking husband. "Such a person would become the greatest hunter and would provide the People with much more meat to eat and fur to wear. A person who knows how to teach this can find someone who wants to learn it!"

"First," the chief's son advised his brother, "you must catch some moose hair from the moose in the woods, roll it into a ball between your forefinger and your thumb, and then save it for a day when the wind loves to whistle. Then, on that day, you must free the fur ball so that the wind can chase it. You will find that the power will grow in you and enable you to see all the moose that are hiding in the woods. And once you can do this, you will always be able to do it!"

To these words, the lazy and unattractive-looking husband replied, "And a person who learns how to do this can decide to catch the hair from the other animals in the woods, roll their hair into fur balls between his forefinger and his thumb, and when the wind loves to whistle, free those fur balls so that the wind can chase them. Then such a person might be able to see all the other animals that are hiding in the woods along with the moose!"

"You may be right about this," the chief's son replied.

So it came to pass that the lazy and unattractive-looking husband became the greatest hunter. He could see all the animals that lived in the woods, no matter where they were hiding, and he could call them to him.

Another day the two young men were standing on the rocks along the river and spearing salmon, when the lazy and unattractive-looking husband said to the chief's son, "Fish do not have hair, but they have bones."

"You are right about this," the chief's son replied. "If a person wanted to learn how to see where all the fish in the river are hiding, it would be possible, although not many know how to teach this skill."

"That would, indeed, be a useful thing to know!" exclaimed the lazy and unattractive-looking husband. "Such a person would become the greatest fisherman and would provide the People with much more food to eat. A person who knows how to teach this can find someone who wants to learn it!"

"First," the chief's son advised his brother, "you must catch a fish and ask if you may have its bones. Next, you must take those bones, pound them into a powder, and save the powder for a day when the wind loves to whistle. Then, on that day, you must free the powder so that the wind can chase it. You will find that the power will grow in you and enable you to see all the fish that are hiding in the river. And once you can do this, you will always be able to do it!"

So it came to pass that the lazy and unattractive-looking husband became a great fisherman. He could see all the fish in the river, no matter where they were hiding, and he could call them to him.

Many moons came and went. One day the two young men were talking together when the lazy and unattractive-looking husband said to the chief's son, "Now I dream dreams about whales and their songs."

To these words, the chief's son replied, "Whales do not die unless a person kills them."

So it came to pass that the lazy and unattractive-looking husband went alone to catch some whalebone by the side of the sea. When he found it, he burned it until he could crush it into a fine powder. He then saved the powder for a day when the wind loved to whistle on its way out to sea.

When that day came, the lazy and unattractive-looking husband walked out upon a rocky outcropping and freed a handful of the powder so that the wind could chase it. He found that the power grew in him and enabled him to see all the whales that were swimming far out in the sea. He freed a second handful of the powder, and as the wind chased the powder out to sea, he called the whales to him, and they came closer. He freed a third handful of the powder, and as the wind chased the powder out to sea, he called the whales to him, and they came even closer.

Three more times the lazy and unattractive-looking husband freed a handful of the powder. Three times, as the wind chased the powder out to sea, he called the whales to him, and with each handful the whales came even closer. The lazy and unattractive-looking husband freed a seventh handful of the powder, and as the wind chased the powder out to sea, he called a huge whale to him. To his surprise, the whale that he had called to him was Whale Person.

"Why have you have called me to you?" Whale Person asked the lazy and unattractive-looking husband.

"I have dreamed about you and about the power that you could give me, if you would be willing to do it," the lazy and unattractive-looking husband replied.

"I will give you the power that you wish to have," Whale Person replied. "When I open my mouth, reach under my tongue and take the medicine that you find there."

The lazy and unattractive-looking husband reached into Whale Person's mouth, found the medicine under his tongue, and removed it.

Once the lazy and unattractive-looking husband held the power medicine in his hand, Whale Person exclaimed, "Now you have the power to be invincible! My medicine will protect you against disease. My medicine will also protect you against the attacks of men and wild animals. My medicine will give you the power to do whatever you wish!"

And with these words, Whale Person dived deep into the sea and disappeared.

So it came to pass that the People in the large camp deep in the woods lived in peace and prosperity. Enemies did not attack them. The animals of the woods and the fish in the rivers permitted themselves to be caught and eaten. Fathers had sons, and, still, there was more than enough for all.

Many, many moons came and went. Finally, the chief was so old that he was not well enough to lead the People. The chief's son came to his brother and asked, "Are you able to return my father's youth and health to him?"

"A person should not tamper with nature," the lazy and unattractive-looking husband replied. "What will come at the end of a person's life should be permitted to come!"

So it came to pass that the chief finally died, leaving the leadership of the People to his son. The chief's son then came to his brother and said, "A chief should be a person who possesses great powers. The husband of my wife's sister is such a man. Maybe he, and not the chief's son, should be the new chief of the People!"

To these words, the lazy and unattractive-looking husband replied, "The new chief will be the son of the old chief! He is a person who also possesses great powers. And his brother will always stand beside him and help him!"

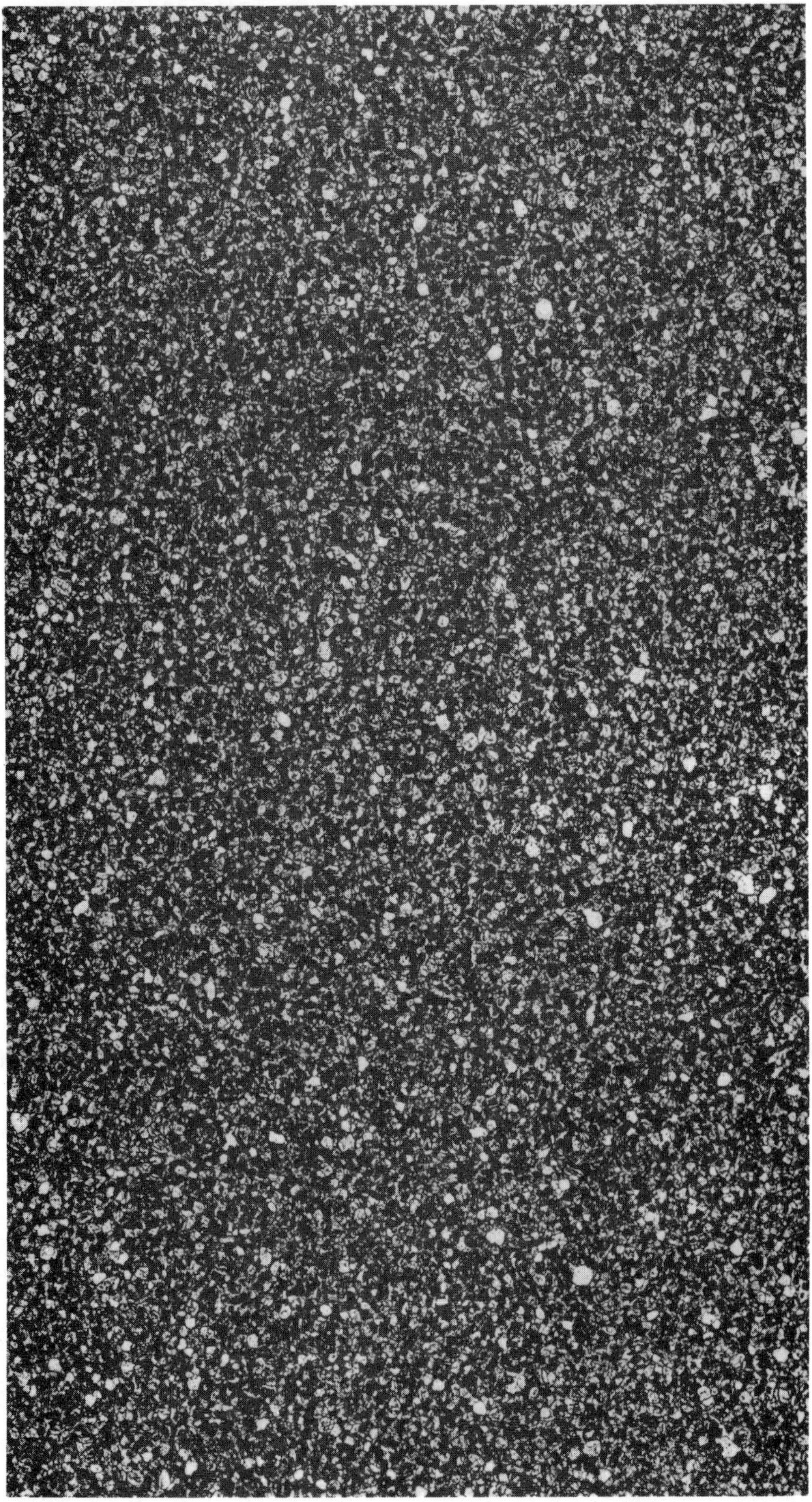

Notes

For each selection, the following Notes will provide you with the titles and publishers of the original sources (in fine translations), my primary sources, and selected supplementary sources for relevant background information, critical study, and further reading pleasure.

You will find additional information about original sources in the Introduction to each myth. The Selected Bibliography provides a detailed listing of all sources mentioned in the Notes.

I have retold each myth in this book from scholarly English translations of the original material. In almost all instances, I have been able to work with at least two different sources. Most of the creation, fertility, and shorter hero myths are complete. However, most of the epics have been abridged because their length was incompatible with the length of this book.

In abridging the epics, my goal has been to retell the principal stories in a way that would preserve the characterization and language of the originals. Consequently, the major characters speak and behave as they do in unabridged editions. Secondary characters and subplots have been eliminated, and since one-third or more of an oral epic usually consists of repeated material, I have often included only one complete passage and then omitted or shortened repetitive passages. Any additions and omissions are explained in the relevant Notes.

GREECE AND ROME
The Creation of the Titans and the Gods
The Greek poet Hesiod (late 8th century B.C.) tells this myth, in poetic form, in the *Theogony*. My primary sources are two

prose versions: *Hesiod, The Homeric Hymns, and Homerica,* translated by Evelyn-White; and Apollodorus' *The Library,* translated by Frazer (both Loeb Classical Library, Harvard Univ. Press). Other excellent translations include poetic versions by Athanassakis (Johns Hopkins Univ. Press) and by Lattimore (Univ. of Michigan Press), and a prose translation by West (Oxford Univ. Press).

The Ages of Man
The Greek poet Hesiod (late 8th century B.C.) tells this myth, in poetic form, in his *Works and Days.* My primary source is *Hesiod, The Homeric Hymns, and Homerica,* translated in prose by Evelyn-White (Loeb Classical Library, Harvard Univ. Press.) Other excellent translations of Hesiod include poetic versions by Athanassakis (Johns Hopkins Univ. Press) and by Lattimore (Univ. of Michigan Press), and a prose translation by West (Oxford Univ. Press).

A helpful resource is Volume 1 of Bonnefoy's *Mythologies* (Univ. of Chicago Press), which contains an elaborate analysis of the Greek gods.

Demeter and Persephone
The most complete version of this myth appears, in poetic form, in *The Homeric Hymns* (8th to 6th centuries B.C.), which were originally attributed to Homer. My primary sources are two prose versions: *Hesiod, The Homeric Hymns, and Homerica,* translated by Evelyn-White; and Apollodorus' *The Library,* translated by Frazer (both Loeb Classical Library, Harvard Univ. Press). Other excellent translations of *The Homeric Hymns* include poetic versions by Athanassakis (John Hopkins Univ. Press), Boer (Spring Publications), and by Hine (Atheneum).

Due to the limitation of space, I have found it necessary to omit the part of this myth in which Demeter nurses Metaneira's infant son, thus limiting my version to those aspects of the myth that best compare with other fertility myths.

The Flood Cycle

The Library (*Bibliotheca*), originally attributed to Athenian writer Apollodorus (writing in about 140 B.C.), contains these myths. (Current scholarship places *The Library* later, in the 1st or 2nd century A.D.) The Roman poet Ovid (43 B.C.–17 A.D.) also tells this group of myths in his *Metamorphoses*.

My primary sources are two prose versions: *The Library*, translated by Frazer; and *Metamorphoses*, translated by Miller (both Loeb Classical Library, Harvard Univ. Press), as well as a poetic version: *Ovid's Metamorphoses*, translated by Sandys (reprinted by Univ. of Nebraska Press). An excellent poetic translation of Ovid's *Metamorphoses* is that by Humphries (Indiana Univ. Press).

The Labors and Death of Heracles

The most complete versions of Heracles' labors appear in *The Library* by Apollodorus and in the *Library of History*, written by the Greek historian Diodorus of Sicily (about 80–20 B.C.). My primary sources are Apollodorus' *The Library*, translated by Frazer, and Diodorus Siculus' *Library of History* (Volume II), translated by Oldfather (both Loeb Classical Library, Harvard Univ. Press). *Gods and Heroes of the Greeks* by Simpson (Univ. of Massachusetts Press) is another excellent translation.

A helpful resource is Volume I of Bonnefoy's *Mythologies* (Univ. of Chicago Press), which contains a detailed analysis of Heracles as the quintessential Greek hero.

Due to the limitation of space, I have found it necessary to omit the birth and youth of Heracles, the myth of Alcestis, Heracles' marriages, and the battle between the gods and the giants. The version contained in this book focuses on those aspects of the myth that best compare with other myths of the traditional hero.

Heracles was the great ancestral hero of Argos. He had such stature in ancient Greece that when Athens was competing with Argos in the 6th century B.C., political and economic supremacy were not considered sufficient. The Athenians felt that they needed a hero from their past who could compete successfully with Heracles. They chose Theseus, who was Heracles' cousin, "found" Theseus' bones on an obscure island, and brought them back to Athens for a proper heroic burial. They also collected a variety of myths, including a series of exploits which imitate those of Heracles, and combined them into one elaborate myth, thus raising Theseus' stature to meet that of Heracles.

The Iliad

Originally written in poetic form, my primary source for *The Iliad* is a prose translation by Murray (Loeb Classical Library, Harvard Univ. Press). Excellent poetic translations include those by Fagles (Viking), Fitzgerald (Anchor/ Doubleday), and Lattimore (Univ of Chicago Press). The Selected Bibliography lists a number of books that are particularly worthwhile as supplementary sources for the study of *The Iliad*. Works whose titles may not immediately identify them as relating to *The Iliad* include: Chadwick's *The Mycenaean World* (Cambridge Univ. Press); Jackson's *The Hero and the King: An Epic Theme* (Columbia Univ. Press); and Vermeule's *Greece in the Bronze Age* (Univ. of Chicago Press).

Due to the limitation of space, I have selected conversations and incidents from the twenty-four books of *The Iliad* with the goal of telling the story simply and directly, while still preserving Homer's characterization of the principals, including their speeches. I have attempted to preserve key elements of Homer's style, occasionally moving suitable Homeric similes from one place in the text to another, in order to keep as much Homeric language as possible.

In order to reduce confusion over a multitude of names, I have omitted epithets that refer to a male character by stating his parent, such as "Son of Atreus," or "Leto's son." Instead, I have substituted other less confusing epithets that also occur frequently in the original.

Because of space, I have had to omit the many anthropomorphic conversations among the gods on Mount Olympus. Moreover, I have found it necessary to omit Diomedes, whom many scholars view as the perfect Homeric hero, as well as Sarpedon and Aeneas. Consequently, I have omitted Homer's often quoted simile that equates the generations of mortals with the growth cycle of leaves (Book VI). In one instance (in Chapter 4), the omission of Diomedes required combining two scenes from the original. Early in Book IX and again in Book XIV, Agamemnon advises the Greek leaders to leave Troy and return home. Diomedes responds in Book IX; Odysseus responds in Book XIV. Given my need to omit Diomedes, I have substituted Odysseus' reply.

The Iliad and *The Odyssey*, along with a later group of six epics (written after *The Iliad* from about 660 B.C. and now lost), became known as the (Trojan) Epic Cycle. Fragments of the six lost epics and Proclus' summaries of them have been published in *Hesiod, The Homeric Hymns, and Homerica* (Loeb Classical Library, Harvard Univ. Press). *The Cypria* (or *Cyprian Lays*) *The Aethiopis*, and the *Little Iliad* are discussed below, in relation to *The Iliad*. *Nostoi* (*The Returns* or *Homecomings*) and *The Telegony* are discussed in my notes to *The Odyssey*. The *Little Iliad* and the *Iliūpe'rsis* (*The Sack of Ilium*) are discussed in my notes to *The Aeneid*.

The Cypria (660 B.C. or slightly earlier), ascribed both to Stasinus of Cyprus and to Hegesinus of Salamis, related the story of the Trojan War up to the beginning of *The Iliad*. It began with Zeus' wish for the Trojan War. It then described the apple of discord, the abduction of Helen, the gathering of the Greek armies, the sacrifice of Iphigeneia, the would of Philoctetes and his desertion by the Greeks, and the first nine years of the Trojan War. It concluded with the events in the tenth year that preceded the argument between Agamemnon and Achilles.

The Aethiopis (776 B.C.), written by Arctinus of Miletus, was the sequel to *The Iliad*. It described Achilles' deeds following Hector's funeral, his death from Paris' arrow, his rescue by Thetis, and his immortality. It concluded with the contest between Ajax and Odysseus for Achilles' armor.

The *Little Iliad* (660 B.C.), ascribed to Lesches of Pyrrha or of Mitylene in Lesbos, described the events that followed the death of Achilles: the contest between Ajax and Odysseus for Achilles' armor; Ajax's madness and suicide following his defeat; and Odysseus' capture of Helenus, the Trojan seer. In the *Little Iliad*, Helenus reveals the four conditions that the Greeks must meet in order to conquer Troy. First, they must bring the bones of Pelops to Troy. (Pelops, a towering figure in Greek myth, is the ancestor of Heracles, Theseus, Eurystheus, Agamemnon, Menelaus, and Aegisthus.) Second, the Greeks must use the bow and arrows of Heracles against the Trojans. (Diomedes and Odysseus persuade Philoctetes, whom the Greeks had abandoned on their way to Troy more than nine years earlier, to rejoin them because he possesses Heracles' bow. His wound is cured, and, in a duel, he kills Paris.) Third, Achilles' son Neoptolemus must fight with the Greeks. (Odysseus brings him to Troy.) Fourth, the Greeks must steal the Palladium from its guarded temple on the fortified acropolis of Troy. (See my notes to *The Aeneid* for the Palladium's significance and its theft.)

Proclus' summary of the *Little Iliad* concludes with Athena's instructing Epeius to build the wooden horse, and its acceptance by the Trojans. However, the epic originally may have concluded with the sack of Troy. (See my notes to *The Aeneid*).

The Odyssey

Originally written in poetic form, my primary source for *The Odyssey* is a prose translation by Murray (Loeb Classical Library, Harvard Univ. Press). Excellent poetic translations include those by Cook (Norton), Fitzgerald (Anchor/Doubleday), and Lattimore (Harper); another excellent prose version is that by Lawrence (Oxford Univ. Press). The Selected Bibiliography lists many books that are helpful supplementary sources for the study of *The Odyssey*. (See also notes to *The Iliad*). Readers may find it interesting that Graves, in his discussion of Nausicaa, supports Butler's theory that *The Odyssey* was written by a gifted Sicilian noblewoman (see Graves, Volume 2.)

Due to the limitation of space, I have selected conversations and incidents from the twenty-four books of *The Odyssey* with the goal of telling the story simply and directly, while still preserving Homer's characterization of the principals, including their speeches. I have attempted to preserve key elements of Homer's style.

In order to reduce confusion over a multitude of names, I have omitted epithets that refer to a male character by stating his parent, such as "Son of Atreus." Instead, I have substituted other less confusing epithets that also occur frequently in the original. In order to make it easier for readers to remember the names of the most important characters, I have also avoided the use of proper names wherever possible, such as Nausicaa (the princess of Phaeacea) and Eumaeus (the swineherd).

Because of space, I have found it necessary to omit Telemachus' role in Ithaca prior to Odysseus' return, and to omit Telemachus' search for his father, including his visits to Nestor and to Helen and Menelaus. Consequently, I

have omitted the descriptions of the wooden horse (Books IV and VIII) and Achilles' funeral (Book XXIV), as well as the themes of Telemachus' development from child to man and Orestes' model of retributive justice. Moreover, I have found it necessary to omit the numerous descriptions of religious rites (sacrifices), hospitality, and entertainment that reveal so much about these aspects of life in ancient Greece.

Two of the lost, post-Homeric epics in the (Trojan) Epic Cycle dealt with events connected with *The Odyssey*. *Nostoi* (*The Returns* or *Homecomings*), written by Agias (or Hegias) of Troezen, described the return of the great Greek heroes, with the notable exception of Odysseus. It included Diomedes, Nestor, Neoptolemus, Agamemnon (including his murder by Clytemnestra and Aegisthus, and Orestes' retribution), and Menelaus (last of all, except for Odysseus). Consequently, *Nostoi* ended where the *Odyssey* begins.

The Telegony (568 B.C.), written by Eugammon of Cyrene as the sequel to *The Odyssey*, began with the burial of Penelope's suitors. According to this epic, after performing the sacrifices the seer Teiresias had said were necessary, Odysseus went to Thesprotis, married its queen Callidice, and remained there until her death. Then he left his and Callidice's son to rule Thesprotis, while he returned to Ithaca. Meanwhile, Telegonus, son of Odysseus and Circe, was searching for his father. Telegonus raided Ithaca without knowing its identity and, when Odysseus fought off his attack, Telegonus inadvertently killed the father for whom he was searching. *The Telegony* ended on Circe's island, with Circe's gifts of immortality and a double marriage: Telemachus to Circe, and Telegonus to Penelope.

Romulus and Remus

The Roman historian Livy (59 B.C.–A.D 17), tells this myth in Book I of his *History of Rome from Its Foundation*. The Greek biographer and historian

Plutarch (A.D. 46–120) also relates this myth in his biography of Romulus in *Parallel Lives*. My primary sources are Livy's *History of Rome from Its Foundation*, translated by Foster; and Plutarch's *Parallel Lives*, translated by Perrin (both Loeb Classical Library, Harvard Univ. Press). These works by Livy and Plutarch are also available in Penguin editions.

It is interesting to note that the ancestor of Romulus and Remus is Aeneas, who is the founder of Rome in Virgil's *Aeneid*. My notes on Heracles, *The Aeneid*, and King Arthur point out that it was a common practice to choose great ancestors to be the patron heroes or the founders of great nations.

The Aeneid

Originally written in poetic form, my primary source for *The Aeneid* is a prose translation by Fairclough (Loeb Classical Library, Harvard Univ. Press). Excellent poetic translations include those by Fitzgerald (Random House) and Mandelbaum (Univ. of California Press); another recommended prose version is by West (Penguin). Excellent supplementary sources for the study of *The Aeneid* include: Beye's *The Iliad, the Odyssey and the Epic Tradition* (Peter Smith); Di Cesare's *The Altar and the City* (Columbia Univ. Press); Galinsky's *Aeneas, Sicily and Rome* (Princeton Univ. Press); Jackson's *The Hero and the King: An Epic Theme* (Columbia Univ. Press); and Lawler's "The Aeneid," in Seidel and Mendelson's *Homer to Brecht* (Yale Univ. Press).

Due to the limitation of space, I have selected conversations and incidents from among the twelve books of *The Aeneid* with the goal of telling the story simply and directly, while still preserving Virgil's characterization of the principals, including their speeches. I have attempted to preserve key elements of Virgil's style. In order to keep as much figurative language as possible, I have moved suitable Homeric similes from one place in Virgil's text to another.

The Aeneid can be divided into two parts: the first includes Aeneas' wanderings and is reminiscent of *The Odyssey*; the second involves the conquest of the Latin people in Italy and is reminiscent of *The Iliad*. From the first part, I have retold the sack of Troy, Aeneas' adventures en route to Italy, and the love affair between Dido and Aeneas — all in great detail. From the second part, I have retold in detail the fight between Turnus and Aeneas that concludes the epic. However, I have condensed the narrative that connects these two sections, and I have omitted many sections that glorify Rome.

As is mentioned in my notes on Heracles and King Arthur, among Western nations in ancient and medieval times, a great city-state or nation was expected to have a great heritage. Homer's Troy was held in such esteem that writers who wished to authenticate their nation's heritage chose their founding fathers from among the heroes of the Trojan War. Consequently, Virgil chose Aeneas to become the founder of Rome.

Although Virgil's account of the wooden horse is famous, he did not create the myth. Two of the lost, post-Homeric epics that dealt with the Trojan War also related this event. The *Little Iliad* (660 B.C.), written by Lesches of Pyrrha or Mitylene in Lesbos, included a description of how the Trojans took the wooden horse into the city, but Proclus' summary of this epic concludes without proceeding further with the fall of Troy. However, it is possible that the *Little Iliad* may originally have concluded with the sack of Troy and that Proclus chose not summarize it because it so closely repeated the versions given in the *Iliūpe'rsis*, which he did summarize.

The *Iliūpe'rsis* (*The Sack of Ilium*) was written in 776 B.C. by Arctinus of Miletus as a sequel to the *Little Iliad*. It described the wooden horse, the death of Laocoon and his son, the role of Sinon, the return of the Greeks from Tenedos, the death of Priam, and the reunion of Menelaus and Helen. It concluded with the murder of Astyanax, the enslavement of the leading Trojan women (prizes of victory for the leading Greek warriors), the burning of Troy, and Athena's plans to punish the returning Greek leaders for their theft of her Palladium.

The Palladium was an object of critical importance in the myth of the Trojan War. According to Apollodorus' *Library*, it was a small wooden statue of the girl Pallas, which Athena created in memory of her dear friend. One day, as the girls were practicing their war skills, they had had an argument. When Zeus saw that Pallas was about to strike Athena, he became worried about his daughter's welfare. He distracted Pallas, thereby causing Athena, in the heat of their practice, inadvertently to give her friend a mortal wound. According to Arctinus' *Iliūpe'rsis*, Zeus gave the Palladium to Dardanus, his favorite mortal son and the earliest ancestor of the Trojan people. From that time forth, the Palladium was highly honored in Troy. In order to protect it, the Trojans secreted the real statue and placed an excellent copy of it on public view in the temple that had been built to honor it.

According to Lesche's *Little Iliad*, when Odysseus captured Helenus, the Trojan seer told him that the Greeks could not conquer Troy as long as the Palladium remained within the city's walls. Consequently, one night Odysseus and Diomedes secretly entered Troy, killed those who guarded the statue, stole the Palladium, and took it to the Greek ships.

Arctinus' *Iliūpe'rsis* states that it was the copy of the Palladium that the Greeks stole. However, the Greeks did conquer Troy. Moreover, Athena's attitude toward the Greeks changes between the end of *The Iliad* and the beginning of *The Odyssey*. Her apparent indifference to the plight of Odysseus as he attempts to return to Ithaca may reflect her anger over his theft of the Palla-

dium. Her attitude is consistent with her plans, related in the *Iliūpe'rsis*, to destroy the Greek leaders as they return home.

The Palladium was such a treasure that accounts differ as to its fate. The Argives claimed that Diomedes took the Palladium home with him to Argos. The Athenians claimed that they raided the Argive ship that was transporting it, and, consequently, that they acquired the Palladium before it reached Argos. However, Virgil takes the Trojan point of view, and, in *The Aeneid*, Aeneas carries the Palladium out of Troy and takes it with him to Italy.

THE MIDDLE EAST
The Enuma elish
Originally written in poetic form on clay tablets, primary sources of the *Enuma elish* provide linear translations of this material. My primary sources are "The Creation Epic," in a linear translation by Speiser, and "The Creation Epic — Additions to Tablets V–VII," in a linear translation by Grayson. Both are included in Pritchard's *Ancient Near Eastern Texts Relating to the Old Testament* (Princeton Univ. Press). *Myths from Mesopotamia*, linear translations by Dalley (Oxford Univ. Press) published after I had written *World Mythology*, appears to be another excellent primary source for the *Enuma elish*. Gaster's *The Oldest Stories in the World* (Beacon) contains an excellent modern version of this epic.

Osiris, Isis, and Horus
The most complete version of this myth is found in Volume I of *Osiris and the Egyptian Resurrection*, by Budge. My primary sources are both by Budge: *Egyptian Religion* (Bell/Crown reprint) and *Osiris and the Egyptian Resurrection* (Dover reprint). Two interesting discussions of this myth can be found in Breasted's *The Dawn of Conscience* (Scribner's) and in Frankfort's *Kingship and the Gods* (Univ. of Chicago Press).

The myth of Osiris, Isis, and Horus was so well known in ancient Egypt that it is depicted on the walls of every major ancient religious structure in Egypt. Consequently, it is possible to understand and appreciate much of the visual art of ancient Egypt with only this one myth in mind.

It is interesting to note that Osiris swallows Horus' eternal eye for the same reason that the Greek warriors stab Hector's corpse with their spears — to gain power through a magical transference. Other peoples have eaten the hearts or drunk the blood of enemies they have killed, thereby expecting to acquire the qualities that made those enemies great.

Telepinu

Originally written on clay tablets, the most complete version of this myth appears in Pritchard's *Ancient Near Eastern Texts Relating to the Old Testament* (Princeton Univ. Press). The myth appears as "The Telepinus Myth" in a linear translation by Goetze, and it is my primary source. Gaster relates an excellent prose version in *The Oldest Stories in the World* (Beacon).

The Hittites were an ancient people who built an empire in Asia Minor that included northern Mesopotamia and parts of Syria. It existed from about 2000 to 1200 B.C., so that the Hittites were contemporaries of the Mycenaean Greeks.

Many versions of the Telepinu myth exist. The particular god who vanishes differs from one version to another, and specific details about the same god differ as well. These variations support the idea that the myth was secondary to the ritual to which it belonged, and that it was recited whenever the ritual was necessary.

Gilgamesh

Originally written in poetic form on clay tablets, primary sources of the *Gilgamesh* epic provide linear translations of this material. My primary sources are included in Pritchard's *Ancient Near Eastern Texts Relating to the Old Testament* (Princeton Univ. Press). The

Sumerian versions of the epic appear as "Gilgamesh and the Land of the Living" and "The Deluge," both in linear translations by Kramer. The Babylonian versions appear as "The Epic of Gilgamesh" and "Atrahasis" (the Babylonian Utanapishtim), both in linear translations by Speiser, and as "The Epic of Gilgamesh — Notes and Additions" and "Atrahasis — Additional Texts," both in linear translations by Grayson.

I have taken additional material from the following translations of *Gilgamesh* tablets: Gardner and Maier (Random House); Kovacs (Stanford Univ. Press); Jacobsen, in his *Treasures of Darkness* (Yale Univ. Press); and Kramer, in his *History Begins at Sumer* (Univ. of Pennsylvania Press).

Myths from Mesopotamia, linear translations by Dalley (Oxford Univ. Press) published after I had written *World Mythology*, appears to be another excellent primary source for the *Gilgamesh* epic. Excellent modern versions of this epic include the poetic versions by Ferry (Farrar Straus) and Mason (New American Library), and the prose versions by Gaster, in his *Oldest Stories in the World* (Beacon); Sandars (Penguin); and Silverberg, in his *Gilgamesh the King* (Arbor House).

Excellent supplementary sources for the study of *Gilgamesh* include: Heidel's *The Gilgamesh Epic and Old Testament Parallels* (Univ. of Chicago Press); Kramer's *History Begins at Sumer* (Univ. of Pennsylvania Press) and *The Sumerians* (Univ. of Chicago Press); Oppenheim's *Letters from Mesopotamia* (Univ. of Chicago Press); and Tigay's *The Evolution of the Gilgamesh Epic* (Univ. of Pennsylvania Press).

In my version of the epic, I have combined Sumerian, Akkadian, and Babylonian material. The Akkadian version of the *Gilgamesh* epic takes its title from its opening words, "He who saw everything" — an appropriate epithet for Gilgamesh. I have added the gods' reasons for the flood from the Old Babylonian and Assyrian texts of the *Atrahasis*. Atrahasis means "exceedingly wise" — an appropriate name for Utanapishtim.

On the other hand, due to the limitation of space, I have found it necessary to shorten this epic. Fortunately, the style is so repetitive that, in most respects, it has been easy to preserve the impact of the original. However, I have had to shorten Gilgamesh's poignant, repetitive reply in which he responds to those who question him by justifying his emaciated, ragged appearance and his search for Utanapishtim. I have handled this problem by elaborating on the reply each time Gilgamesh responds, culminating with his final reply in which he provides his complete statement.

NORTHERN EUROPE
The Creation, Death, and Rebirth of the Universe

Snorri Sturluson (1178–1241), the Icelandic historian and poet, tells the most complete version of this myth in the part of his *Prose Edda* called *Gylfaginning* (*The Deluding of Gylfi*), written in about A.D. 1220. My primary sources are Taylor and Auden's translation of selections from the *Elder Edda* (Random House) and Young's translation of the *Prose Edda* (Univ. of California Press). Other excellent poetic translations of this material include Hollander's *The Poetic Edda* (Univ. of Texas Press) and Terry's *Poems of the Elder Edda* (Univ. of Pennsylvania Press). *The Norse Myths*, retold by Crossley-Holland (Pantheon), contains a fine prose version of this material.

Excellent supplementary sources for the study of Norse myth include Branston's *Gods of the North* (Thomas and Hudson), Dumezil's *Gods of the Ancient Northmen* (Univ. of California Press), and Volume 1 of Bonnefoy's *Mythologies* (Univ. of Chicago Press).

Most scholars think that no unified Germanic religion or mythic tradition existed. Great discrepancies exist within the Icelandic versions of the Norse myths, reflecting contradictory sources for the same subject. The existing Norse myths show similarities to myths from Iran, from other Mediterranean areas, and from the Far East, suggesting the possibility that a group of ancient myths was common to all of these peoples.

Sturluson begins *The Deluding of Gylfi* with a description of the Allfather that does not completely match the description of Odin, who is called the All-Father. Apparently, in an earlier Norse creation myth, a god called Allfather wielded complete power over the universe. Odin, who appears later in Norse mythology, possesses many of the same characteristics as the earlier Allfather, but he has no power over the Norns (the Norse Fates). From Sturluson's tale and earlier material, it is also clear that the Aesir and the Vanir are two distinct groups of gods who fight against one another. As a result, some of the Vanir are adopted by the Aesir.

Situations such as these usually reflect a conflict between two religions. Both the Norse and the Greek myths reveal that the dominant religion adopted part of the religion that it supplanted. Another consideration is the fact that, under Christianity, the oral recitation of pagan literature was suppressed, and most of the written manuscripts were destroyed. Only the people of Iceland were permitted to enjoy pagan literature during the 300 years that followed A.D. 1000. However, they read pagan literature that had been rewritten for a Christian audience, and, consequently, their versions of the Norse myths are more like fairy tales than like the powerful myths of any other culture. It is unfortunate that the Icelandic versions are the only Norse myths that have survived.

It is clear that the topography of the Norse creation myth reflects the topography of the land in which it was rewritten. Even today, Iceland is a land of fire and ice. It is composed of volcanic rock and contains an active volcano, geysers, glaciers, and waterfalls.

The Theft of Idun's Apples

Snorri Sturluson (1178–1241), the Icelandic historian and poet, tells the most complete version of this myth in his *Prose Edda*, written in about A.D. 1220. My primary source is the section called "Poetic Diction" in Young's translation of the *Prose Edda* (Univ. of California Press).

The Death of Balder

Snorri Sturluson (1178–1241), the Icelandic historian and poet, tells the most complete version of this myth in the part of his *Prose Edda* called *Gylfaginning* (*The Deluding of Gylfi*), written in about A.D. 1220. My primary source is Young's translation of the *Prose Edda* (Univ. of California Press).

The Theft of Thor's Hammer

The poem "Thrymskvitha" ("The Lay of Thrym"), in the "Codex Regius" of the *Elder Edda* provides the most complete version of this myth. My primary source is Taylor and Auden's translation of selections from the *Elder Edda* (Random House). Other excellent poetic translations of this material include Hollander's *The Poetic Edda* (Univ. of Texas Press) and Terry's *Poems of the Elder Edda* (Univ. of Pennsylvania Press). *The Norse Myths*, retold by Crossley-Holland (Pantheon), contains a fine prose version of this material.

Sigurd the Volsung

Sigurd the Volsung has an interesting literary history. The story of Sigurd was well-known in Norway between A.D. 600 and 1000. Part of it is related to the defeat of the Burgundians, an eastern Germanic people, whom the Huns defeated in 437. The neighboring Franks observed the event and transformed it into what became a heroic epic.

Four principal versions of the Sigurd epic exist, all based on Norse mythology. The earliest Icelandic version, the *Elder Edda*, was written down in about A.D. 1200 and combines poems from the oral tradition with prose transitions. In about 1241, Snorri Sturluson wrote the second Icelandic version, called the *Younger Edda* or the *Prose Edda*, which he based on the *Elder Edda*. He created passages of narrative to connect the famous poetic dialogues and scenes from the older version. Finally, the *Volsunga Saga* was written in about 1300 by an anonymous poet, and it became the most complete and definitive Icelandic version of the *Sigurd* epic.

Equally famous and complete is the *Nibelungenlied*, the Germanic version of the *Sigurd* epic, written in heroic poetry in about 1200 by an anonymous author who also used Norse sources. In this version, Sigurd is called Siegfried, and the story occurs in a medieval setting among nobles who emphasize knightly behavior and the chivalric code. The poet omitted major incidents in the basic story, so that without prior knowledge of the myth, certain aspects of the *Nibelungenlied* do not make sense.

After a lapse in interest that lasted for hundreds of years, writers once again turned to the epic of Sigurd in the 1800s. In 1857, the Norwegian dramatist Henrik Ibsen adapted material from the *Volsunga Saga* for *The Vikings at Helgeland*, and he continued to borrow ideas and themes from this epic for his later plays as well. In 1860, Richard Wagner wrote his *Ring of the Nibelungen* cycle of operas. Although he called his hero Siegfried, he drew most of his material from the *Elder Edda* and the *Volsunga Saga*, rather than from the *Nibelungenlied*. English poet William Morris translated the *Volsunga Saga* into English and also created his epic, *Sigurd* (1877), from this material.

My version of the *Sigurd* epic follows the Icelandic *Volsunga Saga*, although I have added a few details from the *Prose Edda*. I have taken the idea of Fafnir's protective blood, the linden leaf, and the manner of Sigurd's death from the *Nibelungenlied*, because this type of magic is consistent with the magic found in the *Volsunga Saga*. My primary sources are the *Volsunga Saga*, translated by Morris (Collier), and *The Saga of the Volsungs* by Schlauch (AMS reprint).

Three other editions of the Icelandic version that are of special interest are Anderson's *The Saga of the Volsungs*, which also includes his translation of related material from the *Prose Edda* and other sources (Univ. of Delaware Press); Byock's prose version of *The Saga of the Volsungs*, taken from a 1400 manuscript that includes copies of much older texts (Univ. of California Press); and Smith-Dampier's translation of a version from the Faroe Islands, called *Sigurd the Dragon-Slayer* (Kraus reprint).

Three fine versions of the *Nibelungenlied* exist: two prose versions, translated by Hatto (Viking-Penguin) and by Mustard (Random House), and a poetic version by Ryder (Wayne State Univ. Press.)

Volume 1 of Bonnefoy's *Mythologies* (Univ. of Chicago Press) contains an analysis of Norse myth that is particularly worthwhile. Other excellent supplementary source for the study of *Sigurd the Volsung* are Jackson's *The Hero and the King* and *The Literature of the Middle Ages* (Columbia Univ. Press).

Due to the limitation of space, I have confined my focus to Sigurd. Consequently, I have omitted both the first part of the story, which deals with Sigurd's father (Sigmund), and the last part of the story, which deals with Gudrun's revenge.

In one of the original versions of the epic, Brunhild is two different women: the Valkyrie and the princess. To make the combined woman a more consistent figure, I have omitted the scene in which Brunhild is living with her sister and brother-in-law and is working at handicraft. I have moved the ring gift that occurs in the handicraft scene to the scene in which Brunhild and Sigurd first pledge their love (in Chapter 5).

THE BRITISH ISLES
The Ages of the World

The most complete versions of this myth appear in the following sources: Sjoestedt's *Gods and Heroes of the Celts* (Turtle Island); Squire's *Celtic Myth and Legend* (Newcastle reprint of *The Mythology of the British Islands*); and the recently reissued *Celtic Myths and Legends* by Rolleston (Dover reprint of *Myths & Legends of the Celtic Race*). My primary sources are Sjoestedt's *Gods and Heroes of the Celts* and Squire's *Celtic Myth and Legend*. Excellent supplementary sources for further study of this cycle of Celtic mythology include: Chadwick's *The Celts* (Penguin); MacCulloch's *Celtic Mythology* (Dorset); and Rutherford's *Celtic Mythology* (Sterling).

Dagda the Good

The most complete versions of this myth appear in Squire's *Celtic Myth and Legend* (Newcastle reprint of *The Mythology of the British Islands*), which is my primary source, and also in the recently reissued *Celtic Myths and Legends* by Rolleston (Dover reprint of *Myths & Legends of the Celtic Race*). (See my notes on the Celtic "Ages of the World" for excellent supplementary sources for further study of this cycle of Celtic myths.)

Beowulf

Originally written in Old English (Anglo-Saxon) poetic form, my primary source for *Beowulf* is Child's prose version (Houghton Mifflin). Excellent verse translations include those by Kennedy (Oxford Univ. Press), Osborn (Univ. of California Press), and Raffel (Univ. of Massachusetts Press). Alfred's fine prose translation in *Medieval Epics* (Random House) is accompanied by a superb introduction. A dual-language edition, translated by Chickering (Anchor/Doubleday) makes it possible to see the connections between Old English and modern English.

The Selected Bibliography lists excellent supplementary sources for further study of *Beowulf*. Works whose titles may not immediately identify them as relating to *Beowulf* include: Bruce-Mitford's *Aspects of Anglo-Saxon Archaeology* (Harper's Magazine/Harper); Jackson's *The Hero and the King* and *The Literature of the Middle Ages* (Columbia Univ. Press); Owen's *Rites and Religions of the Anglo-Saxons* (Dorset) and Renoir's essay, "*Beowulf*: A Contextual Introduction to Its Contents and Techniques," in Oinas' *Heroic Epic and Saga* (Indiana Univ. Press).

Due to the limitation of space, I have selected conversations and incidents from *Beowulf* with the goal of telling the story simply and directly, while still preserving the author's characterization of the principals, including their speeches. I have also preserved key elements of Old English poetic style, particularly its use of hyphenated word pairs, such as *whale-road* and *battle-fierce*, and its alliteration.

I have found it necessary to omit the tales chanted by bards in the meadhall. These mini-tales echo the major themes of the *Beowulf* epic, and one is the earliest existing version of *Sigurd the Volsung*.

King Arthur

The definitive version of the King Arthur epic is Malory's *Le Morte d'Arthur*, which combines various sources of Arthurian material. However, I constructed my version of King Arthur from sources that predate Malory. My primary sources are Geoffrey of Monmouth's *Historia Regum Britanniae* (*History of the Kings of Britain*, written in Latin in 1136 (Thorpe translation, Folio Society); Wace's *Roman de Brut*, written in Norman French verse in 1155 (Mason translation, Everyman's Library); Chréten de Troyes' *Lancelot* or *Le Chevalier de la Charrette* (*The Knight of the Cart*), probably written in French in the late 1170s, and part of the Guiot Manuscript copied in the mid-13th century (Comfort translation, Everyman's); Layamon's *Brut*, written in

early Middle English in 1205 (Mason translation, Everyman's); *From Camelot to Joyous Guard: The Old French La Mort le Roi Artu*, composed in approximately 1230 (Carman translation, Univ. Press of Kansas); *Morte Arthure*, written in Middle English alliterative poetry in the mid-14th century (Northwestern Univ. Press); and Caxton's 1485 edition of Malory's *Le Morte D'Arthur* (Univ. of California Press reprint).

Other excellent versions of these works include: Barber's *The Arthurian Legends* (Littlefield Adams); Barron and Weinberg's *Layamon's Arthur* (Univ. of Texas Press); Brengle's *Arthur King of Britain* (Prentice-Hall); Gardner's poetic version of *The Alliterative Morte Arthure* (Southern Illinois Univ. Press); Kibler's translation of Chrétien de Troyes' *Arthurian Romances* (Penguin); Lumiansky's edition of Malory's *Le Morte D'Arthur* (Scribner's); Malory's *Le Mort D'Arthur* (Penguin); and Staines' *The Complete Romances of Chrétien de Troyes* (Indiana Univ. Press).

Excellent supplementary sources for further study of *King Arthur* include: Alcock's *Arthur's Britain* (Penguin); Benson's *Malory's Morte D'Arthur* (Harvard Univ. Press); Jackson's *The Literature of the Middle Ages* (Columbia Univ. Press); Morris' *The Age of Arthur* (Scribner's); and Ross and McLaughlin's *The Portable Medieval Reader* (Viking).

In my version, I have combined two principal plots: Arthur's heroic feats as a warrior-king (the English versions); and the relationship between Arthur, Guinevere, and Lancelot (the French version). However, due to the limitation of space, I have found it necessary to omit the many adventures of the knights of the Round Table that are irrelevant to the principal plot of the love triangle.

As is mentioned in my notes on Heracles and *The Aeneid*, among Western nations in ancient and medieval times, a great city-state or nation was expected to have a great pedigree.

Homer's Troy was held in such esteem that writers who wished to authenticate their nation's heritage chose their founding fathers from among the heroes of the Trojan War. Consequently, in A.D. 1136, Geoffrey of Monmouth, in his *Historia Regum Britanniae*, chose the great-grandson of Aeneas to lead Trojan exiles to England, where they established New Troy (London) and the kingdom of Britain.

THE FAR EAST AND THE PACIFIC ISLANDS

The Creation, Death, and Rebirth of the Universe (India)

This myth is found in the Great Puranas, "stories of ancient times," which were written down between A.D. 300 and 1000 and became accepted throughout India. According to Indian tradition, Vyasa, the Hindu sage and seer, is the author of the Puranas in that he edited and compiled the material from earlier sources. "The Four Ages," "The Origin of Brahma from the Lotus in Vishnu's Navel," and "The Origin of the World from Brahma" are related in the *Kurma*; "The Kali Age" and "The Destruction of the World" are related in the *Vishnu*; and "The Cosmic Egg" is related in the *Vamana Saromahatmya*.

My only primary source of this group of myths is *Classical Hindu Mythology*, translated and edited by Dimmitt and Van Buitenen (Temple Univ. Press). Supplementary sources for further study of Hindu myth are Ions' *Indian Mythology* (Bedrick); *Hindu Myths* (Penguin); and Zimmer's *Myths and Symbols in Indian Art and Civilization* (Princeton Univ. Press).

Indra and the Dragon

"Indra and Vritra" is related in the Rig Veda, an early collection of mythic material that is dedicated to the pre-Hindu gods. Dating from 1500 to 1200 B.C., the Veda was preserved through the oral tradition. Later, "Indra and Vritra" was included, in a Hindu edition, in the Great Purana called the *Bhagvata*. The Great Puranas, "stories of ancient times," were written down between A.D. 300 and 1000 and became accepted throughout India. According to Indian tradition, Vyasa, the Hindu sage and seer, is the author of the Puranas, in that he edited and compiled the material from earlier sources such as the Rig Veda.

My only primary source of "Indra and the Dragon" is *Classical Hindu Mythology*, translated and edited by Dimmitt and Van Buitenen (Temple Univ. Press). (See my notes on the creation myths of India for supplementary sources for further study of Indra.)

The Ramayana

Although the epic poem called *The Ramayana* was composed sometime between 200 B.C. and A.D. 200 by the poet Valmiki, the story of "The Ramayana" is included, also in a Hindu edition, in the Great Purana called the *Garuda*. The Great Puranas, "stories of ancient times," were written down between A.D. 300 and 1000 and became accepted throughout India. According to Indian tradition, Vyasa, the Hindu sage and seer, is the author of the Puranas, in that he edited and compiled the material from earlier sources such as the Rig Veda.

My primary sources for *The Ramayana* are *Myths of the Hindus and Buddhists*, by Coomaraswamy and Nivedita (Dover reprint); *Classical Hindu Mythology*, translated and edited by Dimmitt and Van Buitenen (Temple Univ. Press); and *The Ramayana & The Mahabharata*, a poetic version by Dutt (Everyman's). Other excellent prose translations are those by Buck (Univ. of California Press) and Narayan (Penguin). *The Forest Book of the Ramayana of Kampan*, translated in verse by Hart and Heifetz (Univ. of California Press) is a 12th-century Tamil (South Indian) version of *The Ramayana*. (See my notes on the creation myths of India for supplementary sources for further study of aspects of *The Ramayana*).

I have followed the principal plot of *The Ramayana*, focusing on Rama's marriage to Sita, his banishment, Sita's abduction, the monkeys' search for Sita, Rama's conquest of Ravana, and Rama's two tests of Sita's virtue. I have chosen conversations and incidents with the goal of telling the story simply and directly, while still preserving Valmiki's characterization of the principals. I also have attempted to preserve the beautiful figurative language of the original. Due to the limitation of space, I have found it necessary to omit the stories of such great characters as Sugriva and his brother Vali, and the heroic deeds of Hanuman.

The Creation of the Universe (China)
The first part of the "P'an-ku" creation myth appears in the *San-wu li-chi* (*Record of Cycles in Threes and Fives*), written during the 3rd century B.C. Other, probably later, texts deal with the creative function of his corpse. The best source of the goddess "Nu-kua's" activities can be found in the Han Taoist work, *Huai-nan-tzu*, written during the 2nd century B.C.

My primary sources for this myth are Christie's *Chinese Mythology* (Newnes/Hamlyn); Bodde's essay, "Myths of Ancient China," in Kramer's *Mythologies of the Ancient World* (Anchor/Doubleday); Mackenzie's *Myths of China and Japan* (Gresham); Walls and Walls' *Classical Chinese Myths* (Joint); and Werner's *Ancient Tales and Folklore of China* (Bracken reprint of *Myths and Legends of China*). The myth of Pangu also appears in Sanders' *Dragons, Gods, & Spirits from Chinese Mythology* (Schocken), which is an excellent collection of Chinese myths.

Yi the Archer and the Ten Suns
The ancient Chinese divided each week into ten days, each of which was illuminated by a different sun. The myth that states the problem of the ten suns appears in the Chou texts, *Chuang'tzu* and *Lu-shih sh'un-ch'iu*. The *Huai-nan-tzu*, the Han Taoist work from the 2nd

century B.C., relates how Yi (or Hou Yi) rescues the world by shooting down nine of the suns.

My primary sources for this myth are Christie's *Chinese Mythology* (Newnes/Hamlyn); Bodde's essay, "Myths of Ancient China," in Kramer's *Mythologies of the Ancient World* (Anchor/Doubleday); and Walls and Walls' *Classical Chinese Myths* (Joint). The myth of "Yi the Archer" also appears in Sanders' *Dragons, Gods & Spirits from Chinese Mythology* (Schocken), which is an excellent collection of Chinese myths.

The Quest for the Sun
This myth is called "In Search of the Sun" in Wang Hui-Ming's *Folk Tales of the West Lake* (Foreign Languages), and it is called "Rising Sun Terrace" in Walls and Walls' *West Lake* (Joint). These are my primary sources.

The Creation of the Universe and Japan
This myth is related in *Nihongi: Chronicles of Japan from the Earliest Times to A.D. 697*, translated by Aston (Tuttle), which, being the best, is my only primary source. (The title of this work is also transliterated as *Nihon Shoki*.) This myth also appears in Piggott's *Japanese Mythology* (Bedrick), as well as in Sproul's interesting collection *Primal Myths* (Harper Collins). Mackenzie's *Myths of China and Japan* (Gresham) is an interesting comparative mythological study that includes the Japanese creation and Amaterasu, as well as information about the Ainu.

Amaterasu
This myth is related in *Nihongi: Chronicles of Japan from the Earliest Times to A.D. 697*, translated by Aston (Tuttle), which, being the best, is my only primary source. (The title of this work is also transliterated as *Nihon Shoki*.) The myth of Amaterasu also appears in Davis' *Myths and Legends of Japan* (Graham Brash) and in Piggott's *Japanese Mythology* (Bedrick).

Kotan Utunnai (Ainu)
Batchelor's transcription of *Kotan*

Utunnai was first published, in both Ainu and English, in the *Transactions of the Asiatic Society of Japan* in 1890. My only primary source, which is excellent, is Philippi's poetic translation, in *Songs of Gods, Songs of Humans* (Princeton Univ. Press).

In my prose version, I have retained the first-person narrative perspective because the narrator's limited omniscience recreates his magical world. In the course of the epic, the narrator has seven heroic adventures. Although I have followed the principal plot, I have found it necessary to omit three adventures due to the limitation of space: those involving the Pestilence Deities, the man and woman of Hopuni-santa, and the birdlike monsters.

I have omitted proper names that are infrequently used, such as those of the narrator (Poiyaunpe) and the woman whom he calls "Older Sister" (Chiwashpet-un-mat). "Dangling Nose" is a translation of that famous warrior's real name, Etu-rachichi, and, given his function in the story, I have preferred to use the more colorful translation. "Kotan Utunnai" refers to an isolated location in the land of the Repunkur (people of the sea).

The Creation Cycle (Polynesian/Maori)

Grey relates this myth in the chapter "The Children of Heaven and Earth," in his *Polynesian Mythology and Ancient Traditional History* (Auckland). My primary sources are Alpers' *Maori Myths and Tribal Legends* (Longman Paul), and Sproul's *Primal Myths* (HarperCollins), which is also the best contemporary version.

The Taming of the Sun

Westervelt relates this myth in his *Legends of Ma-ui* (1910). My primary sources are Colum's *Legends of Hawaii* (Yale Univ. Press) and a collection of Westervelt's work, *Myths and Legends of Hawaii* (Mutual). Beckwith's *Hawaiian Mythology* (Univ. of Hawaii Press) is an excellent source of supplementary information. *The Legends of and Myths of*

Hawaii, by His Hawaiian Majesty Kalakaua (Mutual reprint) is stylistically fascinating.

AFRICA
The Creation of the Universe and Ife

Courlander tells this myth in *A Treasury of African Folklore* (Crown), which, being the best, is my only primary source. Other interesting works on this subject are Courlander's *Tales of Yoruba Gods and Heroes* (Crown) and his novel, *The Master of the Forge* (Crown), which is based on Yoruba mythology.

The Quarrel Between Sagbata and Sogbo

Courlander includes this myth in *A Treasury of African Folklore* (Crown), which is my only primary source. Courlander's source is Herskovits and Herskovits' collection of Dahomean or Fon myths, *Dahomean Narrative* (Northwestern Univ. Press). Other excellent sources of African Mythology are Parrinder's *African Mythology* (Hamlyn) and Radin's *African Folktales* (Schocken).

Gassire's Lute

Frobenius and Fox relate *Gassire's Lute* in *African Genesis* (Stackpole), which, in its reprint (Turtle Island), is one of my primary sources. My other sources of this epic, all of which include the Frobenius and Fox version, are Abrahams' *African Folktales* (Pantheon); Courlander's *Treasury of African Folklore* (Crown); and Rothenberg's revised and expanded edition of *Technicians of the Sacred* (Univ. of California Press). *The Heart of the Ngoni*, by Courlander with Ousmane Sako (Crown), is an excellent collection of other West African epics.

Apparently, *Gassire's Lute* is an important part of the existing fragment of the Soninke epic *Dausi*. I have related *Gassire's Lute* in its entirety.

Sunjata

Niane relates the definitive version of this epic in French, as he heard it from Djeli Mamudu Kuyate, a griot from the village of Djeliba Koro (Siguiri), in

Guinea. My primary source of *Sunjata* is Pickett's *Sundiata* (Longman), a prose translation of Niane's *Soundjata, ou l'Epopée Mandingue*.

However, I have incorporated and retold a few incidents from other sources. The second hunter's epic is part of "Lion of Manding: A Wolof Epic," in Courlander's *Treasury of African Folklore* (Crown). It was related to David Ames by Ali Sawse in the village of Ballanghar, Gambia, in 1950.

Okpewho quotes the prophecies of the two prophets in *The Epic in Africa* (Columbia Univ. Press). Okpewho's source is *Sunjata II*, a version from the Gambia River area, which Innes relates in his *Sunjata: Three Mandinka Versions* (School of Oriental and African Studies). Nana Triban's conversation with Sumanguru is quoted in Cavendish's *Legends of the World* (Orbis) as well as in Okpewho's *The Epic of Africa*. Both Cavendish and Okpewho's source is *Sunjata II*. Biebuyck's essay, "The African Heroic Epic," in Oinas' *Heroic Epic and Saga* (Indiana Univ. Press) is worth reading in connection with the study of *Sunjata*.

Although I have followed the principal plot, I have retold the story in chronological order and in the repetitive style that is characteristic of oral epics. I have omitted one of the two hunters in the first hunter's epic and also Sunjata's sister, Djamaru, because they are not important in Niane's version of the epic. I have also omitted songs composed in Sunjata's honor, ostensibly by Balla Fasseke, but according to Niane, by later griots (1307–1332).

Mali and its peoples are known by a variety of related names, depending on the community to which the speaker belongs. I have used *Mandingo* in the context of the Keita nation, Kangaba, the people of Old Mali, and their language; and *Mande-speaking* and *Mandinka* in the broader context of the peoples of the empire of Mali.

Old Mali was located in the area between the Niger and the Sankarani Rivers and was composed of twelve provinces. The empire of Mali was much larger; the modern republic of Mali is much smaller. Today, Mali extends west and south of Bamako, its capital. It includes the Manding mountains and the upper valley of the Niger River, as far as Kurussa, in Guinea.

Niani began as a small village and later became the capital of the empire of Mali. Today Niani is a small village once again. It is located on the Sankarani River, one kilometer from the borders of Mali and Guinea.

Mamadu Kuyate (the griot who relates the Sunjata epic to Niane) alludes to a secret, which may be the cause of Sunjata's death. Some griots say that an arrow killed Sunjata during a public protest in Niani. Others say that Sunjata fought an unjust war against the Wasulu people and that they defeated the emperor and his army in a critical battle by the Sankarani River. Some say that Sunjata jumped into the tumultuous waters of the Sankarani and drowned. Others say that just as Sunjata disappeared beneath the raging waters, a hippopotamus rose to the surface in his place. They proclaim that Sunjata transformed himself into a hippopotamus in order to avoid being captured by the Wasulu. (*Mali* in the Mandingo language means "hippopotamus.")

Mwindo

Biebuyck and Mateene relate this epic in *The Mwindo Epic, from the Banyanga* (Univ. of California Press). My sources of the *Mwindo* epic are Abrahams' *African Folktales* (Pantheon) and Courlander's *Treasury of African Folklore* (Crown). Both authors took the Biebuyck and Mateene version of *Mwindo* as their source.

Biebuyck relates three other versions of *Mwindo* in *Hero and Chief* (Univ. of California Press). Biebuyck's essay, "The African Heroic Epic," in Oinas' *Heroic Epic and Saga* (Indiana Univ. Press) and Okpewho's *The Epic in Africa* (Columbia

Univ. Press) are also worth reading in connection with the study of *Mwindo*.

I have followed the principal plot of Biebuyck's first version of *Mwindo*, focusing on Mwindo's adventures. However, due to the limitation of space, I have found it necessary to omit Mwindo's many songs, even though they are an important part of the performance of the epic. Whenever the words of a song have advanced the plot, I have incorporated them into the narrative.

THE AMERICAS

The Creation (Aymara/Tiahuanaco)

Juan de Betanzos, the official interpreter for the Spanish governor of Peru, took this myth from a Peruvian narrative song, the customary way the Inca historians preserved their nation's history. He relates this myth in his *Suma y Narración de los Incas*. My primary source is Osborne's rendition of de Betanzos' version of the myth, in *South American Mythology* (Newnes/Hamlyn). Osborne also includes an English translation of a related Aymara/Tiahuanaco myth as told by Pedro de Cieza de León in *The Second Part of the Chronicle of Peru* (Hakluyt Society). Another excellent source, published two years after the first edition of *World Mythology*, is Bierhorst's *The Mythology of South America* (Morrow).

Viracocha is discussed in Volume 2 of Bonnefoy's *Mythologies* (Univ. of Chicago Press).

The House of Origin

Pedro de Cieza de León relates this myth in *The Second Part of the Chronicle of the Inca*, which is his sequel to *The Travels of Pedro de Cieza de Leon*. My primary source is Osborne's rendition of this material in his *South American Mythology* (Newnes/Hamlyn).

The Children of the Sun

Inca Garcilaso de la Vega relates this myth in Volume 1 of *The Royal Commentaries of the Inca*, published in Spain in 1609. My primary source is Garcilaso de la Vega's *The Incas*, translated by Jolas

(Avon). Osborne quotes Garcilaso's rendition in *South American Mythology* (Newnes/Hamlyn).

Bierhorst tells this myth and examines its relationship to other myths from this part of the world in *The Mythology of South America* (Morrow). Valdelomar relates creative versions of this and other Inca myths in *Our Children of the Sun* (Southern Illinois Univ. Press).

Paraparawa and Waraku

Rivière relates this myth in *Marriage Among the Trio* (Clarendon). My primary source is Cavendish's *Mythology: An Illustrated Encyclopedia* (Orbis). Roe discusses "Paraparawa and Waraku" in relation to other myths of its type in *The Cosmic Zygote* (Rutgers Univ. Press). In addition, *Watunna* by de Civrieux (North Point) relates an interesting group of myths from northern South America.

The Creation (Maya)

The source of this myth is *The Popol Vuh* of the Quiché Maya, written by an anonymous author. It was translated into alphabetic script during the mid-1500s by Mayan scribes. My primary source is Goetz and Morley's *Popol Vuh* (Univ. of Oklahoma Press).

An excellent version, published after I had first written *World Mythology*, is Tedlock's *Popol Vuh* (Simon and Schuster). Sproul's *Primal Myths* (HarperCollins) contains selections from the opening sections of my primary source, the Goetz and Morley translation.

Bierhorst compares this myth with the *Legend of the Suns* in *The Mythology of Mexico and Central America* (Morrow). Moreover, he enables readers to compare the *Popol Vuh* with other creation myths from this part of the world.

The Creation Cycle (Toltec/Aztec)

"The Five Worlds and Their Suns" can be found in the 16th-century Nahuatl manuscript, the *Chimalpopoca Codex: Annals of Cuauhtitlan and Legend of the Suns*, first recorded in alphabetic script by Aztec scribes in the mid-1500s. The first English edition of this manuscript became available late in 1992, translated by Bierhorst under the title *History and Mythology of the Aztecs* (Univ. of Arizona Press). Bierhorst's edition includes the first translation, in any language, of the complete *Legend of the Suns*. My primary sources are Bierhorst's *Four Masterworks of American Indian Literature* (Univ. of Arizona Press) and Nicholson's *Mexican and Central American Mythology* (Newnes/Hamlyn). Bierhorst compares this myth with the *Popul Vuh* in *The Mythology of Mexican and Central America* (Morrow). Moreover, he enables readers to compare the *Legend of the Suns* with other sun myths from this part of the world.

"The Creation of the Earth" can be found in a 16th-century French manuscript, *Histoyre du Mechique* (*The History of Mexico*), published in a French journal in 1905. Andre Thevet, the translator, took his material from a collection (now lost) compiled by Spanish missionaries in 1543. My primary sources are Bierhorst's version in *The Red Swan* (Farrar Straus; Univ. of New Mexico Press) and Nicholson's version in *Mexican and Central American Mythology* (Newnes/Hamlyn).

"The Creation of Human Beings" can be found in the *Chimalpopoca Codex*. According to Bierhorst, Quetzalcoatl's descent into the Underworld and his use of the bones exists in two other (unspecified) 16th-century versions as well. My primary sources for this myth are Bierhorst's *Four Masterworks of American Indian Literature* and Nicholson's *Mexican and Central American Mythology*.

According to Nicholson, "The Creation of Music" is a poem that can be found in one of the 16th-century Nahuatl manuscripts. It appears in Bierhorst's book *The Hungry Woman* (Morrow), and also in Nicholson's *Mexican and Central American Mythology*, which is my primary source.

Quetzalcoatl
The myths that relate how Quetzalcoatl

is tricked and driven from the Toltec capital by Tezcatlipoca appear in two original sources: the *Chimalpopoca Codex: Annals of Cuauhtitlan and Legend of the Suns*, a 16th-century Nahuatl manuscript, first recorded in alphabetic script by Aztec scribes in the mid-1500s; and also the Nahuatl texts collected and recorded by the 16th-century Spanish priest, Fray Bernardino de Sahagun, under the title *Florentine Codex: General History of the Things of New Spain*. My primary sources are Bierhorst's *Four Masterworks of American Indian Literature* (Univ. of Arizona Press) and Nicholson's *Mexican and Central American Mythology* (Newnes/Hamlyn).

Sahagun's *Florentine Codex* is available in an edition by Anderson and Dibble (Univ. of Utah Press). Sahagun translated the Nahuatl texts known as the *Florentine Codex* in order to study the Nahuatl language, rather than to perpetuate Aztec beliefs. In practice, Christian priests and missionaries learned the Nahuatl language in order to preach about Christianity in the language of their audience. (See my notes on "The Creation Cycle" for information about the first English translation of the *Codex Chimalpopoca*.)

Anaya retells the myth of Quetzalcoatl in the form of a novella in *Lord of the Dawn* (Univ. of New Mexico Press). Bierhorst discusses Quetzalcoatl in terms of other myths from this part of the world in *The Mythology of Mexico and Central America* (Morrow). Brundage analyzes Quetzalcoatl and Tezcatlipoca in *The Fifth Sun* (Univ. of Texas Press).

The Emergence
Matthews' 1897 transcription of the creation myth in his *Navaho Legends* (American Folk-Lore Society) is the classic source of this material. Another version is Klah's *Navajo Creation Myth*, recorded by Wheelwright (Museum of Navaho Ceremonial Art). My primary sources are the versions found in Gilpin's *The Enduring Navajo* (Univ. of Texas Press) and in Newcomb's *Navaho Folk*

Tales (Museum of Navaho Ceremonial Art). The most complete version of this myth since Matthews' is Zolbrod's *Dine bahane: The Navajo Creation Story* (Univ. of New Mexico Press). Burland relates a version of "The Emergence" in *North American Indian Mythology* (Newnes/Hamlyn). Erdoes and Ortiz' *American Indian Myths and Legends* (Pantheon) includes an extensive selection of other Native American creation myths.

Ahaiyuta and the Cloud-Eater

The classic versions of this myth can be found in Benedict's *Zuñi Mythology* (Columbia Univ. Press) and Stevenson's 1904 *The Zuñi Indians* (Bureau of Amercian Ethnology), which are my primary sources. The myth can also be found in Feldmann's *The Storytelling Stone* (Dell) and Wherry's *Indian Masks and Myths of the West* (Bonanza/Crown). Mullett's *Spider Woman* stories (Univ. of Arizona Press) is also an excellent collection of other Native American myths from the Southwest.

Lodge-Boy and Thrown-Away

Simms relates this myth in his 1903 *Traditions of the Crows* (Field Museum Anthropological Series). My primary source is Thompson's classic version, in his *Tales of the North American Indians* (Indiana Univ. Press). Thompson's source is Simms. *Tales of the North American Indians*, originally published in 1929, continues to be reprinted. Moreover, Thompson's versions of the myths, because they are based on primary sources, continue to be reprinted in anthologies compiled by other editors, such as Feldmann's *The Storytelling Stone* (Dell).

Coffin's *Tales of the North American Indians* (American Folklore Society) contains a Wichita version of this myth, entitled "Afterbirth and Lodge Boy." Bierhorst, in *The Mythology of North America* (Morrow), discusses the many variations of the "Lodge-Boy and Thrown-Away" myth. Excellent collections of other Native American myths from the Plains and Rockies

include: Clark's *Indian Legends from the Northern Rockies* (Univ. of Oklahoma Press); Grinnell's *By Cheyenne Campfires* (Univ. of Nebraska Press); Marriott and Rachlin's *American Indian Mythology* and *Plains Indian Mythology* (Crowell); and Walker's *Lakota Myth* (Univ. of Nebraska Press).

The Woman Who Fell from the Sky

Cusick, a Tuscarora Iroquois historian, relates this myth in the 1827 *Sketches of Ancient History of the Six Nations*. The oldest Huron version of this myth was related in 1874 by a seventy-five-year-old Huron sub-chief, and appears in Hale's 1888 "Huron Folk-Lore" (Journal of American Folklore). Hewitt, who was of Tuscarora desent, specialized in the Iroquois creation myth and collected detailed Mohawk, Seneca, and Onondaga versions that appear in his *Introduction to Seneca Fiction, Legends, and Myths 1910–1911* (Bureau of American Ethnology). He also worked with Curtin to write *Seneca Myths and Fictions* (Bureau of American Ethnology), and this is the source of the famous Seneca version of the Iroquois creation myth. Later, Curtin wrote *Seneca Indian Myths* (Dutton).

Each of my three primary sources uses one of the above original sources in relating the Iroquois creation myth. Clark relates Hale's Huron version in her *Indian Legends of Canada* (McClelland & Stewart). Emerson quotes extensively from Cusick's Tuscarora version in her 1884 *Indian Myths or Legends, Traditions and Symbols of the Aborigines of America* (Ross & Haines reprint). Thompson relates Curtin and Hewitt's classic Seneca version in his *Tales of the North American Indians* (Indiana Univ. Press). (See my notes on "Lodge-Boy and Thrown-Away" for information about Thompson's versions of the North American Indian myths.)

Bierhorst presents a detailed discussion of this myth in *The Mythology of North America* (Morrow). A Huron version of this myth is discussed in

Volume 2 of Bonnefoy's *Mythologies* (Univ. of Chicago Press). Feldmann reprints Thompson's Seneca version of this myth in *The Storytelling Stone* (Dell).

The many versions of this myth are very similar in most respects. However, the twins have different names in different versions. In English translation, Cusick calls them "Good Mind" and "Bad Mind." Curtin and Hewitt call them "Little Sprout" and "Flint." Huron versions call them "Good Man" or "Good Brother" and "Like Flint" or "Evil Brother." Moreover, in some versions, Sky Woman does not have a daughter, and she herself gives birth to the twins. In some versions, the twins use bags of corn and beans as weapons in their final battle.

Raven and the Sources of Light

The major Raven myths were all originally published by the Bureau of American Ethnology and are found in Swanton's *Haida Texts and Myths* (1905) and *Tlingit Myths and Texts* (1909), and in Boas' *Tsimshian Mythology* and *Tsimshian Texts*, both published in 1916 and the best known sources. These are my primary sources, as well.

Burland relates "Raven and the Moon," a Haida version, in *North American Indian Mythology* (Newnes/Hamlyn). Clark relates "How Raven Helped the Ancient People," a version from Puget Sound, in her *Indian Legends of the Pacific Northwest* (Univ. of California Press). Coffin relates "Theft of Light," a Tahltan version, in his *Indian Tales of North America* (American Folklore Society). Coffin's version is fascinating in that is combines elements of the Tlingit and Tsimshian versions, while being quite different in many of its details. Erdoes and Ortiz relate "The Theft of Light" (Tsimshian, from Boas/Thompson) in their *American Indian Myths and Legends* (Pantheon). Feldmann relates three raven myths (Boas/Thompson's Tsimshinan, Clark's Puget Sound, and Swanton's Tlingit) in *The Storytelling Stone* (Dell). Goodchild's

Raven Tales (Chicago Review Press) is an excellent source. Wherry relates a raven myth in his *Indian Masks and Myths of the West* (Bonanza/Crown).

The many versions of this myth are very similar in most respects. However, interesting variations exist, and in creating my own version, I have chosen elements and descriptive details from Haida, Tlingit, and Tsimshian versions.

In the major Haida version, the girl swallows Raven in the form of a conifer needle, which is floating in her water-dipper. Raven steals the moon, which is kept in a set of nested boxes, and returns with it under his wing.

In the major Tlingit version, the girl swallows Raven in the form of a small piece of dirt. Raven steals the stars, the moon, and daylight, which are contained in tied, separate, round bundles or bags. He threatens to let the daylight out of a box, and does.

In the major Tsimshian version, Giant removes his Raven-skin and transforms himself into a cedar leaf, which the chief's daughter swallows as it floats in her water-dipper. Giant steals Daylight, which is kept in a box, and, donning his Raven-skin, he escapes. Daylight emerges when Giant is taunted into breaking that box.

Sedna

The most famous version of this myth was originally told to Boas in 1884–1885 by the Oqomiut and the Akudnirmiut people of southern Baffin Island. Boas recorded this material in *The Central Eskimo 1884–1885* (Bureau of American Ethnology). My primary source is Thompson's classic version, related in his *Tales of the North American Indians* (Indiana Univ. Press). Thompson's source is Boas. (See my notes on "Lodge-Boy and Thrown-Away" for information about Thompson's versions of the North American Indian myths.) My second source is Caswell's *Shadows from the Singing House* (Tuttle).

Bierhorst reprints Thompson's versions in *The Red Swan* (Farrar Straus;

Univ. of New Mexico Press). Feldmann does also in *The Storytelling Stone* (Dell). Haviland reprints Caswell's version in *The Faber Book of North American Legends* (Faber and Faber). A version of this myth is discussed in Volume 2 of Bonnefoy's *Mythologies* (Univ. of Chicago Press). Norman's *Northern Tales* (Pantheon) is an excellent collection of Inuit myths. However, it does not include the myth of "Sedna."

Caught by a Hair-String

Rand relates this myth in his 1894 *Legends of the Micmacs* (Longmans), but he does not reveal his source. My primary source is the version beautifully told by Whitehead in her *Stories from the Six Worlds* (Nimbus). Macfarlan's *American Indian Legends* (Heritage) contains another version of this myth.

Clark's *Indian Legends from the Northern Rockies* (Univ. of Oklahoma Press) and *Indian Legends of Canada* (McClelland and Stewart), and Leland's *Algonquin Legends* (Dover reprint of *The Algonquin Legends of New England, or, Myths and Folk Lore of the Micmac, Passamaquoddy, and Penobscot Tribes*) are excellent collections of Canadian Native American myths. However, neither collection includes "Caught by a Hair-String."

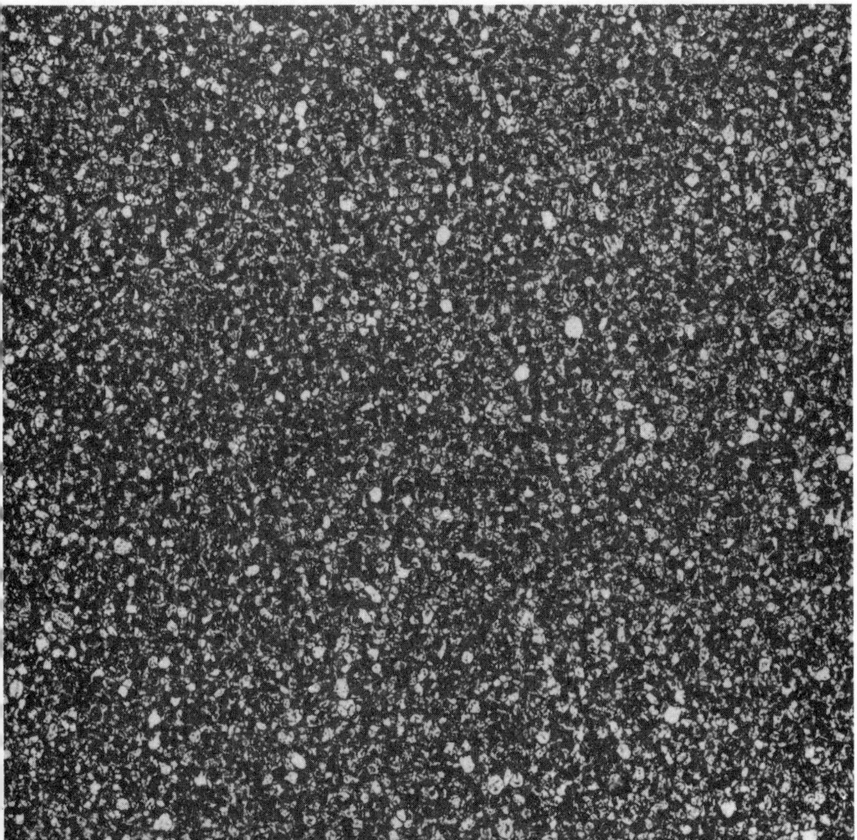

Selected Bibliography

GREECE AND ROME

Agias (or Hegias). "Nostoi." *Hesiod, The Homeric Hymns and Homerica*. Trans. Hugh G. Evelyn-White. Loeb Classical Library. Cambridge: Harvard Univ. Press, 1977.

Apollodorus. *The Library* and *Epitome*. 2 vols. Trans. Sir James George Frazer. Loeb Classical Library. Cambridge: Harvard Univ. Press, 1976; 1970.

———. *The Library: Gods and Heroes of the Greeks*. Trans. Michael Simpson. Amherst: Univ. of Massachusetts Press, 1976.

Arctinus. "The Aethiopis." *Hesiod, The Homeric Hymns and Homerica*. Trans. Hugh G. Evelyn-White. Loeb Classical Library. Cambridge: Harvard Univ. Press, 1977.

———. "The Iliũpe'rsis." *Hesiod, The Homeric Hymns and Homerica*. Trans. Hugh G. Evelyn-White. Loeb Classical Library. Cambridge: Harvard Univ. Press, 1977.

Bespaloff, Rachel. *On the Iliad*. Trans. Mary McCarthy. Princeton: Princeton Univ. Press, 1970.

Beye, Charles Rowan. *The Iliad, the Odyssey and the Epic Tradition*. Gloucester, MA: Peter Smith, 1972.

Burn, Andrew Robert. *The World of Hesiod: A Study of the Greek Middle Ages*. New York: Benjamin Blom, 1966.

Chadwick, John. *The Mycenaean World*. New York: Cambridge Univ. Press, 1976.

Di Cesare, Mario A. *The Altar and the City: A Reading of Virgil's* Aeneid. New York: Columbia Univ. Press, 1974.

Diodorus Siculus. *Library of History*. Vol. II. Trans. C. H. Oldfather. Loeb Classical Library. Cambridge: Harvard Univ. Press, 1967.

Edwards, Mark W. *Homer: Poet of the Iliad*. Baltimore: Johns Hopkins Univ. Press, 1987.

———, ed. *The Iliad: A Commentary*. Volume V. New York: Cambridge Univ. Press, 1991.

Eugammon. "The Telegony." *Hesiod, The Homeric Hymns and Homerica*. Trans. Hugh G. Evelyn-White. Loeb Classical Library. Cambridge: Harvard Univ. Press, 1977.

Finley, John H., Jr. *Homer's Odyssey*. Cambridge: Harvard Univ. Press, 1978.

Galinsky, G. Karl. *Aeneas, Sicily and Rome*. Princeton: Princeton Univ. Press, 1971.

Graves, Robert. *The Greek Myths*. 2 vols. New York: Braziller, 1957.

Hesiod. *Theogony, Works and Days, Shield*. Trans. Apostolos N. Athanassakis. Baltimore: Johns Hopkins Univ. Press, 1983.

———. *Theogony* and *Works and Days*. Trans. M. L. West. New York: Oxford Univ. Press, 1988.

———. "Works and Days." "Theogony." *Hesiod, The Homeric Hymns and Homerica*. Trans. Hugh G. Evelyn-White. Loeb Classical Library. Cambridge: Harvard Univ. Press, 1977.

———. *The Works and Days. Theogony. The Shield of Herakles*. Trans. Richmond Lattimore. Ann Arbor: Univ. of Michigan Press, 1991.

Homer. *The Iliad*. Trans. Robert Fagles. New York: Viking, 1990.

———. *The Iliad*. Trans. Robert Fitzgerald. Garden City, NY.: Anchor/Doubleday, 1974.

———. *The Iliad*. Trans. Richmond Lattimore. Chicago: Univ. of Chicago Press, 1969.

———. *The Iliad*. Trans. A. T. Murray. 2 vols. Loeb Classical Library. Cambridge: Harvard Univ. Press, 1978; 1976.

———. *The Odyssey*. Trans. Albert Cook. New York: Norton, 1974.

———. *The Odyssey*. Trans. Robert Fitzgerald. Garden City, NY: Anchor/Doubleday, 1961.

———. *The Odyssey*. Trans. Richmond Lattimore. New York: Harper & Row, 1977.

———. *The Odyssey*. Trans. T. E. Lawrence. New York: Oxford Univ. Press, 1991.

———. *The Odyssey*. Trans. A. T. Murray. 2 vols. Loeb Classical Library. Cambridge: Harvard Univ. Press, 1976; 1980.

The Homeric Hymns. Trans. Apostolos N. Athanassakis. Baltimore: Johns Hopkins Univ. Press, 1976.

The Homeric Hymns. Trans. Charles Boer. Irving, TX: Spring Publications/Univ. of Dallas, 1979.

"The Homeric Hymns." *Hesiod, The Homeric Hymns and Homerica*. Trans. Hugh G. Evelyn-White. Loeb Classical Library. Cambridge: Harvard Univ. Press, 1977.

The Homeric Hymns and The Battle of the Frogs and the Mice. Trans. Daryl Hine. New York: Atheneum, 1972.

Jackson, W. T. H. *Hero and King*. New York: Columbia Univ. Press, 1986.

Janko, Richard, ed. *The Iliad: A Commentary*. Vol. IV. New York: Cambridge Univ. Press, 1992.

Kirk, G. S., *The Iliad: A Commentary*. Vols. I and II. New York: Cambridge Univ. Press, 1985; 1990.

Kitto, H. D. F. *The Greeks*. New York: Viking Penguin, 1951.

Lamberton, Robert and John J. Keaney, eds. *Homer's Ancient Readers*. Princeton: Princeton Univ. Press, 1992.

Lawler, Traugott. "The *Aeneid*."*Homer to Brecht*. Eds. Michael Seidel and Edward Mendelson. New Haven: Yale Univ. Press, 1977.

Lesches. "The *Little Iliad*." *Hesiod, The Homeric Hymns and Homerica*. Trans. Hugh G. Evelyn-White. Loeb Classical Library. Cambridge: Harvard Univ. Press, 1977.

Livy (Titus Livius). *The Early History of Rome: Books I–V of The History of Rome from Its Foundation*. Trans. Aubrey De Selincourt. New York: Viking Penguin, 1981.

———. *The Roman History: The History of Rome from Its Foundation*. 2 vols. Trans. B. O. Foster. Loeb Classical Library. Cambridge: Harvard Univ. Press, 1988.

Ovid. *Metamorphoses*. Trans. Rolfe Humphries. Bloomington: Indiana Univ. Press, 1967.

———. *Metamorphoses*. Trans. Frank Justus Miller. Loeb Classical Library. Cambridge: Harvard Univ. Press, 1984.

———. *Metamorphoses: Englished, Mythologized, and Represented in Figures*. Trans. George Sandys. Lincoln: Univ. of Nebraska Press, 1970. Reprint of 1632 edition.

Plutarch. *Parallel Lives of Greeks and Romans*. Trans. Bernadotte Perrin. Loeb Classical Library. Cambridge: Harvard Univ. Press, 1967.

Redfield, James M. *Nature and Culture in the Iliad: The Tragedy of Hector*. Chicago: Univ. of Chicago Press, 1978.

Schein, Seth L. *The Mortal Hero: An Introduction to Homer's Iliad*. Berkeley: Univ. of California Press, 1984.

Stasinus (or Hegesinus). "The Cypria." *Hesiod, The Homeric Hymns and Homerica*. Trans. Hugh G. Evelyn-White. Loeb Classical Library.

Cambridge: Harvard Univ. Press, 1977.

Steiner, George and Robert Fagles. *Homer: A Collection of Critical Essays*. Englewood Cliffs: Prentice-Hall, 1962.

Taylor, Charles H., Jr., ed. *Essays on the Odyssey*. Bloomington: Indiana Univ. Press, 1969.

Vermeule, Emily. *Greece in the Bronze Age*. Chicago: Univ. of Chicago Press, 1972.

Versenyi, Laszlo. *Man's Measure: A Study of the Greek Image of Man from Homer to Sophocles*. Albany: State Univ. of New York Press, 1974.

Virgil. *The Aeneid*. Trans. H. R. Fairclough. 2 vols. Loeb Classical Library. Cambridge: Harvard Univ. Press, 1978.

———. *The Aeneid*. Trans. Robert Fitzgerald. New York: Random House, 1983.

———. *The Aeneid*. Trans. Allen Mandelbaum. Berkeley: Univ of California Press, 1973.

———. *The Aeneid*. Trans. David West. New York: Viking Penguin, 1990.

Vivante, Paolo. *Homer*. New Haven: Yale Univ. Press, 1985.

THE MIDDLE EAST

"Atrahasis." (The Flood.) Trans. E. A. Speiser. *Ancient Near Eastern Texts Relating to the Old Testament*. Ed. James B. Pritchard. Third Ed. with Supplement. Princeton: Princeton Univ. Press, 1974.

"Atrahasis — Additional Texts." Trans. A. K. Grayson. *Ancient Near Eastern Texts Relating to the Old Testament*. Ed. James B. Pritchard. Third Ed. with Supplement. Princeton: Princeton Univ. Press, 1974.

Beyerlin, Walter, ed. *Near Eastern Religious Texts Relating to the Old Testament*. Philadelphia: Westminster, 1978. Reprint of London: Medici Society, 1911.

Breasted, James Henry. *The Dawn of Conscience*. New York: Scribner's, 1961.

Budge, E. A. Wallis. *Egyptian Religion*. New York: Bell/Crown, 1959. Reprint of 1900 edition.

———. *Osiris and the Egyptian Resurrection*. Vol. 1. New York: Dover, 1973. Reprint of London: Medici Society, 1911.

"The Creation Epic." Trans. E. A. Speiser. *Ancient Near Eastern Texts Relating to the Old Testament*. Ed. James B. Pritchard. Third Ed. with Supplement. Princeton: Princeton Univ. Press, 1974.

"The Creation Epic — Additions to Tablets V–VII." Trans. A. K. Grayson. *Ancient Near Eastern Texts Relating to the Old Testament*. Ed. James B. Pritchard. Third Ed. with Supplement. Princeton: Princeton Univ. Press, 1974.

"The Deluge." Trans. Samuel Noah Kramer. *Ancient Near Eastern Texts Relating to the Old Testament*. Ed. James B. Pritchard. Third Ed. with Supplement. Princeton: Princeton Univ. Press, 1974.

Frankfort, Henri. *Kingship and the Gods: A Study of Ancient Near Eastern Religion as the Integration of Society and Nature*. Chicago: Univ. of Chicago Press, 1978.

Gaster, Theodor H. *The Oldest Stories in the World*. Boston: Beacon, 1958.

The Epic of Gilgamesh. Trans. Maureen Gallery Kovacs. Stanford: Stanford Univ. Press, 1989.

"The Epic of Gilgamesh: Notes and Additions." Trans. A. K. Grayson. *Ancient Near Eastern Texts Relating to the Old Testament*. Ed. James B. Pritchard. Third Ed. with Supplement. Princeton: Princeton Univ. Press, 1974.

The Epic of Gilgamesh. Trans. N. K. Sandars. New York: Viking Penguin, 1973.

"The Epic of Gilgamesh." Trans. E. A. Speiser. *Ancient Near Eastern Texts Relating to the Old Testament*.

Ed. James B. Pritchard. Third Ed.
with Supplement. Princeton:
Princeton Univ. Press, 1974.

Gilgamesh. Trans. John Gardner and
John Maier. New York: Knopf,
1984.

"Gilgamesh and the Land of the Living."
Trans. Samuel Noah Kramer.
*Ancient Near Eastern Texts Relating
to the Old Testament.* Ed. James B.
Pritchard. Third Ed. with
Supplement. Princeton: Princeton
Univ. Press, 1974.

Gilgamesh: *A New Rendering in English
Verse.* Trans. David Ferry. New
York: Farrar, Straus, 1992.

Gilgamesh: *A Verse Narrative.* Trans.
Herbert Mason. New York: New
American Library, 1972.

Gilgamesh the King: An Epic Tale. Trans.
Robert Silverberg. New York: Arbor
House, 1984.

Heidel, Alexander. *Babylonian Genesis.*
2nd ed. Chicago: Univ. of Chicago
Press, 1966.

———. Gilgamesh *Epic and Old
Testament Parallels.* Chicago: Univ.
of Chicago Press, 1963.

Jacobsen, Thorkild. *The Treasures of
Darkness: A History of
Mesopotamian Religion.* New
Haven: Yale Univ. Press, 1976.

Kramer, Samuel Noah. *History Begins at
Sumer.* Philadelphia: Univ. of
Pennsylvania Press, 1981.

———. *Sumerians: Their History,
Culture, and Character.* Chicago:
Univ. of Chicago Press, 1971.

———, ed. *Mythologies of the Ancient
World.* New York: Doubleday/
Anchor, 1961.

Montet, Pierre. *Everyday Life in Egypt in
the Days of Ramesses the Great.*
Philadelphia: Univ. of Pennsylvania
Press, 1981.

Myths from Mesopotamia. Trans.
Stephanie Dalley. New York:
Oxford Univ. Press, 1991.

Oppenheim, A. Leo. *Letters from
Mesopotamia.* Chicago: Univ. of
Chicago Press, 1967.

Pritchard, James B., ed. *The Ancient Near
East.* Vol. 1. Princeton: Princeton
Univ. Press, 1958.

"The Telepinus Myth." Trans. Albrecht
Goetze. *Ancient Near Eastern Texts
Relating to the Old Testament.* Ed.
James B. Pritchard. Third Ed. with
Supplement. Princeton: Princeton
Univ. Press, 1974.

Tigay, Jeffrey H. *The Evolution of the
Gilgamesh Epic.* Philadelphia: Univ.
of Pennsylvania Press, 1982.

NORTHERN EUROPE

Branston, Brian. *Gods of the North.* New
York: Thames and Hudson, 1980.

Crossley-Holland, Kevin. *The Norse
Myths.* New York: Pantheon, 1981.

Dumezil, Georges. *Gods of the Ancient
Northmen.* Berkeley: Univ. of
California Press, 1974.

The Elder Edda: *A Selection.* Trans. Paul
B. Taylor and W. H. Auden. New
York: Random House, 1969.

Poems of the Elder Edda. Trans. Patricia
Terry. Rev. Ed. Philadelphia: Univ.
of Pennsylvania Press, 1990.

Jackson, W. T. H. *Hero and King.* New
York: Columbia Univ. Press, 1986.

———. *The Literature of the Middle
Ages.* New York: Columbia Univ.
Press, 1962.

The Nibelungenlied. Trans. Arthur
Thomas Hatto. New York: Viking
Penguin, 1975.

The Nibelungenlied. Trans. Helen M.
Mustard. New York: Random
House, 1963.

The Song of the Nibelungs. Trans. Frank
G. Ryder. Detroit: Wayne State
Univ. Press, 1969.

The Poetic Edda. Vol. 1: Heroic Poems.
Trans. Ursula Dronke. New York:
Oxford Univ. Press, 1969.

The Poetic Edda. Trans. Lee M.
Hollander. Rev. Ed. Austin: Univ. of
Texas Press, 1987.

Sturluson, Snorri. *The* Prose Edda: *Tales
from Norse Mythology.* Trans. Jean I.
Young. Berkeley: Univ. of California
Press, 1973.

The Saga of the Volsungs. *Together with Excerpts from the* Nornageststhattr *and Three Chapters from the* Prose Edda. Trans. George K. Anderson. Newark: Univ. of Delaware Press, 1982.

The Saga of the Volsungs: The Norse Epic of Sigurd the Dragon Slayer. Trans. Jesse L. Byock. Berkeley: Univ. of California Press, 1990.

The Saga of the Volsungs; The Saga of Ragnar Lodbrok Together with The Lay of Kraka. Trans. Margaret Schlauch. New York: AMS, 1978. Reprint of New York: American-Scandinavian Foundation/Norton, 1930.

Sigurd the Dragon-Slayer: A Faroese Ballad-Cycle. Trans. E. M. Smith-Dampier. New York: Kraus, 1969. Reprint of Oxford: Basil Blackwell, 1934.

Volsunga Saga: The Story of the Volsungs and Niblungs. Trans. William Morris. New York: Collier Books, 1971.

THE BRITISH ISLES

Alcock, Leslie. *Arthur's Britain: History and Archaeology: A.D. 367–634.* New York: Viking Penguin, 1977.

(Alliterative) Morte Arthure. Ed. John Finlayson. Evanston: Northwestern Univ. Press, 1971.

The Alliterative Morte Arthure, The Owl and the Nightingale, and Five Other Middle English Poems. Trans. John Gardner. Carbondale: Southern Illinois Univ. Press, 1979.

Ashe, Geoffrey and Debrett's Peerage. *The Discovery of King Arthur.* New York: Henry Holt, 1987.

———. *King Arthur: The Dream of the Golden Age.* New York: Thames Hudson, 1990.

———, ed. *The Quest for Arthur's Britain.* Chicago: Academy Chicago, 1988.

Barber, Richard, ed. *Arthurian Legends: An Illustrated Anthology.* Totowa: Littlefield Adams, 1979.

Benson, Larry D. *Malory's Morte*

D'Arthur. Cambridge: Harvard Univ. Press, 1976.

Beowulf. Trans. William Alfred. *Medieval Epics.* New York: Random House, 1963.

Beowulf: A Dual-Language Edition. Trans. Howell D. Chickering, Jr. New York: Anchor/Doubleday, 1977.

Beowulf and the Finnesburh Fragment. Trans. Clarence Griffin Child. Boston: Houghton Mifflin, 1904.

Beowulf: The Oldest English Epic. Trans. Charles W. Kennedy. New York: Oxford Univ. Press, 1977.

Beowulf. Trans. Marijane Osborn. Berkeley: Univ. of California Press, 1983.

Beowulf. Trans. Burton Raffel. Amherst: Univ. of Massachusetts Press, 1971.

Brengle, Richard L., ed. *Arthur King of Britain: History, Chronicle, Romance and Criticism.* Englewood Cliffs: Prentice-Hall, 1964.

Bruce-Mitford, Rupert. *Aspects of Anglo-Saxon Archaeology: Sutton Hoo and Other Discoveries.* New York: Harper's Magazine/Harper & Row, 1974.

Chadwick, Nora. *Celts.* New York: Viking Penguin, 1971.

Chrétien de Troyes. *Arthurian Romances.* Trans. W. W. Comfort. New York: Dutton, 1975.

———. *Arthurian Romances.* Trans. William W. Kibler. New York: Viking Penguin, 1991.

———. *The Complete Romances.* Trans. David Staines. Bloomington: Indiana Univ. Press, 1993.

From Camelot to Joyous Guard: The Old French La Mort le Roi Artu. Trans. J. Neale Carman. Lawrence: Univ. Press of Kansas, 1974.

Geoffrey of Monmouth. *The History of the Kings of Britain.* Trans. Lewis Thorpe. London: Folio Society, 1974.

Irving, Edward B., Jr. *Introduction to Beowulf.* Englewood Cliffs: Prentice Hall, 1969.

————. *A Reading of* Beowulf. New Haven: Yale Univ. Press, 1969.

Jackson, W. T. H. *Hero and King.* New York: Columbia Univ. Press, 1986.

————. *The Literature of the Middle Ages.* New York: Columbia Univ. Press, 1962.

Kiernan, Kevin S. Beowulf *and the* Beowulf Manuscript. New Brunswick: Rutgers Univ. Press, 1981.

Layamon's Arthur: The Arthurian Section of Layamon's Brut. Trans. W. R. J. Barron and S. C. Weinberg. Austin: Univ. of Texas Press, 1989.

MacCulloch, J. A. *Celtic Mythology.* New York: Dorset, 1992.

Malory, Sir Thomas. *Le Morte D'Arthur.* Berkeley: Univ. of California Press, 1983. Reprint of London: Caxton, 1485.

————. *Le Morte D'Arthur.* New York: Viking Penguin, 1983.

————. *Le Morte D'Arthur.* Ed. R. M. Lumiansky. New York: Scribner's, 1982.

Morris, John. *The Age of Arthur: A History of the British Isles from 350 to 650.* New York: Scribner's, 1973.

Nicholson, Lewis E., ed. *An Anthology of* Beowulf *Criticism.* South Bend: Univ. of Notre Dame Press, 1963.

Ogilvy, J. D. A. and Donald C. Baker. *Reading* Beowulf: *An Introduction to the Poem, Its Background, and Its Style.* Norman: Univ. of Oklahoma Press, 1986.

Owen, Gale R. *Rites and Religions of the Anglo-Saxons.* New York: Dorset, 1985.

Renoir, Alain. *"Beowulf: A Contextual Introduction to its Contents and Techniques." Heroic Epic and Saga: An Introduction to the World's Great Folk Epics.* Ed. Felix J. Oinas. Bloomington: Indiana Univ. Press, 1978.

Rolleston, Thomas William. *Celtic Myths and Legends.* New York: Dover, 1990. Reprint of *Myths and Legends of the Celtic Race.* Rev. Ed. London: Harrap, 1917.

Ross, James Bruce and Mary Martin McLaughlin, eds. *The Portable Medieval Reader.* New York: Viking, 1977.

Rutherford, Ward. *Celtic Mythology: The Nature and Influence of Celtic Myth —from Druidism to Arthurian Legend.* New York: Sterling, 1988.

Sjoestedt, Marie-Louise. *Gods and Heroes of the Celts.* Trans. Myles Dillon. Berkeley: Turtle Island Foundation, 1982.

Squire, Charles. *Celtic Myth and Legend.* Hollywood, CA: Newcastle, 1975. Reprint of *The Mythology of the British Islands.* London: Gresham, 19–?

Wace and Layamon. *Arthurian Chronicles.* Trans. Eugene Mason. New York: Dutton, 1976.

THE FAR EAST AND THE PACIFIC ISLANDS

Alpers, Antony. *Maori Myths and Tribal Legends.* Auckland, N.Z.: Longman Paul, 1982.

Beckwith, Martha. *Hawaiian Mythology.* Honolulu: Univ. of Hawaii Press, 1977.

Bodde, Derk. "Myths of Ancient China." *Mythologies of the Ancient World.* Ed. Samuel Noah Kramer. New York: Anchor/Doubleday, 1961.

Christie, Anthony. *Chinese Mythology.* Feltham, Eng.: Newnes/Hamlyn, 1983.

Classical Chinese Myths. Ed. and Trans. Jan Walls and Yvonne Walls. Hong Kong: Joint, 1984.

Classical Hindu Mythology: A Reader in the Sanskrit Puranas. Ed. and Trans. Cornelia Dimmitt and J. A. B. Van Buitenen. Philadelphia: Temple Univ. Press, 1978.

Colum, Padraic. *Legends of Hawaii.* New Haven: Yale Univ. Press, 1987.

Coomaraswamy, Ananda K. and the Sister Nivedita. *Myths of the Hindus and Buddhists.* New York: Dover, 1967. Reprint of London: Harrap, 1913.

Davis, F. Hadland. *Myths and Legends of Japan*. Singapore: Graham Brash, 1989. Reprint of 1913 edition.

Gray, J. E. B. *Indian Tales and Legends*. New York: Oxford Univ. Press, 1989.

Grey, Sir George. *Polynesian Mythology and Ancient Traditional History*. Auckland, N.Z.: H. Brett, 1885.

Hindu Myths. Trans. Wendy Doniger O'Flaherty. New York: Viking Penguin, 1975.

Ions, Veronica. *Indian Mythology*. New York: Bedrick, 1984.

Kalakaua, King David. *The Legends and Myths of Hawaii*. Honolulu: Mutual, 1990. Reprint of New York: Webster, 1888.

Kotan Utunnai. Trans. John Batchelor. *Transactions of the Asiatic Society of Japan* 18, Part 1. April 1890.

Mackenzie, Donald A. *Myths of China and Japan*. London: Gresham, N.D.

Nihongi: Chronicles of Japan from the Earliest Times to A.D. 697. Trans. W. G. Aston. Rutland: Tuttle, 1980.

Piggott, Juliet. *Japanese Mythology*. New York: Bedrick, 1983.

The Ramayana. Ed. and Trans. William Buck. Berkeley: Univ. of California Press, 1976.

The Ramayana and the Mahabharata. Ed. and Trans. Romesh Dutt. New York: Dutton, 1972.

The Ramayana of Kampan, The Forest Book of. Trans. George L. Hart and Hank Heifetz. Berkeley: Univ. of California Press, 1988.

The Ramayana: A Shortened Modern Prose Version (Suggested by the Tamil Version of Kamban). Ed. and Trans. R. K. Narayan. New York: Viking Penguin, 1987.

Sanders, Tao Tao Liu. *Dragons, Gods, and Spirits from Chinese Mythology*. New York: Schocken, 1983.

Songs of Gods, Songs of Humans: The Epic Tradition of the Ainu. Trans. Donald L. Philippi. Princeton: Princeton Univ. Press, 1979.

Werner, Edward T. C. *Ancient Tales and Folklore of China*. London: Bracken, 1986. Reprint of *Myths and Legends of China*. London: Harrap, 1922.

Westervelt, William Drake. *Legends of Ma-ui: A Demi-god of Polynesia, and His Mother Hina*. Honolulu: N.P., 1910.

———. *Myths and Legends of Hawaii*. Ed. A. Grove Day. Honolulu: Mutual, 1987.

West Lake: A Collection of Folktales. Ed. and Trans. Jan Walls and Yvonne Walls. Hong Kong: Joint, 1980.

West Lake: Folk Tales. Ed. and Trans. Wang Hui-ming. Beijing: Foreign Languages, 1982.

Zimmer, Heinrich. *Myths and Symbols in Indian Art and Civilization*. Ed. Joseph Campbell. Princeton: Princeton Univ. Press, 1992.

AFRICA

Abrahams, Roger D. *African Folktales*. (Includes *Gassire's Lute* and *Mwindo*.) New York: Pantheon, 1983.

Ames, David. "Lion of Manding: A Wolof Epic." *A Treasury of African Folklore*. Ed. Harold Courlander. New York: Crown, 1977.

Biebuyck, Daniel. "The African Heroic Epic." *Heroic Epic and Saga: An Introduction to the World's Great Folk Epics*. Ed. Felix J. Oinas. Bloomington: Indiana Univ. Press, 1978.

———. *Hero and Chief: Epic Literature from the Banyanga (Zaire Republic)*. Berkeley: Univ. of California Press, 1978.

———. "The Mwindo Epic (Nyanga)." *A Treasury of African Folklore*. Ed. Harold Courlander. New York: Crown, 1975.

——— and Kohombo C. Mateene. *The Mwindo Epic from the Banyanga*. Berkeley: Univ. of California Press, 1971.

Cavendish, Richard, ed. *Legends of the World*. London: Orbis, 1982.

————, ed. *Mythology: An Illustrated Encyclopedia*. London: Orbis, 1980.

Courlander, Harold. *A Master of the Forge*. New York: Crown, 1983.

————. *Tales of Yoruba Gods and Heroes*. New York: Crown, N.D.

————. *A Treasury of African Folklore*. New York: Crown, 1977.

————, with Ousmane Sako. *The Heart of the Ngoni: Heroes of the African Kingdom of Segu*. New York: Crown, 1982.

De Civrieux, Marc. *Watunna: An Orinoco Creation Cycle*. Ed. and Trans. David M. Guss. San Francisco: North Point, 1980.

Frobenius, Leo and Douglas C. Fox. *African Genesis*. Berkeley: Turtle Island Foundation, 1983. Reprint of New York: Stackpole, 1937.

————. "Gassire's Lute." *Technicians of the Sacred: A Range of Poetries from Africa, America, Asia, Europe & Oceania*. Ed. Jerome Rothenberg. Rev. Ed. Berkeley: Univ. of California Press, 1985.

Herskovits, Melville and Frances Herskovits. *Dahomean Narrative*. Evanston: Northwestern Univ. Press, 1958.

Innes, Gordon. *Sunjata: Three Mandinka Versions*. London: School of Oriental and African Studies, 1974.

Niane, D. T. *Sundiata: An Epic of Old Mali*. Trans. G. D. Pickett. Essex, Eng.: Longman, 1986.

Okpewho, Isidore. *The Epic in Africa: Toward a Poetics of the Oral Performance*. New York: Columbia Univ. Press, 1979.

Parrinder, Geoffrey. *African Mythology*. New York: Bedrick, 1991.

Radin, Paul, ed. *African Folktales*. New York: Schocken, 1983.

Rothenberg, Jerome, ed. *Technicians of the Sacred: A Range of Poetries from Africa, America, Asia, Europe and Oceania*. Rev. Ed. Berkeley: Univ. of California Press, 1985.

Soyinka, Wole. *Myth, Literature and the African World*. New York: Cambridge Univ. Press, 1979.

THE AMERICAS

Anaya, Rudolfo A. *Lord of the Dawn: The Legend of Quetzalcoatl*. Albuquerque: Univ. of New Mexico Press, 1987.

Benedict, Ruth. *Zuñi Mythology*. 2 vols. New York: AMS, 1969. Reprint of 1935 edition.

Betanzos, Juan de. "*Suma y Narración de los Incas*. Cited in Harold Osborne. *South American Mythology*. London: Hamlyn, 1968.

Bierhorst, John. *History and Mythology of the Aztecs: The Codex Chimalpopoca (Annals of Cuauhtitlan and Legend of the Suns)*. Tucson: Univ. of Arizona Press, 1992.

————. *The Hungry Woman: Myths and Legends of the Aztecs*. New York: Morrow, 1984.

————. *The Mythology of Mexico and Central America*. New York: Morrow, 1992.

————. *The Mythology of North America*. New York: Morrow, 1986.

————. *The Mythology of South America*. New York: Morrow, 1988.

————. *Cantares Mexicanos: Songs of the Aztecs*. Palo Alto: Stanford Univ. Press, 1985.

————, ed. *Four Masterworks of American Indian Literature*. Tucson: Univ. of Arizona Press, 1984.

————, ed. *Myths and Tales of the American Indians*. Albuquerque: Univ. of New Mexico Press, 1992. Reprint of *The Red Swan: Myths and Tales of the American Indians*. New York: Farrar Straus, 1976.

Boas, Franz. "The Central Eskimo." *Sixth Annual Report of the Bureau of American Ethnology, 1884–1885*. Washington, DC: Government Printing Office, 1888.

————. "Tsimshian Mythology." *Thirty-First Annual Report of the Bureau of American Ethnology,*

1909–1910. Washington DC: Government Printing Office, 1916.

———. "Tsimshian Texts." *Bureau of American Ethnology Bulletin 27*. Washington, DC: Government Printing Office, 1916.

Brundage, Burr Cartwright. *The Fifth Sun: Aztec Gods, Aztec World*. Austin: Univ. of Texas Press, 1979.

Bunzel, Ruth. *Zuñi Texts*. New York: AMS, 1973. Reprint of 1933 edition.

Burland, Cottie. *North American Indian Mythology*. Rev. Ed. New York: Bedrick, 1985.

———, Irene Nicholson, and Harold Osborne. *Mythology of the Americas*. London: Hamlyn, 1970.

Caswell, Helen. *Shadows from the Singing House: Eskimo Folk Tales*. Tokyo: Tuttle, 1973.

Cavendish, Richard, ed. *Legends of the World*. London: Orbis, 1982.

———, ed. *Mythology: An Illustrated Encyclopedia*. London: Orbis, 1980.

Cieza de León, Pedro de. "*Second Part of the Chronicle of Peru*." Cited in Harold Osborne. *South American Mythology*. London: Hamlyn, 1968. (Source: London: Hakluyt Society, No. 68, 1883.)

———. "*The Travels of Pedro de Cieza de Leon, Contained in the First Part of His Chronicle of Peru, AD 1532– 1550.*" Cited in Harold Osborne. *South American Mythology*. London: Hamlyn, 1968. (Source: London: Hakluyt Society, No. 33, 1864.)

Clark, Ella Elizabeth. *Indian Legends from the Northern Rockies*. Norman: Univ. of Oklahoma Press, 1988.

———. *Indian Legends of Canada*. Toronto: McClelland & Stewart, 1991.

———. *Indian Legends of the Pacific Northwest*. Berkeley: Univ. of California Press, 1953.

Coffin, Tristram, ed. *Indian Tales of North America*. Philadelphia: American Folklore Society, 1961.

Curtin, Jeremiah. *Seneca Indian Myths*. New York: Dutton, 1923.

———, and J. N. B. Hewitt. "Seneca Myths and Fictions." *Thirty-Second Annual Report of the Bureau of American Ethnology*. Washington, DC: Government Printing Office, 1918.

Cusick, David. *Sketches of Ancient History of the Six Nations: A Tale of the Foundation of the Great Island, Now North America, The Two Infants Born, and the Creation of the Universe*. New York: Lewiston, 1827. Cited in Ellen Russell Emerson. *Indian Myths or Legends: Traditions and Symbols of the Aborigines of America*. Minneapolis: Ross & Haines, 1965.

Edmonds, Margot and Ella Elizabeth Clark. *Voices of the Winds: Native American Legends*. New York: Facts on File, 1989.

Emerson, Ellen Russell. *Indian Myths or Legends: Traditions and Symbols of the Aborigines of America*. Minneapolis: Ross Haines, 1965. Reprint of 1884 edition.

Erdoes, Richard and Alfonso Ortiz, eds. *American Indian Myths and Legends*. New York: Pantheon, 1985.

Feldmann, Susan, ed. *The Storytelling Stone: Myths and Tales of the American Indians*. New York: Dell, 1971.

Garcilaso, Inca de la Vega. *The Incas*. (*Royal Commentaries of the Incas*, 1609.) Ed. Alain Gheerbrant. Trans. Maria Jolas. New York: Avon, 1964.

———. *Royal Commentaries of the Incas*. Cited in Emir Rodriguez Monegal. *The Borzoi Anthology of Latin American Literature: From the Time of Colum Rodriguez Monegal. The Borzoi Anthology of Latin American Literature: From the Time of Columus to the Twentieth Century*. Vol. 1. New York: Knopf, 1983.

———. *Royal Commentaries of the Incas*. (Spain, 1609.) Cited in Harold Osborne. *South American Mythology*. London: Hamlyn, 1968

Gilpin, Laura. *The Enduring Navaho*. Austin: Univ. of Texas Press, 1987.

Goodchild, Peter, ed. *The Raven Tales: Traditional Stories of Native Peoples*. Chicago: Chicago Review, 1991.

Grinnell, George Bird. *By Cheyenne Campfires*. Lincoln: Univ. of Nebraska Press, 1971. Reprint of New Haven: Yale Univ. Press, 1926.

Hale, Horatio. "Huron Folk-Lore." *Journal of American Folklore* 1. Boston: American Folk-Lore Society/Houghton Mifflin, 1888.

Haviland, Virginia, ed. *The Faber Book of North American Legends*. Boston: Faber & Faber, 1979.

Hewitt, J. N. B. "Introduction to Seneca Fiction, Legends, and Myths." *Thirty-Fifth Annual Report* of the Bureau of American Ethnology, 1910 –1911. Washington, DC: Government Printing Office, 1918.

"Histoyre du Mechique." ("History of Mexico.") Trans. Andre Thevet. *Journal of the Society of Americanistes*. Paris: 1905.

Josephy, Alvin M., Jr. *The Indian Heritage of America*. Boston: Houghton Mifflin, 1991.

Klah, Hasteen. *Navajo Creation Myth: The Story of Emergence*. New York: AMS, 1976. Reprint of 1942 edition.

Leland, Charles G. *Algonquin Legends*. New York: Dover, 1992. Reprint of *The Algonquin Legends of New England; or, Myths and Folk Lore of the Micmac, Passmaquoddy, and Penobscot Tribes*. Boston: Houghton Mifflin, 1884.

Macfarlan, Allan A., ed. *American Indian Legends*. New York: Heritage, 1968.

Marriott, Alice and Carol K. Rachlin. *American Indian Mythology*. New York: Crowell, 1968.

Matthews, Washington. "Navajo Legends." *Memoirs of the American Folk-Lore Society*. Vol. V. Boston: American Folk-Lore Society/ Houghton Mifflin, 1897.

Monegal, Emir Rodriguez, ed. *The Borzoi Anthology of Latin American Literature: From the Time of Columbus to the Twentieth Century*. Vol. 1. New York: Knopf, 1983.

Mullett, G. M. *Spider Woman Stories: Legends of the Hopi Indians*. Tucson: Univ. of Arizona Press, 1979.

Newcomb, Franc Johnson. *Navaho Folk Tales*. Albuquerque: Univ. of New Mexico Press, 1991.

Nicholson, Irene. *Mexican and Central American Mythology*. New York: Bedrick, 1983.

Norman, Howard, ed. *Northern Tales: Traditional Stories of Eskimo and Indian Peoples*. New York: Pantheon Books, 1990.

Osborne, Harold. *South American Mythology*. New York: Bedrick, 1986.

Popol Vuh: The Definitive Edition of the Mayan Book of the Dawn of Life and the Glories of Gods and Kings. Trans. Dennis Tedlock. New York: Simon & Schuster, 1985.

Popol Vuh: The Sacred Book of the Ancient Quiché Maya. Trans. Delia Goetz and Sylvanus G. Morley. Norman: Univ. of Oklahoma Press, 1983.

Popol Vuh: The Sacred Book of the Ancient Quiché Maya. Trans. Adrian Recinos. Norman: Univ. of Oklahoma Press, 1950.

Rachlan, Carol K. and Alice Marriott. *Plains Indian Mythology*. New York: NAL-Dutton, 1977.

Rand, Silas T. *Legends of the Micmacs*. New York: Longmans, Green, 1984.

Rivière, Peter. *Marriage among the Trio: A Principle of Social Organization*. Oxford: Clarendon, 1969.

Roe, Peter G. *The Cosmic Zygote: Cosmology in the Amazon Basin*. New Brunswick: Rutgers Univ. Press, 1982.

Sahagun, Bernardino de. *Florentine Codex: General History of the Things of New Spain*. Eds. Arthur J. O.

Anderson and Charles E. Dibble. Santa Fe: School of American Research/Univ. of Utah Press, 1950 –1982.

Simms, Stephen Chapman. "Traditions of the Crows." *Field Museum Anthropological Series.* Vol. 2. Chicago: 1903.

Stevenson, Matilda Coxe. "The Zuñi Indians." *Twenty-Third Annual Report of the Bureau of American Ethnology, 1901–1902.* Washington, DC: Government Printing Office, 1904.

Swanton, John Reed. "Haida Texts and Myths." *Bureau of American Ethnology Bulletin* 29. Washington, DC: Government Printing Office, 1905.

———. "Tlingit Myths and Texts." *Bureau of American Ethnology Bulletin* 39. Washington, DC: Government Printing Office, 1909.

Thompson, Stith, ed. *Tales of the North American Indians.* Bloomington: Indiana Univ. Press, 1966. Reprint of 1929 edition.

Underhill, Ruth M. *Red Man's America.* Chicago: Univ. of Chicago Press, 1971.

Valdelomar, Abraham. *Our Children of the Sun: A Suite of Eight Inca Legends.* Carbondale: Southern Illinois Univ. Press, 1968.

Walker, James R. *Lakota Myth.* Ed. Elaine A. Jahner. Lincoln: Univ. of Nebraska Press, 1983.

Wherry, Joseph H. *Indian Masks & Myths of the West.* New York: Bonanza/ Crown, 1969.

Whitehead, Ruth Holmes. *Stories from the Six Worlds: Micmac Legends.* Halifax, N.S.: Nimbus, 1988.

Zolbrod, Paul G. Dine Bahane: *The Navajo Creation Story.* Albuquerque: Univ. of New Mexico Press, 1988.

GENERAL MYTHOLOGY

Bachofen, J. J. *Myth, Religion and Mother Right.* Princeton: Princeton Univ. Press, 1967.

Bonnefoy, Yves. *Mythologies.* 2 vols. Ed. Wendy Doniger. Chicago: Univ. of Chicago Press, 1991.

Burrows, David, Frederick Lapides, and John Shawcross. *Myths and Motifs in Literature.* New York: Free Press, 1973.

Butterworth, E. A. S. *Some Traces of the Pre-Olympian World in Greek Literature and Myth.* Berlin: De Gruyter, 1966.

Campbell, Joseph. *The Masks of God.* 4 vols. New York: Viking Penguin, 1991.

Downing, Christine. *The Goddess: Mythological Images of the Feminine.* New York: Crossroads, 1984.

Dundes, Alan, ed. *The Flood Myth.* Berkeley: Univ. of California Press, 1988.

———. *Sacred Narrative: Readings in the Theory of Myth.* Berkeley: Univ. of California Press, 1984.

Eliade, Mircea. *Myths, Rites, Symbols.* 2 vols. Ed. Wendell C. Beane and William G. Dotz. New York: Harper, 1976.

Feder, Lillian. *Ancient Myth in Modern Poetry.* Princeton: Princeton Univ. Press, 1972.

Frazer, Sir James George. *The Golden Bough: The Roots of Religion and Folklore.* New York: Avenel/Crown, 1981. Reprint of *The Golden Bough: A Study in Comparative Religion.* 2 vols. London: Macmillan, 1890.

Freud, Sigmund. *Totem and Taboo.* Trans. James Strachey. New York: Routledge & Keegan Paul, 1950.

Frye, Northrop. *Anatomy of Criticism.* New York: Atheneum, 1968.

Gaster, Theodor, ed. *The New Golden Bough: A New Abridgment of the Classic Work by Sir James George Frazer.* New York: Phillips, 1972.

Gimbutas, Marija. *Goddesses and Gods of Old Europe, 7000–3500 B.C.: Myths, Legends, and Cult Images.* Rev. Ed. Berkeley: Univ. of California Press, 1982.

———. *Language of the Goddess*. San Francisco: Harper, 1991.

Graves, Robert. *The White Goddess*. Rev. Ed. Magnolia, MA: Peter Smith, 1983.

Harrison, Jane Ellen. *Prolegomena to the Study of Greek Religion*. Princeton: Princeton Univ. Press, 1976. Reprint of 1922 edition.

———. *Themis: A Study of the Social Origins of Greek Religion*. Rev. Ed. Gloucester, MA: Peter Smith, 1974. Reprint of Cambridge: Cambridge Univ. Press, 1912.

Highet, Gilbert. *The Classical Tradition: Greek and Roman Influences on Western Literature*. New York: Oxford Univ. Press, 1949.

Jung, Carl G. *The Archetypes and The Collective Unconscious*. Princeton: Princeton Univ. Press, 1969.

Kirk, G. S. *Myth: Its Meaning and Functions in Ancient and Other Cultures*. Berkeley: Univ. of California Press, 1970.

Leach, Maria, ed. *Funk & Wagnall's Standard Dictionary of Folklore, Mythology, and Legend*. San Francisco: Harper, 1984.

Lévi-Strauss, Claude. *Introduction to a Science of Mythology*. 2 vols. Trans. John Weightman and Doreen Weightman. Chicago: Univ. of Chicago Press, 1983.

———. *Myth and Meaning*. New York: Schocken, 1987.

———. *Mythologiques*. Vols. 3 and 4. Trans. John Weightman and Doreen Weightman. Chicago: Univ. of Chicago Press, 1990.

———. *Structural Anthropology*. Vol. 1. Trans. Claire Jacobson and Brooke Grundfest Schoepf. New York: Basic Books, 1974.

Middleton, John, ed. *Myth & Cosmos: Readings in Mythology and Symbolism*. Austin: Univ. of Texas Press, 1976.

Miller, James E., Jr., ed. *Myth and Method*. Lincoln: Univ. of Nebraska Press, 1960.

Murray, Henry A., ed. *Myth and Myth-making*. Boston: Beacon, 1968.

Neumann, Erich. *The Great Mother: An Analysis of the Archteype*. Princeton: Princeton Univ. Press, 1964.

Olson, Alan M., ed. *Myth, Symbol and Reality*. South Bend: Univ. of Notre Dame Press, 1980.

Porter, Thomas E. *Myth and Modern American Drama*. Detroit: Wayne State Univ. Press, 1969.

Puhvel, Jaan. *Comparative Mythology*. Baltimore: Johns Hopkins Univ. Press, 1989.

Radin, Paul. *Primitive Man as Philosopher*. Rev. Ed. New York: Dover, 1957.

———. *Primitive Religion: Its Nature and Origin*. New York: Dover, 1937.

Raglan, FitzRoy. *The Hero: A Study in Tradition, Myth, and Drama*. New York: New American Library, 1979.

Rank, Otto, FitzRoy Raglan, and Alan Dundes. *In Quest of the Hero*. Princeton: Princeton Univ. Press, 1990.

Rothenberg, Jerome, ed. *Technicians of the Sacred: A Range of Poetries from Africa, America, Asia, Europe, and Oceania*. Rev. Ed. Berkeley: Univ. of California Press, 1985.

Sebeok, Thomas. *Myth: A Symposium*. Bloomington: Indiana Univ. Press, 1972.

Segnec, Jean. *The Survival of the Pagan Gods: The Mythological Tradition and Its Place in Renaissance Humanism and Art*. Princeton: Princeton Univ. Press, 1972.

Slate, Bernice, ed. *Myth and Symbol: Critical Approaches and Applications*. Lincoln: Univ. of Nebraska Press, 1963.

Slochower, Harry. *Mythopoesis: Mythic Patterns in Literary Classics*. Detroit: Wayne State Univ. Press, 1970.

Sproul, Barbara C. *Primal Myths: Creation Myths Around the World*. San Francisco: HarperCollins, 1979

Stone, Merlin. *When God Was a Woman*. New York: Harcourt, 1978.

Vickery, John B. *Myths and Texts: Strategies of Incorporation and Displacement*. Baton Rouge: Louisiana State Univ. Press, 1983.

———, ed. *Myth and Literature: Contemporary Theory and Practice*. Lincoln: Univ. of Nebraska Press, 1969.

Weigle, Marta. *Spiders and Spinsters: Woand Mytho*. Albuquerque: Univ. of New Mexico Native American Studies, 1992.

Index of Characters

Pronunciation Guide

This index provides easy-to-pronounce English approximations of the original languages of the myths. The transcriptions are meant to serve as a guide to English-speaking readers. The following chart shows International Phonetic Alphabet (IPA) and American English values for the symbols used in this index.

[a, A] = IPA [æ]
    cat

[ah, AH] = IPA [ɑ]
    top

[ai, AI] = IPA [ɑɪ]
    pie

[au, AU] = IPA [ɑʊ]
    cow

[b, B]= IPA [b]
    boy

[ch, CH] = IPA [tʃ]
    church

[d, D] = IPA [d]
    did

[dh, DH] = IPA [ð]
    these

[e, E] = IPA [ɛ]
    let

[ee, EE] = IPA [i]
    feed

[ei, EI] = IPA [eɪ]
    pay

[f, F] = IPA [f]
    far

[g, G] = IPA [g]
    get

[h, H] = IPA [h]
    hoot

[i, I] = IPA [ɪ]
    lit

[j, J] = IPA [dʒ]
    judge

[k, K] = IPA [k]
    kid

[l, L] = IPA [l]
    lean

[m, M] = IPA [m]
    my

[n, N] = IPA [n]
    new

[ng, NG] = IPA [ŋ]
    ring

[o, O] = IPA [ɔ]
    law

[oi, OI] = IPA [ɔɪ]
    coy

[oo, OO] = IPA [u]
    moon

[ow, OW] = IPA [ow]
    coat

[p, P] = IPA [p]
    pink

[r, R] = IPA [r, ɚ]
    red

[s, S] = IPA [s]
    suit

[sh, SH] = IPA [ʃ]
    ship

[t, T] = IPA [t]
    tigh**t**

[th, TH] = IPA [θ]
    think

[u, U] = IPA [ʊ]
    p**u**t

[uh, UH] = IPA [ə]
    p**u**tt

[v, V] = IPA [v]
    very

[w, W] = IPA [w]
    what

[y, Y] = IPA [j]
    you

[z, Z] = IPA [z]
    zip

[zh, ZH] = IPA [ʒ]
    gara**ge**

Index

Numbers in italics refer to lists of Principal Characters or Principal Gods.